SPSS

SPSS/PC+
Advanced Statistics™
Version 5.0

Marija J. Norušis/SPSS Inc.

SPSS Inc.
444 N. Michigan Avenue
Chicago, Illinois 60611
Tel: (312) 329-2400
Fax: (312) 329-3668

SPSS Federal Systems (U.S.)
SPSS Latin America
SPSS Benelux BV
SPSS UK Ltd.
SPSS UK Ltd., New Delhi
SPSS GmbH Software
SPSS Scandinavia AB
SPSS Asia Pacific Pte. Ltd.
SPSS Japan Inc.
SPSS Australasia Pty. Ltd.

For more information about SPSS® software products, please write or call

Marketing Department
SPSS Inc.
444 North Michigan Avenue
Chicago, IL 60611
Tel: (312) 329-2400
Fax: (312) 329-3668

SPSS/PC+ Advanced Statistics™, Version 5.0
Copyright © 1992
All rights reserved.
Printed in the United States of America.

2 3 4 5 6 7 8 9 0   95 94 93 92

ISBN 0-923967-68-0

Library of Congress Catalog Card Number: 92-085165

Preface

SPSS/PC+ Release 5 is a powerful software package for microcomputer data management and analysis. The Advanced Statistics option is an add-on enhancement that provides additional statistical analysis techniques. The procedures in Advanced Statistics must be used with the SPSS/PC+ Base system and are completely integrated into that system.

The Advanced Statistics option includes procedures for logistic regression, univariate and multivariate analysis of variance, loglinear analysis, nonlinear regression, probit analysis, and survival analysis. The algorithms are identical to those used in SPSS software on mainframe computers, and the statistical results will be as precise as those computed on a mainframe.

SPSS/PC+ with the Advanced Statistics option will enable you to perform many analyses on your PC that were once possible only on much larger machines. We hope that this statistical power will make SPSS/PC+ an even more useful tool in your work.

Compatibility

SPSS Inc. warrants that SPSS/PC+ and enhancements are designed for personal computers in the IBM PC and IBM PS/2™ lines with a hard disk and at least 640K of RAM. Versions of SPSS/PC+ that support extended memory require additional memory. See the installation instructions that came with your Base System for more information. These products also function on most IBM-compatible machines. Contact SPSS Inc. for details about specific IBM-compatible hardware.

Serial Numbers

Your serial number is your identification number with SPSS Inc. You will need this serial number when you call SPSS Inc. for information regarding support, payment, a defective diskette, or an upgraded system.

The serial number can be found on diskette 3 of your Base System. Before using the system, please copy this number to the **registration card.**

Registration Card

STOP! Before going on, *fill out and send us your registration card.* Until we receive your registration card, you have an unregistered system. Even if you have previously sent a card to us, please fill out and return the card enclosed in your Professional Statistics package. Registering your system entitles you to

- Technical support on our customer hotline.
- Favored customer status.
- New product announcements.

Of course, unregistered systems receive none of the above, so *don't put it off—send your registration card now!*

Replacement Policy

Call Customer Service at 1-800-521-1337 to report a defective diskette. You must provide us with the serial number of your system. (The normal installation procedure will detect any damaged diskettes.) SPSS will ship replacement diskettes the same day we receive notification from you.

Training Seminars

SPSS Inc. provides both public and onsite training seminars for SPSS/PC+. All seminars feature hands-on workshops. SPSS/PC+ seminars will be offered in major U.S. and European cities on a regular basis. For more information on these seminars, call the SPSS Inc. Training Department toll-free at 1-800-543-6607.

Technical Support

The services of SPSS Technical Support are available to registered customers of SPSS/PC+. Customers may call Technical Support for assistance in using SPSS products or for installation help for one of the warranted hardware environments.

To reach Technical Support, call 1-312-329-3410. Be prepared to identify yourself, your organization, and the serial number of your system.

If you are a Value Plus or Customer EXPress customer, use the priority 800 number you received with your materials. For information on subscribing to the Value Plus or Customer EXPress plan, call SPSS Software Sales at 1-800-543-2185 or 1-312-329-3300.

Additional Publications

Additional copies of all SPSS product manuals may be purchased separately. To order additional manuals, just fill out the Publications insert included with your system and send it to SPSS Publications Sales, 444 N. Michigan Avenue, Chicago IL, 60611.

Note: In Europe, additional copies of publications can be purchased by site-licensed customers only. For more information, please contact your local office at the address listed at the end of this preface.

Tell Us Your Thoughts

Your comments are important. So send us a letter and let us know about your experiences with SPSS products. We especially like to hear about new and interesting applications using the SPSS/PC+ system. Write to SPSS Inc. Marketing Department, Attn: Micro Software Products Manager, 444 N. Michigan Avenue, Chicago, IL 60611.

About This Manual

This manual is divided into three sections. The first section provides a guide to the various statistical techniques available with the Professional Statistics option and how to obtain the appropriate statistical analyses. The second section of this manual is a reference guide that provides complete command syntax for all the commands included in the Professional Statistics option. The last section provides annotated examples for each procedure included in the Professional Statistics option. The examples serve to illustrate how actual data are transformed and analyzed.

Contacting SPSS Inc.

If you would like to be on our mailing list, write to us at one of the addresses below. We will send you a copy of our newsletter and let you know about SPSS Inc. activities in your area.

SPSS Inc.
444 North Michigan Ave.
Chicago, IL 60611
Tel: (312) 329-2400
Fax: (312) 329-3668

SPSS Federal Systems
12030 Sunrise Valley Dr.
Suite 300
Reston, VA 22091
Tel: (703) 391-6020
Fax: (703) 391-6002

SPSS Latin America
444 North Michigan Ave.
Chicago, IL 60611
Tel: (312) 329-3556
Fax: (312) 329-3668

SPSS Benelux BV
P.O. Box 115
4200 AC Gorinchem
The Netherlands
Tel: +31.1830.36711
Fax: +31.1830.35839

SPSS UK Ltd.
SPSS House
5 London Street
Chertsey
Surrey KT16 8AP
United Kingdom
Tel: +44.932.566262
Fax: +44.932.567020

SPSS UK Ltd., New Delhi
c/o Ashok Business Centre
Ashok Hotel
50B Chanakyapuri
New Delhi 110 021
India
Tel: +91.11.600121 x1029
Fax: +91.11.6873216

SPSS GmbH Software
Steinsdorfstrasse 19
D-80538 Munich
Germany
Tel: +49.89.2283008
Fax: +49.89.2285413

SPSS Scandinavia AB
Gamla Brogatan 36-38
4th Floor
111 20 Stockholm
Sweden
Tel: +46.8.102610
Fax: +46.8.102550

SPSS Asia Pacific Pte. Ltd.
10 Anson Road, #34-07
International Plaza
Singapore 0207
Singapore
Tel: +65.221.2577
Fax: +65.221.9920

SPSS Japan Inc.
AY Bldg.
3-2-2 Kitaaoyama
Minato-ku
Tokyo 107
Japan
Tel: +81.3.5474.0341
Fax: +81.3.5474.2678

SPSS Australasia Pty. Ltd.
121 Walker Street
North Sydney, NSW 2060
Australia
Tel: +61.2.954.5660
Fax: +61.2.954.5616

Contents

4 Repeated Measures Analysis of Variance   123

5 Hierarchical Loglinear Models   161

1 Logistic Regression Analysis

Predicting whether an event will or will not occur, as well as identifying the variables useful in making the prediction, is important in most academic disciplines as well as the "real" world. Why do some citizens vote and others not? Why do some people develop coronary heart disease and others not? Why do some businesses succeed, while others fail?

There is a variety of multivariate statistical techniques that can be used to predict a binary dependent variable from a set of independent variables. Multiple regression analysis and discriminant analysis are two related techniques that quickly come to mind. However, these techniques pose difficulties when the dependent variable can have only two values—an event occurring or not occurring.

When the dependent variable can have only two values, the assumptions necessary for hypothesis testing in regression analysis are necessarily violated. For example, it is unreasonable to assume that the distribution of errors is normal. Another difficulty with multiple regression analysis is that predicted values cannot be interpreted as probabilities. They are not constrained to fall in the interval between 0 and 1.

Linear discriminant analysis does allow direct prediction of group membership, but the assumption of multivariate normality of the independent variables, as well as equal variance-covariance matrices in the two groups, is required for the prediction rule to be optimal.

In this chapter, we will consider another multivariate technique for estimating the probability that an event occurs: the **logistic regression model**. This model requires far fewer assumptions than discriminant analysis; and even when the assumptions required for discriminant analysis are satisfied, logistic regression still performs well. (See Hosmer and Lemeshow, 1989, for an introduction to logistic regression.)

The Logistic Regression Model

In logistic regression you directly estimate the probability of an event occurring. For the case of a single independent variable, the logistic regression model can be written as

$$\text{Prob (event)} = \frac{e^{B_0 + B_1 X}}{1 + e^{B_0 + B_1 X}} \qquad \text{Equation 1.1}$$

or equivalently

$$\text{Prob (event)} = \frac{1}{1 + e^{-(B_0 + B_1 X)}} \qquad \text{Equation 1.2}$$

where B_0 and B_1 are coefficients estimated from the data, X is the independent variable, and e is the base of the natural logarithms, approximately 2.718.

For more than one independent variable the model can be written as

$$\text{Prob (event)} = \frac{e^Z}{1 + e^Z} \qquad \text{Equation 1.3}$$

or equivalently,

$$\text{Prob (event)} = \frac{1}{1 + e^{-Z}} \qquad \text{Equation 1.4}$$

where Z is the linear combination

$$Z = B_0 + B_1 X_1 + B_2 X_2 + ... + B_p X_p \qquad \text{Equation 1.5}$$

The probability of the event not occurring is estimated as

$$\text{Prob (no event)} = 1 - \text{Prob (event)} \qquad \text{Equation 1.6}$$

Figure 1.1 is a plot of a logistic regression curve when the values of Z are between -5 and $+5$. As you can see, the curve is S-shaped. It closely resembles the curve obtained when the cumulative probability of the normal distribution is plotted. The relationship between the independent variable and the probability is nonlinear. The probability estimates will always be between 0 and 1, regardless of the value of Z.

Figure 1.1   Plot of logistic regression curve

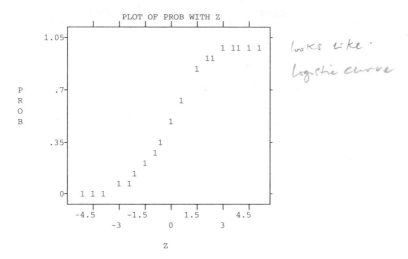

In linear regression, we estimate the parameters of the model using the **least-squares method**. That is, we select regression coefficients that result in the smallest sum of squared distances between the observed and the predicted values of the dependent variable.

In logistic regression, the parameters of the model are estimated using the **maximum-likelihood method**. That is, the coefficients that make our observed results most "likely" are selected. Since the logistic regression model is nonlinear, an iterative algorithm is necessary for parameter estimation.

An Example

The treatment and prognosis of cancer depends on how much the disease has spread. One of the regions to which a cancer may spread is the lymph nodes. If the lymph nodes are involved, the prognosis is generally poorer than if they are not. That's why it's desirable to establish as early as possible whether the lymph nodes are cancerous. For certain cancers, exploratory surgery is done just to determine whether the nodes are cancerous, since this will determine what treatment is needed. If we could predict whether the nodes are affected or not on the basis of data that can be obtained without performing surgery, considerable discomfort and expense could be avoided.

For this chapter, we will use data presented by Brown (1980) for 53 men with prostate cancer. For each patient, he reports the age, serum acid phosphatase (a laboratory value that is elevated if the tumor has spread to certain areas), the stage of the disease (an indication of how advanced the disease is), the grade of the tumor (an indication of malignancy), and x-ray results, as well as whether the cancer had spread to the regional lymph nodes at the time of surgery. The problem is to predict whether the nodes are positive for cancer based on the values of the variables that can be measured without surgery.

Coefficients for the Logistic Model

Figure 1.2 contains the estimated coefficients (under column heading *B*) and related statistics from the logistic regression model that predicts nodal involvement from a constant and the variables *age*, *acid*, *xray*, *stage*, and *grade*. The last three of these variables (*xray*, *stage*, and *grade*) are **indicator variables**, coded 0 or 1. The value of 1 for *xray* indicates positive x-ray findings, the value of 1 for *stage* indicates advanced stage, and the value of 1 for *grade* indicates a malignant tumor.

Figure 1.2   Parameter estimates for the logistic regression model

```
LOGISTIC REGRESSION NODES WITH AGE ACID XRAY GRADE STAGE.

---------------------- Variables in the Equation -----------------------

Variable          B       S.E.     Wald     df     Sig       R     Exp(B)

AGE           -.0693     .0579    1.4320     1    .2314    .0000    .9331
ACID           .0243     .0132    3.4229     1    .0643    .1423   1.0246
XRAY          2.0453     .8072    6.4207     1    .0113    .2509   7.7317
GRADE          .7614     .7708     .9758     1    .3232    .0000   2.1413
STAGE         1.5641     .7740    4.0835     1    .0433    .1722   4.7783
Constant       .0618    3.4599     .0003     1    .9857
```

Given these coefficients, the logistic regression equation for the probability of nodal involvement can be written as

$$\text{Prob (nodal involvement)} = \frac{1}{1 + e^{-Z}}$$

Equation 1.7

where

$$Z = 0.0618 - 0.0693 \, (\text{age}) + 0.0243 \, (\text{acid}) + 2.0453 \, (\text{xray})$$
$$+ 0.7614 \, (\text{grade}) + 1.5641 \, (\text{stage})$$

Equation 1.8

Applying this to a man who is 66 years old, with a serum phosphatase level of 48 and values of 0 for the remaining independent variables, we find:

$$Z = 0.0618 - 0.0693 \, (66) + 0.0243 \, (48) = -3.346$$

Equation 1.9

The probability of nodal involvement is then estimated to be:

$$\text{Prob (nodal involvement)} = \frac{1}{1 + e^{-(-3.346)}} = 0.0340$$

Equation 1.10

Based on this estimate, we would predict that the nodes are unlikely to be malignant. In general, if the estimated probability of the event is less than 0.5, we predict that the event will not occur. If the probability is greater than 0.5, we predict that the event will occur. (In the unlikely event that the probability is exactly 0.5, we can flip a coin for our prediction.)

Testing Hypotheses about the Coefficients

For large sample sizes, the test that a coefficient is 0 can be based on the **Wald statistic**, which has a chi-square distribution. When a variable has a single degree of freedom, the Wald statistic is just the square of the ratio of the coefficient to its standard error. For categorical variables, the Wald statistic has degrees of freedom equal to one less than the number of categories.

For example, the coefficient for age is −0.0693, and its standard error is 0.0579. (The standard errors for the logistic regression coefficients are shown in the column labeled *S.E.* in Figure 1.2.) The Wald statistic is $(-0.0693/0.0579)^2$, or about 1.432. The significance level for the Wald statistic is shown in the column labeled *Sig*. In this example, only the coefficients for *xray* and *stage* appear to be significantly different from 0, using a significance level of 0.05.

Unfortunately, the Wald statistic has a very undesirable property. When the absolute value of the regression coefficient becomes large, the estimated standard error is too large. This produces a Wald statistic that is too small, leading you to fail to reject the null hypothesis that the coefficient is 0, when in fact you should. Therefore, whenever you have a large coefficient, you should not rely on the Wald statistic for hypothesis testing. Instead, you should build a model with and without that variable and base your hypothesis test on the change in the log likelihood (Hauck & Donner, 1977).

Partial Correlation

As is the case with multiple regression, the contribution of individual variables in logistic regression is difficult to determine. The contribution of each variable depends on the other variables in the model. This is a problem, particularly when independent variables are highly correlated.

A statistic that is used to look at the partial correlation between the dependent variable and each of the independent variables is the R statistic, shown in Figure 1.2. R can range in value from −1 to +1. A positive value indicates that as the variable increases in value, so does the likelihood of the event occurring. If R is negative, the opposite is true. Small values for R indicate that the variable has a small partial contribution to the model.

The equation for the R statistic is

$$R = \pm \sqrt{\left(\frac{\text{Wald statistic} - 2K}{-2LL_{(0)}}\right)}$$

Equation 1.11

where K is the degrees of freedom for the variable (Atkinson, 1980). The denominator is -2 times the log likelihood of a base model that contains only the intercept, or a model with no variables if there is no intercept. (If you enter several blocks of variables, the base model for each block is the result of previous entry steps.) The sign of the corresponding coefficient is attached to R. The value of $2K$ in Equation 1.11 is an adjustment for the number of parameters estimated. If the Wald statistic is less than $2K$, R is set to 0.

Interpreting the Regression Coefficients

In multiple linear regression, the interpretation of the regression coefficient is straightforward. It tells you the amount of change in the dependent variable for a one-unit change in the independent variable.

To understand the interpretation of the logistic coefficients, consider a rearrangement of the equation for the logistic model. The logistic model can be rewritten in terms of the odds of an event occurring. (The **odds** of an event occurring are defined as the ratio of the probability that it will occur to the probability that it will not. For example, the odds of getting a head on a single flip of a coin are $0.5/0.5 = 1$. Similarly, the odds of getting a diamond on a single draw from a card deck are $0.25/0.75 = 1/3$. Don't confuse this technical meaning of odds with its informal usage to mean simply the probability.)

First let's write the logistic model in terms of the log of the odds, which is called a **logit**:

$$\log\left(\frac{\text{Prob (event)}}{\text{Prob (no event)}}\right) = B_0 + B_1 X_1 + \ldots + B_p X_p \qquad \text{Equation 1.12}$$

From Equation 1.12, you see that the logistic coefficient can be interpreted as the change in the log odds associated with a one-unit change in the independent variable. For example, from Figure 1.2, you see that the coefficient for *grade* is 0.76. This tells you that when the grade changes from 0 to 1 and the values of the other independent variables remain the same, the log odds of the nodes being malignant increase by 0.76.

Since it's easier to think of odds rather than log odds, the logistic equation can be written in terms of odds as:

$$\frac{\text{Prob (event)}}{\text{Prob (no event)}} = e^{B_0 + B_1 X_1 + \ldots + B_p X_p} = e^{B_0} e^{B_1 X_1} \ldots e^{B_p X_p} \qquad \text{Equation 1.13}$$

Then e raised to the power B_i is the factor by which the odds change when the ith independent variable increases by one unit. If B_i is positive, this factor will be greater than 1, which means that the odds are increased; if B_i is negative, the factor will be less than 1, which means that the odds are decreased. When B_i is 0, the factor equals 1, which leaves the odds unchanged. For example, when *grade* changes from 0 to 1, the odds are increased by a factor of 2.14, as is shown in the *Exp(B)* column in Figure 1.2.

As a further example, let's calculate the odds of having malignant nodes for a 60-year-old man with a serum acid phosphatase level of 62, a value of 1 for x-ray results, and values of 0 for stage and grade of tumor. First, calculate the probability that the nodes are malignant

$$\text{Estimated prob (malignant nodes)} = \frac{1}{1 + e^{-Z}}$$

Equation 1.14

where

$$Z = 0.0618 - 0.0693\,(60) + 0.0243\,(62) + 2.0453\,(1)$$
$$+ 0.7614\,(0) + (1.5641)\,(0) = -0.54$$

Equation 1.15

The estimated probability of malignant nodes is therefore 0.37. The probability of not having malignant nodes is 0.63 (that is, $1 - 0.37$). The *odds* of having a malignant node are then estimated as

$$\text{Odds} = \frac{\text{Prob (event)}}{\text{Prob (no event)}} = \frac{0.37}{1 - 0.37} = 0.59$$

Equation 1.16

and the log odds are -0.53.

What would be the probability of malignant nodes if, instead of 0, the case had a value of 1 for *grade*? Following the same procedure as before, but using a value of 1 for *grade*, the estimated probability of malignant nodes is 0.554. Similarly, the estimated odds are 1.24, and the log odds are 0.22.

By increasing the value of grade by one unit, we have increased the log odds by about 0.75, the value of the coefficient for *grade*. (Since we didn't use many digits in our hand calculations, our value of 0.75 isn't exactly equal to the 0.76 value for grade shown in Figure 1.2. If we carried the computations out with enough precision, we would arrive at exactly the value of the coefficient.)

By increasing the value of grade from 0 to 1, the odds changed from 0.59 to 1.24. That is, they increased by a factor of about 2.1. This is the value of *Exp(B)* for *grade* in Figure 1.2.

Assessing the Goodness of Fit of the Model

There are various ways to assess whether or not the model fits the data. The sections "The Classification Table," below, through "Goodness of Fit with All Variables" on p. 10 discuss the goodness of fit of the model.

The Classification Table

One way to assess how well our model fits is to compare our predictions to the observed outcomes. Figure 1.3 is the classification table for this example.

Figure 1.3   Classification table

LOGISTIC REGRESSION NODES WITH AGE ACID XRAY GRADE STAGE.

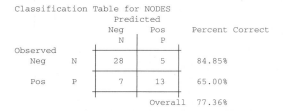

```
Classification Table for NODES
                    Predicted
                 Neg    Pos      Percent Correct
                  N      P
Observed
  Neg    N        28      5        84.85%

  Pos    P         7     13        65.00%

                        Overall  77.36%
```

From the table you see that 28 patients without malignant nodes were correctly predicted by the model not to have malignant nodes. Similarly, 13 men with positive nodes were correctly predicted to have positive nodes. The off-diagonal entries of the table tell you how many men were incorrectly classified. A total of 12 men were misclassified in this example—5 men with negative nodes and 7 men with positive nodes. Of the men without diseased nodes, 85.85% were correctly classified. Of the men with diseased nodes, 65% were correctly classified. Overall, 77.36% of the 53 men were correctly classified.

The classification table doesn't reveal the distribution of estimated probabilities for men in the two groups. For each predicted group, the table shows only whether the estimated probability is greater or less than one-half. For example, you cannot tell from the table whether the 7 patients who had false negative results had predicted probabilities near 50%, or low predicted probabilities. Ideally, you would like the two groups to have very different estimated probabilities. That is, you would like to see small estimated probabilities of positive nodes for all men without malignant nodes and large estimated probabilities for all men with malignant nodes.

Histogram of Estimated Probabilities

Figure 1.4 is a histogram of the estimated probabilities of cancerous nodes. The symbol used for each case designates the group to which the case actually belongs. If you have a model that successfully distinguishes the two groups, the cases for which the event has occurred should be to the right of 0.5, while those cases for which the event has not occurred should be to the left of 0.5. The more the two groups cluster at their respective ends of the plot, the better.

Figure 1.4   Histogram of estimated probabilities

```
LOGISTIC REGRESSION NODES WITH AGE ACID XRAY GRADE STAGE
 /CLASSPLOT.
```

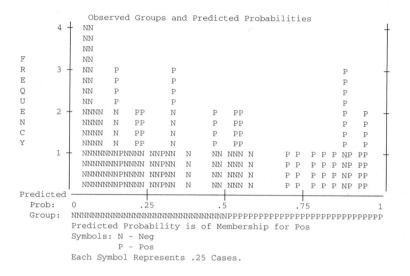

```
                  Observed Groups and Predicted Probabilities
        4 +     NN                                                                 +
                NN
                NN
  F             NN
  R       3 +   NN      P           P                              P               +
  E             NN      P           P                              P
  Q             NN      P           P                              P
  U             NN      P           P                              P
  E       2 +   NNNN  N   PP     N        P    PP                  P     P          +
  N             NNNN  N   PP     N        P    PP                  P     P
  C             NNNN  N   PP     N        P    PP                  P     P
  Y             NNNN  N   PP     N        P    PP                  P     P
          1 +   NNNNNNNPNNNN NNPNN   N    NN NNN N        P P   P P P NP PP          +
                NNNNNNNPNNNN NNPNN   N    NN NNN N        P P   P P P NP PP
                NNNNNNNPNNNN NNPNN   N    NN NNN N        P P   P P P NP PP
                NNNNNNNPNNNN NNPNN   N    NN NNN N        P P   P P P NP PP
Predicted  -----------------------------------------------------------------------
  Prob:    0              .25           .5            .75              1
  Group:   NNNNNNNNNNNNNNNNNNNNNNNNNNNNNNNNNNNNNNPPPPPPPPPPPPPPPPPPPPPPPPPPPPPPPPPP
           Predicted Probability is of Membership for Pos
           Symbols: N - Neg
                    P - Pos
           Each Symbol Represents .25 Cases.
```

From Figure 1.4, you see that there is only one noncancerous case with a high estimated probability of having positive nodes (the case identified with the letter *N* at a probability value of about 0.88.) However, there are four diseased cases with estimated probabilities less than 0.25.

By looking at this histogram of predicted probabilities, you can see whether a different rule for assigning cases to groups might be useful. For example, if most of the misclassifications occur in the region around 0.5, you might decide to withhold judgment for cases with values in this region. In this example, that would mean that you would predict nodal involvement only for cases for which you were reasonably sure the logistic prediction would be correct. You might decide to operate on all questionable cases.

If the consequences of misclassification are not the same in both directions (for example, calling nodes negative when they are really positive is worse than calling nodes positive when they are really negative), the classification rule can be altered to decrease the possibility of making the more severe error. For example, you might decide to call cases "negative" only if their estimated probability is less than 0.3. By looking at the histogram of the estimated probabilities, you can get some idea of how different classification rules might perform. (Of course, when you apply the model to new cases, you can't expect the classification rule to behave exactly the same.)

Goodness of Fit of the Model

Seeing how well the model classifies the observed data is one way of determining how well the logistic model performs. Another way of assessing the goodness of fit of the model is to examine how "likely" the sample results actually are, given the parameter estimates. (Recall that we chose parameter estimates that would make our observed results as likely as possible.)

The probability of the observed results, given the parameter estimates, is known as the **likelihood**. Since the likelihood is a small number less than 1, it is customary to use −2 times the log of the likelihood (−2LL) as a measure of how well the estimated model fits the data. A good model is one that results in a high likelihood of the observed results. This translates to a small value for −2LL. (If a model fits perfectly, the likelihood is 1, and −2 times the log likelihood is 0.)

For the logistic regression model that contains only the constant, −2LL is 70.25, as shown in Figure 1.5.

Figure 1.5   -2LL for model containing only the constant

```
LOGISTIC REGRESSION NODES WITH AGE ACID XRAY GRADE STAGE.

Dependent Variable..    NODES

Beginning Block Number    0.   Initial Log Likelihood Function

-2 Log Likelihood     70.252153

* Constant is included in the model.
```

Another measure of how well the model fits is the **goodness-of-fit statistic**, which compares the observed probabilities to those predicted by the model. The goodness-of-fit statistic is defined as

$$Z^2 = \sum \frac{\text{Residual}_i^2}{P_i(1 - P_i)}$$

Equation 1.17

where the residual is the difference between the observed value, Y_i, and the predicted value, P_i.

Goodness of Fit with All Variables

Figure 1.6 shows the goodness-of-fit statistics for the model with all of the independent variables. For the current model, the value of −2LL is 48.126, which is smaller than the −2LL for the model containing only a constant. The goodness-of-fit statistic is displayed in the second row of the table.

Figure 1.6   Statistics for model containing the independent variables

```
LOGISTIC REGRESSION NODES WITH AGE ACID XRAY GRADE STAGE.

-2 Log Likelihood        48.126
Goodness of Fit          46.790

                    Chi-Square    df Significance

Model Chi-Square        22.126     5      .0005
Improvement             22.126     5      .0005
```

[handwritten annotation: with 53 subjects — maybe 52 d.f.s so G.of is √ mean d.f.s]

There are two additional entries in Figure 1.6. They are labeled *Model Chi-square* and *Improvement*. In this example, the model chi-square is the difference between $-2LL$ for the model with only a constant and $-2LL$ for the current model. (If a constant is not included in the model, the likelihood for the model without any variables is used for comparison. If variables are already in the equation when variable selection begins, the model with these variables is used as the base model.) Thus, the model chi-square tests the null hypothesis that the coefficients for all of the terms in the current model, except the constant, are 0. This is comparable to the overall F test for regression.

In this example, $-2LL$ for the model containing only the constant is 70.25 (from Figure 1.5), while for the complete model, it is 48.126. The model chi-square, 22.126, is the difference between these two values. The degrees of freedom for the model chi-square are the difference between the number of parameters in the two models.

The entry labeled *Improvement* is the change in $-2LL$ between successive steps of building a model. It tests the null hypothesis that the coefficients for the variables added at the last step are 0. In this example, we considered only two models: the constant-only model and the model with a constant and five independent variables. Thus, the model chi-square and the improvement chi-square values are the same. If you sequentially consider more than just these two models, using either forward or backward variable selection, the model chi-square and improvement chi-square will differ. The improvement chi-square test is comparable to the F-change test in multiple regression.

Categorical Variables

In logistic regression, just as in linear regression, the codes for the independent variables must be meaningful. You cannot take a nominal variable like religion, assign arbitrary codes from 1 to 35, and then use the resulting variable in the model. In this situation, you must recode the values of the independent variable by creating a new set of variables that correspond in some way to the original categories.

If you have a two-category variable like sex, you can code each case as 0 or 1 to indicate either female or not female. Or you could code it as being male or not male. This is called **dummy variable** or **indicator variable coding**. *Grade*, *stage*, and *xray* are all examples of two-category variables that have been coded as 0 and 1. The code of 1 indicates that the poorer outcome is present. The interpretation of the resulting coefficients for *grade*, *stage*, and *xray* is straightforward. It tells you the difference between the log odds when a case is a member of the "poor" category and when it is not.

When you have a variable with more than two categories, you must create new variables to represent the categories. The number of new variables required to represent a categorical variable is one less than the number of categories. For example, if instead of the actual values for serum acid phosphatase, you had values of 1, 2, or 3, depending on whether the value was low, medium, or high, you would have to create two new variables to represent the serum phosphatase effect. Two alternative coding schemes are described in "Indicator-Variable Coding Scheme," below, and "Another Coding Scheme" on p. 13.

Indicator-Variable Coding Scheme

One of the ways you can create two new variables for serum acid phosphatase is to use indicator variables to represent the categories. With this method, one variable would represent the low value, coded 1 if the value is low and 0 otherwise. The second variable would represent the medium value, coded 1 if the value is average and 0 otherwise. The value "high" would be represented by codes of 0 for both of these variables. The choice of the category to be coded as 0 for both variables is arbitrary.

With categorical variables, the only statement you can make about the effect of a particular category is in comparison to some other category. For example, if you have a variable that represents type of cancer, you can make only statements such as "lung cancer compared to bladder cancer decreases your chance of survival." Or you might say that "lung cancer compared to all the cancer types in the study decreases your chance of survival." You can't make a statement about lung cancer without relating it to the other types of cancer.

If you use indicator variables for coding, the coefficients for the new variables represent the effect of each category compared to a reference category. The coefficient for the reference category is 0. As an example, consider Figure 1.7. The variable *catacid1* is the indicator variable for low serum acid phosphatase, coded 1 for low levels and 0 otherwise. Similarly, the variable *catacid2* is the indicator variable for medium serum acid phosphatase. The reference category is high levels.

Figure 1.7   Indicator variables

```
COMPUTE CATACID1=0.
COMPUTE CATACID2=0.
IF (ACID LE 50) CATACID1=1.
IF (ACID GT 50 AND ACID LT 75) CATACID2=1.
LOGISTIC REGRESSION NODES WITH AGE CATACID1 CATACID2
   XRAY GRADE STAGE.
```

```
---------------------- Variables in the Equation ----------------------
```

Variable	B	S.E.	Wald	df	Sig	R	Exp(B)
AGE	-.0522	.0630	.6862	1	.4075	.0000	.9492
CATACID			3.8361	2	.1469	.0000	
CATACID(1)	-2.0079	1.0520	3.6427	1	.0563	-.1529	.1343
CATACID(2)	-1.0923	.9264	1.3903	1	.2384	.0000	.3355
XRAY	2.0348	.8375	5.9033	1	.0151	.2357	7.6503
GRADE	.8076	.8233	.9623	1	.3266	.0000	2.2426
STAGE	1.4571	.7683	3.5968	1	.0579	.1508	4.2934
Constant	1.7698	3.8088	.2159	1	.6422		

The coefficient for *catacid1* is the change in log odds when you have a low value compared to a high value. Similarly, *catacid2* is the change in log odds when you have a medium value compared to a high value. The coefficient for the high value is necessarily 0, since it does not differ from itself. In Figure 1.7, you see that the coefficients for both of the indicator variables are negative. This means that compared to high values for serum acid phosphatase, low and medium values are associated with decreased log odds of malignant nodes. The low category decreases the log odds more than the medium category.

The SPSS/PC+ Logistic Regression procedure will automatically create new variables for variables declared as categorical (see "Processing Categorical Variables" on p. 25). You can choose the coding scheme you want to use for the new variables.

Figure 1.8 shows the table that is displayed for each categorical variable. The rows of the table correspond to the categories of the variable. The actual value is given in the column labeled *Value*. The number of cases with each value is displayed in the column labeled *Freq*. Subsequent columns correspond to new variables created by the program. The number in parentheses indicates the suffix used to identify the variable on the output. The codes that represent each original category using the new variables are listed under the corresponding new-variable column.

Figure 1.8   Indicator-variable coding scheme

```
LOGISTIC REGRESSION NODES WITH AGE CATACID XRAY GRADE STAGE
   /CATEGORICAL CATACID
   /CONTRAST(CATACID)=IND.


                              Parameter
               Value   Freq   Coding
                                (1)     (2)
CATACID
                1.00    15   1.000    .000
                2.00    20    .000   1.000
                3.00    18    .000    .000
```

From Figure 1.8, you see that there are 20 cases with a value of 2 for *catacid*. Each of these cases will be assigned a code of 0 for the new variable *catacid(1)* and a code of 1 for the new variable *catacid(2)*. Similarly, cases with a value of 3 for *catacid* will be given the code of 0 for both *catacid(1)* and *catacid(2)*.

Another Coding Scheme

The statement you can make based on the logistic regression coefficients depends on how you have created the new variables used to represent the categorical variable. As shown in the previous section, when you use indicator variables for coding, the coefficients for the new variables represent the effect of each category compared to a reference category. If, on the other hand, you wanted to compare the effect of each category to the average effect of all of the categories, you could have selected the default deviation coding scheme shown in Figure 1.9. This differs from indicator-variable coding only in that the last category is coded as -1 for each of the new variables.

With this coding scheme, the logistic regression coefficients tell you how much better or worse each category is compared to the average effect of all categories, as shown in Figure 1.10. For each new variable, the coefficients now represent the difference from the average effect over all categories. The value of the coefficient for the last category is not displayed, but it is no longer 0. Instead, it is the negative of the sum of the displayed coefficients. From Figure 1.10, the coefficient for "high" level is calculated as $-(-0.9745 - 0.0589) = 1.0334$.

Figure 1.9   Another coding scheme

```
LOGISTIC REGRESSION NODES WITH AGE CATACID XRAY GRADE STAGE
    /CATEGORICAL CATACID
    /CONTRAST(CATACID)=DEV.
```

```
                                  Parameter
                  Value   Freq   Coding
                                  (1)     (2)
CATACID
                  1.00    15   1.000    .000
                  2.00    20    .000   1.000
                  3.00    18  -1.000  -1.000
```

Figure 1.10   New coefficients

```
---------------------- Variables in the Equation ----------------------

Variable            B       S.E.      Wald    df     Sig        R    Exp(B)

AGE               -.0522    .0630     .6862     1    .4075    .0000    .9492
CATACID                               3.8361    2    .1469    .0000
  CATACID(1)      -.9745    .6410    2.3116     1    .1284   -.0666    .3774
  CATACID(2)      -.0589    .5727     .0106     1    .9181    .0000    .9428
XRAY             2.0348    .8375    5.9033     1    .0151    .2357   7.6503
GRADE             .8076    .8233     .9623     1    .3266    .0000   2.2426
STAGE            1.4571    .7683    3.5968     1    .0579    .1508   4.2934
Constant          .7364   3.7352     .0389     1    .8437
```

Different coding schemes result in different logistic regression coefficients, but not in different conclusions. That is, even though the actual values of the coefficients differ between Figure 1.7 and Figure 1.10, they tell you the same thing. Figure 1.7 tells you the effect of category 1 compared to category 3, while Figure 1.10 tells you the effect of category 1 compared to the average effect of all of the categories. You can select the coding scheme to match the type of comparisons you want to make.

Interaction Terms

Just as in linear regression, you can include terms in the model that are products of single terms. For example, if it made sense, you could include a term for the acid-by-age interaction in your model.

Interaction terms for categorical variables can also be computed. They are created as products of the values of the new variables. For categorical variables, make sure that the interaction terms created are those of interest. If you are using categorical variables with indicator coding, the interaction terms generated as the product of the variables are generally not those that you are interested in. Consider, for example, the interaction term between two indicator variables. If you just multiply the variables together, you will obtain a value of 1 only if both of the variables are coded "present." What you would probably like is a code of 1 if both of the variables are present or both are absent. You will obtain this if you use the default coding scheme for category variables instead of specifying the scheme as indicator variables.

Selecting Predictor Variables

In logistic regression, as in other multivariate statistical techniques, you may want to identify subsets of independent variables that are good predictors of the dependent variable. All of the problems associated with variable selection algorithms in regression and discriminant analysis are found in logistic regression as well. None of the algorithms result in a "best" model in any statistical sense. Different algorithms for variable selection may result in different models. It is a good idea to examine several possible models and choose among them on the basis of interpretability, parsimony, and ease of variable acquisition.

As always, the model is selected to fit a particular sample well, so there is no assurance that the same model will be selected if another sample from the same population is taken. The model will always fit the sample better than the population from which it is selected.

The Logistic Regression procedure has several methods available for model selection. You can enter variables into the model at will. You can also use forward stepwise selection and backward stepwise elimination for automated model building. The score statistic is always used for entering variables into a model. The Wald statistic or the change in likelihood can be used for removing variables from a model. All variables that are used to represent the same categorical variable are entered or removed from the model together.

Forward Stepwise Selection

Forward stepwise variable selection in logistic regression proceeds the same way as in multiple linear regression. You start out with a model that contains only the constant unless the option to omit the constant term from the model is selected. At each step, the variable with the smallest significance level for the score statistic, provided it is less than the chosen cutoff value (by default 0.05), is entered into the model. All variables in the forward stepwise block that have been entered are then examined to see if they meet removal criteria. If the Wald statistic is used for deleting variables, the Wald statistics for all variables in the model are examined and the variable with the largest significance level for the Wald statistic, provided it exceeds the chosen cutoff value (by default 0.1), is removed from the model. If no variables meet removal criteria, the next eligible variable is entered into the model.

If a variable is selected for removal and it results in a model that has already been considered, variable selection stops. Otherwise, the model is estimated without the deleted variable and the variables are again examined for removal. This continues until no more variables are eligible for removal. Then variables are again examined for entry into the model. The process continues either until a previously considered model is encountered (which means the algorithm is cycling) or no variables meet entry or removal criteria.

The Likelihood-Ratio Test

A better criterion than the Wald statistic for determining variables to be removed from the model is the **likelihood-ratio (LR) test**. This involves estimating the model with each variable eliminated in turn and looking at the change in the log likelihood when each variable is deleted. The likelihood-ratio test for the null hypothesis that the coefficients of the terms removed are 0 is obtained by dividing the likelihood for the reduced model by the likelihood for the full model.

If the null hypothesis is true and the sample size is sufficiently large, the quantity -2 times the log of the likelihood-ratio statistic has a chi-square distribution with r degrees of freedom, where r is the difference between the number of terms in the full model and the reduced model. (The model chi-square and the improvement chi-square are both likelihood-ratio tests.)

When the likelihood-ratio test is used for removing terms from a model, its significance level is compared to the cutoff value. The algorithm proceeds as previously described but with the likelihood-ratio statistic, instead of the Wald statistic, being evaluated for removing variables.

An Example of Forward Selection

To see what the output looks like for forward selection, consider Figure 1.11, which contains part of the summary statistics for the model when the constant is the only term included. First you see the previously described statistics for the constant. Then you see statistics for variables not in the equation. (The R for variables not in the equation is calculated using the score statistic instead of the Wald statistic.)

Figure 1.11 Variables not in the equation

```
LOGISTIC REGRESSION NODES WITH AGE ACID XRAY GRADE STAGE
    /FSTEP.

--------------------- Variables in the Equation ---------------------

Variable            B        S.E.      Wald      df       Sig        R      Exp(B)

Constant        -.5008     .2834    3.1227      1      .0772

-------------- Variables not in the Equation ----------------
Residual Chi Square      19.451 with        5 df      Sig = .0016

Variable            Score      df       Sig        R

AGE               1.0945      1      .2955     .0000
ACID              3.1168      1      .0775     .1261
XRAY             11.2829      1      .0008     .3635
GRADE             4.0745      1      .0435     .1718
STAGE             7.4381      1      .0064     .2782
```

The residual chi-square statistic tests the null hypothesis that the coefficients for all variables not in the model are 0. (The residual chi-square statistic is calculated from the score statistics, so it is not exactly the same value as the improvement chi-square value that you see in Figure 1.6. In general, however, the two statistics should be similar in value.) If the observed significance level for the residual chi-square statistic is small (that is, if you have reason to reject the hypothesis that all of the coefficients are 0), it is sensible to proceed with variable selection. If you can't reject the hypothesis that the coefficients are 0, you should consider terminating variable selection. If you continue to build a model, there is a reasonable chance that your resulting model will not be useful for other samples from the same population.

In this example, the significance level for the residual chi-square is small, so we can proceed with variable selection. For each variable not in the model, the score statistic and its significance level, if the variable were entered next into the model, is shown. The score statistic is an efficient alternative to the Wald statistic for testing the hypothesis that a coefficient is 0. Unlike the Wald statistic, it does not require the explicit computation of parameter estimates, so it is useful in situations where recalculating parameter estimates for many different models would be computationally prohibitive. The likelihood-ratio statistic, the Wald statistic, and Rao's efficient score statistic are all equivalent in large samples, when the null hypothesis is true (Rao, 1973).

From Figure 1.11, you see that *xray* has the smallest observed significance level less than 0.05, the default value for entry, so it is entered into the model. Statistics for variables not in the model at this step are shown in Figure 1.12. You see that the *stage* variable has the smallest observed significance level and meets entry criteria, so it is entered next. Figure 1.13 contains logistic coefficients when *stage* is included in the model. Since the observed significance levels of the coefficients for both variables in the model are less than 0.1, the default criterion for removal, neither variable is removed from the model.

Figure 1.12   Variables not in the equation

```
LOGISTIC REGRESSION NODES WITH AGE ACID XRAY GRADE STAGE
    /FSTEP.

--------------- Variables not in the Equation ----------------
Residual Chi Square      10.360 with      4 df    Sig = .0348

Variable          Score      df      Sig        R

AGE             1.3524       1     .2449     .0000
ACID            2.0732       1     .1499     .0323
GRADE           2.3710       1     .1236     .0727
STAGE           5.6393       1     .0176     .2276
```

Figure 1.13   Logistic coefficients with variables xray and stage

```
LOGISTIC REGRESSION NODES WITH AGE ACID XRAY GRADE STAGE
    /FSTEP.

--------------------- Variables in the Equation ----------------------

Variable       B      S.E.    Wald    df     Sig      R     Exp(B)

XRAY        2.1194   .7468   8.0537    1   .0045   .2935   8.3265
STAGE       1.5883   .7000   5.1479    1   .0233   .2117   4.8953
Constant   -2.0446   .6100  11.2360    1   .0008
```

The goodness-of-fit statistics for the model with *xray* and *stage* are shown in Figure 1.14. The model chi-square is the difference between $-2LL$ when only the constant is in the model and $-2LL$ when the constant, *xray*, and *stage* are in the model $(70.25 - 53.35 = 16.90)$. The small observed significance level for the model chi-square indicates that you can reject the null hypothesis that the coefficients for *xray* and *stage* are zero. The improvement chi-square is the change in $-2LL$ when *stage* is added to a model containing *xray* and the constant. The small observed significance level indicates that the coefficient for *stage* is not zero. ($-2LL$ for the model with only the constant and *xray* is 59.001, so the improvement chi-square is $59.00 - 53.35 = 5.65$.)

Figure 1.14   Goodness-of-fit statistics with variables stage and xray

```
LOGISTIC REGRESSION NODES WITH AGE ACID XRAY GRADE STAGE
    /FSTEP.

-2 Log Likelihood        53.353
Goodness of Fit          54.018

                    Chi-Square    df Significance

Model Chi-Square      16.899       2      .0002
Improvement            5.647       1      .0175
```

The statistics for variables not in the model after *stage* is entered are shown in Figure 1.15. All three of the observed significance levels are greater than 0.05, so no additional variables are included in the model.

Figure 1.15 Variables not in the model after variable stage

```
LOGISTIC REGRESSION NODES WITH AGE ACID XRAY GRADE STAGE
    /FSTEP.

--------------- Variables not in the Equation ----------------
Residual Chi Square      5.422 with      3 df      Sig = .1434

Variable          Score     df     Sig        R

AGE              1.2678      1    .2602     .0000
ACID             3.0917      1    .0787     .1247
GRADE             .5839      1    .4448     .0000
```

Forward Selection with the Likelihood-Ratio Criterion

If you select the likelihood-ratio statistic for deleting variables, the output will look slightly different from that previously described. For variables in the equation at a particular step, output similar to that shown in Figure 1.16 is produced in addition to the usual coefficients and Wald statistics.

Figure 1.16 Removal statistics

```
LOGISTIC REGRESSION NODES WITH AGE ACID XRAY GRADE STAGE
    /FSTEP (LR).

----------------- Model if Term Removed ------------------

Term       Log                            Significance
Removed    Likelihood    -2 Log LR    df   of Log LR

XRAY        -31.276        9.199       1       .0024
STAGE       -29.500        5.647       1       .0175
```

For each variable in the model, Figure 1.16 contains the log likelihood for the model if the variable is removed from the model; -2 log LR, which tests the null hypothesis that the coefficient of the term is 0; and the observed significance level. If the observed significance level is greater than the cutoff value for remaining in the model, the term is removed from the model and the model statistics are recalculated to see if any other variables are eligible for removal.

Backward Elimination

Forward selection starts without any variables in the model. Backward elimination starts with all of the variables in the model. Then, at each step, variables are evaluated for entry and removal. The score statistic is always used for determining whether variables should be added to the model. Just as in forward selection, the Wald statistic or the likelihood-ratio statistic can be used to select variables for removal.

Diagnostic Methods

Whenever you build a statistical model, it is important to examine the adequacy of the resulting model. In linear regression, we look at a variety of residuals, measures of influence, and indicators of collinearity. These are valuable tools for identifying points for which the model does not fit well, points that exert a strong influence on the coefficient estimates, and variables that are highly related to each other.

In logistic regression, there are comparable diagnostics that should be used to look for problems. The Logistic Regression procedure provides a variety of such statistics.

The **residual** is the difference between the observed probability of the event and the predicted probability of the event based on the model. For example, if we predict the probability of malignant nodes to be 0.80 for a man who has malignant nodes, the residual is $1 - 0.80 = 0.20$.

The **standardized residual** is the residual divided by an estimate of its standard deviation. In this case, it is:

$$Z_i = \frac{\text{Residual}_i}{\sqrt{P_i(1 - P_i)}} \qquad \text{Equation 1.18}$$

For each case, the standardized residual can also be considered a component of the chi-square goodness-of-fit statistic. If the sample size is large, the standardized residuals should be approximately normally distributed, with a mean of 0 and a standard deviation of 1.

For each case, the **deviance** is computed as

$$-2 \times \log(\text{predicted probability for the observed group}) \qquad \text{Equation 1.19}$$

The deviance is calculated by taking the square root of the above statistic and attaching a negative sign if the event did not occur for that case. For example, the deviance for a man without malignant nodes and a predicted probability of 0.8 for nonmalignant nodes is:

$$\text{Deviance} = -\sqrt{-2\log(0.8)} = -0.668 \qquad \text{Equation 1.20}$$

Large values for deviance indicate that the model does not fit the case well. For large sample sizes, the deviance is approximately normally distributed.

The **Studentized residual** for a case is the change in the model deviance if the case is excluded. Discrepancies between the deviance and the Studentized residual may identify unusual cases. Normal probability plots of the Studentized residuals may be useful.

The **logit residual** is the residual for the model if it is predicted in the logit scale. That is,

$$\text{Logit residual}_i = \frac{\text{residual}_i}{P_i(1-P_i)}$$

Equation 1.21

The **leverage** in logistic regression is in many respects analogous to the leverage in least-squares regression. Leverage values are often used for detecting observations that have a large impact on the predicted values. Unlike linear regression, the leverage values in logistic regression depend on both the dependent variable scores and the design matrix. Leverage values are bounded by 0 and 1. Their average value is p/n, where p is the number of estimated parameters in the model, including the constant, and n is the sample size.

Cook's distance is a measure of the influence of a case. It tells you how much deleting a case affects not only the residual for that case, but also the residuals of the remaining cases. Cook's distance (D) depends on the standardized residual for a case, as well as its leverage. It is defined as

$$D_i = \frac{Z_i^2 \times h_i}{(1-h_i)^2}$$

Equation 1.22

where Z_i is the standardized residual and h_i is the leverage.

Another useful diagnostic measure is the change in the logistic coefficients when a case is deleted from the model, or **DfBeta**. You can compute this change for each coefficient, including the constant. For example, the change in the first coefficient when case i is deleted is

$$\text{DfBeta}(B_1^{(i)}) = B_1 - B_1^{(i)}$$

Equation 1.23

where B_1 is the value of the coefficient when all cases are included and $B_1^{(i)}$ is the value of the coefficient when the ith case is excluded. Large values for change identify observations that should be examined.

Plotting Diagnostics

All of the diagnostic statistics described in this chapter can be saved for further analysis. If you save the values for the diagnostics, you can, when appropriate, obtain normal probability plots using the Examine procedure and plot the diagnostics using the Plot procedure (see the *SPSS/PC+ Base System User's Guide* for more information on these procedures).

Figure 1.17 shows a normal probability plot and a detrended normal probability plot of the deviances. As you can see, the deviances do not appear to be normally distributed.

That's because there are cases for which the model just doesn't fit well. In Figure 1.4, you see cases that have high probabilities for being in the incorrect group.

Figure 1.17 Normal probability of the deviances

```
LOGISTIC REGRESSION NODES WITH AGE ACID XRAY GRADE STAGE
   /SAVE DEV LEVER DFBETA ZRESID.
EXAMINE DEV_1/PLOT NPPLOT.
```

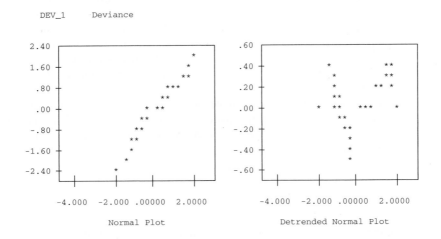

A plot of the standardized residuals against the case sequence numbers is shown in Figure 1.18. Again you see cases with large values for the standardized residuals. Figure 1.19 shows that there is one case with a leverage value that is much larger than the rest. Similarly, Figure 1.20 shows that there is a case that has substantial impact on the estimation of the coefficient for *acid* (case 24). Examination of the data reveals that this case has the largest value for serum acid phosphatase and yet does not have malignant nodes. Since serum acid phosphatase was positively related to malignant nodes, as shown in Figure 1.2, this case is quite unusual. If we remove case 24 from the analysis, the coefficient for serum acid phosphatase changes from 0.0243 to 0.0490. A variable that was, at best, a very marginal predictor becomes much more important.

Figure 1.18   Plot of standardized residual with case ID

```
PLOT PLOT=ZRE_1 LEV_1 DFB2_1 WITH IDENTIF.
```

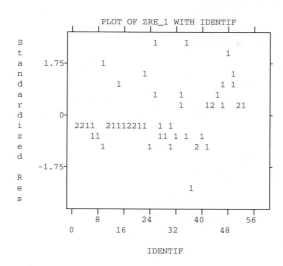

Figure 1.19   Plot of leverage with case ID

```
PLOT PLOT=ZRE_1 LEV_1 DFB2_1 WITH IDENTIF.
```

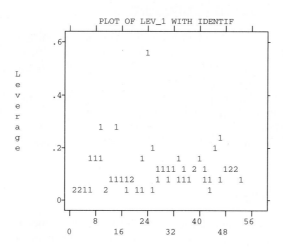

Figure 1.20   Plot of change in acid coefficient with case ID

```
PLOT PLOT=ZRE_1 LEV_1 DFB2_1 WITH IDENTIF.
```

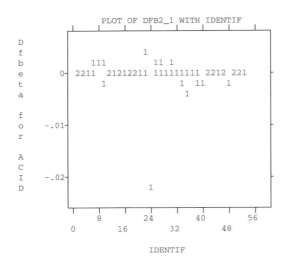

Running the Logistic Regression Procedure

The Logistic Regression procedure builds logistic regression models, which are used to estimate the probability of an event occurring. It allows user-specified entry of variables into the model, as well as forward and backward stepwise entry. It has facilities for automatically converting categorical variables into sets of contrast variables using any of seven contrast types or any user-specified contrast. The subcommands for residual analysis help detect influential data points, outliers, and violations of the model assumptions. The Logistic Regression procedure assumes that data are in case-by-case format. For logistic regression analysis of grouped data, use the Probit procedure, which is described in Chapter 8.

Specifying Variables in the Equation

To build a logistic regression model, use the VARIABLES subcommand to specify the dependent variable, and use either the VARIABLES or the METHOD subcommand to specify independent variables.

VARIABLES Subcommand

The VARIABLES subcommand is required, although the VARIABLES keyword is optional.

- The minimum specification is a dichotomous dependent variable. If the dependent variable does not have exactly two nonmissing values, the analysis terminates.
- You can list the independent variables on VARIABLES subcommand following the keyword WITH. The variable list following WITH must include *all* independent variables (but not necessarily all interaction terms) used in the procedure.
- The independent variables must be individually named. The TO convention is not allowed.
- You can omit WITH and the independent variable list if you specify independent variables (and interaction terms) on *all* METHOD subcommands.
- If some of the independent variables are categorical and you want the program to transform them, name them on the CATEGORICAL subcommand.

Specifying Interaction Terms

You can include interaction terms in the model by joining component variables with the keyword BY. If the component variables are not used by themselves in the procedure, you do not need to specify them individually either on the VARIABLES subcommand or on the METHOD subcommand.

Example

```
LOGISTIC REGRESSION NODES WITH AGE,ACID,XRAY,GRADE,STAGE.
```

- This example produces the default output: a classification table and regression statistics for all of the independent variables.
- See Figure 1.2, Figure 1.3, Figure 1.5, and Figure 1.6 for parts of the output display.

Processing Categorical Variables

Use the CATEGORICAL and CONTRAST subcommands to control processing of categorical independent variables.

CATEGORICAL Subcommand

You can name one or more independent variables on the CATEGORICAL subcommand. A variable thus named is automatically converted into a group of contrasts. The contrasts are entered or removed from the model as a block.

- Variables specified on CATEGORICAL but not on VARIABLES or METHOD are ignored.

- You can specify the contrast type on the CONTRAST subcommand. By default, LO-GISTIC REGRESSION uses deviation contrasts.

- The default contrast type does not give the same results as indicator variable analysis. If your categorical variables are already indicator variables, do not list them on the CATEGORICAL subcommand unless you want to use a different contrast type.

Example

```
LOGISTIC REGRESSION NODES WITH AGE,CATACID,XRAY,STAGE,GRADE
   /CATEGORICAL=CATACID.
```

- This example transforms the independent variable *catacid* using the default contrast type.

- The coding scheme is displayed in Figure 1.9.

CONTRAST Subcommand

When you name a variable with n categories on the CATEGORICAL subcommand, LO-GISTIC REGRESSION converts it into a group of n-1 variables and displays a table showing the values assigned to these variables for each category of the original variable. The variables can be calculated in many different ways, corresponding to different contrasts of the parameters. The choice of contrast type has no effect on the significance of the variable taken as a whole, but it does affect the coefficients and significance levels of the individual parameters.

By default, LOGISTIC REGRESSION uses deviation contrasts with the last category as the reference category. To specify a different contrast type or a different reference category for a categorical variable, use the CONTRAST subcommand followed by the name of the categorical variable in parentheses, an equals sign, and one of eight available keywords.

For deviation, indicator, and simple contrasts, you can specify the sequential number of a reference category in parentheses; the default is the last category.

DEVIATION(refcat)   *Deviations from the overall effect.* The effect for each category of the independent variable except the reference category is compared to the overall effect. This is the default if CONTRAST is not specified.

INDICATOR(refcat)   *Indicator variables.* Contrasts indicate the presence or absence of category membership. This contrast is equivalent to the traditional group of "dummy variables."

SIMPLE(refcat)   *Simple contrasts.* By default, each category of the independent variable (except the last) is compared to the last category.

DIFFERENCE   *Difference or reverse Helmert contrasts.* The effect for each category of the independent variable except the first is compared to the mean effect of the previous categories.

HELMERT   *Helmert contrasts.* The effect for each category of the independent variable except the last is compared to the mean effects of subsequent categories.

POLYNOMIAL(metric)   *Polynomial contrasts.* The first degree of freedom contains the linear effect across the categories of the independent variable, the second contains the quadratic effect, and so on. By default, the categories are assumed to be equally spaced; unequal spacing can be specified by entering a metric consisting of one integer for each category of the independent variable in parentheses after the keyword **POLYNOMIAL**. For example, CONTRAST(STIMULUS) = POLYNOMIAL(1,2,4) indicates that the three levels of *stimulus* are actually in the proportion 1:2:4. The default metric is always $(1,2,...,k)$, where k is the number of categories.

REPEATED   *Comparison of adjacent categories.* Each category of the independent variable except the first is compared to the previous category.

SPECIAL(matrix)   *User-defined contrast.* After this keyword, a matrix is entered in parentheses with $k-1$ rows and k columns, where k is the number of categories of the independent variable.

Example

```
LOGISTIC REGRESSION NODES WITH AGE,CATACID,XRAY,STAGE,GRADE
  /CATEGORICAL=CATACID
  /CONTRAST(CATACID)=INDICATOR.
```

- The independent variable *catacid* is transformed using the indicator contrast type.
- The coding scheme is displayed in Figure 1.8.

Selecting Predictor Variables

Use the METHOD and CRITERIA subcommands to control iteration and statistical criteria in the selection of predictor variables, and use the ORIGIN subcommand to indicate whether the model includes the constant term.

METHOD Subcommand

If you specify the independent variables after the keyword WITH on the VARIABLES subcommand, the METHOD subcommand is optional. If you do not specify them on VARIABLES, you must use a METHOD subcommand to indicate what variables are in the model.

- The keyword METHOD is optional.
- You can combine METHOD subcommands to specify the exact sequence in which model-building proceeds. When multiple METHOD subcommands are used, each method is applied to the equation as it stands at the end of the processing of the previous METHOD subcommand.
- The METHOD subcommand consists of one of the available method keywords followed by an optional list of independent variables.
- If you omit the METHOD subcommand, the default is forced entry of all independent variables named on the VARIABLES subcommand.
- If you omit the variable list, the specified method uses all independent variables named on the VARIABLES subcommand.
- Specifying the METHOD subcommand with no keyword is an error, with or without the variable list.

The following are available method keywords:

ENTER   *Forced entry.* All variables are entered in a single step. This is the default if you omit the METHOD subcommand.

FSTEP   *Forward stepwise.* See "Forward Stepwise Selection" on p. 15. To use the likelihood-ratio statistic as the test for removal from the equation, specify LR in parentheses after the keyword FSTEP. The default uses the Wald statistic.

BSTEP   *Backward stepwise.* See "Backward Elimination" on p. 19. To use the likelihood-ratio statistic, specify LR in parentheses after the keyword BSTEP. The default uses the Wald statistic.

Example

```
LOGISTIC REGRESSION NODES WITH AGE, ACID, XRAY, STAGE, GRADE
  /ENTER AGE STAGE
  /FSTEP.
```

- This example starts with a model containing *age* and *stage* and then continues to build it using the forward-stepwise algorithm.
- By default, both *age* and *stage* are on the FSTEP variable list and are thus eligible for removal. To prevent them from being removed, supply a variable list for FSTEP that does not include them, as in:

```
LOGISTIC REGRESSION NODES WITH AGE, ACID, XRAY, STAGE, GRADE
  /ENTER AGE STAGE
  /FSTEP ACID XRAY GRADE.
```

CRITERIA Subcommand

You can use the CRITERIA subcommand to control stepwise selection of the predictor variables.

Enter a value in parentheses on one or both of the following keywords to specify the criteria by which LOGISTIC REGRESSION enters and removes independent variables from the model:

PIN(value)   *Probability of score statistic for variable entry.* Specifying a larger value makes it easier for variables to enter the model. The default is 0.05.

POUT(value)   *Probability of Wald or LR statistic to remove a variable.* Specifying a larger value makes it easier for variables to remain in the model. The default is 0.10.

Enter a value in parentheses on one or more of the following keywords to control the iterative search for a solution. The iteration terminates when any one of the criteria is met:

BCON(value)   *Change in parameter estimates.* Iteration terminates when the parameters change by less than this value. The default is 0.001.

ITERATE(value)   *Maximum number of iterations.* Iteration terminates after the specified number of iterations. The default is 20.

LCON(value)   *Percentage change in the log-likelihood ratio.* Iteration terminates when the log-likelihood ratio decreases by less than this value. The default percentage change is 0.01.

Enter a value on the following keyword to specify the criterion used in redundancy checking:

EPS(value)   *Epsilon value used for redundancy checking.* The specified value must be less than or equal to 0.05 and greater than or equal to 10^{-12}. Larger values make it more likely that variables will be removed from the model as redundant. The default is 0.00000001.

ORIGIN Subcommand

The logistic regression model contains a constant term. Specify the ORIGIN subcommand to force the constant term to equal 0 and suppress it in the model. ORIGIN has no additional specifications. It affects all METHOD subcommands.

You cannot compare parameter estimates or goodness-of-fit statistics obtained with the ORIGIN subcommand and those obtained without it.

Specify NOORIGIN to include the constant term explicitly.

Selecting Cases

Use SELECT and MISSING subcommands to control the sample used to build the model.

SELECT Subcommand

Use the SELECT subcommand to select a subset of cases for computing the equation. Case selection is based on values of a variable. Specify the variable after SELECT, followed by a relational operator and then a value. Available operators are EQ, NE, LT, LE, GT, and GE. Cases are selected if the logical expression thus formed is true. All valid cases are selected if the SELECT subcommand is omitted. Classification results are reported for both selected and unselected cases.

Example

```
LOGISTIC REGRESSION NODES WITH AGE, ACID, XRAY, STAGE, GRADE
  /SELECT=GROUP LT 5.
```

- This example generates predicted probabilities and residuals for all patients based on a model estimated for patients with values less than 5 for variable *group*.
- For this example, the statistics in the default output are computed from the selected subset of the cases.

MISSING Subcommand

LOGISTIC REGRESSION excludes from the analysis cases with missing values for any variable named in the procedure. Predicted values are still calculated if only the dependent variable is missing. By default, cases with either system-missing or user-missing values are excluded. You can use the MISSING subcommand to include user-missing values in the analysis. Two keywords are available on MISSING:

EXCLUDE   *Exclude cases with user-missing values from the analysis.* This is the default.

INCLUDE   *Include cases with user-missing values.* System-missing values are excluded from analysis.

Requesting Output

Use the PRINT subcommand to obtain additional output or suppress the default output displayed after each step. Use the CLASSPLOT subcommand to obtain a classification plot of the actual and predicted values of the dependent variable at each step.

PRINT Subcommand

By default, LOGISTIC REGRESSION displays classification tables and regression statistics for each step. If you enter one or more of the following keywords after PRINT, only the requested output is displayed. Separate output is displayed for each split file and each METHOD subcommand.

DEFAULT   *Classification tables and statistics for variables in and not in the equation after each step.*

SUMMARY   *Summary information.* Same output as DEFAULT except that the output for each step is not displayed.

CORR   *Correlation matrix of parameter estimates for all parameters estimated in the model.*

ITER(n)   *Parameter estimates reported after each nth iteration during the solution.* Specify the iteration count for reporting parameter estimates in parentheses after ITER. If you omit the iteration count and parentheses, estimates are reported after each iteration.

ALL   *All available output.*

Example

```
LOGISTIC REGRESSION NODES WITH AGE,CATACID,XRAY,STAGE,GRADE
  /CATEGORICAL=CATACID /CONTRAST(CATACID)=INDICATOR.
  /PRINT=ITER(3) CORR.
```

- This example requests parameter estimates after every third iteration, plus a correlation matrix of the final parameter estimates.

CLASSPLOT Subcommand

To obtain a classification plot of the actual and predicted values of the dependent variable at each step, specify the CLASSPLOT subcommand. CLASSPLOT has no additional specifications.

Example

```
LOGISTIC REGRESSION NODES WITH AGE, ACID, XRAY, STAGE, GRADE
  /CLASSPLOT.
```

- This example displays a histogram of estimated probabilities of cancerous nodes. See Figure 1.4.

Requesting Diagnostic Statistics

Once you have built a model, you can display any of the diagnostic statistics or add them to your active file as new variables. Use the CASEWISE subcommand to list diagnostic statistics for each case in your file or for outliers only. Use the SAVE subcommand to add the statistics to your active file as new variables.

Available Diagnostic Statistics

The following diagnostic statistics are available for both the CASEWISE and SAVE subcommands. See "Diagnostic Methods" on p. 20 for discussion of these statistics.

PRED   *Predicted probability.*

PGROUP *Predicted group.*

RESID   *Difference between observed and predicted probability.*

DEV   *Deviance values.*

LRESID   *Logit residual.*

SRESID   *Studentized residual.*

ZRESID   *Standardized residual.*

LEVER   *Leverage value.*

COOK   *Analog of Cook's influence statistic.*

DFBETA *Difference in beta.* One value for DFBETA is produced for each coefficient in the model, including the constant.

CASEWISE Subcommand

Use the CASEWISE subcommand to obtain listings of any of the above statistics for each case in your file or for outliers only. After CASEWISE, enter one or more of the keywords listed in "Available Diagnostic Statistics," above, to display that statistic for all cases.

To obtain a casewise listing for outliers only, enter the following keyword along with one or more of the above:

OUTLIER(value)   *Display only cases for which the absolute value of SRESID, the Studentized residual, is greater than the specified value.* If you omit the value and the parentheses, a value of 2 is used.

Example

```
LOGISTIC REGRESSION NODES WITH AGE, ACID, XRAY, STAGE, GRADE
   /CASEWISE=PRED RESID DFBETA OUTLIER(2.5).
```

- For each case with a Studentized residual greater than 2.5, LOGISTIC REGRESSION displays the predicted probability of being in the second category of *nodes*, the residual, and the difference in each of the six regression coefficients if the case were omitted.

SAVE Subcommand

Use the SAVE subcommand to add any of the statistics listed in "Available Diagnostic Statistics" on p. 32 to your active file as new variables. LOGISTIC REGRESSION generates and reports names for the new variables and adds them to your file. To specify your own new variable names, include the name in parentheses after the corresponding statistics keyword. For the DFBETA keyword, which yields several variables, include a *root name* of seven characters or less in the parentheses.

Example

```
LOGISTIC REGRESSION NODES WITH AGE, ACID, XRAY, STAGE, GRADE
   /SAVE=PRED(NODEPROB) SRESID(RESID) DFBETA(INFL).
```

- This example adds eight new variables to the active file: *nodeprob* contains the estimated probability of the case having the second value for *node*; *resid* contains the case's Studentized residual; and the six variables *infl0* to *infl5* contain the differences in the constant and the five regression coefficients if the case were omitted.

ID Subcommand

Case listings produced by the CASEWISE subcommand are normally identified by case number. You can label the listing with the values or value labels of a variable in the file by using the ID subcommand. After ID, specify the name of a variable in the active file. LOGISTIC REGRESSION will label its casewise listing with the first eight characters of the value labels of that variable, if they are defined, or with the actual values of the variable otherwise.

Processing Large Data Files

Use the EXTERNAL subcommand when you are analyzing large data files to indicate that results should be held in temporary files rather than in memory. This makes it possible to analyze larger problems but increases processing time. There are no additional specifications on EXTERNAL.

2 General Factorial Analysis of Variance

In the *SPSS/PC+ Base System User's Guide*, you saw analysis-of-variance techniques applied to some simple problems. In this and subsequent chapters, you'll see how the SPSS/PC+ MANOVA procedure can be used to analyze simple analysis-of-variance problems in more detail, as well as more complicated problems.

A Simple Factorial Design

When you want to examine the effect of several independent variables (factors)—for example, type of gasoline and car model—on a dependent variable, such as gas mileage or acceleration, you can use a factorial experimental design. For example, if you want to study four types of gasoline and three models of cars, you would take cars of each of the different model types and randomly assign them to the different gasolines. Each type of car is called a **level** of the car factor and, similarly, each brand of gasoline is a level of the gasoline variable. Schematically, this design is shown in Table 2.1.

Table 2.1   A two-factor model

		Cars		
		Model A	Model B	Model C
Gasoline	Brand 1			
	Brand 2			
	Brand 3			
	Brand 4			

Table 2.1 contains 12 cells, one for each combination of the two factor variables: car model and gasoline brand. If you have 80 cars of each model available for your experiment, you would assign 20 of them to each brand of gasoline. You would have 20 different cars in each cell. If the same car is tested using all four brands of gasoline, you have a special type of experiment called a **repeated measures design**. Special statistical techniques are needed for analysis of such data. (See Chapter 4 for discussion of experiments where different levels of the same factor are applied to the same experi-

mental unit.) Why bother with this type of design? Why not do two separate experiments, one to assess the effect of different brands of gasoline on mileage and one to assess the effect of different models of cars on mileage? One of the advantages of a factorial design is that it can answer several important questions at once using the same cars. Not only can you draw conclusions about the effects of the different models and the different brands of gas, you can also test whether there is an interaction of the two factors. That is, do particular brands of gasoline perform better in certain models of cars?

Factorial designs are by no means limited to two factors; you can have many more. For example, if you were also interested in the effect of five different climates on mileage, you would have a three-factor design with 60 cells. There would be a cell for each possible combination of auto model, gas brand, and climate. You could then test not only for the effects of auto, gas, and climate, but also for interactions between all pairs of factors (two-way interactions) and the interaction of all three variables (the three-way interaction).

Where Are We?

To see how you would go about analyzing a factorial design in SPSS/PC+, let's consider a simple example from Winer et al. (1991). You are interested in determining the effectiveness of three instructors who teach map reading using two different methods. You have two factors of interest: the method of teaching (variable *method*), which has two levels, and the instructor (variable *inst*), which has three levels. Five subjects are randomly assigned to each of the six cells in the design. For each, you record a map-reading achievement test score before and after the training. First, we'll analyze just the difference between the post-test and the pretest scores (variable *dif*). In the section "An Analysis-of-Covariance Model" on p. 49, we'll use analysis of covariance to analyze the same type of data.

In all of the examples in this chapter, we will consider what are known as **fixed-effects designs**. These are designs in which the factors and levels under study are the only ones that you are interested in drawing conclusions about. This means that the two methods for teaching are not considered to be a sample from many possible methods for teaching map reading, and the three instructors are not considered to be a sample from a possible pool of instructors. Models in which the factor levels under study are considered a sample of possible levels are called **random-effects designs** (also known as **variance-component designs**). See Winer et al. (1991) for a discussion of such models.

Describing the Data

Before proceeding to a formal analysis of data, it's always a good idea to calculate descriptive statistics and displays. These will help you plan your analyses and interpret your results. Clustered boxplots showing each combination of method and instructor are shown in Figure 2.1. From the boxplots, you see that the median change scores for method 1 are a little lower than for method 2 and that instructor 3 has the smallest change score for both methods.

Figure 2.1   Boxplots for cells

```
SET WIDTH=WIDE.
MANOVA DIF BY METHOD(1,2)  INST(1,3)
 /PLOT=BOXPLOTS
 /DESIGN.
```

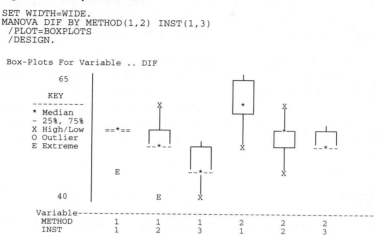

Means and standard deviations for each of the cells are shown in Figure 2.2. You see that all of the instructors have larger average change scores for method 2 than for method 1. You also see that the first instructor has the largest average scores for both methods, while the third instructor has the smallest average scores for both methods. The distribution of means for the six cells is shown in Figure 2.3. You see that three of the cell means are very close to each other, and two are somewhat distant from the rest.

Figure 2.2   Cell means

```
SET WIDTH=WIDE.
MANOVA DIF BY METHOD(1,2)  INST(1,3)
 /PRINT=CELLINFO(MEANS)
 /DESIGN.
```

Cell Means and Standard Deviations
Variable .. DIF

FACTOR	CODE	Mean	Std. Dev.	N	95 percent Conf. Interval	
METHOD	1					
INST	1	53.000	4.472	5	47.447	58.553
INST	2	51.000	7.416	5	41.792	60.208
INST	3	46.000	4.183	5	40.806	51.194
METHOD	2					
INST	1	59.600	6.189	5	51.916	67.284
INST	2	53.000	5.701	5	45.922	60.078
INST	3	52.000	2.739	5	48.600	55.400
For entire sample		52.433	6.328	30	50.070	54.796

Figure 2.3   Histogram of cell means

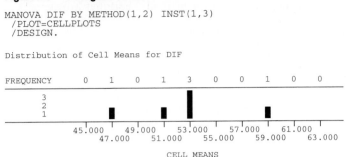

```
MANOVA DIF BY METHOD(1,2) INST(1,3)
  /PLOT=CELLPLOTS
  /DESIGN.

Distribution of Cell Means for DIF


FREQUENCY       0    1    0    1    3    0    0    1    0    0
      3
      2
      1               ▮         ▮    ▮              ▮

          45.000   49.000    53.000    57.000    61.000
             47.000     51.000    55.000    59.000    63.000

                          CELL MEANS
```

Equality of Variances

The assumptions needed for analysis of variance are that for each cell, the data are a random sample for a normal population and that in the population, all of the cell variances are the same. There are several ways to check the equality-of-variance assumption. You can compute the homogeneity-of-variance tests shown in Figure 2.4. For this example, neither test leads you to reject the null hypothesis that all population cell variances are equal. Both of the homogeneity-of-variance tests are sensitive to departures from normality, so you should keep this in mind when interpreting the results.

Figure 2.4   Homogeneity-of-variance tests

```
MANOVA DIF BY METHOD(1,2) INST(1,3)
  /PRINT HOMO(BARTLETT COCHRAN)
  /DESIGN.

Univariate Homogeneity of Variance Tests

  Variable .. DIF

        Cochrans C(4,6) =                  .32201, P =  .520 (approx.)
        Bartlett-Box F(5,741) =            .79055, P =  .557
```

One of the common ways in which the equality-of-variance assumption is violated is when the variances or standard deviations are proportional to the cell means. That is, larger variances are associated with larger values of the dependent variable. To look for a possible relationship between the variability and the cell means, you can plot the variances and standard deviations against the cell means, as shown in Figure 2.5 and Figure

2.6. In this example, there doesn't appear to be a relationship between the measures of variability and the cell means.

Figure 2.5　Plot of cell variances against cell means

```
MANOVA DIF BY METHOD(1,2) INST(1,3)
 /PLOT=CELLPLOTS
 /DESIGN.
```

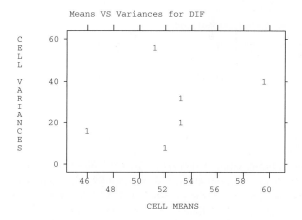

Figure 2.6　Plot of cell standard deviations against cell means

```
MANOVA DIF BY METHOD(1,2) INST(1,3)
 /PLOT=CELLPLOTS
 /DESIGN.
```

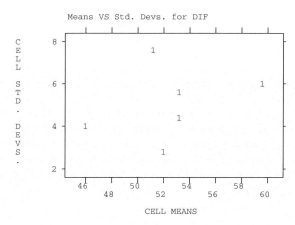

The Analysis-of-Variance Table

When you have a factorial design, you can test hypotheses about the **main effects** (the factor variables individually) and the **interactions** (various combinations of factor variables). Consider Figure 2.7, which is the analysis-of-variance table for the map-reading experiment. (For general discussion of the analysis-of-variance table, see the *SPSS/PC+ Base System User's Guide*.)

Figure 2.7   ANOVA table for full factorial model

```
MANOVA DIF BY METHOD(1,2) INST(1,3)
 /DESIGN.


Tests of Significance for DIF using UNIQUE sums of squares
  Source of Variation          SS        DF        MS          F   Sig of F

  WITHIN CELLS              683.20       24      28.47
  METHOD                    177.63        1     177.63       6.24     .020
  INST                      269.27        2     134.63       4.73     .019
  METHOD BY INST             31.27        2      15.63        .55     .585
```

The first row of the table is labeled *WITHIN CELLS*. The mean square for this term is the estimate of variability derived from the individual cells. The within-cells means square will be the denominator for the *F* tests in the ANOVA table.

The last row of the table, *METHOD BY INST*, provides a test of the method-by-instructor interaction. This tests the hypothesis that the effect of the methods is the same across the instructors. (For a more detailed discussion of interaction terms, see the Analysis of Variance chapter in the *SPSS/PC+ Base System User's Guide*.) This means that there are not particular combinations of methods and instructors that perform better or worse than we would expect based on considering the two effects, method and instructor, individually. In this example, the observed significance level for the interaction term is large ($p = 0.585$), so you cannot reject the null hypothesis that there is no interaction between the two variables. When you find a significant interaction term, you should not perform tests of the main effects, since it makes no sense to say that, overall, the methods or instructors differ or do not. In this situation, effectiveness depends on the combinations of instructors and methods, and you must consider both of the variables together when describing results.

The row labeled *METHOD* tests whether the two methods are equally effective for teaching map reading. Since the observed significance level is small ($p = 0.020$), you can reject the null hypothesis that the two methods are equally effective. The next row, labeled *INST*, is a test of the instructor effect. Again, since the observed significance level is small ($p = 0.019$), you can reject the null hypothesis that the three instructors are equally effective.

Full Factorial Model

In the example we've considered, there were two main-effect terms (method and instructor) and one interaction term (method by instructor). Since these three terms represent all of the possible main effects and the interaction, the model is said to be a **full factorial model**. All possible main-effect and interaction terms are included. When analyzing a factorial design, you need not include all possible terms in a model. Although you will usually include all main-effect terms, when the number of factors is large, you may want to suppress some of the higher-order interactions.

For example, if you have reason to believe that there is no method-by-instructor interaction, you can fit a model that includes only main effects. Figure 2.8 shows the analysis-of-variance table when the method-by-instructor interaction is not tested. Instead, it is included in the within+residual error term, which is now used for the denominator of the F tests.

Figure 2.8   ANOVA table for main-effects model

```
MANOVA DIF BY METHOD(1,2)  INST(1,3)
  /ERROR WITHIN+RESIDUAL
  /DESIGN=METHOD INST.

Tests of Significance for DIF using UNIQUE sums of squares
  Source of Variation          SS       DF       MS          F   Sig of F

  WITHIN+RESIDUAL            714.47     26     27.48
  METHOD                     177.63      1    177.63       6.46      .017
  INST                       269.27      2    134.63       4.90      .016
```

Examining Contrasts

An analysis-of-variance table provides summary results. It tells you whether there is a factor or interaction effect, but it doesn't pinpoint which factor levels are different. One way to examine factor level differences is to construct linear contrasts of their means. For example, you can compare the average of each factor level to the grand mean (the average overall factor levels). These are known as **deviation contrasts**.

To see how this is done, consider Figure 2.9, which shows the overall mean (from the SPSS/PC+ Descriptives procedure), and Figure 2.10, which shows the observed means for each of the method and instructor factor levels. (You'll note that two entries are printed for each level, one labeled *WGT* for weighted mean, the other *UNWGT* for unweighted mean. In this example, both entries are the same, since the same number of subjects is observed in each cell of the design. If there are different numbers of cases in the cells, unweighted means are obtained simply by averaging the means of the individual cells that are part of that effect. All cells contribute equally regardless of how many cases are in a cell. Weighted means take into account the number of cases in a cell, and average the cell means by weighting them by the number of cases in a cell.)

Figure 2.9   Descriptive statistics for change score

```
DESCRIPTIVES VARIABLES=DIF.
                                                  Valid
Variable      Mean    Std Dev   Minimum   Maximum   N   Label

DIF          52.43      6.33     40.00     65.00    30
```

Figure 2.10   Observed means by method and instructor

```
MANOVA DIF BY METHOD(1,2) INST(1,3)
 /OMEANS=TABLES(METHOD,INST)
 /DESIGN.
Combined Observed Means for METHOD
Variable .. DIF
      METHOD
          1           WGT.     50.00000
                      UNWGT.   50.00000
          2           WGT.     54.86667
                      UNWGT.   54.86667

- - - - - - - - - - - - - - - - - - - - - - - - - - - - - - - -
Combined Observed Means for INST
Variable .. DIF
        INST
          1           WGT.     56.30000
                      UNWGT.   56.30000
          2           WGT.     52.00000
                      UNWGT.   52.00000
          3           WGT.     49.00000
                      UNWGT.   49.00000
```

From Figure 2.9 and Figure 2.10, you can calculate the deviation contrasts, which are the differences between the mean for each level of a factor and the overall mean. For example, for method 1, the value of the deviation contrast is 50 (its value) minus 52.43 (the overall mean), or –2.43. For method 2, the deviation contrast is 54.86 minus 52.43, or 2.43. Similarly, for instructor 1, the deviation contrast is 56.30 minus 52.43, or 3.87.

The values for the deviation contrasts (labeled *Estimates for DIF*) are shown in Figure 2.11. The number of parameter estimates printed is one less than the number of levels of the factor. That's because you can always calculate what the values for the omitted factor are, based on the printed values. You can test the null hypothesis that the value of a parameter is 0, using the *t* value and its associated significance level. You can also compute confidence intervals for each of the parameters.

Figure 2.11   Deviation contrasts

```
MANOVA DIF BY METHOD(1,2) INST(1,3)
 /PRINT SIGNIF(EFSIZE)
 /POWER T(.05) F(.05)
 /CINTERVAL=INDIVIDUAL (.95)
 /DESIGN.
```

```
Effect Size Measures and Observed Power at the .0500 Level
                          Partial Noncen-
 Source of Variation      ETA Sqd trality      Power

 METHOD                    .20635 6.24005       .667
 INST                      .28270 9.45902       .736
 METHOD BY INST            .04376 1.09836       .132
```

```
Estimates for DIF
--- Individual univariate .9500 confidence intervals
--- two-tailed observed power taken at .0500 level

METHOD

 Parameter     Coeff.      Std. Err.      t-Value      Sig. t    Lower -95%    CL- Upper    Noncent.    Power

     2     -2.4333333333      .97411      -2.49801      .01974    -4.44380      -.42287      6.24005     .667

INST

 Parameter     Coeff.      Std. Err.      t-Value      Sig. t    Lower -95%    CL- Upper    Noncent.    Power

     3      3.8666666667     1.37760       2.80682      .00977     1.02344      6.70989     7.87822     .766
     4      -.4333333333     1.37760       -.31456      .75582    -3.27656      2.40989      .09895     .053
```

From the parameter estimates in Figure 2.11, you see that method 1 (labeled *Parameter 2*) has a change score significantly worse than average. Similarly, instructor 1 (*Parameter 3*) has an average change score significantly better than the average for the sample. Instructor 2, however, has a change score that does not differ significantly from the average of the change scores. The parameter estimate for instructor 3 is −3.433, since the coefficients for deviation parameter estimates must sum to 0 over all levels of a factor.

Simple Contrasts

The parameter estimates in Figure 2.11 are computed by comparing each level of the factor to the overall mean. This is but one of many types of contrasts that can be computed. (See "Specifying the Contrasts" on p. 111 for other types of contrasts available in SPSS/PC+.) Another type of contrast that is often used is called the **simple contrast**. With simple contrasts, you compare each level of a factor not to the average of all levels, but to a reference level. For example, if you choose the last category as the reference category (the default), you will obtain the parameter estimates shown in Figure 2.12. The values for the coefficients are the differences between each factor level and the last factor level. The coefficients for the last factor level, which are not printed, are all 0, since it is the reference to which the levels are compared.

Figure 2.12   Simple contrasts

```
MANOVA DIF BY METHOD(1,2) INST(1,3)
  /POWER T(.05) F(.05)
  /CONTRAST(INST)=SIMPLE
  /CONTRAST(METHOD)=SIMPLE
  /CINTERVAL=JOINT (.95) UNIVARIATE (BONFER)
  /DESIGN.
```

```
Estimates for DIF
 --- Joint univariate .9500 BONFERRONI confidence intervals
 --- two-tailed observed power taken at .0500 level
```

METHOD

Parameter	Coeff.	Std. Err.	t-Value	Sig. t	Lower -95%	CL- Upper	Noncent.	Power
2	-4.8666667	1.94822	-2.49801	.01974	-8.88759	-.84574	6.24005	.667

INST

Parameter	Coeff.	Std. Err.	t-Value	Sig. t	Lower -95%	CL- Upper	Noncent.	Power
3	7.30000000	2.38607	3.05942	.00539	1.59503	13.00497	9.36007	.834
4	3.00000000	2.38607	1.25730	.22074	-2.70497	8.70497	1.58080	.225

The Problem of Multiple Comparisons

In the One-Way Analysis of Variance chapter in the *SPSS/PC+ Base System User's Guide*, we discussed the problems associated with making many nonindependent comparisons. As the number of comparisons increases, so does the probability that you will call a difference "statistically significant" when, in fact, it is not. The same problem occurs when you examine a set of contrasts. As the number of contrasts you examine increases, so does the likelihood that you will call differences "significant" when they are not. Multiple-comparison procedures similar to those used for comparing all possible pairs of means can be used for contrasts as well. The goal is the same—to provide control over the Type 1 error rate. (Remember, a Type 1 error occurs when you reject the null hypothesis when, in fact, it is true.)

The SPSS/PC+ MANOVA procedure can be used to calculate confidence intervals for parameters using a Bonferroni or Scheffé correction. These intervals are known as **simultaneous confidence intervals** (sometimes called **joint confidence intervals**), since they are constructed for all of the parameters together. Both of these methods result in wider confidence intervals than when no protection for multiple comparisons is made. The Bonferroni method is based on the number of comparisons actually made, while the Scheffé method is based on all possible contrasts. For a large number of contrasts, Bonferroni intervals will be wider than the Scheffé intervals. Both the Scheffé and Bonferroni intervals are computed separately for each term in the design. See Timm (1975) for a discussion of the comparative merits of the intervals.

Once again, consider Figure 2.12. The confidence intervals in the figure are simultaneous Bonferroni confidence intervals. To compute Bonferroni protected tests for each of the parameters, do not use the *Sig. t* entry, but instead determine whether the 95%

confidence interval for a parameter includes 0. If it does, you cannot reject the null hypothesis that in the population the parameter value is 0, using a 5% significance level.

Measuring Effect Size

In a one-way analysis-of-variance design, the **eta-squared statistic** is sometimes used to describe the proportion of the total variability "explained" by the grouping or factor variable. A value close to 1 indicates that all of the total variability is attributable to differences between the groups, while a value close to 0 indicates that the grouping variable explains little of the total variability. Eta squared is sometimes called an **effect-size measure**.

For a factorial design, you can compute several effect size measures based on the eta-squared statistic. The **partial eta-squared statistic** has the same numerator as the eta-squared statistic: the sum of squares for the effect of interest. But instead of the total sum of squares in the denominator, it has the sum of the sum of squares for error and the sum of squares for the effect of interest. From Figure 2.11, you see that the partial eta squared for the method effect is 0.21 ($177.63 / (177.63 + 683.20)$).

Power Computations

Whenever you perform an experiment or conduct a study, you should be concerned with **power** (your ability to reject the null hypothesis when it is false). In general, power depends on the magnitude of the true differences and the sample sizes. If the true differences are very large, even small sample sizes should detect them. If, on the other hand, the true differences are small, you will need large sample sizes to detect them. Your decision on how many experimental units to include in your study should be based on power considerations. That is, you want your sample to be large enough that you stand a good chance of detecting differences you consider important. See Cohen (1977) for a discussion of power analysis.

Sometimes it is also useful to evaluate power after an experiment has been completed. You calculate the probability that you would call your observed difference statistically significant at a chosen alpha level based on the sample size used. For example, consider the simple situation of two independent groups with 10 cases in each. If you found that the difference in average change scores was 7 and the pooled estimate of the standard deviation within a group was 10, you could calculate, based on tables available in Cohen (1977), that your power of detecting this difference, using a 5% significance level for the t test, would be about 0.31. This means that more than half of the time you conducted such an experiment, you would fail to reject the null hypothesis when, in fact, it was false. Thus, even though on the basis of your sample data you failed to reject the null hypothesis that the true difference is 0 (your t value is only 1.57), you know that your experiment had limited power to detect a true difference of 7 points or less.

For analysis-of-variance models, the computation of power is considerably more complicated. However, the basic idea is the same as for the *t* test. You assume that the observed effect size is a true difference, and, based on the sample size you have used and the alpha level you have selected, you calculate the probability that you would have rejected the null hypothesis. If the power is small, you're not very confident about a decision not to reject the null hypothesis. Figure 2.11 shows the power values for the terms in the map-reading example.

Examining Residuals

Once you have estimated an analysis-of-variance model, you can examine the residuals to see how well it fits the data. For each case, you have an observed value and can calculate a predicted value based on the model. (To calculate a predicted value, you estimate parameters for each of the terms in your model.) Figure 2.13 is a listing of the residuals. For each of the cases, you see the observed or actual change score, the score predicted from the model, the raw residual, and the standardized residual. The raw residual is the difference between the observed and predicted values. The standardized residual is the raw residual divided by an estimate of its standard deviation. In this example, the standard deviation is the square root of the within-cells mean square.

Figure 2.13   Residuals listing

```
MANOVA DIF BY METHOD(1,2) INST(1,3)
   /RESIDUAL=CASEWISE
   /DESIGN.

Observed and Predicted Values for Each Case
  Dependent Variable.. DIF

  Case No.      Observed   Predicted Raw Resid. Std Resid.

        1       55.000      53.000      2.000       .375
        2       45.000      53.000     -8.000     -1.499
        3       55.000      53.000      2.000       .375
        4       55.000      53.000      2.000       .375
        5       55.000      53.000      2.000       .375
        6       55.000      51.000      4.000       .750
        7       60.000      51.000      9.000      1.687
        8       40.000      51.000    -11.000     -2.062
        9       50.000      51.000     -1.000      -.187
       10       50.000      51.000     -1.000      -.187
       11       40.000      46.000     -6.000     -1.125
       12       45.000      46.000     -1.000      -.187
       13       50.000      46.000      4.000       .750
       14       50.000      46.000      4.000       .750
       15       45.000      46.000     -1.000      -.187
       16       50.000      59.600     -9.600     -1.799
       17       65.000      59.600      5.400      1.012
       18       60.000      59.600       .400       .075
       19       65.000      59.600      5.400      1.012
       20       58.000      59.600     -1.600      -.300
       21       50.000      53.000     -3.000      -.562
       22       60.000      53.000      7.000      1.312
       23       55.000      53.000      2.000       .375
       24       45.000      53.000     -8.000     -1.499
       25       55.000      53.000      2.000       .375
       26       50.000      52.000     -2.000      -.375
       27       55.000      52.000      3.000       .562
       28       50.000      52.000     -2.000      -.375
       29       55.000      52.000      3.000       .562
       30       50.000      52.000     -2.000      -.375
```

You can also look at various plots of the residuals to see if the analysis-of-variance assumptions have been violated. You should not see a pattern in the plot of residuals against predicted values (Figure 2.14). If the spread of the residuals increases with the magnitude of the predicted values, you have reason to suspect that the variance may not be constant in all cells. If the model fits and the assumption of normality is not violated, the distribution of residuals should be approximately normal. Figure 2.15 is a plot of observed residuals against those expected from a normal distribution. If the normality assumption is not violated, the points should fall more or less on the normal line. Figure 2.16 is a detrended normal plot that shows the distances between the observed points and the expected line. You should not see any pattern in a detrended plot if the assumption of normality is met.

Figure 2.14 Scatterplot matrix of observed and predicted values and residuals

```
MANOVA DIF BY METHOD(1,2) INST(1,3)
  /RESIDUAL=PLOT
  /DESIGN.
```

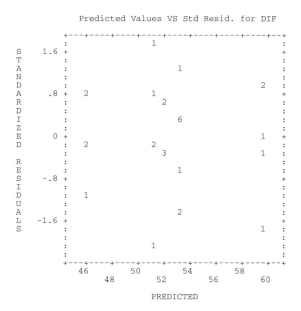

Figure 2.15   Normal probability plot of standardized residuals

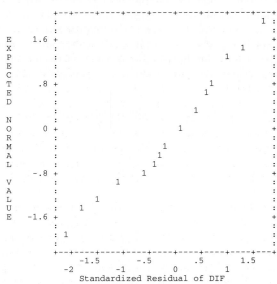

Figure 2.16   Detrended normal plot of standardized residuals

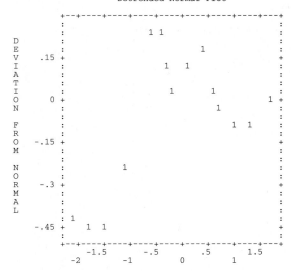

An Analysis-of-Covariance Model

In the map-reading experiment, we had two variables for each subject—the score before the training program and the score after the training program. We had two variables because we knew that differences in final scores are attributable not only to differences between the methods and the instructors but also to differences among the subjects. Everyone did not read maps equally well before the training started. By considering the differences between the two scores, we controlled for some of the initial differences among subjects. In this experiment, the two scores were obtained from similar tests, so computing differences between the two measurements was reasonable.

If we didn't use a pretest but instead recorded a variable, such as IQ or years of education, thought to be related to map-reading aptitude, we couldn't analyze the data by simply computing differences. Instead, we'd need a statistical technique that would allow us to incorporate initial differences among subjects in our analysis.

Analysis of covariance is a statistical technique that can be thought of as a combination of linear regression analysis and analysis of variance. The analysis-of-variance results are adjusted for the linear relationships between the dependent variable and the covariates.

To see how analysis of covariance is used, consider the following example from Winer et al. (1991). Seven subjects are randomly assigned to each of three methods for teaching a course. The dependent variable is a measure of achievement after completing the course. The covariate is an aptitude score obtained prior to the course. Figure 2.17 is a plot of the achievement and aptitude scores for subjects in the three groups. You see that there is a fairly strong linear relationship between the two variables. This is important, since if there were no linear relationship between the two variables, it would make little sense to try to adjust achievement scores based on aptitude scores using a linear regression model. From the plot, it also appears that the relationship between the two variables is similar in the three teaching groups. That is, the three groups have almost parallel regression lines.

Figure 2.17   Plot of achievement against aptitude score

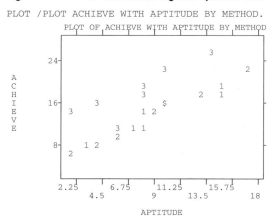

As a first step, let's see what the analysis-of-variance table for achievement looks like when we ignore the aptitude scores (see Figure 2.18). You see that, based on the observed significance level for the method effect, there is not sufficient evidence to reject the null hypothesis that all three teaching methods are equally effective.

Figure 2.18   Analysis-of-variance table for achievement

```
MANOVA ACHIEVE BY METHOD(1,3).

Tests of Significance for ACHIEVE using UNIQUE sums of squares
Source of Variation          SS        DF       MS         F  Sig of F

  WITHIN CELLS            436.57       18      24.25
  METHOD                   94.10        2      47.05       1.94      .173
```

Now let's see what happens when we adjust for initial differences between the aptitudes of the subjects in the three groups. Our goal will be to decrease the error sums of squares by removing the variability due to differences in aptitudes.

Testing for Equal Slopes

Before we perform the analysis of covariance, we have to determine whether it is reasonable to assume that the slopes of the lines relating achievement and aptitude are the same in the three groups. From visual inspection of Figure 2.17, that seemed plausible, but we need a formal test. Figure 2.19 contains the analysis-of-variance table that can be used to test whether the slopes of the regression line are the same in all three groups. The term of interest is the method-by-aptitude interaction. If this interaction is significant, you reject the hypothesis that the slope is the same for all three methods. In this example, the interaction is not significant, so we will fit an analysis-of-covariance model with a common slope. (If the assumption of a common slope is rejected, you can fit separate slopes for each of the cells).

Figure 2.19   Test of homogeneity of slopes

```
MANOVA ACHIEVE BY METHOD(1,3) WITH APTITUDE
  /ANALYSIS ACHIEVE
  /DESIGN APTITUDE METHOD METHOD BY APTITUDE.
Tests of Significance for ACHIEVE using UNIQUE sums of squares
Source of Variation          SS        DF       MS         F  Sig of F

  WITHIN+RESIDUAL          38.11       15       2.54
  APTITUDE               370.97        1     370.97     146.00     .000
  METHOD                  31.24        2      15.62       6.15     .011
  METHOD BY APTITUDE       2.62        2       1.31        .52     .607
```

The Analysis-of-Covariance Table

The analysis-of-covariance table for this example is shown in Figure 2.20. You see that there is a row of the table that is labeled *REGRESSION*. This is a test of the hypothesis that the common slope is 0. Since the observed significance level is very small, you can reject the null hypothesis that the slope is 0.

Figure 2.20   Analysis-of-covariance table for achievement

```
MANOVA ACHIEVE BY METHOD(1,3) WITH APTITUDE
  /ANALYSIS ACHIEVE WITH APTITUDE
  /DESIGN.

Tests of Significance for ACHIEVE using UNIQUE sums of squares
Source of Variation        SS      DF      MS        F   Sig of F

WITHIN CELLS             40.74     17     2.40
REGRESSION              395.84      1   395.84    165.19     .000
METHOD                  169.52      2    84.76     35.37     .000
```

Consider again the row labeled *METHOD*. Looking at the observed significance level, you see that you can now reject the null hypothesis that all three teaching methods are equally effective. Why has the conclusion changed from that obtained in Figure 2.18? The reason is that we have dramatically decreased the within-cells variability, the denominator for the *F* test, by eliminating the variability due to differences in aptitude. Our estimate of variability in each of the cells is now "purer."

From Figure 2.21, you see that the estimate of the common slope is 1.033. This estimate can be used to compute what are called **adjusted means** for each of the cells of the design. The basic idea is to estimate what the mean achievement score for each group would be if the aptitude score were the same for all groups. To compute adjusted means, we must know what the average value of the covariate is in each of the teaching methods. These values, from the SPSS/PC+ Means procedure, are shown in Figure 2.22. For method 1, the average aptitude score was 9.43; for method 2, 8.71; and for method 3, 7.43. The overall average aptitude score was 8.52. So you see that for method 1, the average aptitude score is quite a bit higher than average, while for method 3, it is somewhat less than average. The observed mean achievement scores for each of the groups is shown in Figure 2.23 in the column labeled *Obs. Mean*. To calculate what the mean for each group would be if the average aptitude score were 8.52 (the adjusted mean), you must calculate how much above or below average each group is compared to the overall average and then adjust the observed mean accordingly. The formula is:

$$\text{adjusted mean}_j = \text{observed mean}_j - \text{slope}\,(\text{mean}_j - \text{unweighted grand mean})$$

Equation 2.1

Using Equation 2.1, the adjusted mean for method 1 is:

$$\text{adjusted mean}_{\text{method 1}} = 14.29 - 1.03\,(9.43 - 8.52) = 13.35$$

Equation 2.2

The adjusted mean is less than the observed mean, since the average value of the aptitude score was higher for method 1 than for the other methods. The adjusted means for the three methods are shown in Figure 2.23 in the column labeled *Adj. Mean*. Compar-

isons between groups should be based on these adjusted means, not on the original
means.

Figure 2.21   Regression statistics for aptitude score

```
MANOVA ACHIEVE BY METHOD(1,3) WITH APTITUDE
  /ANALYSIS ACHIEVE WITH APTITUDE
  /PMEANS TABLE(METHOD)
  /DESIGN.
```

```
Regression analysis for WITHIN CELLS error term
--- Individual Univariate .9500 confidence intervals
Dependent variable .. ACHIEVE
```

COVARIATE	B	Beta	Std. Err.	t-Value	Sig. of t	Lower -95% CL- Upper	
APTITUDE	1.03313	.95220	.080	12.853	.000	.864	1.203

Figure 2.22   Means for aptitude score

```
MEANS APTITUDE BY METHOD.
```

```
Summaries of      APTITUDE
By levels of      METHOD
```

Variable	Value Label	Mean	Std Dev	Cases
For Entire Population		8.5238	4.3888	21
METHOD	1.00	9.4286	4.3534	7
METHOD	2.00	8.7143	5.2190	7
METHOD	3.00	7.4286	3.9521	7

```
  Total Cases = 21
```

Figure 2.23   Observed and adjusted means

```
MANOVA ACHIEVE BY METHOD(1,3) WITH APTITUDE
  /ANALYSIS ACHIEVE WITH APTITUDE
  /PMEANS TABLE(METHOD)
  /DESIGN.
```

```
Adjusted and Estimated Means
Variable .. ACHIEVE
```

CELL	Obs. Mean	Adj. Mean	Est. Mean	Raw Resid.	Std. Resid.
1	14.286	13.351	14.286	.000	.000
2	13.429	13.232	13.429	.000	.000
3	18.286	19.417	18.286	.000	.000

More Than One Factor

Although analysis of covariance was illustrated using only one covariate and one grouping
factor, its use is not restricted to these situations. You can include any number of covariates that are linearly related to the dependent variable. Similarly, you can use analysis of
variance for any type of factorial design. When you have several factors, however, testing
for a common slope is more complicated. For further discussion, see MANOVA: Univariate in the Syntax Reference section of this manual.

Types of Sums of Squares

The examples in this chapter had the same number of cases in each of the cells of the design. This greatly simplifies the interpretation of the ANOVA hypotheses. When the number of cases in all of the cells is not equal—that is, when the design is **unbalanced**—several different types of sums of squares can be computed. Different sums of squares correspond to tests of different hypotheses. Two frequently used methods for calculating sums of squares are the **regression method** and the **sequential method**. In the regression method, all effects are adjusted for all other effects in the model. In the sequential method, an effect is adjusted only for effects that precede it in the model.

For any connected design, the hypotheses associated with sequential sums of squares are weighted functions of the population cell means, with weights depending on cell frequencies (Searle, 1971). For designs in which every cell contains observations, the hypotheses corresponding to the regression sums of squares are hypotheses about unweighted cell means. With empty cells, the hypotheses depend on the pattern of missing cells.

When your design contains empty cells, the analysis is greatly complicated. Hypotheses that involve parameters corresponding to empty cells usually cannot be tested. The output from an analysis involving empty cells should be treated with caution (see Milliken & Johnson, 1984).

Running the MANOVA Procedure

See "Running the MANOVA Procedure" on p. 99.

Annotated Example

The following example produces display output shown in Figure 2.1 to Figure 2.16 except Figure 2.8, which illustrates a test of the main effects only, and Figure 2.12, which uses simple contrasts.

```
SET WIDTH=WIDE.
DATA LIST FREE /METHOD INST PRESCORE PSTSCORE.
COMPUTE DIF=PSTSCORE-PRESCORE.
BEGIN DATA
data lines
END DATA.
MANOVA DIF BY METHOD(1,2) INST(1,3)
 /PRINT=CELLINFO(MEANS)  HOMO(BARTLETT COCHRAN)
        PARM(ESTIM) SIGNIF(EFSIZE)
 /POWER=T(.05) F(.05)
 /RESIDUAL=CASEWISE PLOT
 /OMEANS=TABLES(METHOD,INST)
 /PLOT=BOXPLOTS CELLPLOTS
 /DESIGN.
```

- The SET command sets the width of display to 132 characters to permit listing of all statistics, including percentages.
- The DATA LIST command reads in the variables in freefield format.
- The COMPUTE command computes the dependent variable *dif* as the difference between the post-test and the pretest scores (*pstscore* and *prescore*).
- The BEGIN DATA and END DATA commands surround the inline data.
- MANOVA specifies *dif* as the dependent variable and *method* and *inst* as the factors.
- No CONTRAST subcommand is specified. The default deviation contrast is used.
- The PRINT subcommand requests cell means (Figure 2.2), Bartlett and Cochran tests of homogeneity of variance (Figure 2.4), the estimated parameters with their standard errors, *t* tests and confidence levels, and the effect size values (Figure 2.11).
- The POWER subcommand requests observed power values (Figure 2.11).
- The RESIDUAL subcommand requests both casewise listing and plots of observed, predicted, residual, and standardized residual values for *dif* (Figure 2.13 to Figure 2.16).
- The OMEANS subcommand requests a table of observed means of *dif* for levels of both factors, *method* and *inst* (Figure 2.10).
- The PLOT subcommand requests boxplots (Figure 2.1) and cell-means plots (Figure 2.5 and Figure 2.6) for *dif*, useful in checking the assumptions needed in the analysis.

3 Multivariate Analysis of Variance

Tilted houses featured in amusement parks capitalize on the challenge of navigating one's way in the presence of misleading visual cues. It's difficult to maintain balance when walls are no longer parallel and rooms assume strange shapes. We are all dependent on visual information to guide movement, but the extent of this dependence has been found to vary considerably.

Based on a series of experiments, Witkin et al. (1954) classified individuals into two categories: those who can ignore misleading visual cues, termed field-independent, and those who cannot, termed field-dependent. Field dependence has been linked to a variety of psychological characteristics such as self-image and intelligence. Psychologists theorize that it derives from childhood socialization patterns—field-dependent children learn to depend on highly structured environments while field-independent children learn to cope with ambiguous situations.

In this chapter, the relationship between field dependence, sex, and various motor abilities is examined using data reported by Barnard (1973). Students (63 female and 71 male) from the College of Southern Idaho were administered a test of field independence: the rod and frame test. On the basis of this test, subjects were classified as field-dependent, field-independent, or intermediate. Four tests of motor ability were also conducted: two tests of balance, a test of gross motor skills, and a test of fine motor skills.

For the balance test, subjects were required to maintain balance while standing on one foot on a rail. Two trials for each of two conditions, eyes open and eyes closed, were administered, and the average number of seconds a subject maintained balance under each condition was recorded (variables $x10$ to $x13$). Gross motor coordination was assessed with the sidestepping test. For this test, three parallel lines are drawn four feet apart on the floor and a subject stands on the middle line. At the start signal, the subject must sidestep to the left until the left foot crosses the left line. He or she then sidesteps to the right until the right line is crossed. A subject's score is the average number of lines crossed in three ten-second trials (variables $x14$ to $x16$). The Purdue Pegboard Test was used to quantify fine motor skills. Subjects are required to place small pegs into holes using only the left hand, only the right hand, and then both hands simultaneously. The number of pegs placed in two 30-second trials for each condition was recorded and the average over six trials calculated (variables $x17$ to $x22$).

The experiment described above is fairly typical of many investigations. There are several classification, or independent, variables—sex and field independence in this case—and a dependent variable. The goal of the experiment is to examine the relationship between the classification variables and the dependent variable. For example, is motor ability related to field dependence? Does the relationship differ for men and women? Analysis-of-variance techniques are usually used to answer these questions, as discussed in Chapter 2.

In this experiment, however, the dependent variable is not a single measure but four different scores obtained for each student. Although ANOVA tests can be computed separately for each of the dependent variables, this approach ignores the interrelation among the dependent variables. Substantial information may be lost when correlations between variables are ignored. For example, several bivariate regression analyses cannot substitute for a multiple regression model, which considers the independent variables jointly. Only when the independent variables are uncorrelated with each other are the bivariate and multivariate regression results equivalent. Similarly, analyzing multiple two-dimensional tables cannot substitute for an analysis that considers the variables simultaneously.

Multivariate Analysis of Variance

The extension of univariate analysis of variance to the case of multiple dependent variables is termed **multivariate analysis of variance**, abbreviated as MANOVA. Univariate analysis of variance is just a special case of MANOVA, the case with a single dependent variable. The hypotheses tested with MANOVA are similar to those tested with ANOVA. The difference is that sets of means (sometimes called a **vector**) replace the individual means specified in ANOVA. In a one-way design, for example, the hypothesis tested is that the populations from which the groups are selected have the same means for all dependent variables. Thus, the hypothesis might be that the population means for the four motor-ability variables are the same for the three field-dependence categories.

Assumptions

For the case of a single dependent variable, the following assumptions are necessary for the proper application of the ANOVA test: the groups must be random samples from normal populations with the same variance. Similar assumptions are necessary for MANOVA. Since we are dealing with several dependent variables, however, we must make assumptions about their joint distribution—that is, the distribution of the variables considered together. The extension of the ANOVA assumptions to MANOVA requires that the dependent variables have a multivariate normal distribution with the same variance-covariance matrix in each group. A **variance-covariance matrix**, as its name indicates, is a square arrangement of elements with the variances of the variables on the diagonal, and the covariances of pairs of variables off the diagonal. A variance-covariance matrix can be transformed into a correlation matrix by dividing each covariance by the standard deviations of the two variables. Later in this chapter, we present tests for these assumptions.

One-Sample Hotelling's T^2

Before considering more complex generalizations of ANOVA techniques, let's consider the simple one-sample t test and its extension to the case of multiple dependent variables. As you will recall, the one-sample t test is used to test the hypothesis that the sample originates from a population with a known mean. For example, you might want to test the hypothesis that schizophrenics do not differ in mean IQ from the general population, which is assumed to have a mean IQ of 100. If additional variables such as reading comprehension, mathematical aptitude, and motor dexterity are also to be considered, a test that allows comparison of several observed means to a set of constants is required.

A test developed by Hotelling, called Hotelling's T^2, is often used for this purpose. It is the simplest example of MANOVA. To illustrate this test and introduce some of the SPSS/PC+ MANOVA procedure output, we will use the field-dependence and motorability data to test the hypothesis that the observed sample comes from a population with specified values for the means of the four tests. That is, we will assume that normative data are available for the four tests and we will test the hypothesis that our sample is from a population having the normative means.

For illustrative purposes, the standard values are taken to be 13 seconds for balancing with eyes open, 3 seconds for balancing with eyes closed, 18 lines for the sidestepping test, and 10 pegs for the pegboard test. Since the MANOVA procedure automatically tests the hypothesis that a set of means is equal to 0, we subtract the normative values from the observed scores prior to the MANOVA analysis to test the hypothesis that the differences are 0.

Figure 3.1 contains the message displayed by SPSS/PC+ when the cases are processed. It indicates the number of cases to be used in the analysis as well as the number of cases to be excluded. In this example, 134 cases will be included in the analysis. SPSS/PC+ also indicates whether any cases contain missing values for the variables being analyzed or have independent-variable (factor) values outside the designated range. Such cases are excluded from the analysis.

Since the hypothesis being tested involves only a test of a single sample, all observations are members of one **cell**, in ANOVA terminology. If two independent samples, for example, males and females, were compared, two cells would exist. The last line of Figure 3.1 indicates how many different MANOVA models have been specified.

Figure 3.1   Case information

```
COMPUTE  BALOMEAN=((X10+X11)/2)-13.
COMPUTE  BALCMEAN=((X12+X13)/2)-3.
COMPUTE  SSTMEAN=((X14+X15+X16)/3)-18.
COMPUTE  PP=((X17+X18+X19+X20+X21+X22)/6)-10.
MANOVA BALOMEAN BALCMEAN SSTMEAN PP
 /DESIGN.

134 cases accepted.
 0 cases rejected because of out-of-range factor values.
 0 cases rejected because of missing data.
 1 non-empty cell.

 1 design will be processed.
```

Descriptive Statistics

One of the first steps in any statistical analysis, regardless of how simple or complex it may be, is examination of the individual variables. This preliminary screening provides information about a variable's distribution and permits identification of unusual or outlying values.

Of course, when multivariate analyses are undertaken, it is not sufficient just to look at the characteristics of the variables individually. Information about their joint distribution must also be obtained. Similarly, identification of outliers must be based on the joint distribution of variables. For example, a height of six feet is not very unusual, and neither is a weight of 100 pounds, nor being a man. A six-foot-tall male who weighs 100 pounds, however, is fairly atypical and needs to be identified to ascertain that the values have been correctly recorded, and if so, to gauge the effect of such a lean physique on subsequent analyses. (See the discussion on Mahalanobis distance and Cook's distance and deleted residuals in the Multiple Regression chapter in the *SPSS/PC+ Base System User's Guide.*)

Figure 3.2 contains means and confidence intervals for each of the four motor-ability variables after the normative values have been subtracted. The sample exceeds the norm for balancing with eyes closed (*balcmean*) and peg insertion (*pp*) and is poorer than the norm for balancing with eyes open (*balomean*) and sidestepping (*sstmean*). The only confidence interval that includes 0 is for the balancing-with-eyes-closed variable.

Figure 3.2   Cell means and confidence intervals

```
MANOVA BALOMEAN BALCMEAN SSTMEAN PP
  /PRINT= CELLINFO(MEANS)
  /DESIGN.
```

```
Cell Means and Standard Deviations
Variable .. BALOMEAN            Balance Test -- Eyes Open
                                        Mean   Std. Dev.         N    95 percent Conf. Interval

For entire sample                      -1.540     5.860         134    -2.541      -.539

- - - - - - - - - - - - - - - - - - - - - - - - - - - - - - - - - - - - - - - - - - - - - - - -
Variable .. BALCMEAN            Balance Test -- Eyes Closed
                                        Mean   Std. Dev.         N    95 percent Conf. Interval

For entire sample                        .143     1.405         134    -.097       .383

- - - - - - - - - - - - - - - - - - - - - - - - - - - - - - - - - - - - - - - - - - - - - - - -
Variable .. SSTMEAN             Sidestepping Test
                                        Mean   Std. Dev.         N    95 percent Conf. Interval

For entire sample                      -2.597     2.681         134    -3.055     -2.139

- - - - - - - - - - - - - - - - - - - - - - - - - - - - - - - - - - - - - - - - - - - - - - - -
Variable .. PP                  Purdue Pegboard Test
                                        Mean   Std. Dev.         N    95 percent Conf. Interval

For entire sample                       4.973     1.495         134     4.717      5.228
```

The 95% confidence intervals that are displayed are individual confidence intervals. This means that no adjustment has been made for the fact that the confidence intervals for several variables have been computed. We have 95% confidence that each of the individual intervals contains the unknown parameter value. We do not have 95% confidence that *all* intervals considered jointly contain the unknown parameters. The distinction here is closely related to the problem of multiple comparisons in ANOVA.

When many tests are done, the chance that some observed differences appear to be statistically significant when there are no true differences in the populations increases with the number of comparisons made. To protect against calling too many differences "real" when in fact they are not, the criterion for how large a difference must be before it is considered significant is made more stringent. That is, larger differences are required, depending on the number of comparisons made. The larger the number of comparisons, the greater the observed difference must be. Similarly, if a confidence region that simultaneously contains values of observed population parameters with a specified overall confidence level is to be constructed, the confidence interval for each variable must be wider than that needed if only one variable is considered.

Further Displays for Checking Assumptions

Although the summary statistics presented in Figure 3.2 provide some information about the distributions of the dependent variables, more detailed information is often desirable. Figure 3.3 is a stem-and-leaf plot of the pegboard variable. Stem-and-leaf plots provide a convenient way to examine the distribution of a variable.

Figure 3.3   Stem-and-leaf plot for pegboard test

```
EXAMINE PP
 /PLOT STEMLEAF.


     PP         Purdue Pegboard Test


 Frequency    Stem &  Leaf

     3.00         1 .  138
     9.00         2 .  033668888
    23.00         3 .  0133355555556666668888
    31.00         4 .  00111111111135555555556666668888
    31.00         5 .  000001111113335555555556666688888
    23.00         6 .  00001111133335566666668
    12.00         7 .  000001135668
     1.00         8 .  1
     1.00  Extremes   (9.3)

 Stem width:      1.00
 Each leaf:       1 case(s)
```

In Figure 3.3, the numbers to the left of the dotted line are called the **stem**, while those to the right are the **leaves**. Each case is represented by a leaf. For example, the first line of the plot is for a case with a value of 1.1 and a case with a value of 1.3 (the actual values for these cases are 1.17 and 1.33, but the plot uses only the first decimal place). The stem (1) is the same for both cases, while the values of the leaves (1 and 3) differ. When there are several cases with the same values, the leaf value is repeated. For example, there are two cases with a value of 2.6 and four cases with a value of 2.8. In this example, each stem value occurs twice—once for cases with leaves 0 through 4 and once for cases with leaves 5 through 9. This is not always the case, since the stem values depend on the actual data. In this example, the decimal point for each case occurs between the value of the stem and the leaf. This also is not always the case. The SPSS/PC+ Examine procedure scales the variables so that the stem-and-leaf plot is based on the number of significant digits. Since the purpose of the plot is to display the distribution of the variable, the actual scale is not important. The final row of the stem-and-leaf plot, labeled *Extremes*, shows cases with values far removed from the rest. In the frequency column, we see that there is one extreme case that has a pegboard test value of 9.3.

One assumption needed for hypothesis testing in MANOVA is the assumption that the dependent variables have a multivariate normal distribution. If variables have a multivariate normal distribution, each one taken individually must be normally distributed. (However, variables that are normally distributed individually will not necessarily have a multivariate normal distribution when considered together.) The stem-and-leaf plots for each variable allow us to assess the reasonableness of the normality assumption, since if any distribution appears to be markedly non-normal, the assumption of multivariate normality is likely to be violated.

Normal Plots

Although the stem-and-leaf plot gives a rough idea of the normality of the distribution of a variable, other plots that are especially designed for assessing normality can also be obtained. For example, we can assess normality using a normal probability plot, which is obtained by ranking the observed values of a variable from the smallest to the largest and then pairing each value with an expected normal value for a sample of that size from a standard normal distribution.

Figure 3.4 is a normal probability plot of the pegboard variable. If the observed scores are from a normal distribution, points in the plot should be approximately in a straight line. Since the distribution of the pegboard scores appeared fairly normal in the stem-and-leaf plot (Figure 3.3), the normal probability plot should be fairly linear, and it is.

Figure 3.4   Normal probability plot for pegboard test

```
MANOVA BALOMEAN BALCMEAN SSTMEAN PP
   /PLOT NORMAL
   /DESIGN.
```

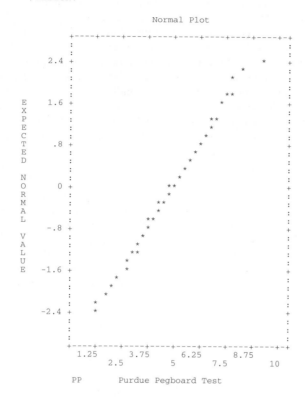

To further assess the linearity of the normal probability plot, we can calculate the difference between the observed point and the expected point under the assumption of normality and plot this difference for each case. If the observed sample is from a normal distribution, these differences should be fairly close to 0 and be randomly distributed.

Figure 3.5 is a plot of the differences for the normal probability plot shown in Figure 3.4. This plot is called a **detrended normal plot**, since the trend in Figure 3.4 has been removed. Note that the values fall roughly in a horizontal band around 0, though there appears to be some pattern. Also notice the two outliers, one in the lower-left corner and the other in the upper-right corner. These correspond to the smallest and largest observations in the sample and indicate that the observed distribution doesn't have quite as much spread in the tails as expected. For the smallest value, the deviation from the expected line is negative, indicating that the smallest value is not quite as large as would be expected. For the largest value, the value is not as small as would be expected. Since most of the points cluster nicely around 0, this small deviation is probably not of too much concern. Nonetheless, it is usually a good idea to check outlying points to make sure that they have been correctly recorded and entered. If the distribution of a variable appears markedly non-normal, transformation of the data should be considered.

Figure 3.5   Detrended normal plot for pegboard test

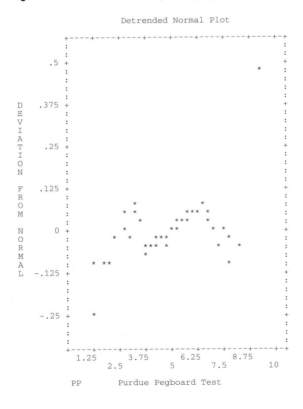

Another Plot

To get a little more practice in interpreting the previously described plots, consider Figure 3.6, which is the plot for the balancing-with-eyes-closed variable. From this stem-and-leaf plot (from the Examine procedure), you can see that the distribution of the data is skewed to the right. That is, there are several large values that are quite removed from the rest.

Figure 3.6   Stem-and-leaf plot for balance variable

```
EXAMINE BALCMEAN
 /PLOT STEMLEAF.


  Frequency     Stem &  Leaf

      2.00        -2 .  00
     25.00        -1 .  0000112222222334444555668
     41.00        -0 .  00111112222233344445555556666666777788889
     38.00         0 .  00000011122223344444455555556778899999
     20.00         1 .  00000112222344555889
      3.00         2 .  244
      1.00         3 .  2
      4.00  Extremes     (4.8),  (6.2),  (6.5)

 Stem width:       1.00
 Each leaf:        1 case(s)
```

Figure 3.7 is the corresponding normal probability plot. Note that the plot is no longer linear but is curved, especially for larger values of the variable. This downward curve indicates that the observed values are larger than predicted by the corresponding expected normal values. This is also seen in the stem-and-leaf plot. The detrended normal plot for this variable is shown in Figure 3.8, which shows that there is a definite pattern to the deviations. The values no longer cluster in a horizontal band around 0. A transformation might be considered.

Figure 3.7   Normal probability plot for balance variable

```
MANOVA BALOMEAN BALCMEAN SSTMEAN PP
  /PLOT=NORMAL
  /DESIGN.
```

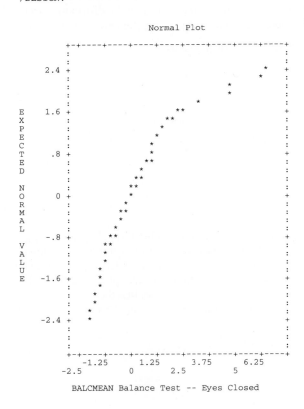

Figure 3.8   Detrended normal plot for balance variable

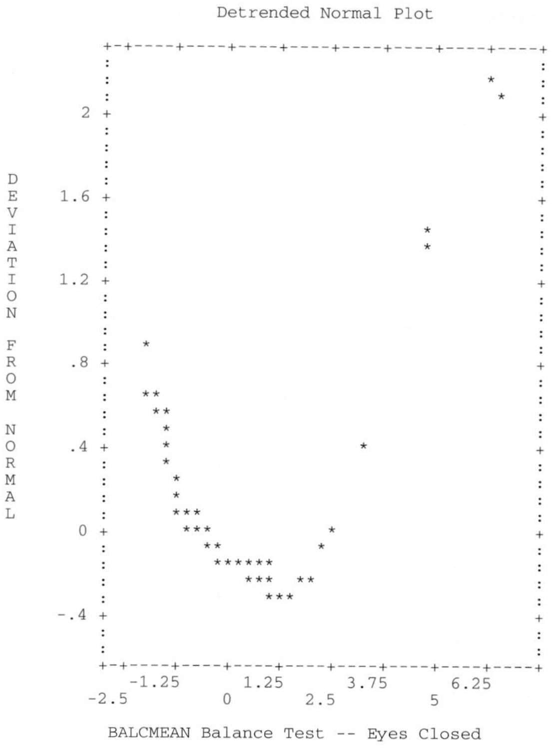

BALCMEAN Balance Test -- Eyes Closed

Bartlett's Test of Sphericity

Since there is no reason to use the multivariate analysis-of-variance procedure if the dependent variables are not correlated, it is useful to examine the correlation matrix of the dependent variables. If the variables are independent, the observed correlation matrix is expected to have small off-diagonal elements. Bartlett's test of sphericity can be used to test the hypothesis that the population correlation matrix is an **identity matrix**—that is, all diagonal terms are 1 and all off-diagonal terms are 0.

The test is based on the determinant of the error correlation matrix. A determinant that is close in value to 0 indicates that one or more of the variables can almost be expressed as a linear function of the other dependent variables. Thus, the hypothesis that the variables are independent is rejected if the determinant is small. Figure 3.9 contains output from Bartlett's test of sphericity. The log of the determinant is displayed first, followed by a transformation of the determinant (which has a chi-square distribution). Since the observed significance level is small (less than 0.0005), the hypothesis that the population correlation matrix is an identity matrix is rejected.

Figure 3.9   Bartlett's test of sphericity

```
MANOVA BALOMEAN BALCMEAN SSTMEAN PP
 /PRINT=ERR(COR)
 /DESIGN.

Statistics for WITHIN CELLS correlations

Log(Determinant) =                  -.18703
Bartlett test of sphericity =    24.46993 with 6 D. F.
Significance =                       .000
```

A graphical test of the hypothesis that the correlation matrix is an identity matrix is described by Everitt (1978). The observed correlation coefficients are transformed using Fisher's Z-transform, and then a half-normal plot of the transformed coefficients is obtained. A half-normal plot is very similar to the normal plot described above. The only difference is that both positive and negative values are treated identically. If the population correlation matrix is an identity matrix, the plot should be fairly linear and the line should pass through the origin.

Figure 3.10 is the plot of the transformed correlation coefficients for the four motor ability variables. The plot shows deviations from linearity, suggesting that the dependent variables are not independent, a result also indicated by Bartlett's test.

Figure 3.10   A half-normal plot of the correlation coefficients

```
MANOVA BALOMEAN BALCMEAN SSTMEAN PP
 /PLOT=ZCORR
 /DESIGN.
```

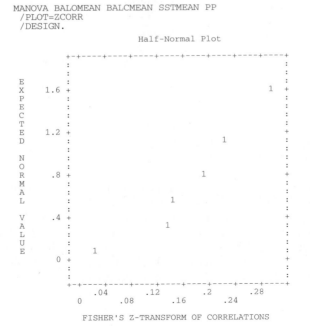

Testing Hypotheses

Once the distributions of the variables have been examined, we are ready to test the hypothesis that there is no difference between the population means and the hypothesized values. To test the various hypotheses of interest, the MANOVA procedure computes a design matrix whose columns correspond to the various effects in the model (see "Parameter Estimates" on p. 78).

To understand how the statistic for testing the hypothesis that all differences are 0 is constructed, recall the one-sample t test. The statistic for testing the hypothesis that the population mean is some known constant, which we will call μ_0, is

$$t = \frac{\bar{X} - \mu_0}{S / \sqrt{N}}$$

Equation 3.1

where $\bar{X}$ is the sample mean, S is the sample standard deviation, and N is the number of cases. The numerator of the t value is a measure of how much the sample mean differs from the hypothesized value, while the denominator is a measure of the variability of the sample mean.

When you simultaneously test the hypothesis that several population means do not differ from a specified set of constants, a statistic that considers all variables together is required. Hotelling's T^2 statistic is usually used for this purpose. It is computed as

$$T^2 = N(\bar{X} - \mu_0)'S^{-1}(\bar{X} - \mu_0)$$

Equation 3.2

where S^{-1} is the inverse of the variance-covariance matrix of the dependent variables and $\bar{X} - \mu_0$ is the vector of differences between the sample means and the hypothesized constants. The two matrices upon which Hotelling's T^2 is based can be displayed by the MANOVA procedure. The matrix that contains the differences between the observed sample means and the hypothesized values is shown in Figure 3.11.

Figure 3.11   The hypothesis sum-of-squares and cross-products matrix

```
MANOVA BALOMEAN BALCMEAN SSTMEAN PP
 /PRINT=SIGNIF(HYPOTH)
 /DESIGN.


EFFECT .. CONSTANT
Adjusted Hypothesis Sum-of-Squares and Cross-Products

                       BALOMEAN         BALCMEAN          SSTMEAN            PP

BALOMEAN            317.76360
BALCMEAN           -29.48957          2.73674
SSTMEAN            535.89403        -49.73284        903.76119
PP               -1026.10361         95.22600      -1730.47761      3313.43367
```

The diagonal elements are just the squares of the sample means minus the hypothesized values, multiplied by the sample size. For example, from Figure 3.2, the difference between the eyes-open balance score and the hypothesized value is -1.54. Squaring this difference and multiplying it by the sample size of 134, we get 317.76, the entry for *balomean* in Figure 3.11. The off-diagonal elements are the product of the differences for the two variables, multiplied by the sample size. For example, the cross-products entry for the *balomean* and *balcmean* is, from Figure 3.2, $-1.54 \times 0.14 \times 134 = -29.49$. For a fixed sample size, as the magnitude of the differences between the sample means and hypothesized values increases, so do the entries of this sums-of-squares and cross-products matrix.

The matrix whose entries indicate how much variability there is in the dependent variables is called the **within-cells sums-of-squares and cross-products matrix**. It is designated as S in the previous formula and is shown in Figure 3.12. The diagonal entries are $(N-1)$ times the variance of the dependent variables. For example, the entry for the pegboard variable is, from Figure 3.2, $1.49^2 \times 133 = 297.12$. The off-diagonal entries are the sums of the cross-products for the two variables. For example, for variables X and Y, the cross-product is:

$$CPSS_{xy} = \sum_{i=1}^{N} (X_i - \bar{X})(Y_i - \bar{Y})$$

Equation 3.3

To compute Hotelling's T^2, the inverse of this within-cells sums-of-squares matrix is required, as well as the hypothesis sums-of-squares matrix in Figure 3.11. The significance level associated with T^2 can be obtained from the F distribution. Figure 3.13 contains the value of Hotelling's T^2 divided by $(N-1)$, its transformation to a variable that has an F distribution, and the degrees of freedom associated with the F statistic. Since there are four dependent variables in this example, the hypothesis degrees of freedom are 4, while the remaining degrees of freedom, 130, are associated with the error sums of squares. Since the observed significance level is small (less than 0.0005), the null hypothesis that the population means do not differ from the hypothesized constants is rejected.

Figure 3.12   Within-cells sums-of-squares and cross-products matrix

```
MANOVA BALOMEAN BALCMEAN SSTMEAN PP
 /PRINT=ERROR(SSCP)
 /DESIGN.

WITHIN CELLS Sum-of-Squares and Cross-Products

                     BALOMEAN        BALCMEAN         SSTMEAN             PP

BALOMEAN          4567.27390
BALCMEAN           311.07957       262.50076
SSTMEAN            459.65597        94.83284       956.23881
PP                  26.79527        40.78234        70.42206      297.12189
```

Figure 3.13   Output containing Hotelling's statistic

```
MANOVA BALOMEAN BALCMEAN SSTMEAN PP
 /DESIGN.

Multivariate Tests of Significance (S = 1, M = 1 , N = 64 )

Test Name       Value     Exact F Hypoth. DF    Error DF  Sig. of F

Pillais         .92961   429.19095      4.00      130.00      .000
Hotellings    13.20588   429.19095      4.00      130.00      .000
Wilks           .07039   429.19095      4.00      130.00      .000
Roys            .92961
```

Univariate Tests

When the hypothesis of no difference is rejected, it is often informative to examine the univariate test results to get some idea of where the differences may be. Figure 3.14 contains the univariate results for the four dependent variables. The hypothesis and error sums of squares are the diagonal terms in Figure 3.11 and Figure 3.12. The mean squares are obtained by dividing the sums of squares by their degrees of freedom, 1 for the hypothesis sums of squares and 133 for the error sums of squares. The ratio of the two mean squares is displayed in the column labeled F. These F values are nothing more than the squares of one-sample t values. Thus, from Figure 3.2, the mean difference for the *balomean* variable is -1.54 and the standard deviation of the difference is 5.86. The corresponding t value is:

$$t = \frac{-1.54}{5.86/\sqrt{134}} = -3.04$$

Equation 3.4

Squaring this produces the value 9.25, which is the entry in Figure 3.14. From Figure 3.2, we can see that the balancing-with-eyes-closed variable is the only one for which the t value is not significant. This is to be expected, since it has a 95% confidence interval that includes 0. The significance levels for the univariate statistics are not adjusted for the fact that several comparisons are being made and thus should be used with a certain amount of caution. For a discussion of the problem of multiple comparisons, see Miller (1981) or Burns (1984).

Figure 3.14   Univariate F tests

```
MANOVA BALOMEAN BALCMEAN SSTMEAN PP
 /PRINT=SIGNIF(UNIV)
 /DESIGN.

Univariate F-tests with (1,133) D. F.

Variable    Hypoth. SS    Error SS Hypoth. MS    Error MS          F  Sig. of F

BALOMEAN     317.76360  4567.27390   317.76360    34.34041    9.25334      .003
BALCMEAN       2.73674   262.50076     2.73674     1.97369    1.38661      .241
SSTMEAN      903.76119   956.23881   903.76119     7.18977  125.70107      .000
PP          3313.43367   297.12189  3313.43367     2.23400 1483.18482      .000
```

The Two-Sample Multivariate T Test

In the previous sections, we were concerned with testing the hypothesis that the sample was drawn from a population with a particular set of means. There was only one sample involved, though there were several dependent variables. In this section, we will consider the multivariate generalization of the two-sample t test. The hypothesis that men and women do not differ on the four motor-ability variables will be tested. It is not necessary to subtract the normative values from the observed scores for this test and, therefore, we recompute the values for the four motor-ability variables.

Figure 3.15 contains descriptive statistics for each variable according to sex. The female subjects are coded as 1's, and the males are coded as 2's. Males appear to maintain balance with eyes open longer than females and cross more lines in the stepping test.

Figure 3.15   Cell means and standard deviations

```
COMPUTE BALOMEAN=(X10+X11)/2.
COMPUTE BALCMEAN=(X12+X13)/2.
COMPUTE SSTMEAN=(X14+X15+X16)/3.
COMPUTE PP=(X17+X18+X19+X20+X21+X22)/6.
MANOVA BALOMEAN BALCMEAN SSTMEAN PP BY SEX(1,2)
 /PRINT CELLINFO(MEANS)
 /DESIGN.
```

```
Cell Means and Standard Deviations
Variable .. BALOMEAN          Balance Test - Eyes Open
     FACTOR            CODE         Mean  Std. Dev.        N   95 percent Conf. Interval

  SEX             Female          9.748     5.707         63     8.311    11.186
  SEX             Male           12.979     5.605         71    11.652    14.306
For entire sample               11.460     5.860        134    10.459    12.461
- - - - - - - - - - - - - - - - - - - - - - - - - - - - - - - - - - - - - - - - - -
Variable .. BALCMEAN          Balance Test - Eyes Closed
     FACTOR            CODE         Mean  Std. Dev.        N   95 percent Conf. Interval

  SEX             Female          3.191     1.518         63     2.809     3.574
  SEX             Male            3.100     1.306         71     2.791     3.409
For entire sample                3.143     1.405        134     2.903     3.383
- - - - - - - - - - - - - - - - - - - - - - - - - - - - - - - - - - - - - - - - - -
Variable .. SSTMEAN           Sidestepping Test
     FACTOR            CODE         Mean  Std. Dev.        N   95 percent Conf. Interval

  SEX             Female         14.095     2.255         63    13.527    14.663
  SEX             Male           16.563     2.501         71    15.972    17.155
For entire sample               15.403     2.681        134    14.945    15.861
- - - - - - - - - - - - - - - - - - - - - - - - - - - - - - - - - - - - - - - - - -
Variable .. PP                Purdue Pegboard Test
     FACTOR            CODE         Mean  Std. Dev.        N   95 percent Conf. Interval

  SEX             Female         15.466     1.453         63    15.100    15.831
  SEX             Male           14.535     1.401         71    14.204    14.867
For entire sample               14.973     1.495        134    14.717    15.228
```

Another way to visualize the distribution of scores in each of the groups is with box-and-whiskers plots from the Examine procedure, as shown in Figure 3.16 for *balomean* and Figure 3.17 for *balcmean*. The upper and lower boundaries of the boxes are the upper and lower quartiles. The box length is the interquartile distance, and the box contains the middle 50% of values in a group. The horizontal line inside the box identifies the group median. The larger the box, the greater the spread of the observations. Any points between 1.5 and 3 interquartile ranges from the end of the box (outliers) are marked with circles. The lines emanating from each box (the whiskers) extend to the smallest and largest observations in a group that are not outliers. Points more than 3 interquartile distances away from the box (extreme values) are marked with asterisks.

Figure 3.16 Box-and-whiskers plots for balomean

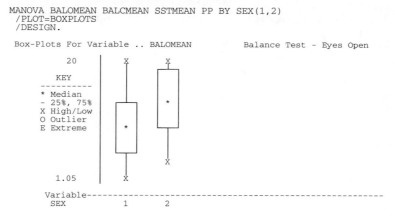

```
MANOVA BALOMEAN BALCMEAN SSTMEAN PP BY SEX(1,2)
 /PLOT=BOXPLOTS
 /DESIGN.

  Box-Plots For Variable .. BALOMEAN          Balance Test - Eyes Open

          20           X        X

          KEY
        ----------
        * Median
        - 25%, 75%
        X High/Low              *
        O Outlier
        E Extreme      *


                                         X


         1.05         X

        Variable------------------------------------------------------------
         SEX          1        2
```

Figure 3.17 Box-and-whiskers plots for balcmean

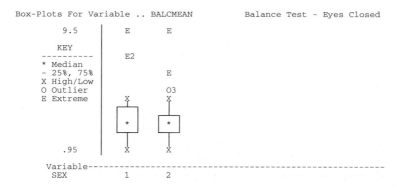

```
  Box-Plots For Variable .. BALCMEAN          Balance Test - Eyes Closed
         9.5          E        E

          KEY
        ----------    E2
        * Median
        - 25%, 75%             E
        X High/Low
        O Outlier              O3
        E Extreme     X        X


                      *        *


          .95         X        X

        Variable------------------------------------------------------------
         SEX          1        2
```

Tests of Homogeneity of Variance

In the one-sample Hotelling's T^2 test, there was no need to worry about the homogeneity of the variance-covariance matrices, since there was only one matrix. In the two-sample test, there are two matrices (one for each group), and tests for their equality are necessary.

The variance-covariance matrices are shown in Figure 3.18. They are computed for each group using the means of the variables within that group. Thus, each matrix indicates how much variability there is in a group. Combining these individual matrices into a common variance-covariance matrix results in the pooled matrix displayed in Figure 3.19.

Figure 3.18   Group variance-covariance matrices for females and males

```
MANOVA BALOMEAN BALCMEAN SSTMEAN PP BY SEX(1,2)
 /PRINT=CELLINFO(COV)
 /DESIGN.

Cell Number .. 1

Variance-Covariance matrix

                    BALOMEAN         BALCMEAN          SSTMEAN              PP
BALOMEAN           32.57185
BALCMEAN            3.39103          2.30400
SSTMEAN              .42704           .55622          5.08397
PP                  1.43677           .36703          1.30888          2.11036

..........

Cell Number .. 2

Variance-Covariance matrix

                    BALOMEAN         BALCMEAN          SSTMEAN              PP
BALOMEAN           31.42090
BALCMEAN            1.58111          1.70536
SSTMEAN             2.38612           .96952          6.25267
PP                   .54349           .21702           .94178          1.96263
```

Figure 3.19   Pooled variance-covariance matrix

```
Pooled within-cells Variance-Covariance matrix

                    BALOMEAN         BALCMEAN          SSTMEAN              PP
BALOMEAN           31.96150
BALCMEAN            2.43122          1.98654
SSTMEAN             1.46594           .77540          5.70374
PP                   .96306           .28748          1.11421          2.03202
```

Figure 3.20 contains two homogeneity-of-variance tests (Cochran's *C* and the Bartlett-Box *F*) for each variable individually. The significance levels indicate that there is no reason to reject the hypotheses that the variances in the two groups are equal. Although these univariate tests are a convenient starting point for examining the equality of the covariance matrices, they are not sufficient. A test that simultaneously considers both the variances and covariances is required.

Box's *M* test, which is based on the determinants of the variance-covariance matrices in each cell as well as of the pooled variance-covariance matrix, provides a multivariate test for the homogeneity of the matrices. However, Box's *M* test is very sensitive to departures from normality. The significance level can be based on either an *F* or a chi-square statistic, and both approximations are given in the output, as shown in Figure 3.21. Given the result of Box's *M* test, there appears to be no reason to suspect the homogeneity-of-dispersion-matrices assumption.

Figure 3.20   Univariate homogeneity-of-variance tests

```
MANOVA BALOMEAN BALCMEAN SSTMEAN PP BY SEX(1,2)
 /PRINT=HOMOGENEITY(COCHRAN BARTLETT)
 /DESIGN.


Univariate Homogeneity of Variance Tests

Variable .. BALOMEAN          Balance Test - Eyes Open

     Cochrans C(66,2) =                         .50899, P =  .884 (approx.)
     Bartlett-Box F(1,51762) =                  .02113, P =  .884

Variable .. BALCMEAN          Balance Test - Eyes Closed

     Cochrans C(66,2) =                         .57466, P =  .224 (approx.)
     Bartlett-Box F(1,51762) =                 1.48033, P =  .224

Variable .. SSTMEAN           Sidestepping Test

     Cochrans C(66,2) =                         .55155, P =  .403 (approx.)
     Bartlett-Box F(1,51762) =                  .69438, P =  .405

Variable .. PP                Purdue Pegboard Test

     Cochrans C(66,2) =                         .51813, P =  .769 (approx.)
     Bartlett-Box F(1,51762) =                  .08603, P =  .769
```

Figure 3.21   Homogeneity-of-dispersion matrices

```
MANOVA BALOMEAN BALCMEAN SSTMEAN PP BY SEX(1,2)
 /PRINT=HOMOGENEITY(BOXM)
 /DESIGN.


Cell Number .. 1

Determinant of Covariance matrix of dependent variables =       538.89812
LOG(Determinant) =                                               6.28953

- - - - - - - - - -

Cell Number .. 2

Determinant of Covariance matrix of dependent variables =       522.34851
LOG(Determinant) =                                               6.25834

- - - - - - - - - -


Determinant of pooled Covariance matrix of dependent vars. =    557.40735
LOG(Determinant) =                                               6.32330


- - - - - - - - - - - - - - - - - - - - - - - - - - - - - - - - - - - - - -

Multivariate test for Homogeneity of Dispersion matrices


Boxs M =                       6.64102
F WITH (10,80608) DF =          .64228, P =   .779 (Approx.)
Chi-Square with 10 DF =        6.42362, P =   .779 (Approx.)
```

Hotelling's T^2 for Two Independent Samples

The actual statistic for testing the equality of several means with two independent samples is also based on Hotelling's T^2. The formula is

$$T^2 = \frac{N_1 N_2}{N_1 + N_2} (\bar{X}_1 - \bar{X}_2)' S^{-1} (\bar{X}_1 - \bar{X}_2)$$

Equation 3.5

where $\bar{X}_1$ is the vector of means for the first group (females), $\bar{X}_2$ is the vector for the second group (males), and S^{-1} is the inverse of the pooled within-groups covariance matrix. The statistic is somewhat similar to the one described for the one-sample test in "Testing Hypotheses" on p. 67.

Again, two matrices are used in the computation of the statistic. The pooled within-groups covariance matrix has been described previously and is displayed in Figure 3.19. The second matrix is the adjusted hypothesis sums-of-squares and cross-products matrix. It is displayed in Figure 3.22. The entries in this matrix are the weighted squared differences of the group means from the combined mean. For example, the entry for the balancing-with-eyes-open variable is

$$SS = 63 (9.75 - 11.46)^2 + 71 (12.98 - 11.46)^2 = 348.36$$

Equation 3.6

where, from Figure 3.15, 9.75 is the mean value for the 63 females, 12.98 is the value for the 71 males, and 11.46 is the mean for the entire sample. The first off-diagonal term for balancing with eyes open (*balomean*) and eyes closed (*balcmean*) is similarly:

$$SS = (9.75 - 11.46) (3.19 - 3.14) 63$$
$$+ (12.98 - 11.46) (3.10 - 3.14) 71 = -9.84$$

Equation 3.7

The diagonal terms should be recognizable to anyone familiar with analysis-of-variance methodology. They are the sums of squares due to groups for each variable.

Figure 3.22   Adjusted hypothesis sums-of-squares and cross-products matrix

```
MANOVA BALOMEAN BALCMEAN SSTMEAN PP BY SEX(1,2)
 /PRINT=SIGNIF(HYPOTH)
 /DESIGN.


EFFECT .. SEX
Adjusted Hypothesis Sum-of-Squares and Cross-Products

                     BALOMEAN       BALCMEAN        SSTMEAN              PP

BALOMEAN            348.35575
BALCMEAN             -9.84206         .27807
SSTMEAN             266.15138       -7.51955      203.34545
PP                 -100.32911        2.83459      -76.65362        28.89555
```

Figure 3.23 contains the value of Hotelling's T^2 statistic divided by $N-2$ for the test of the hypothesis that men and women do not differ on the motor-ability test scores. The significance level is based on the F distribution, with 4 and 129 degrees of freedom. The observed significance level is small (less than 0.0005), so the null hypothesis that men and women perform equally well on the motor-ability tests is rejected.

Figure 3.23   Hotelling's statistic and Wilks' lambda

```
MANOVA BALOMEAN BALCMEAN SSTMEAN PP BY SEX(1,2)
 /PRINT=SIGNIF(MULTIV)
 /DESIGN.

EFFECT .. SEX
Multivariate Tests of Significance (S = 1, M = 1 , N = 63 1/2)

Test Name          Value  Approx. F Hypoth. DF   Error DF  Sig. of F

Pillais           .40103   21.59226      4.00     129.00       .000
Hotellings        .66953   21.59226      4.00     129.00       .000
Wilks             .59897   21.59226      4.00     129.00       .000
Roys              .40103
```

Univariate Tests

To get some idea of where the differences between men's and women's scores occur, the univariate tests for the individual variables may be examined. These are the same as the F values from one-way analyses of variance. In the case of two groups, the F values are just the squares of the two-sample t values.

Figure 3.24   Univariate tests

```
MANOVA BALOMEAN BALCMEAN SSTMEAN PP BY SEX(1,2)
 /PRINT=SIGNIF(UNIV)
 /DESIGN.

Univariate F-tests with (1,132) D. F.

Variable   Hypoth. SS  Error SS Hypoth. MS   Error MS        F  Sig. of F

BALOMEAN    348.35575 4218.91814 348.35575   31.96150 10.89923      .001
BALCMEAN       .27807  262.22270    .27807    1.98654   .13998      .709
SSTMEAN     203.34544  752.89339 203.34544    5.70374 35.65126      .000
PP           28.89555  268.22633  28.89555    2.03202 14.22013      .000
```

From Figure 3.24, we can see that there are significant univariate tests for all variables except balancing with eyes closed. Again, the significance levels are not adjusted for the fact that four tests, rather than one, are being performed.

Discriminant Analysis

In the Discriminant Analysis chapter in *SPSS/PC+ Professional Statistics*, we considered the problem of finding the best linear combination of variables for distinguishing among several groups. Coefficients for the variables are chosen so that the ratio of between-groups sums of squares to total sums of squares is as large as possible. Although the equality-of-means hypotheses tested in MANOVA may initially appear quite unrelated to the discriminant problem, the two procedures are closely related. In fact, MANOVA can be viewed as a problem of first finding linear combinations of the dependent variables that best separate the groups and then testing whether these new variables are significantly different for the groups. For this reason, the usual discriminant analysis statistics can be obtained as part of the MANOVA procedure output.

Figure 3.25 contains the eigenvalues and canonical correlation for the canonical discriminant function that separates males and females. Remember that the **eigenvalue** is the ratio of the between-groups sum of squares to the within-groups sum of squares, while the **square of the canonical correlation** is the ratio of the between-groups sums of squares to the total sum of squares. Thus, about 40% of the variability in the discriminant scores is attributable to between-group differences ($0.633^2 = 0.401$).

Figure 3.25   Eigenvalue and canonical correlation

```
MANOVA BALOMEAN BALCMEAN SSTMEAN PP BY SEX(1,2)
  /PRINT=SIGNIF(EIGEN)
  /DESIGN.

Eigenvalues and Canonical Correlations

Root No.        Eigenvalue          Pct.       Cum. Pct.      Canon Cor.

      1             .66953      100.00000      100.00000          .63327
```

When there are two groups, Wilks' lambda can be interpreted as a measure of the proportion of total variability not explained by group differences. As shown in Figure 3.23, almost 60% of the observed variability is not explained by the group differences. The hypothesis that in the population there are no differences between the group means can be tested using Wilks' lambda. Lambda is transformed to a variable that has an F distribution. For the two-group situation, the F value for Wilks' lambda is identical to that given for Hotelling's T^2.

Both raw and standardized discriminant function coefficients can be displayed by the SPSS/PC+ MANOVA procedure. The **raw coefficients** are the multipliers of the dependent variables in their original units, while the **standardized coefficients** are the multipliers of the dependent variables when the latter have been standardized to a mean of 0 and a standard deviation of 1. Both sets of coefficients are displayed in Figure 3.26.

The sidestepping and pegboard scores have the largest standardized coefficients and, as you will recall from Figure 3.24, they also have the largest univariate F's, suggesting that they are important for separating the two groups. Of course, when variables are correlated, the discriminant function coefficients must be interpreted with care, since highly correlated variables "share" the discriminant weights.

Figure 3.26   Raw and standardized discriminant function coefficients

```
MANOVA BALOMEAN BALCMEAN SSTMEAN PP BY SEX (1,2)
  /DISCRIM=RAW STAN
  /DESIGN.
EFFECT .. SEX (Cont.)
Raw discriminant function coefficients
        Function No.

Variable                   1

BALOMEAN           -.07465
BALCMEAN            .19245
SSTMEAN            -.36901
PP                  .49189


Standardized discriminant function coefficients
        Function No.

Variable                   1

BALOMEAN           -.42205
BALCMEAN            .27125
SSTMEAN            -.88128
PP                  .70118
```

The correlation coefficients for the discriminant scores and each dependent variable, sometimes called **structure coefficients**, are displayed in Figure 3.27. Once again, the sidestepping test and the pegboard test are most highly correlated with the discriminant function, while the correlation coefficient between balancing with eyes closed and the discriminant function is near 0. This is not surprising, since balancing with eyes closed had a nonsignificant univariate F.

Figure 3.27   Structure coefficients

```
MANOVA BALOMEAN BALCMEAN SSTMEAN PP BY SEX(1,2)
  /DISCRIM=CORR
  /DESIGN.

Correlations between DEPENDENT and canonical variables
        Canonical Variable

Variable                   1

BALOMEAN       -.35118
BALCMEAN        .03980
SSTMEAN        -.63514
PP              .40113
```

An additional statistic displayed as part of the discriminant output in the SPSS/PC+ MANOVA procedure is an estimate of the effect for the canonical variable. Consider Figure 3.28 (from the Discriminant procedure described in *SPSS/PC+ Professional Statistics*), which gives the average canonical function scores for the two groups. We can estimate the effect of a canonical variable by measuring its average distance from 0 across all groups. In this example, the average distance is $(0.862 + 0.765)/2 = 0.814$, as shown in Figure 3.29. Canonical variables with small effects do not contribute much to separation between groups.

Figure 3.28   Average canonical function scores

```
DSCRIMINANT GROUPS=SEX(1,2)
 /VARIABLES=BALOMEAN BALCMEAN SSTMEAN PP.

Canonical Discriminant Functions evaluated at Group Means (Group Centroids)

    Group      FUNC   1

       1       -.86214
       2        .76500
```

Figure 3.29   Estimate of effect for canonical variable

```
MANOVA BALOMEAN BALCMEAN SSTMEAN PP BY SEX(1,2)
 /DISCRIM=ESTIM
 /DESIGN.

Estimates of effects for canonical variables
          Canonical Variable

   Parameter            1

        2           .81357
```

Parameter Estimates

As for most other statistical techniques, there is for MANOVA a mathematical model that expresses the relationship between the dependent variable and the independent variables. Recall, for example, that in a univariate analysis-of-variance model with four groups, the mean for each group can be expressed as

$$y_1 = \mu + 1\alpha_1 + 0\alpha_2 + 0\alpha_3 + 0\alpha_4 + e_1$$
$$y_2 = \mu + 0\alpha_1 + 1\alpha_2 + 0\alpha_3 + 0\alpha_4 + e_2$$
$$y_3 = \mu + 0\alpha_1 + 0\alpha_2 + 1\alpha_3 + 0\alpha_4 + e_3$$
$$y_4 = \mu + 0\alpha_1 + 0\alpha_2 + 0\alpha_3 + 1\alpha_4 + e_4$$

Equation 3.8

where y_j is the mean for group j. In matrix form, this can be written as

$$\begin{bmatrix} y_1 \\ y_2 \\ y_3 \\ y_4 \end{bmatrix} = \begin{bmatrix} 1 & 1 & 0 & 0 & 0 \\ 1 & 0 & 1 & 0 & 0 \\ 1 & 0 & 0 & 1 & 0 \\ 1 & 0 & 0 & 0 & 1 \end{bmatrix} \begin{bmatrix} \mu \\ \alpha_1 \\ \alpha_2 \\ \alpha_3 \\ \alpha_4 \end{bmatrix} + \begin{bmatrix} e_1 \\ e_2 \\ e_3 \\ e_4 \end{bmatrix}$$

Equation 3.9

or

$$y = A\theta^* + e$$

Equation 3.10

Since the θ matrix has more columns than rows, it does not have a unique inverse. We are unable to estimate five parameters (μ and α_1 to α_4) on the basis of four sample means. Instead, we can estimate four linear combinations, termed **contrasts**, of the parameters (see Finn, 1974).

Several types of contrasts are available in the SPSS/PC+ MANOVA procedure, resulting in different types of parameter estimates. **Deviation contrasts**, the default, estimate each parameter as its difference from the overall average. This results in parameter estimates of the form $\mu_j - \mu$. Deviation contrasts do not require any particular ordering of the factor levels.

Simple contrasts are useful when one of the factor levels is a comparison or control group. All parameter estimates are then expressed as a deviation from the value of the control group. When factor levels have an underlying metric, **orthogonal polynomial contrasts** may be used to determine whether group means are related to the values of the factor level. For example, if three doses of an agent are administered (10 units, 20 units, and 30 units), you can test whether response is related to dose in a linear or quadratic fashion.

Figure 3.30 contains parameter estimates corresponding to the default deviation contrasts.There are two estimates for the sex parameter, one for females and one for males. The output includes only values for the first parameter (females), since the value for the second parameter is just the negative of the value for the first. The sex effect for females is estimated as the difference between the mean score of females and the overall unweighted mean. For balancing with eyes open, it is $9.75 - 11.36 = -1.61$, the value displayed in Figure 3.30. Confidence intervals and t tests for the null hypothesis that a parameter value is 0 can also be calculated. SPSS/PC+ can calculate either individual or joint confidence intervals for all dependent variables. Note that the t values displayed for each parameter are equal to the square root of the F values (ignoring sign) displayed for the univariate F tests in Figure 3.24.

Figure 3.30   Parameter estimates

```
SET WIDTH=WIDE.
MANOVA BALOMEAN BALCMEAN SSTMEAN PP BY SEX(1,2)
 /PRINT=PARAMETERS(ESTIM)
 /DESIGN.
```

```
Estimates for BALOMEAN
--- Individual univariate .9500 confidence intervals

SEX

  Parameter         Coeff.      Std. Err.       t-Value        Sig. t      Lower -95%     CL- Upper

        2    -1.6152302705         .48926       -3.30140        .00124        -2.58303        -.64743
- - - - - - - - - - - - - - - - - - - - - - - - - - - - - - - - - - - - - - - - - - - - - - - - -
Estimates for BALCMEAN
--- Individual univariate .9500 confidence intervals

SEX

  Parameter         Coeff.      Std. Err.       t-Value        Sig. t      Lower -95%     CL- Upper

        2      .0456349206         .12198         .37413        .70891         -.19564         .28691
- - - - - - - - - - - - - - - - - - - - - - - - - - - - - - - - - - - - - - - - - - - - - - - - -
Estimates for SSTMEAN
--- Individual univariate .9500 confidence intervals

SEX

  Parameter         Coeff.      Std. Err.       t-Value        Sig. t      Lower -95%     CL- Upper

        2    -1.2340710932         .20668       -5.97087        .00000        -1.64291        -.82523
- - - - - - - - - - - - - - - - - - - - - - - - - - - - - - - - - - - - - - - - - - - - - - - - -
Estimates for PP
--- Individual univariate .9500 confidence intervals

SEX

  Parameter         Coeff.      Std. Err.       t-Value        Sig. t      Lower -95%     CL- Upper

        2      .4651985990         .12336        3.77096        .00024         .22117         .70922
```

A Multivariate Factorial Design

So far we have considered two very simple multivariate designs, generalizations of the one- and two-sample t tests to the case of multiple dependent variables. We are now ready to examine a more complex design. Recall that in the experiment conducted by Barnard, the hypothesis of interest concerned the relationship among field dependence, sex, and motor ability. Since subjects are classified into one of three field-dependence categories— low (1), intermediate (2), and high (3)—we have a two-way multivariate factorial design with three levels of field dependence and two categories of sex. The four motor ability variables are the dependent variables.

Some additional plots for cells in the model may be useful. Plotting the mean of a variable for all the cells in the design, as shown in Figure 3.31, gives an idea of the spread of the means. You can see from the plot that there are two cells with means close to 14 seconds, three cells with means less than 11 seconds, and 1 cell with a mean in between.

Figure 3.31   Distribution of cell means for balomean

```
MANOVA BALOMEAN BY SEX(1,2) FIELD(1,3)
 /PLOT=CELLPLOTS
 /DESIGN.
```

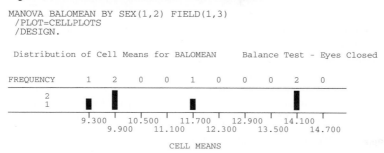

Although both univariate and multivariate analyses of variance require equal variances in the cells, there are many situations in which cell means and standard deviations, or cell means and variances, are proportional. Figure 3.32 shows plots of cell means versus cell variances and cell standard deviations. There appears to be no relationship between the means and the measures of variability. If patterns were evident, transformations of the dependent variables might be used to stabilize the variances.

Figure 3.32   Plots of cell means, cell variances, and cell standard deviations

```
MANOVA BALOMEAN BY SEX(1,2) FIELD(1,3)
 /PLOT=CELLPLOTS
 /DESIGN.
```

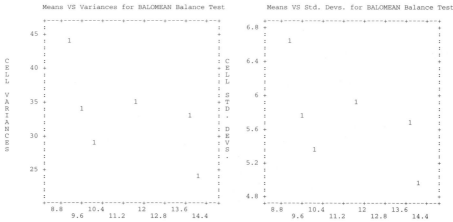

Principal Components Analysis

Bartlett's test of sphericity provides information about the correlations among the dependent variables by testing the hypothesis that the correlation matrix is an identity matrix. Another way to examine dependencies among the dependent variables is to perform a principal components analysis of their within-cells correlation matrix (see Chapter 2 in *SPSS/PC+ Professional Statistics* for a discussion of principal components analysis). If principal components analysis reveals that one of the variables can be expressed as a linear combination of the others, the error sums-of-squares and cross-products matrix will be singular and a unique inverse cannot be obtained.

Figure 3.33 contains the within-cells correlation matrix for the two-way factorial design. The eigenvalues and percentage of variance explained by each are shown in Figure 3.34. The first two principal components account for about two-thirds of the total variance, and the remaining two components account for the rest. None of the eigenvalues is close enough to 0 to cause concern about the error matrix being singular.

Figure 3.33   Within-cells correlation matrix

```
MANOVA BALOMEAN BALCMEAN SSTMEAN PP BY SEX(1,2)FIELD(1,3)
 /PRINT=ERROR(COR)
 /DESIGN.


WITHIN CELLS Correlations with Std. Devs. on Diagonal

                 BALOMEAN         BALCMEAN          SSTMEAN              PP

BALOMEAN          5.67488
BALCMEAN           .30019         1.41485
SSTMEAN            .11506          .24341          2.39327
PP                 .11100          .14334           .34698          1.43842
```

Figure 3.34   Eigenvalues and percentage of variance

```
MANOVA BALOMEAN BALCMEAN SSTMEAN PP BY SEX(1,2)FIELD(1,3)
 /PCOMPS=COR
 /DESIGN.

Eigenvalues of WITHIN CELLS correlation matrix

              Eigenvalue         Pct of Var         Cum Pct

      1         1.63610          40.90257          40.90257
      2         1.02780          25.69499          66.59757
      3          .72258          18.06448          84.66205
      4          .61352          15.33795         100.00000
```

Figure 3.35 contains the loadings, which in this case are equivalent to correlations, between the principal components and dependent variables. The components can be rotated, as shown in Figure 3.36, to increase interpretability. Each variable loads highly on only one of the components, suggesting that none is redundant or highly correlated with the others. When there are many dependent variables, a principal components analysis may indicate how the variables are related to each other. This information is useful for establishing the number of unique dimensions being measured by the dependent variables.

Figure 3.35   Correlations between principal components and dependent variables

```
MANOVA BALOMEAN BALCMEAN SSTMEAN PP BY SEX(1,2)FIELD(1,3)
  /PCOMPS=CORR ROTATE(VARIMAX)
  /DESIGN.

Normalized principal components
        Components
Variables            1            2            3            4

BALOMEAN       -.55200      -.63056      -.48683       .24635
BALCMEAN       -.66950      -.41517       .49417      -.36770
SSTMEAN        -.69880       .41598       .27636       .51212
PP             -.62837       .53366      -.40619      -.39416
```

Figure 3.36   Rotated correlations between components and dependent variables

```
VARIMAX rotated correlations between components and DEPENDENT variable
        Can. Var.
DEP. VAR.            1            2            3            4

BALOMEAN        .98696       .04774       .14699       .04503
BALCMEAN        .15005       .05958       .98016       .11501
SSTMEAN         .04631       .17390       .11606       .97680
PP              .04835       .98230       .05905       .17104
```

Tests of Multivariate Differences

Once the preliminary steps of examining the distribution of the variables for outliers, non-normality, and inequality of variances have been taken and no significant violations have been found, hypothesis testing can begin. In the one- and two-sample test, Hotelling's T^2, a multivariate generalization of the univariate t value, is used. For more complicated designs, an extension of the familiar analysis-of-variance F test to the multivariate case is needed.

The univariate F tests in ANOVA are the ratios of the hypothesis mean squares to the error mean squares. When there is more than one dependent variable, there is no longer a single number that represents the hypothesis and error sums of squares. Instead, as shown in "Testing Hypotheses" on p. 67, there are matrices for the hypothesis and error sums of squares and cross-products. These matrices must be combined into some type of test statistic.

Most multivariate test statistics are based on the determinant of HE^{-1}, where H is the hypothesis sums-of-squares and cross-products matrix and E^{-1} is the inverse of the error sums-of-squares and cross-products matrix. The determinant is a measure of the generalized variance, or dispersion, of a matrix. This determinant can be calculated as the product of the eigenvalues of a matrix, since each eigenvalue represents a portion of the generalized variance. In fact, the process of extracting eigenvalues can be viewed as a principal components analysis on the HE^{-1} matrix.

There are a variety of test statistics for evaluating multivariate differences based on the eigenvalues of HE^{-1}. Four of the most commonly used tests are displayed by the SPSS/PC+ MANOVA procedure:

Pillai's trace:

$$V = \sum_{i=1}^{s} \frac{1}{1 + \lambda_i}$$

Equation 3.11

Wilks' lambda:

$$W = \prod_{i=1}^{s} \frac{1}{1 + \lambda_i}$$

Equation 3.12

Hotelling's trace:

$$T = \Sigma \lambda_i$$

Equation 3.13

Roy's largest root:

$$R = \frac{\lambda_{MAX}}{1 + \lambda_{MAX}}$$

Equation 3.14

where λ_{MAX} is the largest eigenvalue, λ_i is the ith eigenvalue, and s is the number of non-zero eigenvalues of HE^{-1}.

Although the exact distributions of the four criteria differ, they can be transformed into statistics that have approximately an F distribution. Tables of the exact distributions of the statistics are also available.

When there is a single dependent variable, all four criteria are equivalent to the ordinary ANOVA F statistic. When there is a single sample or two independent samples with multiple dependent variables, they are all equivalent to Hotelling's T^2. In both situations, the transformed statistics are distributed exactly as F's.

Two concerns dictate the choice of the multivariate criterion—**power** and **robustness**. That is, the test statistic should detect differences when they exist and not be much affected by departures from the assumptions. For most practical situations, when differences among groups are spread along several dimensions, the ordering of the test criteria in terms of decreasing power is Pillai's, Wilks', Hotelling's, and Roy's. Pillai's trace is also the most robust criterion. That is, the significance level based on it is reasonably correct even when the assumptions are violated. This is important, since a test that results in distorted significance levels in the presence of mild violations of homogeneity of covariance matrices or multivariate normality is of limited use (Olsen, 1976).

Testing the Effects

Since our design is a two-by-three factorial (two sexes and three categories of field dependence), there are three effects to be tested: the sex and field-dependence main effects and the sex-by-field-dependence interaction. As in univariate analysis of variance, the terms are tested in reverse order. That is, higher-order effects are tested before lower-order ones, since it is difficult to interpret lower-order effects in the presence of higher-order interactions. For example, if there is a sex-by-field-dependence interaction, testing for sex and field-dependence main effects is not particularly useful and can be misleading.

The SPSS/PC+ MANOVA procedure displays separate output for each effect. Figure 3.37 shows the label displayed on each page to identify the effect being tested. The hypothesis sums-of-squares and cross-products matrix can be displayed for each effect. The same error matrix (the pooled within-cells sums-of-squares and cross-products matrix) is used to test all effects and is displayed only once before the effect-by-effect output. Figure 3.38 contains the error matrix for the factorial design. Figure 3.39 is the hypothesis sums-of-squares and cross-product matrix. These two matrices are the ones involved in the computation of the test statistics displayed in Figure 3.40.

Figure 3.37   Label for effect being tested

```
EFFECT .. SEX BY FIELD
```

Figure 3.38   Error sums-of-squares and cross-products matrix

```
MANOVA BALOMEAN BALCMEAN SSTMEAN PP BY SEX(1,2)FIELD(1,3)
 /PRINT=ERROR(SSCP)
 /DESIGN.

WITHIN CELLS Sum-of-Squares and Cross-Products

                    BALOMEAN       BALCMEAN        SSTMEAN            PP
BALOMEAN          4122.15200
BALCMEAN           308.51395      256.22940
SSTMEAN            200.02104      105.49895      733.14908
PP                 115.98133       37.33883      152.89508      264.83786
```

Figure 3.39   Hypothesis sums-of-squares and cross-products matrix

```
MANOVA BALOMEAN BALCMEAN SSTMEAN PP BY SEX(1,2)FIELD(1,3)
 /PRINT=SIGNIF(HYPOTH)
 /DESIGN.

Adjusted Hypothesis Sum-of-Squares and Cross-Products

                    BALOMEAN       BALCMEAN        SSTMEAN            PP
BALOMEAN            18.10215
BALCMEAN             8.23621        3.77316
SSTMEAN             2.49483         .55197        13.52286
PP                  -.00368         .21323        -4.85735        1.78988
```

Figure 3.40   Multivariate tests of significance

```
MANOVA BALOMEAN BALCMEAN SSTMEAN PP BY SEX(1,2)FIELD(1,3)
  /PRINT=SIGNIF(MULTIV)
  /DESIGN.


EFFECT .. SEX BY FIELD
Multivariate Tests of Significance (S = 2, M = 1/2, N = 61 1/2)

Test Name        Value  Approx. F Hypoth. DF   Error DF  Sig. of F

Pillais          .05245   .84827       8.00     252.00      .561
Hotellings       .05410   .83848       8.00     248.00      .570
Wilks            .94813   .84339       8.00     250.00      .565
Roys             .03668
```

The first line of Figure 3.40 contains the values of the parameters (S, M, N) used to find significance levels in tables of the exact distributions of the statistics. For the first three tests, the value of the test statistic is given, followed by its transformation to a statistic that has approximately an F distribution. The next two columns contain the numerator (hypothesis) and denominator (error) degrees of freedom for the F statistic. The observed significance level (the probability of observing a difference at least as large as the one found in the sample when there is no difference in the populations) is given in the last column. All of the observed significance levels are large, causing us not to reject the hypothesis that there is no sex-by-field-dependence interaction. There is no straightforward transformation for Roy's largest root criterion to a statistic with a known distribution, so only the value of the largest root is displayed.

Since the multivariate results are not statistically significant, there is no reason to examine the univariate results shown in Figure 3.41. When the multivariate results are significant, however, the univariate statistics may help determine which variables contribute to the overall differences. The univariate F tests for the sex-by-field interaction are the same as the F's for sex by field in a two-way ANOVA. Figure 3.42 contains a two-way analysis of variance for the balancing-with-eyes-open (*balomean*) variable. The within-cells sum of squares is identical to the diagonal entry for *balomean* in Figure 3.38. Similarly, the sex-by-field sum of squares is identical to the diagonal entry for *balomean* in Figure 3.39. The F value for the interaction term, 0.28, is the same as in the first line of Figure 3.41.

Figure 3.41   Univariate F tests

```
MANOVA BALOMEAN BALCMEAN SSTMEAN PP BY SEX(1,2)FIELD(1,3)
  /PRINT=SIGNIF(UNIV)
  /DESIGN.


EFFECT .. SEX BY FIELD (CONT.)
Univariate F-tests with (2,128) D. F.

Variable   Hypoth. SS   Error SS  Hypoth. MS    Error MS        F   Sig. of F

BALOMEAN    18.10215  4122.15200    9.05107    32.20431    .28105      .755
BALCMEAN     3.77316   256.22940    1.88658     2.00179    .94244      .392
SSTMEAN     13.52286   733.14908    6.76143     5.72773   1.18047      .310
PP           1.78988   264.83786     .89494     2.06905    .43254      .650
```

Figure 3.42   Two-way analysis of variance

```
MANOVA BALOMEAN BY SEX(1,2) FIELD(1,3)
  /DESIGN.


Tests of Significance for BALOMEAN using UNIQUE sums of squares
Source of Variation        SS      DF        MS        F  Sig of F

WITHIN CELLS           4122.15     128     32.20
SEX                     389.33       1    389.33    12.09    .001
FIELD                    55.19       2     27.59      .86    .427
SEX BY FIELD             18.10       2      9.05      .28    .755

(Model)                 445.12       5     89.02     2.76    .021
(Total)                4567.27     133     34.34

R-Squared =           .097
Adjusted R-Squared =  .062
```

Discriminant Analysis for the Interaction Effect

As discussed in "Discriminant Analysis" on p. 75, for the two-group situation, the MANOVA problem can also be viewed as one of finding the linear combinations of the dependent variables that best separate the categories of the independent variables. For main effects, the analogy with discriminant analysis is clear: what combinations of the variables distinguish men from women and what combinations distinguish the three categories of field dependence? When interaction terms are considered, we must distinguish among the six (two sex and three field-dependence) categories jointly. This is done by finding the linear combination of variables that maximizes the ratio of the hypothesis to error sums of squares. Since the interaction effect is not significant, there is no particular reason to examine the discriminant analysis results. However, we will consider them for illustrative purposes.

Figure 3.43 contains the standardized discriminant function coefficients for the interaction term. The number of functions that can be derived is equal to the degrees of freedom for that term if it is less than the number of dependent variables. The two variables that have the largest standardized coefficients for function 1 are the sidestepping test and the Purdue Pegboard Test. All warnings concerning the interpretation of coefficients when variables are correlated apply in this situation as well. However, the magnitude of the coefficients may give us some idea of the variables contributing most to group differences.

Figure 3.43   Standardized discriminant function coefficients

```
MANOVA BALOMEAN BALCMEAN SSTMEAN PP BY SEX(1,2)FIELD(1,3)
  /DISCRIM=STAN ALPHA(1)
  /DESIGN.


EFFECT .. SEX BY FIELD
Standardized discriminant function coefficients
        Function No.

Variable            1               2

BALOMEAN          .02621         -.27281
BALCMEAN         -.19519         -.90129
SSTMEAN           .98773          .02420
PP               -.73895          .15295
```

A measure of the strength of the association between the discriminant functions and the grouping variables is the **canonical correlation coefficient**. Its square is the proportion of variability in the discriminant function scores explained by the independent variables. All multivariate significance tests, which were expressed as functions of the eigenvalues in "Tests of Multivariate Differences" on p. 83, can also be expressed as functions of the canonical correlations.

Figure 3.44 contains several sets of statistics for the discriminant functions. The entry under *Eigenvalue* is the dispersion associated with each function. The next column is the percentage of the total dispersion associated with each function. (It is obtained by dividing each eigenvalue by the sum of all eigenvalues and multiplying by 100.) The last column contains the canonical correlation coefficients. The results in Figure 3.44 are consistent with the results of the multivariate significance tests. Both the eigenvalues and canonical correlation coefficients are small, indicating that there is no interaction effect.

Figure 3.44   Eigenvalues and canonical correlations

```
MANOVA BALOMEAN BALCMEAN SSTMEAN PP BY SEX(1,2)FIELD(1,3)
 /PRINT=SIGNIF(EIGEN)
 /DESIGN.

EFFECT .. SEX BY FIELD

- - - - - - - - - - - - - - - - - - - - - - - - - - - - - - - - -


  Eigenvalues and Canonical Correlations

  Root No.      Eigenvalue        Pct.        Cum. Pct.      Canon Cor.

        1          .03808      70.39071        70.39071         .19152
        2          .01602      29.60929       100.00000         .12556
```

When more than one discriminant function can be derived, you should examine how many functions contribute to group differences. The same tests for successive eigenvalues available in the Discriminant procedure can be obtained from the SPSS/PC+ MANOVA procedure. The first line in Figure 3.45 is a test of the hypothesis that all eigenvalues are equal to 0. The value for Wilks' lambda in the first line of Figure 3.45 is equal to the test of multivariate differences in Figure 3.40. Successive lines in Figure 3.45 correspond to tests of the hypothesis that all remaining functions are equal in the groups. These tests allow you to assess the number of dimensions on which the groups differ.

Figure 3.45   Dimension reduction analysis

```
MANOVA BALOMEAN BALCMEAN SSTMEAN PP BY SEX(1,2)FIELD(1,3)
 /PRINT=SIGNIF(DIMENR)
 /DESIGN.

EFFECT .. SEX BY FIELD

- - - - - - - - - - - - - - - - - - - - - - - - - - - - - - - - - - - - - - -
Dimension Reduction Analysis

Roots          Wilks L.          F      Hypoth. DF       Error DF      Sig. of F

1 TO 2           .94813       .84339          8.00         250.00          .565
2 TO 2           .98424       .67273          3.00         126.00          .570
```

Testing for Differences Among Field Dependence and Sex Categories

Since the field-dependence-by-sex interaction term is not significant, the main effects can be tested. Figure 3.46 contains the multivariate tests of significance for the field-dependence variable. All four criteria indicate that there is not sufficient evidence to reject the null hypothesis that the means of the motor-ability variables do not differ for the three categories of field dependence.

Figure 3.46   Multivariate tests of significance for field

```
MANOVA BALOMEAN BALCMEAN SSTMEAN PP BY SEX(1,2)FIELD(1,3)
 /PRINT=SIGNIF(MULTIV)
 /DESIGN.


EFFECT .. FIELD
Multivariate Tests of Significance (S = 2, M = 1/2, N = 61 1/2)

Test Name          Value        Approx. F    Hypoth. DF      Error DF      Sig. of F

Pillais            .04152         .66780         8.00          252.00         .720
Hotellings         .04244         .65789         8.00          248.00         .728
Wilks              .95889         .66285         8.00          250.00         .724
Roys               .02533
Note.. F statistic for WILKS' Lambda is exact.
```

The multivariate tests of significance for the sex variable are shown in Figure 3.47. All four criteria indicate that there are significant differences between men and women on the motor-ability variables. Compare Figure 3.47 with Figure 3.23, which contains Hotelling's statistic for the two-group situation. Note that although the two statistics are close in value—0.669 when *sex* is considered alone and 0.609 when *sex* is included in a model containing field dependence and the sex-by-field-dependence interaction—they are not identical. The reason is that in the second model the sex effect is adjusted for the other effects in the model (see "Different Types of Sums of Squares" on p. 91).

Figure 3.47   Multivariate tests of significance for sex

```
MANOVA BALOMEAN BALCMEAN SSTMEAN PP BY SEX(1,2)FIELD(1,3)
 /PRINT=SIGNIF(MULTIV)
 /DESIGN.


EFFECT .. SEX
Multivariate Tests of Significance (S = 1, M = 1 , N = 61 1/2)


Test Name          Value        Exact F      Hypoth. DF      Error DF      Sig. of F


Pillais            .37871       19.04872        4.00          125.00         .000
Hotellings         .60956       19.04872        4.00          125.00         .000
Wilks              .62129       19.04872        4.00          125.00         .000
Roys               .37871
Note.. F statistics are exact.
```

Stepdown F Tests

If the dependent variables are ordered in some fashion, it is possible to test for group differences of variables adjusting for effects of other variables. This is termed a **stepdown**

procedure. Consider Figure 3.48, which contains the stepdown tests for the motor-ability variables. The first line is just a univariate *F* test for the balancing-with-eyes-open variable. The value is the same as that displayed in Figure 3.49, which contains the univariate *F* tests. The next line in Figure 3.48 is the univariate *F* test for balancing with eyes closed when balancing with eyes open is taken to be a covariate. That is, differences in balancing with eyes open are eliminated from the comparison of balancing with eyes closed. Figure 3.50 is the ANOVA table for the *balcmean* variable when *balomean* is treated as the covariate. Note that the *F* value of 1.77 for *sex* in Figure 3.50 is identical to that for *balcmean* in Figure 3.48.

Figure 3.48   Stepdown tests

```
MANOVA BALOMEAN BALCMEAN SSTMEAN PP BY SEX(1,2)FIELD(1,3)
  /PRINT=SIGNIF(STEPDOWN)
  /DESIGN.

EFFECT .. SEX (Cont.)

Roy-Bargman Stepdown F - tests

Variable     Hypoth. MS    Error MS    StepDown F  Hypoth. DF    Error DF    Sig. of F

BALOMEAN      389.32561    32.20431     12.08924          1          128         .001
BALCMEAN        3.24111     1.83574      1.76556          1          127         .186
SSTMEAN       149.80346     5.46262     27.42335          1          126         .000
PP             44.19767     1.84900     23.90361          1          125         .000
```

Figure 3.49   Univariate F tests

```
MANOVA BALOMEAN BALCMEAN SSTMEAN PP BY SEX(1,2)FIELD(1,3)
  /PRINT=SIGNIF(UNIV)
  /DESIGN.
EFFECT .. SEX (Cont.)
Univariate F-tests with (1,128) D. F.

Variable     Hypoth. SS     Error SS    Hypoth. MS    Error MS          F   Sig. of F

BALOMEAN      389.32561   4122.15200    389.32561    32.20431   12.08924        .001
BALCMEAN         .16537    256.22940       .16537     2.00179     .08261        .774
SSTMEAN       172.11258    733.14908    172.11258     5.72773   30.04902        .000
PP             23.56120    264.83786     23.56120     2.06905   11.38747        .001
```

Figure 3.50   ANOVA table for balcmean with balomean as the covariate

```
MANOVA BALOMEAN BALCMEAN SSTMEAN PP BY SEX(1,2)FIELD(1,3)
  /ANALYSIS=BALCMEAN WITH BALOMEAN
  /DESIGN.


Tests of Significance for BALCMEAN using UNIQUE sums of squares
Source of Variation          SS        DF        MS          F  Sig of F

WITHIN CELLS              233.14       127      1.84
REGRESSION                 23.09         1     23.09      12.58      .001
SEX                         3.24         1      3.24       1.77      .186
FIELD                       2.40         2      1.20        .65      .522
SEX BY FIELD                2.63         2      1.32        .72      .490

(Model)                    29.36         6      4.89       2.67      .018
(Total)                   262.50       133      1.97

R-Squared =          .112
Adjusted R-Squared =  .070
```

The third line of Figure 3.48, the test for the sidestepping variable, is adjusted for both the balancing-with-eyes-open variable and the balancing-with-eyes-closed variable. Similarly, the last line, the Purdue Pegboard Test score, has balancing with eyes open, balancing with eyes closed, and the sidestepping test as covariates. Thus, each variable in Figure 3.48 is adjusted for variables that precede it in the table.

The order in which variables are displayed on the stepdown tests in the SPSS/PC+ MANOVA procedure output depends only on the order in which the variables are specified for the procedure. If this order is not meaningful, the stepdown tests that result will not be readily interpretable or meaningful.

Different Types of Sums of Squares

When there is more than one factor and unequal numbers of cases in each cell in univariate analysis of variance, the total sums of squares cannot be partitioned into additive components for each effect. That is, the sums of squares for all effects do not add up to the total sums of squares. Differences between factor means are "contaminated" by the effects of the other factors.

There are many different algorithms for calculating the sums of squares for unbalanced data. Different types of sums of squares correspond to tests of different hypotheses. Two frequently used methods for calculating the sums of squares are the **unique method**, also known as the **regression method**, in which an effect is adjusted for all other effects in the model, and the **sequential method**, in which an effect is adjusted only for effects that precede it in the model.

In multivariate analysis of variance, unequal sample sizes in the cells lead to similar problems. Again, different procedures for calculating the requisite statistics are available. The SPSS/PC+ MANOVA procedure offers two options: the unique (regression) solution and the sequential solution. All output displayed in this chapter is obtained from the regression solution, the default (see Milliken & Johnson, 1984).

For any connected design, the hypotheses associated with the sequential sums of squares are weighted functions of the population cell means, with weights depending on the cell frequencies (see Searle, 1971). For designs in which every cell is filled, it can be shown that the hypotheses corresponding to the regression model sums of squares are the hypotheses about the unweighted cell means. With empty cells, the hypotheses will depend on the pattern of empty cells.

Problems with Empty Cells

When there are no observations in one or more cells in a design, the analysis is greatly complicated. This is true for both univariate and multivariate designs. Empty cells result in the inability to estimate uniquely all of the necessary parameters. Hypotheses that involve parameters corresponding to the empty cells usually cannot be tested. Thus, the output from an analysis involving empty cells should be treated with caution (see Freund, 1980; Milliken & Johnson, 1984).

Examining Residuals

Residuals—the differences between observed values and those predicted from a model—
provide information about the adequacy of fit of the model and the assumptions. The Multiple Regression chapter in the *SPSS/PC+ Base System User's Guide* discusses residual
analysis for regression models. The same techniques are appropriate for analysis-of-variance models as well.

In the two-factor model with interactions, the equation is

$$\hat{y}_{ij} = \hat{\mu} + \hat{\alpha}_i + \hat{\beta}_j + \hat{\delta}_{ij}$$ **Equation 3.15**

where $\hat{y}_{ij}$ is the predicted value for the cases in the ith category of the first variable and
the jth category of the second. As before, $\hat{\mu}$ is the grand mean, $\hat{\alpha}_i$ is the effect of the ith
category of the first variable, $\hat{\beta}_j$ is the effect of the jth category of the second variable, and
$\hat{\delta}_{ij}$ is their interaction.

Consider Figure 3.51, which contains deviation parameter estimates for the balancing-with-eyes-open variable. From this table and the grand mean (11.42), the predicted
value for females in the low field-dependence category is:

$$\hat{y}_{11} = 11.42 - 1.78 - 0.97 + 0.51 = 9.18$$ **Equation 3.16**

Similarly, the predicted value for males in the high field-dependence category is:

$$\hat{y}_{23} = 11.42 + 1.78 + 0.53 + 0.09 = 13.82$$ **Equation 3.17**

Note that only independent parameter estimates are displayed and that the other estimates
must be derived from these. For example, the parameter estimate displayed for the sex
variable is for the first category, females. The estimate for males is the negative of the estimate for females, since the two values must sum to 0 for the default deviation contrasts.
The value for the third category of field dependence is 0.53, the negative of the sum of the
values for the first two categories. The two parameter estimates displayed for the interaction effects are for females with low field dependence and females with medium field dependence. The remaining estimates can be easily calculated. For example, the value for
males in the low field-dependence category is -0.51, the negative of that for females.
Similarly, the value for females in the high field-dependence category is -0.087, the negative of the sum of the values for females in low and medium field-dependence categories.

Figure 3.51   Parameter estimates for deviation contrasts

```
SET WIDTH=WIDE.
MANOVA BALOMEAN BALCMEAN SSTMEAN PP BY SEX(1,2)FIELD(1,3)
  /PRINT=PARAMETERS(ESTIM)
  /ANALYSIS=BALOMEAN
  /DESIGN.
```

```
Estimates for BALOMEAN
--- Individual univariate .9500 confidence intervals
```

SEX

Parameter	Coeff.	Std. Err.	t-Value	Sig. t	Lower -95%	CL- Upper
2	-1.7790199059	.51166	-3.47696	.00069	-2.79143	-.76661

FIELD

Parameter	Coeff.	Std. Err.	t-Value	Sig. t	Lower -95%	CL- Upper
3	-.9744642465	.74485	-1.30827	.19313	-2.44828	.49935
4	.4457274482	.70743	.63006	.52978	-.95405	1.84551

SEX BY FIELD

Parameter	Coeff.	Std. Err.	t-Value	Sig. t	Lower -95%	CL- Upper
5	.5145658116	.74485	.69083	.49092	-.95925	1.98838
6	-.4273042048	.70743	-.60402	.54690	-1.82709	.97248

Figure 3.52 contains an excerpt of some cases in the study and their observed and predicted values for the balancing-with-eyes-open variable. The fourth column is the **residual**: the difference between the observed and predicted values. Standardized residuals shown in the fifth column are obtained by dividing each raw residual by the error standard deviation.

Figure 3.52   Observed and predicted values

```
MANOVA BALOMEAN BALCMEAN SSTMEAN PP BY SEX(1,2)FIELD(1,3)
  /RESIDUALS=CASEWISE
  /ANALYSIS=BALOMEAN
  /DESIGN.
```

Observed and Predicted Values for Each Case

Dependent Variable.. BALOMEAN   Balance Test - Eyes Open

Case No.	Observed	Predicted	Raw Resid.	Std Resid.
1	4.000	10.082	-6.082	-1.072
2	8.850	9.181	-.331	-.058
3	10.000	9.659	.341	.060
4	3.550	10.082	-6.532	-1.151
5	2.800	9.659	-6.859	-1.209
6	14.500	9.659	4.841	.853
.	.	.	.	.
127	5.000	13.815	-8.815	-1.553
128	20.000	11.710	8.290	1.461
129	20.000	13.815	6.185	1.090
130	19.000	11.710	7.290	1.285
131	16.150	14.072	2.078	.366
132	20.000	14.072	5.928	1.045
.	.	.	.	.

As in regression analysis, a variety of plots is useful for checking the assumptions. Figure 3.53 is a plot of the observed and predicted values for the *balomean* variable. Figure 3.54 is a plot of the standardized residuals against the predicted values. If the spread of the residuals increases with the magnitude of the predicted values, you have reason to suspect that the variance may not be constant in all cells. Standardized residuals are plotted against the case numbers in Figure 3.54. The plot against the case numbers is useful if the data are gathered and entered into the file sequentially. Any patterns in this plot lead to suspicions that the data are not independent of each other. Of course, if the data have been sorted before being entered, a pattern is to be expected.

Figure 3.53 Plot of the observed and predicted values

```
MANOVA BALOMEAN BALCMEAN SSTMEAN PP BY SEX(1,2)FIELD(1,3)
 /RESIDUALS=PLOT
 /ANALYSIS=BALOMEAN
 /DESIGN.
          Observed VS. Predicted Values for BALOMEAN

         +----+----+----+----+----+----+----+----+-+
         :                                         :
         :                                         :
         :                                         :
         :       1 1     1   2 132  1   12   2  15 :
   13.75 +        21         1 12   11 2         6 +
         :                                         :
         :                                         :
         :                                         :
P        :                                         :
R   12.5 +                                         +
E        :                                         :
D        :                                         :
I        :     12 222 11      1 13 3111  1  1  2 5 :
C        :                                         :
T  11.25 +                                         +
E        :                                         :
D        :                                         :
         :                                         :
         :                                         :
      10 +      122  222 2 12 4 11  1            5 +
         : 1 1 2 2 21   1    11    12121 1   1   1 :
         :                                         :
         :   1 111 11  1   11       1          1 2 :
         :                                         :
    8.75 +                                         +
         :                                         :
         +----+----+----+----+----+----+----+----+-+
            2.5       7.5      12.5      17.5
                   5        10        15        20

                          OBSERVED
```

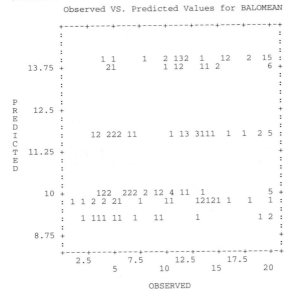

Figure 3.54   Plot of predicted and residual values

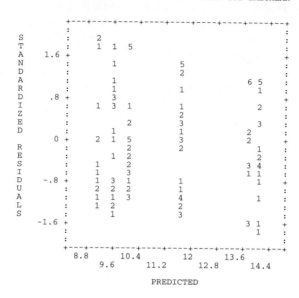

```
                Predicted Values VS Std Resid. for BALOMEAN

         +---+----+----+----+----+----+----+----+--+
   S     :                                         :
   T     :        2                                :
   A     :        1   1   5                         :
   N 1.6 +                                         +
   D     :            1                5           :
   A     :                            2           :
   R     :            1                      6 5   :
   D  .8 :            1                1       1   :
   D  .8 +            3                            +
   I     :        1   3   1           1        2   :
   Z     :                            2           :
   E     :                2           3        3   :
   D     :            1               1      2    :
      0  +        2   1   5           3      2    +
   R     :                2           2       1   :
   E     :            1   2                   2   :
   S     :        1   2                   3 4     :
   I     :        1   3               1 1       :
   D -.8 +        1   3   1           1        1   +
   U     :        2   2   2           1           :
   A     :        1   1   3           4        1   :
   L     :        1   2               2           :
   S     :            1               3           :
    -1.6 +                                   3 1   +
         :                                     1   :
         :                                         :
         +---+----+----+----+----+----+----+----+--+
            8.8       10.4      12       13.6
                 9.6      11.2     12.8       14.4

                            PREDICTED
```

Figure 3.55   Plot of case numbers and residuals for balance test (balomean)

```
              Case Number VS. Std. Residuals for BALOMEAN

         +---+----+----+----+----+----+----+----+--+
   S     :                                         :
   T     :        1           1                    :
   A     :        11 1        2 1   1               :
   N 1.6 +                                         +
   D     :              1       1  1  1      11     :
   A     :                            1     1      :
   R     :                  21 1 11  2   1 111      :
   D  .8 :          1         1            1        :
   D  .8 +    1 1       1              2            +
   I     :        1 1      1 2     1      2         :
   Z     :                    1         1          :
   E     :        1     1  1  1   1    2 1         :
   D     :           1         1   1  1            :
      0  +    2    1  12   11  1   2     2         +
   R     :           1 1            11       1      :
   E     :       1        1 1            2         :
   S     :             11 1     2 1 1   1 11       :
   I     :       1 1   1     1   11                :
   D -.8 +    1 1   2      1 1          1          +
   U     :       1 1   1  11 1 1                   :
   A     :    11 1 1     1     1 1 1 1        1    :
   L     :    1   2          1        1           :
   S     :    1              1   1  1            :
    -1.6 +                  1      1 1   1        +
         :                         1               :
         :                                         :
         +---+----+----+----+----+----+----+----+--+
            20       60        100       140
          0      40        80       120

                            CASE NO.
```

If the assumption of multivariate normality is met, the distribution of the residuals for each variable should be approximately normal. Figure 3.56 is a normal plot of the residuals for the balancing-with-eyes-open variable, while Figure 3.57 is the detrended normal plot of the same variable. Both of these plots suggest that there may be reason to suspect that the distribution of the residuals is not normal.

Figure 3.56   Normal plot of residuals

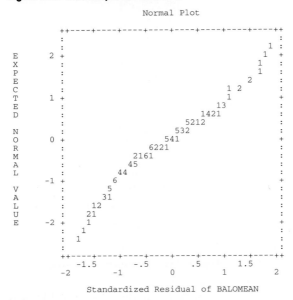

Figure 3.57   Detrended normal plot

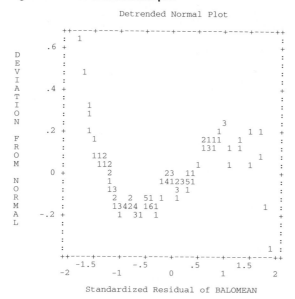

Standardized Residual of BALOMEAN

Predicted Means

Figure 3.58 shows a table that contains observed and predicted means as well as residuals for all cells in the design for the balancing-with-eyes-open variable. The first column of the table, labeled *Obs. Mean,* is the observed mean for that cell. The next value, labeled *Adj. Mean*, is the mean predicted from the model adjusted for the covariates. The column labeled *Est. Mean* contains the predicted means without correcting for covariates. When covariates are present, the differences between the adjusted and estimated means provide an indication of the effectiveness of the covariate adjustment (see Finn, 1974). For a complete factorial design without covariates, the observed, adjusted, and estimated means will always be equal. The difference between them, the residual, will also be equal to 0.

If the design is not a full-factorial model, the observed means and those predicted using the parameter estimates will differ. Consider Figure 3.59, which contains a table of means for the main-effects-only model. The observed cell means are no longer equal to those predicted by the model. The difference between the observed and estimated mean is shown in the column labeled *Raw Resid.* The residual divided by the error standard deviation is shown in the column labeled *Std. Resid.* From this table it is possible to identify cells for which the model does not fit well.

Figure 3.58   Table of predicted means

```
MANOVA BALOMEAN BALCMEAN SSTMEAN PP BY SEX(1,2) FIELD(1,3)
   /PMEANS=TABLES(SEX BY FIELD)
   /DESIGN.
```

Adjusted and Estimated Means
Variable .. BALOMEAN

Factor	Code	Balance Test - Eyes Open Obs. Mean	Adj. Mean	Est. Mean	Raw Resid.	Std. Resid.
SEX Female						
FIELD	1	9.18077	9.18077	9.18077	.00000	.00000
FIELD	2	9.65909	9.65909	9.65909	.00000	.00000
FIELD	3	10.08214	10.08214	10.08214	.00000	.00000
SEX Male						
FIELD	1	11.70968	11.70968	11.70968	.00000	.00000
FIELD	2	14.07174	14.07174	14.07174	.00000	.00000
FIELD	3	13.81471	13.81471	13.81471	.00000	.00000

It is also possible to obtain various combinations of the adjusted means. For example, Figure 3.59 contains the combined adjusted means for the *sex* and *field* variables for the main-effects design. The means are labeled as unweighted, since the sample sizes in the cells are not used when means are combined over the categories of a variable.

Figure 3.59   Table of predicted means

```
MANOVA BALOMEAN BALCMEAN SSTMEAN PP BY SEX(1,2) FIELD(1,3)
   /PMEANS=(TABLES(SEX, FIELD))
   /DESIGN SEX FIELD.
```

Adjusted and Estimated Means
Variable .. BALOMEAN

Factor	Code	Balance Test - Eyes Open Obs. Mean	Adj. Mean	Est. Mean	Raw Resid.	Std. Resid.
SEX Female						
FIELD	1	9.18077	8.40954	8.40954	.77123	.13666
FIELD	2	9.65909	10.06241	10.06241	-.40331	-.07147
FIELD	3	10.08214	10.12332	10.12332	-.04118	-.00730
SEX Male						
FIELD	1	11.70968	12.03310	12.03310	-.32342	-.05731
FIELD	2	14.07174	13.68596	13.68596	.38578	.06836
FIELD	3	13.81471	13.74688	13.74688	.06783	.01202

Combined Adjusted Means for SEX
Variable .. BALOMEAN

SEX		
Female	UNWGT.	9.53176
Male	UNWGT.	13.15531

Combined Adjusted Means for FIELD
Variable .. BALOMEAN

FIELD		
1	UNWGT.	10.22132
2	UNWGT.	11.87418
3	UNWGT.	11.93510

Computation of Power and Effect Size

Whenever you evaluate data, it is important to consider both the magnitude of the observed effect and the power of detecting an effect of the observed magnitude. (Recall that the power of an experiment is the probability of rejecting the null hypothesis when it is false.) The SPSS/PC+ MANOVA procedure will compute power estimates for both univariate and multivariate tests.

Some Final Comments

In this chapter, only the most basic aspects of multivariate analysis of variance have been covered. The SPSS/PC+ MANOVA procedure is capable of testing more elaborate models of several types. Chapter 4 considers a special class of designs called **repeated measures designs**. In such designs, the same variable or variables are measured on several occasions. For further discussion of multivariate analysis of variance, consult Morrison (1976) and Tatsuoka (1971).

Running the MANOVA Procedure

The MANOVA procedure is a generalized analysis of variance and covariance program that performs both univariate and multivariate procedures. You can analyze such designs as block, split-plot, nested, and repeated measures designs. (Repeated measures designs and the MANOVA commands needed to analyze them are discussed in Chapter 4.) MANOVA can also be used to obtain multivariate regression coefficients, principal components, discriminant function coefficients, canonical correlations, and other statistics.

A program with so many facilities naturally has a large number of subcommands available. This section concentrates on the most commonly used subcommands and briefly describes the rest. The repeated measures subcommands WSFACTORS, WSDESIGN, and RENAME are discussed in Chapter 4. For further information and examples, see "MANOVA: Univariate" on p. 318.

Specifying Variables in the Equation

To run MANOVA, you must indicate which variables are dependent variables, which (if any) are factors, and which (if any) are covariates. You also need to specify the design to be used. The simplest MANOVA specification is a list of variables. If no other subcommands or keywords are used, all variables listed are treated as dependent variables and a one-sample Hotelling's T^2 is calculated. Thus, the output in Figure 3.13 was produced by the following command:

```
MANOVA BALOMEAN BALCMEAN SSTMEAN PP.
```

Dependent Variable List

The first variables specified are the dependent variables in the analysis. By default, MANOVA treats a list of dependent variables as jointly dependent and, therefore, uses a multivariate design. This default can be changed by using the ANALYSIS subcommand (see "Specifying the Model" on p. 101).

Specifying the Factor List

Use the BY keyword to specify the factor list. BY must follow the dependent variable list and precede the factor list. Each factor is followed by two integer values, specifying the lowest and highest values for the factor. The two values for each factor must be enclosed in parentheses and separated by a comma.

Example

```
MANOVA BALOMEAN BALCMEAN SSTMEAN PP BY SEX(1,2) FIELD(1,3).
```

- This command specifies two factors: *sex*, with possible values 1 and 2, and *field*, with possible values 1, 2, and 3. Cases with values outside the specified range are excluded from the analysis.
- This command produces the output shown in Figure 3.40 and Figure 3.41.

MANOVA requires factor levels to be integers. You need to recode any non-integer factor values. Factors with empty categories must also be recoded, since MANOVA expects the levels of a factor to be adjacent.

If several factors have the same value range, you can specify a list of factors followed by a single value range, as in the following command:

```
MANOVA SALES BY TVAD RADIOAD MAGAD NEWSPAD(2,5).
```

Certain analyses, such as regression, canonical correlation, and the one-sample Hotelling's T^2, do not require a factor specification. For these analyses, the factor list and the keyword BY should be omitted.

Specifying the Covariate List

Use the WITH keyword to specify the covariate list. WITH must follow the dependent variable list and the factor list (if there is one) and precede the covariate list, as in the following command:

```
MANOVA BALOMEAN BALCMEAN SSTMEAN PP
               BY SEX(1,2) FIELD(1,3) WITH IQ.
```

Specifying the Model

Use the ANALYSIS subcommand to specify a model based on a subset of variables named on the dependent variable and/or the covariate list. You can also use ANALYSIS to change the model specified on the MANOVA command by changing dependent variables to covariates or covariates to dependent variables in the analysis. When ANALYSIS is specified, it completely overrides the dependent variable list and covariate list, but it does not affect the factors. Only variables on the original MANOVA dependent variable list or covariate list can be specified on the ANALYSIS subcommand.

Example

```
MANOVA BALOMEAN BALCMEAN SSTMEAN PP
            BY SEX(1,2) FIELD(1,3) WITH IQ
    /ANALYSIS=BALOMEAN BALCMEAN PP WITH SSTMEAN.
```

- This command changes *sstmean* from a dependent variable to a covariate.

Example

```
MANOVA BALOMEAN BALCMEAN SSTMEAN
            BY SEX(1,2) FIELD(1,3) WITH IQ PP
    /ANALYSIS=BALOMEAN BALCMEAN SSTMEAN PP WITH IQ.
```

- This command changes *pp* from a covariate to a dependent variable.
- The factors *sex* and *field* are still used in the analysis (unless eliminated with a DE-SIGN subcommand; see "Specifying the Design" on p. 102).

Example

```
MANOVA SALES OPINION BY TVAD RADIOAD NEWSPAD(2,5)
        WITH PCTBUSNS
    /ANALYSIS=OPINION.
```

- This command deletes the variables *sales* and *pctbusns* from the analysis.

Only one ANALYSIS subcommand can be specified per DESIGN subcommand, but a single ANALYSIS subcommand can be used to obtain multiple analyses, as long as the lists of dependent variables do not overlap.

Example

```
MANOVA BALOMEAN BALCMEAN SSTMEAN PP
        BY SEX(1,2) FIELD (1,3) WITH EDUC IQ
    /ANALYSIS=(BALOMEAN BALCMEAN /SSTMEAN /PP WITH IQ).
```

- This command specifies three analyses. The first has *balomean* and *balcmean* as dependent variables and no covariates, the second has *sstmean* as the dependent variable and no covariates, and the third has *pp* as the dependent variable and *iq* as a covariate.

- *None of the variable lists overlaps.*

Example

```
MANOVA BALOMEAN BALCMEAN SSTMEAN PP BY SEX (1,2) FIELD(1,3)
      WITH EDUC IQ
  /ANALYSIS=(BALOMEAN BALCMEAN /SSTMEAN /PP WITH IQ) WITH EDUC
  /DESIGN.
```

- This command requests three separate analyses with *educ* as the covariate for all of them.

Although three separate ANALYSIS and DESIGN subcommands could be used to get the same results, it would increase processing time.

When specifying multiple analyses in this fashion, you may sometimes find the keywords CONDITIONAL and UNCONDITIONAL useful. CONDITIONAL indicates that subsequent variable lists should include as covariates all previous dependent variables on that ANALYSIS subcommand. UNCONDITIONAL (the default) indicates that each list should be used as is, independent of the others.

Example

```
MANOVA SALES LEADS OPINIONS CONTRACT
   BY TVAD RADIOAD MAGAD NEWSPAD(2,5) WITH PCTHOMES PCTBUSNS
  /ANALYSIS(CONDITIONAL)=(LEADS OPINIONS CONTRACT/SALES)
   WITH PCTBUSNS
  /DESIGN.
```

This command is equivalent to:

```
MANOVA SALES LEADS OPINIONS CONTRACT
   BY TVAD RADIOAD MAGAD NEWSPAD(2,5) WITH PCTHOMES PCTBUSNS
  /ANALYSIS=LEADS OPINIONS CONTRACT WITH PCTBUSNS
  /DESIGN
  /ANALYSIS=SALES WITH LEADS OPINIONS CONTRACT PCTBUSNS
  /DESIGN.
```

Specifying the Design

Use the DESIGN subcommand to specify the structure of the model. DESIGN must be the *last* subcommand for any given model, and it can be used more than once to specify different models. The default model (obtained when DESIGN is used without further specification) is the full-factorial model.

Because of its importance, the DESIGN subcommand is discussed at this point in the chapter. Remember that the other subcommands discussed later on must *precede* the DESIGN subcommand to which they apply.

Specifying Effects

When a full-factorial model is not desired, the DESIGN subcommand can be used to specify the effects in the model, with the effects separated by blanks or commas.

Example

```
MANOVA BALOMEAN BALCMEAN SSTMEAN PP BY SEX(1,2) FIELD(1,3)
   /DESIGN=SEX FIELD.
```

- This command specifies a model with only main effects.

Specifying Interaction Terms

Use the BY keyword to specify interaction terms on the effect list.

Example

```
MANOVA SALES BY TVAD RADIOAD MAGAD NEWSPAD(2,5)
   /DESIGN=TVAD RADIOAD MAGAD NEWSPAD
          TVAD BY RADIOAD TVAD BY RADIOAD BY NEWSPAD.
```

- This command specifies a model with all main effects, the two-way interaction between *tvad* and *radioad*, and the three-way interaction between *tvad, radioad,* and *newspad*.

Including Single-Degree-of-Freedom Effects

Use the PARTITION subcommand to subdivide the degrees of freedom associated with the factor and specify single-degree-of-freedom effects on DESIGN. You can name the factor on PARTITION before specifying the single-degree-of-freedom effects.

Example

```
MANOVA RELIEF BY DRUG(1,4)
   /CONTRAST(DRUG)=SPECIAL(1 1 1 1,1 -1 0 0,4 4 -8 0,4 4 1 -9)
   /PARTITION(DRUG)
   /DESIGN=DRUG(1) DRUG(2) DRUG(3).
```

This command is equivalent to:

```
MANOVA RELIEF BY DRUG(1,4)
   /CONTRAST(DRUG)=SPECIAL(1 1 1 1,1 -1 0 0,4 4 -8 0,4 4 1 -9)
   /DESIGN=DRUG(1) DRUG(2) DRUG(3).
```

For further information about the PARTITION subcommand, see "Subdividing the Degrees of Freedom" on p. 111. For the CONTRAST subcommand, see "Specifying the Contrasts" on p. 111.

Incorporating Continuous Variables

Use the keyword POOL on DESIGN to incorporate continuous variables into a single effect. The variables to be incorporated cannot be used as dependent variables or covariates in the model. Thus, you must use an ANALYSIS subcommand to redefine the dependent variables and covariates used in the analysis and cannot include in the specification any of the variables to be incorporated by POOL.

Example

```
MANOVA SALES TEST1 TEST2 TEST3 BY TVAD
       RADIOAD MAGAD NEWSPAD(2,5) WITH PCTBUSNS
  /ANALYSIS=SALES WITH PCTBUSNS
  /DESIGN=POOL(TEST1 TEST2 TEST3).
```

- This command incorporates *test1*, *test2*, and *test3* into a single effect with three degrees of freedom.

Specifying Interaction Terms

To specify interactions between factors and continuous variables, simply list these interaction effects on the DESIGN subcommand using the keyword BY. You cannot specify interactions between two continuous variables (including covariates), and you cannot use variables that are included in the model by an ANALYSIS subcommand.

Pooled Effects

Use the plus sign (+) on DESIGN to pool effects together into a single effect. For example, the subcommand

```
  /DESIGN=TVAD + TVAD BY RADIOAD
```

combines the effects of *tvad* and the interaction of *tvad* by *radioad* into a single effect. The BY keyword is evaluated before the plus sign.

Parameters Plus Constant

To obtain estimates that consist of the sum of the constant term and the parameter values, use the MUPLUS keyword. The constant term μ is then combined with the parameter following the MUPLUS keyword. For example, the subcommand

```
  /DESIGN=MUPLUS SEX
```

adds the mean of each dependent variable to the *sex* parameters for that variable. This produces conditional means or "marginals" for each dependent variable. Since these means are adjusted for any covariates in the model, they are also the usual adjusted means when covariates are present. When the adjusted means cannot be estimated, MU-

PLUS produces estimates of the constant and the requested effect. These are no longer the predicted means.

The only way to obtain the standard errors of the conditional means is via the MU-PLUS keyword. However, conditional and adjusted means can be obtained by using the OMEANS and PMEANS subcommands (see "Specifying Printed Output" on p. 112). You can obtain unweighted conditional means for a main effect by specifying the full factorial model and specifying MUPLUS before the effect whose means are to be found. For example, the subcommand

```
/DESIGN=MUPLUS SEX FIELD SEX BY FIELD
```

obtains the unweighted marginal means for *sex* in a two-factor design. For an interaction effect, the DESIGN subcommand should not include any lower-order effects contained in it. For example, the subcommand

```
/DESIGN=MUPLUS SEX BY FIELD
```

obtains the unweighted marginal means for the interaction term *sex* by *field*. Only one MUPLUS keyword may be used per DESIGN subcommand.

Although MANOVA automatically includes the constant term (the correction for the mean), you can change the default by specifying NOCONSTANT on a METHOD subcommand. You can also override the NOCONSTANT specification by specifying CONSTANT on the DESIGN subcommand. *Constant* is not an acceptable variable name in MANOVA (see "MANOVA: Univariate" on p. 318).

Specifying Nested Designs

The WITHIN keyword, or W, indicates that the term to its left is nested in the term to its right. For example, the subcommand

```
/DESIGN=TREATMNT WITHIN TESTCAT
```

indicates that *treatmnt* is nested within *testcat*, while the subcommand

```
/DESIGN=TREATMNT WITHIN TESTCAT BY EDUC BY MOTIVTN
```

indicates that *treatmnt* is nested within the interaction *testcat* by *educ* by *motivtn*.

Specifying Error Terms

Use the keyword VS with one of the following error term keywords to specify error terms for individual effects:

WITHIN   *Within-cells error terms.* Alias W.

RESIDUAL   *Residual error terms.* Alias R.

WITHIN+RESIDUAL   *Combined within-cells and residual error terms.* Alias WR or RW.

To test a term against one of these error terms, specify the term to be tested, followed by the keyword VS and the error term keyword. For example, to test the interaction term *sex* by *field* against the residual error term, specify:

```
/DESIGN=SEX BY FIELD VS RESIDUAL
```

User-Defined Error Terms

You can create up to ten user-defined error terms by declaring any term in the model as an error term. To create such a term, specify the term followed by an equals sign, which is required, and an integer from 1 to 10, as in:

```
/DESIGN=SEX BY FIELD=1 FIELD VS 1 SEX VS 1
```

This command designates the interaction term *sex* by *field* as error term 1, which is then used to test the *sex* and *field* main effects. User-defined error terms can be used either on the left or on the right of the keyword VS.

Any term present in the design but not specified on DESIGN is lumped into the residual error term. The default error term for all tests is WITHIN+RESIDUAL.

Specifying the Default Error Term

Use the ERROR subcommand with one of the following keywords to specify the default error term for each between-subjects effect in subsequent designs:

WITHIN+RESIDUAL   *Pooled within-cells and residual error terms.* Alias WR or RW. This is the default.

WITHIN   *Within-cells error term.* Alias W.

RESIDUAL   *Residual error term.* Alias R.

n   *User-defined error term.*

You can designate a model term *(n)* as the default error term only if you explicitly define error term numbers on the DESIGN subcommand. If the specified error term number is not defined for a particular design, MANOVA does not carry out the significance tests involving that error term, although the parameter estimates and hypothesis sums of squares will be computed.

Example

```
MANOVA BALOMEAN BALCMEAN SSTMEAN PP BY SEX(1,2) FIELD(1,3)
   /ERROR=1
   /DESIGN=SEX FIELD SEX BY FIELD=1
   /DESIGN=SEX FIELD.
```

• This command specifies a user-defined error term (1) as the model error term.

- The first design designates the interaction term *sex* by *field* as error term 1. *Sex* and *field* are tested against the interaction term.
- No significance tests for *sex* or *field* are displayed for the second design, which contains no term defined as error term 1.

Specifying Within-Subjects Factors

Use the WSFACTORS subcommand to specify within-subjects factors for repeated measures analysis (see Chapter 4). You can specify the names and number of levels for within-subjects factors when you use the multivariate data setup. Each name must conform to the naming conventions of SPSS/PC+, and must be unique. That is, a within-subjects factor name cannot be the same as that of any dependent variable, between-subjects factor, or covariate in the MANOVA procedure. The within-subjects factors exist only during the MANOVA analysis.

Example

```
MANOVA DRUG1 TO DRUG4
  /WSFACTORS=TRIAL(4).
```

- This example supplies the name *trial* for the within-subjects factor, with four levels.
- The variable *trial* disappears at the end of the MANOVA procedure.

WSFACTORS must be the first subcommand after the MANOVA specification, and it can be specified only once per MANOVA command. You can specify up to 20 within-subjects and grouping factors altogether. Presence of a WSFACTORS subcommand invokes special repeated measures processing. See Chapter 4 for a complete discussion of the WSFACTORS subcommand.

Specifying a Within-Subjects Model

Use the WSDESIGN subcommand to specify a within-subjects model and a within-subjects transformation matrix based on the ordering of the continuous variables and the levels of the within-subjects factors. See Chapter 4 for a complete discussion of the WSDESIGN subcommand.

Analyzing Doubly Multivariate Designs

You can use the SPSS/PC+ MANOVA procedure to analyze doubly multivariate repeated measures designs, in which subjects are measured on two or more responses on two or more occasions. When the data are entered using the multivariate setup, you can use the MEASURE subcommand to name the multivariate pooled results.

Example

```
MANOVA TEMP1 TO TEMP6, WEIGHT1 TO WEIGHT6 BY GROUP(1,4)
  /WSFACTOR=AMPM(2), DAYS(3)
  /MEASURE=TEMP WEIGHT
  /WSDESIGN=AMPM DAYS, AMPM BY DAYS.
```

See Chapter 4 for a discussion of the MEASURE subcommand.

Specifying Linear Transformations

To specify linear transformations of the dependent variables and covariates, use the TRANSFORM subcommand. The first specification on TRANSFORM is the list of variables to be transformed. The list must be enclosed within parentheses. Multiple variable lists can be used if they are separated by slashes and each list contains the same number of variables. MANOVA then applies the indicated transformation to each list. By default, MANOVA transforms all dependent variables and covariates. If a list is specified, however, only variables named on the list are transformed.

Any number of TRANSFORM subcommands may be specified on a MANOVA command. A TRANSFORM subcommand remains in effect until MANOVA encounters another one. Transformations are *not* cumulative; each transformation applies to the original variables.

Transformed variables should be renamed to avoid possible confusion with the original variables. If you use TRANSFORM but do not supply a RENAME subcommand, MANOVA names the transformed variables *t1, t2,* and so on. You must use the new names for the continuous variables in all subsequent subcommands except OMEANS.

Seven types of transformations are available:

DEVIATION(refcat)	*Compare a dependent variable to the means of the dependent variables on the list.* By default, MANOVA omits the comparison of the last variable to the list of variables. You can omit a variable other than the last by specifying in parentheses the sequential number of the variable to be omitted.
DIFFERENCE	*Compare a dependent variable with the mean of the previous dependent variables on the list.* Also known as reverse Helmert.
HELMERT	*Compare a dependent variable to the means of the subsequent dependent variables on the list.*
SIMPLE(refcat)	*Compare each dependent variable with the last.* You can specify a variable other than the last as the reference variable by giving the sequential number of the variable in parentheses.
REPEATED	*Compare contiguous variable pairs, thereby producing difference scores.*

POLYNOMIAL(metric) *Fit orthogonal polynomials to the variables on the transformation list.* The default metric is equal spacing, but you can specify your own metric.

SPECIAL(matrix) *Fit your own transformation matrix reflecting combinations of interest.* The matrix must be square, with the number of rows and columns equal to the number of variables being transformed.

Example

```
/TRANSFORM(SALES LEADS OPINIONS CONTRACT)=POLYNOMIAL
```

• The subcommand fits orthogonal polynomials to variables *sales, leads, opinions,* and *contract,* with equal spacing assumed.

The type of transformation can be preceded by the keywords CONTRAST, BASIS, or OR-THONORM. CONTRAST and BASIS are alternatives; ORTHONORM may be used with either CONTRAST or BASIS, or alone, which implies CONTRAST.

CONTRAST *Generate the transformation matrix directly from the contrast matrix of the given type.* This is the default if neither CONTRAST nor BASIS is specified.

BASIS *Generate the transformation matrix from the one-way basis corresponding to the specified contrast.*

ORTHONORM *Orthonormalize the transformation matrix by rows before use.* MANOVA does not, by default, orthonormalize rows.

CONTRAST or BASIS can be used with any of the available methods for defining contrasts on the CONTRAST subcommand (see "Specifying the Contrasts" on p. 111). On the TRANSFORM subcommand, keywords CONTRAST and BASIS are used to generate the transformed variables for later analysis, rather than simply to specify the contrasts on which significance testing and parameter estimation will be based.

For further information on the TRANSFORM subcommand, see "MANOVA: Multivariate" on p. 344.

Renaming Transformed Variables

Use the RENAME subcommand to rename dependent variables and covariates after they have been transformed by TRANSFORM or WSFACTORS. Specify the new names after the subcommand keyword RENAME. The number of new names must be equal to the number of dependent variables and covariates. For further information about RENAME, see "MANOVA: Multivariate" on p. 344.

Specifying the Method

Use the METHOD subcommand to control computational aspects of MANOVA.

Method of Partitioning Sums of Squares

You can specify one of two different methods for partitioning the sums of squares. The default is UNIQUE.

UNIQUE   *Regression approach.* Each term is corrected for every other term in the model. With this approach, sums of squares for various components of the model do not add up to the total sum of squares unless the design is balanced. This is the default if the METHOD subcommand is omitted or if neither of the two keywords is specified.

SEQUENTIAL   *Hierarchical decomposition of the sums of squares.* Each term is adjusted only for the terms that precede it on the DESIGN subcommand. This is an orthogonal decomposition, and the sums of squares in the model add up to the total sum of squares.

Method of Estimating Parameters

You can control how parameters are to be estimated by specifying one of the following two keywords available on MANOVA. The default is QR.

QR   *Use modified Givens rotations.* QR bypasses the normal equations and the inaccuracies that can result from creating the cross-products matrix, and it generally results in extremely accurate parameter estimates. This is the default if the METHOD subcommand is omitted or if neither of the two keywords is specified.

CHOLESKY   *Use Cholesky decomposition of the cross-products matrix.* Useful for large data sets with covariates entered on the DESIGN subcommand.

Constant Terms

You can control whether a constant term is included in all models. Two keywords are available on METHOD. The default is CONSTANT.

CONSTANT   *All models include a constant (grand mean) term, even if none is explicitly specified on the DESIGN subcommand.* This is the default if neither of the two keywords is specified.

NOCONSTANT   *Exclude constant terms from models that do not include keyword CONSTANT on the DESIGN subcommand.*

Example

```
MANOVA DEP BY A B C (1,4)
   /METHOD=NOCONSTANT
   /DESIGN=A, B, C
   /METHOD=CONSTANT SEQUENTIAL
   /DESIGN.
```

- For the first design, a main effects model, the METHOD subcommand requests the model to be fitted with no constant.
- The second design requests a full factorial model to be fitted with a constant and with a sequential decomposition of sums of squares.

Subdividing the Degrees of Freedom

The degrees of freedom associated with a factor can be subdivided by using a PARTITION subcommand. Specify the factor name in parentheses, an equals sign, and a list of integers in parentheses indicating the degrees of freedom for each partition. For example, if *educatn* has six values (five degrees of freedom), it can be partitioned into single degrees of freedom by specifying

```
/PARTITION(EDUCATN)=(1,1,1,1,1)
```

or, more briefly, by specifying:

```
/PARTITION(EDUCATN)=(5*1)
```

Since the default degrees-of-freedom partition consists of the single degrees-of-freedom partition, these subcommands are equivalent to:

```
/PARTITION(EDUCATN)
```

On the other hand, the subcommand

```
/PARTITION(EDUCATN)=(2,2,1)
```

partitions *educatn* into three subdivisions, the first two with two degrees of freedom and the third with one degree of freedom. This subcommand can also be specified as

```
/PARTITION(EDUCATN)=(2,2)
```

since MANOVA automatically generates a final partition with the remaining degree(s) of freedom (one in this case). If you then specify ED(1) on the DESIGN subcommand, it will refer to the first partition, which has two degrees of freedom.

Specifying the Contrasts

Use the CONTRAST subcommand to request the desired contrast type for a factor. Specify the factor name in parentheses, followed by an equals sign and a contrast-type keyword. The contrast-type keyword can be any of the following:

DEVIATION(refcat)   *The deviations from the grand mean.* This is the default for between-subjects factors if the subcommand is omitted. To change the category for which the parameter estimate is not printed, specify it in parentheses following the keyword DEVIATION.

DIFFERENCE   *Difference or reverse Helmert contrast.* Compare levels of a factor with the mean of the previous levels of the factor.

SIMPLE(refcat)   *Simple contrasts.* Compare each level of a factor to the last level. To use a value other than the last as the omitted reference category, specify its number in parentheses following the keyword SIMPLE.

HELMERT   *Helmert contrasts.* Compare levels of a factor with the mean of the subsequent levels of the factor.

POLYNOMIAL   *Orthogonal polynomial contrasts.* This is the default for within-subjects factors if the subcommand is omitted.

REPEATED   *Adjacent levels of a factor.*

SPECIAL   *A user-defined contrast.* See the example in "Specifying Effects" on p. 103.

Specifying Printed Output

The PRINT and NOPRINT subcommands control the output produced by MANOVA. PRINT requests specified output, while NOPRINT suppresses it. On both PRINT and NO-PRINT, you specify any of the available keywords followed by keyword options in parentheses.

Example

```
MANOVA DIF BY METHOD(1,2) INST(1,3)
  /PRINT=CELLINFO(MEANS)
  /DESIGN.
```

- This command requests the display of cell means of *dif* for all combinations of values of *method* and *inst*.
- The output is shown in Figure 2.2 of Chapter 2.

The available keywords on PRINT and NOPRINT are listed below, followed by the options available for each keyword.

CELLINFO   *Cell information.*

HOMOGENEITY   *Homogeneity-of-variance tests.*

DESIGN   *Design information.*

ERROR   *Error matrices.*

SIGNIF	*Significance tests.*
PARAMETERS	*Estimated parameters.*
TRANSFORM	*Transformation matrix.*

Cell Information

You can specify any of the following keywords on CELLINFO:

MEANS   *Cell means, standard deviations, and counts.* This is the default if CELLINFO is specified by itself.

SSCP   *Cell sums-of-squares and cross-products matrices.*

COV   *Cell variance-covariance matrices.*

COR   *Cell correlation matrices.*

Homogeneity Tests

You can request appropriate homogeneity tests using one or more of the following keywords on HOMOGENEITY:

BARTLETT   *Bartlett-Box* F *test.*

COCHRAN   *Cochran's* C.

BOXM   *Box's* M. BOXM requires at least two dependent variables. If BOXM is requested when there is only one dependent variable, BARTLETT is printed instead.

Design Information

You can request the following design information on DESIGN:

OVERALL   *The overall reduced-model basis (design matrix).* This is the default if the DESIGN keyword is specified by itself.

ONEWAY   *The one-way basis for each factor.*

DECOMP   *The QR/CHOLESKY decomposition of the design.*

BIAS   *Contamination coefficients displaying the bias present in the design.*

SOLUTION   *Coefficients of the linear combination of the cell means being tested.*

COLLINEARITY   *Collinearity diagnostics for design matrices.*

Error Matrices

You can request the following error matrices on ERROR:

STDDEV *Error standard deviations (univariate case).* This is the default for univariate analysis if ERROR is specified by itself.

COV *Error variance-covariance matrix.* COV, together with COR, is the default for multivariate analysis if ERROR is specified by itself.

COR *Error correlation matrix and standard deviations.* COR, together with COV, is the default for multivariate analysis if ERROR is specified by itself.

SSCP *Error sums-of-squares and cross-product matrix.*

- If COR is specified on ERROR in the multivariate case, MANOVA automatically displays the determinant and Bartlett's test of sphericity.

Significance Tests

You can specify any of the following keywords on SIGNIF to request appropriate significance tests:

MULTIV *Multivariate F tests for group differences.* MULTIV, together with UNIV, is the default if SIGNIF is omitted or if it is specified by itself.

UNIV *Univariate F tests.* UNIV, together with MULTIV, is the default if SIGNIF is omitted or if it is specified by itself.

AVERF *An averaged F test.* Use with repeated measures. When repeated measures analyses are requested, this is the default instead of UNIV.

EIGEN *Eigenvalues of the $S_h S_e^{-1}$ matrix.*

DIMENR *A dimension-reduction analysis.*

HYPOTH *The hypothesis SSCP matrix.*

STEPDOWN *Roy-Bargmann step-down F tests.*

BRIEF *A shortened multivariate output.* BRIEF overrides any of the preceding SIGNIF keywords.

AVONLY *Averaged results only.* Used with repeated measures, AVONLY overrides other SIGNIF keywords. AVONLY and AVERF are mutually exclusive.

SINGLEDF *Single-degree-of-freedom listings of effects.*

- When BRIEF is used, the output consists of a table similar in appearance to a univariate ANOVA table, but with the generalized F and Wilks' lambda instead of the univariate F.

Estimated Parameters

The options available for PARAMETERS are as follows:

ESTIM   *The estimates themselves, along with their standard errors,* t *tests, and confidence intervals.* This is the default if PARAMETERS is specified by itself.

ORTHO   *The orthogonal estimates of parameters used to produce the sums of squares.*

COR   *Correlations between the parameters.*

NEGSUM   *For main effects, the negative sum of the other parameters.* The output represents the parameter for the omitted category.

EFSIZE   *The effect size values.*

OPTIMAL   *Optimal Scheffé contrast coefficients.*

Transformation Matrices

TRANSFORM produces the transformation matrix, which shows how MANOVA transforms variables when a multivariate repeated measures design and a WSFACTORS subcommand are used (see Chapter 4). No further specification is necessary for the TRANSFORM keyword.

Specifying Principal Components Analysis

Use the PCOMPS subcommand to specify a principal components analysis of the error sums-of-squares and cross-products matrices in a multivariate design. The following options are available for the PCOMPS subcommand:

COR   *Principal components analysis of the error correlation matrix.*

COV   *Principal components analysis of the error variance-covariance matrix.*

ROTATE(type)   *Rotation of the principal component loadings.* You can request VARIMAX, EQUAMAX, or QUARTIMAX rotation by specifying the rotation type keyword in parentheses. You can also cancel a rotation requested for a previous design by specifying NOROTATE.

NCOMP(n)   *The number of principal components to be rotated.* Specify *n*, or let *n* default to all components extracted.

MINEIGEN(n)   *The eigenvalue cutoff value for principal components extraction.* Specify the cutoff value in parentheses. The default is 0.

Specifying Canonical Analyses

Use the DISCRIM subcommand to request a canonical analysis of dependent and independent variables in multivariate analyses. If the independent variables are continuous, MANOVA produces a canonical correlation analysis; if they are categorical, MANOVA produces a canonical discriminant analysis. The following options are available on DISCRIM:

RAW   *Raw discriminant function coefficients.*

STAN   *Standardized discriminant function coefficients.*

ESTIM   *Effect estimates in discriminant function space.*

COR   *Correlations between the dependent and canonical variables defined by the discriminant functions.*

ROTATE(type)   *Rotation of the matrix of correlations between dependent and canonical variates.* You can request VARIMAX, EQUAMAX, or QUARTIMAX rotation by specifying the rotation type keyword in parentheses. You can also cancel a rotation requested for a previous design by specifying NOROTATE.

ALPHA(alpha)   *The significance level for the canonical variate.* The default is 0.15.

- MANOVA does not perform rotation unless there are at least two significant canonical variates.

Producing Tables of Combined Observed Means

Use the OMEANS subcommand to request tables of combined observed means. With no specifications, the OMEANS subcommand produces a table of observed means for all of the continuous variables.

- You can use the VARIABLES keyword to specify the continuous variables for which you want the observed means. Name the variables (either dependent variables or covariates) in parentheses. When you explicitly specify variables on the OMEANS subcommand, you must also enter a TABLES specification.

- You can use the TABLES keyword to specify the factors for which you want the observed means displayed. When you specify TABLES but omit VARIABLES, all of the continuous variables are included.

- Always use the original variable names in the VARIABLES specification on OMEANS, even when a transformation has been requested with TRANSFORM or with WSFACTORS (described in Chapter 4). OMEANS produces means of the original, untransformed variables.

Example

```
MANOVA BALOMEAN BALCMEAN SSTMEAN PP BY SEX(1,2) FIELD(1,3)
   /OMEANS VARIABLES(BALOMEAN) TABLES(SEX BY FIELD).
```

- MANOVA displays both weighted and unweighted means for *balomean*. Tables of observed means are displayed by the interaction term *sex* by *field*.

Example

```
MANOVA BALOMEAN BALCMEAN SSTMEAN PP BY SEX(1,2) FIELD(1,3)
   /OMEANS TABLES(SEX,FIELD,SEX BY FIELD).
```

- This example results in three tables, one collapsed over *sex*, one collapsed over *field*, and one showing the observed means themselves.

Computing Predicted and Adjusted Means

Use PMEANS to request predicted and adjusted (for covariates) means, which are displayed for each error term in each design. VARIABLES and TABLES are two specifications that can be used; the format is the same as that for OMEANS. For designs with covariates and multiple error terms, you must specify an error term on the ERROR subcommand. The regression coefficients of the error term are to be used in calculating the predicted means. If no error term is given when one is needed, MANOVA will not calculate predicted means. Predicted means are also suppressed if you specify ESTIM(LASTRES) on the METHOD subcommand or if the design contains the MUPLUS keyword (see "Specifying Effects" on p. 103).

If the WSFACTORS subcommand is used to specify a repeated measures design (see Chapter 4), the means of the orthonormalized variables are displayed when PMEANS is used. If the TRANSFORM or WSFACTORS subcommand is used for a design, PMEANS displays the means of the transformed variables. Therefore, the VARIABLES specification on PMEANS, unlike that on OMEANS, uses the names of the *transformed* variables in analyses using the WSFACTORS or TRANSFORM subcommand. These are either the names you specify on the RENAME subcommand, or the names supplied by SPSS/PC+ (*t1, t2*, etc.). The keyword PLOT on the PMEANS subcommand produces a group-order plot of the estimated, adjusted, and observed means for each dependent variable, and a group-order plot of the mean residuals for each dependent variable. When there is more than one factor in the analysis, the rightmost factor changes most quickly.

Producing Residual Listings and Plots

Use the RESIDUALS subcommand to request listings or plots of predicted values and residuals. Casewise listings of residuals are produced by the keyword CASEWISE. This output includes, for each case, the observed and predicted value of each dependent variable, the residual, and the standardized residual.

- Like PMEANS, RESIDUALS requires an ERROR specification for designs with covariates and multiple error terms.There will be no output if the error term is not specified when needed.
- Predicted observations will be suppressed if you specify ESTIM(LASTRES) on the METHOD subcommand or if the DESIGN subcommand contains the MUPLUS keyword. If the designated error term does not exist for a given design, no predicted values or residuals are calculated.
- The keyword PLOT on the RESIDUALS subcommand displays the following plots: observed values versus standardized residuals, predicted values versus standardized residuals, case number versus standardized residuals, a normal probability plot, and a detrended normal probability plot for the standardized residuals.

Example
```
MANOVA SALES BY TVAD RADIOAD(2,5) WITH PCTBUSNS
  /RESIDUALS=CASEWISE ERROR(WITHIN)
  /DESIGN TVAD VS 1,RADIOAD VS 1, TVAD BY RADIOAD = 1 VS WITHIN.
```

Producing Plots

Use the PLOT subcommand to request plots. The following keywords are available:

CELLPLOTS   *Plot cell statistics.* The output includes a plot of cell means versus cell variances, a plot of cell means versus cell standard deviations, and a histogram of cell means for each of the continuous variables (dependent variables and covariates) defined on the MANOVA command.

BOXPLOTS   *Plot a boxplot for each continuous variable.*

NORMAL   *Plot a normal plot and a detrended normal plot for each continuous variable.*

ZCORR   *Plot a half-normal plot of the within-cells correlations between the dependent variables in a multivariate analysis.*

If there is not enough memory to produce a plot, MANOVA displays a warning and does not produce the requested plot.

Requesting Observed Power Values

Use the POWER subcommand to request observed power values based on fixed-effect assumptions for all univariate and multivariate F and t tests. Both approximate and exact power values can be computed, though exact multivariate power is printed only if there is one hypothesis degree of freedom.

To request power values, specify the appropriate keywords after the POWER subcommand, along with the type of test (either *F* test or *t* test) and the significance level at which the power is to be calculated. If you specify the POWER subcommand without further specification, MANOVA calculates the observed power of all *F* tests at 0.05 significance level.

The following keywords are available on POWER:

APPROXIMATE   *Approximate power values.* This is the default.

EXACT   *Exact power values.*

F(a)   *Alpha level at which the power is to be calculated for* F *tests.* The default is 0.05. You can specify a decimal number between 0 and 1 in parentheses after *F.* The numbers 0 and 1 themselves are not allowed.

T(a)   *Alpha level at which the power is to be calculated for* t *tests.* The default is 0.05. You can specify a decimal number between 0 and 1 in parentheses after *T.* The numbers 0 and 1 themselves are not allowed.

Requesting Simultaneous Confidence Intervals

Use the CINTERVAL subcommand to request simultaneous confidence intervals for each parameter estimate and regression coefficient. Both univariate and multivariate confidence intervals are available. You can request either joint or individual univariate and multivariate confidence intervals, and also vary the confidence level. You can request only one type of confidence interval per design.

To request confidence intervals, specify the CINTERVAL subcommand followed by the appropriate keywords. Without any specifications, CINTERVAL prints individual univariate confidence intervals at the 0.95 level.

The following options are available on CINTERVAL:

INDIVIDUAL(a)   *Individual confidence intervals, and the confidence level desired.* The default is .95. To change the default, specify any decimal number between 0 and 1 in parentheses after INDIVIDUAL. When individual intervals are requested, BONFER and SCHEFFE will have no effect. .

JOINT(a)   *Joint confidence intervals, and the confidence level desired.* The default is .95. To change the default, specify any decimal number between 0 and 1 in parentheses after JOINT.

UNIVARIATE(type)   *Univariate confidence interval, and its type.* Specify either SCHEFFE for Scheffé intervals or BONFER for Bonferroni intervals in parentheses after UNIVARIATE. The default specification is SCHEFFE.

MULTIVARIATE(type)   *Multivariate confidence interval, and its type.* Specify either ROY for Roy's largest root, PILLAI for Pillai's trace, BONFER for Bonferroni intervals, HOTELLING for Hotelling's trace, or WILKS for Wilks' lambda in parentheses after MULTIVARIATE. The default specification is ROY.

Reading and Writing Matrix Materials

MANOVA can write out a set of matrix materials, which it can then use for subsequent jobs. The WRITE subcommand is used to write these materials and it can be specified by itself:

```
/WRITE
```

This sends results to the "results file," which is named *spss.prc* by default.

The READ subcommand reads the materials written with the WRITE subcommand. READ can be specified by itself:

```
/READ
```

READ is used in conjunction with the DATA LIST matrix statement. For details, see DATA LIST: Matrix Materials in the Syntax Reference section of the *SPSS/PC+ Base System User's Guide*.

Missing-Value Treatment

By default, cases with either system- or user-missing values for any of the variables named on MANOVA are excluded from the analysis. To include user-missing values in the analysis, specify the keyword INCLUDE on the subcommand MISSING. The missing subcommand can be used only once.

If you specify INCLUDE on MISSING, you must also include the user-missing values in the ranges specified on the MANOVA factor list in order to include factors with user-missing values in the analysis.

Annotated Example

The following SPSS/PC+ commands produced the output in Figure 3.26 through Figure 3.30:

```
DATA LIST FREE /X1 TO X22.
IF (X1 LT 200) SEX=1.
IF (X1 GE 200) SEX=2.
COMPUTE BALOMEAN=(X10+X11)/2.
COMPUTE BALCMEAN=(X12+X13)/2.
COMPUTE SSTMEAN=(X14+X15+X16)/3.
COMPUTE PP=(X17+X18+X19+X20+X21+X22)/6.
BEGIN DATA
.
. (data records)
.
END DATA.
MANOVA BALOMEAN BALCMEAN SSTMEAN PP BY SEX(1,2)
  /DISCRIM=RAW STAN CORR ESTIM
  /PRINT=SIGNIF(DIMENR) PARAMETERS(ESTIM)
  /DESIGN.
```

- The DATA LIST command reads the variables in freefield format.
- The IF commands set up the variable *sex*.
- The COMPUTE statements compute the dependent variables as averages of the original variables.
- The MANOVA command begins by specifying *balomean, balcmean, sstmean*, and *pp* as the dependent variables and *sex* as a factor. The DISCRIM subcommand requests a canonical analysis of the dependent and independent variables. The PRINT subcommand requests parameter estimates and a dimension-reduction analysis.

4

Repeated Measures Analysis of Variance

Anyone who experiences difficulties sorting through piles of output, stacks of bills, or assorted journals must be awed by the brain's ability to organize, update, and maintain the memories of a lifetime. It seems incredible that someone can instantly recall the name of his first-grade teacher. On the other hand, that same person might spend an entire morning searching for a misplaced shoe.

Memory has two components: storage and retrieval. Many different theories explaining its magical operation have been proposed (see, for example, Eysenck, 1977). In this chapter, an experiment concerned with latency—the length of time required to search a list of items in memory—is examined.

Bacon (1980) conducted an experiment in which subjects were instructed to memorize a number. They were then given a "probe" digit and told to indicate whether it was included in the memorized number. One hypothesis of interest is the relationship between the number of digits in the memorized number and the latency. Is more time required to search through a longer number than a shorter one? Twenty-four subjects were tested on 60 memorized numbers, 20 each of two, three, and four digits in random order. The average latencies, in milliseconds, were calculated for each subject on the two-, three-, and four-digit numbers. Thus, three scores are recorded for each subject, one for each of the number lengths. The probe digit was included in the memorized number in a random position.

Repeated Measures

When the same variable is measured on several occasions for each subject, it is a **repeated measures design**. The simplest repeated measures design is one in which two measurements are obtained for each subject—such as pretest and post-test scores. These types of data are usually analyzed with a paired *t* test.

The advantages of repeated measurements are obvious. Besides requiring fewer experimental units (in this study, human subjects), they provide a control on the differences among units. That is, variability due to differences between subjects can be eliminated from the experimental error. Less attention has been focused on some of the difficulties that may be encountered with repeated measurements. Broadly, these problems can be classified as the carry-over effect, the latent effect, and the order or learning effect.

The carry-over effect occurs when a new treatment is administered before the effect of a previous treatment has worn off. For example, Drug B is given while Drug A still has an effect. The carry-over effect can usually be controlled by increasing the time between treatments. In addition, special designs that allow you to assess directly the carry-over effects are available (Cochran & Cox, 1957).

The latent effect—in which one treatment may activate the dormant effect of the previous treatment or interact with the previous treatment—is not so easily countered. This effect is especially problematic in drug trials and should be considered before using a repeated measures experimental design. Usually, if a latency effect is suspected, a repeated measures design should not be used.

The learning effect occurs when the response may improve merely by repetition of a task, independent of any treatment. For example, subjects' scores on a test may improve each time they take the test. Thus, treatments that are administered later may appear to improve performance, even though they have no effect. In such situations it is important to pay particular attention to the sequencing of treatments. Learning effects can be assessed by including a control group that performs the same tasks repeatedly without receiving any treatment.

Describing the Data

In a repeated measures experiment, as well as any other, the first step is to obtain descriptive statistics. These provide some idea of the distributions of the variables, as well as their average values and dispersions. Figure 4.1 contains cell means and standard deviations for the latency times. The shortest average latency time (520 milliseconds) was observed for the two-digit numbers (*p2digit*). The longest (581 milliseconds) was observed for the four-digit numbers. A plot of the mean latency times against the number of digits is shown in Figure 4.2. Note that there appears to be a linear relationship between the latency time and the number of digits in the memorized number.

Figure 4.1   Means and standard deviations

```
MANOVA  P2DIGIT  P3DIGIT  P4DIGIT
   /PRINT=CELLINFO(MEANS)
   /DESIGN.

Cell Means and Standard Deviations
Variable .. P2DIGIT
                                        Mean   Std. Dev.        N

For entire sample                    520.583    131.366        24

- - - - - - - - - - - - - - - - - - - - - - - - - - - - - - - - - - -
Variable .. P3DIGIT
                                        Mean   Std. Dev.        N

For entire sample                    560.000    118.776        24

- - - - - - - - - - - - - - - - - - - - - - - - - - - - - - - - - - -
Variable .. P4DIGIT
                                        Mean   Std. Dev.        N

For entire sample                    581.250    117.325        24
```

Figure 4.2   Plot of means

```
COMPUTE CONS=1.
AGGREGATE OUTFILE=*
  /BREAK=CONS
  /MPDIG2 MPDIG3 MPDIG4=MEAN(P2DIGIT P3DIGIT P4DIGIT).
COMPUTE C2=2.
COMPUTE C3=3.
COMPUTE C4=4.
PLOT SYMBOLS='***'/VSIZE=15/HSIZE=30
  /FORMAT=OVERLAY
  /TITLE 'MEAN LATENCY TIMES'
  /HORIZONTAL 'NUMBER OF DIGITS'/VERTICAL 'MEAN LATENCY'
  /PLOT=MPDIG2 WITH C2;MPDIG3 WITH C3;MPDIG4 WITH C4.
```

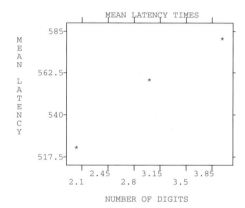

The stem-and-leaf plot of latencies for the *p4digit* is shown in Figure 4.3 (stem-and-leaf plots are available from the Examine procedure). The corresponding normal probability plot is shown in Figure 4.4. From this, it appears that the values are somewhat more "bunched" than you would expect if they were normally distributed. The bunching of the data might occur because of limitations in the accuracy of the measurements. Similar plots can be obtained for the other two variables.

Figure 4.3   Stem-and-leaf plot for p4digit

```
EXAMINE P4DIGIT
 /PLOT=STEMLEAF.


Frequency    Stem &  Leaf

    1.00       3 .  9
    3.00       4 .  247
   11.00       5 .  00011114558
    4.00       6 .  1888
    4.00       7 .  0015
    1.00       8 .  5

Stem width:     100.00
Each leaf:        1 case(s)
```

Figure 4.4   Normal probability plot for p4digit

```
MANOVA  P2DIGIT   P3DIGIT   P4DIGIT
   /PLOT=NORMAL
   /DESIGN.
```

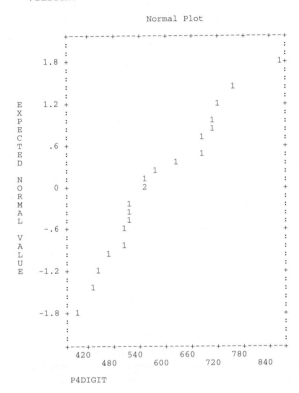

P4DIGIT

Analyzing Differences

Since multiple observations are made on the same experimental unit in a repeated measures design, special procedures that incorporate dependencies within an experimental unit must be used. For example, in the paired *t* test design, instead of analyzing each score separately, we analyze the difference between the two scores. When there are more than two scores for a subject, the analysis becomes somewhat more complicated. For example, if each subject receives three treatments, there are three pairwise differences: the difference between the first two treatments, the difference between the second two treatments, and the difference between the first and third treatments.

Performing three paired t tests of the differences may seem to be the simplest analysis, but it is not, for several reasons, the best strategy. First, the three t tests are not statistically independent, since they involve the same means in overlapping combinations. Some overall protection against calling too many differences significant is needed, especially as the number of treatments increases. Second, since there are three separate t tests, a single test of the hypothesis that there is no difference between the treatments is not available.

There are several approaches for circumventing such problems in the analysis of data from repeated measures experiments. These approaches are described in the remainder of this chapter.

Transforming the Variables

To test the null hypothesis that the mean latencies are the same for the three digit lengths, the original three variables must be transformed. That is, instead of analyzing the original three variables, we analyze linear combinations of their differences. (In the paired t test, the transformation is the difference between the values for each subject or pair.) For certain methods of analysis, these linear combinations, sometimes called **contrasts**, must be chosen so that they are statistically independent (orthogonal) and so that the sum of the squared coefficients is 1 (normalized). Such contrasts are termed **orthonormalized**. The number of statistically independent contrasts that can be formed for a factor is one less than the number of levels of the factor. In addition, a contrast corresponding to the overall mean (the constant term in the model) is always formed. For this example, the contrast for the overall mean is

$$\text{Contrast 1} = \text{p2digit} + \text{p3digit} + \text{p4digit} \qquad \textbf{Equation 4.1}$$

There are many types of transformations that can be used to form contrasts among the means. One is the **difference contrast**, which compares each level of a factor to the average of the levels that precede it. (Another transformation, orthogonal polynomials, is discussed in "Selecting Other Contrasts" on p. 134.)

The first difference contrast for the digit factor (the second contrast for the experiment) is:

$$\text{Contrast 2} = \text{p3digit} - \text{p2digit} \qquad \textbf{Equation 4.2}$$

The second difference contrast is:

$$\text{Contrast 3} = (2 \times \text{p4digit}) - \text{p3digit} - \text{p2digit} \qquad \textbf{Equation 4.3}$$

The contrasts can be normalized by dividing each contrast by the square root of the sum of the squared coefficients. The contrast for the overall mean is divided by

$$\sqrt{1^2 + 1^2 + 1^2} = \sqrt{3}$$

Equation 4.4

and the second difference contrast is divided by

$$\sqrt{2^2 + 1^2 + 1^2} = \sqrt{6}$$

Equation 4.5

Figure 4.5 shows the orthonormalized transformation matrix from MANOVA for creating new variables from *p2digit*, *p3digit*, and *p4digit* with the difference transformation. Each column contains the coefficients for a particular contrast. Each row corresponds to one of the original variables. Thus, the first linear combination is:

Constant = 0.577 (p2digit + p3digit + p4digit)   Equation 4.6

This new variable is, for each case, the sum of the values of the three original variables, multiplied by 0.577. Again, the coefficients are chosen so that the sum of their squared values is 1. The next two variables are the normalized difference contrasts for the digit effect.

Figure 4.5   Orthonormalized transformation matrix for difference contrasts

```
MANOVA  P2DIGIT  P3DIGIT  P4DIGIT
 /WSFACTORS=DIGIT(3)
 /CONTRAST(DIGIT)=DIFFERENCE
 /RENAME=CONS DIF12 DIF12V3
 /PRINT=TRANSFORM
 /DESIGN.

Orthonormalized Transformation Matrix (Transposed)

            CONS      DIF12     DIF12V3

P2DIGIT     .577      -.707      -.408
P3DIGIT     .577       .707      -.408
P4DIGIT     .577       .000       .816
```

What do these new variables represent? The first variable, the sum of the original variables, is the average response over all treatments. It measures latency times over all digit lengths. The hypothesis that the average response, the constant, is equal to 0 is based on this variable. The second two contrasts together represent the treatment (digit) effect. These two contrasts are used to test hypotheses about differences in latencies for the three digit lengths.

Testing for Differences

In Chapter 3, analysis of variance models with more than one dependent variable are described. The same techniques can be used for repeated measures data. For example, we can use the single-sample tests to determine whether particular sets of the transformed variables in the Bacon experiment have means of 0. If the number of digits does not affect latency times, the mean values of the two contrasts for the digit effect are expected to be 0. Different hypotheses are tested using different transformed variables.

Testing the Constant Effect

When a repeated measures design is specified in MANOVA, several hypotheses are automatically tested. The first hypothesis is that the overall mean latency time is 0. It is based on the first transformed variable, which corresponds to the constant effect.

To help identify results, MANOVA displays the names of the transformed variables used to test a hypothesis. In this example, we assigned new names to the transformed variables using the RENAME subcommand (see Figure 4.5). These new names will appear on the output. The first transformed variable is renamed *cons*; the second, *dif12*; and the third, *dif12v3*.

Figure 4.6 shows the explanation displayed when the constant effect is tested. The column labeled *Variates* indicates which transformed variables are involved in the test of a particular effect. Since the test for the constant is based only on variable *cons*, its name appears in that column. When there are no covariates in the analysis, the column labeled *Covariates* is empty, as shown. The note below the table is a reminder that analyses are based on the transformed variables and that the particular analysis is for the constant effect.

Figure 4.6   Renamed variable used in the analysis

```
Order of Variables for Analysis

 Variates      Covariates

 CONS


 1 Dependent Variable
 0 Covariates

- - - - - - - - - - - - - - - - - - - - - - - - - - - - - - - - - - - -

    Note..   TRANSFORMED variables are in the variates column.
             These TRANSFORMED variables correspond to the
             Between-subject effects.
```

The Analysis-of-Variance Table

Since the test for the constant is based on a single variable, the results are displayed in the usual univariate analysis-of-variance table (Figure 4.7). The large F value and the small observed significance level indicate that the hypothesis that the constant is 0 is rejected. This finding is of limited importance here, since we do not expect the time required to search a number to be 0. Tests about the constant might be of interest if the original variables are difference scores—change from baseline, for example—since the test of the constant would then correspond to the test that there has been no overall change from baseline.

Figure 4.7   Analysis-of-variance table

```
Tests of Significance for CONS using UNIQUE sums of squares
Source of Variation          SS        DF        MS         F  Sig of F

WITHIN CELLS            995411.11      23   43278.74
CONSTANT              22093520.22       1   22093520    510.49     .000
```

After the analysis-of-variance table, MANOVA displays parameter estimates and tests of the hypotheses that the individual transformed variables have means of 0. These are shown in Figure 4.8. For the constant effect, the parameter estimate is nothing more than

$$0.57735 \times (520.58 + 560.00 + 581.25) \ = \ 959.46 \qquad \text{Equation 4.7}$$

where the numbers within the parentheses are just the means of the original three variables shown in Figure 4.1. The 0.57735 is the value used to normalize the contrast (the rounded value, 0.577, is shown in Figure 4.5). The test of the hypothesis that the true value of the first parameter is 0 is equivalent to the test of the hypothesis that the constant is 0. Therefore, the t value displayed for the test is the square root of the F value from the analysis-of-variance table (the square root of 510.49 is 22.59). (When the t statistic is squared, it is equal to an F statistic with one degree of freedom for the numerator and the same degrees of freedom for the denominator as the t statistic.)

Figure 4.8   Parameter estimates

```
MANOVA   P2DIGIT   P3DIGIT   P4DIGIT
 /WSFACTORS=DIGIT(3)
 /CONTRAST(DIGIT)=DIFFERENCE
 /RENAME=CONS DIF12 DIF12V3
 /PRINT=PARAM(ESTIM)
 /DESIGN.

Estimates for CONS
--- Individual univariate .9500 confidence intervals
CONSTANT

 Parameter      Coeff.   Std. Err.     t-Value     Sig. t Lower -95%  CL- Upper

        1   959.459922   42.46506    22.59410      .00000  871.61426 1047.30558
```

Testing the Digit Effect

The hypothesis of interest in this study is whether latency time depends on the number of digits in the memorized number. As shown in Figure 4.9, this test is based on the two transformed variables, labeled *dif12* and *dif12v3*. Figure 4.10 contains the multivariate tests of the hypothesis that the means of these two variables are 0. In this situation, all multivariate criteria are equivalent and lead to rejection of the hypothesis that the number of digits does not affect latency time.

Figure 4.9   Transformed variables used

```
Order of Variables for Analysis

  Variates        Covariates

  DIF12
  DIF12V3

  2 Dependent Variables
  0 Covariates

- - - - - - - - - - - - - - - - - - - - - - - - - - - - - - -

     Note..   TRANSFORMED variables are in the variates column.
              These TRANSFORMED variables correspond to the
              'DIGIT' WITHIN-SUBJECT effect.
```

Figure 4.10   Multivariate hypothesis tests

```
EFFECT .. DIGIT

Multivariate Tests of Significance (S = 1, M = 0, N = 10 )
```

Test Name	Value	Exact F	Hypoth. DF	Error DF	Sig. of F
Pillais	.60452	16.81439	2.00	22.00	.000
Hotellings	1.52858	16.81439	2.00	22.00	.000
Wilks	.39548	16.81439	2.00	22.00	.000
Roys	.60452				

Univariate F tests for the individual transformed variables are shown in Figure 4.11. The first row corresponds to a test of the hypothesis that there is no difference in average latency times for numbers consisting of two digits and those consisting of three. (This is equivalent to a one-sample t test that the mean of the second transformed variable *dif12* is 0.) The second row of Figure 4.11 provides a test of the hypothesis that there is no difference between the average response to numbers with two and three digits and numbers with four digits. The average value of this contrast is also significantly different from 0, since the observed significance level is less than 0.0005. (See "Selecting Other Contrasts" on p. 134 for an example of a different contrast type.)

Figure 4.11   Univariate hypothesis tests

```
MANOVA  P2DIGIT  P3DIGIT  P4DIGIT
  /WSFACTORS=DIGIT(3)
  /CONTRAST(DIGIT)=DIFFERENCE
  /RENAME=CONS DIF12 DIF12V3
  /PRINT=SIGNIF(UNIV)
  /DESIGN.

Univariate F-tests with (1,23) D. F.
```

Variable	Hypoth. SS	Error SS	Hypoth. MS	Error MS	F	Sig. of F
DIF12	18644.0833	19800.9167	18644.0833	860.90942	21.65627	.000
DIF12V3	26841.3611	22774.3056	26841.3611	990.18720	27.10736	.000

To estimate the magnitudes of differences among the digit lengths, we can examine the values of each contrast. These are shown in Figure 4.12. The column labeled *Coeff.* is the average value for the normalized contrast. As shown in Figure 4.5, the second contrast is 0.707 times the difference between three- and two-digit numbers, which is $0.707 \times (560 - 520.58) = 27.87$, the value shown in Figure 4.12. To obtain an estimate of the absolute difference between mean response to two and three digits, the parameter estimate must be divided by 0.707. This value is 39.42. Again, the t value for the hypothesis that the contrast is 0 is equivalent to the square root of the F value from the univariate analysis-of-variance table.

Figure 4.12   Estimates for contrasts

```
MANOVA   P2DIGIT   P3DIGIT   P4DIGIT
 /WSFACTORS=DIGIT(3)
 /CONTRAST(DIGIT)=DIFFERENCE
 /RENAME=CONS DIF12 DIF12V3
 /PRINT=PARAM(ESTIM)
 /DESIGN.

--- Individual univariate .9500 confidence intervals
DIGIT

 Parameter      Coeff.   Std. Err.    t-Value     Sig. t Lower -95%  CL- Upper

        1   27.8717923    5.98926    4.65363     .00011   15.48207   40.26152

- - - - - - - - - - - - - - - - - - - - - - - - - - - - - - - - - - - - - -
Estimates for DIF12V3
--- Individual univariate .9500 confidence intervals
DIGIT

 Parameter      Coeff.   Std. Err.    t-Value     Sig. t Lower -95%  CL- Upper

        1   33.4423391    6.42322    5.20647     .00003   20.15489   46.72979
```

Similarly, the parameter estimate for the third contrast, the normalized difference between the average of two and three digits and four digits, is 33.44. The actual value of the difference is 40.96 (33.44 divided by 0.816). The t value, the ratio of the parameter estimate to its standard error, is 5.206, which when squared equals the F value in Figure 4.11. The t values are the same for normalized and non-normalized contrasts.

The parameter estimates and univariate F tests help identify which individual contrasts contribute to overall differences. However, the observed significance levels for the individual parameters are not adjusted for the fact that several comparisons are being made (see Miller, 1981; Burns, 1984). Thus, the significance levels should serve only as guides for identifying potentially important differences. (Simultaneous confidence intervals for the parameters are available using the CINTERVAL keyword.)

Averaged Univariate Results

The individual univariate tests, since they are orthogonal, can be pooled to obtain the averaged F test shown in Figure 4.13. The entries in Figure 4.13 are obtained from Figure 4.11 by summing the hypothesis and error sums of squares and the associated degrees of freedom. In this example, the averaged F test also leads us to reject the hypothesis that average latency times do not differ for numbers of different lengths. This is the same F statistic as that obtained by specifying a repeated measures design as a mixed-model univariate analysis of variance (Winer et al., 1991).

Figure 4.13   Averaged univariate hypothesis test

```
MANOVA  P2DIGIT  P3DIGIT  P4DIGIT
 /WSFACTORS=DIGIT(3)
 /CONTRAST(DIGIT)=DIFFERENCE
 /RENAME=CONS DIF12 DIF12V3
 /PRINT=SIGNIF(AVERF) PARAM(ESTIM)
 /DESIGN.


AVERAGED Tests of Significance for MEAS.1 using UNIQUE sums of squares
Source of Variation         SS        DF      MS         F   Sig of F

WITHIN CELLS            42575.22      46    925.55
DIGIT                   45485.44       2  22742.72     24.57     .000
```

Choosing Multivariate or Univariate Results

In the previous section, we saw that hypothesis tests for the digit effect could be based on multivariate criteria such as Wilks' lambda, or on the averaged univariate F tests. When both approaches lead to similar results, choosing between them is not of much importance. However, there are situations in which the multivariate and univariate approaches lead to different results, and the question of which is appropriate arises.

The multivariate approach considers the measurements on a subject to be a sample from a multivariate normal distribution and makes no assumption about the characteristics of the variance-covariance matrix. The **univariate approach** (sometimes called the mixed-model approach) requires certain assumptions about the variance-covariance matrix. If these conditions are met, especially for small sample sizes, the univariate approach is more powerful than the multivariate approach. That is, it is more likely to detect differences when they exist.

Modifications of the univariate results when the assumptions are violated have also been proposed. These corrected results are approximate and are based on the adjustment of the degrees of freedom of the F ratio (Greenhouse & Geisser, 1959; Huynh & Feldt, 1976). The significance levels for the corrected tests will always be larger than for the uncorrected. Thus, if the uncorrected test is not significant, there is no need to calculate corrected values.

Assumptions Needed for the Univariate Approach

Since subjects in the current example are not subdivided by any grouping characteristics, the only assumption required for using the univariate results is that the variances of all the transformed variables for an effect be equal and that their covariances be 0. (Assumptions required for more complicated designs are described in "Additional Univariate Assumptions" on p. 143.)

Mauchly's test of sphericity is available in the MANOVA procedure for testing the hypothesis that the covariance matrix of the transformed variables has a constant variance on the diagonal and zeros off the diagonal (Morrison, 1967). For small sample sizes, this test is not very powerful. For large sample sizes, the test may be significant even when the impact of the departure on the analysis-of-variance results may be small.

Figure 4.14 contains the correlation matrix with standard deviations on the diagonal for the two transformed variables corresponding to the digit effect, Mauchly's test of sphericity, and the observed significance level based on a chi-square approximation. The observed significance level is 0.150, so the hypothesis of sphericity is not rejected. If the observed significance level is small and the sphericity assumption appears to be violated, an adjustment to the numerator and denominator degrees of freedom can be made. Two estimates of this adjustment, called **epsilon**, are available in the MANOVA procedure. These are also shown in Figure 4.14. Both the numerator and denominator degrees of freedom must be multiplied by epsilon, and the significance of the *F* ratio must be evaluated with the new degrees of freedom. The **Huynh-Feldt epsilon** is an attempt to correct the **Greenhouse-Geisser epsilon**, which tends to be overly conservative, especially for small sample sizes. The lowest value possible for epsilon is also displayed. The Huynh-Feldt epsilon sometimes exceeds the value of 1. When this occurs, MANOVA displays a value of 1.

Figure 4.14 Mauchly's test of sphericity

```
MANOVA   P2DIGIT   P3DIGIT   P4DIGIT
  /WSFACTORS=DIGIT(3)
  /CONTRAST(DIGIT)=DIFFERENCE
  /RENAME=CONS DIF12 DIF12V3
  /PRINT=ERROR(CORR)
  /DESIGN.

WITHIN CELLS Correlations with Std. Devs. on Diagonal

                   DIF12      DIF12V3

DIF12             29.341
DIF12V3             .393      31.467

- - - - - - - - - - - - - - - - - - - - - - - - - - - - - - - - - -

Tests involving 'DIGIT' Within-Subject Effect.

Mauchly sphericity test, W =         .84172
Chi-square approx. =                3.79088 with 2 D. F.
Significance =                       .150

Greenhouse-Geisser Epsilon =         .86335
Huynh-Feldt Epsilon =                .92700
Lower-bound Epsilon =                .50000
```

Selecting Other Contrasts

Based on the orthonormalized transformation matrix shown in Figure 4.5 and the corresponding parameter estimates in Figure 4.12, hypotheses about particular combinations of the means were tested. Remember that the second contrast compared differences between the two- and three-digit numbers, while the third contrast compared the average of the two- and three-digit number to the four-digit number. A variety of other hypotheses can be tested by selecting different orthogonal contrasts.

For example, to test the hypothesis that latency time increases linearly with the number of digits in the memorized number, orthogonal polynomial contrasts can be used. (In fact, polynomial contrasts should have been the first choice for data of this type. Difference contrasts were used for illustrative purposes.) When polynomial contrasts are used, the first contrast for the digit effect represents the linear component, and the second contrast represents the quadratic component. Figure 4.15 contains parameter estimates corresponding to the polynomial contrasts. You can see that there is a significant linear trend, but the quadratic trend is not significant. This is also shown in the plot in Figure 4.3, since the means fall more or less on a straight line, which does not appear to curve upward or downward.

Figure 4.15   Parameter estimates for polynomial contrasts

```
MANOVA  P2DIGIT  P3DIGIT  P4DIGIT
    /WSFACTORS=DIGIT(3)
    /CONTRAST(DIGIT)=POLYNOMIAL
    /RENAME=CONS LIN QUAD
    /PRINT=PARAMETERS(ESTIM)
    /DESIGN.


Estimates for LIN
--- Individual univariate .9500 confidence intervals
DIGIT

 Parameter      Coeff.   Std. Err.     t-Value     Sig. t Lower -95%  CL- Upper

        1    42.8978114    7.27957     5.89290      .00001    27.83887    57.95675


- - - - - - - - - - - - - - - - - - - - - - - - - - - - - - - - - - - - - -
Estimates for QUAD
--- Individual univariate .9500 confidence intervals
DIGIT

 Parameter      Coeff.   Std. Err.     t-Value     Sig. t Lower -95%  CL- Upper

        1    -7.4165106    4.91293    -1.50959      .14476   -17.57968     2.74666
```

The requirement that contrasts be orthonormalized is necessary for the averaged F tests. It is not required for the multivariate approach. MANOVA, however, requires all contrasts for the within-subjects factors to be orthonormal. If nonorthogonal contrasts, such as simple or deviation, are requested, they are orthonormalized prior to the actual analysis. The transformation matrix should always be displayed so that the parameter estimates and univariate F ratios can be properly interpreted.

Adding Another Factor

The experimental design discussed so far is a very simple one. Responses to all levels of one factor (number of digits) were measured for all subjects. However, repeated measures designs can be considerably more complicated. Any factorial design can be applied to a single subject. For example, we can administer several different types of medication at varying dosages and times of day. Such a design has three factors (medication, dosage, and time) applied to each subject.

All of the usual analysis-of-variance hypotheses for factorial designs can be tested when each subject is treated as a complete replicate of the design. However, since observations from the same subject are not independent, the usual analysis-of-variance method is inappropriate. Instead, we need to extend the previously described approach to analyzing repeated measures experiments.

To illustrate the analysis of a two-factor repeated measures design, consider the Bacon data again. The experiment was actually more involved than first described. The single "probe" digit was not always present in the memorized number. Instead, each subject was tested under two conditions—probe digit present and probe digit absent. Presence and absence of the probe digit was randomized. The two conditions were included to test the hypothesis that it takes longer to search through numbers when the probe digit is not present than when it is present. If memory searches are performed sequentially, you would expect that when the probe digit is encountered, searching stops. When the probe digit is not present in a number, searching must continue through all digits of the memorized number.

Thus, each subject has in fact six observations: latency times for the three number lengths when the probe is present, and times for the numbers when the probe is absent. This design has two factors: number of digits, and the probe presence/absence condition. The digit factor has three levels (two, three, and four digits) and the condition factor has two levels (probe present and probe absent).

Testing a Two-Factor Model

The analysis of this modified experiment proceeds similarly to the analysis described for the single-factor design. However, instead of testing only the digit effect, tests for the digit effect, the condition effect, and the digit-by-condition interaction are required. Figure 4.16 is the orthonormalized transformation matrix for the two-factor design.

Figure 4.16 Orthonormalized transformation matrix for the two-factor design

```
MANOVA P2DIGIT P3DIGIT  P4DIGIT   NP2DIGIT  NP3DIGIT  NP4DIGIT
   /WSFACTORS=COND(2) DIGIT(3)
   /CONTRAST(DIGIT)=DIFFERENCE
   /RENAME=CONS  TCONDIF   TDIGIT1   TDIGIT2   TINT1   TINT2
   /PRINT=TRANSFORM
   /DESIGN.
```

Orthonormalized Transformation Matrix (Transposed)

	CONS	TCONDIF	TDIGIT1	TDIGIT2	TINT1	TINT2
P2DIGIT	.408	.408	-.500	-.289	-.500	-.289
P3DIGIT	.408	.408	.500	-.289	.500	-.289
P4DIGIT	.408	.408	.000	.577	.000	.577
NP2DIGIT	.408	-.408	-.500	-.289	.500	.289
NP3DIGIT	.408	-.408	.500	-.289	-.500	.289
NP4DIGIT	.408	-.408	.000	.577	.000	-.577

The Transformed Variables

The coefficients of the transformation matrix indicate that the first contrast is an average of all six variables. The second contrast is the average response under the absent condition compared to the average response under the present condition. The third contrast is the difference between two and three digits averaged over the two conditions. The fourth contrast is the average of two and three digits compared to four digits, averaged over both conditions. As before, these two contrasts jointly provide a test of the digit effect. The last two contrasts are used for the test of interaction. If there is no interaction effect, the difference between the two- and three-digit numbers should be the same for the two probe conditions. Contrast *tint1* is the difference between two and three digits for condition 2, minus two and three digits for condition 1. Similarly, if there is no interaction between probe presence and the number of digits, the average of two and three digits compared to four should not differ for the two probe conditions. Contrast *tint2* is used to test this hypothesis.

Testing Hypotheses

Hypothesis testing for this design proceeds similarly to the single factor design. Each effect is tested individually. Both multivariate and univariate results can be obtained for tests of each effect. (When a factor has only two levels, there is one contrast for the effect, and the multivariate and univariate results are identical.) Since the test of the constant is not of interest, we will proceed to the test of the condition effect.

The Condition Effect

The table in Figure 4.17 explains that variable *tcondif* is being used in the analysis of the condition effect. The analysis-of-variance table in Figure 4.18 indicates that the condition effect is significant. The F value of 52 has an observed significance level of less than 0.0005. The parameter estimate for the difference between the two conditions is -75, as shown in Figure 4.19. The estimate of the actual difference between mean response under the two conditions is obtained by dividing -75 by 0.408, since the contrast is actually

$$\text{Contrast} = 0.408 \times (\text{mean present} - \text{mean absent}) \qquad \textbf{Equation 4.8}$$

Since the contrast value is negative, the latency times for the absent condition are larger than the latency times for the present condition. This supports the notion that memory searching may be sequential, terminating when an item is found rather than continuing until all items are examined.

Figure 4.17   Test of the condition effect

```
Order of Variables for Analysis

 Variates      Covariates

 TCONDIF

  1 Dependent Variable
  0 Covariates

- - - - - - - - - -

Note..  TRANSFORMED variables are in the variates column.
        These TRANSFORMED variables correspond to the
        'COND' WITHIN-SUBJECT effect.
```

Figure 4.18   Analysis-of-variance table for the condition effect

```
Tests of Significance for TCONDIF using UNIQUE sums of squares
Source of Variation        SS       DF       MS          F  Sig of F

WITHIN CELLS           58810.08     23    2556.96
COND                  134322.25      1  134322.25     52.53      .000
```

Figure 4.19   Parameter estimates for the condition effect

```
MANOVA P2DIGIT P3DIGIT  P4DIGIT   NP2DIGIT  NP3DIGIT  NP4DIGIT
    /WSFACTORS=COND(2) DIGIT(3)
    /CONTRAST(DIGIT)=DIFFERENCE
    /RENAME=CONS   TCONDIF   TDIGIT1   TDIGIT2   TINT1   TINT2
    /PRINT=PARAM(ESTIM)
    /DESIGN.

Estimates for TCONDIF
--- Individual univariate .9500 confidence intervals
COND

 Parameter     Coeff.   Std. Err.    t-Value    Sig. t Lower -95%  CL- Upper

       1   -74.811499  10.32182   -7.24790    .00000  -96.16381  -53.45918
```

The Number of Digits

The next effect to be tested is the number of digits in the memorized number. As shown in Figure 4.20, the test is based on the two contrasts labeled *tdigit1* and *tdigit2*. To use the univariate approach, the assumption of sphericity is necessary.

Figure 4.20 Test of the digit effect

```
Order of Variables for Analysis

   Variates        Covariates

   TDIGIT1
   TDIGIT2

   2 Dependent Variables
   0 Covariates
- - - - - - - - - -

Note..  TRANSFORMED variables are in the variates column.
        These TRANSFORMED variables correspond to the
        'DIGIT' WITHIN-SUBJECT effect.
```

Based on the multivariate criteria in Figure 4.21, the hypothesis that there is no digit effect should be rejected. From Figure 4.22, we see that both of the contrasts are also individually different from 0. This can also be seen from Figure 4.23, which contains the parameter estimates for the contrasts. Note that the tests that the parameter values are 0 are identical to the corresponding univariate F tests. The averaged tests of significance for the digit effect, as shown in Figure 4.24, lead to the same conclusion as the multivariate results in Figure 4.21.

Figure 4.21 Multivariate tests of significance

```
MANOVA P2DIGIT P3DIGIT  P4DIGIT  NP2DIGIT  NP3DIGIT  NP4DIGIT
    /WSFACTORS=COND(2) DIGIT(3)
    /CONTRAST(DIGIT)=DIFFERENCE
    /RENAME=CONS  TCONDIF  TDIGIT1  TDIGIT2  TINT1  TINT2
    /PRINT=SIGNIF(MULTIV)
    /DESIGN.


EFFECT .. DIGIT

Multivariate Tests of Significance (S = 1, M = 0, N = 10 )

Test Name        Value      Approx. F      Hypoth. DF      Error DF      Sig. of F

Pillais         .64216      19.73989          2.00           22.00         .000
Hotellings     1.79454      19.73989          2.00           22.00         .000
Wilks           .35784      19.73989          2.00           22.00         .000
Roys            .64216
```

Figure 4.22 Univariate tests of significance

```
MANOVA P2DIGIT P3DIGIT  P4DIGIT  NP2DIGIT  NP3DIGIT  NP4DIGIT
    /WSFACTORS=COND(2) DIGIT(3)
    /CONTRAST(DIGIT)=DIFFERENCE
    /RENAME=CONS  TCONDIF  TDIGIT1  TDIGIT2  TINT1  TINT2
    /PRINT=SIGNIF(UNIV)
    /DESIGN.


Univariate F-tests with (1,23) D. F.

Variable   Hypoth. SS   Error SS  Hypoth. MS    Error MS         F  Sig. of F

TDIGIT1    41002.6667  34710.8333 41002.6667  1509.16667   27.16908       .000
TDIGIT2    53682.7222  30821.4444 53682.7222  1340.06280   40.05986       .000
```

Figure 4.23   Parameter estimates for the digit contrasts

```
MANOVA P2DIGIT P3DIGIT   P4DIGIT   NP2DIGIT   NP3DIGIT   NP4DIGIT
   /WSFACTORS=COND(2) DIGIT(3)
   /CONTRAST(DIGIT)=DIFFERENCE
   /RENAME=CONS   TCONDIF   TDIGIT1   TDIGIT2   TINT1   TINT2
   /PRINT=PARAM(ESTIM)
   /DESIGN.

Estimates for TDIGIT1
--- Individual univariate .9500 confidence intervals
DIGIT

 Parameter      Coeff.   Std. Err.     t-Value      Sig. t Lower -95%   CL- Upper

      1    41.3333333    7.92981    5.21240      .00003    24.92926    57.73740

- - - - - - - - - - - - - - - - - - - - - - - - - - - - - - - - - - - - - -
Estimates for TDIGIT2
--- Individual univariate .9500 confidence intervals
DIGIT

 Parameter      Coeff.   Std. Err.     t-Value      Sig. t Lower -95%   CL- Upper

      1    47.2946096    7.47235    6.32929      .00000    31.83688    62.75233
```

Figure 4.24   Averaged tests of significance

```
MANOVA P2DIGIT P3DIGIT   P4DIGIT   NP2DIGIT   NP3DIGIT   NP4DIGIT
   /WSFACTORS=COND(2) DIGIT(3)
   /CONTRAST(DIGIT)=DIFFERENCE
   /RENAME=CONS   TCONDIF   TDIGIT1   TDIGIT2   TINT1   TINT2
   /PRINT=SIGNIF(AVERF)
   /DESIGN.

AVERAGED Tests of Significance for MEAS.1 using UNIQUE sums of squares
Source of Variation             SS       DF        MS          F  Sig of F

WITHIN CELLS              65532.28       46   1424.61
DIGIT                     94685.39        2  47342.69      33.23     .000
```

The Interaction

The interaction between the number of digits in the memorized number and the presence or absence of the probe digit is based on the last two contrasts, labeled *tint1* and *tint2*, as indicated in Figure 4.25. Based on the multivariate criteria shown in Figure 4.26 and the averaged univariate results in Figure 4.27, the hypothesis that there is no interaction is not rejected.

Figure 4.25   Test of the interaction effect

```
Order of Variables for Analysis

   Variates       Covariates

   TINT1
   TINT2

    2 Dependent Variables
    0 Covariates
- - - - - - - - - -

Note..   TRANSFORMED variables are in the variates column.
         These TRANSFORMED variables correspond to the
         'COND BY DIGIT' WITHIN-SUBJECT effect.
```

Figure 4.26 Multivariate tests of significance

```
MANOVA P2DIGIT P3DIGIT  P4DIGIT  NP2DIGIT  NP3DIGIT  NP4DIGIT
   /WSFACTORS=COND(2) DIGIT(3)
   /CONTRAST(DIGIT)=DIFFERENCE
   /RENAME=CONS  TCONDIF  TDIGIT1  TDIGIT2  TINT1  TINT2
   /PRINT=SIGNIF(MULTIV)
   /DESIGN.


EFFECT .. COND BY DIGIT

Multivariate Tests of Significance (S = 1, M = 0, N = 10 )

Test Name          Value          Exact F        Hypoth. DF        Error DF        Sig. of F

Pillais           .00890          .09873             2.00             22.00            .906
Hotellings        .00898          .09873             2.00             22.00            .906
Wilks             .99110          .09873             2.00             22.00            .906
Roys              .00890
```

Figure 4.27 Averaged tests of significance

```
MANOVA P2DIGIT P3DIGIT  P4DIGIT  NP2DIGIT  NP3DIGIT  NP4DIGIT
   /WSFACTORS=COND(2) DIGIT(3)
   /CONTRAST(DIGIT)=DIFFERENCE
   /RENAME=CONS  TCONDIF  TDIGIT1  TDIGIT2  TINT1  TINT2
   /PRINT=SIGNIF(AVERF)
   /DESIGN.


AVERAGED Tests of Significance for MEAS.1 using UNIQUE sums of squares
Source of Variation        SS        DF        MS        F  Sig of F

WITHIN CELLS          20751.50        46    451.12
COND BY DIGIT            88.17         2     44.08      .10     .907
```

Putting It Together

Consider Figure 4.28, which contains a plot of the average latencies for each of the three number lengths and conditions. Means and standard deviations are shown in Figure 4.29. Note that the average latency times for the absent condition are always higher than those for the present condition. The test for the statistical significance of this observation is based on the condition factor. Figure 4.29 shows that as the number of digits in a number increases, so does the average latency time. The test of the hypothesis that latency time is the same regardless of the number of digits is based on the digit factor. Again, the hypothesis that there is no digit effect is rejected. The relationship between latency time and the number of digits appears to be fairly similar for the two probe conditions. This is tested by the condition-by-digit interaction, which was not found to be statistically significant. If there is a significant interaction, the relationship between latency time and the number of digits would differ for the two probe conditions.

Figure 4.28   Plot of average latencies

```
COMPUTE CONS=1.
AGGREGATE OUTFILE=*/BREAK=CONS/MPDIG2 MPDIG3 MPDIG4
    MNPDIG2 MNPDIG3 MNPDIG4=MEAN(P2DIGIT P3DIGIT P4DIGIT
    NP2DIGIT NP3DIGIT NP4DIGIT).
COMPUTE C2=2.
COMPUTE C3=3.
COMPUTE C4=4.
PLOT SYMBOLS='PPPAAA'
    /VSIZE=45
    /HSIZE=45
    /TITLE 'LATENCY TIMES (P=PROBE PRESENT A=PROBE ABSENT)'
    /FORMAT=OVERLAY
    /HORIZONTAL 'NUMBER OF DIGITS' /VERTICAL 'MEAN LATENCY TIME'
    /PLOT=MPDIG2 WITH C2;MPDIG3 WITH C3;MPDIG4 WITH C4;
    MNPDIG2 WITH C2;MNPDIG3 WITH C3;MNPDIG4 WITH C4.
```

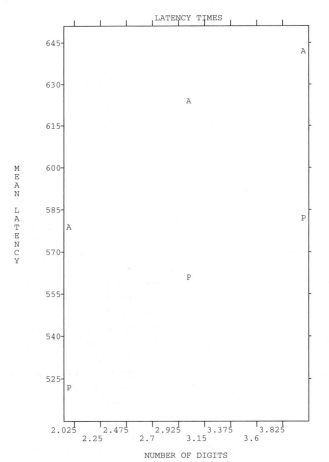

Figure 4.29 Means and standard deviations

```
COMPUTE   DUMMY1=1.
COMPUTE   DUMMY2=1.
VARIABLE  LABEL  DUMMY1  'PRESENT' / DUMMY2  'ABSENT'
   / P2DIGIT  '2 DIGIT'/ P3DIGIT  '3 DIGIT' / P4DIGIT  '4 DIGIT'
   / NP2DIGIT  '2 DIGIT'/ NP3DIGIT  '3 DIGIT' / NP4DIGIT  '4 DIGIT'.
VALUE  LABEL  DUMMY1  DUMMY2 1  ''.
TABLES  OBSERV=P2DIGIT TO  NP4DIGIT
   /TABLE  DUMMY1  BY  P2DIGIT+P3DIGIT+P4DIGIT
   /STATISTICS  MEAN  STDDEV
   /TABLE  DUMMY2  BY  NP2DIGIT+NP3DIGIT+NP4DIGIT
   /STATISTICS  MEAN STDDEV.
```

	2 DIGIT		3 DIGIT		4 DIGIT	
	Mean	Standard Deviation	Mean	Standard Deviation	Mean	Standard Deviation
PRESENT	520.58	131.37	560.00	118.78	581.25	117.32

	2 DIGIT		3 DIGIT		4 DIGIT	
	Mean	Standard Deviation	Mean	Standard Deviation	Mean	Standard Deviation
ABSENT	579.75	132.17	623.00	135.14	642.33	144.81

Within-Subjects and Between-Subjects Factors

Both number of digits and probe status are called **within-subjects factors**, since all combinations occur within each of the subjects. It is also possible to have between-subjects factors in repeated measures designs. **Between-subjects factors** subdivide the sample into discrete subgroups. Each subject has only one value for a between-subjects factor. For example, if cases in the previously described study are subdivided into males and females, sex is a between-subjects factor. Similarly, if cases are classified as those who received "memory enhancers" and those who did not, the memory enhancement factor is a between-subjects factor. If the same subject is tested with and without memory enhancers, memory enhancement would be a within-subjects factor. Thus, the same factor can be either a within-subjects or between-subjects factor, depending on the experimental design. Some factors, such as sex and race, can only be between-subjects factors, since the same subject can be of only one sex or race.

Additional Univariate Assumptions

In a within-subjects design, a sufficient condition for the univariate model approach to be valid is that, for each effect, the variance-covariance matrix of the transformed variables used to test the effect has covariances of 0 and equal variances. Including between-subjects factors in a design necessitates an additional assumption. The variance-covariance matrices for the transformed variables for a particular effect must be equal for all levels of the between-subjects factors. These two assumptions are often called the **symmetry conditions**. If they are not tenable, the F ratios from the averaged univariate results may not be correct.

Back to Memory

In addition to the two within-subjects factors, Bacon's experiment also included a between-subjects factor—the hand subjects used to press the instrument that signaled the presence or absence of the probe digit. All subjects were right-handed, but half were required to signal with the right hand and half with the left. (If a subject had been tested under both conditions, right hand and left hand, hand would be a within-subjects factor.) The hypothesis of interest was whether latency would increase for subjects using the left hand.

The hypothesis that the variance-covariance matrices are equal across all levels of the between-subjects factor can be examined using the multivariate generalization of Box's M test. It is based on the determinants of the variance-covariance matrices for all between-subjects cells in the design. Figure 4.30 contains the multivariate test for equality of the variance-covariance matrices for the two levels of the hand factor (which hand the subject used). Note that in MANOVA, this test is based on all the original variables for the within-subjects effects.

Figure 4.30   Box's M

```
MANOVA  P2DIGIT   P3DIGIT   P4DIGIT   NP2DIGIT   NP3DIGIT   NP4DIGIT
   BY HAND(1,2)
   /WSFACTORS=COND(2)   DIGIT(3)
   /CONTRAST(DIGIT)=DIFFERENCE
   /RENAME=CONS  TCONDIF   TDIGIT1   TDIGIT2   TINT1   TINT2
   /PRINT=HOMOGENEITY(BOXM)
   /DESIGN HAND.


Multivariate test for Homogeneity of Dispersion matrices

Boxs M =                       25.92434
F with (21,1780) DF =            .86321, P =   .641 (Approx.)
Chi-Square with 21 DF =        18.43322, P =   .621 (Approx.)
```

Adding a between-subjects factor to the experiment introduces more terms into the analysis-of-variance model. Besides the digit, condition, and condition-by-digit effects, the model includes the main effect, hand, and the interaction terms hand by digit, hand by condition, and hand by digit by condition.

The analysis proceeds as before. Variables corresponding to the within-subjects factors are again transformed using the transformation matrix shown in Figure 4.31. The between-subjects factors are not transformed.

Figure 4.31   Transformation matrix

```
MANOVA  P2DIGIT  P3DIGIT  P4DIGIT  NP2DIGIT  NP3DIGIT  NP4DIGIT  BY HAND(1,2)
    /WSFACTORS=COND(2)  DIGIT(3)
    /CONTRAST(DIGIT)=DIFFERENCE
    /RENAME=CONS TCONDIF  TDIGIT1  TDIGIT2  TINT1  TINT2
    /PRINT=TRANSFORM
    /DESIGN HAND.
```

Orthonormalized Transformation Matrix (Transposed)

	CONS	TCONDIF	TDIGIT1	TDIGIT2	TINT1	TINT2
P2DIGIT	.408	.408	-.500	-.289	-.500	-.289
P3DIGIT	.408	.408	.500	-.289	.500	-.289
P4DIGIT	.408	.408	.000	.577	.000	.577
NP2DIGIT	.408	-.408	-.500	-.289	.500	.289
NP3DIGIT	.408	-.408	.500	-.289	-.500	.289
NP4DIGIT	.408	-.408	.000	.577	.000	-.577

The within-subjects factors and their interactions are tested as when there were no be-tween-subject factors in the design. Tests of the between-subjects factors and the inter-actions of the between- and within-subjects factors treat the transformed within-subjects variables as dependent variables. For example, the test of the hand effect is identical to a two-sample *t* test, with the transformed variable corresponding to the constant as the dependent variable. The test of the condition-by-hand interaction treats the transformed variable corresponding to the condition effect as the dependent variable. Similarly, the digit-by-hand interaction considers the two transformed variables for the digit effect as dependent variables. The test of the three-way interaction hand by digit by condition treats the two variables corresponding to the interaction of digit by condition as the de-pendent variables. *hand* is always the grouping variable.

The SPSS/PC+ output for a design with both within- and between-subjects factors looks much like before. The variables used for each analysis are first identified, as shown for the constant effect in Figure 4.32.

Figure 4.32   Test of the constant effect

```
Order of Variables for Analysis

  Variates      Covariates

  CONS

    1 Dependent Variable
    0 Covariates

      Note..   TRANSFORMED variables are in the variates column.
               These TRANSFORMED variables correspond to the
               Between-subject effects.
```

All tests based on the same transformed variables are presented together. Since the test of the hand effect is based on the same variable as the test for the constant effect, the tests are displayed together, as shown in Figure 4.33. This is the usual analysis-of-variance table, since there is only one dependent variable in the analyses. From the analysis-of-variance table, it appears that the constant is significantly different from 0, an uninteresting finding we have made before. The hand effect, however, is not statistically significant, since its observed significance level is very close to 1. This means that there is insufficient evidence to reject the null hypothesis that there is no difference in average latency times for subjects who used their right hand and subjects who used their left.

Figure 4.33   Tests of significance using unique sums of squares

```
Tests of Significance for CONS using UNIQUE sums of squares
Source of Variation          SS       DF       MS         F  Sig of F

WITHIN CELLS           2196663.86     22   99848.36
CONSTANT              49193858.03      1   49193858    492.69     .000
HAND                      300.44      1     300.44       .00     .957
```

For the transformed variable used to test the hand effect, the overall mean is 1432. The mean for the right-hand subjects is 1435 and for the left-hand subjects is 1428. The parameter estimates in Figure 4.34 are based on these means. The parameter estimate for constant is the unweighted grand mean, while the parameter estimate for hand is the deviation of the right-hand group from the overall mean. (For between-subjects variables such as *hand*, deviation parameter estimates are the default.)

Figure 4.34   Parameter estimates for the hand contrasts

```
MANOVA  P2DIGIT   P3DIGIT   P4DIGIT   NP2DIGIT   NP3DIGIT   NP4DIGIT
   BY HAND(1,2)
   /WSFACTORS=COND(2)   DIGIT(3)
   /CONTRAST(DIGIT)=DIFFERENCE
   /RENAME=CONS TCONDIF   TDIGIT1   TDIGIT2   TINT1   TINT2
   /PRINT=PARAM(ESTIM)
   /DESIGN HAND.

 Estimates for CONS
--- Individual univariate .9500 confidence intervals
CONSTANT

  Parameter      Coeff.    Std. Err.     t-Value    Sig. t Lower -95%  CL- Upper

     1   1431.69273   64.50076   22.19652     .00000 1297.92634 1565.45913
HAND

  Parameter      Coeff.    Std. Err.     t-Value    Sig. t Lower -95%  CL- Upper

     2   3.53815185   64.50076     .05485     .95675 -130.22824  137.30454
```

Figure 4.35 is the analysis-of-variance table based on the transformed variable for the condition effect. Again, there is a significant effect for condition, but the hand-by-condition effect is not significant.

Figure 4.35 Analysis of variance for the interaction

```
Tests of Significance for TCONDIF using UNIQUE sums of squares
Source of Variation          SS        DF        MS         F  Sig of F

WITHIN CELLS            57889.97        22    2631.36
COND                   134322.25         1  134322.25      51.05     .000
HAND BY COND              920.11         1     920.11        .35     .560
```

Since the digit effect has two degrees of freedom, its test is based on two transformed variables, and both univariate and multivariate results are displayed for hypotheses involving digit. The multivariate results for the hand-by-digit interaction are shown in Figure 4.36. It appears that there is no interaction between number of digits and the hand used to signal the response. The multivariate results for the digit effect are shown in Figure 4.37. Again, they are highly significant. Figure 4.38 shows the averaged univariate results for terms involving the digit effect.

Figure 4.36 Multivariate tests of significance for the hand-by-digit interaction

```
MANOVA  P2DIGIT  P3DIGIT  P4DIGIT  NP2DIGIT  NP3DIGIT  NP4DIGIT
    BY HAND(1,2)
    /WSFACTORS=COND(2)  DIGIT(3)
    /CONTRAST(DIGIT)=DIFFERENCE
    /RENAME=CONS TCONDIF  TDIGIT1  TDIGIT2  TINT1  TINT2
    /PRINT=SIGNIF(MULTIV)
    /DESIGN HAND.


EFFECT .. HAND BY DIGIT
Multivariate Tests of Significance (S = 1, M = 0, N = 9 1/2)

Test Name         Value    Exact F Hypoth. DF   Error DF  Sig. of F

Pillais          .08477    .97258      2.00      21.00       .394
Hotellings       .09263    .97258      2.00      21.00       .394
Wilks            .91523    .97258      2.00      21.00       .394
Roys             .08477
```

Figure 4.37 Multivariate tests of significance for digit effect

```
MANOVA  P2DIGIT  P3DIGIT  P4DIGIT  NP2DIGIT  NP3DIGIT  NP4DIGIT
    BY HAND(1,2)
    /WSFACTORS=COND(2)  DIGIT(3)
    /CONTRAST(DIGIT)=DIFFERENCE
    /RENAME=CONS TCONDIF  TDIGIT1  TDIGIT2  TINT1  TINT2
    /PRINT=SIGNIF(multiv)
    /DESIGN HAND.

EFFECT .. DIGIT
Multivariate Tests of Significance (S = 1, M = 0, N = 9 1/2)

Test Name         Value    Exact F Hypoth. DF   Error DF  Sig. of F

Pillais          .64219  18.84488      2.00      21.00       .000
Hotellings      1.79475  18.84488      2.00      21.00       .000
Wilks            .35781  18.84488      2.00      21.00       .000
Roys             .64219
```

Figure 4.38   Averaged tests of significance

```
MANOVA  P2DIGIT  P3DIGIT  P4DIGIT  NP2DIGIT  NP3DIGIT  NP4DIGIT
    BY HAND(1,2)
    /WSFACTORS=COND(2)  DIGIT(3)
    /CONTRAST(DIGIT)=DIFFERENCE
    /RENAME=CONS TCONDIF  TDIGIT1  TDIGIT2  TINT1  TINT2
    /PRINT=SIGNIF(AVERF)
    /DESIGN HAND.


AVERAGED Tests of Significance for MEAS.1 using UNIQUE sums of squares
Source of Variation        SS        DF        MS          F  Sig of F

WITHIN CELLS          64376.89        44    1463.11
DIGIT                 94685.39         2   47342.69      32.36      .000
HAND BY DIGIT          1155.39         2     577.69        .39      .676
```

Figure 4.39 shows the multivariate results for the hand-by-condition-by-digit effect. Again, these are not significant. The univariate tests, shown in Figure 4.40, agree with the multivariate results.

Figure 4.39   Multivariate tests of significance for the three-way interaction

```
MANOVA  P2DIGIT  P3DIGIT  P4DIGIT  NP2DIGIT  NP3DIGIT  NP4DIGIT
    BY HAND(1,2)
    /WSFACTORS=COND(2)  DIGIT(3)
    /CONTRAST(DIGIT)=DIFFERENCE
    /RENAME=CONS TCONDIF  TDIGIT1  TDIGIT2  TINT1  TINT2
    /PRINT=SIGNIF(MULTIV)
    /DESIGN HAND.
EFFECT .. HAND BY COND BY DIGIT
Multivariate Tests of Significance (S = 1, M = 0, N = 9 1/2)

Test Name       Value      Exact F Hypoth. DF    Error DF  Sig. of F

Pillais         .07632     .86760     2.00         21.00      .434
Hotellings      .08263     .86760     2.00         21.00      .434
Wilks           .92368     .86760     2.00         21.00      .434
Roys            .07632
```

Figure 4.40   Averaged tests of significance for the three-way interaction

```
MANOVA  P2DIGIT  P3DIGIT  P4DIGIT  NP2DIGIT  NP3DIGIT  NP4DIGIT
    BY HAND(1,2)
    /WSFACTORS=COND(2)  DIGIT(3)
    /CONTRAST(DIGIT)=DIFFERENCE
    /RENAME=CONS TCONDIF  TDIGIT1  TDIGIT2  TINT1  TINT2
    /PRINT=SIGNIF(AVERF)
    /DESIGN HAND.


AVERAGED Tests of Significance for MEAS.1 using UNIQUE sums of squares
Source of Variation        SS        DF        MS          F  Sig of F

WITHIN CELLS          20138.11        44     457.68
COND BY DIGIT            88.17         2      44.08        .10      .908
HAND BY COND BY DIGIT   613.39         2     306.69        .67      .517
```

Summarizing the Results

The hand used by the subject to signal the response does not seem to affect overall latency times. It also does not appear to interact with the number of digits in the memorized number or with the presence or absence of the probe digit. This is an interesting finding, since it was conceivable that using a nonpreferred hand would increase the time required to signal. Or subjects using their right hands might have had shorter latency times because of the way different activities are governed by the hemispheres of the brain. Memory is thought to be a function of the left hemisphere, which also governs the activity of the right hand. Thus, using the right hand would not necessitate a "switch" of hemispheres and might result in shorter latency times.

Analysis of Covariance with a Constant Covariate

The speed with which a subject signals that the probe digit is or is not present in the memorized number may depend on various characteristics of the subject. For example, some subjects may generally respond more quickly to stimuli than others. The reaction time or "speed" of a subject may influence performance in the memory experiments. To control for differences in responsiveness, we might administer a reaction-time test to each subject. This time can then be used as a covariate in the analysis. If subjects responding with the right hand are generally slower than subjects responding with the left, we may be able to account for the fact that no differences between the two groups were found.

To adjust for differences in covariates, the regression between the dependent variable and the covariate is calculated. For each subject, the response that would have been obtained if they had the same average speed is then calculated. Further analyses are based on these corrected values.

In a repeated measures design, the general idea is the same. The between-subjects effects are adjusted for the covariates. There is no need to adjust the within-subjects effects for covariates whose values do not change during the course of an experiment, since within-subjects factor differences are obtained from the same subject. That is, a subject's quickness or slowness is the same for all within-subjects factors.

To see how this is done, consider a hypothetical extension of Bacon's experiment. Let's assume that prior to the memory tests, each subject was given a series of trials in which he or she pressed a bar as soon as a light appeared. The interval between the time the light appeared and the time the subject pressed the bar will be termed the reaction time. For each subject, the average reaction time over a series of trials is calculated. This reaction time will be considered a covariate in the analysis.

As in the previous examples, all analyses are based on the transformed within-subjects variables. Figure 4.41 shows the orthonormalized transformation matrix. It is similar to the one used before, except that there are now six additional rows and columns that are used to transform the covariates. Although there is only one covariate in this example, MANOVA requires you to specify a covariate for each within-subjects variable, which is done by repeating the same covariate. The transformation applied to the covariates is the same as the transformation for the within-subjects factors.

Figure 4.41   Transformation matrix with covariates

```
COMPUTE   C1=REACT.
COMPUTE   C2=REACT.
COMPUTE   C3=REACT.
COMPUTE   C4=REACT.
COMPUTE   C5=REACT.
COMPUTE   C6=REACT.
MANOVA  P2DIGIT  P3DIGIT  P4DIGIT  NP2DIGIT  NP3DIGIT  NP4DIGIT  BY  HAND(1,2)
   WITH C1 C2 C3 C4 C5 C6
   /WSFACTORS=COND(2) DIGIT(3)
   /CONTRAST(DIGIT)=DIFFERENCE
   /RENAME=CONS TCONDIF  TDIGIT1  TDIGIT2  TINT1  TINT2
     TC1 TC2 TC3 TC4 TC5 TC6
   /PRINT=TRANSFORM
   /DESIGN  HAND.
```

Orthonormalized Transformation Matrix (Transposed)

	CONS	TCONDIF	TDIGIT1	TDIGIT2	TINT1	TINT2	TC1	TC2
P2DIGIT	.408	.408	-.500	-.289	-.500	-.289	.000	.000
P3DIGIT	.408	.408	.500	-.289	.500	-.289	.000	.000
P4DIGIT	.408	.408	.000	.577	.000	.577	.000	.000
NP2DIGIT	.408	-.408	-.500	-.289	.500	.289	.000	.000
NP3DIGIT	.408	-.408	.500	-.289	-.500	.289	.000	.000
NP4DIGIT	.408	-.408	.000	.577	.000	-.577	.000	.000
C1	.000	.000	.000	.000	.000	.000	.408	.408
C2	.000	.000	.000	.000	.000	.000	.408	.408
C3	.000	.000	.000	.000	.000	.000	.408	.408
C4	.000	.000	.000	.000	.000	.000	.408	-.408
C5	.000	.000	.000	.000	.000	.000	.408	-.408
C6	.000	.000	.000	.000	.000	.000	.408	-.408

	TC3	TC4	TC5	TC6
P2DIGIT	.000	.000	.000	.000
P3DIGIT	.000	.000	.000	.000
P4DIGIT	.000	.000	.000	.000
NP2DIGIT	.000	.000	.000	.000
NP3DIGIT	.000	.000	.000	.000
NP4DIGIT	.000	.000	.000	.000
C1	-.500	-.289	-.500	-.289
C2	.500	-.289	.500	-.289
C3	.000	.577	.000	.577
C4	-.500	-.289	.500	.289
C5	.500	-.289	-.500	.289
C6	.000	.577	.000	-.577

Figure 4.42 is a description of the variables used in the analysis of the constant and the between-subjects variable. The dependent variable is the constant effect, the covariate *tc1*. All of the other variables, including the five transformed replicates of the same covariate labeled *tc2* to *tc6*, are not used for this analysis.

Figure 4.42 Test of the constant effect

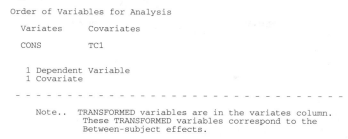

```
Order of Variables for Analysis

  Variates      Covariates

  CONS          TC1


  1 Dependent Variable
  1 Covariate

- - - - - - - - - - - - - - - - - - - - - - - - - - - - - - - -

      Note..  TRANSFORMED variables are in the variates column.
              These TRANSFORMED variables correspond to the
              Between-subject effects.
```

The analysis-of-variance table for the hand and constant effects is shown in Figure 4.43. Notice how the table has changed from Figure 4.33, the corresponding table without the reaction-time covariate. In Figure 4.43, the within-cells error term is subdivided into two components—error sums of squares and sums of squares due to the regression. In an analysis-of-covariance model, we are able to explain some of the variability within a cell of the design by the fact that cases have different values for the covariates. The regression sum of squares is the variability attributable to the covariate. If you were to calculate a regression between the transformed constant term and the transformed covariate, the regression sums of squares would be identical to those in Figure 4.43. The test for the hand effect is thus no longer based on the constant, but on the constant adjusted for the covariate. Thus, differences between the groups in overall reaction time are eliminated. The hand effect is still not significant, however. The sums of squares attributable to hand have also changed. This is because the hypothesis tested is no longer that the overall mean is 0, but that the intercept in the regression equation for the constant and the reaction time is 0.

Figure 4.43 Analysis of covariance

```
Tests of Significance for CONS using UNIQUE sums of squares
Source of Variation         SS      DF       MS         F   Sig of F

WITHIN+RESIDUAL        656243.80     21  31249.70
REGRESSION            1540420.06      1 1540420.1     49.29     .000
HAND                     3745.89      1    3745.89      .12     .733
```

Figure 4.44 shows that the regression coefficient for the transformed reaction time is 97.57. The test of the hypothesis that the coefficient is 0 is identical to the test of the regression effect in the analysis-of-variance table.

Figure 4.44   Regression coefficient for reaction time

```
Regression analysis for WITHIN+RESIDUAL error term
--- Individual Univariate .9500 confidence intervals
Dependent variable .. CONS

COVARIATE            B      Beta   Std. Err.   t-Value   Sig. of t   Lower -95%   CL- Upper

TC1            97.57466   .83788    13.898      7.021       .000       68.673      126.476
```

When constant covariates are specified, messages such as that shown in Figure 4.45 are displayed. All the message says is that since all the covariates are identical, they are linearly dependent. You can simply ignore this message.

Figure 4.45   Linear dependency warning message

```
* * * * * * * * * * * * * * * * * * * * * * * * * * * * * * *
*                     *                                       *
*   W A R N I N G     * For WITHIN CELLS error matrix, these covariates *
*                     * appear LINEARLY DEPENDENT on preceding *
*                     * variables ...                         *
*                     *    TC2                                 *
*                     * 1 D.F. will be returned to this error term. *
*                     *                                       *
* * * * * * * * * * * * * * * * * * * * * * * * * * * * * * *
```

Doubly Multivariate Repeated Measures Designs

There is only one dependent variable in Bacon's experiment, latency time, which was measured for all subjects. In some situations, more than one dependent variable may be measured for each factor combination. For example, to test the effect of different medications on blood pressure, both systolic and diastolic blood pressures may be recorded for each treatment. This is sometimes called a doubly multivariate repeated measures design, since each subject has multiple variables measured at multiple times.

Analysis of doubly multivariate repeated measures data is similar to the analyses above. Each dependent variable is transformed using the same orthonormalized transformation. All subsequent analyses are based on these transformed variables. The tests for each effect are based on the appropriate variables for all dependent variables. For example, in the memory experiment, if two dependent variables had been measured for the three number lengths, the test of the digit effect would be based on four transformed variables, two for the first dependent variable and two for the second. Similarly, the test for constant would have been based on two variables corresponding to averages for each dependent variable.

Running the MANOVA Procedure for Repeated Measures Designs

This section covers only the subcommands needed to specify repeated measures designs. For subcommands or keywords not described here, see "Running the MANOVA Procedure" on p. 99 in Chapter 3.

Specifying Variables in the Equation

The first specification in the MANOVA procedure is the list of variables to be used in the analyses. Dependent variables are named first, followed by the keyword BY and factor names with ranges specified in parentheses. If there are covariates, list them last following keyword WITH. In a repeated measures design, list all variables that correspond to within-subjects factors as dependent variables. Between-subjects variables are considered factors. For example, the command

```
MANOVA P2DIGIT P3DIGIT P4DIGIT.
```

specifies the three variables corresponding to number length when the probe digit is present as the dependent variable. To include the present/absent condition in the analysis as well, specify:

```
MANOVA P2DIGIT P3DIGIT P4DIGIT NP2DIGIT NP3DIGIT NP4DIGIT.
```

To include the between-subjects factor *hand* with two levels coded as 1 and 2, specify:

```
MANOVA P2DIGIT P3DIGIT P4DIGIT NP2DIGIT NP3DIGIT NP4DIGIT
   BY HAND(1,2).
```

When there are additional between-subjects factors, list them all after the BY keyword. Additional rules for specifying variables are given in Chapter 3.

Specifying a Constant Covariate

A covariate that is measured only once is called a **constant covariate**. In a repeated measures design with constant covariates, you must specify as many covariate names as there are dependent variables on the MANOVA command. If there is a single covariate that is measured only once (for example, before the experiment was conducted), use the COMPUTE command to replicate the covariate values. For example, the analysis of covariance described in "Analysis of Covariance with a Constant Covariate" on p. 149, where *react* is the value of the reaction time, can be specified as:

```
COMPUTE C1=REACT.
COMPUTE C2=REACT.
COMPUTE C3=REACT.
COMPUTE C4=REACT.
COMPUTE C5=REACT.
COMPUTE C6=REACT.
MANOVA P2DIGIT P3DIGIT P4DIGIT NP2DIGIT NP3DIGIT NP4DIGIT
   BY HAND(1,2)
   WITH C1 C2 C3 C4 C5 C6.
```

Specifying the Structure of the Design

For a repeated measures design, you must also specify the structure of the design. For example, if there are six variables on the dependent variable list, they may have originated from a variety of repeated measures designs. There may be one within-subjects factor—say, *treatment*—which has six values representing six different agents administered to the same subject. Or there may be two within-subjects factors, such as *treatment* and *dose*, one having three levels and the other having two. For example, each subject receives three different treatments at two dosage levels; or perhaps two treatments at each of three dosage levels are given.

Identifying Within-Subjects Factors

Use the WSFACTORS subcommand to identify the correspondence between the variable list and the within-subjects factors. Specify the name of each factor on WSFACTOR, followed by the number of levels in parentheses. The product of the number of levels of the factors must equal the number of dependent variables (except in doubly multivariate repeated measures; see "Labeling the Display of Averaged Results" on p. 156). WSFACTORS must be the first subcommand after the variable list.

For example, to indicate that the three variables *p2digit, p3digit,* and *p4digit* correspond to three levels of a within-subjects factor that is to be assigned the name *digit*, specify:

```
MANOVA P2DIGIT P3DIGIT P4DIGIT
  /WSFACTORS=DIGIT(3).
```

The names assigned to the within-subjects factors must follow the SPSS/PC+ variable-naming conventions. Each name must be unique. The names exist only during the MANOVA analysis in which they are defined.

A name must be assigned to each within-subjects factor. For example, to define the two within-subjects factors for number length and presence/absence condition, specify:

```
MANOVA P2DIGIT P3DIGIT P4DIGIT NP2DIGIT NP3DIGIT NP4DIGIT
  /WSFACTORS=COND(2) DIGIT(3).
```

Each variable named on the variable list corresponds to a particular combination of within-subjects factor levels. For example, variable *p2digit* is the latency time for a two-digit number when the probe digit is present.

The order in which factors are named on WSFACTORS must correspond to the sequence of variables on the variable list. The first factor named on WSFACTORS changes most slowly. Thus, in the example above, values of the *digit* factor change faster than values of the *cond* factor. For example, *p2digit* is the response at the first level of *cond* and the first level of *digit*, and *p3digit* is the response at the first level of *cond* and the second level of *digit*. If the order of the variables on the MANOVA command is changed, the order of factor names on the WSFACTORS subcommand must also be changed, as in:

```
MANOVA P2DIGIT NP2DIGIT P3DIGIT NP3DIGIT P4DIGIT NP4DIGIT
   /WSFACTORS=DIGIT(3) COND(2).
```

In general, the variables must be arranged on the variable list in such a way that their structure can be represented on a WSFACTORS subcommand. For example, it is not possible to represent the following list of variables on a WSFACTORS subcommand, since the variables are not arranged in a predictable sequence. *Do not use variable lists like this:*

```
MANOVA P2DIGIT P3DIGIT NP2DIGIT NP3DIGIT P4DIGIT NP4DIGIT
```

Renaming the Transformed Variables

When a repeated measures design is specified, the original variables are transformed using an orthonormal transformation matrix, and the transformed variables are then analyzed. To make the MANOVA output easier to interpret, it is a good idea to assign names to the new variables. This is done with the RENAME subcommand.

For example, the following command created the transformation matrix shown in Figure 4.31:

```
MANOVA P2DIGIT P3DIGIT P4DIGIT NP2DIGIT NP3DIGIT NP4DIGIT
   BY HAND(1,2)
   /WSFACTORS=COND(2) DIGIT(3)
   /CONTRAST (DIGIT)=DIFFERENCE
   /RENAME=CONS TCONDIF TDIGIT1 TDIGIT2 TINT1 TINT2
   /PRINT=TRANSFORM.
```

The name *cons* is assigned to the constant effect, the name *tcondif* to the condition effect, the names *tdigit1* and *tdigit2* to the two transformed variables for the *digit* effect, and *tint1* and *tint2* to the two transformed variables that represent the interaction of condition and digit length.

The number of names listed on the RENAME subcommand must equal the number of dependent variables and covariates on the variable list. To retain a variable's original name, specify either the original name or an asterisk. For example, to retain the names of the covariates in the following command, specify:

```
MANOVA P2DIGIT P3DIGIT P4DIGIT NP2DIGIT NP3DIGIT NP4DIGIT
   BY HAND(1,2)
   WITH C1 C2 C3 C4 C5 C6
   /WSFACTORS=COND(2) DIGIT(3)
   /RENAME=CONS TCONDIF TDIGIT1 TDIGIT2 TINT1 TINT2 * * * * * *.
```

If you do not supply a RENAME subcommand in a situation where the variables are being transformed, as in repeated measures analysis, MANOVA automatically assigns the names *t1, t2,* and so on, to the transformed variables. You must use the new names on all subsequent subcommands except on OMEANS, which produces tables of observed means of the *untransformed* variables and accepts only the original variable names.

Labeling the Display of Averaged Results

In a doubly multivariate repeated measures design (when more than one variable is measured at each combination of the factor levels), you can use the MEASURE subcommand to differentiate sets of dependent variables. In a doubly multivariate design, the arrangement of the within-subjects factors must be the same for all sets of variables. For example, if both systolic and diastolic blood pressure are measured at three points in time, you can specify:

```
MANOVA SYS1 SYS2 SYS3 DIAS1 DIAS2 DIAS3
  /WSFACTORS=TIME(3)
  /MEASURE=SYSTOL DIASTOL.
```

This command names one factor, *time*, which has three levels for two sets of dependent variables. Variables *sys1, sys2,* and *sys3* are in the *systol* set, and *dias1, dias2,* and *dias3* are in the *diastol* set. Note that the number of variables named on the MEASURE subcommand times the product of the levels of factors named on the WSFACTORS subcommand equals the number of dependent variables used in the design.

If you omit MEASURE from the above command, MANOVA will automatically generate a doubly multivariate design based on the three levels of the *time* factor. The advantage of using MEASURE is that the display of averaged results (produced by SIGNIF(AVERF) on the PRINT subcommand) will be labeled with the names you specify. If you do not use MEASURE, MANOVA displays the results but uses its own labeling. Thus, the MEASURE subcommand is optional, but it is recommended for clarity.

Specifying the Contrasts

All of the contrast types described in Chapter 3 can be used for between-subjects factors in repeated measures designs. In the case of within-subjects factors, nonorthogonal contrasts such as deviation and simple are orthonormalized prior to the repeated measures analysis. If the contrast requested is not orthogonal, the parameter estimates obtained for terms involving the within-subjects factors will not correspond to the contrast requested. Therefore, it is recommended that only orthogonal contrasts be specified on the CONTRAST subcommand for within-subjects factors. Orthogonal contrast types are DIFFERENCE, HELMERT, and POLYNOMIAL.

The default contrast for within-subjects factors is POLYNOMIAL. If nonorthogonal contrasts are requested, the transformation matrix should always be displayed to ascertain what orthonormalized contrasts are used.

Specifying the Design for Within-Subjects Factors

Use the WSDESIGN subcommand to specify the design for the within-subjects factors. Its specification is similar to the DESIGN subcommand discussed in Chapter 3. For example, to request a complete factorial design for the *digit* and *cond* within-subjects factors, specify:

```
MANOVA P2DIGIT P3DIGIT P4DIGIT NP2DIGIT NP3DIGIT NP4DIGIT
   /WSFACTORS=COND(2) DIGIT(3)
   /WSDESIGN=COND DIGIT COND BY DIGIT.
```

As is the case for between-subjects factors, the complete factorial design is the default and can be obtained by omitting the WSDESIGN subcommand altogether or by entering it with no specifications. To suppress estimation of the condition-by-digit interaction and specify a main-effects model, specify:

```
MANOVA P2DIGIT P3DIGIT P4DIGIT NP2DIGIT NP3DIGIT NP4DIGIT
   /WSFACTORS=COND(2) DIGIT(3)
   /WSDESIGN=COND DIGIT.
```

Specifications Unavailable on WSDESIGN

The following specifications, which can be used on the DESIGN subcommand, are not permitted on the WSDESIGN subcommand:

- Error term references and definitions.
- The MUPLUS and CONSTANT keywords.
- Continuous variables.
- Between-subjects factors.

WSDESIGN and Other Subcommands

The WSDESIGN specification signals the beginning of within-subjects design processing, so if you explicitly enter a WSDESIGN subcommand, all other subcommands that affect the within-subjects design must appear before it. For example, if a HELMERT contrast is to be used for the *digit* effect instead of the default POLYNOMIAL contrast, this must be indicated prior to the WSDESIGN subcommand, as in:

```
MANOVA P2DIGIT P3DIGIT P4DIGIT NP2DIGIT NP3DIGIT NP4DIGIT
   /WSFACTORS=COND(2) DIGIT(3)
   /CONTRAST(DIGIT)=HELMERT
   /WSDESIGN COND DIGIT.
```

Repeated Measures Processing

In a repeated measures analysis of variance, all dependent variables are not tested together as is usually done in MANOVA. Instead, sets of transformed variables that correspond to particular effects are tested. For example, in the memory experiment, the constant is tested first, then the variable that represents the condition effect, then the two variables that represent the digit effect, and, finally, the two variables that represent the digit-by-condition interaction. The cycling through the dependent variables is automatically accomplished when you enter a WSFACTORS subcommand.

For example, to obtain a test of the full-factorial within-subjects design, specify:

```
MANOVA P2DIGIT P3DIGIT P4DIGIT NP2DIGIT NP3DIGIT NP4DIGIT
  /WSFACTORS=COND(2) DIGIT(3)
  /RENAME=CONS TCONDIF TDIGIT1 TDIGIT2 TINT1 TINT2.
```

Specifying the Between-Subjects Factors

Use the DESIGN subcommand according to the rules defined in Chapter 3 to list between-subjects effects to be tested. If no effects are listed on the DESIGN subcommand, the default is a full-factorial design. Thus, the complete memory experiment can be analyzed with the command:

```
MANOVA P2DIGIT P3DIGIT P4DIGIT NP2DIGIT NP3DIGIT NP4DIGIT
  BY HAND(1,2)
  /WSFACTORS=COND(2) DIGIT(3)
  /RENAME=CONS TCONDIF TDIGIT1 TDIGIT2 TINT1 TINT2
  /WSDESIGN=COND DIGIT COND BY DIGIT
  /DESIGN=HAND.
```

Here, both the WSDESIGN and the DESIGN subcommands are optional, since complete factorial designs are the default. In a repeated measures analysis, interactions between the within-subjects factors and the between-subjects factors are always included.

Requesting Optional Output

All statistics and plots described in Chapter 3 are available for repeated measures designs. However, some output is particularly useful for repeated measures designs. The orthonormalized transformation matrix used to generate the transformed variables is requested with the keyword TRANSFORM on PRINT. The averaged univariate F tests are displayed by default but can be explicitly requested with the keywords AVERF on SIGNIF. For example, to display the transformation matrix, specify:

```
/PRINT=TRANSFORM
```

Homogeneity-of-variance tests and Mauchly's test of sphericity may be used to analyze departures from the symmetry assumptions necessary for a univariate (averaged F test) analysis. Use BARTLETT, COCHRAN, and/or BOXM on keyword HOMOGENEITY to request the homogeneity tests, as in:

```
/PRINT=TRANSFORM SIGNIF(AVERF) HOMOGENEITY(BARTLETT BOXM)
```

Mauchly's test is always displayed for a repeated measures analysis.

Annotated Example

The following SPSS/PC+ commands produced the output shown in Figure 4.5 to Figure 4.10 and Figure 4.12:

```
DATA LIST FREE
  /HAND P2DIGIT P3DIGIT P4DIGIT NP2DIGIT NP3DIGIT NP4DIGIT
REACT.
BEGIN DATA.
.
data records
.
END DATA.
MANOVA P2DIGIT P3DIGIT P4DIGIT
  /WSFACTORS=DIGIT(3)
  /CONTRAST(DIGIT)=DIFFERENCE
  /RENAME=CONS DIF12 DIF12V3
  /WSDESIGN
  /PRINT=PARAMETERS(ESTIM) TRANSFORM
  /DESIGN.
```

- The DATA LIST command gives the variable names and tells SPSS/PC+ that the data will be found in freefield format.

- Three dependent variables are specified on the MANOVA command, each corresponding to a number length when the probe digit is present.

- The WSFACTORS subcommand indicates that the three variables *p2digit*, *p3digit*, and *p4digit* correspond to three levels of a within-subjects factor assigned the name *digit*.

- The CONTRAST subcommand requests DIFFERENCE orthogonal contrasts.

- The RENAME subcommand gives new names to the transformed variables.

- The WSDESIGN requests a complete factorial design.

- The PRINT subcommand requests the parameter estimates and the transformation matrix as part of the display.

5 Hierarchical Loglinear Models

> There is only one way to achieve
> happiness on this terrestrial ball,
> And that is to have either a clear
> conscience or, none at all.

> Ogden Nash

Ignoring Nash's warning, many of us continue to search for happiness in terrestrial institutions and possessions. Marriage, wealth, and health are all hypothesized to contribute to happiness. But do they really? And how can you investigate possible associations?

Consider Figure 5.1, which is a two-way classification of marital status and score on a happiness scale. The data are from the 1982 General Social Survey conducted by the National Opinion Research Center. Of the 854 currently married respondents, 92% indicated that they were very happy or pretty happy, while only 79% of the 383 divorced, separated, or widowed people classified themselves as very happy or pretty happy.

Figure 5.1   Two-way crosstabulation

```
CROSSTABS TABLES=HAPPY BY MARITAL
   /CELLS=COLUMN COUNT.

HAPPY  by  MARITAL
```

	Count Col Pct	MARITAL MARRIED 1.00	SINGLE 2.00	SPLIT 3.00	Row Total
HAPPY	1.00	787	221	301	1309
YES		92.2	82.5	78.6	87.0
	2.00	67	47	82	196
NO		7.8	17.5	21.4	13.0
	Column Total	854	268	383	1505
		56.7	17.8	25.4	100.0

Although the results in Figure 5.1 are interesting, they suggest many new questions. What role does income play in happiness? Are poor married couples happier than affluent singles? What about health? Determining the relationship among such variables is potentially complicated. If family income is recorded in three categories and condition of health in two, a separate two-way table of happiness score and marital status is obtained for each of the six possible combinations of health and income. As additional variables are included in the cross-classification tables, the number of cells rapidly increases and it is difficult, if not impossible, to unravel the associations among the variables by examining only the cell entries.

The usual response of researchers faced with crosstabulated data is to compute a chi-square test of independence for each subtable. This strategy is fraught with problems and usually does not result in a systematic evaluation of the relationship among the variables. The classical chi-square approach also does not provide estimates of the effects of the variables on each other, and its application to tables with more than two variables is complicated.

Loglinear Models

The advantages of statistical models that summarize data and test hypotheses are well recognized. Regression analysis, for example, examines the relationship between a dependent variable and a set of independent variables. Analysis-of-variance techniques provide tests for the effects of various factors on a dependent variable. But neither technique is appropriate for categorical data, where the observations are not from populations that are normally distributed with constant variance.

A special class of statistical techniques, called **loglinear models**, has been formulated for the analysis of categorical data (Haberman, 1978; Bishop, Fienberg, & Holland, 1975). These models are useful for uncovering the potentially complex relationships among the variables in a multiway crosstabulation. Loglinear models are similar to multiple regression models. In loglinear models, all variables that are used for classification are independent variables, and the dependent variable is the number of cases in a cell of the crosstabulation.

A Fully Saturated Model

Consider Figure 5.1 again. Using a loglinear model, the number of cases in each cell can be expressed as a function of marital status, degree of happiness, and the interaction between degree of happiness and marital status. To obtain a linear model, the natural logs of the cell frequencies, rather than the actual counts, are used. The natural logs of the cell frequencies in Figure 5.1 are shown in Table 5.1. (Recall that the natural log of a number is the power to which the number e (approximately 2.718) is raised to give that number. For example, the natural log of the first cell entry is 6.668, since $e^{6.668} = 787$.)

Table 5.1   Natural logs

Happy	Married	Single	Split	Average
Yes	6.668	5.398	5.707	5.924
No	4.205	3.850	4.407	4.154
Average	5.436	4.624	5.057	5.039

The loglinear model for the first cell in Table 5.1 is:

$$\log (787) = \mu + \lambda_{yes}^{happy} + \lambda_{married}^{marital} + \lambda_{yes\ married}^{happy\ marital}$$

Equation 5.1

The term denoted as μ is comparable to the grand mean in the analysis of variance. It is the average of the logs of the frequencies in all table cells. The lambda parameters represent the increments or decrements from the base value (μ) for particular combinations of values of the row and column variables.

Each individual category of the row and column variables has an associated lambda. The term $\lambda_{married}^{marital}$ indicates the effect of being in the *married* category of the marital status variable, and similarly λ_{yes}^{happy} is the effect of being in the *happy* category. The term $\lambda_{yes\ married}^{happy\ marital}$ represents the interaction of being happy and married. Thus, the number of cases in a cell is a function of the values of the row and column variables and their interactions.

In general, the model for the log of the observed frequency in the *i*th row and the *j*th column is given by

$$\ln (F_{ij}) = \mu + \lambda_i^H + \lambda_j^S + \lambda_{ij}^{HS}$$

Equation 5.2

where F_{ij} is the observed frequency in the cell, λ_i^H is the effect of the *i*th happiness category, λ_j^S is the effect of the *j*th marital status category, and λ_{ij}^{HS} is the interaction effect for the *i*th value of the happiness category and the *j*th value of the marital status variable.

The lambda parameters and μ are estimated from the data. The estimate for μ is simply the average of the logs of the frequencies in all table cells. From Table 5.1, the estimated value of μ is 5.039. Estimates for the lambda parameters are obtained in a manner similar to analysis of variance. For example, the effect of the *happy* category is estimated as

$$\lambda_{yes}^{happy} = 5.924 - 5.039 = 0.885$$

Equation 5.3

where 5.924 is the average of the logs of the observed counts in the *happy* cells. The lambda parameter is just the average log of the frequencies in a particular category minus the grand mean. In general, the effect of the *i*th category of a variable, called a **main effect**, is estimated as

$$\lambda_i = \mu_i - \mu \qquad\qquad \text{Equation 5.4}$$

where μ_i is the mean of the logs in the *i*th category and μ is the grand mean. Positive values of lambda occur when the average number of cases in a row or a column is larger than the overall average. For example, since there are more married people in the sample than single or separated people, the lambda for *married* is positive. Similarly, since there are fewer unhappy people than happy people, the lambda for *not happy* is negative.

The interaction parameters indicate how much difference there is between the sums of the effects of the variables taken individually and collectively. They represent the "boost" or "interference" associated with particular combinations of the values. For example, if marriage does result in bliss, the number of cases in the *happy* and *married* cell would be larger than the number expected based only on the frequency of married people ($\lambda^{\text{marital}}_{\text{married}}$) and the frequency of happy people ($\lambda^{\text{happy}}_{\text{yes}}$). This excess would be represented by a positive value for $\lambda^{\text{happy}}_{\text{yes}}{}^{\text{marital}}_{\text{married}}$. If marriage decreases happiness, the value for the interaction parameter would be negative. If marriage neither increases nor decreases happiness, the interaction parameter would be 0.

The estimate for the interaction parameter is the difference between the log of the observed frequency in a particular cell and the log of the predicted frequency using only the lambda parameters for the row and column variables. For example,

$$\lambda^{\text{happy}}_{\text{yes}}{}^{\text{marital}}_{\text{married}} = \ln(F_{11}) - (\mu + \lambda^{\text{happy}}_{\text{yes}} + \lambda^{\text{marital}}_{\text{married}}) \qquad\qquad \text{Equation 5.5}$$
$$= 6.668 - (5.039 + 0.885 + 0.397) = 0.347$$

where F_{11} is the observed frequency in the *married* and *happy* cell. Table 5.2 contains the estimates of the lambda parameters for the main effects (marital status and happiness) and their interactions.

To uniquely estimate the lambda parameters, we need to impose certain constraints on them. The lambdas must sum to 0 across the categories of a variable. For example, the sum of the lambdas for marital status is $0.397 + (-0.415) + 0.018 = 0$. Similar constraints are imposed on the interaction terms. They must sum to 0 over all categories of a variable.

Table 5.2   Estimates of lambda parameters

$\lambda_{\text{yes}}^{\text{happy}} = 5.924 - 5.039 = 0.885$

$\lambda_{\text{no}}^{\text{happy}} = 4.154 - 5.039 = -0.885$

$\lambda_{\text{married}}^{\text{marital}} = 5.436 - 5.039 = 0.397$

$\lambda_{\text{single}}^{\text{marital}} = 4.624 - 5.039 = -0.415$

$\lambda_{\text{split}}^{\text{marital}} = 5.057 - 5.039 = 0.018$

$\lambda_{\text{YM}}^{\text{HM}} = 6.668 - (5.039 + 0.885 + 0.397) = 0.347$

$\lambda_{\text{NM}}^{\text{HM}} = 4.205 - (5.039 - 0.885 + 0.397) = -0.347$

$\lambda_{\text{YSi}}^{\text{HM}} = 5.398 - (5.039 + 0.885 - 0.415) = -0.111$

$\lambda_{\text{NSi}}^{\text{HM}} = 3.850 - (5.039 - 0.885 - 0.415) = 0.111$

$\lambda_{\text{YSp}}^{\text{HM}} = 5.707 - (5.039 + 0.885 + 0.018) = -0.235$

$\lambda_{\text{NSp}}^{\text{HM}} = 4.407 - (5.039 - 0.885 + 0.018) = 0.235$

Each of the observed cell frequencies is reproduced exactly by a model that contains all main-effect and interaction terms. This type of model is called a **saturated model**. For example, the observed log frequency in cell 1 of Table 5.1 is given by:

$$\ln(F_{11}) = \mu + \lambda_{\text{yes}}^{\text{happy}} + \lambda_{\text{married}}^{\text{marital}} + \lambda_{\text{yes married}}^{\text{happy marital}}$$

$$= 5.039 + 0.885 + 0.397 + 0.346 = 6.67$$

Equation 5.6

All other observed cell frequencies can be similarly expressed as a function of the lambdas and the grand mean.

Output for the Cells

Consider Figure 5.2, which contains the observed and expected (predicted from the model) counts for the data shown in Figure 5.1. The first column gives the names of the variables used in the analysis, and the second contains the value labels for the cells in the table. The next column indicates the number of cases in each of the cells. For example, 787 people who classify themselves as *happy* are married, which is 52.29% of all respondents in the survey (787 out of 1505). This percentage is listed in the next column. Since the number of cases in each cell is expressed as a percentage of the total cases, the sum of all the percentages is 100. The saturated model reproduces the observed cell frequencies exactly, so the expected and observed cell counts and percentages are equal. For the same reason, the next two columns, which compare the observed and expected counts, are all zeros. (Models that do not exactly reproduce the observed cell counts are examined later.)

Figure 5.2   Observed and expected frequencies for saturated model

```
HILOGLINEAR HAPPY (1,2) MARITAL (1,3)
  /CRITERIA=DELTA(0)
  /DESIGN=HAPPY*MARITAL.
```
Observed, Expected Frequencies and Residuals.

Factor	Code	OBS. count	& PCT.	EXP. count	& PCT.	Residual	Std. Resid.
HAPPY	YES						
MARITAL	MARRIED	787.00	(52.29)	787.00	(52.29)	.000	.000
MARITAL	SINGLE	221.00	(14.68)	221.00	(14.68)	.000	.000
MARITAL	SPLIT	301.00	(20.00)	301.00	(20.00)	.000	.000
HAPPY	NO						
MARITAL	MARRIED	67.00	(4.45)	67.00	(4.45)	.000	.000
MARITAL	SINGLE	47.00	(3.12)	47.00	(3.12)	.000	.000
MARITAL	SPLIT	82.00	(5.45)	82.00	(5.45)	.000	.000

Parameter Estimates

The estimates of the loglinear model parameters are also displayed as part of the output from the SPSS/PC+ Hierarchical Loglinear procedure. Figure 5.3 contains parameter estimates for the data in Figure 5.1. The parameter estimates are displayed in blocks for each effect.

Parameter estimates for the interaction effects are displayed first. Because estimates must sum to 0 across the categories of each variable, only two parameter estimates need to be displayed for the interaction effects: those for $\lambda_{yes\ married}^{happy\ marital}$ and for $\lambda_{yes\ single}^{happy\ marital}$. All other interaction parameter estimates can be derived from these.

After the interaction terms, parameter estimates for the main effects of the variables are displayed. The first estimate is for λ_{yes}^{happy} and is identical to the value given in Table 5.2 (0.885). Again, only one parameter estimate is displayed, since we can infer that the parameter estimate for λ_{no}^{happy} is −0.885 (the two estimates must sum to 0). Two parameter estimates and associated statistics are displayed for the marital status variable, since it has three categories. The estimate for the third parameter, $\lambda_{split}^{marital}$, is the negative of the sum of the estimates for $\lambda_{married}^{marital}$ and $\lambda_{single}^{marital}$. Thus, $\lambda_{split}^{marital}$ is estimated to be 0.0178, as shown in Table 5.2.

Figure 5.3   Estimates for parameters

```
HILOGLINEAR HAPPY(1,2) MARITAL(1,3)
  /CRITERIA=DELTA(O)
  /PRINT=ESTIM
  /DESIGN=HAPPY*MARITAL.
```

```
Estimates for Parameters.

 HAPPY*MARITAL
```

Parameter	Coeff.	Std. Err.	Z-Value	Lower 95 CI	Upper 95 CI
1	.3464441901	.05429	6.38147	.24004	.45285
2	-.1113160745	.06122	-1.81833	-.23131	.00867

```
 HAPPY
```

Parameter	Coeff.	Std. Err.	Z-Value	Lower 95 CI	Upper 95 CI
1	.8853236244	.03997	22.14946	.80698	.96367

```
 MARITAL
```

Parameter	Coeff.	Std. Err.	Z-Value	Lower 95 CI	Upper 95 CI
1	.3972836534	.05429	7.31793	.29088	.50369
2	-.4150216289	.06122	-6.77930	-.53501	-.29503

Since the individual parameter estimates in Figure 5.3 are not labeled, the following rules for identifying the categories to which they correspond may be helpful. For main effects, the parameter estimates correspond to the first $K - 1$ categories of the variable, where K is the total number of categories. For interaction parameters, the number of estimates displayed is the product of the number of categories, minus 1, of each variable in the interaction, multiplied together. For example, marital status has three categories and happiness has two, so the number of estimates displayed is $(3 - 1) \times (2 - 1) = 2$.

To identify individual parameters, first look at the order in which the variable labels are listed in the heading. In this case, the heading is *HAPPY*MARITAL*. The first estimate corresponds to the first category of both variables, which is happy–yes and marital–married. The next estimate corresponds to the first category of the first variable (*happy*) and the second category of the second variable (*marital*). In general, the categories of the last variable rotate most quickly and those of the first variable most slowly. Terms involving the last categories of the variables are omitted.

Figure 5.3 also displays the standard error for each estimate. For the $\lambda_{\text{yes}}^{\text{happy}}$ parameter, the standard error is 0.03997. The ratio of the parameter estimate to its standard error is given in the column labeled *Z-Value*. For sufficiently large sample sizes, the test of the null hypothesis that lambda is 0 can be based on this Z value, since the standardized lambda is approximately normally distributed with a mean of 0 and a standard deviation of 1 if the model fits the data. Lambdas with Z values greater than 1.96 in absolute value can be considered significant at the 0.05 level. When tests for many lambdas are calculated, however, the usual problem of multiple comparisons arises. That is, when many comparisons are made, the probability that some are found to be significant when there is no effect increases rapidly. Special multiple-comparison procedures for testing the lambdas are discussed in Goodman (1984).

Individual confidence intervals can be constructed for each lambda. The 95% confidence interval for $\lambda_{\text{yes}}^{\text{happy}}$ is $0.885 \pm (1.96 \times 0.03997)$, which results in a lower limit of 0.80698 and an upper limit of 0.96367. Since the confidence interval does not include 0, the hypothesis that the population value is 0 can be rejected. These values are displayed in the last two columns of Figure 5.3.

The Independence Model

Representing an observed-frequency table with a loglinear model that contains as many parameters as there are cells (a saturated model) does not result in a parsimonious description of the relationship between the variables. It may, however, serve as a good starting point for exploring other models that could be used to represent the data. Parameters that have small values can be excluded from subsequent models.

To illustrate the general procedure for fitting a model that does not contain all possible parameters (an unsaturated model), consider the familiar independence hypothesis for a two-way table. If variables are independent, they can be represented by a loglinear model that does not have any interaction terms. For example, if happiness and marital status are independent,

$$\log (\hat{F}_{ij}) = \mu + \lambda_i^{\text{happy}} + \lambda_j^{\text{marital}} \qquad \textbf{Equation 5.7}$$

Note that $\hat{F}_{ij}$ is no longer the observed frequency in the (i,j)th cell, but is now the expected frequency based on the model. The estimates for the expected frequencies must be obtained using an iterative algorithm. Each time an estimate is obtained, it is called an **iteration**, while the largest amount by which successive estimates differ is called the **convergence criterion**.

The message shown in Figure 5.4 gives the number of iterations required for convergence. For this example, two iterations were required for convergence. The observed and expected counts in each of the cells of the table are shown in Figure 5.5.

Figure 5.4   Message indicating number of iterations required for convergence

```
HILOGLINEAR HAPPY(1,2) MARITAL(1,3)
  /DESIGN=HAPPY MARITAL.

DESIGN 1 has generating class

    MARITAL
    HAPPY

The Iterative Proportional Fit algorithm converged at iteration 2.
The maximum difference between observed and fitted marginal totals is      .000
and the convergence criterion is      .787
```

Figure 5.5   Observed and expected frequencies for unsaturated model

```
Observed, Expected Frequencies and Residuals.
        Factor          Code      OBS. count  & PCT.    EXP. count  & PCT.    Residual   Std. Resid.

    HAPPY              YES
      MARITAL          MARRIED      787.00 (52.29)       742.78 (49.35)        44.219        1.622
      MARITAL          SINGLE       221.00 (14.68)       233.10 (15.49)       -12.098        -.792
      MARITAL          SPLIT        301.00 (20.00)       333.12 (22.13)       -32.121       -1.760

    HAPPY              NO
      MARITAL          MARRIED       67.00 ( 4.45)       111.22 ( 7.39)       -44.219       -4.193
      MARITAL          SINGLE        47.00 ( 3.12)        34.90 ( 2.32)        12.098        2.048
      MARITAL          SPLIT         82.00 ( 5.45)        49.88 ( 3.31)        32.121        4.548
```

The expected values are identical to those obtained from the usual formulas for expected values in a two-way crosstabulation, as shown in Figure 5.6. For example, from Figure 5.1, the estimated probability of an individual being happy is $1309/1505$, and the estimated probability of an individual being married is $854/1505$. If marital status and happiness are independent, the probability of being a happy, married person is estimated to be:

$$\frac{1309}{1505} \times \frac{854}{1505} = 0.4935 \qquad \textbf{Equation 5.8}$$

The expected number of happy, married people in a sample of 1505 is then:

$$0.4935 \times 1505 = 742.78 \qquad \textbf{Equation 5.9}$$

This is the value displayed in the expected-count column in Figure 5.5. Since the independence model is not saturated, the observed and expected counts are no longer equal, as was the case in Figure 5.2.

Figure 5.6   Crosstabulation of happiness by marital status

```
CROSSTABS TABLE=HAPPY BY MARITAL
   /CELLS=EXPECTED COUNT
   /STATISTICS=CHISQ.
HAPPY  by  MARITAL
```

		MARITAL			
	Count Exp Val	MARRIED	SINGLE	SPLIT	
		1.00	2.00	3.00	Row Total
HAPPY	1.00	787	221	301	1309
YES		742.8	233.1	333.1	87.0%
	2.00	67	47	82	196
NO		111.2	34.9	49.9	13.0%
	Column Total	854 56.7%	268 17.8%	383 25.4%	1505 100.0%

Chi-Square	Value	DF	Significance
Pearson	48.81639	2	.00000
Likelihood Ratio	48.01178	2	.00000
Mantel-Haenszel test for linear association	47.18692	1	.00000

Chi-square Goodness-of-Fit Tests

The test of the hypothesis that a particular model fits the observed data can be based on the familiar **Pearson chi-square statistic**, which is calculated as

$$\chi^2 = \sum_i \sum_j \frac{(F_{ij} - \hat{F}_{ij})^2}{\hat{F}_{ij}}$$

Equation 5.10

where the subscripts i and j include all cells in the table. An alternative statistic is the **likelihood-ratio chi-square**, which is calculated as:

$$L^2 = 2 \sum_i \sum_j F_{ij} ln \frac{F_{ij}}{\hat{F}_{ij}}$$

Equation 5.11

For large sample sizes, these statistics are equivalent. The advantage of the likelihood-ratio chi-square statistic is that it, like the total sums of squares in analysis of variance, can be subdivided into interpretable parts that add up to the total (see "Partitioning the Chi-square Statistic" on p. 174).

Figure 5.7 shows that the value of the Pearson chi-square statistic is 48.82 and the likelihood-ratio chi-square is 48.01. The degrees of freedom associated with a particular model equal the number of cells in the table minus the number of independent parameters in the model. In this example, there are six cells and four independent parameters to be estimated (the grand mean, λ_{yes}^{happy}, $\lambda_{married}^{marital}$, $\lambda_{split}^{marital}$), so there are two degrees of free-dom. (There are only four independent parameters because of the constraint that parameter estimates must sum to 0 over the categories of a variable. Therefore, the value for one of the categories is determined by the values of the others and is not, in a statistical sense, independent.)

Because the observed significance level associated with both chi-square statistics is very small (less than 0.0005), the independence model is rejected. Note that both the Pearson and likelihood-ratio chi-square statistics displayed for the independence model are the same as the chi-square value displayed by the SPSS/PC+ Crosstabs procedure, as shown in Figure 5.6.

Figure 5.7   Chi-square goodness-of-fit test

```
Goodness-of-fit test statistics

    Likelihood ratio chi square =      48.01187    DF = 2   P =   .000
              Pearson chi square =      48.81639    DF = 2   P =   .000
```

Residuals

Another way to assess how well a model fits the data is to examine the differences between the observed and expected cell counts based on the model. If the model fits the observed data well, these differences, called **residuals**, should be fairly small in value and not have any discernible pattern. The column labeled *Residual* in Figure 5.5 shows the differences between the observed and expected counts in each cell. For example, 787 individuals were found to be very happy and married, while 742.78 are expected to fall into this category if the independence model is correct. The residual is $787 - 742.78 = 44.22$.

As in regression analysis, it is useful to standardize the residuals by dividing them by their standard error, in this case the square root of the expected cell count. For example, the standardized residual for the first cell in Figure 5.5 is:

$$\frac{44.2}{\sqrt{742.8}} = 1.6 \qquad \text{Equation 5.12}$$

This value is displayed in the column labeled *Std. Resid.* in Figure 5.5. If the model is adequate, the standardized residuals are approximately normally distributed with a mean of 0 and standard deviation close to 1. Standardized residuals greater than 1.96 or less than −1.96 suggest important discrepancies, since they are unlikely to occur if the model is adequate. Particular combinations of cells with large standardized residuals may suggest which other models might be more appropriate.

The same types of diagnostics for residuals used in regression analysis can be used in loglinear models (see the Linear Regression Analysis chapter in the *SPSS/PC+ Base System User's Guide*). Figure 5.8 and Figure 5.9 are plots of the standardized residuals against the observed and expected cell frequencies, respectively. If the model is adequate, there should be no discernible pattern in the plots. Patterns suggest that the chosen loglinear model, or the loglinear representation in general, may not be appropriate for the data.

Figure 5.8   Plot of standardized residuals against observed counts

```
HILOGLINEAR HAPPY(1,2) MARITAL(1,3)
 /PLOT=RESID
 /DESIGN=MARITAL HAPPY.
```

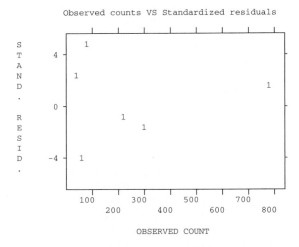

Figure 5.9   Plot of standardized residuals against expected counts

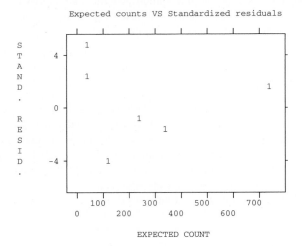

If the standardized residuals are normally distributed, the normal probability plot (Figure 5.10) should be approximately linear. In this plot, the standardized residuals are plotted against expected residuals from a normal distribution.

Figure 5.10   Plot of standardized residuals versus expected residuals

```
HILOGLINEAR HAPPY(1,2) MARITAL(1,3)
 /PLOT=NORMPROB
 /DESIGN=MARITAL HAPPY.
```

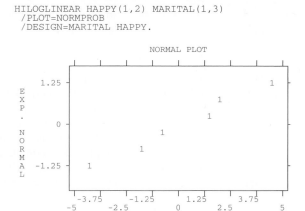

Hierarchical Models

A saturated loglinear model contains all possible effects. For example, a saturated model for a two-way table contains terms for the row main effects, the column main effects, and their interaction. Different models can be obtained by deleting terms from a saturated model. The independence model is derived by deleting the interaction effect. Although it is possible to delete any particular term from a model, in loglinear analysis attention is often focused on a special class of models called **hierarchical models**.

In a hierarchical model, if a term exists for the interaction of a set of variables, there must be lower-order terms for all possible combinations of these variables. For a two-variable model, this means that the interaction term can be included only if both main effects are present. For a three-variable model, if the term λ^{ABC} is included in a model, the terms λ^A, λ^B, λ^C, λ^{AB}, λ^{BC}, and λ^{AC} must also be included.

To describe a hierarchical model, it is sufficient to list the highest-order terms in which variables appear. This is called the **generating class** of a model. For example, the specification A*B*C indicates that a model contains the term λ^{ABC} and all its lower-order relations. (Terms are "relatives" if all variables that are included in one term are also included in the other. For example, the term λ^{ABCD} is a higher-order relative of the terms

λ^{ABC}, λ^{BCD}, λ^{ACD}, λ^{BAD}, as well as all other lower-order terms involving variables A, B, C, or D. Similarly, λ^{AB} is a lower-order relative of both λ^{ABC} and λ^{ABD}.) The model

$$\ln (\hat{F}_{ijk}) = \mu + \lambda_i^A + \lambda_j^B + \lambda_k^C + \lambda_{ij}^{AB}$$

Equation 5.13

can be represented by the generating class (A*B)(C), since AB is the highest-order term in which A and B occur, and C is included in the model only as a main effect.

Model Selection

Even if attention is restricted to hierarchical models, many different models are possible for a set of variables. How do you choose among them? The same guidelines discussed for model selection in regression analysis apply to loglinear models (see the Linear Regression Analysis chapter in the *SPSS/PC+ Base System User's Guide*). A model should fit the data and be substantively interpretable and as simple (parsimonious) as possible. For example, if models with and without higher-order interaction terms fit the data well, the simpler models are usually preferable, since higher-order interaction terms are difficult to interpret.

A first step in determining a suitable model might be to fit a saturated model and examine the standardized values for the parameter estimates. Effects with small estimated values can usually be deleted from a model. Another strategy is to systematically test the contribution to a model made by terms of a particular order. For example, you might fit a model with interaction terms and then with main effects only. The change in the chi-square value between the two models is attributable to the interaction effects.

Partitioning the Chi-square Statistic

In regression analysis, the change in multiple R^2 when a variable is added to a model indicates the additional information conveyed by the variable. Similarly, in loglinear analysis, the decrease in the value of the likelihood-ratio chi-square statistic when terms are added to the model signals their contribution to the model. (Remember that R^2 increases when additional variables are added to a model, since large values of R^2 are associated with good models. Chi-square decreases when terms are added, since small values of chi-square are associated with good models.)

As an example, consider the happiness and marital status data when two additional variables, total income in 1982 and the condition of one's health, are included. Figure 5.11 contains goodness-of-fit statistics for three different models. Design 3 contains all terms except the four-way interaction of *happy*, *marital*, *income82*, and *health*. Design 2 contains main effects and second-order interactions only, and design 1 is a main-effects-only model.

Design 1 has a large chi-square value and an observed significance level less than 0.0005, so it definitely does not fit well. To judge the adequacy of designs 2 and 3, consider the changes in the chi-square goodness-of-fit statistic as terms are removed from the model.

Figure 5.11 Goodness-of-fit statistics for three models

```
HILOGLINEAR HAPPY(1,2) MARITAL(1,3) INCOME82(1,3) HEALTH(1,2)
  /DESIGN=HAPPY MARITAL INCOME82 HEALTH
  /DESIGN=HAPPY*MARITAL  HAPPY*INCOME82  HAPPY*HEALTH  MARITAL*INCOME82
        MARITAL*HEALTH  INCOME82*HEALTH
  /DESIGN=HAPPY*MARITAL*INCOME82  HAPPY*MARITAL*HEALTH
        MARITAL*INCOME82*HEALTH  HAPPY*INCOME82*HEALTH.

DESIGN 1 has generating class

    HAPPY
    MARITAL
    INCOME82
    HEALTH

The Iterative Proportional Fit algorithm converged at iteration 2.

  Goodness-of-fit test statistics

    Likelihood ratio chi square =    404.07126    DF = 29  P =  .000
                Pearson chi square =    592.88539    DF = 29  P =  .000


DESIGN 2 has generating class

    HAPPY*MARITAL
    HAPPY*INCOME82
    HAPPY*HEALTH
    MARITAL*INCOME82
    MARITAL*HEALTH
    INCOME82*HEALTH

The Iterative Proportional Fit algorithm converged at iteration 5.

  Goodness-of-fit test statistics

    Likelihood ratio chi square =     12.60513    DF = 16  P =  .701
                Pearson chi square =     12.31678    DF = 16  P =  .722


DESIGN 3 has generating class

    HAPPY*MARITAL*INCOME82
    HAPPY*MARITAL*HEALTH
    MARITAL*INCOME82*HEALTH
    HAPPY*INCOME82*HEALTH

The Iterative Proportional Fit algorithm converged at iteration 3.

  Goodness-of-fit test statistics

    Likelihood ratio chi square =      3.99376    DF = 4  P =  .407
                Pearson chi square =      3.97331    DF = 4  P =  .410
```

For a saturated model, the value of the chi-square statistic is always 0. Eliminating the fourth-order interaction (design 3) results in a likelihood-ratio chi-square value of 3.99. The change in chi-square from 0 to 3.99 is attributable to the fourth-order interaction. The change in the degrees of freedom between the two models equals 4, since a saturated model has 0 degrees of freedom and the third-order interaction model has 4. The change in the chi-square value can be used to test the hypothesis that the fourth-order interaction term is 0. If the observed significance level for the change is small, the hypothesis that the fourth-order term is 0 is rejected, since this indicates that the model without the fourth-order term does not fit well. A chi-square value of 3.99 has an observed significance of 0.41, so the hypothesis that the fourth-order term is 0 is not rejected.

The likelihood-ratio chi-square value for design 2, the second-order interaction model, is 12.61. This value provides a test of the hypothesis that all third- and fourth-order interaction terms are 0. The difference between 12.61 and 3.99 (8.62) provides a test of the hypothesis that all third-order terms are 0. In general, the test of the hypothesis that the kth order terms are 0 is based on

$$\chi^2 = \chi^2_{k-1} - \chi^2_k$$

Equation 5.14

where χ^2_k is the value for the model that includes the kth-order effect or effects, and χ^2_{k-1} is the chi-square value for the model without the kth-order effects.

The SPSS/PC+ Hierarchical Loglinear procedure automatically calculates tests of two types of hypotheses: the hypothesis that all kth- and higher-order effects are 0 and the hypothesis that the kth-order effects are 0. Figure 5.12 contains the tests for the hypothesis that k- and higher-order effects are 0.

Figure 5.12   Tests that k-way and higher-order effects are 0

```
HILOGLINEAR HAPPY(1,2) MARITAL(1,3) INCOME82(1,3) HEALTH(1,2)
   /DESIGN.
```

Tests that K-way and higher order effects are zero.

K	DF	L.R. Chisq	Prob	Pearson Chisq	Prob	Iteration
4	4	3.994	.4069	3.973	.4097	3
3	16	12.605	.7014	12.317	.7219	5
2	29	404.071	.0000	592.885	.0000	2
1	35	2037.780	.0000	2938.739	.0000	0

The first line of Figure 5.12 is a test of the hypothesis that the fourth-order interaction is 0. Note that the likelihood-ratio chi-square value of 3.99 is the same as the value displayed for design 3 in Figure 5.11. This is the goodness-of-fit statistic for a model without the fourth-order interaction. Similarly, the entry for the k of 3 is the goodness-of-fit test for a model without third- and fourth-order effects, as shown in design 2 in Figure 5.11. The last line, $k = 1$, corresponds to a model that has no effects except the grand mean. That is, the expected value for all cells is the same—the average of the logs of the observed frequencies in all cells.

The column labeled *Prob* in Figure 5.12 gives the observed significance levels for the tests that k- and higher-order effects are 0. Small observed significance levels indicate that the hypothesis that terms of particular orders are 0 should be rejected. Note in Figure 5.12 that the hypotheses that all effects are 0 and that second-order and higher effects are 0 should be rejected. Since the observed significance level for the test that third- and higher-order terms are 0 is large (0.72), the hypothesis that third- and fourth-order interactions are 0 should not be rejected. Thus, it appears that a model with first- and second-order effects is adequate to represent the data.

It is sometimes also of interest to test whether interaction terms of a particular order are 0. For example, rather than asking if all effects greater than two-way are 0, the question is whether two-way effects are 0. Figure 5.13 gives the tests for the hypothesis that k-way effects are 0.

Figure 5.13   Tests that k-way effects are 0

```
Tests that K-way effects are zero.

      K     DF    L.R. Chisq    Prob   Pearson Chisq     Prob    Iteration
      1      6     1633.708    .0000      2345.854      .0000        0
      2     13      391.466    .0000       580.568      .0000        0
      3     12        8.612    .7357         8.345      .7576        0
      4      4        3.994    .4069         3.973      .4097        0
```

From Figure 5.12, the likelihood-ratio chi-square for a model with only the mean is 2037.78. The value for a model with first-order effects is 404.07. The difference between these two values, 1633.71, is displayed on the first line of Figure 5.13. The difference is an indication of how much the model improves when first-order effects are included. The observed significance level for a chi-square value of 1634 with six degrees of freedom $(35 - 29)$ is small, less than 0.00005, so the hypothesis that first-order effects are 0 is rejected. The remaining entries in Figure 5.13 are obtained in a similar fashion. The test that third-order effects are 0 is the difference between a model without third-order terms ($\chi^2_{LR} = 12.61$) and a model with third-order terms ($\chi^2_{LR} = 3.99$). The resulting chi-square value of 8.61 with 12 degrees of freedom has a large observed significance level (0.76), so the hypothesis that third-order terms are 0 is not rejected.

Testing Individual Terms in the Model

The two tests described in the previous section provide an indication of the collective importance of effects of various orders. They do not, however, test the individual terms. That is, although the overall hypothesis that second-order terms are 0 may be rejected, that does not mean that every second-order effect is present.

One strategy for testing individual terms is to fit two models differing only in the presence of the effect to be tested. The difference between the two likelihood-ratio chi-square values, sometimes called the **partial chi-square**, also has a chi-square distribution and can be used to test the hypothesis that the effect is 0. For example, to test that the happy-by-marital-by-income82 effect is 0, a model with all three-way interactions can be fit. From Figure 5.11, the likelihood-ratio chi-square value for this model is 3.99. When a model without the *happy* by *marital* by *income82* effect is fit (Figure 5.14), the likelihood ratio is 7.36. Thus, the partial chi-square value with four $(8 - 4)$ degrees of freedom is 3.37 $(7.36 - 3.99)$.

Figure 5.14 Model without happy by marital by income82

```
HILOGLINEAR HAPPY(1,2) MARITAL(1,3) INCOME82(1,3) HEALTH(1,2)
    /DESIGN=HAPPY*MARITAL*HEALTH
         MARITAL*INCOME82*HEALTH
         HAPPY*INCOME82*HEALTH.

DESIGN 1 has generating class

    HAPPY*MARITAL*HEALTH
    MARITAL*INCOME82*HEALTH
    HAPPY*INCOME82*HEALTH

The Iterative Proportional Fit algorithm converged at iteration 4.

 Goodness-of-fit test statistics

    Likelihood ratio chi square =      7.36366    DF = 8  P =  .498
                 Pearson chi square =      7.50538    DF = 8  P =  .483
```

Figure 5.15 contains the partial chi-square values and their observed significance levels for all effects in the *happy* by *marital* by *health* by *income82* table. Note that the observed significance levels are large for all three-way effects, confirming that first- and second-order effects are sufficient to represent the data. The last column indicates the number of iterations required to achieve convergence.

Figure 5.15 Partial chi-squares for happy by marital by health by income82

```
HILOGLINEAR HAPPY(1,2) MARITAL(1,3) INCOME82(1,3) HEALTH(1,2)
 /PRINT=ASSOCIATION
 /DESIGN=HAPPY*MARITAL*HEALTH*INCOME82.


 Tests of PARTIAL associations.
```

Effect Name	DF	Partial Chisq	Prob	Iter
HAPPY*MARITAL*INCOME82	4	3.370	.4979	4
HAPPY*MARITAL*HEALTH	2	.458	.7955	4
HAPPY*INCOME82*HEALTH	2	.955	.6205	3
MARITAL*INCOME82*HEALTH	4	3.652	.4552	5
HAPPY*MARITAL	2	15.050	.0005	5
HAPPY*INCOME82	2	16.120	.0003	5
MARITAL*INCOME82	4	160.738	.0000	4
HAPPY*HEALTH	1	55.696	.0000	5
MARITAL*HEALTH	2	8.391	.0151	5
INCOME82*HEALTH	2	35.600	.0000	4
HAPPY	1	849.537	.0000	2
MARITAL	2	343.395	.0000	2
INCOME82	2	86.115	.0000	2
HEALTH	1	354.662	.0000	2

Model Selection Using Backward Elimination

As in regression analysis, another way to arrive at a "best" model is by using variable-selection algorithms. Forward selection adds effects to a model, while backward elimination starts with all effects in a model and then removes those that do not satisfy the criterion for remaining in the model. Since backward elimination appears to be the better procedure for model selection in hierarchical loglinear models (Benedetti & Brown, 1978), it is the only procedure described here.

The initial model for backward elimination need not be saturated but can be any hierarchical model. At the first step, the effect whose removal results in the least significant change in the likelihood-ratio chi-square is eligible for elimination, provided that the observed significance level is larger than the criterion for remaining in the model. To ensure a hierarchical model, only effects corresponding to the generating class are examined at each step. For example, if the generating class is *marital*happy*income82*health*, the first step examines only the fourth-order interaction.

Figure 5.16 shows output at the first step. Elimination of the fourth-order interaction results in a chi-square change of 3.99, which has an associated significance level of 0.41. Since this significance level is not less than 0.05 (the default criterion for remaining in the model), the effect is removed. The new model has all three-way interactions as its generating class.

Figure 5.16   First step in backward elimination

```
HILOGLINEAR HAPPY(1,2) MARITAL(1,3) INCOME82(1,3) HEALTH(1,2)
 /METHOD=BACKWARD
 /MAXSTEPS=6
 /DESIGN=HAPPY*MARITAL*INCOME82*HEALTH.

Backward Elimination for DESIGN 1 with generating class

  HAPPY*MARITAL*INCOME82*HEALTH

 Likelihood ratio chi square =      .00000   DF = 0  P = 1.000


If Deleted Simple Effect is             DF   L.R. Chisq Change   Prob   Iter

 HAPPY*MARITAL*INCOME82*HEALTH          4               3.994   .4069    3

Step 1

  The best model has generating class

        HAPPY*MARITAL*INCOME82
        HAPPY*MARITAL*HEALTH
        HAPPY*INCOME82*HEALTH
        MARITAL*INCOME82*HEALTH

  Likelihood ratio chi square =      3.99367   DF = 4  P =   .407
```

Figure 5.17 contains the statistics for the second step. The effects eligible for removal are all three-way interactions. The *happy*marital*health* interaction has the largest observed significance level for the change in the chi-square if it is removed, so it is eliminated from the model. The likelihood-ratio chi-square for the resulting model is 4.45.

Figure 5.17   Statistics used to eliminate second effect

```
If Deleted Simple Effect is              DF   L.R. Chisq Change    Prob   Iter

  HAPPY*MARITAL*INCOME82                  4            3.370      .4979    4
  HAPPY*MARITAL*HEALTH                    2             .458      .7955    4
  HAPPY*INCOME82*HEALTH                   2             .955      .6205    3
  MARITAL*INCOME82*HEALTH                 4            3.652      .4552    5

Step 2

  The best model has generating class

      HAPPY*MARITAL*INCOME82
      HAPPY*INCOME82*HEALTH
      MARITAL*INCOME82*HEALTH

  Likelihood ratio chi square =     4.45127    DF = 6   P =  .616
```

At the next three steps, the remaining third-order interactions are removed from the model. The sixth step begins with all second-order items in the model, as shown in Figure 5.18.

Figure 5.18   Sixth step in backward elimination

```
If Deleted Simple Effect is              DF   L.R. Chisq Change    Prob   Iter

  HAPPY*HEALTH                            1           55.697      .0000    5
  HAPPY*MARITAL                           2           15.051      .0005    5
  HAPPY*INCOME82                          2           16.120      .0003    5
  MARITAL*INCOME82                        4          160.738      .0000    5
  MARITAL*HEALTH                          2            8.392      .0151    5
  INCOME82*HEALTH                         2           35.601      .0000    4

Step 6

  The best model has generating class

      HAPPY*HEALTH
      HAPPY*MARITAL
      HAPPY*INCOME82
      MARITAL*INCOME82
      MARITAL*HEALTH
      INCOME82*HEALTH

  Likelihood ratio chi square =    12.60482    DF = 16   P =  .701

The final model has generating class

      HAPPY*HEALTH
      HAPPY*MARITAL
      HAPPY*INCOME82
      MARITAL*INCOME82
      MARITAL*HEALTH
      INCOME82*HEALTH
```

Since the observed significance level for removal of any of the two-way interactions is smaller than 0.05, no more effects are removed from the model. The final model contains all second-order interactions and has a chi-square value of 12.60. This is the same model suggested by the partial-association table.

At this point, it is a good idea to examine the residuals to see if any anomalies are apparent. The largest standardized residual is 1.34, which suggests that there are not cells with bad fits. The residual plots also show nothing suspicious.

Running the Hierarchical Loglinear Procedure

The SPSS/PC+ Hierarchical Loglinear procedure allows you to fit, test, and estimate parameters of hierarchical loglinear models. Using HILOGLINEAR, you can examine and compare a variety of hierarchical models, either by specifying tests of partial association or by requesting backward elimination. HILOGLINEAR also provides estimates of the parameters for saturated models.

HILOGLINEAR operates via a variable list and subcommands. None of the subcommands is required; the minimum specification on HILOGLINEAR is simply the variable list. The output for the minimum specification includes observed and expected frequencies for a k-way table and parameter estimates for the saturated model.

Specifying Variables in the Equation

The variable list identifies the categorical variables used in the model or models you fit. Variables must be numeric and integer.

- Each variable in the list must be accompanied by minimum and maximum values in parentheses, as in the command:

```
HILOGLINEAR SEX(1,2) RACE(1,2) HAPPY(1,2)
            MARITAL(1,3) INCOME82(1,3).
```

- If several consecutive variables in the variable list have the same minimum and maximum values, the range can be listed after the last variable with these values. Thus, the following command is equivalent to the previous one:

```
HILOGLINEAR SEX RACE HAPPY(1,2) MARITAL INCOME82(1,3).
```

- The values of the variables should be consecutive positive integers, since HILOGLINEAR assumes there is a category for every integer value in the specified range. For example, the values 1, 2, and 3 are preferable to the values 5, 10, and 15. If necessary, recode variables using the RECODE command prior to the HILOGLINEAR command.

Specifying the Generating Class

Use the DESIGN subcommand to specify the generating class for the terms in a model. Asterisks are used to specify the highest-order interactions in a generating class. For example, the command

```
HILOGLINEAR SEX RACE HAPPY(1,2) MARITAL INCOME82(1,3)
  /DESIGN=HAPPY*MARITAL*INCOME82 SEX.
```

specifies a hierarchical model with the main effects *happy*, *marital*, *income82*, and *sex*; all second-order effects involving *happy*, *marital*, and *income82*; and the third-order interaction term *happy *marital*income82*. Similarly, the command

```
HILOGLINEAR HAPPY(1,2) MARITAL(1,3)
   /DESIGN=HAPPY*MARITAL.
```

specifies a hierarchical model with the main effects *happy* and *marital* and the second-order interaction of *happy* by *marital*.

You can use multiple DESIGN subcommands on a HILOGLINEAR command. If you omit the DESIGN subcommand or use it without specifications, a default saturated model is fit.

SPSS/PC+ produces parameter estimates only for saturated models. If you request an unsaturated model, the output will contain only the goodness-of-fit test for the model, the observed and expected frequencies, and the residuals and standardized residuals.

Building a Model

Use the MAXORDER, CRITERIA, METHOD, and CWEIGHT subcommands to control computational and design aspects of a model and to perform model selection. Each of these subcommands remains in effect for any subsequent DESIGN subcommands unless overridden by new specifications.

Specifying the Maximum Order of the Model

Use the MAXORDER subcommand to specify the maximum order of terms in a model. HILOGLINEAR fits a model with all terms of the maximum order or less. Thus, MAXORDER provides an abbreviated way of specifying models. For example, the command

```
HILOGLINEAR MARITAL(1,3) HAPPY RACE SEX(1,2)
   /MAXORDER=2.
```

is equivalent to:

```
HILOGLINEAR MARITAL(1,3) HAPPY RACE SEX(1,2)
   /DESIGN=MARITAL*HAPPY
          MARITAL*RACE
          MARITAL*SEX
          HAPPY*RACE
          HAPPY*SEX
          RACE*SEX.
```

The MAXORDER subcommand can be used to restrict the model stated on the DESIGN subcommand. If MAXORDER specifies an order less than the total number of variables (that is, if an unsaturated model is fit), HILOGLINEAR does not display parameter estimates but does produce a goodness-of-fit test and the observed and expected frequencies for the model.

Specifying the Estimation Criteria

HILOGLINEAR uses an iterative procedure to fit models. Use the CRITERIA subcommand to specify the values of constants in the iterative proportional-fitting and model-selection routines. The following keywords are available for CRITERIA:

CONVERGE(n)   *Convergence criterion.* The default is 0.25 or 10^{-3} times the largest cell size, whichever is larger. Iterations stop when the change in fitted frequencies is less than the specified value.

ITERATE(n)   *Maximum number of iterations.* The default is 20.

P(p)   *Probability of chi-square for removal.* The default value is 0.05.

MAXSTEPS(n)   *Maximum number of steps.* The default is 10.

DELTA(d)   *Cell delta value.* The value of delta is added to each cell frequency for the first iteration. It is left in the cells for saturated models only. The default value is 0.5. You can specify any value for delta that is equal to 0 or greater (generally, delta should be less than 1). HILOGLINEAR does not display parameter estimates or the covariance matrix of parameter estimates if any zero cells (either structural or sampling) exist in the expected table after delta is added.

DEFAULT   *Default values.* Use DEFAULT to restore defaults altered by a previous CRITERIA subcommand.

The value for each keyword must be enclosed in parentheses. You can specify more than one keyword on a CRITERIA subcommand. Only those criteria specifically altered are changed. The keywords P and MAXSTEPS apply only to model selection and, therefore, must be used with an accompanying METHOD subcommand.

Requesting Backward Elimination

Use the METHOD subcommand to request backward elimination of terms from the model. This is the default if the subcommand METHOD is used with no keyword or with the keyword BACKWARD.

If you omit the METHOD subcommand, HILOGLINEAR tests the model requested on the DESIGN subcommand but does not perform any model selection.

You can use the METHOD subcommand with DESIGN or MAXORDER to obtain backward elimination that begins with the specified hierarchical model. For example, the command

```
HILOGLINEAR RACE SEX HAPPY(1,2) MARITAL INCOME82(1,3)
  /MAXORDER=3
  /METHOD=BACKWARD.
```

requests backward elimination beginning with a hierarchical model that contains all three-way interactions and excludes all four- and five-way interactions.

You can use the CRITERIA subcommand with METHOD to specify the removal criterion and maximum number of steps for a backward-elimination analysis. Thus, the command

```
HILOGLINEAR MARITAL INCOME(1,3) SEX HAPPY(1,2)
  /METHOD=BACKWARD
  /CRITERIA=P(.01) MAXSTEPS(25).
```

specifies a removal probability criterion of 0.01 and a maximum of 25 steps. The command

```
HILOGLINEAR HAPPY(1,2) MARITAL(1,3) INCOME82(1,3) HEALTH(1,2)
  /METHOD=BACKWARD
  /CRITERIA=MAXSTEPS(6)
  /DESIGN=HAPPY*MARITAL*INCOME82*HEALTH.
```

requests a backward elimination of terms with a maximum of six steps, producing the output in Figure 5.16, Figure 5.17, and Figure 5.18.

Setting Structural Zeros

Use the CWEIGHT subcommand to specify cell weights for a model. To weight aggregated input data, however, do not use the CWEIGHT subcommand; use the WEIGHT command before you invoke HILOGLINEAR.

CWEIGHT allows you to impose structural zeros on a model. HILOGLINEAR ignores the CWEIGHT subcommand with a saturated model.

There are two ways to specify cell weights. First, you can specify a numeric variable whose values are the cell weights. The command

```
HILOGLINEAR MARITAL(1,3) SEX HAPPY(1,2)
  /CWEIGHT=CELLWGT
  /DESIGN=MARITAL*SEX SEX*HAPPY MARITAL*HAPPY.
```

weights a cell by the value of the variable *cellwgt* when a case containing the frequency for that cell is read.

Alternatively, you can specify a matrix of weights enclosed in parentheses on the CWEIGHT subcommand. You can use the prefix $n*$ to indicate that a cell weight is repeated n times in the matrix. The command

```
HILOGLINEAR MARITAL(1,3) INCOME(1,3)
  /CWEIGHT=(0 1 1 1 0 1 1 1 0)
  /DESIGN=MARITAL INCOME.
```

is equivalent to:

```
HILOGLINEAR MARITAL(1,3) INCOME(1,3)
  /CWEIGHT=(0 3*1 0 3*1 0)
  /DESIGN=MARITAL INCOME.
```

You must specify a weight for every cell in the table. Cell weights are indexed by the levels of the variables in the order they are specified on the variable list. The index values of the rightmost variable change the most quickly.

Requesting Output

By default, HILOGLINEAR displays observed and expected cell frequencies, residuals and standardized residuals, and, for saturated models, parameter estimates. Use the following keywords on the PRINT command to change the default or request desired output:

FREQ   *Observed and expected cell frequencies.*

RESID   *Residuals and standardized residuals.*

ESTIM   *Parameter estimates, standard errors of estimates, and confidence intervals for parameters.* These are calculated only for saturated models.

ASSOCIATION   *Tests of partial association.* These are calculated only for saturated models.

DEFAULT   *Default display.* FREQ and RESID for all models plus ESTIM for saturated models.

ALL   *All available output.*

If you specify PRINT with no keyword, the default output is displayed. If you specify PRINT with any keyword, only explicitly requested output is displayed. The PRINT subcommand affects all subsequent DESIGN subcommands unless a new PRINT subcommand is specified. For example, the command

```
HILOGLINEAR HAPPY(1,2) MARITAL (1,3)
  /PRINT=ESTIM
  /CRITERIA=DELTA(0)
  /DESIGN=HAPPY*MARITAL.
```

limits the display to parameter estimates, standard errors of estimates, and confidence intervals for the saturated model. This command produces the output in Figure 5.3.

Requesting Plots

Use the PLOT subcommand to obtain plots of residuals. The following keywords are available on PLOT:

RESID   *Plot of standardized residuals against observed and expected counts.*

NORMPLOT   *Normal and detrended normal probability plots of the standardized residuals.*

NONE   *No plots.* Suppresses any plots requested on a previous PLOT subcommand. This is the default if the subcommand is omitted.

DEFAULT   *Default plots.* RESID and NORMPLOT are plotted when PLOT is used without keyword specifications or with keyword DEFAULT. No plots are produced if the subcommand is omitted entirely.

ALL   *All available plots.*

The PLOT subcommand affects all subsequent DESIGN subcommands unless a new PLOT subcommand is specified.

Missing Values

By default, HILOGLINEAR deletes from the analysis all cases with missing values for any variable named on the variable list. Use the MISSING subcommand to include cases with user-missing values or to specify the default explicitly. The keywords are:

LISTWISE   *Delete cases with missing values listwise.* This is the default.

INCLUDE   *Include cases with user-missing values.*

DEFAULT   *Same as LISTWISE.*

The MISSING subcommand can be specified only once on each HILOGLINEAR command and applies to all the designs specified on that command.

Annotated Example

The following SPSS/PC+ commands produced the output in Figure 5.16, Figure 5.17, and Figure 5.18.

```
DATA LIST /
     MARITAL 8 AGE 15-16 RACE 24 INCOME82 31-32
     SEX 40 HAPPY 48 HEALTH 56.
RECODE MARITAL (1=1)(5=2)(2 THRU 4=3)(ELSE=SYSMIS)/
     INCOME82 (1 THRU 10=1)(11 THRU 14=2)(15 THRU 17=3)
              (ELSE=SYSMIS)/
     SEX (1=2)(2=1)/HAPPY (1 THRU 2=1)(3=2)(ELSE=SYSMIS)/
     HEALTH (1 THRU 2=1)(3 THRU 4=2)(ELSE=SYSMIS).
VALUE LABELS MARITAL 1 'MARRIED' 2 'SINGLE' 3 'SPLIT'/
             INCOME82 1 'LOW' 2 'MIDDLE' 3 'HIGH'/
             SEX 1 'FEMALE' 2 'MALE'/
             HAPPY 1 'YES' 2 'NO'/
             HEALTH 1 'GOOD+' 2 'FAIR-'.
BEGIN DATA.
data records
END DATA.
HILOGLINEAR HAPPY(1,2) MARITAL(1,3) INCOME82(1,3) HEALTH(1,2)
   /PLOT=ALL
   /METHOD=BACKWARD
   /MAXSTEPS=6
   /DESIGN=HAPPY*MARITAL*INCOME82*HEALTH.
```

- The DATA LIST command gives the variable names and column locations of the variables used in the analysis.

- The RECODE command recodes the variables into consecutive integers to assure efficient processing.
- The VALUE LABELS command assigns descriptive labels to the recoded values of variables *marital, income82, sex, happy,* and *health.*
- The HILOGLINEAR command requests a backward elimination of the model with a maximum number of six steps. It also requests plots of the standardized residuals against observed and expected counts, as well as the normal and detrended normal probability plots of the standardized residuals.

6 Further Topics in Loglinear Models

Why do some people slip on banana peels while others glide through life unscathed? Why are some people Pollyannas and others Ebenezer Scrooges? Throughout history, many theories have been proposed to explain such differences. The ancient Greeks believed that the human body was composed of four humors: phlegm, blood, yellow bile, and black bile. The predominant humor determined the personality. For example, black bile is associated with melancholia, and phlegm with a phlegmatic disposition.

The Babylonians and Egyptians looked to the positions of the stars and planets to explain differences among people. The position of the sun and planets at the time of one's birth determined destiny. Though the four-humors theory has few followers today, astrology continues to intrigue many. Even the most serious scientist may on occasion sneak a look at the horoscope page, just for fun, of course...

The ultimate test of any theory is how well it withstands the rigors of scientific testing. The General Social Survey in 1984 recorded the zodiac signs of 1,462 persons, along with a variety of other information, ranging from views on the after life to the mother's employment status when the respondent was 16 years old. In this chapter, the Loglinear procedure is used to test a variety of hypotheses about zodiac signs and their relationships to other variables.

Loglinear Models

Chapter 5 described the Hierarchical Loglinear procedure for testing hypotheses about hierarchical loglinear models. In this chapter, additional types of models (including nonhierarchical models) estimated by the Loglinear procedure are examined. This chapter assumes familiarity with the hierarchical loglinear models described in Chapter 5.

Frequency Table Models

One of the first hypotheses you might want to test is whether all 12 zodiac signs appear to be equally likely in the population from which the General Social Survey draws its sample. Figure 6.1 contains the observed and expected cell counts under the equiprobability model. For example, as shown in the column labeled *OBS. count*, there are 113 Ariens. If all zodiac signs are equally likely, 121.83 (1462/12) respondents are expected in each cell, as shown in the column labeled *EXP. count & PCT*. The differences between the observed and expected counts are shown in the column labeled *Residual*.

Figure 6.1   Frequencies and residuals for the equiprobability model

```
SET WIDTH=WIDE.
COMPUTE X=1.
LOGLINEAR ZODIAC(1,12) WITH X
  /DESIGN=X.
```

Observed, Expected Frequencies and Residuals

Factor	Code	OBS. count & PCT.	EXP. count & PCT.	Residual	Std. Resid.	Adj. Resid.
ZODIAC	ARIES	113.00 (7.73)	121.83 (8.33)	-8.8333	-.8003	-.8359
ZODIAC	TAURUS	115.00 (7.87)	121.83 (8.33)	-6.8333	-.6191	-.6466
ZODIAC	GEMINI	137.00 (9.37)	121.83 (8.33)	15.1667	1.3741	1.4352
ZODIAC	CANCER	121.00 (8.28)	121.83 (8.33)	-.8333	-.0755	-.0789
ZODIAC	LEO	122.00 (8.34)	121.83 (8.33)	.1667	.0151	.0158
ZODIAC	VIRGO	133.00 (9.10)	121.83 (8.33)	11.1667	1.0117	1.0567
ZODIAC	LIBRA	144.00 (9.85)	121.83 (8.33)	22.1667	2.0082	2.0975
ZODIAC	SCORPIO	114.00 (7.80)	121.83 (8.33)	-7.8333	-.7097	-.7412
ZODIAC	SAGITTAR	116.00 (7.93)	121.83 (8.33)	-5.8333	-.5285	-.5520
ZODIAC	CAPRICOR	131.00 (8.96)	121.83 (8.33)	9.1667	.8305	.8674
ZODIAC	AQUARIUS	93.00 (6.36)	121.83 (8.33)	-28.8333	-2.6122	-2.7284
ZODIAC	PISCES	123.00 (8.41)	121.83 (8.33)	1.1667	.1057	.1104

Goodness-of-Fit test statistics

```
Likelihood Ratio Chi Square =    16.58881     DF = 11   P =   .121
           Pearson Chi Square =    16.28181     DF = 11   P =   .131
```

As in regression analysis, it is useful to normalize the residuals by dividing them by their standard deviations. Standardized residuals are obtained by dividing each residual by the square root of the expected count. Adjusted residuals are calculated by dividing each residual by an estimate of its standard error. For large sample sizes, the distribution of adjusted residuals is approximately standard normal.

By examining residuals, we can identify patterns of deviation from the model. The only noticeable deviations from the equiprobability model occur for the Libras and Aquarians. Both of these zodiac signs have adjusted residuals greater than 2 in absolute value. The value 2 is a rule of thumb for "suspiciousness" since, in a standard normal distribution, only 5% of the absolute values exceed 1.96.

From the chi-square goodness-of-fit statistics shown in Figure 6.1, it appears that there is not sufficient evidence to reject the hypothesis that all zodiac signs are equally likely. The likelihood-ratio chi-square value is 16.59 with 11 degrees of freedom. The observed significance level is 0.12.

Fitting a Quadratic Function

Figure 6.1 shows the results for each zodiac sign individually. It might be interesting to collapse the signs into four categories based on seasons of the year and see whether a relationship exists between seasons and number of births. For example, if the number of births steadily increases from spring to winter, we might consider a linear relationship. From Figure 6.2, you can see that the relationship between the number of births and the seasons does not appear linear. Instead, a function that "peaks" and then decreases again is needed.

Let's consider a quadratic function. For this analysis, factor variable *seasons*, coded 1 (spring) through 4 (winter), defines the cells of the table. The model contains linear and quadratic terms, which are entered as covariates. The linear term (*lin*) is equal to the value of *seasons* for a case, and the quadratic term *(lin2)* is computed as the square of *seasons*. Figure 6.2 contains the expected frequencies for each of the seasons when the expected number of cases for a season is expressed as a quadratic function.

Figure 6.2   Frequencies and residuals for the quadratic model

```
SET WIDTH=WIDE.
COMPUTE SEASON=ZODIAC.
RECODE SEASON(1,2,3=1) (4,5,6=2) (7,8,9=3) (10,11,12=4).
VALUE LABELS SEASON 1 'Spring' 2 'Summer' 3 'Fall' 4 'Winter'.
COMPUTE LIN=SEASON.
COMPUTE LIN2=SEASON*SEASON.
LOGLINEAR SEASON(1,4) WITH LIN LIN2
  /DESIGN=LIN LIN2.
```

Observed, Expected Frequencies and Residuals

Factor	Code	OBS. count & PCT.	EXP. count & PCT.	Residual	Std. Resid.	Adj. Resid.
SEASON	Spring	365.00 (24.97)	364.36 (24.92)	.6447	.0338	.1493
SEASON	Summer	376.00 (25.72)	377.93 (25.85)	-1.9342	-.0995	-.1493
SEASON	Fall	374.00 (25.58)	372.07 (25.45)	1.9342	.1003	.1493
SEASON	Winter	347.00 (23.73)	347.64 (23.78)	-.6447	-.0346	-.1493

Note that the expected values are not equal for each season. Summer has the largest expected frequency, 377.93, while winter has the smallest. This is true for the observed frequencies as well. The statistics for the overall fit of the quadratic model are shown in Figure 6.3. Note that the chi-square value is very small (0.02), indicating that the model fits quite well. However, Figure 6.4 shows that the coefficients for the linear and quadratic terms for the log frequencies are not large, compared to their standard errors. In addition, both 95% confidence intervals include 0, leading us not to reject the hypothesis that the linear and quadratic coefficients are 0.

Figure 6.3   Goodness of fit for the quadratic model

```
Goodness-of-Fit test statistics

      Likelihood Ratio Chi Square =      .02229   DF = 1   P =   .881
             Pearson Chi Square =      .02229   DF = 1   P =   .881
```

Figure 6.4   Parameter estimates for the linear and quadratic terms

```
COMPUTE SEASON=ZODIAC.
RECODE SEASON(1,2,3=1) (4,5,6=2) (7,8,9=3) (10,11,12=4).
VALUE LABELS SEASON 1 'Spring' 2 'Summer' 3 'Fall' 4 'Winter'.
COMPUTE LIN=SEASON.
COMPUTE LIN2=SEASON*SEASON.
LOGLINEAR SEASON(1,4) WITH LIN LIN2
  /PRINT=ESTIM
  /DESIGN=LIN LIN2.
```

```
Estimates for Parameters

  LIN

    Parameter       Coeff.      Std. Err.    Z-Value    Lower 95 CI    Upper 95 CI

          1     .1149510016      .13261      .86681       -.14497         .37487

  LIN2

    Parameter       Coeff.      Std. Err.    Z-Value    Lower 95 CI    Upper 95 CI

          2    -.0261200872      .02616     -.99829       -.07740         .02516
```

An equiprobability model also fits the data reasonably well, as shown in Figure 6.5. It has an observed significance level for goodness of fit of 0.694. Note that the goodness-of-fit statistics for this are not the same as for the individual zodiac signs.

Including additional terms in the model improves the fit, but not by much. The additional parameters decrease the degrees of freedom and should be used only if they substantially improve the fit. In other words, a good model should fit the data well and be as simple as possible.

Figure 6.5   Statistics for the equiprobability model

```
SET WIDTH=WIDE.
COMPUTE SEASON=ZODIAC.
RECODE SEASON(1,2,3=1) (4,5,6=2) (7,8,9=3) (10,11,12=4).
VALUE LABELS SEASON 1 'Spring' 2 'Summer' 3 'Fall' 4 'Winter'.
COMPUTE X=1.
LOGLINEAR SEASON(1,4) WITH X
  /DESIGN=X.
```

```
Observed, Expected Frequencies and Residuals

    Factor          Code        OBS. count & PCT.    EXP. count & PCT.    Residual    Std. Resid.    Adj. Resid.

    SEASON         Spring        365.00 (24.97)       365.50 (25.00)       -.5000        -.0262         -.0302
    SEASON         Summer        376.00 (25.72)       365.50 (25.00)      10.5000         .5492          .6342
    SEASON         Fall          374.00 (25.58)       365.50 (25.00)       8.5000         .4446          .5134
    SEASON         Winter        347.00 (23.73)       365.50 (25.00)     -18.5000        -.9677        -1.1174
```

- -

```
Goodness-of-Fit test statistics

    Likelihood Ratio Chi Square =    1.44824    DF = 3    P =  .694
               Pearson Chi Square =    1.43639    DF = 3    P =  .697
```

The Zodiac and Job Satisfaction

Now that we've established that there is no reason to disbelieve that all zodiac signs are equally likely (Figure 6.1), let's consider the possible relationship of zodiac sign to various aspects of life. Since zodiac sign is thought to influence everything from love to numerical aptitude, it might be associated with characteristics such as income, education, happiness, and job satisfaction.

Consider Figure 6.6, which is a crosstabulation of zodiac sign and response to a question about job satisfaction (for information on how to obtain a crosstabulation, see the chapter Crosstabulation and Measures of Association in the *SPSS/PC+ Base System User's Guide*). Respondents are grouped into two categories: those who are very satisfied with their jobs and those who are less enthusiastic. The row percentages show quite a bit of variability among the signs. The irrepressible Aquarians are most likely to be satisfied with their jobs, while Virgos are the least likely to be content.

Figure 6.6   Zodiac sign by job satisfaction

```
RECODE SATJOB(1=1) (2,3,4=2) (ELSE=SYSMIS).
VALUE LABELS SATJOB 1 'Very Sat' 2 'Not Very Sat'.
CROSSTABS ZODIAC BY SATJOB
  /CELLS=ROW COUNT.
```

ZODIAC   RESPONDENT'S ASTROLOGICAL SIGN   by   SATJOB   JOB OR HOUSEWORK

		SATJOB		
Count Row Pct		Very Sat 1	Not Very Sat 2	Row Total
ZODIAC				
ARIES	1	45 49.5	46 50.5	91 7.6
TAURUS	2	42 43.3	55 56.7	97 8.1
GEMINI	3	61 53.0	54 47.0	115 9.6
CANCER	4	48 48.5	51 51.5	99 8.2
LEO	5	48 48.0	52 52.0	100 8.3
VIRGO	6	41 38.0	67 62.0	108 9.0
LIBRA	7	51 42.5	69 57.5	120 10.0
SCORPIO	8	37 38.9	58 61.1	95 7.9
SAGITTARIUS	9	46 47.9	50 52.1	96 8.0
CAPRICORN	10	46 42.2	63 57.8	109 9.1
AQUARIUS	11	49 63.6	28 36.4	77 6.4
PISCES	12	37 38.9	58 61.1	95 7.9
Column Total		551 45.8	651 54.2	1202 100.0

Fitting a Logit Model

To test whether zodiac sign and job satisfaction are independent, a loglinear model can be fit to the data in Figure 6.6. If the two variables are independent, a model without the interaction term should be sufficient. In such models, no distinction is made between independent and dependent variables. Both zodiac sign and job satisfaction are used to estimate the expected number of cases in each cell.

When one variable is thought to depend on the others, a special class of loglinear models, called **logit models**, can be used to examine the relationship between a dichotomous dependent variable, such as job satisfaction, and one or more independent variables. Let's examine the relationship between job satisfaction and zodiac sign, considering job satisfaction as the dependent variable and zodiac sign as the independent variable.

In many statistical procedures, a dichotomous dependent variable is coded as having values of 0 or 1, and subsequent calculations are based on these values. In a logit model, the dependent variable is not the actual value of the variable but the **log odds**. Odds are the ratio of the frequency that an event occurs to the frequency that it does not occur. For example, from Figure 6.6, the observed frequency of an Arien's being very satisfied with his job is 45, while the observed frequency of an Arien's being not very satisfied with his job is 46. The estimated odds that an Arien is very satisfied are 45 to 46, or 0.98. This means that an Arien is about equally likely to be very satisfied or not very satisfied. Similarly, the odds for an Aquarian of being very satisfied are 1.75 (49/28), indicating that Aquarians are more likely to be very satisfied than unsatisfied. The odds can also be interpreted as the ratio of two probabilities—the probability that an Arien is very satisfied and the probability that an Arien is not very satisfied.

Let's consider how a logit model can be derived from the usual loglinear model. In a saturated loglinear model, the log of the number of very satisfied Ariens can be expressed as:

$$\ln (F_{11}) = \mu + \lambda^{\text{very satisfied}} + \lambda^{\text{Arien}} + \lambda^{\text{very satisfied * Arien}} \qquad \text{Equation 6.1}$$

Similarly, the log of the number of unsatisfied Ariens is:

$$\ln (F_{12}) = \mu + \lambda^{\text{unsatisfied}} + \lambda^{\text{Arien}} + \lambda^{\text{unsatisfied * Arien}} \qquad \text{Equation 6.2}$$

The log of the ratio of the two frequencies is called a **logit**. Recalling that the log of the ratio is

$$\ln \left(\frac{F_{11}}{F_{12}} \right) = ln (F_{11}) - ln (F_{12}) \qquad \text{Equation 6.3}$$

we can compute the logit for Ariens as:

$$\ln\left(\frac{F_{11}}{F_{12}}\right) = (\mu - \mu) + (\lambda^{\text{very satisfied}} - \lambda^{\text{unsatisfied}}) + (\lambda^{\text{Arien}} - \lambda^{\text{Arien}})$$

Equation 6.4

$$+ (\lambda^{\text{very satisfied} * \text{Arien}} - \lambda^{\text{unsatisfied} * \text{Arien}})$$

Equation 6.4 can be considerably simplified. Note first that all the μ and λ^{Arien} terms cancel. Next, remember that the lambda terms must sum to 0 over all categories of a variable. For a variable that has two categories, this means that the values of the lambda parameters are equal in absolute value but opposite in sign. Thus, $\lambda^{\text{very satisfied}} = -\lambda^{\text{unsatisfied}}$, and $\lambda^{\text{very satisfied} * \text{Arien}} = -\lambda^{\text{unsatisfied} * \text{Arien}}$. Using these observations, the previous equation can be expressed as:

$$\ln\left(\frac{F_{11}}{F_{12}}\right) = 2(\lambda^{\text{very satisfied}} + \lambda^{\text{very satisfied} * \text{Arien}})$$

Equation 6.5

Thus, the logit is a function of the same lambda parameters that appear in the general loglinear model. As shown in Figure 6.7, since the logit model is saturated, the observed and expected frequencies are equal and all of the residuals are 0.

Figure 6.7   Observed and expected frequencies for the saturated logit model

```
SET WIDTH=WIDE.
LOGLINEAR SATJOB(1,2) BY ZODIAC(1,12)
 /CRITERIA=DELTA(0)
 /DESIGN SATJOB SATJOB BY ZODIAC.
```

Observed, Expected Frequencies and Residuals

Factor	Code	OBS. count & PCT.	EXP. count & PCT.	Residual	Std. Resid.	Adj. Resid.
SATJOB	Very Sat					
ZODIAC	ARIES	45.00 (49.45)	45.00 (49.45)	.0000	.0000	.0000
ZODIAC	TAURUS	42.00 (43.30)	42.00 (43.30)	.0000	.0000	.0000
ZODIAC	GEMINI	61.00 (53.04)	61.00 (53.04)	.0000	.0000	.0000
ZODIAC	CANCER	48.00 (48.48)	48.00 (48.48)	.0000	.0000	.0000
ZODIAC	LEO	48.00 (48.00)	48.00 (48.00)	.0000	.0000	.0000
ZODIAC	VIRGO	41.00 (37.96)	41.00 (37.96)	.0000	.0000	.0000
ZODIAC	LIBRA	51.00 (42.50)	51.00 (42.50)	.0000	.0000	.0000
ZODIAC	SCORPIO	37.00 (38.95)	37.00 (38.95)	.0000	.0000	.0000
ZODIAC	SAGITTAR	46.00 (47.92)	46.00 (47.92)	.0000	.0000	.0000
ZODIAC	CAPRICOR	46.00 (42.20)	46.00 (42.20)	.0000	.0000	.0000
ZODIAC	AQUARIUS	49.00 (63.64)	49.00 (63.64)	.0000	.0000	.0000
ZODIAC	PISCES	37.00 (38.95)	37.00 (38.95)	.0000	.0000	.0000
SATJOB	Not Very					
ZODIAC	ARIES	46.00 (50.55)	46.00 (50.55)	.0000	.0000	.0000
ZODIAC	TAURUS	55.00 (56.70)	55.00 (56.70)	.0000	.0000	.0000
ZODIAC	GEMINI	54.00 (46.96)	54.00 (46.96)	.0000	.0000	.0000
ZODIAC	CANCER	51.00 (51.52)	51.00 (51.52)	.0000	.0000	.0000
ZODIAC	LEO	52.00 (52.00)	52.00 (52.00)	.0000	.0000	.0000
ZODIAC	VIRGO	67.00 (62.04)	67.00 (62.04)	.0000	.0000	.0000
ZODIAC	LIBRA	69.00 (57.50)	69.00 (57.50)	.0000	.0000	.0000
ZODIAC	SCORPIO	58.00 (61.05)	58.00 (61.05)	.0000	.0000	.0000
ZODIAC	SAGITTAR	50.00 (52.08)	50.00 (52.08)	.0000	.0000	.0000
ZODIAC	CAPRICOR	63.00 (57.80)	63.00 (57.80)	.0000	.0000	.0000
ZODIAC	AQUARIUS	28.00 (36.36)	28.00 (36.36)	.0000	.0000	.0000
ZODIAC	PISCES	58.00 (61.05)	58.00 (61.05)	.0000	.0000	.0000

Parameter Estimates

In the logit model, the parameter estimates displayed (Figure 6.8) are the actual lambdas, not twice lambda. Thus, the values are identical to those obtained in the loglinear model. No coefficient is displayed for the *zodiac* variable, since it does not directly appear in the logit model (see Equation 6.5).

Figure 6.8   Parameter estimates for the logit model

```
LOGLINEAR SATJOB(1,2) BY ZODIAC(1,12)
 /CRITERIA=DELTA(0)
 /DESIGN SATJOB SATJOB BY ZODIAC.


Estimates for Parameters

 SATJOB

  Parameter          Coeff.      Std. Err.      Z-Value    Lower 95 CI    Upper 95 CI

         1       -.0767137815       .02943      -2.60689       -.13439        -.01904

 SATJOB BY ZODIAC

  Parameter          Coeff.      Std. Err.      Z-Value    Lower 95 CI    Upper 95 CI

         2        .0657243282       .10012        .65644       -.13052         .26197
         3       -.0581180019       .09805       -.59273       -.25030         .13406
         4        .1376586903       .09022       1.52584       -.03917         .31449
         5        .0464014706       .09639        .48139       -.14252         .23533
         6        .0366924277       .09598        .38228       -.15143         .22482
         7       -.1688464948       .09517      -1.77422       -.35537         .01768
         8       -.0744266544       .08928       -.83367       -.24941         .10055
         9       -.1480487674       .10044      -1.47398       -.34491         .04882
        10        .0350229771       .09778        .35817       -.15663         .22668
        11       -.0805328834       .09328       -.86331       -.26337         .10230
        12        .3565216755       .11206       3.18144        .13688         .57617
```

As in the general loglinear model, the deviation parameter estimates (the default) can be used to predict the expected cell frequencies. However, in a logit model, instead of predicting individual cell frequencies, the log odds are predicted. For example, the predicted log odds for the Ariens are:

$$\ln\left(\frac{F_{11}}{F_{12}}\right) = 2 \times (\lambda^{\text{very satisfied}} + \lambda^{\text{very satisfied * Arien}})$$

$$= 2\,(-0.0767 + 0.0657)$$

$$= -0.022$$

Equation 6.6

We can obtain the predicted odds by raising each side of the equation to the power of *e*:

$$\frac{F_{11}}{F_{12}} = e^{-0.022}$$

$$= 0.98$$

Equation 6.7

Since this is a saturated model, the predicted odds equal the observed odds, or the ratio of satisfied to dissatisfied Ariens $(45/46)$.

Measures of Dispersion and Association

When a model is formulated with one classification variable considered as dependent, it is possible to analyze the dispersion or spread in the dependent variable. Two statistics that are used to measure the spread of a nominal variable are **Shannon's entropy measure,**

$$H = \Sigma p_j \log p_j \qquad \text{Equation 6.8}$$

and **Gini's concentration measure,**

$$C = 1 - \Sigma p_j^2 \qquad \text{Equation 6.9}$$

Using either of these measures, it is possible to subdivide the total dispersion of the dependent variable into that explained by the model and the residual, or unexplained, variance. Figure 6.9 contains the analysis of dispersion for the satisfaction and zodiac sign variables when a saturated logit model is fit.

Figure 6.9   Analysis of dispersion

```
Analysis of Dispersion

                                 Dispersion
    Source of Variation      Entropy  Concentration      DF

        Due to Model          10.564         10.450
        Due to Residual      818.434        586.390
        Total                828.998        596.840      1201


- - - - - - - - - - - - - - - - - - - - - - - - - - - - - - - - - - -


Measures of Association

            Entropy =     .012744
      Concentration =     .017509
```

Based on the analysis of dispersion, it is possible to calculate statistics similar to R^2 in regression that indicate what proportion of the total dispersion in the dependent variable is attributable to the model (Magidson, 1981). In Figure 6.9, when dispersion is measured by the entropy criterion, the ratio of the dispersion "explained" by the model to the total dispersion is 0.013. When measured by the concentration criterion, it is 0.0175. These values can be interpreted as measures of association. Although it is tempting to interpret the magnitudes of these measures similarly to R^2 in regression, this may be misleading, since the coefficients may be small even when the variables are strongly related (Haberman, 1982). It appears that the coefficients are best interpreted in the light of experience.

Fitting an Unsaturated Logit Model

As discussed in Chapter 5, a saturated model fits the data exactly. This is also true for a logit model, which contains all interaction terms between the dependent variable and all combinations of the independent variables. Alternative models can be formed by deleting some terms from the saturated logit model. For example, to ascertain whether job satisfaction and zodiac sign are independent, we need to fit a logit model without the interaction term between job satisfaction and zodiac sign. Figure 6.10 contains the statistics for the cells and the chi-square values when the interaction term is eliminated.

Figure 6.10   Statistics for the unsaturated model

```
SET WIDTH=WIDE.
LOGLINEAR SATJOB(1,2) BY ZODIAC(1,12)
    /DESIGN=SATJOB.
```

Observed, Expected Frequencies and Residuals

Factor	Code	OBS. count & PCT.	EXP. count & PCT.	Residual	Std. Resid.	Adj. Resid.
SATJOB	Very Sat					
ZODIAC	ARIES	45.00 (49.45)	41.71 (45.84)	3.2854	.5087	.7189
ZODIAC	TAURUS	42.00 (43.30)	44.47 (45.84)	-2.4651	-.3697	-.5239
ZODIAC	GEMINI	61.00 (53.04)	52.72 (45.84)	8.2837	1.1409	1.6302
ZODIAC	CANCER	48.00 (48.48)	45.38 (45.84)	2.6181	.3886	.5513
ZODIAC	LEO	48.00 (48.00)	45.84 (45.84)	2.1597	.3190	.4527
ZODIAC	VIRGO	41.00 (37.96)	49.51 (45.84)	-8.5075	-1.2091	-1.7222
ZODIAC	LIBRA	51.00 (42.50)	55.01 (45.84)	-4.0083	-.5404	-.7740
ZODIAC	SCORPIO	37.00 (38.95)	43.55 (45.84)	-6.5483	-.9923	-1.4050
ZODIAC	SAGITTAR	46.00 (47.92)	44.01 (45.84)	1.9933	.3005	.4257
ZODIAC	CAPRICOR	46.00 (42.20)	49.97 (45.84)	-3.9659	-.5611	-.7995
ZODIAC	AQUARIUS	49.00 (63.64)	35.30 (45.84)	13.7030	2.3065	3.2395
ZODIAC	PISCES	37.00 (38.95)	43.55 (45.84)	-6.5483	-.9923	-1.4050
SATJOB	Not Very					
ZODIAC	ARIES	46.00 (50.55)	49.29 (54.16)	-3.2854	-.4680	-.7189
ZODIAC	TAURUS	55.00 (56.70)	52.53 (54.16)	2.4651	.3401	.5239
ZODIAC	GEMINI	54.00 (46.96)	62.28 (54.16)	-8.2837	-1.0496	-1.6302
ZODIAC	CANCER	51.00 (51.52)	53.62 (54.16)	-2.6181	-.3575	-.5513
ZODIAC	LEO	52.00 (52.00)	54.16 (54.16)	-2.1597	-.2935	-.4527
ZODIAC	VIRGO	67.00 (62.04)	58.49 (54.16)	8.5075	1.1124	1.7222
ZODIAC	LIBRA	69.00 (57.50)	64.99 (54.16)	4.0083	.4972	.7740
ZODIAC	SCORPIO	58.00 (61.05)	51.45 (54.16)	6.5483	.9129	1.4050
ZODIAC	SAGITTAR	50.00 (52.08)	51.99 (54.16)	-1.9933	-.2764	-.4257
ZODIAC	CAPRICOR	63.00 (57.80)	59.03 (54.16)	3.9659	.5162	.7995
ZODIAC	AQUARIUS	28.00 (36.36)	41.70 (54.16)	-13.7030	-2.1219	-3.2395
ZODIAC	PISCES	58.00 (61.05)	51.45 (54.16)	6.5483	.9129	1.4050

- -

Goodness-of-Fit test statistics

```
Likelihood Ratio Chi Square =    21.12888    DF = 11   P =  .032
         Pearson Chi Square =    21.04523    DF = 11   P =  .033
```

The chi-square values indicate that an independence model does not fit the data well. The observed significance level is about 0.03. The adjusted residuals for the Aquarians are particularly large, so the model fits very poorly for this zodiac sign. The proportion of very satisfied Aquarians is substantially larger than expected.

Figure 6.11 is a plot of the observed values against the adjusted residuals. Two residuals are large in absolute value, and there may be a linear trend.

Figure 6.11 Plot of observed counts and adjusted residuals

```
LOGLINEAR SATJOB(1,2) BY ZODIAC(1,12)
   /PLOT=RESID
   /DESIGN=SATJOB.
```

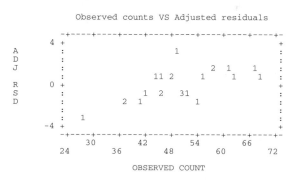

```
               Observed counts VS Adjusted residuals

         -+----+----+----+----+----+----+----+----+-
      4  +                                          +
   A     :                        1                 :
   D     :                                          :
   J     :                            2  1    1     :
         :              11 2     1        1    1     :
   R  0  +                                          +
   S     :            1  2   31                     :
   D     :         2  1              1              :
         :                                          :
         :     1                                    :
     -4  +                                          +
         -+----+----+----+----+----+----+----+----+-
             30        42        54        66
         24        36        48        60        72

                       OBSERVED COUNT
```

The results obtained from fitting a logit model without the interaction term are exactly identical to those that would be obtained if the usual loglinear model of independence were fit. The only difference is that, in the logit model, the parameter estimates for the zodiac values are not displayed, since they do not appear directly in the model. (The Loglinear procedure, unlike the Hierarchical Loglinear procedure, produces parameter estimates for unsaturated models.)

Fitting a More Complicated Logit Model

Since earning money is usually an important reason for working, it is interesting to see what happens when income is included in the logit model of job satisfaction.

For the analysis, respondents' income is grouped into four categories, each containing roughly the same number of cases. Figure 6.12 contains the observed frequencies for the crosstabulation of job satisfaction with zodiac sign and income level.

Figure 6.12   Three-way crosstabulation from SPSS/PC+ Tables option

```
SET WIDTH=WIDE LENGTH=NONE.
TABLES /FORMAT=CWIDTH(15,7)
   /FTOTAL=T1'Column Total' T2 'Row Total'
   /TABLE=ZODIAC + T1 BY SATJOB > (RINCOME+ T2)
   /STATISTICS=COUNT(ZODIAC'') CPCT(ZODIAC' ':ZODIAC SATJOB).
```

	JOB OR HOUSEWORK									
	Very Satisfied					Not Very Satisfied				
	RESPONDENT'S INCOME				Row Total	RESPONDENT'S INCOME				Row Total
	< $6000	$6000 to $14,999	$15,000 to $24,999	$25,000 and up		< $6000	$6000 to $14,999	$15,000 to $24,999	$25,000 and up	
RESPONDENT'S ASTROLOGICAL SIGN										
ARIES	8 29.6%	9 33.3%	2 7.4%	8 29.6%	27 100.0%	9 31.0%	10 34.5%	5 17.2%	5 17.2%	29 100.0%
TAURUS	7 25.0%	10 35.7%	10 35.7%	1 3.6%	28 100.0%	9 20.5%	21 47.7%	6 13.6%	8 18.2%	44 100.0%
GEMINI	8 17.4%	17 37.0%	9 19.6%	12 26.1%	46 100.0%	16 36.4%	14 31.8%	9 20.5%	5 11.4%	44 100.0%
CANCER	8 20.0%	11 27.5%	14 35.0%	7 17.5%	40 100.0%	11 28.9%	14 36.8%	10 26.3%	3 7.9%	38 100.0%
LEO	7 20.6%	13 38.2%	8 23.5%	6 17.6%	34 100.0%	12 33.3%	11 30.6%	9 25.0%	4 11.1%	36 100.0%
VIRGO	6 16.7%	9 25.0%	12 33.3%	9 25.0%	36 100.0%	5 10.4%	16 33.3%	23 47.9%	4 8.3%	48 100.0%
LIBRA	4 12.5%	10 31.3%	9 28.1%	9 28.1%	32 100.0%	15 26.8%	19 33.9%	11 19.6%	11 19.6%	56 100.0%
SCORPIO	7 25.9%	10 37.0%	6 22.2%	4 14.8%	27 100.0%	10 23.3%	11 25.6%	15 34.9%	7 16.3%	43 100.0%
SAGITTARIUS	7 18.9%	9 24.3%	12 32.4%	9 24.3%	37 100.0%	7 18.9%	13 35.1%	10 27.0%	7 18.9%	37 100.0%
CAPRICORN	3 8.6%	8 22.9%	12 34.3%	12 34.3%	35 100.0%	10 22.7%	14 31.8%	9 20.5%	11 25.0%	44 100.0%
AQUARIUS	12 30.8%	10 25.6%	11 28.2%	6 15.4%	39 100.0%	5 22.7%	9 40.9%	5 22.7%	3 13.6%	22 100.0%
PISCES	5 17.2%	8 27.6%	8 27.6%	8 27.6%	29 100.0%	15 31.3%	12 25.0%	10 20.8%	11 22.9%	48 100.0%
Column Total	82 20.0%	124 30.2%	113 27.6%	91 22.2%	410 100.0%	124 25.4%	164 33.5%	122 24.9%	79 16.2%	489 100.0%

Consider a logit model that includes only the effects of job satisfaction, job satisfaction by income, and job satisfaction by zodiac. Based on the statistics displayed in Figure 6.13, it appears that the logit model without the three-way interaction of job satisfaction, income, and zodiac sign fits the data well. The observed significance level for the goodness-of-fit statistic is about 0.5. The diagnostic plots of adjusted residuals (not shown) give no indication that there are suspicious departures from the model.

Figure 6.13   Goodness of fit for the expanded logit model

```
LOGLINEAR SATJOB(1,2) BY ZODIAC(1,12) RINCOME(1,4)
  /DESIGN=SATJOB, SATJOB BY ZODIAC, SATJOB BY RINCOME.

Goodness-of-Fit test statistics

   Likelihood Ratio Chi Square =     31.62898    DF = 33   P =  .535
                Pearson Chi Square =     30.67426    DF = 33   P =  .583
```

Deviation parameter estimates for the logit model are shown in Figure 6.14. The *satjob* parameter estimate is negative, indicating that, overall, the proportion of people highly satisfied with their jobs is less than the proportion that are dissatisfied. The coefficients corresponding to the *satjob* by *rincome* effect show the increase or decrease in the log odds ratio associated with each income category. The parameter estimate shows that there is a progression from a fairly large negative value, -0.145, to a fairly large positive value, 0.166. (The estimate for the last income category is not displayed. It is obtained as the negative of the sum of the previous estimates.) Thus, it appears that people in the lower income categories experience less job satisfaction than people in the higher income categories. The parameter estimates for the *satjob* by *zodiac* interaction give the contribution of each zodiac sign to job satisfaction. Again, negative values are associated with dissatisfied zodiac signs while positive values are associated with more content signs. The largest positive parameter estimate (parameter 12) is for the Aquarians, who as a group are the most satisfied.

Figure 6.14   Parameter estimates for the expanded logit model

```
LOGLINEAR SATJOB(1,2) BY ZODIAC(1,12) RINCOME(1,4)
  /PRINT=ESTIM
  /DESIGN=SATJOB, SATJOB BY ZODIAC, SATJOB BY RINCOME.

Estimates for Parameters

SATJOB

  Parameter      Coeff.       Std. Err.     Z-Value    Lower 95 CI   Upper 95 CI

         1    -.0704541613      .03499     -2.01344      -.13904       -.00187

SATJOB BY ZODIAC

  Parameter      Coeff.       Std. Err.     Z-Value    Lower 95 CI   Upper 95 CI

         2     .0564737768      .12811       .44083      -.19462        .30757
         3    -.1279033527      .11635     -1.09932      -.35594        .10014
         4     .1140066820      .10289      1.10807      -.08765        .31567
         5     .1178086027      .10963      1.07465      -.09706        .33267
         6     .0689561722      .11512       .59900      -.15667        .29459
         7    -.0802959724      .10761      -.74615      -.29122        .13063
         8    -.2077153468      .10751     -1.93201      -.41844        .00301
         9    -.1492020965      .11786     -1.26593      -.38021        .08180
        10     .0683122274      .11222       .60873      -.15164        .28826
        11    -.0634811554      .11004      -.57688      -.27916        .15220
        12     .3845323775      .12723      3.02224       .13515        .63391

SATJOB BY RINCOME

  Parameter      Coeff.       Std. Err.     Z-Value    Lower 95 CI   Upper 95 CI

        13    -.1451090801      .06216     -2.33441      -.26694       -.02327
        14    -.0643412033      .05513     -1.16708      -.17240        .04371
        15     .0435190304      .05889       .73898      -.07191        .15894
```

Note that the logit is calculated as the ratio of the number of cases in the first category to the number of cases in the second category. If *satjob* had been coded so that the first value was for the *dissatisfied* category, positive parameter estimates would occur for dissatisfied signs.

The predicted log odds for each combination of income and zodiac sign can be obtained from the coefficients in Figure 6.14. For example, the predicted log odds for Ariens with incomes less than $6,000 is:

$$2(-0.0704 - 0.145 + 0.0565) = -0.318 \qquad \text{Equation 6.10}$$

The expected odds are $e^{-0.318}$, or 0.728. Thus, Ariens in low income categories are less likely to be highly satisfied than dissatisfied. Predicted odds values for the other cells are found in a similar fashion.

The Equivalent Loglinear Model

As previously discussed, logit models can also be formulated as loglinear models. However, not all terms that are in the loglinear model appear in the logit model, since logit models do not include relationships among the independent variables. When the odds ratios are formed, terms involving only the independent variables cancel, since for a particular combination of values of the independent variables, the effects are the same for both categories of the dependent variable.

Thus, the loglinear representation of a logit model contains additional terms for the independent variables. For example, the loglinear model that corresponds to the logit model described above has three additional terms: the main effect for zodiac sign, the main effect for income category, and the interaction between zodiac sign and income category. Goodness-of-fit statistics for the equivalent loglinear model are identical to those in Figure 6.13.

Models for Ordinal Data

In many situations, the categorical variables used in loglinear models are ordinal in nature. For example, income levels range from low to high, as does interest in a product, or severity of a disease. Ordinal variables may result from grouping values of interval variables such as income or education, or they may arise when ordering (but not distance) between categories can be established. Happiness, interest, and opinions on various issues are measured on ordinal scales. Although "a lot" is more than "some," the actual distance between the two response categories cannot be determined. The additional information contained in the ordering of the categories can be incorporated into loglinear models, which may result in a more parsimonious representation of the data (see Agresti, 1984).

Let's consider some common models for ordinal data using the job satisfaction and income variables. Although only two categories of job satisfaction were used to illustrate logit models, there were actually four possible responses to the question: *very satisfied*, *moderately satisfied*, *a little dissatisfied*, and *very dissatisfied*. Figure 6.15 is the crosstabulation of job satisfaction and income categories. You can see that as salary increases, so does job satisfaction, especially at the ends of the salary scale. Almost 10% of people earning less than $6,000 were very dissatisfied with their jobs, while only 4% of those earning $25,000 or more were very dissatisfied with theirs. Similarly, almost 54% of those earning over $25,000 were very satisfied with their jobs, while only 40% of those earning less than $6,000 were very satisfied.

Figure 6.15   Job satisfaction by income level

```
RECODE SATJOB (1=4)(2=3)(3=2)(4=1)(ELSE=SYSMIS).
VALUE LABELS SATJOB 1 'Very Dis' 2 'A Little' 3 'Mod Sat' 4 'Very Sat'.
RECODE RINCOME(1 THRU 5=1)(6 THRU 9=2)(10,11=3) (12=4) (ELSE=SYSMIS).
VALUE LABELS RINCOME 1 '< 6000' 2 '6-15' 3 '15-25' 4 '25+'.
CROSSTABS SATJOB BY RINCOME
   /CELLS=COLUMN COUNT
   /STATISTICS=CHISQ.
```

SATJOB   JOB OR HOUSEWORK   by   RINCOME   RESPONDENT'S INCOME

		RINCOME				
Count Col Pct		< 6000	6-15	15-25	25+	Row
		1	2	3	4	Total
SATJOB						
Very Dis	1	20 9.7	22 7.6	13 5.5	7 4.1	62 6.9
A Little	2	24 11.7	38 13.1	28 11.9	18 10.5	108 12.0
Mod Sat	3	80 38.8	104 36.0	81 34.5	54 31.6	319 35.4
Very Sat	4	82 39.8	125 43.3	113 48.1	92 53.8	412 45.7
Column Total		206 22.9	289 32.1	235 26.1	171 19.0	901 100.0

Chi-Square	Value	DF	Significance
Pearson	11.98857	9	.21395
Likelihood Ratio	12.03690	9	.21124
Mantel-Haenszel test for linear association	9.54552	1	.00200

Minimum Expected Frequency -   11.767

A variety of loglinear models that use the ordering of the job satisfaction and income variables can be considered. Some of the models depend on the "scores" assigned to each category of response. Sometimes these are arbitrary, since the actual distances between the categories are unknown. In this example, scores from 1 to 4 are assigned to both the income and job satisfaction categories. Other scores, such as the midpoints of the salary categories, might also be considered.

Three types of models will be considered for these data. One is the **linear-by-linear association model**, which uses the ordering of both variables. Another is the **row-effects model**, which uses only the ordering of the column variable. The third is the **column-effects model**, which uses the ordering of the row variable.

The Linear-by-Linear Association Model

The linear-by-linear association model for two variables can be expressed as

$$\ln(\hat{F}_{ij}) = \mu + \lambda_i^X + \lambda_j^Y + B(U_i - \overline{U})(V_j - \overline{V})$$

Equation 6.11

where the scores U_i and V_j are assigned to rows and columns. In this model, μ and the two lambda parameters are the usual loglinear terms for the overall mean and the main effects of income and job satisfaction. What differs is the inclusion of the term involving B. The coefficient B is essentially a regression coefficient that, for a particular cell, is multiplied by the scores assigned to that cell for income and job satisfaction. If the two variables are independent, the coefficient should be close to 0. (However, a coefficient of 0 does not necessarily imply independence, since the association between the two variables may be nonlinear.) If the coefficient is positive, more cases are expected to fall in cells with large scores or small scores for both variables than would be expected if the two variables were independent. If the coefficient is negative, an excess of cases is expected in cells that have small values for one variable and large values for the other.

Consider Figure 6.16, which contains the deviation parameter estimates for the linear-by-linear association model for job satisfaction and income. The coefficient labeled B is the regression coefficient. The coefficient is positive and large when compared to its standard error, indicating that there is a positive association between income and job satisfaction. That is, as income increases or decreases, so does job satisfaction. The goodness-of-fit statistics displayed in Figure 6.17 indicate that the linear-by-linear interaction model fits the data very well. Inclusion of one additional parameter in the model has changed the observed significance level from 0.21 for the independence model (see Figure 6.15) to 0.97 for the linear-by-linear interaction model (see Figure 6.17).

Figure 6.16 Parameter estimates for the linear-by-linear model

```
COMPUTE B=RINCOME*SATJOB.
LOGLINEAR SATJOB(1,4) RINCOME(1,4) WITH B
  /PRINT=ESTIM
  /DESIGN=SATJOB RINCOME B.
```

```
Estimates for Parameters

 SATJOB

   Parameter          Coeff.          Std. Err.         Z-Value       Lower 95 CI       Upper 95 CI

          1       -.6373902979            .15514        -4.10855          -.94146           -.33332
          2       -.3298650538            .09273        -3.55723          -.51162           -.14811
          3        .4926713610            .06961         7.07754           .35623            .62911

 RINCOME

   Parameter          Coeff.          Std. Err.         Z-Value       Lower 95 CI       Upper 95 CI

          4        .4628350833            .18277         2.53232           .10460            .82107
          5        .4523050202            .08199         5.51637           .29160            .61301
          6       -.1140864252            .07981        -1.42945          -.27052            .04234

 B

   Parameter          Coeff.          Std. Err.         Z-Value       Lower 95 CI       Upper 95 CI

          7        .1119394092            .03641         3.07462           .04058            .18330
```

Figure 6.17 Goodness of fit for the linear-by-linear model

```
Goodness-of-Fit test statistics

   Likelihood Ratio Chi Square =      2.38592     DF = 8   P =   .967
               Pearson Chi Square =      2.32965     DF = 8   P =   .969
```

Row- and Column-Effects Models

In a row-effects model, only the ordinal nature of the column variable is used. For each row, a separate slope based on the values of the column variables is estimated. The magnitude and sign of the coefficient indicates whether cases are more or less likely to fall in a column with a high or low score, as compared to the independence model.

Consider the row-effects model when job satisfaction is the row variable. The coefficients for each row are displayed in Figure 6.18 under the heading *SATJOB BY COV*. The first coefficient is negative, indicating that very dissatisfied people are less likely to be in high income categories than the independence model would predict. The next two coefficients are positive but small, indicating that there is not much difference from the independence model in these rows. The fourth coefficient, which is not displayed, is the negative of the sum of the previous three coefficients (see "Parameter Estimates" on p. 216). Its value is 0.17, indicating that there is an excess of respondents in the high income category who classify themselves as very satisfied. Overall, the row-effects model fits quite well, as shown in the goodness-of-fit statistics in Figure 6.19. The observed significance level, 0.998, is quite large.

Figure 6.18   Parameter estimates for the row-effects model

```
COMPUTE COV=RINCOME.
LOGLINEAR SATJOB(1,4) RINCOME(1,4) WITH COV
  /PRINT=ESTIM
  /DESIGN=SATJOB, RINCOME, SATJOB BY COV.
```

```
Estimates for Parameters

SATJOB
```

Parameter	Coeff.	Std. Err.	Z-Value	Lower 95 CI	Upper 95 CI
1	-.5315173884	.23757	-2.23727	-.99716	-.06587
2	-.5365551858	.20123	-2.66635	-.93097	-.14214
3	.6100166132	.14540	4.19540	.32503	.89500

```
RINCOME
```

Parameter	Coeff.	Std. Err.	Z-Value	Lower 95 CI	Upper 95 CI
4	.0324159194	.07298	.44420	-.11062	.17545
5	.3101582155	.05654	5.48563	.19934	.42098
6	.0299955391	.05864	.51154	-.08493	.14493

```
SATJOB BY COV
```

Parameter	Coeff.	Std. Err.	Z-Value	Lower 95 CI	Upper 95 CI
7	-.2159732482	.10077	-2.14329	-.41348	-.01847
8	.0340580646	.07897	.43129	-.12072	.18884
9	.0071007552	.05807	.12228	-.10671	.12092

Figure 6.19   Goodness of fit for the row-effects model

```
Goodness-of-Fit test statistics

    Likelihood Ratio Chi Square =    .52562    DF = 6  P =  .998
              Pearson Chi Square =    .52573    DF = 6  P =  .998
```

The column-effects model, which treats job satisfaction as an ordinal variable and ignores the ranking of the income categories, also fits the data reasonably well, as shown in Figure 6.20. The observed significance level is 0.91. In fact, all three models that incorporate the ordinal nature of the classification variables result in good fit. Of the three, the linear-by-linear model is the most parsimonious because when it is compared to the independence model, it estimates only one additional parameter. The row- and column-effects models are particularly useful when only one classification variable is ordinal or when both variables are ordinal but a linear trend across categories exists for only one.

Figure 6.20 Goodness of fit for the column-effects model

```
COMPUTE COV=SATJOB.
LOGLINEAR SATJOB(1,4) RINCOME(1,4) WITH COV
    /DESIGN=SATJOB, RINCOME, COV BY RINCOME.


    Likelihood Ratio Chi Square =      2.13725   DF = 6   P =  .907
              Pearson Chi Square =      2.11052   DF = 6   P =  .909
```

Incomplete Tables

All models examined so far have been based on complete tables. That is, all cells of the crosstabulations can have nonzero observed frequencies. This is not necessarily the case. For example, if you are studying the association between types of surgery and sex of the patient, the cell corresponding to caesarean sections for males must be 0. This is termed a **fixed-zero cell**, since no cases can ever fall into it. Also, certain types of models "ignore" cells by treating them as if they were fixed zeros. Fixed-zero cells lead to incomplete tables, and special provisions must be made during analysis.

Cells in which the observed frequency is 0 but in which it is *possible* to have cases are sometimes called **random zeros**. For example, in a cross-classification of occupation and ethnic origin, the cell corresponding to Lithuanian sword-swallowers would probably be a random zero.

If a table has many cells with small expected values (say, less than 5), the chi-square approximation for the goodness-of-fit statistics may be inadequate. In this case, pooling of categories should be considered.

There are many types of models for analyzing incomplete tables. In the next section, we will consider one of the simplest, the quasi-independence model, which considers the diagonal entries of a square table to be fixed zeros.

Testing Real Against Ideal

What is the "ideal" number of children? The answer to the question is obviously influenced by various factors, including the size of the family in which one was raised. The 1982 General Social Survey asked respondents how many siblings they have as well as how many children should be in the ideal family. Figure 6.21 contains the crosstabulation of the number of children in the respondent's family and the number of children perceived as ideal.

Figure 6.21   Actual number of children by ideal number of children

```
CROSSTABS IDEAL BY REAL
     /CELLS=COLUMN COUNT
     /STATISTICS=CHISQ.

IDEAL   IDEAL NUMBER OF CHILDREN  by  REAL  Actual Number of Children
```

Count Col Pct		REAL 0-1 1.00	2 2.00	3-4 3.00	5 + 4.00	Row Total
IDEAL						
0-1	1	2 2.7	6 3.0	20 4.5	26 3.9	54 3.9
2	2	55 74.3	138 68.7	278 62.3	335 49.7	806 57.8
3-4	3	16 21.6	48 23.9	139 31.2	287 42.6	490 35.1
5 +	4	1 1.4	9 4.5	9 2.0	26 3.9	45 3.2
Column Total		74 5.3	201 14.4	446 32.0	674 48.3	1395 100.0

Chi-Square	Value	DF	Significance
Pearson	46.30172	9	.00000
Likelihood Ratio	47.48080	9	.00000
Mantel-Haenszel test for linear association	23.46950	1	.00000

```
Minimum Expected Frequency -     2.387
Cells with Expected Frequency < 5 -      2 OF    16 ( 12.5%)
```

To test the hypothesis that the actual (real) number of children and the ideal number are independent, the chi-square test of independence can be used. From Figure 6.21, the chi-square value is 46 with nine degrees of freedom. The observed significance level is very small, indicating that it is unlikely that the numbers of real children and ideal children are independent.

Quasi-Independence

There are many reasons why the independence model may not fit the data. One possible explanation is that, in fact, the real and ideal sizes are fairly close to one another. However, if we ignore the diagonal entries of the table, we may find that the remaining cells are independent—in other words, that there is no tendency for children from small families to want large families or children from large families to want small families.

This hypothesis may be tested by ignoring the diagonal entries of the table and testing independence for the remaining cells using the test of **quasi-independence** (cell weighting is used to impose **structural zeros** on diagonal cells). Figure 6.22 contains the observed and expected cell frequencies for this model. Notice that all diagonal entries have values of 0 for observed and expected cell frequencies. However, the residuals and goodness-of-fit statistics indicate that the quasi-independence model does not fit well either.

Figure 6.22   Statistics for the quasi-independence model

```
SET WIDTH=WIDE.
COMPUTE WEIGHT=1.
IF (IDEAL EQ REAL) WEIGHT=0.
LOGLINEAR REAL IDEAL(1,4)
  /CWEIGHT=WEIGHT
  /DESIGN=REAL IDEAL.
```

Observed, Expected Frequencies and Residuals

Factor	Code	OBS. count & PCT.	EXP. count & PCT.	Residual	Std. Resid.	Adj. Resid.
REAL	0-1					
IDEAL	0-1	.00 (.00)	.00 (.00)	.0000	.0000	.0000
IDEAL	2	55.00 (5.05)	39.97 (3.67)	15.0308	2.3775	3.7476
IDEAL	3-4	16.00 (1.47)	30.06 (2.76)	-14.0590	-2.5643	-3.5402
IDEAL	5 +	1.00 (.09)	1.97 (.18)	-.9718	-.6921	-.7423
REAL	2					
IDEAL	0-1	6.00 (.55)	5.34 (.49)	.6554	.2835	.3143
IDEAL	2	.00 (.00)	.00 (.00)	.0000	.0000	.0000
IDEAL	3-4	48.00 (4.40)	54.11 (4.96)	-6.1061	-.8301	-2.3969
IDEAL	5 +	9.00 (.83)	3.55 (.33)	5.4508	2.8933	3.3175
REAL	3-4					
IDEAL	0-1	20.00 (1.83)	20.30 (1.86)	-.2973	-.0660	-.0879
IDEAL	2	278.00 (25.50)	273.22 (25.07)	4.7763	.2890	1.2556
IDEAL	3-4	.00 (.00)	.00 (.00)	.0000	.0000	.0000
IDEAL	5 +	9.00 (.83)	13.48 (1.24)	-4.4790	-1.2200	-2.3296
REAL	5 +					
IDEAL	0-1	26.00 (2.39)	26.36 (2.42)	-.3580	-.0697	-.1025
IDEAL	2	335.00 (30.73)	354.81 (32.55)	-19.8071	-1.0515	-3.7838
IDEAL	3-4	287.00 (26.33)	266.83 (24.48)	20.1652	1.2345	4.4107
IDEAL	5 +	.00 (.00)	.00 (.00)	.0000	.0000	.0000

- -

Goodness-of-Fit test statistics

```
     Likelihood Ratio Chi Square =    24.61341    DF = 5   P =  .000
               Pearson Chi Square =    26.05831    DF = 5   P =  .000
```

Symmetry Models

If the diagonal terms of Figure 6.21 are ignored, the table can be viewed as consisting of two triangles. The lower triangle, shown in Table 6.1, consists of cells in which the ideal number of children is larger than the actual number of children. The upper triangle, shown in Table 6.2, consists of cells in which the ideal number is smaller than the actual number.

Table 6.1   Lower-left triangle 1 (real < ideal)

		Real		
		0-1	2	3-4
	2	55		
Ideal	3-4	16	48	
	5+	1	9	9

Table 6.2   Upper-right (rotated) triangle 2 (real > ideal)

		Ideal		
		0-1	2	3-4
	2	6		
Real	3-4	20	278	
	5+	26	335	287

Several hypotheses about the two triangles may be of interest. One is the symmetry hypothesis. That is, are the corresponding entries of the two triangles equal? In a loglinear model framework, symmetry implies that the main effects for the row and column variables, as well as their interaction, are the same for the two triangles. The loglinear representation of this model is:

$$\ln\,(\hat{F}_{ijk}) \;=\; \mu + \lambda_i^{\text{real}} + \lambda_j^{\text{ideal}} + \lambda_{ij}^{\text{real}*\text{ideal}} \hspace{3cm} \textbf{Equation 6.12}$$

Figure 6.23 contains the Loglinear procedure output for the symmetry hypothesis. The expected values are simply the average of the observed frequencies for the two cells. Thus, the expected values for corresponding cells are always equal. For example, the first expected frequency, 30.5, is the average of 55 and 6. Notice also that the second triangle has been "rotated" into lower-triangular form without changing the variable names, so that the variables are mislabeled in triangle 2. For example, the entry labeled *TRIANGLE 2, IDEAL 2, REAL 0-1* is really the entry for an ideal number of children of 0 or 1 and an actual number of 2.

Figure 6.23 Statistics for the symmetry model

```
SET WIDTH=WIDE.
COMPUTE TRIANGLE=2.
IF (IDEAL GE REAL) TRIANGLE=1.
COMPUTE TEMP=IDEAL.
IF (TRIANGLE EQ 2) IDEAL=REAL.
IF (TRIANGLE EQ 2) REAL=TEMP.
LOGLINEAR TRIANGLE(1,2) IDEAL(2,4) REAL(1,3)
   /CWEIGHT=(1 0 0
             1 1 0
             1 1 1
             1 0 0
             1 1 0
             1 1 1)
      /DESIGN=REAL, IDEAL, REAL BY IDEAL.
```

Observed, Expected Frequencies and Residuals

Factor	Code	OBS. count & PCT.	EXP. count & PCT.	Residual	Std. Resid.	Adj. Resid.
TRIANGLE	1					
IDEAL	2					
REAL	0-1	55.00 (5.05)	30.50 (2.80)	24.5000	4.4363	6.2738
REAL	2	.00 (.00)	.00 (.00)	.0000	.0000	.0000
REAL	3-4	.00 (.00)	.00 (.00)	.0000	.0000	.0000
IDEAL	3-4					
REAL	0-1	16.00 (1.47)	18.00 (1.65)	-2.0000	-.4714	-.6667
REAL	2	48.00 (4.40)	163.00 (14.95)	-115.0000	-9.0075	-12.7385
REAL	3-4	.00 (.00)	.00 (.00)	.0000	.0000	.0000
IDEAL	5 +					
REAL	0-1	1.00 (.09)	13.50 (1.24)	-12.5000	-3.4021	-4.8113
REAL	2	9.00 (.83)	172.00 (15.78)	-163.0000	-12.4286	-17.5767
REAL	3-4	9.00 (.83)	148.00 (13.58)	-139.0000	-11.4257	-16.1584
TRIANGLE	2					
IDEAL	2					
REAL	0-1	6.00 (.55)	30.50 (2.80)	-24.5000	-4.4363	-6.2738
REAL	2	.00 (.00)	.00 (.00)	.0000	.0000	.0000
REAL	3-4	.00 (.00)	.00 (.00)	.0000	.0000	.0000
IDEAL	3-4					
REAL	0-1	20.00 (1.83)	18.00 (1.65)	2.0000	.4714	.6667
REAL	2	278.00 (25.50)	163.00 (14.95)	115.0000	9.0075	12.7385
REAL	3-4	.00 (.00)	.00 (.00)	.0000	.0000	.0000
IDEAL	5 +					
REAL	0-1	26.00 (2.39)	13.50 (1.24)	12.5000	3.4021	4.8113
REAL	2	335.00 (30.73)	172.00 (15.78)	163.0000	12.4286	17.5767
REAL	3-4	287.00 (26.33)	148.00 (13.58)	139.0000	11.4257	16.1584

- -

Goodness-of-Fit test statistics

```
Likelihood Ratio Chi Square =   977.41822    DF = 6   P =  .000
           Pearson Chi Square =   795.25964    DF = 6   P =  .000
```

The goodness-of-fit statistics, as well as the large residuals, indicate that the symmetry model fits poorly. This is not very surprising, since examination of Table 6.1 shows that the number of cases in each triangle is quite disparate.

The symmetry model provides a test of whether the probability of falling into cell (i,j) of triangle 1 is the same as the probability of falling into cell (i,j) of triangle 2. It does not take into account the fact that the overall observed probability of membership in triangle 2 is much greater than the probability of membership in triangle 1.

Since the triangle totals are so disparate, a more reasonable hypothesis to test is whether the probability of falling into corresponding cells in the two triangles is equal, adjusting for the observed totals in the two triangles. In other words, we test whether the probability of falling in cell (i,j) is the same for triangle 1 and triangle 2, assuming that the probability of membership in the two triangles is equal. The expected value for each cell is no longer the average of the observed frequencies for the two triangles but is a weighted average. The weights are the proportion of cases in each triangle. The expected value is the product of the expected probability and the sample size in the triangle.

The symmetry model that preserves triangle totals is represented by the following loglinear model:

$$\ln(\hat{F}_{ijk}) = \mu + \lambda_i^{\text{real}} + \lambda_j^{\text{ideal}} + \lambda_k^{\text{triangle}} + \lambda_{ij}^{\text{real * ideal}} \qquad \text{Equation 6.13}$$

This differs from the previous symmetry model in that the term $\lambda_k^{\text{triangle}}$, which preserves triangle totals, is included.

Figure 6.24 shows a symmetry model that preserves triangle totals. Note that the expected number of cases in the first cell is 7.72. This is 5.59% of the total number of cases in triangle 1. Similarly for triangle 2, the expected number of cases in the first cell is 53.28. This is 5.59% of the cases in triangle 2. Thus, the estimated probabilities are the same for the two triangles, although the actual numbers differ. The residuals and goodness-of-fit tests, however, suggest that a symmetry model preserving the observed totals in the two triangles does not fit the data well either.

Figure 6.24   Statistics for the symmetry model preserving observed totals

```
SET WIDTH=WIDE.
LOGLINEAR TRIANGLE(1,2) IDEAL(2,4) REAL(1,3)
    /CWEIGHT=(1 0 0
             1 1 0
             1 1 1
             1 0 0
             1 1 0
             1 1 1)
    /DESIGN=TRIANGLE, IDEAL, REAL, IDEAL BY REAL.
```

Observed, Expected Frequencies and Residuals

Factor		Code	OBS. count & PCT.	EXP. count & PCT.	Residual	Std. Resid.	Adj. Resid.
TRIANGLE		1					
IDEAL	2						
REAL		0-1	55.00 (5.05)	7.72 (.71)	47.2771	17.0122	18.7353
REAL		2	.00 (.00)	.00 (.00)	.0000	-.0002	-.0002
REAL		3-4	.00 (.00)	.00 (.00)	.0000	.0000	.0000
IDEAL	3-4						
REAL		0-1	16.00 (1.47)	4.56 (.42)	11.4422	5.3596	5.8320
REAL		2	48.00 (4.40)	41.27 (3.79)	6.7266	1.0470	1.3382
REAL		3-4	.00 (.00)	.00 (.00)	.0000	-.0001	-.0001
IDEAL	5+						
REAL		0-1	1.00 (.09)	3.42 (.31)	-2.4183	-1.3080	-1.4173
REAL		2	9.00 (.83)	43.55 (4.00)	-34.5523	-5.2357	-6.7719
REAL		3-4	9.00 (.83)	37.48 (3.44)	-28.4752	-4.6515	-5.8317
TRIANGLE		2					
IDEAL	2						
REAL		0-1	6.00 (.55)	53.28 (4.89)	-47.2771	-6.4771	-18.7353
REAL		2	.00 (.00)	.00 (.00)	.0000	-.0004	-.0004
REAL		3-4	.00 (.00)	.00 (.00)	.0000	-.0001	.0000
IDEAL	3-4						
REAL		0-1	20.00 (1.83)	31.44 (2.88)	-11.4422	-2.0406	-5.8320
REAL		2	278.00 (25.50)	284.73 (26.12)	-6.7266	-.3986	-1.3382
REAL		3-4	.00 (.00)	.00 (.00)	.0000	-.0004	-.0004
IDEAL	5+						
REAL		0-1	26.00 (2.39)	23.58 (2.16)	2.4183	.4980	1.4173
REAL		2	335.00 (30.73)	300.45 (27.56)	34.5523	1.9934	6.7719
REAL		3-4	287.00 (26.33)	258.52 (23.72)	28.4752	1.7710	5.8317

Goodness-of-Fit test statistics

```
Likelihood Ratio Chi Square =   294.50141    DF = 5  P =  .000
           Pearson Chi Square =   423.62825    DF = 5  P =  .000
```

Adjusted Quasi-Symmetry

The previously described symmetry model preserves only totals in each triangle. It does not require that the row and column sums for the expected values equal the observed row and column sums. The original crosstabulation shows that the marginal distributions of real and ideal children are quite different. The **adjusted quasi-symmetry model** can be used to test whether the pattern of association in the two triangles is similar when row and column totals are preserved in each triangle.

The loglinear model for adjusted quasi-symmetry is:

$$\ln\left(\hat{F}_{ijk}\right) = \mu + \lambda_i^{\text{real}} + \lambda_j^{\text{ideal}} + \lambda_k^{\text{triangle}} + \lambda_{ij}^{\text{real}*\text{ideal}}$$
$$+ \lambda_{ik}^{\text{real}*\text{triangle}} + \lambda_{jk}^{\text{ideal}*\text{triangle}}$$

Equation 6.14

This model differs from the completely saturated model for the three variables only in that it does not contain the three-way interaction among number of real children, number of ideal children, and triangle number. Thus, the adjusted quasi-symmetry model tests whether the three-way interaction is significantly different from 0.

Figure 6.25 contains the goodness-of-fit statistics for the quasi-symmetry model. The small chi-square value suggests that there is no reason to believe that the model does not fit well. However, there is only one degree of freedom for the model, since many parameters have been estimated.

Figure 6.25   Statistics for the adjusted quasi-symmetry model

```
SET WIDTH=WIDE.
LOGLINEAR TRIANGLE (1,2) IDEAL(2,4) REAL(1,3)
 /CWEIGHT=(1 0 0
           1 1 0
           1 1 1
           1 0 0
           1 1 0
           1 1 1)
 /DESIGN=TRIANGLE, REAL, IDEAL, REAL BY IDEAL, TRIANGLE BY REAL, TRIANGLE BY IDEAL.
```

Observed, Expected Frequencies and Residuals

Factor	Code	OBS. count & PCT.	EXP. count & PCT.	Residual	Std. Resid.	Adj. Resid.
TRIANGLE	1					
IDEAL	2					
REAL	0-1	55.00 (5.05)	55.00 (5.05)	.0000	.0000	.0004
REAL	2	.00 (.00)	.00 (.00)	.0000	-.0004	-.0004
REAL	3-4	.00 (.00)	.00 (.00)	.0000	-.0001	.0000
IDEAL	3-4					
REAL	0-1	16.00 (1.47)	14.76 (1.35)	1.2352	.3215	1.0756
REAL	2	48.00 (4.40)	49.24 (4.52)	-1.2352	-.1760	-1.0756
REAL	3-4	.00 (.00)	.00 (.00)	.0000	-.0002	-.0002
IDEAL	5+					
REAL	0-1	1.00 (.09)	2.24 (.21)	-1.2352	-.8262	-1.0756
REAL	2	9.00 (.83)	7.76 (.71)	1.2352	.4433	1.0756
REAL	3-4	9.00 (.83)	9.00 (.83)	.0000	.0000	.0002
TRIANGLE	2					
IDEAL	2					
REAL	0-1	6.00 (.55)	6.00 (.55)	.0000	.0000	.0002
REAL	2	.00 (.00)	.00 (.00)	.0000	-.0002	-.0002
REAL	3-4	.00 (.00)	.00 (.00)	.0000	.0000	.0000
IDEAL	3-4					
REAL	0-1	20.00 (1.83)	21.24 (1.95)	-1.2352	-.2681	-1.0756
REAL	2	278.00 (25.50)	276.76 (25.39)	1.2352	.0742	1.0756
REAL	3-4	.00 (.00)	.00 (.00)	.0000	-.0004	-.0004
IDEAL	5+					
REAL	0-1	26.00 (2.39)	24.76 (2.27)	1.2352	.2482	1.0756
REAL	2	335.00 (30.73)	336.24 (30.85)	-1.2352	-.0674	-1.0756
REAL	3-4	287.00 (26.33)	287.00 (26.33)	.0000	.0000	.0004

Goodness-of-Fit test statistics

```
      Likelihood Ratio Chi Square =    1.32440    DF = 1  P =  .250
              Pearson Chi Square =     1.15697    DF = 1  P =  .282
```

An Ordinal Model for Real versus Ideal

Although the various symmetry models provide information about the relationship between the two triangles of a square table, we might wish to develop a more general model for the association between number of siblings in a family and one's view on the ideal number of children. The ordinal models considered in "Models for Ordinal Data" on p. 202 through "Row- and Column-Effects Models" on p. 205 might be a good place to start.

Figure 6.21 reveals that two children seems to be the most popular number. However, as the number of real children in a family increases, so does the tendency toward a larger ideal family size. For example, only 21.6% of only children consider three to four children to be ideal. Almost 43% of those from families of five or more children consider three or four children to be optimal. Thus, we might consider a row-effects model that incorporates the ordinal nature of the real number of children. Figure 6.26 contains the statistics for the row-effects model. The large observed significance level and small residuals indicate that the model fits reasonably well.

Figure 6.26   Statistics for the row-effects ordinal model

```
SET WIDTH=WIDE.
COMPUTE COV=REAL.
LOGLINEAR IDEAL REAL (1,4) WITH COV
  /DESIGN=IDEAL, REAL, COV BY IDEAL.
```

Observed, Expected Frequencies and Residuals

Factor		Code	OBS. count & PCT.	EXP. count & PCT.	Residual	Std. Resid.	Adj. Resid.
IDEAL		0-1					
REAL		0-1	2.00 (.14)	2.26 (.16)	-.2621	-.1742	-.2196
REAL		2	6.00 (.43)	7.02 (.50)	-1.0168	-.3838	-.5189
REAL		3-4	20.00 (1.43)	17.18 (1.23)	2.8197	.6803	.8651
REAL		5 +	26.00 (1.86)	27.54 (1.97)	-1.5409	-.2936	-.8027
IDEAL		2					
REAL		0-1	55.00 (3.94)	56.98 (4.08)	-1.9848	-.2629	-.6737
REAL		2	138.00 (9.89)	139.41 (9.99)	-1.4129	-.1197	-.2885
REAL		3-4	278.00 (19.93)	269.22 (19.30)	8.7801	.5351	1.0663
REAL		5 +	335.00 (24.01)	340.38 (24.40)	-5.3824	-.2917	-1.1155
IDEAL		3-4					
REAL		0-1	16.00 (1.15)	13.08 (.94)	2.9156	.8060	1.0759
REAL		2	48.00 (3.44)	49.11 (3.52)	-1.1141	-.1590	-.2443
REAL		3-4	139.00 (9.96)	145.52 (10.43)	-6.5184	-.5404	-.8302
REAL		5 +	287.00 (20.57)	282.28 (20.24)	4.7170	.2808	1.0304
IDEAL		5 +					
REAL		0-1	1.00 (.07)	1.67 (.12)	-.6687	-.5177	-.6410
REAL		2	9.00 (.65)	5.46 (.39)	3.5438	1.5172	2.0459
REAL		3-4	9.00 (.65)	14.08 (1.01)	-5.0814	-1.3541	-1.7244
REAL		5 +	26.00 (1.86)	23.79 (1.71)	2.2063	.4523	1.2775

Goodness-of-Fit test statistics

```
Likelihood Ratio Chi Square =    6.71177    DF = 6   P =  .348
            Pearson Chi Square =    6.83537    DF = 6   P =  .336
```

Parameter Estimates

Once an adequate model has been identified, you can examine the parameter estimates to assess the effects of the individual categories of the variables. Several different types of parameter estimates, corresponding to different types of contrasts, can be obtained. Consider Table 6.3, which contains the expected cell frequencies for the row-effects model previously described. The natural logs of the expected cell frequencies are displayed in Table 6.4.

Table 6.3   Expected cell frequencies for the row-effects model

		Real			
		0–1	2	3–4	5
	0–1	2.26	7.02	17.18	27.54
	2	56.98	139.41	269.22	340.38
Ideal	3–4	13.08	49.11	145.52	282.28
	5+	1.67	5.46	14.08	23.79

Table 6.4   Natural logs of the expected cell frequencies

		Real				
		0–1	2	3–4	5	Average
	0–1	0.815	1.949	2.844	3.316	
	2	4.043	4.937	5.595	5.830	
Ideal	3–4	2.571	3.894	4.980	5.643	
	5+	0.513	1.697	2.645	3.169	
	Average	1.986	3.119	4.016	4.4895	3.403

From Table 6.4, parameter estimates can be obtained for both variables. We will restrict our attention to estimates for the *real* variable, since they can be obtained from the column averages and the grand mean. Estimates for the *ideal* variable are a little more complicated to obtain, since the covariate effect must be eliminated from the row entries.

Often it is desirable to compare each effect to the grand mean. The parameter estimate for a category is its difference from the overall mean. These types of estimates are called **deviation parameter estimates**. (They are included in the default Loglinear procedure output if parameter estimates are requested.) For the first category of the *real* variable, the value of the deviation parameter estimate is $1.986 - 3.403 = -1.417$. Similarly, for the second category, it is $3.119 - 3.403 = -0.284$. These values are shown in the output displayed in Figure 6.27. The value for the last category is not displayed and must be estimated as the negative of the sum of the previous values, since the sum of deviations about the mean is 0.

Figure 6.27 Deviation parameter estimates

```
COMPUTE COV=REAL.
LOGLINEAR IDEAL REAL(1,4) WITH COV
 /CONTRAST(REAL)=DEVIATION
 /PRINT=ESTIM
 /DESIGN=IDEAL REAL COV BY IDEAL.

REAL
```

Parameter	Coeff.	Std. Err.	Z-Value	Lower 95 CI	Upper 95 CI
4	-1.4169683119	.12503	-11.33288	-1.66203	-1.17191
5	-.2834476028	.06767	-4.18893	-.41607	-.15082
6	.6135052404	.05876	10.44092	.49834	.72867

Difference contrasts are obtained by comparing the level of a factor with the average effects of the previous levels of the factor. For example, the first parameter estimate in Figure 6.28 is just the difference between the mean of the second category and the mean of the first category, or $3.119 - 1.986 = 1.133$. Similarly, the second parameter estimate is obtained by comparing the third category of the *real* variable to the average of the first two categories. Thus, the difference parameter estimate for the third level of the *real* variable is calculated as:

$$-0.5 \times 1.986 - 0.5 \times 3.119 + 4.016 = 1.463 \qquad \text{Equation 6.15}$$

This value is displayed in Figure 6.28 as the fifth parameter estimate. For the fourth category, the value is:

$$-0.33 \times 1.986 - 0.33 \times 3.119 - 0.33 \times 4.016 + 4.4895 = 1.449 \qquad \text{Equation 6.16}$$

Note that difference parameter estimates, unlike deviation parameter estimates, do not sum to 0 over all categories of a variable.

Figure 6.28 Difference parameter estimates

```
COMPUTE COV=REAL.
LOGLINEAR IDEAL REAL(1,4) WITH COV
 /CONTRAST(REAL)=DIFFERENCE
 /PRINT=ESTIM
 /DESIGN=IDEAL REAL COV BY IDEAL.

REAL
```

Parameter	Coeff.	Std. Err.	Z-Value	Lower 95 CI	Upper 95 CI
4	1.1335207090	.14907	7.60383	.84134	1.42570
5	1.4637131978	.11986	12.21180	1.22879	1.69864
6	1.4492142324	.12597	11.50452	1.20231	1.69611

When the last category of a variable is considered a reference category—for example, when it corresponds to a control group—all parameter estimates can be expressed as deviations from it. These are called **simple contrasts**. For example, for the first category of the *real* variable, the parameter estimate corresponding to a simple contrast is

$1.986 - 4.490 = -2.504$. Similarly, for the second category, it is $3.119 - 4.490 = -1.370$. The value for the fourth category, which is not displayed, is 0, since this category is the comparison category (see Figure 6.29).

Figure 6.29   Simple parameter estimates

```
COMPUTE COV=REAL.
LOGLINEAR IDEAL REAL(1,4) WITH COV
 /CONTRAST(REAL)=SIMPLE
 /PRINT=ESTIM
 /DESIGN=IDEAL REAL COV BY IDEAL.

REAL
```

Parameter	Coeff.	Std. Err.	Z-Value	Lower 95 CI	Upper 95 CI
4	-2.5038789861	.20842	-12.01359	-2.91238	-2.09537
5	-1.3703582771	.13527	-10.13055	-1.63549	-1.10523
6	-.4734054338	.08097	-5.84648	-.63211	-.31470

When the categories of a variable are ordered, parameter estimates corresponding to linear, quadratic, and higher-order **polynomial effects** can be obtained, as shown in Figure 6.30. The first coefficient is for the linear effect, the second is for the quadratic effect, and the third is for the cubic effect. From the large Z value, it appears that there is a significant linear and quadratic component.

Figure 6.30   Polynomial parameter estimates

```
COMPUTE COV=REAL.
LOGLINEAR IDEAL REAL(1,4) WITH COV
 /CONTRAST(REAL)=POLYNOMIAL
 /PRINT=ESTIM
 /DESIGN=IDEAL REAL COV BY IDEAL.

REAL
```

Parameter	Coeff.	Std. Err.	Z-Value	Lower 95 CI	Upper 95 CI
4	1.8802178391	.15137	12.42113	1.58353	2.17691
5	-.3300576376	.07536	-4.38000	-.47775	-.18236
6	-.0418098970	.06323	-.66123	-.16574	.08212

The Design Matrix

The Loglinear procedure also displays a design matrix, as shown in Figure 6.31. The columns of the matrix correspond to the parameter estimates for an effect. The number of columns for an effect is equal to its degrees of freedom. As indicated in the table labeled *Correspondence Between Effects and Columns of Design*, the first three columns of Figure 6.31 are for the *ideal* variable, the next three are for the *real* variable (for which polynomial contrasts are shown), and the last three are for the *ideal*-by-*cov* (the cell covariate) effect.

Figure 6.31   Design matrix

```
SET WIDTH=WIDE.
COMPUTE COV=REAL.
LOGLINEAR IDEAL REAL(1,4) WITH COV
  /CONTRAST(REAL)=POLYNOMIAL
  /PRINT=ALL
  /DESIGN=IDEAL REAL COV BY IDEAL.
```

Correspondence Between Effects and Columns of Design/Model 4

Starting Column	Ending Column	Effect Name
1	3	IDEAL
4	6	REAL
7	9	COV BY IDEAL

- -

Design Matrix

1-IDEAL   2-REAL

Factor		Parameter								
1	2	1	2	3	4	5	6	7	8	9
1	1	1.00000	.00000	.00000	-.67082	.50000	-.22361	1.00000	.00000	.00000
1	2	1.00000	.00000	.00000	-.22361	-.50000	.67082	2.00000	.00000	.00000
1	3	1.00000	.00000	.00000	.22361	-.50000	-.67082	3.00000	.00000	.00000
1	4	1.00000	.00000	.00000	.67082	.50000	.22361	4.00000	.00000	.00000
2	1	.00000	1.00000	.00000	-.67082	.50000	-.22361	.00000	1.00000	.00000
2	2	.00000	1.00000	.00000	-.22361	-.50000	.67082	.00000	2.00000	.00000
2	3	.00000	1.00000	.00000	.22361	-.50000	-.67082	.00000	3.00000	.00000
2	4	.00000	1.00000	.00000	.67082	.50000	.22361	.00000	4.00000	.00000
3	1	.00000	.00000	1.00000	-.67082	.50000	-.22361	.00000	.00000	1.00000
3	2	.00000	.00000	1.00000	-.22361	-.50000	.67082	.00000	.00000	2.00000
3	3	.00000	.00000	1.00000	.22361	-.50000	-.67082	.00000	.00000	3.00000
3	4	.00000	.00000	1.00000	.67082	.50000	.22361	.00000	.00000	4.00000
4	1	-1.00000	-1.00000	-1.00000	-.67082	.50000	-.22361	-1.00000	-1.00000	-1.00000
4	2	-1.00000	-1.00000	-1.00000	-.22361	-.50000	.67082	-2.00000	-2.00000	-2.00000
4	3	-1.00000	-1.00000	-1.00000	.22361	-.50000	-.67082	-3.00000	-3.00000	-3.00000
4	4	-1.00000	-1.00000	-1.00000	.67082	.50000	.22361	-4.00000	-4.00000	-4.00000

When orthogonal contrasts are requested for a variable (when the sum of the product of corresponding coefficients for any two contrasts is 0), the numbers in the columns are the coefficients of the linear combinations of the logs of the predicted cell frequencies. For example, since polynomial contrasts are requested in Figure 6.31 for the *real* variable and they are orthogonal, column 4 contains the coefficients for the linear effect, column 5 contains the coefficients for the quadratic effect, and column 6 contains the coefficients for the cubic effect. The parameter estimate for the quadratic effect is calculated as:

$$(0.5(0.815 + 3.316 + 4.043 + 5.830 + 2.571 + 5.643 + 0.513 \\ + 3.169) - 0.5(1.949 + 2.844 + 4.937 + 5.595 + 3.894 + 4.980 \\ + 1.697 + 2.645))/4 = -0.33$$

Equation 6.17

The linear combination of the cell means is divided by the sum of all of the coefficients squared. In this example, that sum is $16 \times 0.5^2 = 4$. The value of -0.33 corresponds to the parameter estimate for the quadratic effect displayed in Figure 6.30. The estimates for the linear and cubic effects can be obtained in a similar fashion using the coefficients in columns 4 and 6.

The Loglinear procedure uses a **reparameterized model**. When nonorthogonal contrasts, such as deviation and simple, are requested for an effect, the columns of the design matrix for that effect are not the contrast coefficients. Instead, they are the *basis* for the requested contrasts (see Bock, 1975; Finn, 1974). For example, in Figure 6.31, the default deviation contrasts are used for the *ideal* variable. The three columns for the *ideal* effect, however, contain coefficients for simple contrasts, the basis for deviation contrasts. The parameter estimates displayed correspond to those requested in the contrast specification; in this case, deviation for the *ideal* variable and polynomial for the *real* variable.

When covariates are included in a model, they also occur in the design matrix. In this example the covariate values are just the scores from 1 to 4. For each cell, these scores are multiplied by the corresponding entries of the first three columns to obtain the entries for the covariate-by-*ideal* interaction effects in Figure 6.31. Covariates in the Loglinear procedure are treated as cell covariates. That is, all cases in the cell are assumed to have the same value for the covariate. If all cases in the cell do not have the same covariate value, the cell average is used to represent all cases in that cell. This will, in general, give different results from models that adjust for covariates on a case-by-case basis.

Running the Loglinear Procedure

The Loglinear procedure can be used to fit many different types of models, including logit models and nonhierarchical loglinear models. Parameter estimates can be obtained for all types of models. For hierarchical models, the Hierarchical Loglinear procedure, which uses an iterative proportional fitting algorithm, may require less computing time. However, parameter estimates for unsaturated models cannot be obtained in HILOGLINEAR.

The LOGLINEAR command must begin with a list of variables, optionally followed by one or more subcommands. One model is produced for each DESIGN subcommand. All subcommands can be used more than once and, with the exception of the DESIGN subcommand, are carried from model to model unless explicitly overridden. The subcommands that affect a DESIGN subcommand should be placed before that DESIGN subcommand. If the last specified subcommand is not DESIGN, LOGLINEAR generates a saturated model as the last design.

Specifying Variables in the Equation

The only required specification for LOGLINEAR is a list of all variables used in the models specified on the command. LOGLINEAR analyzes two classes of variables: categorical and continuous. Categorical variables are used to define the cells of the table. Continuous variables can be used as covariates.

Categorical variables must be numeric and integer. You must specify a range in parentheses indicating the minimum and maximum values, as in:

```
LOGLINEAR ZODIAC(1,12) RINCOME(1,4).
```

This command builds a 12 × 4 frequency table for analysis. The model produced is a general loglinear model, since no BY keyword appears. The design defaults to a saturated model in which all main effects and interaction effects are fitted.

Cases with values outside the specified range are excluded from the analysis, and non-integer values within the range are truncated for purposes of building the table. The value range specified must match the values in the data. That is, if the range specified for a variable is 1 and 4, there should be cases for values 1, 2, 3, and 4. Empty categories are not allowed. Use the RECODE command to assign successive integer values to factor levels.

If several variables have the same range, you can specify the range following the last variable in the list, as in

```
LOGLINEAR ZODIAC(1,12) REAL IDEAL(1,4).
```

where *zodiac* has twelve values ranging from 1 to 12, and both *real* and *ideal* have four values ranging from 1 to 4.

Specifying Independent Variables: BY Keyword

Use the BY keyword to separate the independent variables from the dependent variables in a logit model, as in:

```
LOGLINEAR SATJOB(1,2) BY ZODIAC(1,12).
```

Categorical variables preceding the keyword BY are the dependent variables; categorical variables following the keyword BY are the independent variables. Usually, you also specify a DESIGN subcommand to request the desired logit model (see "Specifying the Design" on p. 222).

Specifying Cell Covariates: WITH Keyword

Use the WITH keyword to specify cell covariates at the end of the variables specification, as in:

```
LOGLINEAR ZODIAC(1,12) SATJOB(1,2) WITH B.
```

To enter cell covariates into the model, you must specify them on the DESIGN subcommand (see "Specifying the Design" on p. 222). "The Design Matrix" on p. 218 discusses computations involving covariates in LOGLINEAR.

Specifying the Design

Use the DESIGN subcommand to specify the model or models to fit. If you do not specify the DESIGN subcommand or if you specify it without naming any variables on it, the default is a saturated model, in which all interaction effects are fit.

You can use multiple DESIGN subcommands, each specifying one model. Variables named on DESIGN must have been specified on the initial list of variables (see "Specifying Variables in the Equation" on p. 221).

Main-Effects Models

To test for independence, a model with only main effects is fit. For example, to test that *zodiac* and *satjob* are independent, specify:

```
LOGLINEAR ZODIAC(1,12) SATJOB(1,2)
   /DESIGN=ZODIAC SATJOB.
```

Interactions

Use the BY keyword to specify interaction terms. For example, to fit the saturated model that consists of the *zodiac* main effect, the *satjob* main effect, and the interaction of *zodiac* by *satjob*, specify:

```
LOGLINEAR ZODIAC(1,12) SATJOB(1,2)
   /DESIGN=ZODIAC, SATJOB, ZODIAC BY SATJOB.
```

For the general loglinear model, this DESIGN specification is the same as the default model. Thus, the specification

```
LOGLINEAR ZODIAC(1,12) SATJOB(1,2)
   /DESIGN.
```

is equivalent to the preceding one.

Including Covariates in the Design

To include covariates, you must first identify them on the LOGLINEAR variable list by naming them after the keyword WITH. Then, simply specify the covariate on the DESIGN subcommand, as in:

```
LOGLINEAR ZODIAC(1,12) SATJOB(1,2) WITH COV
   /DESIGN=ZODIAC SATJOB COV.
```

You can specify an interaction of a covariate and an independent variable. However, a covariate-by-covariate interaction is not allowed. Instead, use the COMPUTE command to create interaction variables (see "The Linear-by-Linear Association Model" on p. 204). For example, for a linear-by-linear association model, specify:

```
COMPUTE B=SATJOB*RINCOME.
LOGLINEAR SATJOB(1,2) RINCOME(1,4) WITH B
  /DESIGN=SATJOB RINCOME B.
```

To specify an equiprobability model, use a covariate that is actually a constant of 1, as in:

```
COMPUTE X=1.
LOGLINEAR ZODIAC(1,12) WITH X
  /DESIGN=X.
```

This model tests whether the frequencies in the 12-cell table are equal (see "Frequency Table Models" on p. 189).

Single-Degree-of-Freedom Partitions

A variable followed by an integer in parentheses refers to a single-degree-of-freedom partition of a specified contrast. For example, you can specify the row-effects model described in "Row- and Column-Effects Models" on p. 205, as in

```
LOGLINEAR SATJOB(1,4) RINCOME(1,4)
  /CONTRAST(RINCOME)=POLYNOMIAL
  /PRINT=ESTIM
  /DESIGN=SATJOB, RINCOME, SATJOB BY RINCOME(1).
```

where RINCOME(1) refers to the first partition of *rincome*, which is the linear effect of *rincome*, since a polynomial contrast is specified.

Similarly, to fit the quadratic model for the season data (see "Fitting a Quadratic Function" on p. 190), specify:

```
LOGLINEAR SEASON(1,4)
  /CONTRAST(SEASON)=POLYNOMIAL
  /PRINT=ESTIM
  /DESIGN=SEASON(1) SEASON(2).
```

The actual parameter estimates for SEASON(1) and SEASON(2) will differ from those displayed in Figure 6.4, since the polynomial contrasts are orthonormalized. The ratio of the estimate to the standard error and other statistics will be the same for the two specifications.

Specifying Cell Weights

Use the CWEIGHT subcommand to specify cell weights for the model. By default, cell weights are equal to 1. You can specify either a matrix of weights or a numeric variable, as in:

```
LOGLINEAR REAL IDEAL(1,4)
  /CWEIGHT=CWT.
```

This is useful for specifying structural zeros.

Only one variable can be named as a weight variable. You can specify multiple CWEIGHT subcommands per LOGLINEAR command, but if you do, you cannot name a weight variable. The CWEIGHT subcommands must all specify matrices of weights.

If you specify a matrix of weights, the matrix is enclosed in parentheses and its elements are separated by blanks, commas, or both. The matrix must contain the same number of elements as the product of the levels of the categorical variables. If you specify weights for a multiple-variable model, the index value of the rightmost variable increases most rapidly. For example, the command

```
LOGLINEAR TRIANGLE(1,2)  IDEAL(2,4)  REAL(1,3)
  /CWEIGHT=(1 0 0
            1 1 0
            1 1 1
            1 0 0
            1 1 0
            1 1 1).
```

assigns cell weights as follows:

TRIANGLE	IDEAL	REAL	Weight	TRIANGLE	IDEAL	REAL	Weight
1	2	1	1	2	2	1	1
1	2	2	0	2	2	2	0
1	2	3	0	2	2	3	0
1	3	1	1	2	3	1	1
1	3	2	1	2	3	2	1
1	3	3	0	2	3	3	0
1	4	1	1	2	4	1	1
1	4	2	1	2	4	2	1
1	4	3	1	2	4	3	1

You can use the notation $n*c$ to indicate that value c is repeated n times, as in:

```
LOGLINEAR TRIANGLE(1,2)  IDEAL(2,4)  REAL(1,3)
  /CWEIGHT=(1 0 0 1 1 0 3*1 1 0 0 1 1 0 3*1).
```

The CWEIGHT specification remains in effect until explicitly overridden with another CWEIGHT subcommand. For example, the command

```
LOGLINEAR A B (1,4)
  /CWEIGHT=(0 4*1 0 4*1 0 4*1 0)
  /DESIGN=A B
  /CWEIGHT=(16*1)
  /DESIGN=A B.
```

uses a second CWEIGHT subcommand to return to the default cell weights.

You can use CWEIGHT to impose fixed zeros on the model (see "Incomplete Tables" on p. 207). This feature is useful in the analysis of incomplete tables. For example, to impose fixed zeros on the diagonal of a symmetric crosstabulation table, specify:

```
COMPUTE CWT=1.
IF (REAL EQ IDEAL) CWT=0.
LOGLINEAR REAL IDEAL(1,4)
  /CWEIGHT=CWT.
```

These commands set *cwt* equal to 0 when *real* equals *ideal*. Alternatively, you can specify a CWEIGHT matrix, as in:

```
/CWEIGHT=(0 4*1 0 4*1 0 4*1 0)
```

Calculating Generalized Residual

Use the GRESID subcommand to produce linear combinations of observed cell frequencies, expected cell frequencies, and adjusted residuals. Specify one or more variables, or a matrix whose contents are the coefficients of the desired linear combinations. The matrix specification for GRESID is the same as for CWEIGHT (see "Specifying Cell Weights" on p. 223). You can specify multiple GRESID subcommands, only one of which can specify a variable name. If you specify a matrix, it must contain as many elements as the number of cells implied by the variables specification, as in:

```
LOGLINEAR ZODIAC(1,12)
  /GRESID=(3*1 9*0)
  /GRESID=(3*0 3*1 6*0)
  /GRESID=(6*0 3*1 3*0)
  /GRESID=(9*0 3*1).
```

The first GRESID subcommand combines the first three signs into a spring effect, the second subcommand combines the second three signs into a summer effect, and the last two subcommands form the fall and winter effects. For each effect, LOGLINEAR displays the observed and expected counts, the residual, the standardized residual, and the adjusted residual.

Requesting or Suppressing Output

Use the PRINT and NOPRINT subcommands to control the statistical output. PRINT displays the named statistics, and NOPRINT suppresses them. You can use the following keywords on both the PRINT and NOPRINT subcommands:

FREQ   *Observed and expected cell frequencies and percentages.* This is the default if neither subcommand is specified.

RESID   *Raw, standardized, and adjusted residuals.* This is the default if neither subcommand is specified.

DESIGN   *The design matrix of the model, showing the basis matrix corresponding to the contrasts used in the model.*

ESTIM   *The parameter estimates of the model.* If you do not specify a design on the DESIGN subcommand, LOGLINEAR generates a saturated model and displays the parameter estimates for the saturated model by default. SPSS/PC+ centers all covariates, so parameter estimates for constant covariates are always 0.

COR   *The correlation matrix of the parameter estimates.*

ALL   *All available output.*

DEFAULT   *FREQ and RESID.* ESTIM is also displayed by default if the DESIGN subcommand is not used.

NONE   *None of the available output.* NONE on PRINT suppresses all statistics except goodness-of-fit. NONE on NOPRINT displays all available output.

You can specify multiple PRINT and NOPRINT subcommands. The effect is cumulative.

Example

```
LOGLINEAR SATJOB(1,2) RINCOME(1,4)
  /PRINT=ESTIM
  /DESIGN=SATJOB, RINCOME, SATJOB BY RINCOME
  /PRINT=ALL
  /DESIGN=SATJOB RINCOME.
```

- The first design is the saturated model. Since it fits the data exactly, you do not want to see the frequencies and residuals. Instead, you want to see parameter estimates, which are requested by `PRINT=ESTIM`.

- The second design is the main-effects model, which implicitly tests the hypothesis of independence. The PRINT subcommand displays all available display output for this model.

Requesting Plots

Use the PLOT subcommand to request optional plots. No plots are displayed if PLOT is not specified.

RESID   *Plots of adjusted residuals against observed and expected counts.*

NORMPROB   *Normal and detrended normal plots of the adjusted residuals.*

NONE   *No plots.* This is the default if the PLOT subcommand is omitted.

DEFAULT   *RESID and NORMPROB.* These are the defaults if you specify PLOT without keywords.

You can use multiple PLOT subcommands on one LOGLINEAR command. The effect is cumulative. For example,

```
LOGLINEAR RESPONSE(1,2) BY TIME(1,4)
  /CONTRAST(TIME)=SPECIAL(4*1 7 14 27 51 8*1)
  /PLOT=RESID NORMPROB
  /DESIGN=RESPONSE TIME(1) BY RESPONSE
  /PLOT=NONE
  /DESIGN.
```

displays residual and normal probability plots for the first design and no plots for the second design.

Processing Categorical Variables

Use the CONTRAST subcommand to specify the type of contrast for a categorical variable. Specify the variable name in parentheses after the CONTRAST subcommand, followed by the name of the contrast type. For example,

```
LOGLINEAR SATJOB(1,2) RINCOME(1,4)
  /CONTRAST(RINCOME)=POLYNOMIAL.
```

applies a polynomial contrast to *rincome*.

In LOGLINEAR, contrasts do not have to sum to 0 or be orthogonal. The following contrasts are available:

DEVIATION(refcat)   *Deviations from the overall effect.* These are the default parameter estimates in LOGLINEAR. Refcat is the category for which parameter estimates are not displayed (they must be obtained as the negative of the sum of the others). By default, refcat is the last category of the variable.

DIFFERENCE   *Compare levels of a variable with the average effect of previous levels of a variable.* Also known as reverse Helmert contrasts.

HELMERT   *Compare levels of a variable with the average effect of subsequent levels of a variable.*

SIMPLE(refcat)   *Compare each level of a variable to the last level.* You can specify a value for refcat enclosed in parentheses after the keyword SIMPLE. By default, it is the last category of the variable.

REPEATED   *Compare adjacent levels of a variable.*

POLYNOMIAL(metric)   *Orthogonal polynomial contrasts.* The default metric is equal spacing (see "Parameter Estimates" on p. 216 and "The Design Matrix" on p. 218). Optionally, you can specify the coefficients of the linear polynomial in parentheses, indicating the spacing between levels of the treatment measured by the contrast variable.

[BASIS]	*User-defined contrast.* You must specify as many elements as
SPECIAL(matrix)	square of the number of categories. If BASIS is specified, a basis
	matrix is generated for the special contrast. Otherwise, the matrix
	specified is the basis matrix.

For further illustration of contrast types, see Appendix A.

Only one contrast is in effect for each variable on a DESIGN subcommand. If you do not use the CONTRAST subcommand, the contrast defaults to DEVIATION. You must use separate CONTRAST subcommands for each variable for which you specify contrasts. A contrast specification remains in effect for subsequent designs until explicitly overridden with another CONTRAST subcommand, as in:

```
LOGLINEAR SATJOB(1,2) RINCOME(1,4)
  /CONTRAST(RINCOME)=POLYNOMIAL
  /DESIGN=SATJOB, RINCOME, SATJOB BY RINCOME(1)
  /CONTRAST(RINCOME)=SIMPLE
  /DESIGN=SATJOB, RINCOME.
```

The first CONTRAST subcommand requests polynomial contrasts of *rincome* for the first design. The second CONTRAST subcommand, for the second DESIGN subcommand, requests SIMPLE contrasts of *rincome*, with the last category (value 4) used as the reference category.

You can display the design matrix used for the contrasts by specifying the DESIGN keyword on the PRINT subcommand (see "The Design Matrix" on p. 218).

Specifying Parameters

Use the CRITERIA subcommand to specify the values of some constants in the Newton-Raphson algorithm, the estimation algorithm used in LOGLINEAR.

CONVERGE(n)	*Convergence criterion.* Specify the convergence criterion n in parentheses. The default is 0.001.
ITERATION(n)	*Maximum number of iterations.* Specify n as the maximum number of iterations for the algorithm. The default is 20.
DELTA(d)	*Cell delta value.* The value d is added to each cell frequency before analysis. The default value is 0.5. Delta remains in the cells only for saturated models.
DEFAULT	*Default values.* Use DEFAULT to reset the parameters to the default.

For example, to increase the maximum number of iterations to 50, specify:

```
LOGLINEAR DPREF(2,3) BY RACE ORIGIN CAMP(1,2)
  /CRITERIA=ITERATION(50).
```

Defaults or specifications remain in effect until overridden by another CRITERIA subcommand.

Specifying Display Width

By default, the display width is the width specified on the SET command (see *SPSS/PC+ Base System User's Guide*). Use the WIDTH subcommand to specify a different display width. For example, if you have a 132-character printer, you can specify a width of 132 to obtain the wide format output. Only one width can be in effect at a time and it controls all display. The WIDTH subcommand can be placed anywhere after the variables specification, as in:

```
LOGLINEAR ZODIAC(1,12) SATJOB(1,2)
  /WIDTH=72.
```

A narrow format suppresses the display of percentages and standardized residuals in frequencies tables.

Including User-Missing Values

By default, LOGLINEAR deletes cases with missing values for any variable listed on the variables specification. To include cases with user-missing values, specify INCLUDE on the MISSING subcommand. Cases with system-missing values are always deleted from the analysis. Note that if you specify INCLUDE on MISSING, you must also include the user-missing values in the value range specification for the variables.

7 Nonlinear Regression

Many real-world relationships are approximated with linear models, especially in the absence of theoretical models that can serve as guides. We would be unwise to model the relationship between speed of a vehicle and stopping time with a linear model, since the laws of physics dictate otherwise. However, nothing deters us from modeling salary as a linear function of variables such as age, education, and experience. In general, we choose the simplest model that fits an observed relationship. Another reason that explains our affinity to linear models is the accompanying simplicity of statistical estimation and hypothesis testing. Algorithms for estimating parameters of linear models are straightforward; direct solutions are available; iteration is not required. There are, however, situations in which it is necessary to fit nonlinear models. Before considering the steps involved in nonlinear model estimation, let's consider what makes a model nonlinear.

What Is a Nonlinear Model?

There is often confusion about the characteristics of a nonlinear model. Consider the following equation:

$$Y = B_0 + B_1 X_1^2$$

Equation 7.1

Is this a linear or nonlinear model? The equation is certainly not that of a straight line—it is the equation for a parabola. However, the word *linear,* in this context, does not refer to whether the equation is that of a straight line or a curve. It refers to the functional form of the equation. That is, can the dependent variable be expressed as a linear combination of parameter values times values of the independent variables? The parameters must be linear. The independent variables can be transformed in any fashion. They can be raised to various powers, logged, and so on. The transformation cannot involve the parameters in any way, however.

The previous model is a linear model, since it is nonlinear in only the independent variable X. It is linear in the parameters B_0 and B_1. In fact, we can write the model as

$$Y = B_0 + B_1 X'$$

Equation 7.2

where X' is the square of X_1. The parameters in the model can be estimated using the usual linear model techniques.

Transforming Nonlinear Models

Consider the model:

$$Y = e^{B_0 + B_1 X_1 + B_2 X_2 + E}$$

Equation 7.3

The model, as it stands, is not of the form

$$Y = B_0 + B_1 Z_1 + B_2 Z_2 + \ldots + B_p Z_p + E$$

Equation 7.4

where the B's are the parameters and the Z's are functions of the independent variables, so it is a nonlinear model. However, if we take natural logs of both sides of Equation 7.3, we get the model:

$$\ln(Y) = B_0 + B_1 X_1 + B_2 X_2 + E$$

Equation 7.5

The transformed equation is linear in the parameters, and we can use the usual techniques for estimating them. Models that initially appear to be nonlinear but that can be transformed to a linear form are sometimes called **intrinsically linear models**. It is a good idea to examine what appears to be a nonlinear model to see if it can be transformed to a linear one. Transformation to linearity makes estimation much easier.

Another example of a transformable nonlinear model is:

$$Y = e^B X + E$$

Equation 7.6

The transformation $B' = e^B$ results in the model:

$$Y = B'X + E$$

Equation 7.7

We can use the usual methods to estimate B' and then take its natural log to get the values of B.

Error Terms in Transformed Models

In both linear and nonlinear models, we assume that the error term is additive. When we transform a model to linearity, we must make sure that the transformed error term satisfies the requisite assumptions. For example, if our original model is

$$Y = e^{BX} + E$$

Equation 7.8

taking natural logs does not result in a model that has an additive error term. To have an additive error term in the transformed model, our original model would have had to be:

$$Y = e^{BX+E} = e^{BX}e^{E}$$

Equation 7.9

Intrinsically Nonlinear Models

A model such as

$$Y = B_0 + e^{B_1 X_1} + e^{B_2 X_2} + e^{B_3 X_3} + E$$

Equation 7.10

is **intrinsically nonlinear**. We can't apply a transformation to linearize it. We must estimate the parameters using nonlinear regression. In nonlinear regression, just as in linear regression, we choose values for the parameters so that the sum of squared residuals is a minimum. There is not, however, a closed solution. We must solve for the values iteratively. There are several algorithms for the estimation of nonlinear models (see Fox, 1984; Draper & Smith, 1981).

Fitting the Logistic Population Growth Model

As an example of fitting a nonlinear equation, we will consider a model for population growth. Population growth is often modeled using a logistic population growth model of the form

$$Y_i = \frac{C}{1 + e^{A + BT_i}} + E_i$$

Equation 7.11

where Y_i is the population size at time T_i. Although the model often fits the observed data reasonably well, the assumptions of independent error and constant variance may be violated, since with time-series data errors are not independent and the size of the error may be dependent on the magnitude of the population. Since the logistic population growth model is not transformable to a linear model, we will have to use nonlinear regression to estimate the parameters.

Figure 7.1 contains a listing of decennial populations (in millions) of the United States from 1790 to 1960, as found in Fox (1984). Figure 7.2 is a plot of the same data. For the nonlinear regression, we will use the variable *decade*, which represents the number of decades since 1790, as the independent variable. This should prevent possible computational difficulties arising from large data values (see "Computational Problems" on p. 240).

Figure 7.1   Decennial population of the United States

```
LIST POP YEAR DECADE.

      POP YEAR DECADE

    3.895 1790      0
    5.267 1800      1
    7.182 1810      2
    9.566 1820      3
   12.834 1830      4
   16.985 1840      5
   23.069 1850      6
   31.278 1860      7
   38.416 1870      8
   49.924 1880      9
   62.692 1890     10
   75.734 1900     11
   91.812 1910     12
  109.806 1920     13
  122.775 1930     14
  131.669 1940     15
  150.697 1950     16
  178.464 1960     17
```

Figure 7.2   Plot of decennial population of the United States

```
PLOT PLOT=POP WITH YEAR.
```

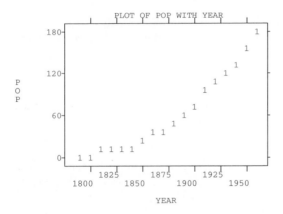

In order to start the nonlinear estimation algorithm, we must have initial values for the parameters. Unfortunately, the results of nonlinear estimation often depend on having good starting values for the parameters. There are several ways for obtaining starting values (see "Estimating Starting Values" on p. 239 through "Use Properties of the Non-linear Model" on p. 239).

For this example, we can obtain starting values by making some simple assumptions. In the logistic growth model, the parameter C represents the asymptote. We'll arbitrarily choose an asymptote that is not too far from the largest observed value. Let's take an asymptote of 200, since the largest observed value for the population is 178.

Using the value of 200 for C, we can estimate a value for A based on the observed population at time 0:

$$3.895 = \frac{200}{1 + e^A}$$

Equation 7.12

So,

$$A = \ln\left(\frac{200}{3.895} - 1\right) = 3.9$$

Equation 7.13

To estimate a value for B, we can use the population at time 1, and our estimates of C and A. This gives us

$$5.267 = \frac{200}{1 + e^{B + 3.9}}$$

Equation 7.14

from which we derive

$$B = \ln\left(\frac{200}{5.27} - 1\right) - 3.9 = -0.29$$

Equation 7.15

We use these values as initial values in the nonlinear regression routine.

Estimating the Parameters

Figure 7.3 shows the residual sums of squares and parameter estimates at each iteration. At step 1, the parameter estimates are the starting values that we have supplied. At the major iterations, which are identified with integer numbers, the derivatives are evaluated and the direction of the search determined. At the minor iterations, the distance is established. As the note at the end of the table indicates, iteration stops when the relative change in residual sums of squares between iterations is less than or equal to the convergence criterion.

Figure 7.3 Parameter estimates for nonlinear regression

```
MODEL PROGRAM A=3.9 B=-.3 C=200.
COMPUTE PRED=C/(1+EXP(A+B*DECADE)).
NLR POP WITH DECADE
 /SAVE=PRED RESID.

  Iteration   Residual SS          A              B              C
      1       969.6898219     3.90000000    -.30000000    200.000000
     1.1      240.3756732     3.87148503    -.27852484    237.513991
      2       240.3756732     3.87148503    -.27852484    237.513991
     2.1      186.5020615     3.89003377    -.27910189    243.721558
      3       186.5020615     3.89003377    -.27910189    243.721558
     3.1      186.4972404     3.88880285    -.27886478    243.975465
      4       186.4972404     3.88880285    -.27886478    243.975465
     4.1      186.4972278     3.88885122    -.27886164    243.985983
      5       186.4972278     3.88885122    -.27886164    243.985983
     5.1      186.4972277     3.88884856    -.27886059    243.987297

Run stopped after 10 model evaluations and 5 derivative evaluations.
Iterations have been stopped because the relative reduction between successive
residual sums of squares is at most SSCON = 1.000E-08
```

Summary statistics for the nonlinear regression are shown in Figure 7.4. For a nonlinear model, the tests used for linear models are not appropriate. In this situation, the residual mean square is not an unbiased estimate of the error variance, even if the model is correct. For practical purposes, we can still compare the residual variance with an estimate of the total variance, but the usual F statistic cannot be used for testing hypotheses.

The entry in Figure 7.4 labeled *Uncorrected Total* is the sum of the squared values of the dependent variable. The entry labeled *Corrected Total* is the sum of squared deviations around the mean. The *Regression* sum of squares is the sum of the squared predicted values. The entry labeled *R squared* is the coefficient of determination. It may be interpreted as the proportion of the total variation of the dependent variable around its mean that is explained by the fitted model. For nonlinear models, its value can be negative if the selected model fits worse than the mean. (For a discussion of this statistic, see Kvalseth, 1985.) It appears from the R^2 value of 0.9965 that the model fits the observed values well. Figure 7.5 is a plot of the observed and predicted values for the model.

Figure 7.4 Summary statistics for nonlinear regression

```
Nonlinear Regression Summary Statistics      Dependent Variable POP

   Source            DF   Sum of Squares   Mean Square

   Regression         3    123053.53112    41017.84371
   Residual          15       186.49723       12.43315
   Uncorrected Total 18    123240.02834

   (Corrected Total) 17     53293.92477

   R squared = 1 - Residual SS / Corrected SS =      .99650
```

Figure 7.5   Observed and predicted values for nonlinear model

```
VARIABLE LABELS POP 'OBSERVED VALUE' PRED 'PREDICTED'.
PLOT FORMAT=OVERLAY
 /SYMBOLS 'OP'
 /PLOT=POP PRED WITH YEAR.
```

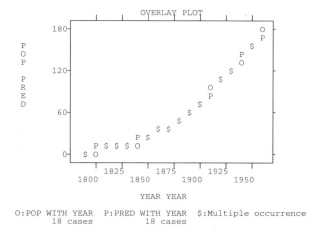

Approximate Confidence Intervals for the Parameters

In the case of nonlinear regression, it is not possible to obtain exact confidence intervals for each of the parameters. Instead, we must rely on **asymptotic** (large sample) approximations. Figure 7.6 shows the estimated parameters, standard errors, and asymptotic 95% confidence intervals. The asymptotic correlation matrix of the parameter estimates is shown in Figure 7.7. If there are very large positive or negative values for the correlation coefficients, it is possible that the model is **overparameterized**. That is, a model with fewer parameters may fit the observed data as well. This does not necessarily mean that the model is inappropriate; it may mean that the amount of data is not sufficient to estimate all of the parameters.

Figure 7.6   Estimated parameters and confidence intervals

Parameter	Estimate	Asymptotic Std. Error	Asymptotic 95 % Confidence Interval Lower	Upper
A	3.888848558	.093704405	3.689122348	4.088574768
B	-.278860587	.015593951	-.312098307	-.245622868
C	243.98729731	17.967400515	205.69068964	282.28390497

Figure 7.7   Asymptotic correlation matrix of parameter estimates

```
Asymptotic Correlation Matrix of the Parameter Estimates

                    A          B          C

   A             1.0000     -.7244     -.3762
   B             -.7244     1.0000      .9042
   C             -.3762      .9042     1.0000
```

Examining the Residuals

The SPSS/PC+ Nonlinear Regression procedure allows you to save predicted values and residuals that can be used for exploring the goodness of fit of the model. Figure 7.8 is a plot of residuals against the observed year values. You will note that the errors appear to be correlated and that the variance of the residuals increases with time.

Figure 7.8   Plot of residuals against observed values

```
PLOT PLOT=RESID WITH YEAR.
```

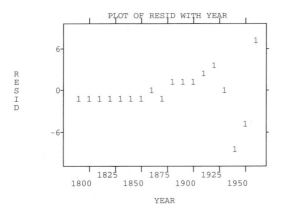

To compute asymptotic standard errors of the predicted values and statistics used for outlier detection and influential case analysis, you can use the Regression procedure, specifying the residuals from the Nonlinear Regression procedure as the dependent variable and the derivatives (see "Saving Predicted Values, Residuals, and Derivatives" on p. 245) as the independent variables.

Estimating Starting Values

As previously indicated, you must specify initial values for all parameters. Good initial values are important and may provide a better solution in fewer iterations. In addition, computational difficulties can sometimes be avoided by a good choice of initial values. Poor initial values can result in nonconvergence, a local rather than global solution, or a physically impossible solution.

There are a number of ways to determine initial values for nonlinear models. Milliken (1987) and Draper and Smith (1981) describe several approaches, which are summarized in the following sections. Generally, a combination of techniques will be most useful. If you don't have starting values, don't just set them all to 0. Use values in the neighborhood of what you expect to see.

If you ignore the error term, sometimes a linear form of the model can be derived. Linear regression can then be used to obtain initial values. For example, consider the model:

$$Y = e^{A + BX} + E \qquad \qquad \text{Equation 7.16}$$

If we ignore the error term and take the natural log of both sides of the equation, we obtain the model:

$$\ln (Y) = A + BX \qquad \qquad \text{Equation 7.17}$$

We can use linear regression to estimate A and B and specify these values as starting values in nonlinear regression.

Use Properties of the Nonlinear Model

Sometimes we know the values of the dependent variable for certain combinations of parameter values. For example, if in the model

$$Y = e^{A + BX} \qquad \qquad \text{Equation 7.18}$$

we know that when X is 0, Y is 2, we would select the natural log of 2 as a starting value for A. Examination of an equation at its maximum, minimum, and when all the independent variables approach 0 or infinity may help in selection of initial values.

Solve a System of Equations

By taking as many data points as you have parameters, you can solve a simultaneous system of equations. For example, in the previous model, we could solve the equations:

$$\ln (Y_1) = A + BX_1$$
$$\ln (Y_2) = A + BX_2$$

Equation 7.19

Using subtraction,

$$\ln (Y_1) - \ln (Y_2) = BX_1 - BX_2$$

Equation 7.20

we can solve for the values of the parameters

$$B = \frac{\ln (Y_1) - \ln (Y_2)}{X_1 - X_2}$$

Equation 7.21

and

$$A = \ln (Y_1) - BX_1$$

Equation 7.22

Computational Problems

Computationally, nonlinear regression problems can be difficult to solve. Models that require exponentiation or powers of large data values may cause underflows or overflows. (An **overflow** is caused by a number that is too large for the computer to handle, while an **underflow** is caused by a number that is too small for the computer to handle.) Sometimes the program may continue and produce a reasonable solution, especially if only a few data points caused the problem. If this is not the case, you must eliminate the cause of the problem. If your data values are large—for example, years—you can subtract the smallest year from all of the values. That's what was done with the population example. Instead of using the actual years, we used decades since 1790 (to compute the number of decades, we subtracted the smallest year from each year value and divided the result by 10). You must, however, consider the effect of rescaling on the parameter values. Many nonlinear models are not scale invariant. You can also consider rescaling the parameter values.

If the program fails to arrive at a solution—that is, if it doesn't converge—you might consider choosing different starting values. You can also change the criterion used for convergence.

Running the Nonlinear Regression Procedure

The Nonlinear Regression procedure is used to estimate parameter values and goodness-of-fit statistics for models which are not linear in their parameters. NLR estimates the values of the parameters for the model and, optionally, computes and saves predicted values, residuals, and derivatives. Final parameter estimates can be saved in a system file and used in subsequent analyses.

To run NLR, you need to specify more than one command. The commands used for the procedure fall into three categories:

- *Model specification.* Use the MODEL PROGRAM command to specify the model to fit and initial parameter estimates. This command, followed by computational statements for the model, is required.

- *Derivatives specification.* Use the DERIVATIVES command to specify the derivatives with respect to each parameter. This command is optional. If derivatives are provided by the user, computational time is reduced, and sometimes a better solution is possible.

- *Regression specification.* Use the NLR command to specify the dependent and independent variables for the nonlinear regression, the criteria for termination of iteration and, optionally, the output to be displayed or saved. This command is required.

Example

```
MODEL PROGRAM A=3.9 B=-.3 C=200.
COMPUTE PRED=C/(1 + EXP (A + B * DECADE)).
NLR POP WITH DECADE.
```

- The MODEL PROGRAM command assigns starting values to the three parameters (*a, b,* and *c*) to be estimated.

- The COMPUTE command gives the nonlinear function to fit, which is the logistic model: $Y = C/(1 + e^{A + B*\text{decade}})$.

- The NLR command displays the default nonlinear regression statistics. The dependent variable is *pop*, and the independent variable is *decade*. Both *pop* and *decade* are variables in your active file.

- By default, the procedure assumes that the variable name assigned to the model to be estimated is *pred.* If you use a different name you must specify the name on the PRED subcommand (see "Specifying the Variable that Identifies the Model" on p. 244).

Identifying the Model

The first step in estimating a nonlinear regression model is to determine which model you wish to fit. Any nonlinear model can be estimated with this program. There is no default model; you must specify the equation that best describes your data. The equation is specified in the model program. The model program serves two purposes:

- Assignment of variable names and initial values to the parameters.
- Specification of the equation using the transformation language.

Specifying the Parameters

Use the MODEL PROGRAM command to assign variable names and initial values to the parameters.

Consider the following equation, which is the sum of two exponentials: $Y = Ae^{BX} + Ce^{DX}$. The equation has four parameters *(a, b, c,* and *d)* which must be estimated from the data. The data in this case consist of values for the independent variable *x* and the dependent variable *y.* To estimate the model using NLR, you must assign variable names and starting values to each of the parameters. Any acceptable SPSS/PC+ variable name can be used for a parameter. To assign the variable names *a, b, c,* and *d* and starting values of 10, 0, 5, and 0 to the parameters, specify:

```
MODEL PROGRAM  A=10 B=0 C=5 D=0.
```

You must specify each parameter individually on the MODEL PROGRAM command; you cannot use the TO keyword.

Specifying the Equation

To specify the equation to be fit, you must use the SPSS/PC+ transformation commands described in the *SPSS/PC+ Base System User's Guide.* Your specified equation is used to calculate predicted values for the dependent variable. Based on the parameter estimates and the values of the independent variables, the program assumes by default that the variable name *pred* is assigned to the result of the transformation. If you use a different variable name, you must supply it on the PRED subcommand (see "Saving Predicted Values, Residuals, and Derivatives" on p. 245).

For example, you can use the following MODEL PROGRAM to assign starting values and names to the four parameters *a, b, c,* and *d,* and to define the model to fit as the sum of two exponentials:

```
MODEL PROGRAM A=10 B=0 C=5 D=0.
COMPUTE PRED= A*EXP(B*X) + C*EXP(D*X).
```

All of the variables created in the model program are temporary. They will not be automatically saved in the active file. In the model program, you can assign variable names and formats to any of the temporary variables you create.

In a model program, you can use all of the capabilities of the transformation language. For example, the following commands specify a segmented model in which join points are to be estimated. The form of the model is different for different ranges of the independent variable.

```
MODEL PROGRAM B0=14 B1=.01 K1=25 K2=55.
IF (X LE K1) PRED=B0.
IF (X GT K1 AND X LE K2) PRED=B0 + B1*(X-K1)*(X-K1).
IF (X GT K2) PRED=B0+B1*((K2-K1)*(K2-K1)+K2*(X-K2)).
```

Specifying Derivatives

Nonlinear estimation is iterative and requires determination of direction and step size at each iteration based on the values of the derivatives with respect to each of the parame-ters. You can supply some or all of the derivatives using the derivatives program, or you can allow the program to numerically estimate the derivatives. If you supply the deriv-atives, computational time is reduced. In some situations, if you supply derivatives the solution may actually be better.

The derivatives program consists of the DERIVATIVES command followed by COM-PUTE statements for each of the derivatives. The DERIVATIVES command must follow the model program. To name the derivatives, attach the prefix *d.* to each parameter name. For example, the derivative name for the parameter named *parm1* would be *d.parm1*. The following derivatives program can be used to specify derivatives for the previously described sum-of-two-exponentials model:

```
DERIVATIVES.
COMPUTE D.A = EXP (B * X).
COMPUTE D.B = A * EXP (B * X) * X.
COMPUTE D.C = EXP (D * X).
COMPUTE D.D = C * EXP (D * X) * X.
```

Defined derivatives can be used on the right of the equals sign. Thus, the previous pro-gram can also be written as:

```
DERIVATIVES.
COMPUTE D.A = EXP (B * X).
COMPUTE D.B = A * X * D.A.
COMPUTE D.C = EXP (D * X).
COMPUTE D.D = C* X * D.C.
```

You need not supply all of the derivatives. Those that are not supplied will be numeri-cally estimated by the program. During the first iteration of the nonlinear estimation, de-rivatives calculated in the DERIVATIVES program are compared with numerically calculated derivatives. This serves as a check on the values you supply. See "Controlling Iteration" on p. 245 for a description of the CKDER option for controlling this check.

NLR Command

Once you have specified the model and, optionally, the derivatives, use the NLR command to provide information about the dependent and independent variables to be used in the regression. The NLR command must follow the model program and the derivatives program, if one is included.

On the NLR command, you can use optional subcommands to request output that is not displayed by default, to identify the name of the model expression if it is not named *pred*, to save variables in the active file, or to modify the criteria used by the estimation algorithm.

Specifying Regression Variables

After the command NLR, give the name of the dependent variable. You can specify only one numeric variable as the dependent variable. Independent variables must be specified after the keyword WITH. For example, in the command

```
NLR Y WITH X.
```

the observed dependent variable is named *y* and the independent variable is named *x*.

Among the independent variables, you must include all variables on your active file that you have used in the model program and derivatives program. Do not list variables you have created in the model or derivatives programs. For example, in the following analysis, *x* is the only variable that must be included in the list. It is the only variable from the active file used in the model and derivatives programs; all of the other variables are temporary variables created for the nonlinear task.

```
DATA LIST FREE / Y X.
BEGIN DATA
data records
END DATA.
MODEL PROGRAM A=10 B=0 C=5 D=0.
COMPUTE PRED = A*EXP(B*X) + C*EXP(D*X).
DERIVATIVES.
COMPUTE D.A = EXP (B * X).
COMPUTE D.B = A * EXP(B*X) * X.
COMPUTE D.C = EXP (D * X).
COMPUTE D.D = C * EXP(D*X) * X.
NLR Y WITH X.
```

Specifying the Variable that Identifies the Model

Use the PRED subcommand to specify the variable created in the model program for identifying the model. By default, the variable is assumed to be *pred*. If you have used a name other than this in the model program, supply the name on the PRED subcommand.

Example

```
MODEL PROGRAM A=10 B=0 C=5 D=0.
COMPUTE VALUE=A*EXP(B*X) + C*EXP(D*X).
NLR Y WITH X/PRED=VALUE.
```

- COMPUTE names *value* as the variable used to define the model.
- PRED is required on NLR to specify the name.

Saving Predicted Values, Residuals, and Derivatives

By default, none of the variables created in the model program are saved in the active file. If you wish to save predicted values for the dependent variable, residuals, or derivatives, use the SAVE subcommand. The following keywords can be specified on SAVE:

PRED
: *Predicted values.* The variable name you used to define the model in the model program is the name assigned to the predicted values.

RESID(varname)
: *Residuals.* Specify the variable name for the residuals in parentheses after the keyword RESID. If no variable name is specified, the name *resid* will be used. If the residual cannot be computed, it is assigned the system-missing value.

DERIVATIVES
: *The derivatives for each parameter.* Derivative names are created by adding *d.* to the parameter names. Derivatives are saved for all parameters.

Example

```
NLR Y WITH X/SAVE PRED RESID.
```

- This command saves two new variables in the active file. The variable *pred* contains predicted values; the variable *resid* contains residuals.

Controlling Iteration

Use the CRITERIA subcommand to control the values of the five cutoff points used to stop iterative calculations in NLR. You can specify as many as you want of the following keywords. Those you don't specify retain their default values.

ITER n
: *Maximum number of iterations allowed.* The default is 100 iterations per parameter.

SSCON n
: *Convergence criterion for the sum of squares.* If successive iterations fail to reduce the sum of squares by this proportion or more, the procedure stops. The default is $1E - 8$. Specify 0 to disable this criterion.

PCON n   *Convergence criterion for the parameter values.* If successive iterations fail to change any of the parameter values by this proportion or more, the procedure stops. The default is $1E - 8$. Specify 0 to disable this criterion.

RCON n   *Convergence criterion for the correlation between the residuals and the derivatives.* If the largest value for the correlation between the residuals and the derivatives is less than or equal to *n*, the procedure stops because it lacks the information it needs to estimate a direction for its next move. This criterion is often referred to as a **gradient convergence criterion**. The default is $1E - 8$. Specify 0 to disable this criterion.

CKDER n   *Critical value for derivative checking.* If any score falls below the CKDER value on the first iteration, NLR terminates and issues an error message. You can specify a number between 0 and 1 for *n*. The default is 0.5. Specify 0 to disable this criterion.

Example

```
MODEL PROGRAM A=.5 B=1.6.
COMPUTE PRED=A*SPEED**B.
NLR STOP WITH SPEED /CRITERIA=ITER(80) SSCON=(.000001).
```

- CRITERIA changes two of the five iteration cutoff values, ITER and SSCON, and leaves the remaining three, PCON, RCON, and CKDER, at their default values.

Writing Parameter Estimates to a System File

You can save the final parameter estimates, the residual sum of squares, and the number of cases used in the analysis to a system file. Use the keyword OUTFILE followed by a filename. The resulting file has one case. The names for the parameters are those used in the model program, the name *sse* is used for the sum of squared residuals, and the name *ncases* for the unweighted number of cases in the analysis. For example, the following command will create the file *nlr.sys*, which you can read in with the FILE subcommand on NLR:

```
NLR Y WITH X/OUTFILE='NLR.SYS'.
```

Reading Parameter Estimates from a System File

Use the subcommand FILE to indicate that initial parameter estimates are on a system file saved in a previous NLR run. When starting values are read from a system file, the model program need list only the names of the variables in that file, in any order.

Example

```
MODEL PROGRAM A B C.
   ...
NLR Y WITH X/FILE='ESTIM.SYS'.
```

- NLR reads the initial values for parameters *a, b,* and *c* from the file *estim.sys.*
- If for certain parameters you want to specify a starting value that differs from the value in the system file, or you wish to include additional parameters and their starting values, list starting values for those parameters only.

Case Weights

If a WEIGHT command is in effect, NLR uses case weights to calculate the residual sum of squares and derivatives. When the model program is first executed for each case, the value of the weight variable is that in the active file. The weight value can be changed by computing a new value in the model program. NLR uses the weight variable's value after each execution of the model program. The degrees of freedom in the ANOVA table, however, are based on unweighted cases.

Example

```
COMPUTE WT=1.
WEIGHT BY WT.
MODEL PROGRAM
B0=2.3 B1=1.6 B2=.014
COMPUTE PRED=B0 +B1x1+B2X2
COMPUTE Z=(Y-PRED)/1.63
COMPUTE WT=EXP(-.3*ABS(Z)).
NLR Y WITH X1 X2.
```

- These commands can be used to perform a robust regression via iteratively reweighted least squares.
- The weight for each case is a function of the scaled residuals, where 1.63 is the estimate of scale obtained from a preliminary linear least-squares regression.
- The model in this case is linear. We are using NLR to obtain iteratively reweighted least squares.

8 Probit Analysis

How much insecticide does it take to kill a pest? How low does a sale price have to be to induce a consumer to buy a product? In both of these situations, we are concerned with evaluating the potency of a stimulus. In the first example, the stimulus is the amount of insecticide; in the second, it is the sale price of an object. The response we are interested in is all-or-none. An insect is either dead or alive, a sale made or not. Since all insects and shoppers do not respond in the same way—that is, they have different tolerances for insecticides and sale prices—the problem must be formulated in terms of the proportion responding at each level of the stimulus.

Different mathematical models can be used to express the relationship between the proportion responding and the "dose" of one or more stimuli. In this chapter, we will consider two commonly used models: the probit response model and the logit response model. We will assume that we have one or more stimuli of interest and that each stimulus can have several doses. We expose different groups of individuals to the desired combinations of stimuli. For each combination, we record the number of individuals exposed and the number who respond.

Probit and Logit Response Models

In probit and logit models, instead of regressing the actual proportion responding on the values of the stimuli, we transform the proportion responding using either a logit or probit transformation. For a probit transformation, we replace each of the observed proportions with the value of the standard normal curve below which the observed proportion of the area is found.

For example, if half (0.5) of the subjects respond at a particular dose, the corresponding probit value is 0, since half of the area in a standard normal curve falls below a Z score of 0. If the observed proportion is 0.95, the corresponding probit value is 1.64.

If the logit transformation is used, the observed proportion P is replaced by:

$$\ln\left(\frac{P}{1-P}\right)$$

Equation 8.1

This quantity is called a **logit**. If the observed proportion is 0.5, the logit-transformed value is 0, the same as the probit-transformed value. Similarly, if the observed proportion is 0.95, the logit-transformed value is 1.47. This differs somewhat from the corresponding probit value of 1.64. (In most situations, analyses based on logits and probits give very similar results.)

The regression model for the transformed response can be written as

$$\text{Transformed } P_i = A + BX_i \qquad\qquad\qquad \textbf{Equation 8.2}$$

where P_i is the observed proportion responding at dose X_i. (Usually, the log of the dose is used instead of the actual dose.) If there is more than one stimulus variable, terms are added to the model for each of the stimuli. The Probit procedure obtains maximum-likelihood estimates of the regression coefficients.

An Example

Finney (1971) presents data showing the effect of a series of doses of rotenone (an insecticide) when sprayed on *Macrosiphoniella sanborni*. Table 8.1 contains the concentration, the number of insects tested at each dose, the proportion dying, and the probit transformation of each of the observed proportions.

Table 8.1   Effects of rotenone

Dose	Number observed	Number dead	Proportion dead	Probit
10.2	50	44	0.88	1.18
7.7	49	42	0.86	1.08
5.1	46	24	0.52	0.05
3.8	48	16	0.33	-0.44
2.6	50	6	0.12	-1.18

Figure 8.1 is a plot of the observed probits against the logs of the concentrations. (You specify *died* as the response frequency variable, *total* as the observation frequency variable, and *dose* as the predictor. The variable *dose* is transformed using the log 10 transformation, which is the default in the Probit procedure.) You can see that the relationship between the two variables is linear. If the relationship did not appear linear, the concentrations would have to be transformed in some other way in order to achieve linearity. If a suitable transformation could not be found, fitting a straight line would not be a reasonable strategy for modeling the data.

Figure 8.1   Plot of observed probits against logs of concentrations

```
SET LENGTH=40.
PROBIT DIED OF TOTAL WITH DOSE.
```

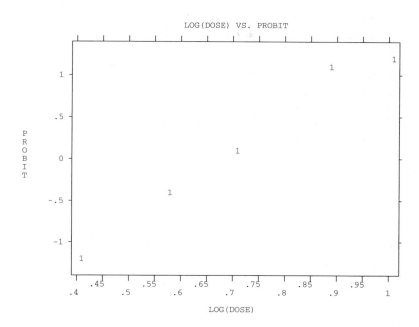

The parameter estimates and standard errors for this example are shown in Figure 8.2.

Figure 8.2   Parameter estimates and standard errors

```
Parameter estimates converged after 10 iterations.
Optimal solution found.

Parameter Estimates (PROBIT model:  (PROBIT(p)) = Intercept + BX):

          Regression Coeff.   Standard Error    Coeff./S.E.

   DOSE          4.16914           .47306          8.81306


              Intercept   Standard Error  Intercept/S.E.

              -2.85940        .34717         -8.23640

Pearson  Goodness-of-Fit  Chi Square =     1.621    DF = 3    P =  .655

Since Goodness-of-Fit Chi square is NOT significant, no heterogeneity
factor is used in the calculation of confidence limits.
```

The regression equation is:

$$\text{Probit } (P_i) = -2.86 + 4.17 \, (\log_{10} (\text{dose}_i))$$ **Equation 8.3**

To see how well this model fits, consider Figure 8.3, which contains observed and expected frequencies, residuals, and the predicted probability of a response for each of the log concentrations.

Figure 8.3   Statistics for each concentration

```
Observed and Expected Frequencies


          Number of    Observed     Expected
  DOSE    Subjects     Responses    Responses    Residual       Prob

  1.01       50.0        44.0         45.586       -1.586      .91172
   .89       49.0        42.0         39.330        2.670      .80265
   .71       46.0        24.0         24.845        -.845      .54010
   .58       48.0        16.0         15.816         .184      .32950
   .41       50.0         6.0          6.253        -.253      .12506
```

You can see that the model appears to fit the data reasonably well. A goodness-of-fit test for the model, based on the residuals, is shown in Figure 8.1. The chi-square goodness-of-fit test is calculated as

$$\chi^2 = \sum \frac{(\text{residual}_i)^2}{n_i \hat{P}_i (1 - \hat{P}_i)}$$ **Equation 8.4**

where n_i is the number of subjects exposed to dose i and $\hat{P}_i$ is the predicted proportion responding at dose i. The degrees of freedom are equal to the number of doses minus the number of estimated parameters. In this example, we have five doses and two estimated parameters, so there are three degrees of freedom for the chi-square statistic. Since the observed significance level for the chi-square statistic is large—0.655—there is no reason to doubt the model.

When the significance level of the chi-square statistic is small, several explanations are possible. It may be that the relationship between the concentration and the probit is not linear. Or it may be that the relationship is linear but the spread of the observed points around the regression line is unequal. That is, the data are heterogeneous. If this is the case, a correction must be applied to the estimated variances for each concentration group (see "Confidence Intervals for Expected Dosages," below).

Confidence Intervals for Expected Dosages

Often you want to know what the concentration of an agent must be in order to achieve a certain proportion of response. For example, you may want to know what the concentration would have to be in order to kill half of the insects. This is known as the **median**

lethal dose. It can be obtained from the previous regression equation by solving for the concentration that corresponds to a probit value of 0. For this example,

$$\log_{10}(\text{median lethal dose}) = 2.86/4.17$$

$$\text{median lethal dose} = 4.85$$

Equation 8.5

Confidence intervals can be constructed for the median lethal dose as well as for the dose required to achieve any response. The Probit procedure calculates 95% intervals for the concentrations required to achieve various levels of response. The values for this example are shown in Figure 8.4.

Figure 8.4   Confidence intervals

```
Confidence Limits for Effective DOSE


                                 95% Confidence Limits
      Prob           DOSE          Lower         Upper

      .01          1.34232        .90152       1.73955
      .02          1.56042       1.09195       1.97144
      .03          1.71682       1.23282       2.13489
      .04          1.84473       1.35041       2.26709
      .05          1.95577       1.45411       2.38094
      .06          2.05553       1.54847       2.48260
      .07          2.14718       1.63607       2.57552
      .08          2.23270       1.71858       2.66189
      .09          2.31344       1.79709       2.74314
      .10          2.39033       1.87239       2.82033
      .15          2.73686       2.21737       3.16638
      .20          3.04775       2.53300       3.47603
      .25          3.34246       2.83556       3.77074
      .30          3.63134       3.13342       4.06251
      .35          3.92126       3.43173       4.36004
      .40          4.21775       3.73415       4.67105
      .45          4.52592       4.04368       5.00346
      .50          4.85119       4.36322       5.36609
      .55          5.19983       4.69624       5.76942
      .60          5.57976       5.04753       6.22651
      .65          6.00164       5.42413       6.75456
      .70          6.48081       5.83681       7.37806
      .75          7.04092       6.30250       8.13488
      .80          7.72177       6.84956       9.08968
      .85          8.59893       7.53102      10.36751
      .90          9.84550       8.46614      12.26163
      .91         10.17274       8.70644      12.77237
      .92         10.54059       8.97434      13.35269
      .93         10.96042       9.27744      14.02276
      .94         11.44911       9.62693      14.81270
      .95         12.03312      10.04028      15.77021
      .96         12.75742      10.54699      16.97720
      .97         13.70788      11.20286      18.59208
      .98         15.08186      12.13489      20.98491
      .99         17.53233      13.75688      25.40958
```

The column labeled *Prob* is the proportion responding. The column labeled *DOSE* is the estimated dosage required to achieve this proportion. The 95% confidence limits for the dose are shown in the next two columns. If the chi-square goodness-of-fit test has a significance level less than 0.15 (the program default), a heterogeneity correction is automatically included in the computation of the intervals (Finney, 1971).

Comparing Several Groups

In the previous example, only one stimulus at several doses was studied. If you want to compare several different stimuli, each measured at several doses, additional statistics may prove useful. Consider the inclusion of two additional insecticides in the previously described problem. Besides rotenone at five concentrations, we also have five concentrations of deguelin and four concentrations of a mixture of the two. Figure 8.5 shows a listing of these data. As in the previous example, variable *dose* contains the insecticide concentration (again, *dose* is log-transformed), *total* contains the total number of cases, and *died* contains the number of deaths. Grouping variable *agent* is coded 1 (rotenone), 2 (deguelin), or 3 (mixture).

Figure 8.5   Data for rotenone and deguelin

DOSE	AGENT	TOTAL	DIED
2.57	1.00	50.00	6.00
3.80	1.00	48.00	16.00
5.13	1.00	46.00	24.00
7.76	1.00	49.00	42.00
10.23	1.00	50.00	44.00
10.00	2.00	48.00	18.00
20.42	2.00	48.00	34.00
30.20	2.00	49.00	47.00
40.74	2.00	50.00	47.00
50.12	2.00	48.00	48.00
10.00	3.00	46.00	27.00
15.14	3.00	48.00	38.00
20.42	3.00	46.00	43.00
25.12	3.00	50.00	48.00

Figure 8.6 is a plot of the observed probits against the logs of the concentrations for each of the three groups separately.

You can see that there appears to be a linear relationship between the two variables for all three groups. One of the questions of interest is whether all three lines are parallel. If so, it would make sense to estimate a common slope for them. Figure 8.7 contains the estimate of the common slope, separate intercept estimates for each of the groups, and a test of parallelism.

Figure 8.6   Plot of observed probits against logs of concentrations

```
SET WIDTH=40.
PROBIT DIED OF TOTAL WITH DOSE BY AGENT(1,3).
```

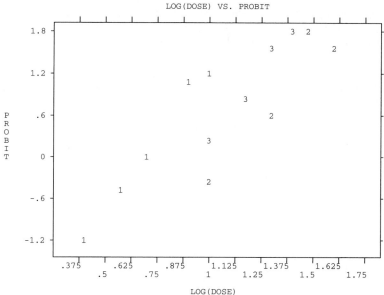

```
PROBIT DIED OF TOTAL WITH DOSE BY AGENT(1,3)
 /PRINT=PARALL.
```

Figure 8.7   Intercept estimates and test of parallelism

Parameter Estimates (PROBIT model: (PROBIT(p)) = Intercept + BX):

	Regression Coeff.	Standard Error	Coeff./S.E.	
DOSE	3.90635	.30691	12.72803	

	Intercept	Standard Error	Intercept/S.E.	AGENT
	-2.67343	.23577	-11.33913	rotenone
	-4.36573	.40722	-10.72071	deguelin
	-3.71153	.37491	-9.89977	mixture

```
Pearson  Goodness-of-Fit  Chi Square =     7.471   DF = 10   P =  .680
         Parallelism Test Chi Square =     1.162   DF = 2    P =  .559
```

Since Goodness-of-Fit Chi square is NOT significant, no heterogeneity
factor is used in the calculation of confidence limits.

The observed significance level for the test of parallelism is large—0.559—so there is no reason to reject the hypothesis that all three lines are parallel. Thus, the equation for rotenone is estimated to be

$$\text{Probit } (P_i) = -2.67 + 3.91 \, (\log_{10} (\text{dose}_i))$$

Equation 8.6

The equation for deguelin is

$$\text{Probit } (P_i) = -4.37 + 3.91 \, (\log_{10} (\text{dose}_i))$$

Equation 8.7

and for the mixture is

$$\text{Probit } (P_i) = -3.71 + 3.91 \, (\log_{10} (\text{dose}_i))$$

Equation 8.8

Comparing Relative Potencies of the Agents

The relative potency of two stimuli is defined as the ratio of two doses that are equally effective. For example, the relative median potency is the ratio of two doses that achieve a response rate of 50%. In the case of parallel regression lines, there is a constant relative potency at all levels of response. For example, consider Figure 8.8, which shows some of the doses needed to achieve a particular response for each of the three agents.

For rotenone, the expected dosage to kill half of the insects is 4.83; for deguelin, it is 13.11; and for the mixture, it is 8.91. The relative median potency for rotenone compared to deguelin is 4.83/13.11, or 0.37; for rotenone compared to the mixture, it is 0.54; and for deguelin compared to the mixture, it is 1.47. These relative median potencies and their confidence intervals are shown in Figure 8.9.

Figure 8.8   Expected doses

```
Confidence Limits for Effective DOSE

AGENT        1  rotenone

                            95% Confidence Limits
Prob         DOSE         Lower            Upper

.25        3.24875       2.82553          3.65426
.30        3.54926       3.11581          3.97227
.35        3.85249       3.40758          4.29636
.40        4.16414       3.70545          4.63356
.45        4.48965       4.01370          4.99083
.50        4.83482       4.33680          5.37586
.55        5.20654       4.68002          5.79788
.60        5.61352       5.05003          6.26880
.65        6.06764       5.45592          6.80487
.70        6.58603       5.91086          7.42974
.75        7.19524       6.43524          8.18030

AGENT        2  deguelin

                            95% Confidence Limits
Prob         DOSE         Lower            Upper

.25        8.80913       7.24085         10.32755
.30        9.62399       8.00041         11.20430
.35       10.44620       8.76976         12.09054
.40       11.29127       9.56202         13.00451
.45       12.17389      10.38960         13.96387
.50       13.10986      11.26577         14.98799
.55       14.11778      12.20605         16.10010
.60       15.22135      13.23000         17.33026
.65       16.45271      14.36393         18.71981
.70       17.85833      15.64554         20.32922
.75       19.51024      17.13277         22.25327

AGENT        3  mixture

                            95% Confidence Limits
Prob         DOSE         Lower            Upper

.25        5.99049       4.82754          7.12052
.30        6.54462       5.33737          7.72006
.35        7.10375       5.85480          8.32478
.40        7.67843       6.38880          8.94696
.45        8.27864       6.94795          9.59841
.50        8.91512       7.54150         10.29194
.55        9.60054       8.18034         11.04290
.60       10.35100       8.87822         11.87107
.65       11.18837       9.65364         12.80367
.70       12.14424      10.53309         13.88054
.75       13.26759      11.55720         15.16421
```

Figure 8.9   Relative potencies and their confidence intervals

```
                              95% Confidence Limits
AGENT        Estimate       Lower          Upper

1 VS.  2       .3688        .23353          .52071
1 VS.  3       .5423        .38085          .71248
2 VS.  3      1.4705       1.20619         1.85007
```

If a confidence interval does not include the value of 1, we have reason to suspect the hypothesis that the two agents are equally potent.

Estimating the Natural Response Rate

In some situations, the response of interest is expected to occur even if the stimulus is not present. For example, if the organism of interest has a very short life span, you would expect to observe deaths even without the agent. In such situations, you must adjust the observed proportions to reflect deaths due to the agent alone.

If the natural response rate is known, it can be entered into the Probit procedure. It can also be estimated from the data, provided that data for a dose of 0 are entered together with the other doses. If the natural response rate is estimated from the data, an additional degree of freedom must be subtracted from the chi-square goodness-of-fit degrees of freedom.

More than One Stimulus Variable

If several stimuli are evaluated simultaneously, an additional term is added to the regression model for each stimulus. Regression coefficients and standard errors are displayed for each stimulus. In the case of several stimuli, relative potencies and confidence intervals for the doses needed to achieve a particular response cannot be calculated in the usual fashion, since you need to consider various combinations of the levels of the stimuli.

Running the Probit Procedure

The Probit procedure performs either probit or logit analysis with a dichotomous dependent variable. It is designed for use with aggregated data, where each case gives the number of responses and the number of total observations for a specific level of the predictor variable(s) and for a specific value of a grouping variable, if there is one. To use PROBIT with unaggregated data, where each case represents a single observation, you must use the AGGREGATE command (see "Using Case-by-Case Data" on p. 259).

Specifying Variables in the Equation

The PROBIT command requires at least three variable specifications: a variable containing the number of cases responding to a stimulus, a second variable, following the keyword OF, containing the number of cases to which the stimulus was applied, and a third variable, following the keyword WITH, containing the level of the stimulus. For example, in the command

```
PROBIT R OF N WITH DOSE.
```

the *r* variable is the number of cases that responded to the treatment, *n* is the total number of cases that received the treatment, and *dose* is the treatment level. The values of *r* and *n* must be positive, and *r* must be less than *n* for each case. The command

```
PROBIT DIED OF TOTAL WITH DOSE.
```

produces a default analysis using the probit response model, with a base-10 logarithmic transformation of *dose*. This command produces the probit plot in Figure 8.1, the parameter estimates in Figure 8.2, the observed and expected frequencies in Figure 8.3, and the confidence intervals in Figure 8.4.

You can name more than one predictor variable after the keyword WITH, as in:

```
PROBIT DIED OF TOTAL WITH DOSE AGE WEIGHT.
```

Using a Grouping Variable

To indicate a grouping variable in your data, use the keyword BY followed by the name of the grouping variable with a range of values in parentheses. You can specify the grouping variable either before or after the predictor variable, but you can specify only one grouping variable, as in:

```
PROBIT DIED OF TOTAL WITH DOSE BY AGENT(1,3).
```

With this command, each case corresponds to a group of observations at a specific level of *dose* in one of the three groups defined by *agent*. The default output includes a plot of transformed proportions, parameter estimates, fiducial confidence intervals for each group, a chi-square goodness-of-fit test, and relative median potencies for all pairs of groups. This command produces the output in Figure 8.6, Figure 8.8, and Figure 8.9.

Using Case-by-Case Data

When your data file contains individual observations, you should aggregate it before using PROBIT, if possible. First, recode the response variable for individual cases, if necessary, to 0 (no response) or 1 (response). Then, use commands modeled after these:

```
AGGREGATE OUTFILE=* /BREAK=AGENT DOSE
 /N=N(RESPONSE) /R=SUM(RESPONSE).
PROBIT R OF N WITH DOSE BY AGENT(1,3).
```

The aggregate variable *n* contains the number of nonmissing observations of the original variable *response*, and the aggregate variable *r* contains the number of observations that responded to the stimulus (coded 1 for *response*).

When it is not possible to aggregate your data, you can still use PROBIT. The response variable (*r*) should again be coded 0 or 1. Then, you must compute a variable equal to the constant 1 to indicate that each case represents a single observation.

```
COMPUTE N=1.
PROBIT R OF N WITH DOSE BY AGENT(1,3).
```

When you use unaggregated data in PROBIT, the goodness-of-fit tests will be based on the number of individual cases, not the number of levels of the stimuli.

Specifying the Model

Use the MODEL subcommand to specify the response model to be used to transform the response probabilities (see "Probit and Logit Response Models" on p. 249). Specify one of the following:

PROBIT   *Probit response model.* This is the default.

LOGIT   *Logit response model.*

BOTH   *Both response models.*

Specifying Natural Response Rate

Use the NATRES subcommand to indicate that there is a natural response rate even in the absence of the stimulus. There are two methods for indicating the natural response rate.

If you have data indicating the response rate at 0 level of the stimulus, enter the NATRES subcommand without any additional specifications, as in:

```
PROBIT R OF N WITH DOSE /NATRES.
```

Assuming that the data contain a case for which *dose* is 0, PROBIT estimates the natural response rate based on the proportion of observations represented by that case that showed the response.

If you know the natural response rate, you do not need to supply data with a 0 stimulus level. Simply indicate the natural response rate on the NATRES subcommand, as in:

```
PROBIT R OF N WITH DOSE /NATRES=0.1.
```

PROBIT adjusts its estimates for the fact that the response occurs 10% of the time even if *dose* is 0.

Requesting Statistical Output

Use the PRINT subcommand to control statistical output. After PRINT, enter one or more of the following keywords:

FREQ   *Observed and predicted frequencies for each case.*

CI   *Fiducial confidence intervals for models with a single predictor variable.* If you specify a grouping variable, PROBIT displays a table of confidence intervals for each group. The confidence intervals are calculated with a heterogeneity factor if the goodness-of-fit test is significant (see "Controlling Estimation" on p. 261).

RMP   *Relative median potency.* This is available only when a grouping variable is used.

PARALL   *Parallelism test for regression lines across categories of the grouping variable, if any.*

ALL   *All of the above that are applicable.*

DEFAULT   *FREQ, CI, and when a grouping variable is used, RMP.*

NONE   *Only the PROBIT plot (for a single-predictor model), the parameter estimates, and the covariances.*

For example, the command

```
PROBIT DIED OF TOTAL WITH DOSE BY AGENT(1,3)
  /PRINT=PARALL.
```

produces the parallelism test in Figure 8.7.

If you use the PRINT subcommand, only the statistical output you specifically request will be displayed.

Specifying Logarithmic Transformations

Use the LOG subcommand to control the logarithmic transformations that are normally applied to predictor variables in a probit model. By default, the base-10 logarithms of all predictors are used to estimate the model. You can specify another base for the logarithmic transformation on the LOG subcommand:

base   *Base for the log transformation.* If you specify LOG without additional specifications, base is assumed to be *e* (approximately 2.718).

NONE   *No logarithmic transformation.* To transform some, but not all, of the predictors, specify NONE on the LOG subcommand and use COMPUTE statements to carry out the transformations. If you specify that the natural response rate is to be estimated and do not request a log transformation, the control group is included in the analysis.

Controlling Estimation

Use CRITERIA to specify the values of control parameters for the PROBIT algorithm. You can specify any or all of the keywords below. Defaults remain in effect for parameters that are not changed.

OPTOL(n)   *Optimality tolerance.* Alias CONVERGE. If an iteration point is a feasible point and the next step will not produce a relative change in either the parameter vector or the log-likelihood function of more than the square root of n, an optimal solution has been found. OPTOL can also be thought of as the number of significant digits in the log-likelihood function at the solution. For example, if OPTOL$=10^{-6}$, the log-likelihood function should have approximately six significant digits of accuracy. The default value is machine epsilon**0.8.

ITERATE(n) *Iteration limit.* Specify the maximum number of iterations. The default is max $(50, 3(p+1))$, where p is the number of parameters in the model.

P(p) *Heterogeneity criterion probability.* Specify a cutoff value between 0 and 1 for the significance of the goodness-of-fit test. The cutoff value determines whether a heterogeneity factor is included in calculations of confidence levels for effective levels of a predictor. If the significance of chi-square is greater than the cutoff, the heterogeneity factor is not included. If you specify 0, this criterion is disabled; if you specify 1, a heterogeneity factor is automatically included. The default is 0.15.

STEPLIMIT(n) *Step limit.* The PROBIT algorithm does not allow changes in the length of the parameter vector to exceed a factor of n. This limit prevents very early steps from going too far from good initial estimates. Specify any positive value. The default value is 0.1.

CONVERGE(n) *Alias of OPTOL.*

Missing-Value Treatment

PROBIT always excludes cases with system-missing values for any variable in the analysis. You can control the inclusion of cases with user-missing values by specifying one of the following keywords after the MISSING subcommand:

EXCLUDE *Exclude cases with any system- or user-missing values.* This is the default.

INCLUDE *Include cases with user-missing values.*

9

Survival Analysis

How long do marriages last? How long do people work for a company? How long do patients with a particular cancer live? To answer these questions, you must evaluate the interval between two events—marriage and divorce, hiring and departure, diagnosis and death. Solution of the problem is complicated by the fact that the event of interest (divorce, termination, or death) may not occur for all people during the period in which they are observed, and the actual period of observation may not be the same for all people. That is, not everyone gets divorced or quits a job, and not everyone gets married or starts a job on the same day.

These complicating factors eliminate the possibility of doing something simple, such as calculating the average time between the two events. In this chapter, we will consider special statistical techniques for looking at the interval between two events when the second event does not necessarily happen to everyone and when people are observed for different periods of time.

The Follow-up Life Table

A statistical technique useful for these types of data is called a follow-up **life table**. (The technique was first applied to the analysis of survival data, from which the term life table originates.) The basic idea of the life table is to subdivide the period of observation after a starting point, such as beginning work at a company, into smaller time intervals—say, single years. For each interval, all people who have been observed at least that long are used to calculate the probability of a **terminal event**, such as leaving the company, occurring in that interval. The probabilities estimated from each of the intervals are then used to estimate the overall probability of the event occurring at different time points. All available data are used for the computations.

A Personnel Example

As an example of life table techniques, consider the following problem. As personnel director of a small company, you are asked to prepare a report on the longevity of employees in your company. You have available in the corporate database information on the date that employees started employment and the last date they worked. You know that it is wrong to look at just the average time on the job for people who left. It doesn't tell you anything about the length of employment for people who are still employed. For example, if your only departures were 10 people who left during their first year with the company, an average employment time based only on them would be highly misleading. You need a way to use information from both the people who left and those who are still with the company.

The employment times for people who are still with the company are known as **censored observations**, since you don't know exactly how long these people will work for the company. You do know, however, that their employment time will be at least as long as the time they have already been at the company. People who have already left the company are **uncensored**, since you know their employment times exactly.

Organizing the Data

As a first step in analyzing the data, you must construct a summary table like that shown in Table 9.1. Each row of the table corresponds to a time interval of one year. (You can choose any interval length you want. For a rapid-turnover company, you might want to consider monthly intervals; for a company with minimal turnover, you might want to consider intervals of several years.) The first interval corresponds to a time period of less than one year, the second interval corresponds to a time period of one year or more but less than two, and so on. The starting point of each interval is shown in the column labeled *Start of Interval*.

For each interval, you count the number of people who left within that interval (*Left*). Similarly, you count the number of people who have worked that long and are still working for the company. For them, this is the latest information available. For each interval, you can also count the number of people who were observed in each of the intervals. That is, you can count how many people worked at least one year, at least two years, and so on.

Table 9.1   Summary table

Start of Interval (years)	Left	Current employees working this long	Employees working at least this long	At risk
0	2	2	100	99
1	1	2	96	95
2	7	16	93	85
3	6	15	70	62
4	5	12	49	43
5	5	10	32	27
6	4	9	17	12.5
7	1	1	4	3.5
8	0	2	2	1.0
TOTAL	31	69		

From Table 9.1, for example, you see that you have information for 100 people, of whom 31 have left the company and 69 are still with the company. You see that two people left the company during their first year, and two current employees have been employed for less than one year. Since four people have been observed for one year or less, all of the rest, 96 people, have worked for one year or more (this is the entry in the second to the last column for the interval that starts at 1).

Calculating Probabilities

Based on the data shown in Table 9.1, you can calculate some useful summary statistics to describe the longevity of the employees. These statistics will make maximum use of the available information by estimating a series of probabilities, each based on as much data as possible.

The first probability you want to estimate is the probability that an employee will quit during the first year of employment. You have observations on 100 employees, 2 of whom quit during the first year. Initially, you may think that the estimate of the probability of leaving in the first year should be 2 out of 100. However, such a calculation does not take into account the fact that you have on staff two employees who have not yet completed their first year. They haven't been observed for the entire interval. You can assume, for simplicity, that they have been observed, on average, for half of the length of the interval. Thus, each is considered as contributing only half of an observation. So for the first interval, instead of having observations for 100 people, we have observations for 99 ($100 - (0.5 \times 2)$). The column labeled *At risk* in Table 9.1 shows the number of observations for each interval when the number is adjusted for the current employees who are assumed to be observed for half of the interval.

The probability of an employee leaving during the first year, using the number in the *At risk* column as the denominator, is $2/99$, or 0.0202. The probability of staying until the end of the first interval is 1 minus the probability of leaving. For the first interval, it is 0.9798.

The next probability you must estimate is that of an employee leaving during the second year, assuming that the employee did not leave during the first year. All employees who have been employed at least one year contribute information to this calculation. From Table 9.1, you see that 1 employee out of 95 at risk left during the second year. The probability of leaving during the second year, given that an employee made it through the first, is then $1/95$, which is 0.0105. The probability of staying to the end of the second year, if the employee made it to the beginning of the second year, is 0.9895.

From these two probabilities (the probability of making it through the first year, and the probability of making it through the second year given that an employee has made it through the first), you can estimate the probability that the employee will make it to the end of the second year of employment. The formula is:

$$P \text{ (second)} = P \text{ (first)} \times P \text{ (second given first)} \qquad \text{Equation 9.1}$$

For this example, the probability of surviving to the end of the second year is 0.9798×0.9895, or 0.9695. This is the cumulative probability of surviving to the end of the second interval.

The Life Table

Figure 9.1 is the life table computed by the SPSS/PC+ Survival procedure for the personnel data. The contents of the columns of the life table are as follows:

Interval Start Time. The beginning value for the each interval. Each interval extends from its start time up to the start time of the next interval.

Number Entering This Interval. The number of cases that have survived to the beginning of the current interval.

Number Withdrawn during This Interval. The number of cases entering the interval for which follow-up ends somewhere in the interval. These are censored cases; that is, these are cases for which the event of interest has not occurred at the time of last contact.

Number Exposed to Risk. This is calculated as the number of cases entering the interval minus one half of those withdrawn during the interval.

Number of Terminal Events. The number of cases for which the event of interest occurs within the interval.

Proportion of Terminal Events. An estimate of the probability of the event of interest occurring in an interval for a case that has made it to the beginning of that interval. It is computed as the number of terminal events divided by the number exposed to risk.

Proportion Surviving. The proportion surviving is 1 minus the proportion of terminal events.

Cumulative Proportion Surviving at End. This is an estimate of the probability of surviving to the end of an interval. It is computed as the product of the proportion surviving this interval and the proportion surviving all previous intervals.

Probability Density. The probability density is an estimate of the probability per unit time of experiencing an event in the interval.

Hazard Rate. The hazard rate is an estimate of the probability per unit time that a case that has survived to the beginning of an interval will experience an event in that interval.

Standard Error of the Cumulative Proportion Surviving. This is an estimate of the variability of the estimate of the cumulative proportion surviving.

Standard Error of the Probability Density. This is an estimate of the variability of the estimated probability density.

Standard Error of the Hazard Rate. This is an estimate of the variability of the estimated hazard rate.

Figure 9.1   Life table

```
SURVIVAL TABLES=LENGTH
 /INTERVALS=THRU 10 BY 1
 /STATUS=EMPLOY(0).

SURVIVAL VARIABLE  LENGTH
```

INTVL START TIME	NUMBER ENTRNG THIS INTVL	NUMBER WDRAWN DURING INTVL	NUMBER EXPOSD TO RISK	NUMBER OF TERMNL EVENTS	PROPN TERMI- NATING	PROPN SURVI- VING	CUMUL PROPN SURV AT END	PROBA- BILITY DENSTY	HAZARD RATE	SE OF CUMUL SURV- IVING	SE OF PROB- ABILTY DENS	SE OF HAZRD RATE
.0	100.0	2.0	99.0	2.0	.0202	.9798	.9798	.0202	.0204	.014	.014	.014
1.0	96.0	2.0	95.0	1.0	.0105	.9895	.9695	.0103	.0106	.017	.010	.011
2.0	93.0	16.0	85.0	7.0	.0824	.9176	.8896	.0798	.0859	.033	.029	.032
3.0	70.0	15.0	62.5	6.0	.0960	.9040	.8042	.0854	.1008	.045	.033	.041
4.0	49.0	12.0	43.0	5.0	.1163	.8837	.7107	.0935	.1235	.056	.040	.055
5.0	32.0	10.0	27.0	5.0	.1852	.8148	.5791	.1316	.2041	.070	.054	.091
6.0	17.0	9.0	12.5	4.0	.3200	.6800	.3938	.1853	.3810	.090	.080	.187
7.0	4.0	1.0	3.5	1.0	.2857	.7143	.2813	.1125	.3333	.115	.099	.329
8.0	2.0	2.0	1.0	.0	.0000	1.0000	.2813	.0000	.0000	.115	.000	.000

```
THE MEDIAN SURVIVAL TIME FOR THESE DATA IS   6.43
```

Median Survival Time

An estimate of the median survival time is displayed below the life table. The median survival time is the time point at which the value of the cumulative survival function is 0.5. That is, it is the time point by which half of the cases are expected to experience the event. Linear interpolation is used to calculate this value. If the cumulative proportion surviving at the end of the last interval is greater than 0.5, the start time of the last interval is identified with a plus sign (+) to indicate that the median time exceeds the start value of the last interval.

From Figure 9.1, you see that the median survival time for the personnel data is 6.43 years. This means that half of the people have left the company after 6.43 years. At six years, almost 58% of the employees remain. At seven years, only 39% remain.

Assumptions Needed to Use the Life Table

The basic assumption underlying life table calculations is that survival experience does not change during the course of the study. For example, if the employment possibilities or work conditions change during the period of the study, it makes no sense to combine all of the cases into a single life table. To use a life table, you must assume that a person hired today will behave the same way as a person who was hired five years ago. You must also assume that observations that are censored do not differ from those that are not censored. These are critical assumptions that determine whether life table analysis is an appropriate technique.

Lost to Follow-up

In the personnel example, we had information available for all employees in the company. We knew who left and when. This is not always the case. If you are studying the survival experience of patients who have undergone a particular therapeutic procedure, you may have two different types of censored observations. You will have patients whose length of survival is not known because they are still alive. You may also have patients with whom you have lost contact and for whom you know only that they were alive at some date in the past. If patients with whom you have lost contact differ from patients who remain in contact, the results of a life table analysis will be misleading.

Consider the situation in which patients with whom you have lost contact are healthier than patients who remain in contact. By assuming that patients who are lost to follow-up behave the same way as patients who are not, the life table will underestimate the survival experience of the group. Similarly, if sicker patients lose contact, the life table will overestimate the proportion surviving at various time points. It cannot be emphasized too strongly that no statistical procedure can atone for problems associated with incomplete follow-up.

Plotting Survival Functions

The survival functions displayed in the life table can also be plotted. This allows you to better examine the functions. It also allows you to compare the functions for several groups. For example, Figure 9.2 is a plot of the cumulative percentage surviving when the employees from Figure 9.1 are subdivided into two groups: clerical and professional. You see that clerical employees have shorter employment times than professional employees.

Comparing Survival Functions

If two or more groups in your study can be considered as samples from some larger population, you may want to test the null hypothesis that the survival distributions are the same for the subgroups. The SPSS/PC+ Survival procedure uses the Wilcoxon (Gehan) test (Lee, 1992).

As shown in Figure 9.3, the number of censored and uncensored cases, as well as an average score, are displayed for each group. The average score is calculated by comparing each case to all others and incrementing the score for a case by 1 if the case has a longer survival time than another case and decrementing it by 1 if the case has a shorter survival time.

In Figure 9.3, the observed significance level for the test that all groups come from the same distribution is less than 0.00005, leading you to reject the null hypothesis that the groups do not differ.

Figure 9.2   Plot of surviving clerical employees against professionals

```
SURVIVAL TABLES=LENGTH BY TYPE(1,2)
 /INTERVALS=THRU 10 BY 1
 /STATUS=EMPLOY(0)
 /PLOTS (SURVIVAL).
```

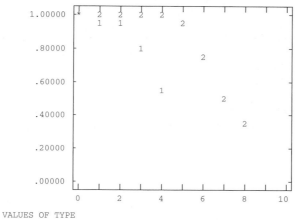

```
 GRAPH OF SURVIVAL FUNCTION
   SURVIVAL VARIABLE   LENGTH
          GROUPED BY   TYPE
```

```
VALUES OF TYPE                                           AND GRAPH SYMBOLS

            GRAPH   VALUE                        GRAPH   VALUE
    VALUE   SYMBOL  LABEL            VALUE        SYMBOL  LABEL
      1      1      Clerical           2           2      Professional
```

Figure 9.3   Comparing subgroups

```
SURVIVAL TABLES=LENGTH BY TYPE(1,2)
 /INTERVALS=THRU 10 BY 1
 /STATUS=EMPLOY(0)
 /COMPARE.
```

```
COMPARISON OF SURVIVAL EXPERIENCE USING THE WILCOXON (GEHAN) STATISTIC
   SURVIVAL VARIABLE   LENGTH
          GROUPED BY   TYPE
```

OVERALL COMPARISON	STATISTIC	26.786	D.F.	1	PROB.	.0000

GROUP	LABEL	TOTAL N	UNCEN	CEN	PCT CEN	MEAN SCORE
1	Clerical	54	19	35	64.81	-15.4444
2	Professional	46	12	34	73.91	18.1304

Running the Survival Procedure

The SPSS/PC+ Survival procedure produces actuarial life tables, plots, and related statistics for examining the length of time to the occurrence of an event, often known as survival times. Cases can be classified into groups for separate analyses and comparisons. Time intervals can be calculated with the SPSS/PC+ date-conversion function YRMODA (see the *SPSS/PC+ Base System User's Guide*).

SURVIVAL requires a TABLES subcommand for naming a survival variable, an INTERVALS subcommand for setting the period to be examined, and a STATUS subcommand for identifying the variable that indicates the survival status. The remaining subcommands are optional and can appear in any order, but they must be placed after the required subcommands.

Specifying Variables in the Equation

Use the TABLES subcommand to list the survival variables and control variables that you want to include in the analysis. For example, the following command produces Figure 9.1:

```
SURVIVAL TABLES=LENGTH
  /INTERVALS=THRU 10 BY 1
  /STATUS=EMPLOY(0).
```

Specifying Control Variables

Use the BY keyword to separate the survival variables from the first-order control variables. Use a second BY keyword to separate the first- and second-order control variable lists. Each control variable must be followed by a value range in parentheses. These values must be integers separated by a comma or a blank. Non-integer values in the data are truncated, and cases are assigned to subgroups based on the integer portion of their values on the variable. To specify only one value for a control variable, use the same value for the minimum and maximum, as in GROUP(1,1).

Example

```
SURVIVAL TABLES=TIME BY GROUP(1,3) BY SEX(1,2)
  /INTERVALS=THRU 60 BY 12
  /STATUS=CENSOR(1).
```

• This example produces a separate life table for each combination of *group* and *sex*, for a total of six life tables.

Specifying Intervals

The survival variables are measured in units of time such as days, weeks, months, or years. You must use the INTERVALS subcommand to specify which period of time is to be examined and how the time period is divided for the analysis. The INTERVALS subcommand has two required keyword specifications:

- Use the keyword THRU to indicate the period of time to be examined. For example, if your data are recorded in yearly intervals, a specification of THRU 10 indicates a time period of 0 through 10 years.

- Use the keyword BY to specify the time intervals for the analysis. For example, if your data are recorded in monthly intervals, but you are concerned only with yearly changes, the specification BY 12 groups the monthly data into yearly intervals.

Even if your data are already recorded in the intervals you want to use, you *must* specify both THRU and BY, as in:

```
SURVIVAL TABLES=LENGTH
   /INTERVALS=THRU 10 BY 1
   /STATUS=EMPLOY(0).
```

This example produces Figure 9.1.

You can divide the period into intervals of varying lengths with multiple THRU and BY keywords, as in:

```
SURVIVAL TABLES=LENGTH
   /INTERVALS=THRU 10 BY 1 THRU 20 BY 2
   /STATUS=EMPLOY(0).
```

The first interval always begins at 0. Subsequent intervals begin after the value specified on the preceding THRU keyword. So the second THRU specification above applies to values from 11 to 20. THRU values must be specified in ascending order, without any overlap in ranges.

Only one INTERVALS subcommand can be used on a SURVIVAL command. The interval specifications apply to all the survival variables listed on the TABLES subcommand.

Specifying the Status Variables

For each survival variable listed on the TABLES subcommand, you must provide a variable that indicates the survival status of each case. The codes on these status variables distinguish between cases for which the terminal event has occurred and those that either survived to the end of the study or were dropped for some reason (censored cases).

Use the STATUS subcommand to specify a status variable with a value or value range enclosed in parentheses, optionally followed by the keyword FOR and the name of one or more of the survival variables. The value range identifies the codes that indicate that the terminal event has occurred. All observations that do not have a code in the value range are classified as censored cases.

Example

```
SURVIVAL TABLES=LENGTH
  /INTERVALS=THRU 10 BY 1
  /STATUS=EMPLOY(0).
```

- The STATUS subcommand in this example specifies that a code of 0 on *employ* means the terminal event for the survival variable *length* has occurred.

- Cases with any other code on *employ* are treated as censored.

Only one status variable can be listed on a STATUS subcommand. Use separate STATUS subcommands for each of the survival variables or, if appropriate, list more than one survival variable after the FOR keyword. If the FOR keyword is not specified, the status variable specification applies to any of the survival variables not named on another STATUS subcommand.

Controlling Output Display

By default, SURVIVAL displays life tables with its output. If you are interested only in the plots and the subgroup comparisons available in SURVIVAL, you can use the PRINT subcommand to suppress the display of the life tables.

TABLE   *Display the life tables.* This is the default.

NOTABLE   *Suppress the life tables.* Only plots and comparisons are displayed. If you specify NOTABLE and yet do not include either a PLOTS or a COMPARE subcommand, no output is generated and SPSS/PC+ displays an error message.

Requesting Plots

You can request plots of the three survival functions by specifying in parentheses any of five keywords available on the PLOT subcommand:

ALL   *Produce all available function plots.* This is the default if PLOT is specified by itself.

LOGSURV   *Produce a plot of the cumulative survival distribution on a logarithmic scale.*

SURVIVAL   *Plot the cumulative survival distribution on a linear scale.*

HAZARD   *Plot the hazard function.*

DENSITY   *Plot the density function.*

Example

```
SURVIVAL TABLES=LENGTH BY TYPE(1,2)
   /INITIAL=THRU 10 BY 1
   /STATUS=EMPLOY (0)
   /PLOTS (SURVIVAL).
```

- This example produces Figure 9.2.

You can specify more than one type of plot on the same PLOT subcommand, as in:

```
   /PLOT (SURVIVAL HAZARD).
```

By default, each function requested is plotted for each survival variable listed on the TABLES subcommand. Optionally, you can limit the plots to specific variables by specifying an equals sign followed by a variable list, as in:

```
   /PLOT (SURVIVAL HAZARD)=LENGTH.
```

You can use the TO keyword to imply consecutive variables. The order of variables is determined by their order on the TABLES subcommand, not their order in the active file.

Comparing Subgroups

Use the COMPARE subcommand to compare the survival of subgroups defined by the control variables. COMPARE with no variable list produces a default set of comparisons using the TABLES variable list. At least one survival and one first-order control variable must be specified to make comparisons possible.

Example

```
SURVIVAL TABLES=LENGTH BY TYPE(1,2)
   /INTERVALS=THRU 10 BY 1
   /STATUS=EMPLOY(0)
   /COMPARE.
```

- This example produces Figure 9.3.

Specifying Ways of Comparison

Use the CALCULATE subcommand to indicate how survival comparisons for subgroups of cases are to be calculated. The default is EXACT, for exact comparisons. You can specify any of the following keywords on CALCULATE:

EXACT   *Exact comparisons.* This is the default.

PAIRWISE   *Pairwise comparisons.* Comparisons of each possible pair of values of every first-order control variable are produced along with an overall comparison.

CONDITIONAL   *Approximate comparisons if memory is insufficient for exact comparisons.*

APPROXIMATE   *Approximate comparisons only.*

COMPARE   *Comparisons only.* Survival tables specified on the TABLES subcommand are not computed and requests for plots are ignored. This allows all available workspace to be used for comparisons. You cannot use the WRITE subcommand when this specification is in effect.

Exact and Approximate Comparisons

SURVIVAL accepts either individual or aggregated data. With individual data, you can obtain exact comparisons, for which survival scores are calculated on the basis of the survival experience of each observation. While this method is the most accurate, it requires all data to be in memory simultaneously. When exact comparisons become impractical because of the large sample size or when individual data are not available (see "Entering Aggregated Data" on p. 274), you should request approximate comparisons.

Use the keyword APPROXIMATE to request approximate comparisons. Use the keyword CONDITIONAL to produce approximate comparisons only if there is insufficient memory available for exact comparisons. The approximate comparison approach assumes that all events—termination, withdrawal, and so forth—occur at the midpoint of the interval. Under exact comparisons, some of these midpoint ties can be resolved. However, if interval widths are not too great, the difference between exact and approximate comparisons should be small.

Entering Aggregated Data

When data are recorded for the entire sample at set points in time instead of on an individual basis, it is necessary to enter aggregated data for SURVIVAL analysis. When aggregated data are used, two records are entered for each interval, one for censored cases and one for uncensored cases. The number of cases included on each record is used as the weight variable (see the *SPSS/PC+ Base System User's Guide* for a discussion of the WEIGHT command). If control variables are used, there must be a pair of records (one for censored and one for uncensored cases) for each value of the control variable in each interval. These records must contain the value of the control variable and the number of cases that belong in the particular category as well as values for survival time and status.

Example

```
DATA LIST FREE /SURVEVAR  STATVAR  SEX  CASES.
BEGIN DATA
1 1 1 0
1 2 1 1
1 1 2 2
1 2 2 1
2 1 1 1
2 2 1 2
2 1 2 1
2 2 2 3
 . . .
END DATA.
VALUE LABELS  STATVAR 1 'DECEASED' 2 'ALIVE'
  /SEX 1 'FEMALE' 2 'MALE'.
WEIGHT BY CASES.
SURVIVAL TABLES=SURVEVAR BY SEX (1,2)
  /INTERVALS=THRU 10 BY 1
  /STATUS=STATVAR (1).
```

- DATA LIST reads in aggregated data.

- SURVIVAL uses a control variable with two values. The first data record has a code of 1 on the status variable *statvar*, indicating it is an uncensored case, and a code of 1 on *sex*, the control variable. The number of cases for this subset is 0, the value of the variable *cases*.

- *Cases* is not used in SURVIVAL but is the weight variable.

- In this example, each interval requires four records to provide all the data for each *survevar* interval.

Missing-Value Treatment

Use the MISSING subcommand to control missing-value treatment. The default keyword on MISSING is GROUPWISE, which excludes cases with missing values on a variable from any calculation involving that variable. The MISSING subcommand can also exclude cases listwise. With either groupwise or listwise treatment of missing values, you can include user-missing values in the analysis.

With any missing-value treatment, negative values on the survival variables are automatically treated as missing data. In addition, cases outside the value range on a control variable are excluded.

GROUPWISE   *Exclude missing values groupwise.* Cases with missing values on a variable are excluded from any calculation involving that variable. This is the default.

LISTWISE   *Exclude missing values listwise.* Cases missing on any variables named are excluded from the analysis.

INCLUDE   *Include cases with user-missing values.* Only cases with system-missing values are excluded.

You can specify INCLUDE with GROUPWISE or LISTWISE, as in:

```
/MISSING=LISTWISE INCLUDE.
```

This subcommand excludes cases with system-missing values on a listwise basis. Cases with user-missing values are included.

Saving Survival Tables

Use the WRITE subcommand to save data in the survival tables to an output file. This file can be used for further analyses or to produce graphic displays. You can specify one of the following keywords:

NONE   *Do not write survival tables to file.* This is the default if the WRITE subcommand is not specified.

TABLES   *Write out survival table data records.* All survival table statistics are written to the file. This is the default when you specify the WRITE subcommand without additional specifications.

BOTH   *Write out survival table data and label records.* Variable names, variable labels, and value labels are written out along with the survival table statistics.

When you specify the WRITE subcommand with SURVIVAL, the data are written to the results file. The default results file is *spss.prc*. The SURVIVAL data will overwrite any previous contents of the results file. Before running the SURVIVAL command, you can change the name of the results file with the SET command.

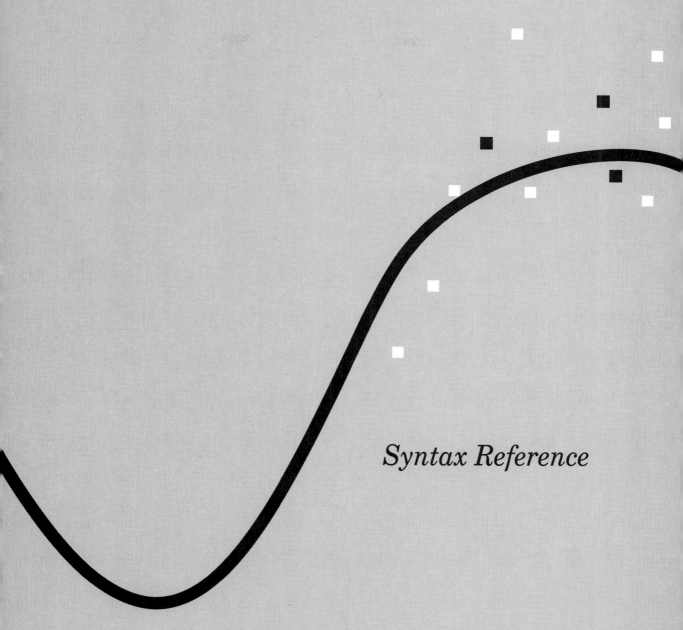

Syntax Reference

HILOGLINEAR

```
HILOGLINEAR {varlist} (min,max) [varlist ...]
            {ALL    }

[/METHOD [= BACKWARD]]

[/MAXORDER = k]

[/CRITERIA = [CONVERGE({0.25**})] [ITERATE({20**})] [P({0.05**})]
                       {n      }            {n    }     {prob   }
              [DELTA({0.5**})] [MAXSTEPS({10**})]
                     {d    }             {n   }
              [DEFAULT] ]

[/CWEIGHT = {varname }]
            {(matrix)}

[/PRINT = {[FREQ**] [RESID**] [ESTIM**][ASSOCIATION]}]
          {DEFAULT**                                }
          {ALL                                      }
          {NONE                                     }

[/PLOT = [{NONE**            }]
          {DEFAULT           }
          {[RESID] [NORMPROB]}
          {ALL               }

[/MISSING = [{EXCLUDE**}]]
             {INCLUDE  }

[/DESIGN = effectname effectname*effectname ...]
```

** Default if subcommand or keyword is omitted.

Example:

```
HILOGLINEAR V1(1,2) V2(1,2)
  /DESIGN=V1*V2.
```

Overview

HILOGLINEAR fits hierarchical loglinear models to multidimensional contingency tables using an iterative proportional-fitting algorithm. HILOGLINEAR also estimates parameters for saturated models. These techniques are described in Everitt (1977), Bishop et al. (1975), and Goodman (1978). HILOGLINEAR is much more efficient for these models than the Loglinear procedure because HILOGLINEAR uses an iterative proportional-fitting algorithm rather than the Newton-Raphson method used in LOGLINEAR.

Options

Design Specification. You can request automatic model selection using backward elimination with the METHOD subcommand. You can also specify any hierarchical design and request multiple designs using the DESIGN subcommand.

Design Control. You can control the criteria used in the iterative proportional-fitting and model-selection routines with the CRITERIA subcommand. You can also limit the order of effects in the model with the MAXORDER subcommand and specify structural zeros for cells in the tables you analyze with the CWEIGHT subcommand.

Display and Plots. You can select the display for each design with the PRINT subcommand. For saturated models, you can request tests for different orders of effects as well. With the PLOT subcommand, you can request residuals plots or normal probability plots of residuals.

Basic Specification

- The basic specification is a variable list with at least two variables followed by their minimum and maximum values.
- HILOGLINEAR estimates a saturated model for all variables in the analysis.
- By default, HILOGLINEAR displays parameter estimates, goodness of fit, frequencies, and residuals for the saturated model.

Subcommand Order

- The variable list must be specified first.
- Subcommands affecting a given DESIGN must appear before the DESIGN subcommand. Otherwise, subcommands can appear in any order.
- MISSING can be placed anywhere after the variable list.

Syntax Rules

- DESIGN is optional. If DESIGN is omitted or the last specification is not a DESIGN subcommand, a default saturated model is estimated.
- You can specify multiple PRINT, PLOT, CRITERIA, MAXORDER, and CWEIGHT subcommands. The last of each type specified is in effect for subsequent designs.
- PRINT, PLOT, CRITERIA, MAXORDER, and CWEIGHT specifications remain in effect until they are overridden by new specifications on these subcommands.
- You can specify multiple METHOD subcommands, but each one affects only the next design.
- MISSING can be specified only once.

Operations

- HILOGLINEAR builds a contingency table using all variables on the variable list. The table contains a cell for each possible combination of values within the range specified for each variable.
- HILOGLINEAR assumes that there is a category for every integer value in the range of each variable. Empty categories waste space and can cause computational problems. If there

are empty categories, use the RECODE command to create consecutive integer values for categories.

- Cases with values outside the range specified for a variable are excluded.

- If the last subcommand is not a DESIGN subcommand, HILOGLINEAR displays a warning and generates the default model. This is the saturated model unless MAXORDER is specified. This model is in addition to any that are explicitly requested.

- If the model is not saturated (for example, when MAXORDER is less than the number of factors), SPSS/PC+ displays only the goodness of fit, observed and expected frequencies, and residuals.

- The display uses the WIDTH subcommand defined on the SET command. If the defined width is less than 132, some portions of the display may be deleted.

Limitations

HILOGLINEAR cannot estimate all possible frequency models, and it produces limited output for unsaturated models.

- It can estimate only hierarchical loglinear models.

- It treats all table variables as nominal. (You can use LOGLINEAR to fit nonhierarchical models to tables involving variables that are ordinal.)

- It can produce parameter estimates for saturated models only (those with all possible main-effect and interaction terms).

- It can estimate partial associations for saturated models only.

- It can handle tables with no more than 10 factors.

Example

```
HILOGLINEAR V1(1,2) V2(1,2) V3(1,3) V4(1,3)
  /DESIGN=V1*V2*V3, V4.
```

- HILOGLINEAR builds a $2 \times 2 \times 3 \times 3$ contingency table for analysis.

- DESIGN specifies the generating class for a hierarchical model. This model consists of main effects for all four variables, two-way interactions among V1, V2, and V3, and the three-way interaction term V1 by V2 by V3.

Variable List

The required variable list specifies the variables in the analysis. The variable list must precede all other subcommands.

- Variables must be numeric and have integer values. If a variable has a fractional value, the fractional portion is truncated.

- Keyword ALL can be used to refer to all user-defined variables in the active file.

- A range must be specified for each variable, with the minimum and maximum values separated by a comma and enclosed in parentheses.

- If the same range applies to several variables, the range can be specified once after the last variable to which it applies.
- If ALL is specified, all variables must have the same range.

METHOD Subcommand

By default, HILOGLINEAR tests the model specified on the DESIGN subcommand (or the default model) and does not perform any model selection. All variables are entered and none removed. Use METHOD to specify automatic model selection using backward elimination for the next design specified.

- You can specify METHOD alone or with keyword BACKWARD for an explicit specification.
- When the backward-elimination method is requested, a step-by-step output is displayed regardless of the specification on the PRINT subcommand.
- METHOD affects only the next design.

BACKWARD   *Backward elimination.* Perform backward elimination of terms in the model. All terms are entered. Those that do not meet the P criterion specified on the CRITERIA subcommand (or the default P, if P is not specified) are removed one at a time.

MAXORDER Subcommand

MAXORDER controls the maximum order of terms in the model estimated for subsequent designs. If MAXORDER is specified, HILOGLINEAR tests a model only with terms of that order or less.

- MAXORDER specifies the highest-order term that will be considered for the next design. MAXORDER can thus be used to abbreviate computations for the BACKWARD method.
- If the integer on MAXORDER is less than the number of factors, parameter estimates and measures of partial association are not available. Only the goodness of fit, observed and expected frequencies, and residuals are displayed.
- You can use MAXORDER with backward elimination to find the best model with terms of a certain order or less. This is computationally much more efficient than eliminating terms from the saturated model.

Example

```
HILOGLINEAR V1 V2 V3(1,2)
  /MAXORDER=2
  /DESIGN=V1 V2 V3
  /DESIGN=V1*V2*V3.
```

- HILOGLINEAR builds a $2 \times 2 \times 2$ contingency table for *V1, V2,* and *V3*.
- MAXORDER has no effect on the first DESIGN subcommand because the design requested considers only main effects.
- MAXORDER restricts the terms in the model specified on the second DESIGN subcommand to two-way interactions and main effects.

CRITERIA Subcommand

Use the CRITERIA subcommand to change the values of constants in the iterative proportional-fitting and model-selection routines for subsequent designs.

- The default criteria are in effect if the CRITERIA subcommand is omitted (see below).
- You cannot specify the CRITERIA subcommand without any keywords.
- Specify each CRITERIA keyword followed by a criterion value in parentheses. Only those criteria specifically altered are changed.
- You can specify more than one keyword on CRITERIA, and they can be in any order.

DEFAULT   *Reset parameters to their default values.* If you have specified criteria other than the defaults for a design, use this keyword to restore the defaults for subsequent designs.

CONVERGE(n)   *Convergence criterion.* The default is 10^{-3} times the largest cell size, or 0.25, whichever is larger.

ITERATE(n)   *Maximum number of iterations.* The default is 20.

P(n)   *Probability for change in chi-square if term is removed.* Specify a value between 0 and 1 for the significance level. The default is 0.05. P is in effect only when you request BACKWARD on the METHOD subcommand.

MAXSTEPS(n)   *Maximum number of steps for model selection.* Specify an integer between 1 and 99, inclusive. The default is 10.

DELTA(d)   *Cell delta value.* The value of delta is added to each cell frequency for the first iteration. It is left in the cells for saturated models only. The default value is 0.5. You can specify any value for delta that is equal to 0 or greater (generally, delta should be less than 1). HILOGLINEAR does not display parameter estimates or the covariance matrix of parameter estimates if any zero cells (either structural or sampling) exist in the expected table after delta is added.

CWEIGHT Subcommand

CWEIGHT specifies cell weights for a model. CWEIGHT is typically used to specify structural zeros in the table. You can also use CWEIGHT to adjust tables to fit new margins.

- You can specify the name of a variable whose values are cell weights, or provide a matrix of cell weights enclosed in parentheses.
- If you use a variable to specify cell weights, you are allowed only one CWEIGHT subcommand.
- If you specify a matrix, you must provide a weight for every cell in the contingency table, where the number of cells equals the product of the number of values of all variables.
- Cell weights are indexed by the values of the variables in the order in which they are specified on the variable list. The index values of the rightmost variable change the most quickly.
- You can use the notation $n * cw$ to indicate that cell weight cw is repeated n times in the matrix.

Example

```
HILOGLINEAR V1(1,2) V2(1,2) V3(1,3)
  /CWEIGHT=CELLWGT
  /DESIGN=V1*V2, V2*V3, V1*V3.
```

- This example uses the variable *CELLWGT* to assign cell weights for the table. Only one CWEIGHT subcommand is allowed.

Example

```
HILOGLINEAR V4(1,3) V5(1,3)
  /CWEIGHT=(0 1 1  1 0 1  1 1 0)
  /DESIGN=V4, V5.
```

- The HILOGLINEAR command sets the diagonal cells in the model to structural zeros. This type of model is known as a **quasi-independence model**.
- Because both *V4* and *V5* have three values, weights must be specified for nine cells.
- The first cell weight is applied to the cell in which *V4* is 1 and *V5* is 1; the second weight is applied to the cell in which *V4* is 1 and *V5* is 2; and so forth.

Example

```
HILOGLINEAR V4(1,3) V5(1,3)
  /CWEIGHT=(0 3*1 0 3*1 0)
  /DESIGN=V4,V5.
```

- This example is the same as the previous example except that the *n*cw* notation is used.

Example

```
* An Incomplete Rectangular Table

DATA LIST FREE / LOCULAR RADIAL FREQ.
WEIGHT BY FREQ.
BEGIN DATA
1 1 462
1 2 130
1 3 2
1 4 1
2 1 103
2 2 35
2 3 1
2 4 0
3 5 614
3 6 138
3 7 21
3 8 14
3 9 1
4 5 443
4 6 95
4 7 22
4 8 8
4 9 5
END DATA.
HILOGLINEAR LOCULAR (1,4) RADIAL (1,9)
  /CWEIGHT=(4*1 5*0   4*1 5*0   4*0 5*1   4*0 5*1)
  /DESIGN LOCULAR RADIAL.
```

- This example uses aggregated table data as input.
- The DATA LIST command defines three variables. The values of *LOCULAR* and *RADIAL* index the levels of those variables, so that each case defines a cell in the table. The values of *FREQ* are the cell frequencies.
- The WEIGHT command weights each case by the value of the variable *FREQ*. Because each case represents a cell in this example, the WEIGHT command assigns the frequencies for each cell.
- The BEGIN DATA and END DATA commands enclose the inline data.
- The HILOGLINEAR variable list specifies two variables. *LOCULAR* has values 1, 2, 3, and 4. *RADIAL* has integer values 1 through 9.
- The CWEIGHT subcommand identifies a block rectangular pattern of cells that are logically empty. There is one weight specified for each cell of the 36-cell table.
- In this example, the matrix form needs to be used in CWEIGHT because the structural zeros do not appear in the actual data. (For example, there is no case corresponding to *LOCULAR*=1, *RADIAL*=5.)
- The DESIGN subcommand specifies main effects only for *LOCULAR* and *RADIAL*. Lack of fit for this model indicates an interaction of the two variables.
- Because there is no PRINT or PLOT subcommand, HILOGLINEAR produces the default output for an unsaturated model.

PRINT Subcommand

PRINT controls the display produced for the subsequent designs.

- If PRINT is omitted or included with no specifications, the default display is produced.
- If any keywords are specified on PRINT, only output specifically requested is displayed.
- HILOGLINEAR displays Pearson and likelihood-ratio chi-square goodness-of-fit tests for models. For saturated models, it also provides tests that the k-way effects and the k-way and higher-order effects are zero.
- Both adjusted and unadjusted degrees of freedom are displayed for tables with sampling or structural zeros. K-way and higher-order tests use the unadjusted degrees of freedom.
- The unadjusted degrees of freedom are not adjusted for zero cells, and they estimate the upper bound of the true degrees of freedom. These are the same degrees of freedom you would get if all cells were filled.
- The adjusted degrees of freedom are calculated from the number of non-zero-fitted cells minus the number of parameters that would be estimated if all cells were filled (that is, unadjusted degrees of freedom minus the number of zero-fitted cells). This estimate of degrees of freedom may be too low if some parameters do not exist because of zeros.

DEFAULT   *Default displays.* This option includes FREQ and RESID output for nonsaturated models, and FREQ, RESID, and ESTIM output for saturated models. For saturated models, the observed and expected frequencies are equal, and the residuals are zeros.

FREQ   *Observed and expected cell frequencies.*

RESID	*Raw and standardized residuals.*
ESTIM	*Parameter estimates for a saturated model.*
ASSOCIATION	*Partial associations.* You can request partial associations of effects only when you specify a saturated model. This option is computationally expensive for tables with many factors.
ALL	*All available output.*
NONE	*Design information and goodness-of-fit statistics only.* Use of this option overrides all other specifications on PRINT.

PLOT Subcommand

Use PLOT to request residuals plots.
- If PLOT is included without specifications, standardized residuals and normal probability plots are produced.
- No plots are displayed for saturated models, since all residuals are 0 for saturated models.
- If PLOT is omitted, no plots are produced.

RESID	*Standardized residuals against observed and expected counts.*
NORMPLOT	*Normal probability plots of adjusted residuals.*
NONE	*No plots.* Specify NONE to suppress plots requested on a previous PLOT subcommand. This is the default if PLOT is omitted.
DEFAULT	*Default plots.* Includes RESID and NORMPLOT. This is the default when PLOT is specified without keywords.
ALL	*All available plots.*

MISSING Subcommand

By default, a case with either system-missing or user-missing values for any variable named on the HILOGLINEAR variable list is omitted from the analysis. Use MISSING to change the treatment of cases with user-missing values.
- MISSING can be named only once and can be placed anywhere following the variable list.
- MISSING cannot be used without specifications.
- A case with a system-missing value for any variable named on the variable list is always excluded from the analysis.

EXCLUDE	*Delete cases with missing values.* This is the default if the subcommand is omitted. You can also specify keyword DEFAULT.
INCLUDE	*Include user-missing values as valid.* Only cases with system-missing values are deleted.

DESIGN Subcommand

By default, HILOGLINEAR uses a saturated model that includes all variables on the variable list. The model contains all main effects and interactions for those variables. Use DESIGN to specify a different generating class for the model.

- If DESIGN is omitted or included without specifications, the default model is estimated. When DESIGN is omitted, SPSS/PC+ issues a warning message.

- To specify a design, list the highest-order terms, using variable names and asterisks (*) to indicate interaction effects.

- In a hierarchical model, higher-order interaction effects imply lower-order interaction and main effects. $V1*V2*V3$ implies the three-way interaction $V1$ by $V2$ by $V3$, two-way interactions $V1$ by $V2$, $V1$ by $V3$, and $V2$ by $V3$, and main effects for $V1$, $V2$, and $V3$. The highest-order effects to be estimated are the generating class.

- Any PRINT, PLOT, CRITERIA, METHOD, and MAXORDER subcommands that apply to a DESIGN subcommand must appear before it.

- All variables named on DESIGN must be named or implied on the variable list.

- You can specify more than one DESIGN subcommand. One model is estimated for each DESIGN subcommand.

- If the last subcommand on HILOGLINEAR is not DESIGN, the default model will be estimated in addition to models explicitly requested. SPSS/PC+ issues a warning message for a missing DESIGN subcommand.

Annotated Example

For a complete example with output, see the Annotated Examples following the Syntax Reference section of this manual.

LOGISTIC REGRESSION

```
LOGISTIC REGRESSION [VARIABLES =] dependent var
          [WITH independent varlist [BY var [BY var] ... ]]

[/CATEGORICAL = var1, var2, ... ]

[/CONTRAST (categorical var) = [{DEVIATION [(refcat)]    }]]
                                {SIMPLE [(refcat)]        }
                                {DIFFERENCE               }
                                {HELMERT                  }
                                {REPEATED                 }
                                {POLYNOMIAL[({1,2,3...})]  }
                                {            {metric   }  }
                                {SPECIAL (matrix)         }
                                {INDICATOR [(refcat)]     }

[/METHOD = {ENTER**       }  [{ALL    }]]
           {BSTEP [{WALD}]}   {varlist}
           {       {LR  }}
           {FSTEP [{WALD}]}
           {       {LR  }}

[/SELECT = {ALL**                  }]
           {varname relation value}

[/{NOORIGIN**}]
  {ORIGIN   }

[/ID = [variable]]

[/PRINT = [DEFAULT**] [SUMMARY] [CORR] [ALL] [ITER [({1})]]]
                                                    {n}

[/CRITERIA = [BCON ({0.001**})] [ITERATE({20**})] [LCON({0.01**})]
                    {value  }            {n   }         {value }

             [PIN({0.05**})] [POUT({0.10**})] [EPS({.00000001**})]]]
                  {value }          {value }        {value      }

[/CLASSPLOT]

[/MISSING = {EXCLUDE **}]
            {INCLUDE   }

[/CASEWISE = [tempvarlist]  [OUTLIER({2**  })]]]
                                     {value}

[/SAVE = tempvar[(newname)] tempvar[(newname)]...]

[/EXTERNAL]
```

** Default if subcommand or keyword is omitted.

Temporary variables created by LOGISTIC REGRESSION are:

PRED	LEVER	COOK
PGROUP	LRESID	DFBETA
RESID	SRESID	
DEV	ZRESID	

Example:

```
LOGISTIC REGRESSION PROMOTED WITH AGE, JOBTIME, JOBRATE.
```

Overview

LOGISTIC REGRESSION regresses a dichotomous dependent variable on a set of independent variables (Aldrich & Nelson, 1984; Fox, 1984; Hosmer & Lemeshow, 1989; McCullagh & Nelder, 1989; Agresti, 1990). Categorical independent variables are replaced by sets of contrast variables, each set entering and leaving the model in a single step.

Options

Processing of Independent Variables. You can specify which independent variables are categorical in nature on the CATEGORICAL subcommand. You can control treatment of categorical independent variables by the CONTRAST subcommand. Five methods are available for building a model. You can specify any one of them on the METHOD subcommand. You can also use the keyword BY between variable names to enter interaction terms.

Selecting Cases. You can use the SELECT subcommand to define subsets of cases to be used in estimating a model.

Regression Through the Origin. You can use the ORIGIN subcommand to exclude a constant term from a model.

Specifying Termination and Model-building Criteria. You can further control computations when building the model by specifying criteria on the CRITERIA subcommand.

Adding New Variables to the Active File. You can SAVE the residuals, predicted values, and diagnostics generated by LOGISTIC REGRESSION in the active file.

Output. You can use the PRINT subcommand to print optional output, use the CASEWISE subcommand to request analysis of residuals, and use the ID subcommand to specify a variable whose values or value labels identify cases in output. You can request plots of the actual and predicted values for each case with the CLASSPLOT subcommand.

Basic Specification

- The minimum specification is the VARIABLES subcommand with one dichotomous dependent variable. You must specify a list of independent variables either following the keyword WITH on the VARIABLES subcommand or on a METHOD subcommand.
- The default output includes goodness-of-fit tests for the model and a classification table for the predicted and observed group memberships. The regression coefficient, standard error of the regression coefficient, Wald statistic and its significance level, and a multiple correlation coefficient adjusted for the number of parameters (Atkinson, 1980) are displayed for each variable in the equation.

Subcommand Order

- Subcommands can be named in any order. If the VARIABLES subcommand is not specified first, a slash (/) must precede it.

- The ordering of METHOD subcommands determines the order in which models are estimated. Different sequences may result in different models.

Syntax Rules

- Only one dependent variable can be specified for each LOGISTIC REGRESSION.
- Any number of independent variables may be listed. The dependent variable may not appear on this list.
- The independent variable list is required if any of the METHOD subcommands are used without a variable list or if the METHOD subcommand is not used. Keyword TO cannot be used on any variable list.
- If you specify keyword WITH on the VARIABLES subcommand, all independent variables must be listed.
- If keyword WITH is used on the VARIABLES subcommand, interaction terms do not have to be specified on the variable list, but the individual variables that make up the interactions must be listed.
- Multiple METHOD subcommands are allowed.
- The minimum truncation for this command is LOGI REG.

Operations

- Independent variables specified on the CATEGORICAL subcommand are replaced by sets of contrast variables. In stepwise analyses, the set of contrast variables associated with a categorical variable is entered or removed from the model as a single step.
- Independent variables are screened to detect and eliminate redundancies.
- If the linearly dependent variable is one of a set of contrast variables, the set will be reduced by the redundant variable or variables. A warning will be issued, and the reduced set will be used.
- For the forward stepwise method, redundancy checking is done when a variable is to be entered into the model.
- When backward stepwise or direct-entry methods are requested, all variables for each METHOD subcommand are checked for redundancy before that analysis begins.

Limitations

- The dependent variable must be dichotomous. Specifying a dependent variable with more or less than two nonmissing values will result in an error.

Example

```
LOGISTIC REGRESSION PASS WITH GPA, MAT, GRE.
```

- *PASS* is specified as the dependent variable.

- *GPA, MAT,* and *GRE* are specified as independent variables.
- LOGISTIC REGRESSION produces the default output for the logistic regression of *PASS* on *GPA, MAT,* and *GRE.*

VARIABLES Subcommand

VARIABLES specifies the dependent variable and, optionally, all independent variables in the model. The dependent variable appears first on the list and is separated from the independent variables by keyword WITH.

- One VARIABLES subcommand is allowed for each Logistic Regression procedure.
- The dependent variable must be dichotomous—that is, it must have exactly two values other than system-missing and user-missing values.
- The dependent variable may be a string variable if its two values can be differentiated by their first eight characters.
- You can indicate an interaction term on the variable list by using keyword BY to separate the individual variables.
- If all METHOD subcommands are accompanied by independent variable lists, keyword WITH and the list of independent variables may be omitted.
- If keyword WITH is used, *all* independent variables must be specified. For interaction terms, only the individual variable names that make up the interaction (for example, X1, X2) need to be specified if they are to be used by themselves in the procedure. Specifying the actual interaction term (for example, X1 BY X2) on the VARIABLES subcommand is optional if you specify it on a METHOD subcommand.

Example

```
LOGISTIC REGRESSION PROMOTED WITH AGE,JOBTIME,JOBRATE,
    AGE BY JOBTIME.
```

- *PROMOTED* is specified as the dependent variable.
- *AGE, JOBTIME, JOBRATE,* and the interaction *AGE* by *JOBTIME* are specified as the independent variables.
- Because no METHOD subcommand is specified, all three single independent variables and the interaction term are entered into the model.
- LOGISTIC REGRESSION produces the default output.

CATEGORICAL Subcommand

CATEGORICAL identifies independent variables that are nominal or ordinal. Variables that are declared to be categorical are automatically transformed into a set of contrast variables as specified on the CONTRAST subcommand. If a variable coded as {0,1} is declared as categorical, its coding scheme will be changed to deviation contrasts by default.

- Independent variables not specified on the CATEGORICAL subcommand are assumed to be at least interval level, except for string variables.

- Any variable specified on CATEGORICAL is ignored if it does not appear either after WITH on the VARIABLES subcommand or on any METHOD subcommand.
- Variables specified on CATEGORICAL are replaced by sets of contrast variables. If the categorical variable has n distinct values, there will be $n - 1$ contrast variables generated. The set of contrast variables associated with a categorical variable is entered or removed from the model as a step.
- If any one of the variables in an interaction term is specified on CATEGORICAL, the interaction term is replaced by contrast variables.
- All string variables are categorical. Only the first eight characters of each value of a string variable are used in distinguishing between values. Thus, if two values of a string variable are identical for the first eight characters, the values are treated as though they were the same.

Example

```
LOGISTIC REGRESSION PASS WITH GPA, GRE, MAT, CLASS, TEACHER
/CATEGORICAL = CLASS,TEACHER.
```

- The dichotomous dependent variable *PASS* is regressed on the interval-level independent variables *GPA*, *GRE*, and *MAT* and the categorical variables *CLASS* and *TEACHER*.

CONTRAST Subcommand

CONTRAST specifies the type of contrast used for categorical independent variables. The interpretation of the regression coefficients for categorical variables depends on the contrasts used. The default is DEVIATION. The categorical independent variable is specified in parentheses following CONTRAST. The closing parenthesis is followed by one of the contrast-type keywords.

- If the categorical variable has n values, there will be $n - 1$ rows in the contrast matrix. Each contrast matrix is treated as a set of independent variables in the analysis.
- Only one categorical independent variable can be specified per CONTRAST subcommand, but multiple CONTRAST subcommands can be specified.

The following contrast types are available. See Finn (1974) and Kirk (1982) for further information on a specific type. For illustration of contrast types, see Appendix A.

DEVIATION(refcat)   *Deviations from the overall effect.* This is the default. The effect for each category of the independent variable except one is compared to the overall effect. Refcat is the category for which parameter estimates are not displayed (they must be calculated from the others). By default, refcat is the last category. To omit a category other than the last, specify the sequence number of the omitted category (which is not necessarily the same as its value) in parentheses after the keyword DEVIATION.

SIMPLE(refcat)   *Each category of the independent variable except the last is compared to the last category.* To use a category other than the last as the omitted reference category, specify its sequence number (which is not necessarily the same as its value) in parentheses following the keyword SIMPLE.

DIFFERENCE	*Difference or reverse Helmert contrasts.* The effect for each category of the independent variable except the first is compared to the mean effects of the previous categories.
HELMERT	*Helmert contrasts.* The effect for each category of the independent variable except the last is compared to the mean effects of subsequent categories.
POLYNOMIAL(metric)	*Polynomial contrasts.* The first degree of freedom contains the linear effect across the categories of the independent variable, the second contains the quadratic effect, and so on. By default, the categories are assumed to be equally spaced; unequal spacing can be specified by entering a metric consisting of one integer for each category of the independent variable in parentheses after the keyword POLYNOMIAL. For example, CONTRAST(STIMULUS)=POLYNOMIAL(1,2,4) indicates that the three levels of STIMULUS are actually in the proportion 1:2:4. The default metric is always $(1,2,...,k)$, where k categories are involved. Only the relative differences between the terms of the metric matter: (1,2,4) is the same metric as (2,3,5) or (20,30,50), because the difference between the second and third numbers is twice the difference between the first and second in each instance.
REPEATED	*Comparison of adjacent categories.* Each category of the independent variable except the first is compared to the previous category.
SPECIAL(matrix)	*A user-defined contrast.* After this keyword, a matrix is entered in parentheses with $k - 1$ rows and k columns (where k is the number of categories of the independent variable). The rows of the contrast matrix contain the special contrasts indicating the desired comparisons between categories. If the special contrasts are linear combinations of each other, LOGISTIC REGRESSION reports the linear dependency and stops processing. If k rows are entered, the first row is discarded and only the last $k - 1$ rows are used as the contrast matrix in the analysis.
INDICATOR(refcat)	*Indicator variables.* Contrasts indicate the presence or absence of category membership. By default, refcat is the last category (represented in the contrast matrix as a row of zeros). To omit a category other than the last, specify the sequence number of the omitted category (which is not necessarily the same as its value) in parentheses after the keyword INDICATOR.

Example

```
LOGISTIC REGRESSION PASS WITH GRE, CLASS
 /CATEGORICAL = CLASS
 /CONTRAST(CLASS)=HELMERT.
```

- A logistic regression analysis of the dependent variable *PASS* is performed on the interval independent variable *GRE* and the categorical independent variable *CLASS*.

- *PASS* is a dichotomous variable representing course pass/fail status, and *CLASS* identifies whether a student is in one of three classrooms. A HELMERT contrast is requested.

Example

```
LOGISTIC REGRESSION PASS WITH GRE, CLASS
 /CATEGORICAL = CLASS
 /CONTRAST(CLASS)=SPECIAL(2 -1 -1
                          0  1 -1).
```

- In this example, the contrasts are specified with keyword SPECIAL.

METHOD Subcommand

METHOD indicates how the independent variables enter the model. The specification is the METHOD subcommand followed by a single method keyword. Keyword METHOD can be omitted. Optionally, specify the independent variables and interactions for which the method is to be used. Use keyword BY between variable names of an interaction term.

- If no variable list is specified or if keyword ALL is used, all the independent variables following keyword WITH on the VARIABLES subcommand are eligible for inclusion in the model.
- If no METHOD subcommand is specified, the default method is ENTER.
- Variables specified on CATEGORICAL are replaced by sets of contrast variables. The set of contrast variables associated with a categorical variable is entered or removed from the model as a single step.
- Any number of METHOD subcommands can appear in a Logistic Regression procedure. METHOD subcommands are processed in the order in which they are specified. Each method starts with the results from the previous method. If BSTEP is used, all remaining eligible variables are entered at the first step. All variables are then eligible for entry and removal unless they have been excluded from the METHOD variable list.
- The beginning model for the first METHOD subcommand is either the constant variable (by default or if NOORIGIN is specified) or an empty model (if ORIGIN is specified).

The available METHOD keywords are:

ENTER   *Forced entry.* All variables are entered in a single step. This is the default if the METHOD subcommand is omitted.

FSTEP   *Forward stepwise.* The variables (or interaction terms) specified on FSTEP are tested for entry into the model one by one, based on the significance level of the score statistic. The variable with the smallest significance less than PIN is entered into the model. After each entry, variables that are already in the model are tested for possible removal, based on the significance of the Wald statistic or the likelihood-ratio criterion. The variable with the largest probability greater than the specified POUT value is removed and the model is reestimated. Variables in the model are then evaluated again for removal. Once no more variables satisfy the removal criterion, covariates not in the model are evaluated for entry. Model building stops when no more variables meet entry or removal criteria, or when the current model is the same as a previous one.

BSTEP   *Backward stepwise.* As a first step, the variables (or interaction terms) specified on BSTEP are entered into the model together and are tested for removal one by one. Stepwise removal and entry then follow the same process as described for FSTEP until no more variables meet entry or removal criteria, or when the current model is the same as a previous one.

The statistic used in the test for removal can be specified by an additional keyword in parentheses following FSTEP or BSTEP. If FSTEP or BSTEP is specified by itself, the default is WALD.

WALD   *Wald statistic.* The removal of a variable from the model is based on the significance of the Wald statistic.

LR   *Likelihood ratio.* The removal of a variable from the model is based on the significance of the change in the log likelihood. If LR is specified, the model must be re-estimated without each of the variables in the model. This can substantially increase computational time. However, the likelihood-ratio statistic is the best criterion for deciding which variables are to be removed.

Example

```
LOGISTIC REGRESSION PROMOTED WITH AGE JOBTIME JOBRATE RACE SEX AGENCY
 /CATEGORICAL RACE SEX AGENCY
 /METHOD ENTER AGE   JOBTIME
 /METHOD BSTEP (LR) RACE SEX JOBRATE AGENCY.
```

- *AGE, JOBTIME, JOBRATE, RACE, SEX*, and *AGENCY* are specified as independent variables. *RACE, SEX*, and *AGENCY* are specified as categorical independent variables.
- The first METHOD subcommand enters *AGE* and *JOBTIME* into the model.
- Variables in the model at the termination of the first METHOD subcommand are included in the model at the beginning of the second METHOD subcommand.
- The second METHOD subcommand adds the variables *RACE, SEX, JOBRATE*, and *AGENCY* to the previous model.
- Backward stepwise logistic regression analysis is then done with only the variables on the BSTEP variable list tested for removal using the LR statistic.
- The procedure continues until all variables from the BSTEP variable list have been removed or the removal of a variable will not result in a decrease in the log likelihood with a probability larger than POUT.

SELECT Subcommand

By default, all cases in the active file are considered for inclusion in LOGISTIC REGRESSION. Use the optional SELECT subcommand to include a subset of cases in the analysis.

- The specification is either a logical expression or keyword ALL. ALL is the default. Variables named on VARIABLES, CATEGORICAL, or METHOD subcommands cannot appear on SELECT.
- In the logical expression on SELECT, the relation can be EQ, NE, LT, LE, GT, or GE. The variable must be numeric and the value can be any number.
- Only cases for which the logical expression on SELECT is true are included in calculations. All other cases, including those with missing values for the variable named on SELECT, are unselected.

- Diagnostic statistics and classification statistics are reported for both selected and unselected cases.
- Cases deleted from the active file with the SELECT IF or SAMPLE command are not included among either the selected or unselected cases.

Example

```
LOGISTIC REGRESSION VARIABLES=GRADE WITH GPA,TUCE,PSI
/SELECT SEX EQ 1 /CASEWISE=RESID.
```

- Only cases with the value 1 for *SEX* are included in the logistic regression analysis.
- Residual values generated by CASEWISE are displayed for both selected and unselected cases.

ORIGIN and NOORIGIN Subcommands

ORIGIN and NOORIGIN control whether or not the constant is included. NOORIGIN (the default) includes a constant term (intercept) in all equations. ORIGIN suppresses the constant term and requests regression through the origin. (NOCONST can be used as an alias for ORIGIN.)

- The only specification is either ORIGIN or NOORIGIN.
- ORIGIN or NOORIGIN can be specified only once per Logistic Regression procedure, and it affects all METHOD subcommands.

Example

```
LOGISTIC REGRESSION VARIABLES=PASS WITH GPA,GRE,MAT /ORIGIN.
```

- ORIGIN suppresses the automatic generation of a constant term.

ID Subcommand

ID specifies a variable whose values or value labels identify the casewise listing. By default, cases are labeled by their case number.

- The only specification is the name of a single variable that exists in the active file. If multiple variables are specified, only the first is used.
- Only the first eight characters of the variable's value labels are used to label cases. If the variable has no value labels, the values are used.
- Only the first eight characters of a string variable are used to label cases.

PRINT Subcommand

PRINT controls the display of optional output. If PRINT is omitted, DEFAULT output (defined below) is displayed.

- The minimum specification is PRINT followed by a single keyword.
- If PRINT is used, only the requested output is displayed.

DEFAULT   *Classification tables and statistics for the variables in and not in the equation at each step.* Tables and statistics are displayed for each METHOD subcommand.

SUMMARY   *Summary information.* Same output as DEFAULT, except that the output for each step is not displayed.

CORR   *Correlation matrix of parameter estimates for the variables in the model.*

ITER(value) *Iterations at which parameter estimates are to be displayed.* The value in parentheses controls the spacing of iteration reports. If the value is n, the parameter estimates are displayed for every nth iteration starting at 0. If a value is not supplied, intermediate estimates are displayed at each iteration.

ALL   *All available output.*

Example

```
LOGISTIC REGRESSION VARIABLES=PASS WITH GPA,GRE,MAT
 /METHOD FSTEP
 /PRINT CORR SUMMARY ITER(2).
```

- A forward stepwise logistic regression analysis of *PASS* on *GPA*, *GRE*, and *MAT* is specified.
- The PRINT subcommand requests the display of the correlation matrix of parameter estimates for the variables in the model (CORR), classification tables and statistics for the variables in and not in the equation for the final model (SUMMARY), and parameter estimates at every second iteration (ITER(2)).

CRITERIA Subcommand

CRITERIA controls the statistical criteria used in building the logistic regression models. The way in which these criteria are used depends on the method specified on the METHOD subcommand. The default criteria are noted in the description of each keyword below. Iterations will stop if the criterion for BCON, LCON, or ITERATE is satisfied.

BCON(value) *Change in parameter estimates to terminate iteration.* Iteration terminates when the parameters change by less than the specified value. The default is 0.001. To eliminate this criterion, specify a value of 0.

ITERATE   *Maximum number of iterations.* The default is 20.

LCON(value) *Percentage change in the log likelihood ratio for termination of iterations.* If the log likelihood decreases by less than the specified value, iteration terminates. The default is 0.01. To eliminate this criterion, specify a value of 0.

PIN(value)   *Probability of score statistic for variable entry.* The default is 0.05. The larger the specified probability, the easier it is for a variable to enter the model.

POUT(value) *Probability of Wald or LR statistic to remove a variable.* The default is 0.1. The larger the specified probability, the easier it is for a variable to remain in the model.

EPS(value)   *Epsilon value used for redundancy checking.* The specified value must be less than or equal to 0.05 and greater than or equal to 10^{-12}. The default is 10^{-8}. Larger values make it harder for variables to pass the redundancy check—that is, they are more likely to be excluded from the analysis.

Example

```
LOGISTIC REGRESSION PROMOTED WITH AGE JOBTIME RACE
 /CATEGORICAL RACE
 /METHOD BSTEP
 /CRITERIA BCON(0.01) ITERATE(10) PIN(0.01) POUT(0.05).
```

- A backward stepwise logistic regression analysis is performed for the dependent variable *PROMOTED* and the independent variables *AGE, JOBTIME,* and *RACE.*
- CRITERIA alters four of the statistical criteria that control the building of a model.
- BCON specifies that if the change in the absolute value of all of the parameter estimates is less than 0.01, the iterative estimation process should stop. Larger values lower the number of iterations required. Notice that the ITER and LCON criteria remain unchanged and that if either of them is met before BCON, iterations will terminate. (LCON can be set to 0 if only BCON and ITER are to be used.)
- ITERATE specifies that the maximum number of iterations is 10.
- POUT requires that the probability of the statistic used to test whether a variable should remain in the model be smaller than 0.05. This is more stringent than the default value of 0.1.
- PIN requires that the probability of the score statistic used to test whether a variable should be included be smaller than 0.01. This makes it more difficult for variables to be included in the model than the default value of 0.05.

CLASSPLOT Subcommand

CLASSPLOT generates a classification plot of the actual and predicted values of the dichotomous dependent variable at each step.

- Keyword CLASSPLOT is the only specification.
- If CLASSPLOT is not specified, plots are not generated.

Example

```
LOGISTIC REGRESSION PROMOTED WITH JOBTIME RACE
 /CATEGORICAL RACE
 /CLASSPLOT.
```

- A logistic regression model is constructed for the dichotomous dependent variable *PROMOTED* and the independent variables *JOBTIME* and *RACE.*
- CLASSPLOT produces a classification plot for the dependent variable *PROMOTED.* The vertical axis of the plot is the frequency of the variable *PROMOTED.* The horizontal axis is the predicted probability of membership in the second of the two levels of *PROMOTED.*

CASEWISE Subcommand

CASEWISE produces a casewise listing of the values of the temporary variables created by LOGISTIC REGRESSION.

The following keywords are available for specifying temporary variables (see Fox, 1984). When CASEWISE is specified by itself, the default lists *PRED, PGROUP, RESID*, and *ZRESID*. If a list of variable names is given, only those named temporary variables are displayed.

PRED   *Predicted probability.* For each case, the predicted probability of having the second of the two values of the dichotomous dependent variable.

PGROUP   *Predicted group.* The group to which a case is assigned based on the predicted probability.

RESID   *Difference between observed and predicted probability.*

DEV   *Deviance values.* For each case, a log-likelihood-ratio statistic is computed which measures how well the model fits the case.

LRESID   *Logit residual.* Residual divided by the product of *PRED* and $1 - PRED$.

SRESID   *Studentized residual.*

ZRESID   *Standardized residual.* Residual divided by the square root of the product of *PRED* and $1 - PRED$.

LEVER   *Leverage value.* A measure of the relative influence of each observation on the model's fit.

COOK   *Analog of Cook's influence statistic.*

DFBETA   *Difference in beta.* The difference in the estimated coefficients for each model term if the case is omitted.

The following keyword is available for restricting the cases to be displayed, based on the absolute value of *SRESID*:

OUTLIER (value)   *Cases with absolute values of SRESID greater than or equal to the specified value are displayed.* If OUTLIER is specified with no value, the default is 2.

Example

```
LOGISTIC REGRESSION PROMOTED WITH JOBTIME SEX RACE
 /CATEGORICAL SEX RACE
 /METHOD ENTER
 /CASEWISE SRESID LEVER DFBETA.
```

- CASEWISE produces a casewise listing of the temporary variables *SRESID, LEVER*, and *DFBETA*.

- There will be one *DFBETA* value for each parameter in the model. The continuous variable *JOBTIME*, the two-level categorical variable *SEX*, and the constant each require one parameter, while the four-level categorical variable *RACE* requires three parameters. Thus, six values of *DFBETA* will be produced for each case.

MISSING Subcommand

LOGISTIC REGRESSION excludes all cases with missing values on any of the independent variables. For a case with a missing value on the dependent variable, predicted values are calculated if it has nonmissing values on all independent variables. The MISSING subcommand controls the processing of user-missing values. If the subcommand is not specified, the default is EXCLUDE.

EXCLUDE   *Delete cases with user-missing values as well as system-missing values.* This is the default.

INCLUDE   *Include user-missing values in the analysis.*

SAVE Subcommand

SAVE saves the temporary variables created by LOGISTIC REGRESSION. To specify variable names for the new variables, assign the new names in parentheses following each temporary variable name. If new variable names are not specified, LOGISTIC REGRESSION generates default names.

- Assigned variable names must be unique in the active file. System variable names (that is, names that begin with $) cannot be used.
- A temporary variable can be saved only once on the same SAVE subcommand.

Example

```
LOGISTIC REGRESSION PROMOTED WITH JOBTIME AGE
 /SAVE PRED (PREDPRO) DFBETA (DF).
```

- A logistic regression analysis of *PROMOTED* on the independent variables *JOBTIME* and *AGE* is performed.
- SAVE adds four variables to the active file: one variable named *PREDPRO*, containing the predicted value from the specified model for each case, and three variables named *DF0, DF1,* and *DF2* containing, respectively, the *DFBETA* values for each case of the constant, the independent variable *JOBTIME*, and the independent variable *AGE*.

EXTERNAL Subcommand

EXTERNAL indicates that the data should be held in an external scratch file during processing. This can help conserve memory resources when running complex analyses or analyses with large data sets.

- Keyword EXTERNAL is the only specification.
- Specifying EXTERNAL may result in slightly longer processing time.
- If EXTERNAL is not specified, all data are held internally and no scratch file is written.

Annotated Example

For a complete example with output, see the Annotated Examples following the Syntax Reference section of this manual.

LOGLINEAR

```
LOGLINEAR varlist(min,max)...[BY] varlist(min,max)

          [WITH covariate varlist]

  [/CWEIGHT={varname }] [/CWEIGHT=(matrix)...]
           {(matrix)}

  [/GRESID={varlist }]  [/GRESID=(matrix)...]
           {(matrix)}

  [/CONTRAST (varname)={DEVIATION** [(refcat)]  } [/CONTRAST...]]
                       {DIFFERENCE               }
                       {HELMERT                  }
                       {SIMPLE [(refcat)]        }
                       {REPEATED                 }
                       {POLYNOMIAL [({1,2,3,...})]}
                       {            {metric    } }
                       {[BASIS] SPECIAL(matrix)  }

  [/CRITERIA=[CONVERGE({0.001**})] [ITERATE({20**})] [DELTA({0.5**})]
                      {n      }            {n   }          {n    }
             [DEFAULT]]

  [/{PRINT  } = {[FREQ**][RESID**][DESIGN][ESTIM][COR]} ]
    {NOPRINT}    {DEFAULT                             }
                 {ALL                                 }
                 {NONE                                }

  [/PLOT={NONE**  }]
         {DEFAULT }
         {RESID   }
         {NORMPROB}

  [/WIDTH={132}]
          { n }

  [/MISSING=[{EXCLUDE**}]]
            {INCLUDE  }

  [/DESIGN=effect[(n)] effect[(n)]... effect BY effect...] [/DESIGN...]
```

**Default if subcommand or keyword is omitted.

Example:

```
LOGLINEAR JOBSAT (1,2) ZODIAC (1,12) /DESIGN=JOBSAT.
```

Overview

LOGLINEAR is a general procedure for model fitting, hypothesis testing, and parameter estimation for any model that has categorical variables as its major components. LOGLINEAR subsumes a variety of related techniques, including general models of multi-way-contingency tables, logit models, logistic regression on categorical variables, and quasi-independence models.

LOGLINEAR models cell frequencies using the multinomial response model and produces maximum likelihood estimates of parameters by means of the Newton-Raphson algorithm (Haberman, 1978). HILOGLINEAR, which uses an iterative proportional fitting algorithm, is more efficient for hierarchical models, but it cannot produce parameter estimates for unsaturated models, does not permit specification of contrasts for parameters, and does not display a correlation matrix of the parameter estimates.

Options

Model Specification. You can specify the model or models to be fit using the DESIGN subcommand.

Cell Weights. You can specify cell weights, such as structural zeros, for the model with the CWEIGHT subcommand.

Output Display. You can control the output display with the PRINT and NOPRINT subcommands.

Optional Plots. You can produce plots of adjusted residuals against observed and expected counts, normal plots, and detrended normal plots with the PLOT subcommand.

Linear Combinations. You can calculate linear combinations of observed cell frequencies, expected cell frequencies, and adjusted residuals using the GRESID subcommand.

Contrasts. You can indicate the type of contrast desired for a factor using the CONTRAST subcommand.

Criteria for Algorithm. You can control the values of algorithm-tuning parameters with the CRITERIA subcommand.

Formatting Options. You can control the width of the display output using the WIDTH subcommand.

Basic Specification

The basic specification is two or more variables that define the crosstabulation. The minimum and maximum values for each variable must be specified in parentheses after the variable name.

By default, LOGLINEAR estimates the saturated model for a multidimensional table. Output includes the factors or effects, their levels, and any labels; observed and expected frequencies and percentages for each factor and code; residuals, standardized residuals, and adjusted residuals; two goodness-of-fit statistics (the likelihood-ratio chi-square and Pearson's chi-square); and estimates of the parameters with accompanying Z values and 95% confidence intervals.

Limitation

- Maximum 10 independent (factor) variables.

Subcommand Order

- The variables specification must come first.
- The subcommands that affect a specific model must be placed before the DESIGN subcommand specifying the model.
- All subcommands can be used more than once and, with the exception of the DESIGN subcommand, are carried from model to model unless explicitly overridden.
- If the last subcommand is not DESIGN, LOGLINEAR generates a saturated model in addition to the explicitly requested model(s).

Example

```
LOGLINEAR JOBSAT (1,2) ZODIAC (1,12)
  /DESIGN=JOBSAT, ZODIAC.
```

- The variable list specifies two categorical variables, *JOBSAT* and *ZODIAC*. *JOBSAT* has values 1 and 2. *ZODIAC* has values 1 through 12.
- DESIGN specifies a model with main effects only.

Example

```
LOGLINEAR DPREF (2,3) RACE CAMP (1,2).
```

- *DPREF* is a categorical variable with values 2 and 3. *RACE* and *CAMP* are categorical variables with values 1 and 2.
- This is a general loglinear model because no BY keyword appears. The design defaults to a saturated model that includes all main effects and interaction effects.

Example

```
LOGLINEAR GSLEVEL (4,8) EDUC (1,4) SEX (1,2)
  /DESIGN=GSLEVEL EDUC SEX.
```

- *GSLEVEL* is a categorical variable with values 4 through 8. *EDUC* is a categorical variable with values 1 through 4. *SEX* has values 1 and 2.
- DESIGN specifies a model with main effects only.

Example

```
LOGLINEAR GSLEVEL (4,8) BY EDUC (1,4) SEX (1,2)
  /DESIGN=GSLEVEL, GSLEVEL BY EDUC, GSLEVEL BY SEX.
```

- Keyword BY on the variable list specifies a logit model in which *GSLEVEL* is the dependent variable and *EDUC* and *SEX* are the independent variables.
- DESIGN specifies a model that can test for the absence of joint effect of *SEX* and *EDUC* on *GSLEVEL*.

Variable List

The variable list specifies the variables to be included in the model. LOGLINEAR analyzes two classes of variables: categorical and continuous. Categorical variables are used to define the cells of the table. Continuous variables are used as cell covariates. Continuous variables can be specified only after the keyword WITH following the list of categorical variables.

- The list of categorical variables must be specified first. Categorical variables must be numeric and integer.

- A range must be defined for each categorical variable by specifying, in parentheses after each variable name, the minimum and maximum values for that variable. Separate the two values with at least one space or a comma.

- To specify the same range for a list of variables, specify the list of variables followed by a single range. The range applies to all variables in the list.

- To specify a logit model, use keyword BY (see Logit Model, below). A variable list without keyword BY generates a general loglinear model.

- Cases with values outside the specified range are excluded from the analysis. Non-integer values within the range are truncated for the purpose of building the table.

Logit Model

- To separate the independent (factor) variables from the dependent variable in a logit model, use the keyword BY. The categorical variable preceding BY is the dependent variable; the categorical variables following BY are the independent variables.

- Up to nine variables can be included as independent variables following the keyword BY.

- A DESIGN subcommand should be used to request the desired logit model.

- LOGLINEAR displays an analysis of dispersion and two measures of association: entropy and concentration. These measures are discussed in Haberman (1982) and can be used to quantify the magnitude of association among the variables. Both are proportional reduction in error measures. The entropy statistic is analogous to Theil's entropy measure, while the concentration statistic is analogous to Goodman and Kruskal's tau-*b*. Both statistics measure the strength of association between the dependent variable and the predictor variable set.

Cell Covariates

- Continuous variables can be used as covariates. When used, the covariates must be specified after the keyword WITH following the list of categorical variables. Ranges are not specified for the continuous variables.

- A variable cannot be named as both a categorical variable and a cell covariate.

- To enter cell covariates into a model, the covariates must be specified on the DESIGN subcommand.

- Cell covariates are not applied on a case-by-case basis. The mean covariate value for a cell in the contingency table is applied to that cell.

Example

```
LOGLINEAR DPREF(2,3) RACE CAMP (1,2) WITH COVAR
  /DESIGN=DPREF RACE CAMP COVAR.
```

- Variable *COVAR* is a continuous variable specified as a cell covariate. Cell covariates must be specified after keyword WITH following the variable list. No range is defined for cell covariates.
- To include the cell covariate in the model, variable *COVAR* is specified on DESIGN.

CWEIGHT Subcommand

CWEIGHT specifies cell weights, such as structural zeros, for a model. By default, cell weights are equal to 1.

- The specification is either one numeric variable or a matrix of weights enclosed in parentheses.
- If a matrix of weights is specified, the matrix must contain the same number of elements as the product of the levels of the categorical variables. An asterisk can be used to signify repetitions of the same value.
- If weights are specified for a multiple-factor model, the index value of the rightmost factor increments the most rapidly.
- If a variable is used to specify the weights, only one CWEIGHT subcommand can be used on LOGLINEAR.
- To use multiple cell weights on the same LOGLINEAR, specify all weights in matrix format. Each matrix must be specified on a separate CWEIGHT subcommand, and each CWEIGHT specification remains in effect until explicitly overridden by another CWEIGHT subcommand.
- CWEIGHT can be used to impose structural, or *a priori*, zeros on the model. This feature is useful in the analysis of symmetric tables.

Example

```
COMPUTE  CWT=1.
IF (HUSED EQ WIFED) CWT=0.
LOGLINEAR HUSED WIFED(1,4) WITH DISTANCE
  /CWEIGHT=CWT
  /DESIGN=HUSED WIFED DISTANCE.
```

- COMPUTE initially assigns *CWT* the value 1 for all cases.
- IF assigns *CWT* the value 0 when *HUSED* equals *WIFED*.
- CWEIGHT imposes structural zeros on the diagonal of the symmetric crosstabulation. Because a variable name is specified, only one CWEIGHT can be used.

Example

```
LOGLINEAR  HUSED WIFED(1,4) WITH DISTANCE
  /CWEIGHT=(0, 4*1, 0, 4*1, 0, 4*1, 0)
  /DESIGN=HUSED WIFED DISTANCE
  /CWEIGHT=(16*1)
  /DESIGN=HUSED WIFED DISTANCE.
```

- The first CWEIGHT matrix specifies the same values as variable *CWT* provided in the first example. The specified matrix is as follows:

```
0 1 1 1
1 0 1 1
1 1 0 1
1 1 1 0
```

- The same matrix can be specified in full as (0 1 1 1 1 0 1 1 1 1 0 1 1 1 1 0).
- By using the matrix format on CWEIGHT rather than a variable name, a different CWEIGHT subcommand can be used for the second model.

GRESID Subcommand

GRESID (Generalized Residual) calculates linear combinations of observed cell frequencies, expected cell frequencies, and adjusted residuals.

- The specification is either a numeric variable or a matrix whose contents are coefficients of the desired linear combinations.
- If a matrix of coefficients is specified, the matrix must contain the same number of elements as the number of cells implied by the variables specification. An asterisk can be used to signify repetitions of the same value.
- Each GRESID subcommand specifies a single linear combination. Each matrix or variable must be specified on a separate GRESID subcommand. All GRESID subcommands specified are displayed for each design.

Example

```
LOGLINEAR  MONTH(1,18) WITH Z
 /GRESID=(6*1,12*0)
 /GRESID=(6*0,6*1,6*0)
 /GRESID=(12*0,6*1)
 /DESIGN=Z.
```

- The first GRESID subcommand combines the first six months into a single effect. The second GRESID subcommand combines the second six months, and the third GRESID subcommand combines the last six months.
- For each effect, LOGLINEAR displays the observed and expected counts, the residual, the standardized residual, and the adjusted residual.

CONTRAST Subcommand

CONTRAST indicates the type of contrast desired for a factor, where a factor is any categorical dependent or independent variable. The default contrast is DEVIATION for each factor.

- The specification is CONTRAST, which is followed by a variable name in parentheses and the contrast-type keyword.
- To specify a contrast for more than one factor, use a separate CONTRAST subcommand for each specified factor. Only one contrast can be in effect for each factor on each DESIGN.

- A contrast specification remains in effect for subsequent designs until explicitly overridden by another CONTRAST subcommand.
- The design matrix used for the contrasts can be displayed by specifying keyword DESIGN on the PRINT subcommand. However, this matrix is the basis matrix that is used to determine contrasts; it is not the contrast matrix itself.
- CONTRAST can be used for a multinomial logit model, in which the dependent variable has more than two categories.
- CONTRAST can be used for fitting linear logit models. Keyword BASIS is not appropriate for such models.
- In a logit model, CONTRAST is used to transform the independent variable into a metric variable. Again, keyword BASIS is not appropriate.

The following contrast types are available. For illustration of contrast types, see Appendix A.

DEVIATION(refcat) *Deviations from the overall effect.* DEVIATION is the default contrast if the CONTRAST subcommand is not used. Refcat is the category for which parameter estimates are not displayed (they are the negative of the sum of the others). By default, refcat is the last category of the variable.

DIFFERENCE *Comparison of levels of a factor with the average effect of previous levels.* Also known as reverse Helmert contrasts.

HELMERT *Comparison of levels of a factor with the average effect of subsequent levels.*

SIMPLE(refcat) *Comparison of each level of a factor to the reference level.* By default, LOGLINEAR uses the last category of the factor variable as the reference category. Optionally, any level can be specified as the reference category enclosed in parentheses after keyword SIMPLE. The sequence of the level, not the actual value, must be specified.

REPEATED *Adjacent comparisons across levels of a factor.*

POLYNOMIAL(metric) *Orthogonal polynomial contrasts.* The default is equal spacing. Optionally, the coefficients of the linear polynomial can be specified in parentheses, indicating the spacing between levels of the treatment measured by the factor.

[BASIS]SPECIAL(matrix) *User-defined contrast.* As many elements as the number of categories squared must be specified. If BASIS is specified before SPECIAL, a basis matrix is generated for the special contrast, which makes the coefficients of the contrast equal to the special matrix. Otherwise, the matrix specified is the basis matrix used to determine coefficients for the contrast matrix.

Example

```
LOGLINEAR  A(1,4) BY B(1,4)
 /CONTRAST(B)=POLYNOMIAL
 /DESIGN=A A BY B(1)
 /CONTRAST(B)=SIMPLE
 /DESIGN=A A BY B(1).
```

- The first CONTRAST subcommand requests polynomial contrasts of *B* for the first design.
- The second CONTRAST subcommand requests the simple contrast of *B*, with the last category (value 4) used as the reference category for the second DESIGN subcommand.

Example

```
* Multinomial logit model

LOGLINEAR  PREF(1,5) BY RACE ORIGIN CAMP(1,2)
 /CONTRAST(PREF)=SPECIAL(5*1, 1 1 1 1 -4, 3 -1 -1 -1 0,
        0 1 1 -2 0, 0 1 -1 0 0).
```

- LOGLINEAR builds special contrasts among the five categories of the dependent variable *PREF*, which measures preference for training camps among Army recruits. For *PREF*, 1=stay, 2=move to north, 3=move to south, 4=move to unnamed camp, and 5=undecided.
- The four contrasts are: (1) move or stay versus undecided, (2) stay versus move, (3) named camp versus unnamed, and (4) northern camp versus southern. Because these contrasts are orthogonal, SPECIAL and BASIS SPECIAL produce equivalent results.

Example

```
* Contrasts for a linear logit model

LOGLINEAR RESPONSE(1,2) BY YEAR(0,20)
 /PRINT=ESTIM
 /CONTRAST(YEAR)=SPECIAL(21*1, -10, -9, -8, -7, -6, -5, -4,
                    -3, -2, -1, 0, 1, 2, 3, 4, 5, 6, 7,
                     8, 9, 10, 399*1)
 /DESIGN=RESPONSE RESPONSE BY YEAR(1).
```

- *YEAR* measures years of education and ranges from 0 through 20. Therefore, allowing for the constant effect, *YEAR* has 20 estimable parameters associated with it.
- The SPECIAL contrast specifies the constant—that is, 21*1—and the linear effect of *YEAR*—that is, –10 to 10. The other 399 1's fill out the 21*21 matrix.

Example

```
* Contrasts for a logistic regression model

LOGLINEAR RESPONSE(1,2) BY TIME(1,4)
 /CONTRAST(TIME) = SPECIAL(4*1, 7 14 27 51, 8*1)
 /PRINT=ALL
 /PLOT=DEFAULT
 /DESIGN=RESPONSE, TIME(1) BY RESPONSE.
```

- CONTRAST is used to transform the independent variable into a metric variable.
- *TIME* represents elapsed time in days. Therefore, the weights in the contrast represent the metric of the passage of time.

CRITERIA Subcommand

CRITERIA specifies the values of some constants in the Newton-Raphson algorithm. Defaults or specifications remain in effect until overridden with another CRITERIA subcommand.

CONVERGE(n) *Convergence criterion.* Specify a value for the convergence criterion. The default is 0.001.

ITERATION(n) *Maximum number of iterations.* Specify the maximum number of iterations for the algorithm. The default number is 20.

DELTA(n) *Cell delta value.* The value of delta is added to each cell frequency for the first iteration. Delta remains in the cells only for saturated models. The default value is 0.5. LOGLINEAR does not display parameter estimates or correlation matrices of parameter estimates if any sampling zero cells exist in the expected table after delta is added. Parameter estimates and correlation matrices can be displayed in the presence of structural zeros.

DEFAULT *Default values are used.* DEFAULT can be used to reset the parameters to the default.

Example

```
LOGLINEAR  DPREF(2,3) BY RACE ORIGIN CAMP(1,2)
 /CRITERIA=ITERATION(50) CONVERGE(.0001).
```

- ITERATION increases the maximum number of iterations to 50.
- CONVERGE lowers the convergence criterion to 0.0001.

PRINT and NOPRINT Subcommands

PRINT requests statistics that are not produced by default. NOPRINT suppresses the display of specified output.

- By default, LOGLINEAR displays the frequency table and residuals. The parameter estimates of the model are also displayed if DESIGN is not used. To turn off these defaults, use NOPRINT.
- Multiple PRINT and NOPRINT subcommands are permitted. The specifications are cumulative.

The following keywords can be used on both PRINT and NOPRINT:

FREQ *Observed and expected cell frequencies and percentages.* This is displayed by default.

RESID *Raw, standardized, and adjusted residuals.* This is displayed by default.

DESIGN *The design matrix of the model, showing the basis matrix corresponding to the contrasts used in the model.*

ESTIM *The parameter estimates of the model.* If you do not specify a design on the DESIGN subcommand, LOGLINEAR generates a saturated model and displays the parameter estimates for the saturated model. LOGLINEAR does not display parameter estimates or correlation matrices of parameter estimates if any sampling zero cells exist in the expected table after delta is added. Parameter estimates and a correlation matrix are displayed when structural zeros are present. SPSS/PC+ centers all covariates, so parameter estimates for constant covariates are always 0.

COR   *The correlation matrix of the parameter estimates.* Alias COV.

ALL   *All available output.*

DEFAULT   *FREQ and RESID.* ESTIM is also displayed by default if the DESIGN subcommand is not used.

NONE   *The design information and goodness-of-fit statistics only.* This option overrides all other specifications on the PRINT subcommand. The NONE option applies only to the PRINT subcommand.

Example

```
LOGLINEAR A(1,2) B(1,2)
 /PRINT=ESTIM
 /NOPRINT=DEFAULT
 /DESIGN=A,B,A BY B
 /PRINT=ALL
 /DESIGN=A,B.
```

- The first design is the saturated model. Because it fits the data exactly, there is no need to see the frequencies or residuals. NOPRINT suppresses the default. The parameter estimates are displayed with ESTIM specified on PRINT.
- The second design is the main-effects model, which tests the hypothesis of no interaction. The second PRINT subcommand displays all available display output for this model.

PLOT Subcommand

PLOT produces optional plots. No plots are displayed if PLOT is not specified or is specified without any keyword. Multiple PLOT subcommands can be used. The specifications are cumulative.

RESID   *Plots of adjusted residuals against observed and expected counts.*

NORMPROB   *Normal and detrended normal plots of the adjusted residuals.*

NONE   *No plots.*

DEFAULT   *RESID and NORMPROB.*

Example

```
LOGLINEAR  RESPONSE(1,2) BY TIME(1,4)
  /CONTRAST(TIME)=SPECIAL(4*1, 7 14 27 51, 8*1)
  /PLOT=DEFAULT
  /DESIGN=RESPONSE TIME(1) BY RESPONSE
  /PLOT=NONE
  /DESIGN.
```

- RESID and NORMPROB plots are displayed for the first design.
- No plots are displayed for the second design.

WIDTH Subcommand

WIDTH specifies the display width. The default display uses the width specified on SET.

- Only one width is in effect at a time, and it controls all display.
- WIDTH can be placed anywhere after the variables specification.
- With narrow width settings, the frequency table displays fewer statistics and has fewer decimal places. In addition, observed and expected percentages are omitted.

Example

```
LOGLINEAR  DPREF(2,3) RACE CAMP(1,2)
 /WIDTH=72.
```

- WIDTH sets the display width to 72 columns.

MISSING Subcommand

MISSING controls missing values. By default, LOGLINEAR excludes all cases with system- or user-missing values on any variable. You can specify INCLUDE to include user-missing values. If INCLUDE is specified, user-missing values must also be included in the value range specification.

EXCLUDE   *Delete cases with user-missing values.* This is the default if the subcommand is omitted. You can also specify keyword DEFAULT.

INCLUDE   *Include user-missing values.* Only cases with system-missing values are deleted.

Example

```
MISSING VALUES A(0).
LOGLINEAR A(0,2) B(1,2)
 /MISSING=INCLUDE
 /DESIGN=B.
```

- Even though 0 was specified as missing, it is treated as a nonmissing category of *A* in this analysis.

DESIGN Subcommand

DESIGN specifies the model or models to be fit. If DESIGN is omitted or used with no specifications, the saturated model is produced. The saturated model fits all main effects and all interaction effects.

- To specify more than one model, use more than one DESIGN subcommand. Each DESIGN specifies one model.

- To obtain main effects models, name all the variables listed on the variables specification.
- To obtain interactions, use keyword BY to specify each interaction, as in A BY B and C BY D. To obtain the single-degree-of-freedom partition of a specified contrast, specify the partition in parentheses following the factor (see the example below).
- To include cell covariates in the model, first identify them on the variable list by naming them after keyword WITH, then specify the variable names on DESIGN.
- To specify an equiprobability model, name a cell covariate that is actually a constant of 1.

Example

```
* Testing the linear effect of the dependent variable

COMPUTE X=MONTH.
LOGLINEAR MONTH (1,12) WITH X
  /DESIGN X.
```

- The variable specification identifies *MONTH* as a categorical variable with values 1 through 12. Keyword WITH identifies *X* as a covariate.
- DESIGN tests the linear effect of *MONTH*.

Example

```
* Specifying main effects models

LOGLINEAR A(1,4) B(1,5)
  /DESIGN=A
  /DESIGN=A,B.
```

- The first design tests the homogeneity of category probabilities for *B*; it fits the marginal frequencies on *A*, but assumes that membership in any of the categories of *B* is equiprobable.
- The second design tests the independence of *A* and *B*. It fits the marginals on both *A* and *B*.

Example

```
* Specifying interactions

LOGLINEAR A(1,4) B(1,5) C(1,3)
  /DESIGN=A,B,C, A BY B.
```

- This design consists of the *A* main effect, the *B* main effect, the *C* main effect, and the interaction of *A* and *B*.

Example

```
* Single-degree-of-freedom partitions

LOGLINEAR A(1,4) BY B(1,5)
  /CONTRAST(B)=POLYNOMIAL
  /DESIGN=A,A BY B(1).
```

- The value 1 following *B* refers to the first partition of *B*, which is the linear effect of *B*; this follows from the contrast specified on the CONTRAST subcommand.

Example

```
* Specifying cell covariates

LOGLINEAR HUSED WIFED(1,4) WITH DISTANCE
   /DESIGN=HUSED WIFED DISTANCE.
```

- The continuous variable *DISTANCE* is identified as a cell covariate by specifying it after WITH on the variable list. The cell covariate is then included in the model by naming it on DESIGN.

Example

```
* Equiprobability model

COMPUTE  X=1.
LOGLINEAR  MONTH(1,12) WITH X
   /DESIGN=X.
```

- This model tests whether the frequencies in the 12-cell table are equal by using a cell covariate that is a constant of 1.

Annotated Example

For a complete example with output, see the Annotated Examples following the Syntax Reference section of this manual.

MANOVA: Overview

```
MANOVA dependent varlist [BY factor list (min,max)[factor list...]
                         [WITH covariate list]]

  [/WSFACTORS=varname (levels) [varname...] ]

  [/WSDESIGN]*

  [/TRANSFORM [(dependent varlist [/dependent varlist])]=
                      [ORTHONORM] [ {CONTRAST} ] {DEVIATION (refcat)    } ]
                                  { BASIS    }   {DIFFERENCE            }
                                                 {HELMERT               }
                                                 {SIMPLE (refcat)       }
                                                 {REPEATED              }
                                                 {POLYNOMIAL [({1,2,3...})]}
                                                 {            {metric  } }
                                                 {SPECIAL (matrix)      }

  [/MEASURE=newname newname...]

  [/RENAME= {newname} {newname}...]
           {*      } {*      }


  [/ERROR= {WITHIN + RESIDUAL**} ]
           {WITHIN             }
           {RESIDUA            }
           {n                  }

  [/CONTRAST (factorname)= {DEVIATION** [(refcat)]       }] †
                           {POLYNOMIAL**[({1,2,3...})]   }
                           {            {metric     }    }
                           {SIMPLE [(refcat)]            }
                           {DIFFERENCE                   }
                           {HELMERT                      }
                           {REPEATED                     }
                           {SPECIAL (matrix)             }

  [/PARTITION (factorname)[=({1,1...  })]]
                           {n1,n2...}

  [/METHOD=[ {UNIQUE**  } ] [ {CONSTANT**} ] [ {QR**    }]]
            {SEQUENTIAL}     {NOCONSTANT}     {CHOLESKY}

  [/ {PRINT  } = [CELLINFO [({MEANS] [SSCP] [COV] [COR] [ALL])]]
     {NOPRINT}    [HOMOGENEITY [([ALL] [BARTLETT] [COCHRAN] [BOXM])]]
                  [DESIGN [([OVERALL] [ONEWAY] [DECOMP] [BIAS] [SOLUTION]
                          [REDUNDANCY] [COLLINEARITY] [ALL])]]
                  [PARAMETERS [([ESTIM] [ORTHO][COR][NEGSUM][EFSIZE][OPTIMAL][ALL])]]
                  [SIGNIF [[(SINGLEDF)]
                          [(MULTIV**)] [(EIGEN)] [(DIMENR)]
                          [(UNIV**)] [(HYPOTH)][(STEPDOWN)] [(BRIEF)]
                          [{(AVERF**)}] [(HF)] [(GG)] [(EFSIZE)]]
                          {(AVONLY) }
                          [ERROR[(STDDEV)][(COR)][(COV)][(SSCP)]] [(ALL)]]

  [/OMEANS =[VARIABLES(varlist)] [TABLES ({factor name    }] ]
                                         {factor BY factor}
                                         {CONSTANT        }

  [/PMEANS =[VARIABLES(varlist)] [TABLES ({factor name    })] [PLOT]] ]
                                         {factor BY factor}
                                         {CONSTANT        }

  [/RESIDUALS=[CASEWISE] [PLOT] ]

  [/POWER=[T({.05**})] [F({.05**})] [ {APPROXIMATE}]]
            {a    }      {a    }      {EXACT      }
```

```
[/CINTERVAL=[{INDIVIDUAL}][({.95}) ]
             {JOINT     }    {a  }
             [UNIVARIATE ({SCHEFFE})]
                          {BONFER }
             [MULTIVARIATE  ({ROY      })]  ]
                             {PILLAI   }
                             {BONFER   }
                             {HOTELLING}
                             {WILKS    }
[/PCOMPS [COR] [COV] [ROTATE(rottype)]
         [NCOMP(n)] [MINEIGEN(eigencut)] [ALL] ]

[/PLOT=[BOXPLOTS] [CELLPLOTS] [NORMAL] [ZCORR] [ALL] ]

[/DISCRIM [RAW] [STAN] [ESTIM] [COR] [ALL]
          [ROTATE(rottype)] [ALPHA({.25**})]]
                                   {a    }

[/MISSING=[LISTWISE**] [{EXCLUDE**}] ]
                        {INCLUDE  }

[/MATRIX=[IN({file})]  [OUT({file})]]
             {[*] }        {[*] }

[/ANALYSIS [({UNCONDITIONAL**})]=[()dependent varlist
             {CONDITIONAL     }        [WITH covariate varlist]
                                       [/dependent varlist...][)][WITH varlist] ]

[/DESIGN={factor [(n)]  }[BY factor[(n)]] [WITHIN factor[(n)]][WITHIN...]
         {POOL(varlist) }

         [+ {factor [(n)]  }...]
            {POOL(varlist) }

         [[= n] {AGAINST} {WITHIN  }
                {VS     } {RESIDUAL}
                          {WR      }
                          {n       }

         [{factor [(n)]  } ... ]
          {POOL(varlist) }

         [MWITHIN factor(n)]
         [MUPLUS]
         [CONSTANT [=n] ]
```

* WSDESIGN uses the same specification as DESIGN, with only within-subjects factors.

† DEVIATION is the default for between-subjects factors while POLYNOMIAL is the default for within-subjects factors.

** Default if subcommand or keyword is omitted.

Example 1:
```
* Analysis of Variance

MANOVA RESULT BY TREATMNT(1,4) GROUP(1,2).
```

Example 2:
```
* Analysis of Covariance

MANOVA RESULT BY TREATMNT(1,4) GROUP(1,2) WITH RAINFALL.
```

Example 3:

```
* Repeated Measures Analysis

MANOVA SCORE1 TO SCORE4 BY CLASS(1,2)
  /WSFACTORS=MONTH(4).
```

Example 4:

```
* Parallelism Test with Crossed Factors

MANOVA YIELD BY PLOT(1,4) TYPEFERT(1,3) WITH FERT
  /ANALYSIS YIELD
  /DESIGN FERT, PLOT, TYPEFERT, PLOT BY TYPEFERT,
  FERT BY PLOT + FERT BY TYPEFERT
  + FERT BY PLOT BY TYPEFERT.
```

Overview

Multivariate analysis of variance (MANOVA) is a generalized procedure for analysis of variance and covariance. MANOVA is the most powerful of the analysis-of-variance procedures in SPSS/PC+ and can be used for both univariate and multivariate designs. Only MANOVA allows you to perform the following tasks:

- Specify nesting of effects.
- Specify individual error terms for effects in mixed-model analyses.
- Estimate covariate-by-factor interactions to test the assumption of homogeneity of regressions.
- Obtain parameter estimates for a variety of contrast types, including irregularly spaced polynomial contrasts with multiple factors.
- Test user-specified special contrasts with multiple factors.
- Partition effects in models.
- Pool effects in models.

To simplify the presentation, reference material on MANOVA is divided into three sections: *univariate* designs with one dependent variable, *multivariate* designs with several interrelated dependent variables, and *repeated measures* designs in which the dependent variables represent the same types of measurements taken at more than one time.

If you are unfamiliar with the models, assumptions, and statistics used in MANOVA, consult Chapters 2, 3, and 4.

The full syntax diagram for MANOVA is presented here. The three sections that follow include partial syntax diagrams showing the MANOVA subcommands and specifications discussed in each section. Individually, those diagrams are incomplete. Subcommands listed for univariate designs are available for any analysis, and subcommands listed for multivariate designs can be used in any multivariate analysis, including repeated measures.

MANOVA was designed and programmed by Philip Burns of Northwestern University.

Annotated Example

For a complete example with output, see the Annotated Examples following the Syntax Reference section of this manual.

MANOVA: Univariate

```
MANOVA dependent var [BY factor list (min,max)][factor list...]
                     [WITH covariate list]

[/ERROR={WITHIN + RESIDUAL**}  ]
        {WITHIN              }
        {RESIDUAL            }
        {n                   }
[/CONTRAST (factorname)={DEVIATION**  [(refcat)]        }]
                        {POLYNOMIAL   [({1,2,3...})]    }
                        {                    {metric  } }
                        {SIMPLE [(refcat)]              }
                        {DIFFERENCE                     }
                        {HELMERT                        }
                        {REPEATED                       }
                        {SPECIAL (matrix)               }
[/PARTITION (factorname)[=({1,1...  })]]
                           {n1,n2...}
[/METHOD=[{UNIQUE**    }] [{CONSTANT**}] [{QR**    }]]
          {SEQUENTIAL}    {NOCONSTANT}   {CHOLESKY}
[/{PRINT  } = [CELLINFO [([MEANS] [SSCP] [COV] [COR] [ALL])]]
  {NOPRINT}   [HOMOGENEITY [([ALL] [BARTLETT] [COCHRAN])]]
              [DESIGN [([OVERALL] [ONEWAY] [DECOMP] [BIAS] [SOLUTION]
                        [REDUNDANCY] [COLLINEARITY])]]
              [PARAMETERS [([ESTIM][ORTHO][COR][NEGSUM][EFSIZE][OPTIMAL][ALL])]]
              [SIGNIF[(SINGLEDF)]]
              [ERROR[(STDDEV)]]                                              ]
[/OMEANS =[VARIABLES(varlist)] [TABLES ({factor name  }] ]
                                        {factor BY factor}
                                        {CONSTANT        }
[/PMEANS =[TABLES ({factor name  })] [PLOT]] ]
                   {factor BY factor}
                   {CONSTANT        }
[/RESIDUALS=[CASEWISE] [PLOT]]
[/POWER=[T({.05**})] [F({.05**})] [{APPROXIMATE}]]
          {a    }      {a    }    {EXACT      }
[/CINTERVAL=[{INDIVIDUAL}][({.95}) ]] [UNIVARIATE ({SCHEFFE})]]
            {JOINT     }    {a  }                {BONFER }
[/PLOT=[BOXPLOTS] [CELLPLOTS] [NORMAL]  [ALL] ]
[/MISSING=[LISTWISE**] [{EXCLUDE**}] ]
                       {INCLUDE  }
[/MATRIX=[IN({file})]  [OUT({file})]]
             {*   }        {*   }
[/ANALYSIS=dependent var [WITH covariate list]]
[/DESIGN={factor [(n)]  }[BY factor[(n)]] [WITHIN factor[(n)]][WITHIN...]
         {POOL(varlist)}
         [+ {factor [(n)]  }...]
            {POOL(varlist)}
         [[= n] {AGAINST} {WITHIN  }
                {VS     } {RESIDUAL}
                          {WR      }
                          {n       }

         [{factor [(n)]  } ... ]
          {POOL(varlist)}
         [MUPLUS]
         [MWITHIN factor(n)]
         [CONSTANT [=n] ]
```

** Default if subcommand or keyword is omitted.

Example:

```
MANOVA YIELD BY SEED(1,4) FERT(1,3)
   /DESIGN.
```

318

Overview

This section describes the use of MANOVA for univariate analyses. However, the subcommands described here can be used in any type of analysis with MANOVA. For additional subcommands used in those types of analysis, see MANOVA: Multivariate and MANOVA: Repeated Measures. For basic specification, syntax rules, and limitations of the MANOVA procedures, see MANOVA: Overview. If you are unfamiliar with the models, assumptions, and statistics used in MANOVA, consult Chapter 2.

Options

Design Specification. You can specify which terms to include in the design on the DESIGN subcommand. This allows you to estimate a model other than the default full factorial model, incorporate factor-by-covariate interactions, indicate nesting of effects, and indicate specific error terms for each effect in mixed models. You can specify a different continuous variable as a dependent variable or work with a subset of the continuous variables with the ANALYSIS subcommand.

Contrast Types. You can specify contrasts other than the default deviation contrasts on the CONTRAST subcommand. You can also subdivide the degrees of freedom associated with a factor using the PARTITION subcommand and test the significance of a specific contrast or group of contrasts.

Optional Output. You can choose from a wide variety of optional output on the PRINT subcommand or suppress output using the NOPRINT subcommand. Output appropriate to univariate designs includes cell means, design or other matrices, parameter estimates, and tests for homogeneity of variance across cells. Using the OMEANS, PMEANS, RESIDUAL, and PLOT subcommands, you can also request tables of observed or predicted means, casewise values and residuals for your model, and various plots useful in checking assumptions. In addition, you can request observed power values based on fixed-effect assumptions using the POWER subcommand and request simultaneous confidence intervals for each parameter estimate and regression coefficient using the CINTERVAL subcommand.

Matrix Materials. You can write matrices of intermediate results to a matrix data file, and you can read such matrices in performing further analyses using the MATRIX subcommand.

Basic Specification

- The basic specification is a variable list identifying the dependent variable, the factors (if any), and the covariates (if any).
- By default, MANOVA uses a full factorial model, which includes all main effects and all possible interactions among factors. Estimation is performed using the cell-means model and UNIQUE (regression-type) sums of squares, adjusting each effect for all other effects in the model. Parameters are estimated using DEVIATION contrasts to determine if their categories differ significantly from the mean.

Subcommand Order

- The variable list must be specified first.
- Subcommands applicable to a specific design must be specified before that DESIGN subcommand. Otherwise, subcommands can be used in any order.

Syntax Rules

- For many analyses, the MANOVA variable list and the DESIGN subcommand are the only specifications needed. If a full factorial design is desired, DESIGN can be omitted.
- All other subcommands apply only to designs that follow. If you do not enter a DESIGN subcommand or if the last subcommand is not DESIGN, MANOVA will use a full factorial model.
- Unless replaced, MANOVA subcommands other than DESIGN and ERROR remain in effect for all subsequent models.
- MISSING can be specified only once.
- The following words are reserved as keywords or internal commands in the MANOVA procedure: AGAINST, CONSPLUS, CONSTANT, CONTIN, MUPLUS, MWITHIN, POOL, R, RESIDUAL, RW, VERSUS, VS, W, WITHIN, and WR. Variable names that duplicate these words should be changed before you invoke MANOVA.
- If you enter one of the multivariate specifications in a univariate analysis, MANOVA will ignore it.

Limitations

- Maximum 20 factors.
- Memory requirements depend primarily on the number of cells in the design. For the default full factorial model, this equals the product of the number of levels or categories in each factor.

Example

```
MANOVA YIELD BY SEED(1,4) FERT(1,3) WITH RAINFALL
  /PRINT=CELLINFO(MEANS) PARAMETERS(ESTIM)
  /DESIGN.
```

- *YIELD* is the dependent variable; *SEED* (with values 1, 2, 3, and 4) and *FERT* (with values 1, 2, and 3) are factors; *RAINFALL* is a covariate.
- The PRINT subcommand requests the means of the dependent variable for each cell and the default deviation parameter estimates.
- The DESIGN subcommand requests the default design, a full factorial model. This subcommand could have been omitted or could have been specified in full as:

```
/DESIGN = SEED, FERT, SEED BY FERT.
```

MANOVA Variable List

The variable list specifies all variables that will be used in any subsequent analyses.

- The dependent variable must be the first specification on MANOVA.
- By default, MANOVA treats a list of dependent variables as jointly dependent, implying a multivariate design. However, you can change the role of a variable or its inclusion status in the analysis on the ANALYSIS subcommand.
- The names of the factors follow the dependent variable. Use the keyword BY to separate the factors from the dependent variable.
- Factors must have adjacent integer values, and you must supply the minimum and maximum values in parentheses after the factor name(s).
- If several factors have the same value range, you can specify a list of factors followed by a single value range in parentheses.
- Certain one-cell designs, such as univariate and multivariate regression analysis, canonical correlation, and one-sample Hotelling's T^2, do not require a factor specification. To perform these analyses, omit keyword BY and the factor list.
- Enter the covariates, if any, following the factors and their ranges. Use keyword WITH to separate covariates from factors (if any) and the dependent variable.

Example

```
MANOVA DEPENDNT BY FACTOR1 (1,3) FACTOR2, FACTOR3 (1,2).
```

- In this example, three factors are specified.
- *FACTOR1* has values 1, 2, and 3, while *FACTOR2* and *FACTOR3* have values 1 and 2.
- A default full factorial model is used for the analysis.

Example

```
MANOVA Y BY A(1,3) WITH X
    /DESIGN.
```

- In this example, the *A* effect is tested after adjusting for the effect of the covariate *X*. It is a test of equality of adjusted *A* means.
- The test of the covariate *X* is adjusted for *A*. It is a test of the pooled within-groups regression of *Y* on *X*.

ERROR Subcommand

ERROR allows you to specify or change the error term used to test all effects for which you do not explicitly specify an error term on the DESIGN subcommand. ERROR affects all terms in all subsequent designs, except terms for which you explicitly provide an error term.

WITHIN+RESIDUAL   *Terms are tested against the pooled within-cells and residual sum of squares.* This specification can be abbreviated to WR or RW. This is the default.

WITHIN   *Terms in the model are tested against the within-cell sum of squares.* This specification can be abbreviated to W.

RESIDUAL   *Terms in the model are tested against the residual sum of squares.* This specification can be abbreviated to R. This includes all terms not named on the DESIGN subcommand.

error number   *Terms are tested against a numbered error term.* The error term must be defined on each DESIGN subcommand (for a discussion of error terms, see DESIGN Subcommand).

- If you specify ERROR=WITHIN+RESIDUAL and one of the components does not exist, MANOVA uses the other component alone.
- If you specify your own error term by number and a design does not have an error term with the specified number, MANOVA does not carry out significance tests. It will, however, display hypothesis sums of squares and, if requested, parameter estimates.

Example

```
MANOVA DEP BY A(1,2) B(1,4)
   /ERROR = 1
   /DESIGN = A, B, A BY B = 1 VS WITHIN
   /DESIGN = A, B.
```

- ERROR defines error term 1 as the default error term.
- In the first design, *A* by *B* is defined as error term 1 and is therefore used to test the *A* and *B* effects. The *A* by *B* effect itself is explicitly tested against the within-cells error.
- In the second design, no term is defined as error term 1, so no significance tests are carried out. Hypothesis sums of squares are displayed for *A* and *B*.

CONTRAST Subcommand

CONTRAST specifies the type of contrast desired among the levels of a factor. For a factor with *k* levels or values, the contrast type determines the meaning of its $k - 1$ degrees of freedom. If the subcommand is omitted or is specified with no keyword, the default is DEVIATION for between-subjects factors.

- Specify the factor name in parentheses following the subcommand CONTRAST.
- You can specify only one factor per CONTRAST subcommand, but you can enter multiple CONTRAST subcommands.
- After closing the parentheses, enter an equals sign followed by one of the contrast keywords.
- To obtain *F* tests for individual degrees of freedom for the specified contrast, enter the factor name followed by a number in parentheses on the DESIGN subcommand. The number refers to a partition of the factor's degrees of freedom. If you do not use the PARTITION subcommand, each degree of freedom is a distinct partition.

The following contrast types are available:

DEVIATION(refcat)   *Deviations from the grand mean.* This is the default for between-subjects factors. Each level of the factor except one is compared to the grand mean. One category (by default the last) must be omitted so that the effects will be independent of one another. To omit a category other than the last, specify the number of the omitted category (which is not necessarily the same as its value) in parentheses after keyword DEVIATION. For example:

```
MANOVA A BY B(2,4)
    /CONTRAST(B)=DEVIATION(1).
```

The specified contrast omits the first category, in which *B* has the value 2. Deviation contrasts are not orthogonal.

POLYNOMIAL(metric)   *Polynomial contrasts.* This is the default for within-subjects factors. The first degree of freedom contains the linear effect across the levels of the factor, the second contains the quadratic effect, and so on. In a balanced design, polynomial contrasts are orthogonal. By default, the levels are assumed to be equally spaced; you can specify unequal spacing by entering a metric consisting of one integer for each level of the factor in parentheses after keyword POLYNOMIAL. For example:

```
MANOVA RESPONSE BY STIMULUS (4,6)
    /CONTRAST(STIMULUS) = POLYNOMIAL(1,2,4).
```

The specified contrast indicates that the three levels of *STIMULUS* are actually in the proportion 1:2:4. The default metric is always $(1,2,...,k)$, where k levels are involved. Only the relative differences between the terms of the metric matter (1,2,4) is the same metric as (2,3,5) or (20,30,50) because, in each instance, the difference between the second and third numbers is twice the difference between the first and second.

DIFFERENCE   *Difference or reverse Helmert contrasts.* Each level of the factor except the first is compared to the mean of the previous levels. In a balanced design, difference contrasts are orthogonal.

HELMERT   *Helmert contrasts.* Each level of the factor except the last is compared to the mean of subsequent levels. In a balanced design, Helmert contrasts are orthogonal.

SIMPLE(refcat)   *Each level of the factor except the last is compared to the last level.* To use a category other than the last as the omitted reference category, specify its number (which is not necessarily the same as its value) in parentheses following keyword SIMPLE. For example:

```
MANOVA A BY B(2,4)
    /CONTRAST(B)=SIMPLE(1).
```

The specified contrast compares the other levels to the first level of *B*, in which *B* has the value 2. Simple contrasts are not orthogonal.

REPEATED   *Comparison of adjacent levels.* Each level of the factor except the first is compared to the previous level. Repeated contrasts are not orthogonal.

SPECIAL   *A user-defined contrast.* After this keyword, enter a square matrix in parentheses with as many rows and columns as there are levels in the factor. The first row represents the mean effect of the factor and is generally a vector of 1's. It represents a set of weights indicating how to collapse over the categories of this factor in estimating parameters for other factors. The other rows of the contrast matrix contain the special contrasts indicating the desired comparisons between levels of the factor. If the special contrasts are linear combinations of each other, MANOVA reports the linear dependency and stops processing.

Orthogonal contrasts are particularly useful. In a balanced design, contrasts are orthogonal if the sum of the coefficients in each contrast row is 0 and if, for any pair of contrast rows, the products of corresponding coefficients sum to 0. DIFFERENCE, HELMERT, and POLYNOMIAL contrasts always meet these criteria in balanced designs. For illustration of contrast types, see Appendix A.

Example

```
MANOVA DEP BY FAC(1,5)
  /CONTRAST(FAC)=DIFFERENCE
  /DESIGN=FAC(1) FAC(2) FAC(3) FAC(4).
```

- The factor *FAC* has five categories and therefore four degrees of freedom.
- CONTRAST requests DIFFERENCE contrasts, which compare each level (except the first) with the mean of the previous levels.
- Each of the four degrees of freedom is tested individually on the DESIGN subcommand.

PARTITION Subcommand

PARTITION subdivides the degrees of freedom associated with a factor. This permits you to test the significance of the effect of a specific contrast or group of contrasts of the factor instead of the overall effect of all contrasts of the factor. The default is a single degree of freedom for each partition.

- Specify the factor name in parentheses following the PARTITION subcommand.
- Specify an integer list in parentheses after the optional equals sign to indicate the degrees of freedom for each partition.
- Each value in the partition list must be a positive integer, and the sum of the values cannot exceed the degrees of freedom for the factor.
- The degrees of freedom available for a factor are one less than the number of levels of the factor.
- The meaning of each degree of freedom depends upon the contrast type for the factor. For example, with deviation contrasts (the default for between-subjects factors), each degree of freedom represents the deviation of the dependent variable in one level of the factor from its grand mean over all levels. With polynomial contrasts, the degrees of freedom represent the linear effect, the quadratic effect, and so on.
- If your list does not account for all the degrees of freedom, MANOVA adds one final partition containing the remaining degrees of freedom.

- You can use a repetition factor of the form $n*$ to specify a series of partitions with the same number of degrees of freedom.
- To specify a model that tests only the effect of a specific partition of a factor in your design, include the number of the partition in parentheses on the DESIGN subcommand (see example below).
- If you want the default single degree-of-freedom partition, you can omit the PARTITION subcommand and simply enter the appropriate term on the DESIGN subcommand.

Example

```
MANOVA OUTCOME BY TREATMNT(1,12)
  /PARTITION(TREATMNT) = (3*2,4)
  /DESIGN TREATMNT(2).
```

- The factor *TREATMNT* has 12 categories, hence 11 degrees of freedom.
- PARTITION divides the effect of *TREATMNT* into four partitions, containing respectively two, two, two, and four degrees of freedom. A fifth partition is formed to contain the remaining one degree of freedom.
- DESIGN specifies a model in which only the second partition of *TREATMNT* is tested. This partition contains the third and fourth degrees of freedom.
- Since the default contrast type for between-subjects factors is DEVIATION, this second partition represents the deviation of the third and fourth levels of *TREATMNT* from the grand mean.

METHOD Subcommand

METHOD controls the computational aspects of the MANOVA analysis. You can specify one of two different methods for partitioning the sums of squares. The default is UNIQUE.

UNIQUE
: *Regression approach.* Each term is corrected for every other term in the model. With this approach, sums of squares for various components of the model do not add up to the total sum of squares unless the design is balanced. This is the default if the METHOD subcommand is omitted or if neither of the two keywords is specified.

SEQUENTIAL
: *Hierarchical decomposition of the sums of squares.* Each term is adjusted only for the terms that precede it on the DESIGN subcommand. This is an orthogonal decomposition, and the sums of squares in the model add up to the total sum of squares.

You can control how parameters are to be estimated by specifying one of the following two keywords available on MANOVA. The default is QR.

QR
: *Use modified Givens rotations.* QR bypasses the normal equations and the inaccuracies that can result from creating the cross-products matrix, and it generally results in extremely accurate parameter estimates. This is the default if the METHOD subcommand is omitted or if neither of the two keywords is specified.

CHOLESKY   *Use Cholesky decomposition of the cross-products matrix.* Useful for large data sets with covariates entered on the DESIGN subcommand.

You can also control whether a constant term is included in all models. Two keywords are available on METHOD. The default is CONSTANT.

CONSTANT   *All models include a constant (grand mean) term, even if none is explicitly specified on the DESIGN subcommand.* This is the default if neither of the two keywords is specified.

NOCONSTANT   *Exclude constant terms from models that do not include keyword CONSTANT on the DESIGN subcommand.*

Example

```
MANOVA DEP BY A B C (1,4)
  /METHOD=NOCONSTANT
  /DESIGN=A, B, C
  /METHOD=CONSTANT SEQUENTIAL
  /DESIGN.
```

- For the first design, a main effects model, the METHOD subcommand requests the model to be fitted with no constant.
- The second design requests a full factorial model to be fitted with a constant and with a sequential decomposition of sums of squares.

PRINT and NOPRINT Subcommands

PRINT and NOPRINT control the display of optional output.
- Specifications on PRINT remain in effect for all subsequent designs.
- Some PRINT output, such as CELLINFO, applies to the entire MANOVA procedure and is displayed only once.
- You can turn off optional output that you have requested on PRINT by entering a NOPRINT subcommand with the specifications originally used on the PRINT subcommand.
- Additional output can be obtained on the PCOMPS, DISCRIM, OMEANS, PMEANS, PLOT, and RESIDUALS subcommands.
- Some optional output greatly increases the processing time. Request only the output you want to see.

The following specifications are appropriate for univariate MANOVA analyses. For information on PRINT specifications appropriate for other MANOVA models, see MANOVA: Multivariate and MANOVA: Repeated Measures.

CELLINFO   *Basic information about each cell in the design.*

PARAMETERS   *Parameter estimates.*

HOMOGENEITY   *Tests of homogeneity of variance.*

DESIGN   *Design information.*

ERROR   *Error standard deviations.*

CELLINFO Keyword

You can request any of the following cell information by specifying the appropriate keyword(s) in parentheses after CELLINFO. The default is MEANS.

MEANS *Cell means, standard deviations, and counts for the dependent variable and covariates.* Confidence intervals for the cell means are displayed if you have set width wide. This is the default when CELLINFO is requested with no further specification.

SSCP *Within-cell sum-of-squares and cross-products matrices for the dependent variable and covariates.*

COV *Within-cell variance-covariance matrices for the dependent variable and covariates.*

COR *Within-cell correlation matrices, with standard deviations on the diagonal, for the dependent variable and covariates.*

ALL *MEANS, SSCP, COV, COR.*

- Output from CELLINFO is displayed once before the analysis of any particular design. Specify CELLINFO only once.
- When you specify SSCP, COV, or COR, the cells are numbered for identification, beginning with cell 1.
- The levels vary most rapidly for the factor named last on the MANOVA variables specification.
- Empty cells are neither displayed nor numbered.
- A table showing the levels of each factor corresponding to each cell number is displayed at the beginning of MANOVA output.

Example

```
MANOVA DEP BY A(1,4) B(1,2) WITH COV
  /PRINT=CELLINFO(MEANS COV)
  /DESIGN.
```

- For each combination of levels of *A* and *B*, MANOVA displays separately the means and standard deviations of *DEP* and *COV*. Beginning with cell 1, it will then display the variance-covariance matrix of *DEP* and *COV* within each non-empty cell.
- A table of cell numbers will be displayed to show the factor levels corresponding to each cell.
- Keyword COV, as a parameter of CELLINFO, is not confused with variable *COV*.

PARAMETERS Keyword

Keyword PARAMETERS displays information relating to the estimated size of the effects in the model. You can specify any of the following keywords in parentheses on PARAMETERS. The default is ESTIM.

ESTIM	*The estimated parameters themselves, along with their standard errors, t tests, and confidence intervals.* Only nonredundant parameters are displayed. This is the default if PARAMETERS is requested without further specification.
NEGSUM	*The negative of the sum of parameters for each effect.* For DEVIATION main effects, this equals the parameter for the omitted (redundant) contrast. NEGSUM is displayed along with the parameter estimates.
ORTHO	*The orthogonal estimates of parameters used to produce the sums of squares.*
COR	*Covariance factors and correlations among the parameter estimates.*
EFSIZE	*The effect size values.*
OPTIMAL	*Optimal Scheffé contrast coefficients.*
ALL	*ESTIM, NEGSUM, ORTHO, COR, EFSIZE, and OPTIMAL.*

SIGNIF Keyword

SIGNIF requests special significance tests, most of which apply to multivariate designs (see MANOVA: Multivariate). The following specification is useful in univariate applications of MANOVA:

SINGLEDF	*Significance tests for each single degree of freedom making up each effect for analysis-of-variance tables.*

- When nonorthogonal contrasts are requested or when the design is unbalanced, the SINGLEDF effects will differ from single degree-of-freedom partitions. SINGLEDEF effects are orthogonal within an effect; single degree-of-freedom partitions are not.

Example

```
MANOVA DEP BY FAC(1,5)
  /CONTRAST(FAC)=POLY
  /PRINT=SIGNIF(SINGLEDF)
  /DESIGN.
```

- POLYNOMIAL contrasts are applied to *FAC*, testing the linear, quadratic, cubic, and quartic components of its five levels. POLYNOMIAL contrasts are orthogonal in balanced designs.
- The SINGLEDF specification on SIGNIF requests significance tests for each of these four components.

HOMOGENEITY Keyword

HOMOGENEITY requests tests for the homogeneity of variance of the dependent variable across the cells of the design. You can specify one or more of the following specifications in parentheses. If HOMOGENEITY is requested without further specification, the default is ALL.

BARTLETT	*Bartlett-Box* F *test.*
COCHRAN	*Cochran's* C.
ALL	*Both BARTLETT and COCHRAN.* This is the default.

DESIGN Keyword

You can request the following by entering one or more of the specifications in parentheses following keyword DESIGN. If DESIGN is requested without further specification, the default is OVERALL.

The DECOMP and BIAS matrices can provide valuable information on the confounding of the effects and the estimability of the chosen contrasts. If two effects are confounded, the entry corresponding to them in the BIAS matrix will be non-zero; if they are orthogonal, the entry will be zero. This is particularly useful in designs with unpatterned empty cells. For further discussion of the matrices, see Bock (1985).

OVERALL *The overall reduced-model design matrix (not the contrast matrix).* This is the default.

ONEWAY *The one-way basis matrix (not the contrast matrix) for each factor.*

DECOMP *The upper triangular QR/CHOLESKY decomposition of the design.*

BIAS *Contamination coefficients displaying the bias present in the design.*

SOLUTION *Coefficients of the linear combinations of the cell means used in significance testing.*

REDUNDANCY *Exact linear combinations of parameters that form a redundancy.* This keyword displays a table only if QR (the default) is the estimation method.

COLLINEARITY *Collinearity diagnostics for design matrices.* These diagnostics include the singular values of the normalized design matrix (which are the same as those of the normalized decomposition matrix), condition indexes corresponding to each singular value, and the proportion of variance of the corresponding parameter accounted for by each principal component. For greatest accuracy, use the QR method of estimation whenever you request collinearity diagnostics.

ALL *All available options.*

ERROR Keyword

Generally, keyword ERROR on PRINT produces error matrices. In univariate analyses, the only valid specification for ERROR is STDDEV, which is the default if ERROR is specified by itself.

STDDEV *The error standard deviation.* Normally, this is the within-cells standard deviation of the dependent variable. If you specify multiple error terms on DESIGN, this specification will display the standard deviation for each.

OMEANS Subcommand

OMEANS (observed means) displays tables of the means of continuous variables for levels or combinations of levels of the factors.

- Use keywords VARIABLES and TABLES to indicate which observed means you want to display.
- With no specifications, the OMEANS subcommand is equivalent to requesting CELLINFO (MEANS) on PRINT.
- OMEANS displays confidence intervals for the cell means if you have set width to 132.
- Output from OMEANS is displayed once before the analysis of any particular design. This subcommand should be specified only once.

VARIABLES *Continuous variables for which you want means.* Specify the variables in parentheses after the keyword VARIABLES. You can request means for the dependent variable or any covariates. If you omit the VARIABLES keyword, observed means are displayed for the dependent variable and all covariates. If you enter the keyword VARIABLES, you must also enter the keyword TABLES, discussed below.

TABLES *Factors for which you want the observed means displayed.* List in parentheses the factors, or combinations of factors, separated with BY. Observed means are displayed for each level, or combination of levels, of the factors named (see example below). Both weighted means and unweighted means (where all cells are weighted equally, regardless of the number of cases they contain) are displayed. If you enter the keyword CONSTANT, the grand mean is displayed.

Example

```
MANOVA DEP BY A(1,3) B(1,2)
  /OMEANS=TABLES(A,B)
  /DESIGN.
```

- Because there is no VARIABLES specification on the OMEANS subcommand, observed means are displayed for all continuous variables. *DEP* is the only dependent variable here, and there are no covariates.
- The TABLES specification on the OMEANS subcommand requests tables of observed means for each of the three categories of *A* (collapsing over *B*) and for both categories of *B* (collapsing over *A*).
- MANOVA displays both weighted means, in which all cases count equally, and unweighted means, in which all cells count equally.

PMEANS Subcommand

PMEANS (predicted means) displays a table of the predicted cell means of the dependent variable, both adjusted for the effect of covariates in the cell and unadjusted for covariates. For comparison, it also displays the observed cell means.

- Output from PMEANS can be computationally expensive.
- PMEANS without any additional specifications displays a table showing for each cell the observed mean of the dependent variable, the predicted mean adjusted for the effect of covariates in that cell (adjusted mean), the predicted mean unadjusted for covariates (estimated mean), and the raw and standardized residuals from the estimated means.

- Cells are numbered in output from PMEANS so that the levels vary most rapidly on the factor named last in the MANOVA variables specification. A table showing the levels of each factor corresponding to each cell number is displayed at the beginning of the MANOVA output.
- Predicted means are suppressed for any design in which the MUPLUS keyword appears.
- Covariates are not predicted.
- In designs with covariates and multiple error terms, use the ERROR subcommand to designate which error term's regression coefficients are to be used in calculating the standardized residuals.

For univariate analysis, the following keywords are available on the PMEANS subcommand:

TABLES   *Additional tables showing adjusted predicted means for specified factors or combinations of factors.* Enter the names of factors or combinations of factors in parentheses after this keyword. For each factor or combination, MANOVA displays the predicted means (adjusted for covariates) collapsed over all other factors.

PLOT   *A plot of the predicted means for each cell.*

Example

```
MANOVA DEP BY A(1,4) B(1,3)
  /PMEANS TABLES(A, B, A BY B)
  /DESIGN = A, B.
```

- PMEANS displays the default table of observed and predicted means for *DEP* and raw and standardized residuals in each of the 12 cells in the model.
- The TABLES specification on PMEANS displays tables of predicted means for *A* (collapsing over *B*), for *B* (collapsing over *A*), and all combinations of *A* and *B*.
- Because *A* and *B* are the only factors in the model, the means for *A* by *B* in the TABLES specification come from every cell in the model. They are identical to the adjusted predicted means in the default PMEANS table, which always includes all non-empty cells.
- Predicted means for *A* by *B* can be requested in the TABLES specification, even though the *A* by *B* effect is not in the design.

Example

```
MANOVA DEP BY A B C(1,3)
  /PMEANS
  /ERROR=1
  /DESIGN A, B WITHIN A = 1, C VS W.
```

- Two error terms are used in this design: the *B* within *A* sum of squares, which is defined as error term 1 (to test the *A* effect), and the within-cells sum of squares (to test *B* within *A* itself as well as the *C* effect).
- To use *B* within *A* as the error term for standardized residuals, the PMEANS subcommand requires an error specification on the ERROR subcommand. If the ERROR subcommand is omitted, MANOVA uses the within-cells plus residual error term.

- Since there is no TABLES keyword on the PMEANS subcommand, the default table of predicted means for each cell is produced.

RESIDUALS Subcommand

Use RESIDUALS to display and plot casewise values and residuals for your models.

- Use the ERROR subcommand to specify an error term other than the default to be used to standardize the residuals.
- If a designated error term does not exist for a given design, no predicted values or residuals are calculated.
- If you specify RESIDUALS without any keyword, CASEWISE output is displayed.

The following keywords are available:

CASEWISE   *A case-by-case listing of the observed, predicted, residual, and standardized residual values for each dependent variable.*

PLOT   *A plot of observed values, predicted values, and case numbers versus the standardized residuals, plus normal and detrended normal probability plots for the standardized residuals (five plots in all).*

POWER Subcommand

POWER requests observed power values based on fixed-effect assumptions for all univariate and multivariate F tests and t tests. Both approximate and exact power values can be computed, although exact multivariate power is displayed only when there is one hypothesis degree of freedom. If POWER is specified by itself, with no keywords, MANOVA calculates the approximate observed power values of all F tests at 0.05 significance level.

The following keywords are available on the POWER subcommand:

APPROXIMATE   *Approximate power values.* This is the default if POWER is specified without any keyword. Approximate power values for univariate tests are derived from an Edgeworth-type normal approximation to the noncentral beta distribution. Approximate values are normally accurate to three decimal places and are much cheaper to compute than exact values.

EXACT   *Exact power values.* Exact power values for univariate tests are computed from the noncentral incomplete beta distribution.

F(a)   *Alpha level at which the power is to be calculated for* F *tests.* The default is 0.05. To change the default, specify a decimal number between 0 and 1 in parentheses after F. The numbers 0 and 1 themselves are not allowed. F test at 0.05 significance level is the default when POWER is omitted or specified without any keyword.

T(a)   *Alpha level at which the power is to be calculated for* t *tests.* The default is 0.05. To change the default, specify a decimal number between 0 and 1 in parentheses after T. The numbers 0 and 1 themselves are not allowed.

- For univariate F tests and t tests, MANOVA computes a measure of the effect size based on partial η^2:

$$\text{partial } \eta^2 = (ssh) / (ssh + sse)$$

where ssh is hypothesis sum of squares and sse is error sum of squares. The measure is an overestimate of the actual effect size. However, it is consistent and is applicable to all F tests and t tests. For a discussion of effect size measures, see Cohen (1977) or Hays (1981).

CINTERVAL Subcommand

CINTERVAL requests simultaneous confidence intervals for each parameter estimate and regression coefficient. MANOVA provides either individual or joint confidence intervals at any desired confidence level. You can compute joint confidence intervals using either Scheffé or Bonferroni intervals. Scheffé intervals are based on all possible contrasts, while Bonferroni intervals are based on the number of contrasts actually made. For a large number of contrasts, Bonferroni intervals will be larger than Scheffé intervals. Timm (1975) provides a good discussion of which intervals are best for certain situations. Both Scheffé and Bonferroni intervals are computed separately for each term in the design. You can request only one type of confidence interval per design.

The following keywords are available on the CINTERVAL subcommand. If the subcommand is specified without any keyword, CINTERVAL automatically displays individual univariate confidence intervals at the 0.95 level.

INDIVIDUAL(a)   *Individual confidence intervals.* Specify the desired confidence level in parentheses following the keyword. The default is 0.95. The desired confidence level can be any decimal number between 0 and 1. When individual intervals are requested, BONFER and SCHEFFE have no effect.

JOINT(a)   *Joint confidence intervals.* Specify the desired confidence level in parentheses after the keyword. The default is 0.95. The desired confidence level can be any decimal number between 0 and 1.

UNIVARIATE(type)   *Univariate confidence interval.* Specify either SCHEFFE for Scheffé intervals or BONFER for Bonferroni intervals in parentheses after the keyword. The default specification is SCHEFFE.

PLOT Subcommand

MANOVA can display a variety of plots useful in checking the assumptions needed in the analysis. Plots are produced only once in the MANOVA procedure, regardless of how many DESIGN subcommands you enter. Use the following keywords on the PLOT subcommand to request plots. If the PLOT subcommand is specified by itself, the default is BOX-PLOT.

BOXPLOTS   *Boxplots.* Plots are displayed for each continuous variable (dependent or covariate) named on the MANOVA variable list. Boxplots provide a simple graphical means of comparing the cells in terms of mean location and spread. The data must be stored in memory for these plots; if there is not enough memory, boxplots are not produced and a warning message is issued. This is the default if the PLOT subcommand is specified without a keyword.

CELLPLOTS   *Cell statistics, including a plot of cell means versus cell variances, a plot of cell means versus cell standard deviations, and a histogram of cell means.* Plots are produced for each continuous variable (dependent or covariate) named on the MANOVA variable list. The first two plots aid in detecting heteroscedasticity (nonhomogeneous variances) and in determining an appropriate data transformation if one is needed. The third plot gives distributional information for the cell means.

NORMAL   *Normal and detrended normal plots.* Plots are produced for each continuous variable (dependent or covariate) named on the MANOVA variable list. MANOVA ranks the scores and then plots the ranks against the expected normal deviate, or detrended expected normal deviate, for that rank. These plots aid in detecting non-normality and outlying observations. All data must be held in memory to compute ranks. If not enough memory is available, MANOVA displays a warning and skips the plots.

- ZCORR, an additional plot available on the PLOT subcommand, is described in MANOVA: Multivariate.
- You can request other plots on PMEANS and RESIDUALS (see respective subcommands).

MISSING Subcommand

By default, cases with missing values for any of the variables on the MANOVA variable list are excluded from the analysis. The MISSING subcommand allows you to include cases with user-missing values. If MISSING is not specified, the defaults are LISTWISE and EXCLUDE.

- The same missing-value treatment is used to process all designs in a single execution of MANOVA.
- If you enter more than one MISSING subcommand, the last one entered will be in effect for the entire procedure, including designs specified before the last MISSING subcommand.
- Pairwise deletion of missing data is not available in MANOVA.
- Keywords INCLUDE and EXCLUDE are mutually exclusive; either can be specified with LISTWISE.

LISTWISE   *Cases with missing values for any variable named on the MANOVA variable list are excluded from the analysis.* This is always true in the MANOVA procedure.

EXCLUDE   *Exclude both user-missing and system-missing values.* This is the default when MISSING is not specified.

INCLUDE	*User-missing values are treated as valid.* For factors, you must include the missing-value codes within the range specified on the MANOVA variable list. It may be necessary to recode these values so that they will be adjacent to the other factor values. System-missing values cannot be included in the analysis.

WRITE Subcommand

MANOVA allows you to write intermediate results to the resulting file and then read them back into a later run for further analysis. This can significantly reduce processing time when you are analyzing large numbers of cases or variables.

- The WRITE subcommand writes matrix materials to the resulting file (by default, *SPSS.PRC*) in a format that can be read in by the READ subcommand.
- WRITE requires no specifications.
- Six types of records are written to the resulting file.

The formats of the output records are as follows:

Type 1	*Design information.* Four 10-character fields containing, respectively, the number of non-empty cells, the number of observations, the number of factors, and the number of continuous variables (dependent variables and covariates).
Type 2	*Factor codes for cells.* For each non-empty cell, a Type 2 record lists the value of each factor. These values are written in 8-character fields. Each Type 2 record is followed by the corresponding Type 3 records.
Type 3	*Cell means for continuous variables.* Each number occupies 16 characters. Means for continuous variables are written in the order variables were named on the MANOVA variables specification.
Type 4	*Cell n's.* Following the pairs of Type 2 and 3 records, MANOVA writes out case counts for all cells on Type 4 records, using 10 characters per count.
Type 5	*Within-cell error correlation matrix for continuous variables.* The matrix is written in lower-triangular form, with ones on the diagonal and correlations in F10.6 format. The order of variables is that on the MANOVA variables specification.
Type 6	*Within-cell standard deviations for continuous variables.* Standard deviations are written in the order variables were named on the MANOVA variables specification.

READ Subcommand

The READ subcommand reads matrix materials formatted as described for the WRITE subcommand. Starting an analysis with these intermediate results can significantly reduce processing time. READ requires no specifications.

The Active File

MANOVA reads matrix materials only from the active file. When using the READ subcommand in MANOVA, you must precede the MANOVA command by a DATA LIST MATRIX command.

- DATA LIST MATRIX does not have to specify the same variable names as those used when the matrix materials were written.
- The order in which you list variables on DATA LIST MATRIX does not matter, except in determining the order of variables in the active file.
- The active file created for MANOVA using matrix input cannot be used by any other procedure.

Limitations

Since READ reads in matrix materials rather than a case file, you cannot obtain statistics based on case information.

- You cannot use the RESIDUALS subcommand when you use matrix input.
- The only plot you can obtain is ZCORR.
- You cannot specify continuous variables or factor-by-covariate interactions on the DESIGN subcommand.
- The homogeneity-of-variance tests are not available with matrix input. Do not request HOMOGENEITY on PRINT.

Example

```
GET FILE='MYFILE.SYS'.
SET RESULTS 'MANOVA.MAT'.
MANOVA V1 V2 V3 V4 BY SEX(1,2) CLASS(1,3)
   /WRITE
   /DESIGN SEX CLASS.

DATA LIST MATRIX FILE='MANOVA.MAT'
   /X1 TO X4 SEX CLASS.

MANOVA X1 X2 X3 X4 BY SEX(1,2) CLASS(1,3)
   /READ
   /ANALYSIS X1 WITH X2 X3
   /PRINT=PARAM(ESTIM)
   /DESIGN=SEX, CLASS, SEX BY CLASS.
```

- The SET command specifies the result file name. The matrix materials are to be written to the file *MANOVA.MAT*.
- In the first MANOVA procedure, the WRITE subcommand sends formatted matrix materials to *MANOVA.MAT*. These materials describe the four continuous variables *V1* to *V4* in the six cells defined by *SEX* and *CLASS*.
- The DATA LIST MATRIX command names the *MANOVA.MAT* file and assigns names to the variables. The names *X1*, *X2*, *X3*, and *X4* will now be used for the variables originally known as *V1*, *V2*, *V3*, and *V4*. The order in which variables are named on DATA LIST MATRIX does not matter.

- The second MANOVA command uses the new names. The variables specification defines four continuous variables and two factors. The number and order of continuous variables, the number and order of factors, and the levels of each factor must be the same as those in the MANOVA command that wrote the matrix materials. The names of the six variables must be chosen from among the names on the DATA LIST MATRIX command.
- The ANALYSIS subcommand redefines *X2* and *X3* as covariates and omits *X4* entirely from the analysis.
- The DESIGN subcommand specifies a design that is different from the one in the original analysis.
- Any analysis using these four continuous variables and two factors can be performed. However, the RESIDUALS subcommand, most plots, the homogeneity-of-variance tests, and continuous variables on the DESIGN subcommand cannot be specified.

ANALYSIS Subcommand

ANALYSIS allows you to work with a subset of the continuous variables (dependent variable and covariates) you have named on the MANOVA variable list. In univariate analysis of variance, you can use ANALYSIS to allow factor-by-covariate interaction terms in your model (see DESIGN Subcommand). You can also use it to switch the roles of the dependent variable and a covariate.

- In general, ANALYSIS gives you complete control over which continuous variables are to be dependent variables, which are to be covariates, and which are to be neither.
- ANALYSIS specifications are like the MANOVA variables specification, except that factors are not named. Enter the dependent variable and, if there are covariates, the keyword WITH and the covariates.
- Only variables listed as dependent variables or covariates on the MANOVA variable list can be entered on the ANALYSIS subcommand.
- In a univariate analysis of variance, the most important use of ANALYSIS is to omit covariates altogether from the analysis list, thereby making them available for inclusion on DESIGN (see example below and DESIGN Subcommand examples).
- For more information on ANALYSIS, refer to MANOVA: Multivariate.

Example

```
MANOVA DEP BY FACTOR(1,3) WITH COV
  /ANALYSIS DEP
  /DESIGN FACTOR, COV, FACTOR BY COV.
```

- *COV*, a continuous variable, is included on the MANOVA variable list as a covariate.
- *COV* is not mentioned on ANALYSIS, so it will not be included in the model as a dependent variable or covariate. It can, therefore, be explicitly included on the DESIGN subcommand.
- DESIGN includes the main effects of *FACTOR* and *COV* and the *FACTOR* by *COV* interaction.

DESIGN Subcommand

DESIGN specifies the effects included in a specific model. It must be the last subcommand entered for any model.

The cells in a design are defined by all of the possible combinations of levels of the factors in that design. The number of cells equals the product of the number of levels of all the factors. A design is *balanced* if each cell contains the same number of cases. MANOVA can analyze both balanced and unbalanced designs.

- Specify a list of terms to be included in the model, separated by spaces or commas.
- The default design, if the DESIGN subcommand is omitted or is specified by itself, is a full factorial model containing all main effects and all orders of factor-by-factor interaction.
- If the last subcommand specified is not DESIGN, a default full factorial design is estimated.
- To include a term for the main effect of a factor, enter the name of the factor on the DESIGN subcommand.
- To include a term for an interaction between factors, use the keyword BY to join the factors involved in the interaction.
- Terms are entered into the model in the order in which you list them on DESIGN. If you have specified SEQUENTIAL on the METHOD subcommand to partition the sums of squares in a hierarchical fashion, this order may affect the significance tests.
- You can specify other types of terms in the model, as described in the following sections.
- Multiple DESIGN subcommands are accepted. An analysis of one model is produced for each DESIGN subcommand.

Example

```
MANOVA Y BY A(1,2) B(1,2) C(1,3)
  /DESIGN
  /DESIGN A, B, C
  /DESIGN A, B, C, A BY B, A BY C.
```

- The first DESIGN produces the default full factorial design, with all main effects and interactions for factors *A*, *B*, and *C*.
- The second DESIGN produces an analysis with main effects only for *A*, *B*, and *C*.
- The third DESIGN produces an analysis with main effects and the interactions between *A* and the other two factors. The interaction between *B* and *C* is not in the design, nor is the interaction between all three factors.

Partitioned Effects: Number in Parentheses

You can specify a number in parentheses following a factor name on the DESIGN subcommand to identify individual degrees of freedom or partitions of the degrees of freedom associated with an effect.

- If you specify PARTITION, the number refers to a partition. Partitions can include more than one degree of freedom (see PARTITION Subcommand). For example, if the first partition of *SEED* includes two degrees of freedom, the term SEED(1) on a DESIGN subcommand tests the two degrees of freedom.

- If you do not use PARTITION, the number refers to a single degree of freedom associated with the effect.
- The number refers to an individual level for a factor if that factor follows the keyword WITHIN or MWITHIN (see the sections on nested effects and pooled effects below).
- A factor has one less degree of freedom than it has levels or values.

Example

```
MANOVA YIELD BY SEED(1,4) WITH RAINFALL
  /PARTITION(SEED)=(2,1)
  /DESIGN=SEED(1) SEED(2).
```

- Factor *SEED* is subdivided into two partitions, one containing the first two degrees of freedom and the other the last degree of freedom.
- The two partitions of *SEED* are treated as independent effects.

Nested Effects: WITHIN Keyword

Use the WITHIN keyword (alias W) to nest the effects of one factor within those of another factor or an interaction term.

Example

```
MANOVA YIELD BY SEED(1,4) FERT(1,3) PLOT (1,4)
  /DESIGN = FERT WITHIN SEED BY PLOT.
```

- The three factors in this example are type of seed (*SEED*), type of fertilizer (*FERT*), and location of plots (*PLOT*).
- The DESIGN subcommand nests the effects of *FERT* within the interaction term of *SEED* by *PLOT*. The levels of *FERT* are considered distinct for each combination of levels of *SEED* and *PLOT*.

Simple Effects: WITHIN and MWITHIN Keywords

A factor can be nested within one specific level of another factor by indicating the level in parentheses. This allows you to estimate simple effects or the effect of one factor within only one level of another. Simple effects can be obtained for higher-order interactions as well.
Use WITHIN to request simple effects of between-subjects factors.

Example

```
MANOVA YIELD BY SEED(2,4) FERT(1,3) PLOT (1,4)
  /DESIGN = FERT WITHIN SEED (1).
```

- This example requests the simple effect of *FERT* within the first level of *SEED*.
- The number (*n*) specified after a WITHIN factor refers to the level of that factor. It is the ordinal position, which is not necessarily the value of that level. In this example, the first level is associated with value 2.
- The number does *not* refer to the number of partitioned effects (see Partitioned Effects).

Example

```
MANOVA YIELD BY SEED(2,4) FERT(1,3) PLOT (3,5)
 /DESIGN = FERT WITHIN PLOT(1) WITHIN SEED(2)
```

- This example requests the effect of *FERT* within the second *SEED* level of the first *PLOT* level.
- The second *SEED* level is associated with value 3 and the first *PLOT* level is associated with value 3.

Use MWITHIN to request simple effects of within-subjects factors in repeated measures analysis (see MANOVA: Repeated Measures).

Pooled Effects: Plus Sign

To pool different effects for the purpose of significance testing, join the effects with a plus sign (+). A single test is made for the combined effect of the pooled terms.

- Keyword BY is evaluated before effects are pooled together.
- Parentheses are not allowed to change the order of evaluation. For example, it is illegal to specify `(A + B) BY C`. You must specify `/DESIGN=A BY C + B BY C`.

Example

```
MANOVA Y BY A(1,3) B(1,4) WITH X
 /ANALYSIS=Y
 /DESIGN=A, B, A BY B, A BY X + B BY X + A BY B BY X.
```

- This example shows how to test homogeneity of regressions in a two-way analysis of variance.
- The + signs are used to produce a pooled test of all interactions involving the covariate *X*. If this test is significant, the assumption of homogeneity of variance is questionable.

MUPLUS Keyword

MUPLUS combines the constant term (μ) in the model with the term specified after it. The normal use of this specification is to obtain parameter estimates that represent weighted means for the levels of some factor. For example, `MUPLUS SEED` represents the constant, or overall, mean plus the effect for each level of *SEED*. The significance of such effects is usually uninteresting, but the parameter estimates represent the weighted means for each level of *SEED*, adjusted for any covariates in the model.

- MUPLUS cannot appear more than once on a given DESIGN subcommand.
- MUPLUS is the only way to get standard errors for the predicted mean for each level of the factor specified.
- Parameter estimates are not displayed by default; you must explicitly request them on the PRINT subcommand or via a CONTRAST subcommand.
- You can obtain the unweighted mean by specifying the full factorial model, excluding those terms contained by an effect, and prefixing the effect whose mean is to be found by MUPLUS.

Effects of Continuous Variables

Usually you name factors but not covariates on the DESIGN subcommand. The linear effects of covariates are removed from the dependent variable before the design is tested. However, the design can include variables measured at the interval level and originally named as covariates or as additional dependent variables.

- Continuous variables on a DESIGN subcommand must be named as dependents or covariates on the MANOVA variable list.

- Before you can name a continuous variable on a DESIGN subcommand, you must supply an ANALYSIS subcommand that does *not* name the variable. This excludes it from the analysis as a dependent variable or covariate and makes it eligible for inclusion on DESIGN.

- More than one continuous variable can be pooled into a single effect (provided that they are all excluded on an ANALYSIS subcommand) with keyword POOL(varlist). For a single continuous variable, POOL(VAR) is equivalent to VAR.

- The TO convention in the variable list for POOL refers to the order of continuous variables (dependent variables and covariates) on the original MANOVA variable list, which is not necessarily their order on the active file. This is the only allowable use of keyword TO on a DESIGN subcommand.

- You can specify interaction terms between factors and continuous variables. If *FAC* is a factor and *COV* is a covariate that has been omitted from an ANALYSIS subcommand, FAC BY COV is a valid specification on a DESIGN statement.

- You cannot specify an interaction between two continuous variables. Use the COMPUTE command to create a variable representing the interaction prior to MANOVA.

Example

```
*   This example tests whether the regression of the dependent
    variable Y on the two variables X1 and X2 is the same across
    all the categories of the factors AGE and TREATMNT.

MANOVA Y BY AGE(1,5) TREATMNT(1,3) WITH X1, X2
   /ANALYSIS = Y
   /DESIGN = POOL(X1,X2),
             AGE, TREATMNT, AGE BY TREATMNT,
             POOL(X1,X2) BY AGE + POOL(X1,X2) BY TREATMNT
                + POOL(X1,X2) BY AGE BY TREATMNT.
```

- ANALYSIS excludes *X1* and *X2* from the standard treatment of covariates, so that they can be used in the design.

- DESIGN includes five terms. POOL(X1,X2), the overall regression of the dependent variable on *X1* and *X2*, is entered first, followed by the two factors and their interaction.

- The last term is the test for equal regressions. It consists of three factor-by-continuous-variable interactions pooled together. POOL(X1,X2) BY AGE is the interaction between *AGE* and the combined effect of the continuous variables *X1* and *X2*. It is combined with similar interactions between *TREATMNT* and the continuous variables and between the *AGE* by *TREATMNT* interaction and the continuous variables.

- If the last term is not statistically significant, there is no evidence that the regression of *Y* on *X1* and *X2* is different across any combination of the categories of *AGE* and *TREATMNT*.

Error Terms for Individual Effects

The "error" sum of squares against which terms in the design are tested is specified on the ERROR subcommand. For any particular term on a DESIGN subcommand, you can specify a different error term to be used in the analysis of variance. To do so, name the term followed by keyword VS (or AGAINST) and the error term keyword.

- To test a term against only the within-cells sum of squares, specify the term followed by VS WITHIN on the DESIGN subcommand. For example, `GROUP VS WITHIN` tests the effect of the factor *GROUP* against only the within-cells sum of squares.

- To test a term against only the residual sum of squares (the sum of squares for all terms not included in your DESIGN), specify the term followed by VS RESIDUAL.

- To test against the combined within-cells and residual sums of squares, specify the term followed by VS WITHIN+RESIDUAL.

- To test against any other sum of squares in the analysis of variance, include a term corresponding to the desired sum of squares in the design and assign it to an integer between 1 and 10. You can then test against the number of the error term. It is often convenient to test against the term before you define it. This is perfectly acceptable as long as you define the error term on the same DESIGN subcommand.

Example

```
MANOVA DEP BY A, B, C (1,3)
   /DESIGN=A VS 1,
          B WITHIN A = 1 VS 2,
          C WITHIN B WITHIN A = 2 VS WITHIN.
```

- In this example, the factors *A*, *B*, and *C* are completely nested; levels of *C* occur within levels of *B*, which occur within levels of *A*. Each factor is tested against everything within it.

- *A*, the outermost factor, is tested against the *B* within *A* sum of squares, to see if it contributes anything beyond the effects of *B* within each of its levels. The *B* within *A* sum of squares is defined as error term number 1.

- *B* nested within *A*, in turn, is tested against error term number 2, which is defined as the *C* within *B* within *A* sum of squares.

- Finally, *C* nested within *B* nested within *A* is tested against the within-cells sum of squares.

User-defined error terms are specified simply by inserting = n after a term, where *n* is an integer from 1 to 10. The equals sign is required. Keywords used in building a design term, such as BY or WITHIN, are evaluated first. For example, error term number 2 in the above example consists of the entire term C WITHIN B WITHIN A. An error term *number,* but not an error term *definition,* can follow keyword VS.

CONSTANT Keyword

By default, the constant (grand mean) term is included as the first term in the model.

- If you have specified NOCONSTANT on the METHOD subcommand, a constant term will not be included in any design unless you request it with the CONSTANT keyword on DESIGN.
- You can specify an error term for the constant.
- A factor named CONSTANT will not be recognized on the DESIGN subcommand.

Annotated Example

For a complete example with output, see the Annotated Examples following the Syntax Reference section of this manual.

MANOVA: Multivariate

```
MANOVA dependent varlist [BY factor list (min,max) [factor list...]]
[WITH covariate list]

[/TRANSFORM [(dependent varlist [/dependent varlist])]=
             [ORTHONORM] [{CONTRAST}] {DEVIATIONS (refcat)        }]
                         {BASIS    }  {DIFFERENCE                 }
                                      {HELMERT                    }
                                      {SIMPLE (refcat)            }
                                      {REPEATED                   }
                                      {POLYNOMIAL[({1,2,3...})]]  }
                                      {           {metric }       }
                                      {SPECIAL (matrix)           }

[/RENAME={newname} {newname}...]
         {*      } {*      }

[/{PRINT  }=[HOMOGENEITY [(BOXM)]]
  {NOPRINT} [ERROR [(([COV] [COR] [SSCP] [STDDEV])]]
            [SIGNIF [(([MULTIV**] [EIGEN] [DIMENR]
                       [UNIV**] [HYPOTH][STEPDOWN] [BRIEF])]]
            [TRANSFORM]                                     ]

[/PCOMPS=[COR] [COV] [ROTATE(rottype)]
         [NCOMP(n)] [MINEIGEN(eigencut)] [ALL]]

[/PLOT=[ZCORR]]

[/DISCRIM [RAW] [STAN] [ESTIM] [COR] [ALL]
          [ROTATE(rottype)] [ALPHA({.25**})]]
                                   {a    }

[/POWER=[T({.05**})] [F({.05**})] [{APPROXIMATE}]]
           {a    }      {a    }    {EXACT      }

[/CINTERVAL=[MULTIVARIATE  ({ROY     })]]
                           {PILLAI  }
                           {BONFER  }
                           {HOTELLING}
                           {WILKS   }

[/ANALYSIS [({UNCONDITIONAL**})]=[()dependent varlist
            {CONDITIONAL    }      [WITH covariate varlist]
                                        [/dependent varlist...][()][WITH varlist]]

[/DESIGN...]*
```

* The DESIGN subcommand has the same syntax as is described in MANOVA: Univariate.

**Default if subcommand or keyword is omitted.

Example:
```
MANOVA SCORE1 TO SCORE4 BY METHOD(1,3).
```

Overview

This section discusses the subcommands that are used in multivariate analysis of variance and covariance designs with several interrelated dependent variables. The discussion focuses on subcommands and keywords that do not apply, or apply in different manners, to univariate analyses. It does not contain information on all the subcommands you will need to specify the design. For subcommands not covered here, see MANOVA: Univariate.

Options

Dependent Variables and Covariates. You can specify subsets and reorder the dependent variables and covariates using the ANALYSIS subcommand. You can specify linear transformations of the dependent variables and covariates using the TRANSFORM subcommand. When transformations are performed, you can rename the variables using the RENAME subcommand and request the display of a transposed transformation matrix currently in effect using the PRINT subcommand.

Optional Output. You can request or suppress output on the PRINT and NOPRINT subcommands. Additional output appropriate to multivariate analysis includes error term matrices, Box's M statistic, multivariate and univariate F tests, and other significance analyses. You can also request predicted cell means for specific dependent variables on the PMEANS subcommand, produce a canonical discriminant analysis for each effect in your model with the DISCRIM subcommand, specify a principal components analysis of each error sum-of-squares and cross-product matrix in a multivariate analysis on the PCOMPS subcommand, display multivariate confidence intervals using the CINTERVAL subcommand, and generate a half-normal plot of the within-cells correlations among the dependent variables with the PLOT subcommand.

Basic Specification

- The basic specification is a variable list identifying the dependent variables, with the factors (if any) named after BY and the covariates (if any) named after WITH.
- By default, MANOVA produces multivariate and univariate F tests.

Subcommand Order

- The variable list must be specified first.
- Subcommands applicable to a specific design must be specified before that DESIGN subcommand. Otherwise, subcommands can be used in any order.

Syntax Rules

- All syntax rules applicable to univariate analysis apply to multivariate analysis. See Syntax Rules in MANOVA: Univariate.
- If you enter one of the multivariate specifications in a univariate analysis, MANOVA ignores it.

MANOVA Variable List

- Multivariate MANOVA calculates statistical tests that are valid for analyses of dependent variables that are correlated with one another. The dependent variables must be specified first.
- The factor and covariate lists follow the same rules as in univariate analyses.
- If the dependent variables are uncorrelated, the univariate significance tests have greater statistical power.

TRANSFORM Subcommand

TRANSFORM performs linear transformations of some or all of the continuous variables (dependent variables and covariates). Specifications on TRANSFORM include an optional list of variables to be transformed, optional keywords to describe how to generate a transformation matrix from the specified contrasts, and a required keyword specifying the transformation contrasts.

- Transformations apply to all subsequent designs unless replaced by another TRANSFORM subcommand.
- TRANSFORM subcommands are not cumulative. Only the transformation specified most recently is in effect at any time. You can restore the original variables in later designs by specifying SPECIAL with an identity matrix.
- You should not use TRANSFORM when you use the WSFACTORS subcommand to request repeated measures analysis; a transformation is automatically performed in repeated measures analysis (see MANOVA: Repeated Measures).
- Transformations are in effect for the duration of the MANOVA procedure only. After the procedure is complete, the original variables remain in the active file.
- By default, the transformation matrix is not displayed. Specify the keyword TRANSFORM on the PRINT subcommand to see the matrix generated by the TRANSFORM subcommand.
- If you do not use the RENAME subcommand with TRANSFORM, the variables specified on TRANSFORM are renamed temporarily (for the duration of the procedure) as *T1, T2,* etc. Explicit use of RENAME is recommended.
- Subsequent references to transformed variables should use the new names. The only exception is when you supply a VARIABLES specification on the OMEANS subcommand after using TRANSFORM. In this case, specify the original names. OMEANS displays observed means of original variables (see OMEANS Subcommand in MANOVA: Univariate).

Variable Lists

- By default, MANOVA applies the transformation you request to all continuous variables (dependent variables and covariates).
- You can enter a variable list in parentheses following the TRANSFORM subcommand. If you do, only the listed variables are transformed.

- You can enter multiple variable lists, separated by slashes, within a single set of parentheses. Each list must have the same number of variables, and the lists must not overlap. The transformation is applied separately to the variables on each list.
- In designs with covariates, transform only the dependent variables, or, in some designs, apply the same transformation separately to the dependent variables and the covariates.

CONTRAST, BASIS, and ORTHONORM Keywords

You can control how the transformation matrix is to be generated from the specified contrasts. If none of these three keywords is specified on TRANSFORM, the default is CONTRAST.

CONTRAST   *Generate the transformation matrix directly from the contrast matrix specified* (see CONTRAST Subcommand in MANOVA: Univariate). This is the default.

BASIS   *Generate the transformation matrix from the one-way basis matrix corresponding to the specified contrast matrix.* BASIS makes a difference only if the transformation contrasts are not orthogonal.

ORTHONORM   *Orthonormalize the transformation matrix by rows before use.* MANOVA eliminates redundant rows. By default, orthonormalization is not done.

- CONTRAST and BASIS are alternatives and are mutually exclusive.
- ORTHONORM is independent of the CONTRAST/BASIS choice; you can enter it before or after either of those keywords.

Transformation Methods

To specify a transformation method, use one of the following keywords available on the TRANSFORM subcommand. Note that these are identical to the keywords available for the CONTRAST subcommand (see CONTRAST Subcommand in MANOVA: Univariate). However, in univariate designs, they are applied to the different levels of a factor. Here they are applied to the continuous variables in the analysis. This reflects the fact that the different dependent variables in a multivariate MANOVA setup can often be thought of as corresponding to different levels of some factor.

- The transformation keyword (and its specifications, if any) must follow all other specifications on the TRANSFORM subcommand.

DEVIATION(refcat)   *Deviations from the mean of the variables being transformed.* The first transformed variable is the mean of all variables in the transformation. Other transformed variables represent deviations of individual variables from the mean. One of the original variables (by default the last) is omitted as redundant. To omit a variable other than the last, specify the number of the variable to be omitted in parentheses after the DEVIATION keyword. For example,

```
/TRANSFORM (A B C) = DEVIATION(1)
```

omits *A* and creates variables representing the mean, the deviation of *B* from the mean, and the deviation of *C* from the mean. A DEVIATION transformation is not orthogonal.

DIFFERENCE   *Difference or reverse Helmert transformation.* The first transformed variable is the mean of the original variables. Each of the original variables except the first is then transformed by subtracting the mean of those (original) variables that precede it. A DIFFERENCE transformation is orthogonal.

HELMERT   *Helmert transformation.* The first transformed variable is the mean of the original variables. Each of the original variables except the last is then transformed by subtracting the mean of those (original) variables that follow it. A HELMERT transformation is orthogonal.

SIMPLE(refcat)   *Each original variable, except the last, is compared to the last of the original variables.* To use a variable other than the last as the omitted reference variable, specify its number in parentheses following keyword SIMPLE. For example,

```
/TRANSFORM(A B C) = SIMPLE(2)
```

specifies the second variable, *B*, as the reference variable. The three transformed variables represent the mean of *A, B,* and *C*, the difference between *A* and *B*, and the difference between *C* and *B*. A SIMPLE transformation is not orthogonal.

POLYNOMIAL(metric)   *Orthogonal polynomial transformation.* The first transformed variable represents the mean of the original variables. Other transformed variables represent the linear, quadratic, and higher-degree components. By default, values of the original variables are assumed to represent equally spaced points. You can specify unequal spacing by entering a metric consisting of one integer for each variable in parentheses after keyword POLYNOMIAL. For example,

```
/TRANSFORM(RESP1 RESP2 RESP3) = POLYNOMIAL(1,2,4)
```

might indicate that three response variables correspond to levels of some stimulus that are in the proportion 1:2:4. The default metric is always (1,2,...,*k*), where *k* variables are involved. Only the relative differences between the terms of the metric matter: (1,2,4) is the same metric as (2,3,5) or (20,30,50) because in each instance the difference between the second and third numbers is twice the difference between the first and second.

REPEATED   *Comparison of adjacent variables.* The first transformed variable is the mean of the original variables. Each additional transformed variable is the difference between one of the original variables and the original variable that followed it. Such transformed variables are often called **difference scores**. A REPEATED transformation is not orthogonal.

SPECIAL   *A user-defined transformation.* After keyword SPECIAL, enter a square matrix in parentheses with as many rows and columns as there are variables to transform. MANOVA multiplies this matrix by the vector of original variables to obtain the transformed variables (see examples below).

Example

```
MANOVA X1 TO X3 BY A(1,4)
  /TRANSFORM(X1 X2 X3) = SPECIAL( 1  1  1,
                                  1  0 -1,
                                  2 -1 -1)
  /DESIGN.
```

- The given matrix will be post-multiplied by the three continuous variables (considered as a column vector) to yield the transformed variables. The first transformed variable will therefore equal $X1 + X2 + X3$, the second will equal $X1 - X3$, and the third will equal $2X1 - X2 - X3$.
- The variable list is optional in this example, since all three interval-level variables are transformed.
- You do not need to enter the matrix one row at a time, as shown above. For example,

```
/TRANSFORM = SPECIAL(1 1 1 1 0 -1 2 -1 -1)
```

is equivalent to the TRANSFORM specification in the above example.

- You can specify a repetition factor followed by an asterisk to indicate multiple consecutive elements of a SPECIAL transformation matrix. For example,

```
/TRANSFORM = SPECIAL (4*1 0 -1 2 2*-1)
```

is again equivalent to the TRANSFORM specification above.

Example

```
MANOVA X1 TO X3, Y1 TO Y3 BY A(1,4)
  /TRANSFORM (X1 X2 X3/Y1 Y2 Y3) = SPECIAL( 1  1  1,
                                            1  0 -1,
                                            2 -1 -1)
  /DESIGN.
```

- Here the same transformation shown in the previous example is applied to *X1, X2, X3* and to *Y1, Y2, Y3*.

RENAME Subcommand

Use RENAME to assign new names to transformed variables. Renaming variables after a transformation is strongly recommended. If you transform but do not rename the variables, the names *T1, T2,..., TN* are used as names for the transformed variables.

- Follow RENAME with a list of new variable names.
- You must enter a new name for each dependent variable and covariate on the MANOVA variable list.

- Enter the new names in the order in which the original variables appeared on the MANOVA variable list.
- To retain the original name for one or more of the interval variables, you can either enter an asterisk or reenter the old name as the new name.
- References to dependent variables and covariates on subcommands following RENAME must use the new names. The original names will not be recognized within the MANOVA procedure. The only exception is the OMEANS subcommand, which displays observed means of the original (untransformed) variables. Use the original names on OMEANS.
- The new names exist only during the MANOVA procedure that created them. They do not remain in the active file after the procedure is complete.

Example

```
MANOVA A, B, C, V4, V5 BY TREATMNT(1,3)
  /TRANSFORM(A, B, C) = REPEATED
  /RENAME = MEANABC, AMINUSB, BMINUSC, *, *
  /DESIGN.
```

- The REPEATED transformation produces three transformed variables, which are then assigned mnemonic names *MEANABC, AMINUSB*, and *BMINUSC*.
- *V4* and *V5* retain their original names.

Example

```
MANOVA WT1, WT2, WT3, WT4 BY TREATMNT(1,3) WITH COV
  /TRANSFORM (WT1 TO WT4) = POLYNOMIAL
  /RENAME = MEAN, LINEAR, QUAD, CUBIC, *
  /ANALYSIS = MEAN, LINEAR, QUAD WITH COV
  /DESIGN.
```

- After the polynomial transformation of the four *WT* variables, RENAME assigns appropriate names to the various trends.
- Even though only four variables were transformed, RENAME applies to all five continuous variables. An asterisk is required to retain the original name for *COV*.
- The ANALYSIS subcommand following RENAME refers to the interval variables by their new names.

PRINT and NOPRINT Subcommands

All of the PRINT specifications described in MANOVA: Univariate are available in multivariate analyses. The following additional output can be requested. To suppress any optional output, specify the appropriate keyword on NOPRINT.

ERROR *Error matrices.* Three types of matrices are available.

SIGNIF *Significance tests.*

TRANSFORM *Transformation matrix.* It is available if you have transformed the dependent variables with the TRANSFORM subcommand.

HOMOGENEITY *Test for homogeneity of variance.* BOXM is available for multivariate analyses.

ERROR Keyword

In multivariate analysis, error terms consist of entire matrices, not single values. You can display any of the following error matrices on a PRINT subcommand by requesting them in parentheses following the keyword ERROR. If you specify ERROR by itself, without further specifications, the default is to display COV and COR.

SSCP   *Error sums-of-squares and cross-products matrix.*

COV   *Error variance-covariance matrix.*

COR   *Error correlation matrix with standard deviations on the diagonal.* This also displays the determinant of the matrix and Bartlett's test of sphericity, a test of whether the error correlation matrix is significantly different from an identity matrix.

SIGNIF Keyword

You can request any of the optional output listed below by entering the appropriate specification in parentheses after the keyword SIGNIF on the PRINT subcommand. Further specifications for SIGNIF are described in MANOVA: Repeated Measures.

MULTIV   *Multivariate* F *tests for group differences.* MULTIV is always printed unless explicitly suppressed with the NOPRINT subcommand.

EIGEN   *Eigenvalues of the* $S_h S_e^{-1}$ *matrix.* This matrix is the product of the hypothesis sums-of-squares and cross-products (SSCP) matrix and the inverse of the error SSCP matrix. To print EIGEN, request it on the PRINT subcommand.

DIMENR   *A dimension-reduction analysis.* To print DIMENR, request it on the PRINT subcommand.

UNIV   *Univariate* F *tests.* UNIV is always printed except in repeated measures analysis. If the dependent variables are uncorrelated, univariate tests have greater statistical power. To suppress UNIV, use the NOPRINT subcommand.

HYPOTH   *The hypothesis SSCP matrix.* To print HYPOTH, request it on the PRINT subcommand.

STEPDOWN   *Roy-Bargmann stepdown* F *tests.* To print STEPDOWN, request it on the PRINT subcommand.

BRIEF   *Abbreviated multivariate output.* This is similar to a univariate analysis of variance table but with Wilks' multivariate *F* approximation (lambda) replacing the univariate *F*. BRIEF overrides any of the SIGNIF specifications listed above.

SINGLEDF   *Significance tests for the single degree of freedom making up each effect for ANOVA tables.* Results are displayed separately corresponding to each hypothesis degree of freedom. See MANOVA: Univariate.

- If neither PRINT nor NOPRINT is specified, MANOVA displays the results corresponding to MULTIV and UNIV for a multivariate analysis not involving repeated measures.

- If you enter any specification except BRIEF or SINGLEDF for SIGNIF on the PRINT sub-command, the requested output is displayed in addition to the default.
- To suppress the default, specify the keyword(s) on the NOPRINT subcommand.

TRANSFORM Keyword

The keyword TRANSFORM specified on PRINT displays the transposed transformation matrix in use for each subsequent design. This matrix is helpful in interpreting a multivariate analysis in which the interval-level variables have been transformed with either TRANS-FORM or WSFACTORS.

- The matrix displayed by this option is the transpose of the transformation matrix.
- Original variables correspond to the rows of the matrix, and transformed variables correspond to the columns.
- A **transformed variable** is a linear combination of the original variables using the coefficients displayed in the column corresponding to that transformed variable.

HOMOGENEITY Keyword

In addition to the BARTLETT and COCHRAN specifications described in MANOVA: Univariate, the following test for homogeneity is available for multivariate analyses:

BOXM   *Box's* M *statistic.* BOXM requires at least two dependent variables. If there is only one dependent variable when BOXM is requested, MANOVA prints Bartlett-Box *F* test statistic and issues a note.

PLOT Subcommand

In addition to the plots described in MANOVA: Univariate, the following is available for multivariate analyses:

ZCORR   *A half-normal plot of the within-cells correlations among the dependent variables.* MANOVA first transforms the correlations using Fisher's *Z* transformation. If errors for the dependent variables are uncorrelated, the plotted points should lie close to a straight line.

PCOMPS Subcommand

PCOMPS requests a principal components analysis of each error matrix in a multivariate analysis. You can display the principal components of the error correlation matrix, the error variance-covariance matrix, or both. These principal components are corrected for differences due to the factors and covariates in the MANOVA analysis. They tend to be more useful than principal components extracted from the raw correlation or covariance matrix when there are significant group differences between the levels of the factors or when a significant amount of error variance is accounted for by the covariates. You can specify any of the keywords listed below on PCOMPS.

| COR | *Principal components analysis of the error correlation matrix.* |

| COV | *Principal components analysis of the error variance-covariance matrix.* |

ROTATE *Rotate the principal components solution.* By default, no rotation is performed. Specify a rotation type (either VARIMAX, EQUAMAX, or QUARTIMAX) in parentheses after keyword ROTATE. To cancel a rotation specified for a previous design, enter NOROTATE in the parentheses after ROTATE.

NCOMP(n) *The number of principal components to rotate.* Specify a number in parentheses. The default is the number of dependent variables.

MINEIGEN(n) *The minimum eigenvalue for principal component extraction.* Specify a cutoff value in parentheses. Components with eigenvalues below the cutoff will not be retained in the solution. The default is 0: all components (or the number specified on NCOMP) are extracted.

ALL *COR, COV, and ROTATE.*

- You must specify either COR or COV (or both). Otherwise, MANOVA will not produce any principal components.
- Both NCOMP and MINEIGEN limit the number of components that are rotated.
- If the number specified on NCOMP is less than two, two components are rotated provided that at least two components have eigenvalues greater than any value specified on MINEIGEN.
- Principal components analysis is computationally expensive if the number of dependent variables is large.

DISCRIM Subcommand

DISCRIM produces a canonical discriminant analysis for each effect in a design. (For covariates, DISCRIM produces a canonical correlation analysis.) These analyses aid in the interpretation of multivariate effects. You can request the following statistics by entering the appropriate keywords after the subcommand DISCRIM:

RAW *Raw discriminant function coefficients.*

STAN *Standardized discriminant function coefficients.*

ESTIM *Effect estimates in discriminant function space.*

COR *Correlations between the dependent variables and the canonical variables defined by the discriminant functions.*

ROTATE *Rotation of the matrix of correlations between dependent and canonical variables.* Specify rotation type VARIMAX, EQUAMAX, or QUARTIMAX in parentheses after this keyword.

ALL *RAW, STAN, ESTIM, COR, and ROTATE.*

By default, the significance level required for the extraction of a canonical variable is 0.25. You can change this value by specifying keyword ALPHA and a value between 0 and 1 in parentheses:

ALPHA   *The significance level required before a canonical variable is reported.* The default is 0.25. To change the default, specify a decimal number between 0 and 1 in parentheses after ALPHA.

- The correlations between dependent variables and canonical functions are not rotated unless at least two functions are significant at the level defined by ALPHA.
- If you set ALPHA to 1.0, all discriminant functions are reported (and rotated, if you so request).
- If you set ALPHA to 0, no discriminant functions are reported.

POWER Subcommand

The following specifications are available for POWER in multivariate analysis. For applications of POWER in univariate analysis, see MANOVA: Univariate.

APPROXIMATE   *Approximate power values.* This is the default. Approximate power values for multivariate tests are derived from procedures presented by Muller and Peterson (1984). Approximate values are normally accurate to three decimal places and are much cheaper to compute than exact values.

EXACT   *Exact power values.* Exact power values for multivariate tests are computed from the non-central F distribution. Exact multivariate power values will be displayed only if there is one hypothesis degree of freedom, where all the multivariate criteria have identical power.

- For information on the multivariate generalizations of power and effect size, see Muller and Peterson (1984), Green (1977), and Huberty (1972).

CINTERVAL Subcommand

In addition to the specifications described in MANOVA: Univariate, the keyword MULTIVARIATE is available for multivariate analysis. You can specify a type in parentheses after the MULTIVARIATE keyword. The following type keywords are available on MULTIVARIATE:

ROY   *Roy's largest root.* An approximation given by Pillai (1967) is used. This approximation is accurate for upper percentage points (0.95 to 1), but it is not as good for lower percentage points. Thus, for Roy intervals, the user is restricted to the range 0.95 to 1.

PILLAI   *Pillai's trace.* The intervals are computed by approximating the percentage points with percentage points of the F distribution.

WILKS   *Wilks' lambda.* The intervals are computed by approximating the percentage points with percentage points of the F distribution.

HOTELLING   *Hotelling's trace.* The intervals are computed by approximating the percentage points with percentage points of the F distribution.

BONFER   *Bonferroni intervals.* This approximation is based on Student's t distribution.

- The Wilks', Pillai's, and Hotelling's approximate confidence intervals are thought to match exact intervals across a wide range of alpha levels, especially for large sample sizes (Burns, 1984). Use of these intervals, however, has not been widely investigated.
- To obtain multivariate intervals separately for each parameter, choose individual multivariate intervals. For individual multivariate confidence intervals, the hypothesis degree of freedom is set to 1, in which case Hotelling's, Pillai's, Wilks', and Roy's intervals will be identical and equivalent to those computed from percentage points of Hotelling's T^2 distribution. Individual Bonferroni intervals will differ and, for a small number of dependent variables, will generally be shorter.
- If you specify MULTIVARIATE on CINTERVAL, you must specify a type keyword. If you specify CINTERVAL without any keyword, the default is the same as with univariate analysis: CINTERVAL displays individual-univariate confidence intervals at the 0.95 level.

ANALYSIS Subcommand

ANALYSIS is discussed in MANOVA: Univariate as a means of obtaining factor-by-covariate interaction terms. In multivariate analyses, it is considerably more useful.

- ANALYSIS specifies a subset of the continuous variables (dependent variables and covariates) listed on the MANOVA variable list and completely redefines which variables are dependent and which are covariates.
- All variables named on an ANALYSIS subcommand must have been named on the MANOVA variable list. It does not matter whether they were named as dependent variables or as covariates.
- Factors cannot be named on an ANALYSIS subcommand.
- After keyword ANALYSIS, specify the names of one or more dependent variables and, optionally, keyword WITH followed by one or more covariates.
- An ANALYSIS specification remains in effect for all designs until you enter another ANALYSIS subcommand.
- Continuous variables named on the MANOVA variable list but omitted from the ANALYSIS subcommand currently in effect can be specified on the DESIGN subcommand. See DESIGN Subcommand in MANOVA: Univariate.
- You can use an ANALYSIS subcommand to request analyses of several groups of variables provided that the groups do not overlap. Separate the groups of variables with slashes and enclose the entire ANALYSIS specification in parentheses.

CONDITIONAL and UNCONDITIONAL Keywords

When several analysis groups are specified on a single ANALYSIS subcommand, you can control how each list is to be processed by specifying CONDITIONAL or UNCONDITIONAL in the parentheses immediately following the ANALYSIS subcommand. The default is UNCONDITIONAL.

UNCONDITIONAL   *Process each analysis group separately, without regard to other lists.* This is the default.

CONDITIONAL   *Use variables specified in one analysis group as covariates in subsequent analysis groups.*

- CONDITIONAL analysis is not carried over from one ANALYSIS subcommand to another.
- You can specify a final covariate list outside the parentheses. These covariates apply to every list within the parentheses, regardless of whether you specify CONDITIONAL or UNCONDITIONAL. The variables in this global covariate list must not be specified in any individual lists.

Example

```
MANOVA A B C BY FAC(1,4) WITH D, E
  /ANALYSIS = (A, B / C / D WITH E)
  /DESIGN.
```

- The first analysis uses *A* and *B* as dependent variables and uses no covariates.
- The second analysis uses *C* as a dependent variable and uses no covariates.
- The third analysis uses *D* as the dependent variable and uses *E* as a covariate.

Example

```
MANOVA A, B, C, D, E BY FAC(1,4) WITH F G
  /ANALYSIS = (A, B / C / D WITH E) WITH F G
  /DESIGN.
```

- A final covariate list `WITH F G` is specified outside the parentheses. The covariates apply to every list within the parentheses.
- The first analysis uses *A* and *B*, with *F* and *G* as covariates.
- The second analysis uses *C*, with *F* and *G* as covariates.
- The third analysis uses *D*, with *E*, *F*, and *G* as covariates.
- Factoring out *F* and *G* is the only way to use them as covariates in all three analyses, since no variable can be named more than once on an ANALYSIS subcommand.

Example

```
MANOVA A B C BY FAC(1,3)
  /ANALYSIS(CONDITIONAL) = (A WITH B / C)
  /DESIGN.
```

- In the first analysis, *A* is the dependent variable, *B* is a covariate, and *C* is not used.
- In the second analysis, *C* is the dependent variable, and both *A* and *B* are covariates.

Annotated Example

For a complete example with output, see the Annotated Examples following the Syntax Reference section of this manual.

MANOVA: Repeated Measures

```
MANOVA dependent varlist [BY factor list (min,max)[factor list...]
                         [WITH covariate list]]

  /WSFACTORS = varname (levels) [varname...]

[/WSDESIGN = [effect effect...]]

[/MEASURE = newname newname...]

[/RENAME = newname newname...]

[/ {PRINT  }=[SIGNIF**({AVERF**})(MULTIV**) (HF) (GG) (EFSIZE)]]
   {NOPRINT}           {AVONLY }

[/DESIGN]*
```

* The DESIGN subcommand has the same syntax as is described in MANOVA: Univariate.

** Default if subcommand or keyword is omitted.

Example:

```
MANOVA Y1 TO Y4 BY GROUP(1,2)
  /WSFACTORS=YEAR(4).
```

Overview

This section discusses the subcommands that are used in repeated measures designs, in which the dependent variables represent measurements of the same variable (or variables) at different times. This section does not contain information on all subcommands you will need to specify the design. For some subcommands or keywords not covered here, such as DESIGN, see MANOVA: Univariate. For information on optional output and the multivariate significance tests available, see MANOVA: Multivariate.

- In a simple repeated measures analysis, all dependent variables represent different measurements of the same variable for different values (or levels) of a within-subjects factor. Between-subjects factors and covariates can also be included in the model, just as in analyses not involving repeated measures.

- A within-subjects factor is simply a factor that distinguishes measurements made on the same subject or case, rather than distinguishing different subjects or cases.

- MANOVA permits more complex analyses, in which the dependent variables represent levels of two or more within-subjects factors.

- MANOVA also permits analyses in which the dependent variables represent measurements of several variables for the different levels of the within-subjects factors. These are known as **doubly multivariate designs**.

- A repeated measures analysis includes a within-subjects design describing the model to be tested with the within-subjects factors, as well as the usual between-subjects design describing the effects to be tested with between-subjects factors. The default for both types of design is a full factorial model.

- MANOVA always performs an orthonormal transformation of the dependent variables in a repeated measures analysis. By default, MANOVA renames them as *T1, T2,* and so forth.

Basic Specification

- The basic specification is a variable list followed by the WSFACTORS subcommand.
- By default, MANOVA performs special repeated measures processing. Default output includes SIGNIF(AVERF) but not SIGNIF(UNIV). In addition, for any within-subjects effect involving more than one transformed variable, the Mauchly test of sphericity is displayed to test the assumption that the covariance matrix of the transformed variables is constant on the diagonal and 0 off the diagonal. The Greenhouse-Geiser epsilon and the Huynh-Feldt epsilon are also displayed for use in correcting the significance tests in the event that the assumption of sphericity is violated. These tests are discussed in the relevant chapters of this manual.

Subcommand Order

- The list of dependent variables, factors, and covariates must be first.
- WSFACTORS must be the first subcommand used after the variable list.

Syntax Rules

- The WSFACTORS (within-subjects factors), WSDESIGN (within-subjects design), and MEASURE subcommands are used only in repeated measures analysis.
- WSFACTORS is required for any repeated measures analysis.
- If WSDESIGN is not specified, a full factorial within-subjects design consisting of all main effects and interactions among within-subjects factors is used by default.
- The MEASURE subcommand is used for doubly multivariate designs, in which the dependent variables represent repeated measurements of more than one variable.
- Do not use the TRANSFORM subcommand with the WSFACTORS subcommand because WSFACTORS automatically causes an orthonormal transformation of the dependent variables.
- WSFACTORS determines how the dependent variables on the MANOVA variable list will be interpreted.
- The number of cells in the within-subjects design is the product of the number of levels for all within-subjects factors.
- The number of dependent variables on the MANOVA variable list must be a multiple of the number of cells in the within-subjects design. If there are six cells in the within-subjects design, each group of six dependent variables represents a single variable that has been measured in each of the six cells.
- Normally, the number of dependent variables should equal the number of cells in the within-subjects design multiplied by the number of variables named on the MEASURE subcommand (if one is used). If you have more groups of dependent variables than are accounted for by the MEASURE subcommand, MANOVA will choose variable names to label the output, which may be difficult to interpret.
- If you use covariates in a repeated measures analysis, the number of covariates must be an integer multiple of the number of dependent variables. If covariates are measured only once, dummy copies must be created via COMPUTE and named on the MANOVA variable list.

Example

```
MANOVA Y1 TO Y4 BY GROUP(1,2)
  /WSFACTORS=YEAR(4)
  /CONTRAST(YEAR)=POLYNOMIAL
  /RENAME=CONST, LINEAR, QUAD, CUBIC
  /PRINT=TRANSFORM PARAM(ESTIM)
  /WSDESIGN=YEAR
  /DESIGN=GROUP.
```

- WSFACTORS immediately follows the MANOVA variable list and specifies a repeated measures analysis in which the four dependent variables represent a single variable measured at four levels of the within-subjects factor. The within-subjects factor is called *YEAR* for the duration of the MANOVA procedure.
- CONTRAST requests polynomial contrasts for the levels of *YEAR*. Because the four variables *Y1, Y2, Y3, Y4* in the active file represent the four levels of *YEAR*, the effect is to perform an orthonormal polynomial transformation of these variables.
- RENAME assigns names to the dependent variables to reflect the transformation.
- PRINT requests that the transformation matrix and the parameter estimates be displayed.
- WSDESIGN specifies a within-subjects design that includes only the effect of the *YEAR* within-subjects factor. Because *YEAR* is the only within-subjects factor specified, this is the default design and WSDESIGN could have been omitted.
- DESIGN specifies a between-subjects design that includes only the effect of the *GROUP* between-subjects factor. This subcommand could have been omitted.

WSFACTORS Subcommand

WSFACTORS names the within-subjects factors and specifies the number of levels for each.

- For repeated measures designs, WSFACTORS must be the first subcommand after the MANOVA variable list.
- Only one WSFACTORS subcommand is permitted per execution of MANOVA.
- Names for the within-subjects factors are specified on the WSFACTORS subcommand. Factor names must not duplicate any of the dependent variables, factors, or covariates named on the MANOVA variable list.
- If there are more than one within-subjects factors, they must be named in the order corresponding to the order of the dependent variables on the MANOVA variable list. MANOVA varies the levels of the last-named within-subjects factor most rapidly when assigning dependent variables to within-subjects cells (see example below).
- Levels of the factors must be represented in the data by the dependent variables named on the MANOVA variable list.
- Enter a number in parentheses after each factor to indicate how many levels the factor has. If two or more adjacent factors have the same number of levels, you can enter the number of levels in parentheses after all of them.
- Enter only the number of levels for within-subjects factors, not a range of values.

Example

```
MANOVA X1Y1 X1Y2 X2Y1 X2Y2 X3Y1 X3Y2 BY TREATMNT(1,5) GROUP(1,2)
  /WSFACTORS=X(3) Y(2)
  /DESIGN.
```

- The MANOVA variable list names six dependent variables and two between-subjects factors, *TREATMNT* and *GROUP*.
- WSFACTORS identifies two within-subjects factors whose levels distinguish the six dependent variables. *X* has three levels and *Y* has two. Thus, there are $3 \times 2 = 6$ cells in the within-subjects design, corresponding to the six dependent variables.
- Variable *X1Y1* corresponds to levels 1,1 of the two within-subjects factors; variable *X1Y2* corresponds to levels 1,2; *X2Y1* to levels 2,1; and so on up to *X3Y2*, which corresponds to levels 3,2. The first within-subjects factor named, *X*, varies most slowly, and the last within-subjects factor named, *Y*, varies most rapidly on the list of dependent variables.
- Because there is no WSDESIGN subcommand, the within-subjects design will include all main effects and interactions: *X*, *Y*, and *X* by *Y*.
- Likewise, the between-subjects design includes all main effects and interactions: *TREATMNT*, *GROUP*, and *TREATMNT* by *GROUP*.
- In addition, a repeated measures analysis always includes interactions between the within-subjects factors and the between-subjects factors. There are three such interactions for each of the three within-subjects effects.

CONTRAST for WSFACTORS

The levels of a within-subjects factor are represented by different dependent variables. Therefore, contrasts between levels of such a factor compare these dependent variables. Specifying the type of contrast amounts to specifying a transformation to be performed on the dependent variables.

- An orthonormal transformation is automatically performed on the dependent variables in a repeated measures analysis.
- To specify the type of orthonormal transformation, use the CONTRAST subcommand for the within-subjects factors.
- Regardless of the contrast type you specify, the transformation matrix is orthonormalized before use.
- If you do not specify a contrast type for within-subjects factors, the default contrast type is orthogonal POLYNOMIAL. Intrinsically orthogonal contrast types are recommended for within-subjects factors if you wish to examine each degree-of-freedom test. Other orthogonal contrast types are DIFFERENCE and HELMERT. MULTIV and AVERF tests are identical, no matter what contrast was specified.
- To perform non-orthogonal contrasts, you must use the TRANSFORM subcommand instead of CONTRAST. The TRANSFORM subcommand is discussed in MANOVA: Multivariate.
- When you implicitly request a transformation of the dependent variables with CONTRAST for within-subjects factors, the same transformation is applied to any covariates in the

analysis. The number of covariates must be an integer multiple of the number of dependent variables.

- You can display the transpose of the transformation matrix generated by your within-subjects contrast using keyword TRANSFORM on the PRINT subcommand.

Example

```
MANOVA SCORE1 SCORE2 SCORE3 BY GROUP(1,4)
  /WSFACTORS=ROUND(3)
  /CONTRAST(ROUND)=DIFFERENCE
  /CONTRAST(GROUP)=DEVIATION
  /PRINT=TRANSFORM PARAM(ESTIM).
```

- This analysis has one between-subjects factor, *GROUP*, with levels 1, 2, 3, and 4, and one within-subjects factor, *ROUND*, with three levels that are represented by the three dependent variables.
- The first CONTRAST subcommand specifies difference contrasts for *ROUND*, the within-subjects factor.
- There is no WSDESIGN subcommand, so a default full factorial within-subjects design is assumed. This could also have been specified as WSDESIGN=ROUND, or simply WSDE-SIGN.
- The second CONTRAST subcommand specifies deviation contrasts for *GROUP*, the between-subjects factor. This subcommand could have been omitted because deviation contrasts are the default.
- PRINT requests the display of the transformation matrix generated by the within-subjects contrast and the parameter estimates for the model.
- There is no DESIGN subcommand, so a default full factorial between-subjects design is assumed. This could also have been specified as DESIGN=GROUP, or simply DESIGN.

Example

```
COMPUTE SES1 = SES.
COMPUTE SES2 = SES.
COMPUTE SES3 = SES.
COMPUTE SES4 = SES.
MANOVA SCORE1 TO SCORE4 BY METHOD(1,2) WITH SES1 TO SES4
  /WSFACTORS=SEMESTER(4)
  /CONTRAST(SEMESTER)=DIFFERENCE
  /RENAME=MEAN,DIF2 TO DIF4,*,*,*,*.
```

- The four dependent variables represent a score measured four times (corresponding to the four levels of *SEMESTER*).
- The four COMPUTE commands create four copies of the constant covariate *SES* so that there will be one covariate for each within-subjects cell.
- RENAME supplies names for the difference transformation of the within-subjects factor *SEMESTER*. Because the MANOVA variable specification includes eight continuous variables, eight names are specified. The four asterisks indicate that the existing names are kept for the covariates.
- Covariates are transformed in the same way as the dependent variables. However, because these covariates are identical, the orthonormal transformation results in one con-

stant multiple of the original and three new covariates that are identically 0. The 0 covariates play no role in the analysis.

PARTITION for WSFACTORS

The PARTITION subcommand also applies to factors named on WSFACTORS. (See PARTITION Subcommand in MANOVA: Univariate.)

WSDESIGN Subcommand

WSDESIGN specifies the design for within-subjects factors. Its specifications are like those of the DESIGN subcommand, but it uses the within-subjects factors rather than the between-subjects factors.

- The default WSDESIGN is a full factorial design, which includes all main effects and all interactions for within-subjects factors. The default is in effect whenever a design is processed without a preceding WSDESIGN or when the preceding WSDESIGN subcommand has no specifications.

- A WSDESIGN specification can include main effects, factor-by-factor interactions, nested terms (term within term), terms using keyword MWITHIN, and pooled effects using the plus sign. The specification is the same as on the DESIGN subcommand but involves only within-subjects factors.

- A WSDESIGN specification cannot include between-subjects factors or terms based on them, nor does it accept interval-level variables, keywords MUPLUS or CONSTANT, or error-term definitions or references.

- The WSDESIGN specification applies to all subsequent within-subjects designs until another WSDESIGN subcommand is encountered.

Example

```
MANOVA JANLO,JANHI,FEBLO,FEBHI,MARLO,MARHI BY SEX(1,2)
    /WSFACTORS MONTH(3) STIMULUS(2)
    /WSDESIGN MONTH, STIMULUS
    /DESIGN SEX
    /WSDESIGN.
```

- There are six dependent variables, corresponding to three months and two different levels of stimulus.

- The dependent variables are named on the MANOVA variable list in such an order that the level of stimulus varies more rapidly than the month. Thus, *STIMULUS* is named last on the WSFACTORS subcommand.

- The first WSDESIGN subcommand specifies only the main effects for within-subjects factors. There is no *MONTH* by *STIMULUS* interaction term.

- The second WSDESIGN subcommand has no specifications and, therefore, invokes the default within-subjects design, which includes the main effects and their interaction.

- Because the last subcommand is not DESIGN, MANOVA generates a full factorial design at the end. In this example, there is only one between-subjects factor, *SEX*, so the last design is identical to the one specified by DESIGN=SEX. The last design, however, will include the *MONTH* by *STIMULUS* within-subjects interaction. It will automatically include the interaction between *SEX* and *MONTH* by *STIMULUS*. You do not need to specify (and, indeed, cannot specify) such interactions between elements of the within-subjects and the between-subjects designs.

MWITHIN Keyword for Simple Effects

You can use MWITHIN on either the WSDESIGN or the DESIGN subcommand in a model with both between- and within-subjects factors to estimate simple effects for factors nested within factors of the opposite type.

Example

```
MANOVA WEIGHT1 WEIGHT2 BY TREAT(1,2)
 /WSFACTORS=WEIGHT(2)
 /DESIGN=MWITHIN TREAT(1) MWITHIN TREAT(2)
 /WSDESIGN=MWITHIN WEIGHT(1) MWITHIN WEIGHT(2)
 /DESIGN.
```

- The first DESIGN tests the simple effects of *WEIGHT* within each level of *TREAT*.
- The second DESIGN tests the simple effects of *TREAT* within each level of *WEIGHT*.

MEASURE Subcommand

In a doubly multivariate analysis, the dependent variables represent multiple variables measured under the different levels of the within-subjects factors. Use MEASURE to assign names to the variables that you have measured for the different levels of within-subjects factors.

- Specify a list of one or more variable names to be used in labeling the averaged results. If no within-subjects factor has more than two levels, MEASURE has no effect.
- The number of dependent variables on the DESIGN subcommand should equal the product of the number of cells in the within-subjects design and the number of names on MEASURE.
- If you do not enter a MEASURE subcommand and there are more dependent variables than cells in the within-subjects design, MANOVA assigns names (normally *MEAS.1, MEAS.2,* etc.) to the different measures.
- All of the dependent variables corresponding to each measure should be listed together and ordered so that the within-subjects factor named last on the WSFACTORS subcommand varies most rapidly.

Example

```
MANOVA TEMP1 TO TEMP6, WEIGHT1 TO WEIGHT6 BY GROUP(1,2)
 /WSFACTORS=DAY(3) AMPM(2)
 /MEASURE=TEMP WEIGHT
 /WSDESIGN=DAY, AMPM, DAY BY AMPM
 /PRINT=SIGNIF(HYPOTH AVERF)
 /DESIGN.
```

- There are twelve dependent variables: six temperatures and six weights, corresponding to morning and afternoon measurements on three days.
- WSFACTORS identifies the two factors (*DAY* and *AMPM*) that distinguish the temperature and weight measurements for each subject. These factors define six within-subjects cells.
- MEASURE indicates that the first group of six dependent variables correspond to *TEMP* and the second group of six dependent variables correspond to *WEIGHT*.
- These labels, *TEMP* and *WEIGHT*, are used on the output requested by PRINT.
- WSDESIGN requests a full factorial within-subjects model. Because this is the default, WSDESIGN could have been omitted.

RENAME Subcommand

Because any repeated measures analysis involves a transformation of the dependent variables, it is always a good idea to rename the dependent variables. Choose appropriate names depending on the type of contrast specified for within-subjects factors. This is easier to do if you are using one of the orthogonal contrasts. The most reliable way to assign new names is to inspect the transformation matrix.

Example

```
MANOVA LOW1 LOW2 LOW3 HI1 HI2 HI3
   /WSFACTORS=LEVEL(2) TRIAL(3)
   /CONTRAST(TRIAL)=DIFFERENCE
   /RENAME=CONST LEVELDIF TRIAL21 TRIAL312 INTER1 INTER2
   /PRINT=TRANSFORM
   /DESIGN.
```

- This analysis has two within-subjects factors and no between-subjects factors.
- Difference contrasts are requested for *TRIAL*, which has three levels.
- Because all orthonormal contrasts produce the same F test for a factor with two levels, there is no point in specifying a contrast type for *LEVEL*.
- New names are assigned to the transformed variables based on the transformation matrix. These names correspond to the meaning of the transformed variables: the mean or constant, the average difference between levels, the average effect of trial 2 compared to 1, the average effect of trial 3 compared to 1 and 2; and the two interactions between *LEVEL* and *TRIAL*.
- The transformation matrix requested by the PRINT subcommand looks like Figure 1.

Figure 1   Transformation matrix

	CONST	LEVELDIF	TRIAL21	TRIAL312	INTER1	INTER2
LOW1	0.408	0.408	-0.500	-0.289	-0.500	-0.289
LOW2	0.408	0.408	0.500	-0.289	0.500	-0.289
LOW3	0.408	0.408	0.000	0.577	0.000	0.577
HI1	0.408	-0.408	-0.500	-0.289	0.500	0.289
HI2	0.408	-0.408	0.500	-0.289	-0.500	0.289
HI3	0.408	-0.408	0.000	0.577	0.000	-0.577

PRINT Subcommand

The following additional specifications on PRINT are useful in repeated measures analysis:

SIGNIF(AVERF)   *Averaged* F *tests for use with repeated measures.* This is the default display in repeated measures analysis. The averaged *F* tests in the multivariate setup for repeated measures are equivalent to the univariate (or split-plot or mixed-model) approach to repeated measures.

SIGNIF(AVONLY)   *Only the averaged* F *test for repeated measures.* AVONLY produces the same output as AVERF and suppresses all other SIGNIF output.

SIGNIF(HF)   *The Huynh-Feldt corrected significance values for averaged univariate* F *tests.*

SIGNIF(GG)   *The Greenhouse-Geisser corrected significance values for averaged univariate* F *tests.*

SIGNIF(EFSIZE)   *The effect size for the univariate* F *and* t *tests.*

- Keywords AVERF and AVONLY are mutually exclusive.
- When you request repeated measures analysis with the WSFACTORS subcommand, the default display includes SIGNIF(AVERF) but does not include the usual SIGNIF(UNIV).
- The averaged *F* tests are appropriate in repeated measures because the dependent variables that are averaged actually represent contrasts of the WSFACTOR variables. When the analysis is not doubly multivariate, as discussed above, you can specify `PRINT=SIGNIF(UNIV)` to obtain significance tests for each degree of freedom, just as in univariate MANOVA.

Annotated Example

For a complete example with output, see the Annotated Examples following the Syntax Reference section of this manual.

NLR

```
MODEL PROGRAM parameter=value [parameter=value ...]
transformation commands

[DERIVATIVES
transformation commands]

NLR dependent var WITH independent vars

 [/FILE=file]    [/OUTFILE=file]

 [/PRED=varname]

 [/SAVE [PRED] [RESID [(varname)] [DERIVATIVES]]]

 [/CRITERIA=[ITER {100**}] [CKDER {0.5**}]
                  {n    }         {n   }
            [SSCON {1E-8**}]  [PCON {1E-8**}]  [RCON {1E-8**}]]
                   {n     }        {n     }          {n     }
```

**Default if subcommand or keyword is omitted.

Example:
```
MODEL PROGRAM A=.6.
COMPUTE PRED=EXP(A*X).
NLR Y WITH X.
```

Overview

Nonlinear regression is used to estimate parameter values and regression statistics for models that are not linear in their parameters. The SPSS/PC+ Nonlinear Regression procedure, which uses a Levenberg-Marquardt algorithm, estimates the values of the parameters for the model and, optionally, computes and saves predicted values, residuals, and derivatives. Final parameter estimates can be saved in a system file and used in subsequent analyses.

Options

The Model. You can use any number of transformation commands under MODEL PROGRAM to define complex models.

Derivatives. You can use any number of transformation commands under DERIVATIVES to supply derivatives.

Adding Variables to Active File. You can add predicted values, residuals, and derivatives to the active file with the SAVE subcommand.

Writing Parameter Estimates to a New System File. You can save final parameter estimates as a system file using the OUTFILE subcommand and retrieve them in subsequent analyses using the FILE subcommand.

Controlling Model-building Criteria. You can control the iteration process used in the regression with the CRITERIA subcommand.

Basic Specification

The basic specification requires three commands: MODEL PROGRAM, COMPUTE (or any other computational transformation command), and NLR.

- The MODEL PROGRAM command assigns initial values to the parameters and signifies the beginning of the model program.

- The computational transformation command generates a new variable to define the model. The variable can take any legitimate name, but if the name is not *PRED*, the PRED subcommand will be required.

- The NLR command provides the regression specifications. The minimum specification is the dependent variable followed by the keyword WITH and one or more independent variables.

- By default, the residual sum of squares and estimated values of the model parameters are displayed for each iteration. Statistics generated include regression and residual sums of squares and mean squares, corrected and uncorrected total sums of squares, R^2, parameter estimates with their asymptotic standard errors and 95% confidence intervals, and an asymptotic correlation matrix of the parameter estimates.

Command Order

- The model program, beginning with the MODEL PROGRAM command, must precede the NLR command and be followed by one or more transformation commands. The transformations in the MODEL PROGRAM block must follow any permanent transformations in a program because the SPSS/PC+ variables created by the MODEL PROGRAM transformations do not become a part of the active system file.

- The derivatives program (when used), beginning with the DERIVATIVES command, must follow the model program but precede the NLR command.

- Subcommands on NLR can be named in any order.

Operations

- By default, the predicted values, residuals, and derivatives are created as temporary variables. To save these variables, use the SAVE subcommand.

Weighting Cases

- If case weighting is in effect, NLR uses case weights when calculating the residual sum of squares and derivatives. However, the degrees of freedom in the ANOVA table are always based on unweighted cases.

- When the model program is first invoked for each case, the weight variable's value is set equal to its value in the active file. The model program may recalculate that value. For example, to effect a robust estimation, the model program may recalculate the weight variable's value as an inverse function of the residual magnitude. NLR uses the weight variable's value after the model program is executed.

Missing Values

Cases with missing values for any of the dependent or independent variables named on the NLR command are excluded.

- Predicted values, but not residuals, can be calculated for cases with missing values on the dependent variable.

- NLR ignores cases that have missing, negative, or zero weights. The procedure displays a warning message if it encounters any negative or zero weights at any time during its execution.

- If a variable used in the model program or the derivatives program is omitted from the independent variable list on the NLR command, the predicted value and some or all of the derivatives may be missing for every case. If this happens, SPSS/PC+ generates an error message.

Example

```
MODEL PROGRAM A=.5 B=1.6.
COMPUTE PRED=A*SPEED**B.

DERIVATIVES.
COMPUTE D.A=SPEED**B.
COMPUTE D.B=A*LN(SPEED)*SPEED**B.

NLR STOP WITH SPEED.
```

- MODEL PROGRAM assigns values to the model parameters *A* and *B*.

- COMPUTE generates the variable *PRED* to define the nonlinear model using parameters *A* and *B* and the variable *SPEED* from the active file. Because this variable is named *PRED*, the PRED subcommand is not required on NLR.

- DERIVATIVES indicates that calculations for derivatives are being supplied.

- The two COMPUTE statements on the DERIVATIVES transformations list calculate the derivatives for the parameters *A* and *B*. If either one had been omitted, NLR would have calculated it numerically.

- NLR specifies *STOP* as the dependent variable and *SPEED* as the independent variable.

MODEL PROGRAM Command

The MODEL PROGRAM command assigns initial values to the parameters and signifies the beginning of the model program. The model program specifies the nonlinear equation chosen to model the data. There is no default model.

- The model program is required and must precede the NLR command.

- The MODEL PROGRAM command must specify all parameters in the model program. Each parameter must be individually named. Keyword TO is not allowed.

- Parameters can be assigned any acceptable SPSS/PC+ variable name. However, if you intend to write the final parameter estimates to a file with the OUTFILE subcommand, do not use the name *SSE* or *NCASES* (see "OUTFILE Subcommand" on p. 371).

- Each parameter in the model program must have an assigned value. The value can be specified on MODEL PROGRAM or read from an existing parameter data file named on the FILE subcommand.

- Zero should be avoided as an initial value because it provides no information on the scale of the parameters.

- The model program must include at least one command that uses the parameters and the independent variables (or preceding transformations of these) to calculate the predicted value of the dependent variable. This predicted value defines the nonlinear model. There is no default model.

- By default, the program assumes that *PRED* is the name assigned to the variable for the predicted values. If you use a different variable name in the model program, you must supply the name on the PRED subcommand (see "PRED Subcommand" on p. 372).

- In the model program, you can assign a label to the variable holding predicted values and also change its print and write formats, but you should not specify missing values for this variable.

- You can use any computational or output commands (such as COMPUTE, IF, RECODE, COUNT, or WRITE) in the model program, but you cannot use input commands (such as DATA LIST or GET).

- Transformations in the model program are used only by NLR. They do not affect the active file. The parameters created by the model program do not become a part of the active file. Permanent transformations should be specified before the model program.

Caution

- The selection of good initial values for the parameters in the model program is very important to the operation of NLR. The selection of poor initial values can result in no solution, a local rather than a general solution, or a physically impossible solution.

Example

```
MODEL PROGRAM A=10 B=1 C=5 D=1.
COMPUTE PRED= A*exp(B*X) + C*exp(D*X).
```

- The MODEL PROGRAM command assigns starting values to the four parameters *A, B, C,* and *D*.

- COMPUTE defines the model to be fit as the sum of two exponentials.

DERIVATIVES Command

The optional DERIVATIVES command signifies the beginning of the derivatives program. The derivatives program contains transformation statements for computing some or all of the derivatives of the model. The derivatives program must follow the model program but precede the NLR command.

If the derivatives program is not used, NLR numerically estimates derivatives for all the parameters. Providing derivatives reduces computation time and, in some situations, may result in a better solution.

- The DERIVATIVES command has no further specifications but must be followed by the set of transformation statements that calculate the derivatives.
- You can use any computational or output commands (such as COMPUTE, IF, RECODE, COUNT, or WRITE) in the derivatives program, but you cannot use input commands (such as DATA LIST or GET).
- To name the derivatives, specify the prefix D. before each parameter name. For example, the derivative name for the parameter *PARM1* would be *D.PARM1*.
- Once a derivative has been calculated by a transformation, the variable for that derivative can be used in subsequent transformations.
- You do not need to supply all of the derivatives. Those that are not supplied will be estimated by the program. During the first iteration of nonlinear estimation, derivatives calculated in the derivatives program are compared with numerically calculated derivatives. This serves as a check on the supplied values (see "CRITERIA Subcommand" on p. 374).
- Transformations in the derivatives program are used by NLR only and do not affect the active file.

Example

```
DERIVATIVES.
COMPUTE D.A = exp (B * X).
COMPUTE D.B = A * exp (B * X) * X.
COMPUTE D.C = exp (D * X).
COMPUTE D.D = C * exp (D * X) * X.
```

- The derivatives program specifies derivatives for the sum of the two exponentials in the model described by the following equation:

$$Y = Ae^{Bx} + Ce^{Dx}$$

Example

```
DERIVATIVES.
COMPUTE D.A = exp (B * X).
COMPUTE D.B = A * X * D.A.
COMPUTE D.C = exp (D * X).
COMPUTE D.D = C * X * D.C.
```

- This is an alternative way to express the same derivatives program specified in the previous example.

NLR Command

The NLR command is required to specify the dependent and independent variables for the nonlinear regression.

- The minimum specification is a dependent variable followed by keyword WITH and a list of independent variables.
- Only one dependent variable can be specified. It must be a numeric variable in the active file and cannot be a variable generated by the model or the derivatives program.

- The list of independent variables is required and must include every variable from the active file used in the transformation commands associated with the MODEL PROGRAM and DERIVATIVES commands.

OUTFILE Subcommand

OUTFILE stores final parameter estimates for use on a subsequent NLR command. The only specification on OUTFILE is the target file. Some or all of the values from this file can be read into a subsequent Nonlinear Regression procedure with the FILE subcommand. The parameter data file created by OUTFILE stores the following variables:

- All the parameters named on the MODEL PROGRAM command.
- The sum of squared residuals (named *SSE*). *SSE* has no labels or missing values. The print and write format for *SSE* is F10.8.
- The number of cases on which the analysis was based (named *NCASES*). *NCASES* has no labels or missing values. The print and write format for *NCASES* is F8.0.

When OUTFILE is used, the model program cannot create variables named *SSE* or *NCASES*.

Example

```
MODEL PROGRAM A=.5 B=1.6.
COMPUTE PRED=A*SPEED**B.
NLR STOP WITH SPEED
 /OUTFILE='PARAM.SYS'.
```

- OUTFILE generates a parameter data file containing one case for four variables: *A*, *B*, *SSE*, and *NCASES*.

FILE Subcommand

FILE reads starting values for the parameters from a parameter data file created by an OUTFILE subcommand from a previous Nonlinear Regression procedure. When starting values are read from a file, they do not have to be specified on the MODEL PROGRAM command. Rather, the MODEL PROGRAM command simply names the parameters that correspond to the parameters in the data file.

- The only specification on FILE is the file that contains the starting values.
- Some new parameters may be specified for the model on the MODEL PROGRAM command while others are read from the file specified on the FILE subcommand.
- You do not have to name the parameters on MODEL PROGRAM in the order they occur in the parameter data file. In addition, you can name a partial list of the variables contained in the file.
- If the starting value for a parameter is specified on MODEL PROGRAM, the specification overrides the value read from the parameter data file.
- To read starting values from a parameter data file and then replace those values with the final results from NLR, specify the same file on the FILE and OUTFILE subcommands. The input file is read completely before anything is written in the output file.

Example

```
MODEL PROGRAM A B C=1 D=3.
COMPUTE PRED=A*SPEED**B + C*SPEED**D.
NLR STOP WITH SPEED /FILE='PARAM.SYS' /OUTFILE='PARAM.SYS'.
```

- MODEL PROGRAM names four of the parameters used to calculate *PRED*, but assigns values to only *C* and *D*. The values of *A* and *B* are read from the existing data file *PARAM.SYS*.
- After NLR computes the final estimates of the four parameters, OUTFILE writes over the old input file. If, in addition to these new final estimates, the former starting values of *A* and *B* are still desired, specify a different file on the OUTFILE subcommand.

PRED Subcommand

PRED identifies the variable holding the predicted values.

- The only specification is a variable name, which must be identical to the variable name used to calculate predicted values in the model program.
- If the model program names the variable *PRED*, the PRED subcommand can be omitted. Otherwise, the PRED subcommand is required.
- The variable for predicted values is not saved in the active file unless the SAVE subcommand is used.

Example

```
MODEL PROGRAM A=.5 B=1.6.
COMPUTE PSTOP=A*SPEED**B.
NLR STOP WITH SPEED /PRED=PSTOP.
```

- COMPUTE in the model program creates a variable named *PSTOP* to temporarily store the predicted values for the dependent variable *STOP*.
- PRED identifies *PSTOP* as the variable used to define the model for the Nonlinear Regression procedure.

SAVE Subcommand

SAVE is used to save the temporary variables for the predicted values, residuals, and derivatives created by the model and the derivatives programs.

- The minimum specification is a single keyword.
- The variables to be saved must have unique names in the active file. If a naming conflict exists, the variables are not saved.
- Parameters specified by the model program are not saved in the active file. They will not cause naming conflicts.

The following keywords are available and can be used in any combination and in any order. The new variables are always appended to the active file in the order in which these keywords are presented here:

PRED *Save the predicted values.* The variable's name, label, and formats are those specified for it (or assigned by default) in the model program.

RESID (varname) *Save the residuals.* You can specify a variable name in parentheses following the keyword. If no variable name is specified, the name of this variable is the same as the specification you use for this keyword. For example, if you use the three-character abbreviation RES, the default variable name will be *RES*. The variable has the same print and write format as the predicted values variable created by the model program. It has no variable label and no user-defined missing values. It is system-missing for any case in which either the dependent variable is missing or the predicted value cannot be computed.

DERIVATIVES *Save the derivatives.* The derivative variables are named with the prefix *D.* to the first six characters of the parameter names. Derivative variables use the print and write formats of the predicted values variable and have no value labels or user-defined missing values. Derivative variables are saved in the same order as the parameters named on MODEL PROGRAM. Derivatives are saved for all parameters, whether or not the derivative was supplied in the derivatives program.

Asymptotic standard errors of predicted values and residuals, and special residuals used for outlier detection and influential case analysis are not provided by the Nonlinear Regression procedure. However, the asymptotically correct values for all these statistics can be calculated using the SAVE subcommand with NLR and then using the Regression procedure. In REGRESSION, the dependent variable is still the same, and derivatives of the model parameters are used as independent variables. Casewise plots, standard errors of prediction, partial regression plots, and other diagnostics of the regression are valid for the nonlinear model.

Example

```
MODEL PROGRAM A=.5 B=1.6.
COMPUTE PSTOP=A*SPEED**B.
NLR STOP WITH SPEED /PRED=PSTOP
  /SAVE=RESID(RSTOP) DERIVATIVES PRED.
REGRESSION VARIABLES=STOP D.A D.B /ORIGIN
  /DEPENDENT=STOP /ENTER D.A D.B /RESIDUALS.
```

- The SAVE subcommand creates the residuals variable *RSTOP* and the derivative variables *D.A* and *D.B*.

- Because the PRED subcommand identifies *PSTOP* as the variable for predicted values in the nonlinear model, keyword PRED on SAVE adds the variable *PSTOP* to the active file.

- The new variables are added to the active file in the following order: *PSTOP, RSTOP, D.A,* and *D.B*.

- The subcommand RESIDUALS for REGRESSION produces the default analysis of residuals.

CRITERIA Subcommand

CRITERIA controls the values of the cutoff points used to stop the iterative calculations in NLR.

- The minimum specification is any of the CRITERIA keywords and an appropriate value. The value can be specified in parentheses after an equals sign, a space, or a comma. Multiple keywords can be specified in any order. Defaults are in effect for keywords not specified.

Checking Derivatives

Upon entering the first iteration, NLR always checks any derivatives calculated on the derivatives program by comparing them with numerically calculated derivatives. For each comparison, it computes an agreement score. A score of 1 indicates agreement to machine precision; a score of 0 indicates definite disagreement. If a score is less than 1, either an incorrect derivative was supplied or there were numerical problems in estimating the derivative. The lower the score, the more likely it is that the supplied derivatives are incorrect. Highly correlated parameters may cause disagreement even when a correct derivative is supplied. Be sure to check the derivatives if the agreement score is not 1.

During the first iteration, NLR checks each derivative score. If any score is below 1, it begins displaying a table to show the worst (lowest) score for each derivative. If any score is below the critical value, the program stops.

To specify the critical value, use the following keyword on CRITERIA:

CKDER n   *Critical value for derivative checking.* Specify a number between 0 and 1 for *n*. The default is 0.5. Specify 0 to disable this criterion.

Iteration Criteria

The Nonlinear Regression procedure uses an adaptation of subroutine LMSTR from the MINPACK package by Garbow et al. NLR computes parameter estimates using the Levenberg-Marquardt method. At each iteration, NLR evaluates the estimates against a set of control criteria. The iterative calculations continue until one of five cutoff points is met, at which point the iterations stop and the reason for stopping is displayed.

The CRITERIA subcommand has the following keywords:

ITER n   *Maximum number of iterations allowed.* Specify any positive integer for *n*. The default is 100 iterations per parameter. If the search for a solution stops because this limit is exceeded, NLR issues a warning message.

SSCON n   *Convergence criterion for the sum of squares.* Specify any non-negative number for *n*. The default is $1E - 8$. If successive iterations fail to reduce the sum of squares by this proportion, the procedure stops. Specify 0 to disable this criterion.

PCON n   *Convergence criterion for the parameter values.* Specify any non-negative number for *n*. The default is $1E - 8$. If successive iterations fail to change any of the parameter values by this proportion, the procedure stops. Specify 0 to disable this criterion.

RCON n   *Convergence criterion for the correlation between the residuals and the derivatives.* Specify any non-negative number for *n*. The default is $1E - 8$. If the largest value for the correlation between the residuals and the derivatives equals this value, the procedure stops because it lacks the information it needs to estimate a direction for its next move. This criterion is often referred to as a gradient convergence criterion. Specify 0 to disable this criterion.

Example

```
MODEL PROGRAM A=.5 B=1.6.
COMPUTE PRED=A*SPEED**B.
NLR STOP WITH SPEED /CRITERIA=ITER(80) SSCON=.000001.
```

- CRITERIA changes two of the five cutoff values affecting iteration, ITER and SSCON, and leaves the remaining three, PCON, RCON, and CKDER, at their default values.

Annotated Example

For a complete example with output, see the Annotated Examples following the Syntax Reference section of this manual.

PROBIT

```
PROBIT response-count varname OF observation-count varname
       WITH varlist [BY varname(min,max)]

[/MODEL={PROBIT**}]
       {LOGIT  }
       {BOTH   }

[/LOG=[{10**  }]]
       {2.718 }
       {value }
       {NONE  }

[/CRITERIA=[{OPTOL   }({epsilon**0.8})][P({0.15**})][STEPLIMIT({0.1**})]
            {CONVERGE} {n          }   {p      }             {n     }

            [ITERATE({max(50,3(p+1)**})]]
                     {n              }

[/NATRES[=value]]

[/PRINT={[CI**] [FREQ**] [RMP**]} [PARALL] [NONE] [ALL]]
        {DEFAULT**               }

[/MISSING=[{EXCLUDE**}]  ]
           {INCLUDE  }
```

**Default if subcommand or keyword is omitted.

Example:

```
PROBIT  R OF N BY ROOT(1,2) WITH X
   /MODEL = BOTH.
```

Overview

PROBIT can be used to estimate the effects of one or more independent variables on a dichotomous dependent variable (such as dead or alive, employed or unemployed, product purchased or not). The program is designed for dose-response analyses and related models, but PROBIT also estimates logistic regression models for grouped data. (For logistic regression analysis when data are in case-by-case format, use the Logistic Regression procedure. See Chapter 1 for more information.)

Options

The Model. You can request a probit or logit response model, or both, for the observed response proportions with the MODEL subcommand.

Transform Predictors. You can control the base of the log transformation applied to the predictors or request no log transformation with the LOG subcommand.

Natural Response Rates. You can instruct PROBIT to estimate the natural response rate (threshold) of the model or you can supply a known natural response rate to be used in the solution with the NATRES subcommand.

Algorithm Control Parameters. You can specify values of algorithm control parameters, such as the limit on iterations, using the CRITERIA subcommand.

Statistics. By default, PROBIT calculates frequencies, fiducial confidence intervals, and the relative median potency. It also produces a plot of the transformed observed proportions against the values of a single independent variable. Optionally, you can use the PRINT subcommand to request a test of the parallelism of regression lines for different levels of the grouping variable or to suppress any or all of these statistics.

Basic Specification

- The basic specification is the response-count variable, keyword OF, the observation-count variable, keyword WITH, and at least one independent variable.
- PROBIT calculates maximum-likelihood estimates for the parameters of the default probit response model and automatically displays estimates of the regression coefficient and intercept terms, their standard errors, a covariance matrix of parameter estimates, and a Pearson chi-square goodness-of-fit test of the model.

Subcommand Order

- The variable specification must be first.
- Subcommands can be named in any order.

Syntax Rules

- The variables must include a response count, an observation count, and at least one predictor. A categorical grouping variable is optional.
- All subcommands are optional and each can appear only once.
- Generally, data should not be entered for individual observations. PROBIT expects predictor values, response counts, and the total number of observations as the input case.
- If the data are available only in a case-by-case form, use AGGREGATE first to compute the required response and observation counts.

Operations

- The transformed response variable is predicted as a linear function of other variables using the nonlinear-optimization method. Note that the previous releases used the iteratively weighted least-squares method and a different way of transforming the response variables. See "MODEL Subcommand" on p. 380.
- If individual cases are entered in the data, PROBIT skips the plot of transformed response proportions and predictor values.
- If individual cases are entered, the degrees of freedom for the chi-square goodness-of-fit statistic are based on the individual cases.

Limitations

- Only one prediction model can be tested on a single PROBIT command, although both probit and logit response models can be requested for that prediction.
- Confidence limits, the plot of transformed response proportions and predictor values, and computation of relative median potency are necessarily limited to single-predictor models.

Example

```
PROBIT  R OF N BY ROOT(1,2) WITH X
  /MODEL = BOTH.
```

- This example specifies that both the probit and logit response models be applied to the response frequency *R*, given *N* total observations and the predictor *X*.
- By default, the predictor is log transformed.

Example

```
* Using data in a case-by-case form

DATA LIST FREE / PREPARTN DOSE RESPONSE.
BEGIN DATA
1 1.5 0
  ...
4 20.0 1
END DATA.
COMPUTE SUBJECT = 1.
PROBIT RESPONSE OF SUBJECT BY PREPARTN(1,4) WITH DOSE.
```

- This dose-response model (Finney, 1971) illustrates a case-by-case analysis. A researcher tests four different preparations at varying doses and observes whether each subject responds. The data are individually recorded for each subject, with 1 indicating a response and 0 indicating no response. The number of observations is always 1 and is stored in variable *SUBJECT*.
- PROBIT warns that the data are in a case-by-case form and that the plot is therefore skipped.
- Degrees of freedom for the goodness-of-fit test are based on individual cases, not dosage groups.
- PROBIT displays predicted and observed frequencies for all individual input cases.

Example

```
* Aggregating case-by-case data

DATA LIST FREE /PREPARTN DOSE RESPONSE.
BEGIN DATA
     1.00      1.50       .00
     ...
     4.00     20.00      1.00
END DATA.
AGGREGATE OUTFILE=*
  /BREAK=PREPARTN DOSE
  /SUBJECTS=N(RESPONSE)
  /NRESP=SUM(RESPONSE).
PROBIT NRESP OF SUBJECTS BY PREPARTN(1,4) WITH DOSE.
```

- This example analyzes the same dose-response model as the previous example, but the data are first aggregated.
- AGGREGATE summarizes the data by cases representing all subjects who received the same preparation (*PREPARTN*) at the same dose (*DOSE*).
- The number of cases having a nonmissing response is recorded in the aggregated variable *SUBJECTS*.
- Because *RESPONSE* is coded 0 for no response and 1 for a response, the sum of the values gives the number of observations with a response.
- PROBIT requests a default analysis.
- The parameter estimates for this analysis are the same as those calculated for individual cases in the example above. The chi-square test, however, is based on the number of dosages.

Variable Specification

The variable specification on PROBIT identifies the variables for response count, observation count, groups, and predictors. The variable specification is required.

- The variables must be specified first. The specification must include the response-count variable, followed by the keyword OF and then the observation-count variable.
- If the value of the response-count variable exceeds that of the observation-count variable, a procedure error occurs and PROBIT is not executed.
- At least one predictor (covariate) must be specified following the keyword WITH. The number of predictors is limited only by available workspace. All predictors must be continuous variables.
- You can specify a grouping variable (factor) after the keyword BY. Only one variable can be specified. It must be numeric and can contain only integer values. You must specify, in parentheses, a range indicating the minimum and maximum values for the grouping variable. Each integer value in the specified range defines a group.
- Cases with values for the grouping variable that are outside the specified range are excluded from the analysis.

- Keywords BY and WITH can appear in either order. However, both must follow the response- and observation-count variables.

Example

```
PROBIT R OF N WITH X.
```

- The number of observations having the measured response appears in variable R, and the total number of observations is in N. The predictor is X.

Example

```
PROBIT  R OF N BY ROOT(1,2) WITH X.

PROBIT  R OF N WITH X BY ROOT(1,2).
```

- Because keywords BY and WITH can be used in either order, these two commands are equivalent. Each command specifies X as a continuous predictor and $ROOT$ as a categorical grouping variable.
- Groups are identified by the levels of variable $ROOT$, which may be 1 or 2.
- For each combination of predictor and grouping variables, the variable R contains the number of observations with the response of interest, and N contains the total number of observations.

MODEL Subcommand

MODEL specifies the form of the dichotomous-response model. Response models can be thought of as transformations (T) of response rates, which are proportions or probabilities (p). Note the difference in the transformations between the current version and the previous versions.

- A **probit** is the inverse of the cumulative standard normal distribution function. Thus, for any proportion, the probit transformation returns the value below which that proportion of standard normal deviates is found. For the probit response model, the program uses $T(p) = \text{PROBIT}(p)$. Hence:

$$T(0.025) = \text{PROBIT}(0.025) = -1.96$$

$$T(0.400) = \text{PROBIT}(0.400) = -0.25$$

$$T(0.500) = \text{PROBIT}(0.500) = 0.00$$

$$T(0.950) = \text{PROBIT}(0.950) = 1.64$$

- A **logit** is simply the natural log of the odds ratio, $p/(1-p)$. In the Probit procedure, the response function is given as $T(p) = \log_e(p/(1-p))$. Hence:

$$T(0.025) = \text{LOGIT}(0.025) = -3.66$$

$$T(0.400) = \text{LOGIT}(0.400) = -0.40$$

$$T(0.500) = \text{LOGIT}(0.500) = 0.00$$

$$T(0.950) = \text{LOGIT}(0.950) = 2.94$$

You can request one or both of the models on the MODEL subcommand. The default is PRO-BIT if the subcommand is not specified or is specified with no keyword.

PROBIT   *Probit response model.* This is the default.

LOGIT   *Logit response model.*

BOTH   *Both probit and logit response models.* PROBIT displays all the output for the logit model followed by the output for the probit model.

- If subgroups and multiple-predictor variables are defined, PROBIT estimates a separate intercept, a_j, for each subgroup and a regression coefficient, b_i, for each predictor.

LOG Subcommand

LOG specifies the base of the logarithmic transformation of the predictor variables or suppresses the default log transformation.

- LOG applies to all predictors.
- To transform only selected predictors, use COMPUTE commands before the Probit procedure. Then specify NONE on the LOG subcommand.
- If LOG is omitted, a logarithm base of 10 is used.
- If LOG is used without a specification, the natural logarithm base *e* (approximately 2.718) is used.
- If you have a control group in your data and specify NONE on the LOG subcommand, the control group is included in the analysis. See "NATRES Subcommand" on p. 382.

You can specify one of the following on LOG:

value   *Logarithm base to be applied to all predictors.*

NONE   *No transformation of the predictors.*

Example

```
PROBIT R OF N BY ROOT (1,2) WITH X
    /LOG = 2.
```

- LOG specifies a base-2 logarithmic transformation.

CRITERIA Subcommand

Use CRITERIA to specify the values of control parameters for the PROBIT algorithm. You can specify any or all of the keywords below. Defaults remain in effect for parameters that are not changed.

OPTOL(n)   *Optimality tolerance.* Alias CONVERGE. If an iteration point is a feasible point and the next step will not produce a relative change in either the parameter vector or the log-likelihood function of more than the square root of *n*, an optimal solution has been found. OPTOL can also be thought of as the number of significant digits in the log-likelihood function at the solution. For example, if OPTOL$=10^{-6}$, the log-likelihood function should have approximately six significant digits of accuracy. The default value is machine epsilon**0.8.

ITERATE(n)   *Iteration limit.* Specify the maximum number of iterations. The default is max $(50, 3(p+1))$, where p is the number of parameters in the model.

P(p)   *Heterogeneity criterion probability.* Specify a cutoff value between 0 and 1 for the significance of the goodness-of-fit test. The cutoff value determines whether a heterogeneity factor is included in calculations of confidence levels for effective levels of a predictor. If the significance of chi-square is greater than the cutoff, the heterogeneity factor is not included. If you specify 0, this criterion is disabled; if you specify 1, a heterogeneity factor is automatically included. The default is 0.15.

STEPLIMIT(n)   *Step limit.* The PROBIT algorithm does not allow changes in the length of the parameter vector to exceed a factor of n. This limit prevents very early steps from going too far from good initial estimates. Specify any positive value. The default value is 0.1.

CONVERGE(n)   *Alias of OPTOL.*

NATRES Subcommand

You can use NATRES either to supply a known natural response rate to be used in the solution or to instruct PROBIT to estimate the natural (threshold) response rate of the model.

- To supply a known natural response rate as a constraint on the model solution, specify a value less than 1 on NATRES.

- To instruct PROBIT to estimate the natural response rate of the model, you can indicate a control group by giving a 0 value to any of the predictor variables. PROBIT displays the estimate of the natural response rate and the standard error and includes the estimate in the covariance/correlation matrix as *NAT RESP*.

- If no control group is indicated and NATRES is specified without a given value, PROBIT estimates the natural response rate from the entire data and informs you that no control group has been provided. The estimate of the natural response rate and the standard error are displayed and *NAT RESP* is included in the covariance/correlation matrix.

- If you have a control group in your data and specify NONE on the LOG subcommand, the control group is included in the analysis.

Example

```
DATA LIST FREE / SOLUTION DOSE NOBSN NRESP.
BEGIN DATA
1   5 100 20
1  10   80 30
1   0 100 10
. . .
END DATA.

PROBIT NRESP OF NOBSN BY SOLUTION(1,4) WITH DOSE
   /NATRES.
```

- This example reads four variables and requests a default analysis with an estimate of the natural response rate.
- The predictor variable, *DOSE*, has a value of 0 for the third case.
- The response count (10) and the observation count (100) for this case establish the initial estimate of the natural response rate.
- Because the default log transformation is performed, the control group is not included in the analysis.

Example

```
DATA LIST FREE / SOLUTION DOSE NOBSN NRESP.
BEGIN DATA
1   5 100 20
1  10   80 30
1   0 100 10
   . . .
END DATA.

PROBIT NRESP OF NOBSN BY SOLUTION(1,4) WITH DOSE
   /NATRES = 0.10.
```

- This example reads four variables and requests an analysis in which the natural response rate is set to 0.10. The values of the control group are ignored.
- The control group is excluded from the analysis because the default log transformation is performed.

PRINT Subcommand

Use PRINT to control the statistics calculated by PROBIT.

- PROBIT always displays the plot (for a single-predictor model) and the parameter estimates and covariances for the probit model.
- If PRINT is used, the requested statistics are calculated and displayed in addition to the parameter estimates and plot.
- If PRINT is not specified or is specified without any keyword, FREQ, CI, and RMP are calculated and displayed in addition to the parameter estimates and plot.

DEFAULT *FREQ, CI, and RMP.* This is the default if PRINT is not specified or is specified by itself.

FREQ   *Frequencies.* Display a table of observed and predicted frequencies with their residual values. If observations are entered on a case-by-case basis, this listing can be quite lengthy.

CI   *Fiducial confidence intervals.* Print Finney's (1971) fiducial confidence intervals for the levels of the predictor needed to produce each proportion of responses. PROBIT displays this default output for single-predictor models only. If a categorical grouping variable is specified, PROBIT produces a table of confidence intervals for each group. If the Pearson chi-square goodness-of-fit test is significant ($p < 0.15$ by default), PROBIT uses a heterogeneity factor to calculate the limits.

RMP   *Relative median potency.* Display the relative median potency (RMP) of each pair of groups defined by the grouping variable. PROBIT displays this default output for single-predictor models only. For any pair of groups, the RMP is the ratio of the stimulus tolerances in those groups. **Stimulus tolerance** is the value of the predictor necessary to produce a 50% response rate. If the derived model for one predictor and two groups estimates that a predictor value of 21 produces a 50% response rate in the first group, and that a predictor value of 15 produces a 50% response rate in the second group, the relative median potency would be 21/15 = 1.40. In biological assay analyses, RMP measures the comparative strength of preparations.

PARALL   *Parallelism test.* Produce a test of the parallelism of regression lines for different levels of the grouping variable. This test displays a chi-square value and its associated probability. It requires an additional pass through the data and, thus, additional processing time.

NONE   *Display only the unconditional output.* This option can be used to override any other specification on the PRINT subcommand for PROBIT.

ALL   *All available output.* This is the same as requesting FREQ, CI, RMP, and PARALL.

MISSING Subcommand

PROBIT always deletes cases having a missing value for any variable. In the output, PROBIT indicates how many cases it rejected because of missing data. This information is displayed with the data information that prints at the beginning of the output. You can use the MISSING subcommand to control the treatment of user-missing values.

EXCLUDE   *Delete cases with user-missing values.* This is the default. You can also make it explicit by using the keyword DEFAULT.

INCLUDE   *Include user-missing values.* PROBIT treats user-missing values as valid. Only cases with system-missing values are rejected.

Annotated Example

For a complete example with output, see the Annotated Examples following the Syntax Reference section of this manual.

SURVIVAL

```
SURVIVAL TABLES=survival varlist
                 [BY varlist (min, max)...][BY varlist (min, max)...]

  /INTERVALS=THRU n BY a [THRU m BY b ...]

  /STATUS=status variable({min, max}) FOR {ALL               }
                          {value     }     {survival varlist}
[/STATUS=...]

[/PLOTS ({ALL     })={ALL             } BY {ALL    }   BY {ALL    }]
        {LOGSURV }   {survival varlis}    {varlist}      {varlist}
        {SURVIVAL}
        {HAZARD  }
        {DENSITY }

[/PRINT={TABLE** }]
        {NOTABLE }

[/COMPARE={ALL             } BY {ALL    } BY {ALL    }]
          {survival varlist}    {varlist}    {varlist}

[/CALCULATE=[{EXACT**     }] [PAIRWISE] [COMPARE] ]
            {CONDITIONAL }
            {APPROXIMATE }

[/MISSING={GROUPWISE**}   [INCLUDE] ]
          {LISTWISE   }

[/WRITE=[{NONE** }] ]
        {TABLES }
        {BOTH   }
```

**Default if subcommand or keyword is omitted.

Example:
```
SURVIVAL TABLES=MOSFREE BY TREATMNT(1,3)
  /STATUS = PRISON (1)
  /INTERVALS=THRU 24 BY 3.
```

Overview

SURVIVAL produces actuarial life tables, plots, and related statistics for examining the length of time to the occurrence of an event, often known as **survival time**. Cases can be classified into groups for separate analyses and comparisons. Time intervals can be calculated with the SPSS/PC+ date-conversion function YRMODA (see the *SPSS/PC+ Base System User's Guide*).

Options

Life Tables. You can list the variables to be used in the analysis, including any control variables on the TABLES subcommand. You can also suppress the life tables in the output with the PRINT subcommand.

Intervals. SURVIVAL reports the percentage alive at various times after the initial event. You can select the time points for reporting with the INTERVALS subcommand.

Plots. You can plot the survival functions for all cases or separately for various subgroups with the PLOTS subcommand.

Comparisons. When control variables are listed on the TABLES subcommand, you can compare groups using the COMPARE subcommand. You can request pairwise or approximate comparisons with the CALCULATE subcommand.

Writing a File. You can write the life tables, including the labeling information, to a file with the WRITE subcommand.

Basic Specification

- The basic specification requires three subcommands: TABLES, INTERVALS, and STATUS. TABLES identifies at least one survival variable from the active file, INTERVALS divides the time period into intervals, and STATUS names a variable that indicates whether the event occurred for a particular observation.
- The basic specification prints one or more life tables, depending on the number of survival and control variables specified.

Subcommand Order

- TABLES must be first.
- Remaining subcommands can be named in any order.

Syntax Rules

- Only one TABLES subcommand can be specified, but multiple survival variables can be named. A survival variable cannot be specified as a control variable on any subcommands.
- Only one INTERVALS subcommand can be in effect on a SURVIVAL command. The interval specifications apply to all the survival variables listed on TABLES. If multiple INTERVALS subcommands are used, the last specification supersedes all previous ones.
- Only one status variable can be listed on each STATUS subcommand. To specify multiple status variables, use multiple STATUS subcommands.
- You can specify multiple control variables on one BY keyword. Use a second BY keyword to specify second-order control variables to interact with the first-order control variables.
- All variables, including survival variables, control variables, and status variables, must be numeric. SURVIVAL does not process string variables.

Operations

- SURVIVAL computes time intervals according to specified interval widths, calculates the survival functions for each interval, and builds one life table for each group of survival variables. The life table is displayed unless explicitly suppressed.
- When the PLOT subcommand is specified, SURVIVAL plots the survival functions for all cases or separately for various groups.
- When the COMPARE subcommand is specified, SURVIVAL compares survival-time distributions of different groups based on the Wilcoxon (Gehan) statistic.

Limitations

- Maximum 20 survival variables.
- Maximum 100 control variables total on the first- and second-order control-variable lists combined.
- Maximum 20 THRU and BY specifications on INTERVALS.
- Maximum 35 values can appear on a plot.

Example

```
SURVIVAL TABLES=MOSFREE BY TREATMNT(1,3)
  /STATUS = PRISON (1)
  /INTERVALS = THRU 24 BY 3.
```

- The survival analysis is used to examine the length of time between release from prison and return to prison for prisoners in three treatment programs. The variable *MOSFREE* is the length of time in months a prisoner stayed out of prison. The variable *TREATMNT* indicates the treatment group for each case.
- A value of 1 on the variable *PRISON* indicates a terminal outcome—that is, cases coded as 1 have returned to prison. Cases with other non-negative values for *PRISON* have not returned. Because we don't know their final outcome, such cases are called censored.
- Life tables are produced for each of the three subgroups. INTERVALS specifies that the survival experience be described every three months for the first two years.

TABLES Subcommand

TABLES identifies the survival and control variables to be included in the analysis.
- The minimum specification is one or more survival variables.
- To specify one or more first-order control (or factor) variables, use keyword BY followed by the control variable(s). First-order control variables are processed in sequence. For example, BY A(1,3) B(1,2) results in five groups (A=1, A=2, A=3, B=1, and B=2).
- You can specify one or more second-order control variables following a second BY keyword. Separate life tables are generated for each combination of values of the first-order

and second-order controls. For example, BY A(1,3) BY B(1,2) results in six groups (*A*=1 *B*=1, *A*=1 *B*=2, *A*=2 *B*=1, *A*=2 *B*=2, *A*=3 *B*=1, and *A*=3 *B*=2).

- Each control variable must be followed by a value range in parentheses. These values must be integers separated by a comma or a blank. Non-integer values in the data are truncated, and the case is assigned to a subgroup based on the integer portion of its value on the variable. To specify only one value for a control variable, use the same value for the minimum and maximum.

- To generate life tables for all cases combined, as well as for control variables, use COMPUTE to create a variable that has the same value for all cases. With this variable as a control, tables for the entire set of cases, as well as for the control variables, will be produced.

Example

```
SURVIVAL TABLES = MOSFREE BY TREATMNT(1,3) BY RACE(1,2)
 /STATUS = PRISON(1)
 /INTERVAL = THRU 24 BY 3.
```

- *MOSFREE* is the survival variable, and *TREATMNT* is the first-order control variable. The second BY defines *RACE* as a second-order control group having a value of 1 or 2.

- Six life tables with the median survival time are produced, one for each pair of values for the two control variables.

INTERVALS Subcommand

INTERVALS determines the period of time to be examined and how the time will be grouped for the analysis. The interval specifications apply to all the survival variables listed on TABLES.

- SURVIVAL always uses 0 as the starting point for the first interval. Do not specify the 0. The INTERVALS specification *must* begin with keyword THRU.

- Specify the terminal value of the time period after the keyword THRU. The final interval includes any observations that exceed the specified terminal value.

- The grouping increment, which follows keyword BY, must be in the same units as the survival variable.

- The period to be examined can be divided into intervals of varying lengths by repeating the THRU and BY keywords. The period must be divided in ascending order. If the time period is not a multiple of the increment, the endpoint of the period is adjusted upward to the next even multiple of the grouping increment.

- When the period is divided into intervals of varying lengths by repeating the THRU and BY specifications, the adjustment of one period to produce even intervals changes the starting point of subsequent periods. If the upward adjustment of one period completely overlaps the next period, no adjustment is made and the procedure terminates with an error.

Example

```
SURVIVAL TABLES = MOSFREE BY TREATMNT(1,3)
 /STATUS = PRISON(1)
 /INTERVALS = THRU 12 BY 1 THRU 24 BY 3.
```

- INTERVALS produces life tables computed from 0 to 12 months at one-month intervals and from 13 to 24 months at three-month intervals.

Example

```
SURVIVAL TABLES = ONSSURV BY TREATMNT (1,3)
  /STATUS = OUTCOME (3,4)
  /INTERVALS = THRU 50 BY 6.
```

- On the INTERVALS subcommand, the value following BY (6) does not divide evenly into the period to which it applies (50). Thus, the endpoint of the period is adjusted upward to the next even multiple of the BY value, resulting in a period of 54 with 9 intervals of 6 units each.

Example

```
SURVIVAL TABLES = ONSSURV BY TREATMNT (1,3)
  /STATUS = OUTCOME (3,4)
  /INTERVALS = THRU 50 BY 6 THRU 100 BY 10 THRU 200 BY 20.
```

- Multiple THRU and BY specifications are used on the INTERVAL subcommand to divide the period of time under examination into intervals of different lengths.
- The first THRU and BY specifications are adjusted to produce even intervals as in the previous example. As a result, the following THRU and BY specifications are automatically readjusted to generate 5 intervals of 10 units (through 104), followed by 5 intervals of 20 units (through 204).

STATUS Subcommand

To determine whether the terminal event has occurred for a particular observation, SURVIVAL checks the value of a status variable. STATUS lists the status variable associated with each survival variable and the codes that indicate that a terminal event occurred.

- Specify a status variable followed by a value range enclosed in parentheses. The value range identifies the codes that indicate that the terminal event has taken place. All cases with non-negative times that do not have a code in the value range are classified as **censored cases**, which are cases for which the terminal event has not yet occurred.
- If the status variable does not apply to all the survival variables, specify FOR and the name of the survival variable(s) to which the status variable applies.
- Each survival variable on TABLES must have an associated status variable identified by a STATUS subcommand.
- Only one status variable can be listed on each STATUS subcommand. To specify multiple status variables, use multiple STATUS subcommands.
- If FOR is omitted on the STATUS specification, the status-variable specification applies to all of the survival variables not named on another STATUS subcommand.
- If more than one STATUS subcommand omits keyword FOR, the final STATUS subcommand without FOR applies to all survival variables not specified by FOR on other STATUS subcommands. No warning is printed.

Example

```
SURVIVAL TABLES = ONSSURV BY TREATMNT (1,3)
  /INTERVALS = THRU 50 BY 5, THRU 100 BY 10
  /STATUS = OUTCOME (3,4).
```

- STATUS specifies that a code of 3 or 4 on *OUTCOME* means that the terminal event for the survival variable *ONSSURV* occurred.

Example

```
SURVIVAL TABLES = NOARREST MOSFREE BY TREATMNT(1,3)
  /STATUS = ARREST (1) FOR NOARREST
  /STATUS = PRISON (1)
  /INTERVAL=THRU 24 BY 3.
```

- STATUS defines the terminal event for *NOARREST* as a value of 1 for *ARREST*. Any other value for *ARREST* is considered censored.
- The second STATUS subcommand defines the value of 1 for *PRISON* as the terminal event. Keyword FOR is omitted. Thus, the status-variable specification applies to *MOSFREE*, which is the only survival variable not named on another STATUS subcommand.

PLOT Subcommand

PLOT produces plots of the cumulative survival distribution, the hazard function, and the probability density function. The PLOT subcommand can plot only the survival functions generated by the TABLES subcommand; PLOT cannot eliminate control variables.

- When specified by itself, the PLOT subcommand produces all available plots for each survival variable. Points on each plot are identified by values of the first-order control variables. If second-order controls are used, a separate plot is generated for every value of the second-order control variables.
- To request specific plots, specify, in parentheses following PLOT, any combination of the keywords defined below.
- Optionally, you can generate plots for only a subset of the requested life tables. Use the same syntax as used on the TABLES subcommand for specifying survival and control variables, omitting the value ranges. Each survival variable named on PLOT must have as many control levels as were specified for that variable on TABLES. However, only one control variable needs to be present for each level. If a required control level is missing on the PLOT specification, the default BY ALL is used for that level. Keyword ALL can be used to refer to an entire set of survival or control variables.
- To determine the number of plots that will be produced, multiply the number of functions plotted by the number of survival variables times the number of first-order controls times the number of distinct values represented in all of the second-order controls.

ALL   *Plot all available functions.* ALL *is the default if PLOT is used without specifications.*

LOGSURV   *Plot the cumulative survival distribution on a logarithmic scale.*

SURVIVAL   *Plot the cumulative survival distribution on a linear scale.*

HAZARD   *Plot the hazard function.*

DENSITY   *Plot the density function.*

Example

```
SURVIVAL TABLES = NOARREST MOSFREE BY TREATMNT(1,3)
  /STATUS = ARREST (1) FOR NOARREST
  /STATUS = PRISON (1) FOR MOSFREE
  /INTERVALS = THRU 24 BY 3
  /PLOT (SURVIVAL,HAZARD) = MOSFREE.
```

- Separate life tables are produced for each of the survival variables (*NOARREST* and *MOS-FREE*) for each of the three values of the control variable *TREATMNT*.
- PLOTS produces plots of the cumulative survival distribution and the hazard rate for *MOS-FREE* for the three values of *TREATMNT* (even though *TREATMNT* is not included on the PLOT specification).
- Because plots are requested only for the survival variable *MOSFREE*, no plots are generated for variable *NOARREST*.

PRINT Subcommand

By default, SURVIVAL prints life tables. PRINT can be used to suppress the life tables.

TABLE   *Print the life tables.* This is the default.

NOTABLE   *Suppress the life tables.* Only plots and comparisons are printed. The WRITE subcommand, which is used to write the life tables to a file, can be used when NOTABLE is in effect.

Example

```
SURVIVAL TABLES = MOSFREE BY TREATMNT(1,3)
  /STATUS = PRISON (1)
  /INTERVALS = THRU 24 BY 3
  /PLOT (ALL)
  /PRINT = NOTABLE.
```

- PRINT NOTABLE suppresses the printing of life tables.

COMPARE Subcommand

COMPARE compares the survival experience of subgroups defined by the control variables. At least one first-order control variable is required for calculating comparisons.

- When specified by itself, the COMPARE subcommand produces comparisons using the TABLES variable list.
- Alternatively, specify the survival and control variables for the comparisons. Use the same syntax as used on the TABLES subcommand for specifying survival and control variables, omitting the value ranges. Only variables that appear on the TABLES subcommand can be listed on COMPARE, and their role as survival, first-order, and second-order control

variables cannot be altered. Keyword TO can be used to refer to a group of variables, and keyword ALL can be used to refer to an entire set of survival or control variables.

- By default, COMPARE calculates exact comparisons between subgroups. Use the CALCULATE subcommand to obtain pairwise comparisons or approximate comparisons.

Example

```
SURVIVAL TABLES = MOSFREE BY TREATMNT(1,3)
  /STATUS = PRISON (1)
  /INTERVAL = THRU 24 BY 3
  /COMPARE.
```

- COMPARE computes the Wilcoxon (Gehan) statistic, degrees of freedom, and observed significance level for the hypothesis that the three survival curves based on the values of *TREATMNT* are identical.

Example

```
SURVIVAL TABLES=ONSSURV,RECSURV BY TREATMNT(1,3)
  /STATUS = RECURSIT(1,9) FOR RECSURV
  /STATUS = STATUS(3,4) FOR ONSSURV
  /INTERVAL = THRU 50 BY 5 THRU 100 BY 10
  /COMPARE = ONSSURV BY TREATMNT.
```

- COMPARE requests a comparison of *ONSSURV* by *TREATMNT*. No comparison is made of *RECSURV* by *TREATMNT*.

CALCULATE Subcommand

CALCULATE controls the comparisons of survival for subgroups specified on the COMPARE subcommand.

- The minimum specification is the subcommand keyword by itself. EXACT is the default.
- Only one of the keywords EXACT, APPROXIMATE, and CONDITIONAL can be specified. If more than one keyword is used, only one is in effect. The order of precedence is APPROXIMATE, CONDITIONAL, and EXACT.
- The keywords PAIRWISE and COMPARE can be used with any of the EXACT, APPROXIMATE, or CONDITIONAL keywords.
- If CALCULATE is used without the COMPARE subcommand, CALCULATE is ignored. However, if the keyword COMPARE is specified on CALCULATE and the COMPARE subcommand is omitted, SPSS/PC+ generates an error message.
- Data can be entered into SURVIVAL for each individual case or aggregated for all cases in an interval. The way in which data are entered determines whether an exact or an approximate comparison is most appropriate. See "Using Aggregated Data" on p. 393.

EXACT   *Calculate exact comparisons.* This is the default. You can obtain exact comparisons based on the survival experience of each observation with individual data. While this method is the most accurate, it requires that all of the data be in memory simultaneously. Thus, exact comparisons may be impractical for large samples. It is also inappropriate when individual data are not available and data aggregated by interval must be used.

APPROXIMATE   *Calculate approximate comparisons only.* Approximate comparisons are appropriate for aggregated data. The approximate-comparison approach assumes that all events occur at the midpoint of the interval. With exact comparisons, some of these midpoint ties can be resolved. However, if interval widths are not too great, the difference between exact and approximate comparisons should be small.

CONDITIONAL   *Calculate approximate comparisons if memory is insufficient.* Approximate comparisons are produced only if there is insufficient memory available for exact comparisons.

PAIRWISE   *Perform pairwise comparisons.* Comparisons of all pairs of values of the first-order control variable are produced along with the overall comparison.

COMPARE   *Produce comparisons only.* Survival tables specified on the TABLES subcommand are not computed, and requests for plots are ignored. This allows all available workspace to be used for comparisons. The WRITE subcommand cannot be used when this specification is in effect.

Example

```
SURVIVAL TABLES = MOSFREE BY TREATMNT(1,3)
  /STATUS = PRISON (1)
  /INTERVAL = THRU 24 BY 3
  /COMPARE
  /CALCULATE = PAIRWISE.
```

- PAIRWISE on CALCULATE computes the Wilcoxon (Gehan) statistic, degrees of freedom, and observed significance levels for each pair of values of *TREATMNT*, as well as for an overall comparison of survival across all three *TREATMNT* subgroups.
- All comparisons are exact comparisons.

Example

```
SURVIVAL TABLES = MOSFREE BY TREATMNT(1,3)
  /STATUS = PRISON (1)
  /INTERVAL = THRU 24 BY 3
  /COMPARE
  /CALCULATE = APPROXIMATE COMPARE.
```

- APPROXIMATE on CALCULATE computes the Wilcoxon (Gehan) statistic, degrees of freedom, and probability for the overall comparison of survival across all three *TREATMNT* subgroups using the approximate method.
- Because keyword COMPARE is specified on CALCULATE, survival tables are not computed.

Using Aggregated Data

When aggregated survival information is available, the number of censored and uncensored cases at each time point must be entered. Up to two records can be entered for each interval, one for censored cases and one for uncensored cases. The number of cases included on each record is used as the weight factor. If control variables are used, there will be up to two records (one for censored and one for uncensored cases) for each value of the control variable in each interval. These records must contain the value of the control variable and the number of cases that belong in the particular category as well as values for survival time and status.

Example

```
DATA LIST   / SURVEVAR 2 STATVAR 4 SEX 6 COUNT 8.
VALUE LABELS  STATVAR 1 'DECEASED' 2 'ALIVE'
              /SEX 1 'FEMALE' 2 'MALE'.
BEGIN DATA
 1 1 1 6
 1 1 1 1
 1 2 2 2
 1 1 2 1
 2 2 1 1
 2 1 1 2
 2 2 2 1
 2 1 2 3
   ...
END DATA.
WEIGHT COUNT.
SURVIVAL TABLES = SURVEVAR BY SEX (1,2)
   /INTERVALS = THRU 10 BY 1
   /STATUS = STATVAR (1).
```

- This example reads aggregated data and performs a SURVIVAL analysis when a control variable with two values is used.
- The first data record has a code of 1 on the status variable *STATVAR*, indicating it is an uncensored case, and a code of 1 on *SEX*, the control variable. The number of cases for this interval is 6, the value of the variable *COUNT*. Intervals with weights of 0 do not have to be included.
- *COUNT* is not used in SURVIVAL but is the weight variable. In this example, each interval requires four records to provide all the data for each *SURVEVAR* interval.

MISSING Subcommand

MISSING controls missing-value treatments. The default is GROUPWISE.

- Negative values on the survival variables are automatically treated as missing data. In addition, cases outside the value range on a control variable are excluded.
- GROUPWISE and LISTWISE are mutually exclusive. However, each can be used with INCLUDE.

GROUPWISE   *Exclude missing values groupwise.* Cases with missing values on a variable are excluded from any calculation involving that variable. This is the default.

LISTWISE   *Exclude missing values listwise.* Cases missing on any variables named on TABLES are excluded from the analysis.

INCLUDE   *Include user-missing values.* User-missing values are included in the analysis.

WRITE Subcommand

WRITE writes data in the survival tables to a file. This file can be used for further analyses or to produce graphics displays.

- When WRITE is omitted, the default is NONE. No output file is created.
- When WRITE is specified without a keyword, the default is TABLES.

NONE   *Do not write procedure output to a file.* This is the default when WRITE is omitted.

TABLES   *Write survival table data records.* All survival table statistics are written to a file.

BOTH   *Write out survival table data and label records.* Variable names, variable labels, and value labels are written out along with the survival table statistics.

When you specify the WRITE subcommand with SURVIVAL, the data are written to the results file. The default results file is *SPSS.PRC*. The SURVIVAL data will overwrite any previous contents of the results file. Before running the SURVIVAL command, you can change the name of the results file with the SET command (see the *SPSS/PC+ Base System User's Guide*).

Format

WRITE writes five types of records. Keyword TABLES writes record types 30, 31, and 40. Keyword BOTH writes record types 10, 20, 30, 31, and 40. The format of each record type is described in the following tables:

Table 1   Record type 10, produced only by keyword BOTH

Columns	Content	Format
1–2	Record type (10)	F2.0
3–7	Table number	F5.0
8–15	Name of survival variable	A8
16–55	Variable label of survival variable	A40
56	Number of BY's (0, 1, or 2)	F1.0
57–60	Number of rows in current survival table	F4.0

- One type-10 record is produced for each life table.
- Column 56 specifies the number of orders of control variables (0, 1, or 2) that have been applied to the life table.
- Columns 57–60 specify the number of rows in the life table. This number is the number of intervals in the analysis that show subjects entering; intervals in which no subjects enter are not noted in the life tables.

Table 2   Record type 20, produced by keyword BOTH

Columns	Content	Format
1–2	Record type (20)	F2.0
3–7	Table number	F5.0
8–15	Name of control variable	A8
16–55	Variable label of control variable	A40
56–60	Value of control variable	F5.0
61–80	Value label for this value	A20

- One type-20 record is produced for each control variable in each life table.
- If only first-order controls have been placed in the survival analysis, one type-20 record will be produced for each table. If second-order controls have also been applied, two type-20 records will be produced per table

Table 3   Record type 30, produced by both keywords TABLES and BOTH

Columns	Content	Format
1–2	Record type (30)	F2.0
3–7	Table number	F5.0
8–13	Beginning of interval	F6.2
14–21	Number entering interval	F8.2
22–29	Number withdrawn in interval	F8.2
30–37	Number exposed to risk	F8.2
38–45	Number of terminal events	F8.2

- Information on record type 30 continues on record type 31. Each pair of type-30 and type-31 records contains the information from one line of the life table.

Table 4   Record type 31, continuation of record type 30

Columns	Content	Format
1–2	Record type (31)	F2.0
3–7	Table number	F5.0
8–15	Proportion terminating	F8.6
16–23	Proportion surviving	F8.6
24–31	Cumulative proportion surviving	F8.6
32–39	Probability density	F8.6
40–47	Hazard rate	F8.6
48–54	S.E. of cumulative proportion surviving	F7.4
55–61	S.E. of probability density	F7.4
62–68	S.E. of hazard rate	F7.4

- Record type 31 is a continuation of record type 30.
- As many type-30 and type-31 record pairs are output for a table as it has lines (this number is noted in columns 57-60 of the type-10 record for the table)

.

Table 5   Record type 40, produced by both keywords TABLES and BOTH

Columns	Content	Format
1–2	Record type (40)	F2.0

- Type-40 records indicate the completion of the series of records for one life table.

Record Order

The SURVIVAL output file contains records for each of the life tables specified on the TABLES subcommand. All records for a given table are produced together in sequence. The records for the life tables are produced in the same order as the tables themselves. All life tables for the first survival variable are written first. The values of the first- and second-order control variables rotate, with the values of the first-order controls changing more rapidly.

Example

```
SURVIVAL TABLES = MOSFREE BY TREATMNT(1,3)
  /STATUS = PRISON (1) FOR MOSFREE
  /INTERVAL = THRU 24 BY 3
  /WRITE = BOTH.
```

- WRITE generates an output file containing life tables, variable names and labels, and value labels stored as record types 10, 20, 30, 31, and 40.

Annotated Example

For a complete example with output, see the Annotated Examples following the Syntax Reference section of this manual.

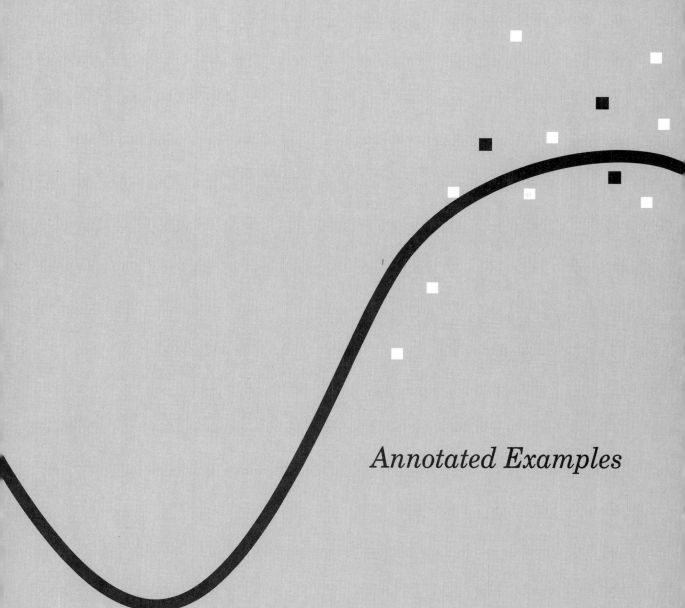

Annotated Examples

HILOGLINEAR

In this example, we will consider a market research analysis of laundry detergent preferences. Consumers in the survey prefer either Brand M or Brand X detergent. This analysis examines the relationship among brand preference and three other variables. The variables are:

- *BRANDPRF*—preference for either Brand M or Brand X detergent.
- *WATSOFT*—water softness.
- *PREVUSE*—previous use of Brand M.
- *TEMP*—washing temperature.

The data are in an external file named *AHILOG.DAT*. The SPSS/PC+ command file that performs the hierarchical loglinear analysis is as follows:

```
TITLE Detergent Preferences Ries & Smith (1963).

DATA LIST FREE FILE='AHILOG.DAT'
  / WATSOFT BRANDPRF PREVUSE TEMP FREQ.
VARIABLE LABELS WATSOFT  'WATER SOFTNESS'
                BRANDPRF 'BRAND PREFERENCE'
                PREVUSE  'PREVIOUS USE OF M'
                TEMP     'WATER TEMPERATURE'
                FREQ     'NUMBER IN CONDITION'.
VALUE LABELS WATSOFT 1 'SOFT' 2 'MEDIUM' 3 'HARD' /
             BRANDPRF 1 'BRAND X' 2 'BRAND M' /
             PREVUSE 1 'YES' 2 'NO' /
             TEMP 1 'HIGH' 2 'LOW'.
WEIGHT BY FREQ.
HILOGLINEAR WATSOFT (1,3) BRANDPRF PREVUSE TEMP (1,2)
  /PRINT=ALL
  /PLOT=DEFAULT
  /METHOD=BACKWARD
  /CRITERIA=MAXSTEPS(24)
  /DESIGN.
```

- The TITLE command puts the title *Detergent Preferences Ries & Smith (1963)* at the top of each page of output for this session.
- DATA LIST names the file that contains the data and defines the variables. Keyword FREE indicates that the data are in freefield format.
- The VARIABLE LABELS and VALUE LABELS commands complete the variable definition.
- The WEIGHT command weights the observations by FREQ, the variable containing the number of observations for each combination of values.
- HILOGLINEAR specifies four variables. The variable *WATSOFT* has three levels and the other three variables each have two.

- The PRINT subcommand requests all available displays: observed, expected, and residual values (display not shown); the result of the iterative proportional-fitting algorithm and tests of effects for the saturated model and for each order (Figure 1); measures of partial association for effects (Figure 2); and parameter estimates (Figure 3).
- The PLOT subcommand requests the default plots: residuals against observed and expected values, and a normal probability plot (partial display in Figure 6).
- The METHOD subcommand requests backward elimination. The CRITERIA subcommand specifies a maximum of 24 steps, and the DESIGN subcommand successively eliminates terms from the default saturated model (partial display in Figure 4). The observed and expected frequencies for the final model are also displayed (Figure 5).

Portions of the display are shown in Figure 1 through Figure 6. The exact appearance of printed display depends on the characters available on your printer.

Figure 1   Tests of effects for the saturated model and for each order

```
Tests that K-way and higher order effects are zero.

        K      DF    L.R. Chisq    Prob    Pearson Chisq    Prob    Iteration

        4       2          .737   .6917             .738   .6915           3
        3       9         9.846   .3631            9.871   .3611           3
        2      18        42.929   .0008           43.902   .0006           2
        1      23       118.627   .0000          115.714   .0000           0

Tests that K-way effects are zero.

        K      DF    L.R. Chisq    Prob    Pearson Chisq    Prob    Iteration

        1       5        75.698   .0000           71.812   .0000           0
        2       9        33.082   .0001           34.032   .0001           0
        3       7         9.109   .2449            9.133   .2433           0
        4       2          .737   .6917             .738   .6915           0
```

Figure 2   Partial associations

```
Tests of PARTIAL associations.

Effect Name                              DF    Partial Chisq    Prob    Iter

WATSOFT*BRANDPRF*PREVUSE                   2           4.571   .1017      3
WATSOFT*BRANDPRF*TEMP                      2            .162   .9223      3
WATSOFT*PREVUSE*TEMP                       2           1.377   .5023      3
BRANDPRF*PREVUSE*TEMP                      1           2.222   .1361      3
WATSOFT*BRANDPRF                           2            .216   .8978      3
WATSOFT*PREVUSE                            2           1.005   .6050      3
BRANDPRF*PREVUSE                           1          19.892   .0000      3
WATSOFT*TEMP                               2           6.095   .0475      3
BRANDPRF*TEMP                              1           3.739   .0532      3
PREVUSE*TEMP                               1            .740   .3898      3
WATSOFT                                    2            .502   .7782      2
BRANDPRF                                   1            .064   .8008      2
PREVUSE                                    1           1.921   .1657      2
TEMP                                       1          73.212   .0000      2
```

Figure 3   Partial display of parameter estimates for saturated model

```
Estimates for Parameters.

WATSOFT*BRANDPRF*PREVUSE*TEMP

    Parameter        Coeff.       Std. Err.       Z-Value       Lower 95 CI      Upper 95 CI

         1      -.0085755197        .04794        -.17888        -.10254           .08539
         2      -.0291703076        .04698        -.62095        -.12124           .06290

WATSOFT*BRANDPRF*PREVUSE

    Parameter        Coeff.       Std. Err.       Z-Value       Lower 95 CI      Upper 95 CI

         1       .0915571370        .04794        1.90983        -.00241           .18552
         2      -.0313716378        .04698        -.66781        -.12345           .06070

WATSOFT*BRANDPRF*TEMP

    Parameter        Coeff.       Std. Err.       Z-Value       Lower 95 CI      Upper 95 CI

         1      -.0199148627        .04794        -.41541        -.11388           .07405
         2       .0046079493        .04698         .09809        -.08747           .09668

WATSOFT*PREVUSE*TEMP

    Parameter        Coeff.       Std. Err.       Z-Value       Lower 95 CI      Upper 95 CI

         1      -.0466770430        .04794        -.97366        -.14064           .04729
         2       .0480797596        .04698        1.02348        -.04399           .14015

BRANDPRF*PREVUSE*TEMP

    Parameter        Coeff.       Std. Err.       Z-Value       Lower 95 CI      Upper 95 CI

         1      -.0492537407        .03337       -1.47605        -.11466           .01615
```

Figure 4   Partial display of final statistics

```
Backward Elimination for DESIGN 1 with generating class

   WATSOFT*BRANDPRF*PREVUSE*TEMP

 Likelihood ratio chi square =        .00000    DF = 0  P = 1.000

.........

Step 8

   The best model has generating class

         WATSOFT*TEMP
         BRANDPRF*TEMP
         BRANDPRF*PREVUSE

   Likelihood ratio chi square =     11.88644    DF = 14  P =  .615

If Deleted Simple Effect is                        DF  L.R. Chisq Change   Prob  Iter

WATSOFT*TEMP                                         2            6.099   .0474    2
BRANDPRF*TEMP                                        1            4.362   .0368    2
BRANDPRF*PREVUSE                                     1           20.581   .0000    2

Step 9

   The best model has generating class

         WATSOFT*TEMP
         BRANDPRF*TEMP
         BRANDPRF*PREVUSE

   Likelihood ratio chi square =     11.88644    DF = 14  P =  .615

The final model has generating class

         WATSOFT*TEMP
         BRANDPRF*TEMP
         BRANDPRF*PREVUSE

The Iterative Proportional Fit algorithm converged at iteration 0.
The maximum difference between observed and fitted marginal totals is     .000
and the convergence criterion is      .250
```

Figure 5 Observed and expected frequencies for final model

Observed, Expected Frequencies and Residuals.

Factor	Code	OBS count	EXP count	Residual	Std Resid
WATSOFT	SOFT				
BRANDPRF	BRAND X				
PREVUSE	YES				
TEMP	HIGH	19.0	19.5	-.52	-.12
TEMP	LOW	57.0	47.8	9.15	1.32
PREVUSE	NO				
TEMP	HIGH	29.0	28.4	.61	.11
TEMP	LOW	63.0	69.6	-6.58	-.79
BRANDPRF	BRAND M				
PREVUSE	YES				
TEMP	HIGH	29.0	30.8	-1.85	-.33
TEMP	LOW	49.0	57.5	-8.52	-1.12
PREVUSE	NO				
TEMP	HIGH	27.0	25.2	1.76	.35
TEMP	LOW	53.0	47.1	5.94	.87
WATSOFT	MEDIUM				
BRANDPRF	BRAND X				
PREVUSE	YES				
TEMP	HIGH	23.0	23.7	-.65	-.13
TEMP	LOW	47.0	47.0	.01	.00
PREVUSE	NO				
TEMP	HIGH	33.0	34.4	-1.40	-.24
TEMP	LOW	66.0	68.3	-2.32	-.28
BRANDPRF	BRAND M				
PREVUSE	YES				
TEMP	HIGH	47.0	37.4	9.63	1.57
TEMP	LOW	55.0	56.5	-1.48	-.20
PREVUSE	NO				
TEMP	HIGH	23.0	30.6	-7.58	-1.37
TEMP	LOW	50.0	46.2	3.79	.56
WATSOFT	HARD				
BRANDPRF	BRAND X				
PREVUSE	YES				
TEMP	HIGH	24.0	26.1	-2.09	-.41
TEMP	LOW	37.0	42.9	-5.89	-.90
PREVUSE	NO				
TEMP	HIGH	42.0	37.9	4.06	.66
TEMP	LOW	68.0	62.4	5.63	.71
BRANDPRF	BRAND M				
PREVUSE	YES				
TEMP	HIGH	43.0	41.2	1.77	.28
TEMP	LOW	52.0	51.6	.44	.06
PREVUSE	NO				
TEMP	HIGH	30.0	33.7	-3.73	-.64
TEMP	LOW	42.0	42.2	-.18	-.03

Goodness-of-fit test statistics

```
Likelihood ratio chi square =    11.88644   DF = 14   P =   .615
          Pearson chi square =    11.91780   DF = 14   P =   .613
```

Figure 6   HILOGLINEAR residuals plots

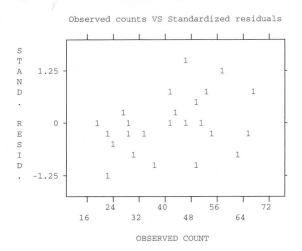

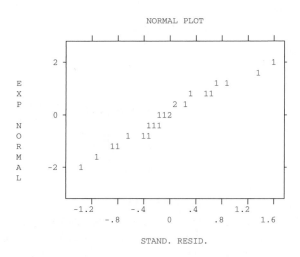

LOGISTIC REGRESSION

This example illustrates the use of logistic regression to predict students' grades in a class. The data are from Aldrich & Nelson (1984). The variables are

- *GPA* — entering grade point average.
- *TUCE* — score on the pretest.
- *PSI* — teaching method, coded as 0 if the traditional method was used and 1 if the new method was used.
- *GRADE* — coded as 1 if the student received an A, 0 otherwise. This is the dependent variable.
- *INITIAL* — student's initials used for identification purposes.

The SPSS/PC+ commands are as follows:

```
DATA LIST / GPA 1-4(2) TUCE 6-7 PSI 9 GRADE 11 INITIAL 13-14(A).
BEGIN DATA
(data records)
END DATA.

VARIABLE LABELS
    GPA "ENTERING GRADE POINT AVERAGE"
    TUCE "PRETEST SCORE"
    PSI "TEACHING METHOD"
    GRADE "FINAL GRADE".
VALUE LABELS PSI 1 "PSI USED" 0 "OTHER METHOD"
  /GRADE 1 "A" 0 "NOT A".
COMPUTE ID=$CASENUM.
LOGISTIC REGRESSION GRADE WITH GPA TUCE PSI
  /CLASSPLOT
  /ID=INITIAL
  /METHOD=ENTER GPA
  /METHOD=FSTEP(LR) TUCE PSI
  /PRINT=ITER(2)
  /CASEWISE=PGROUP PRED RESID
  /SAVE=DFBETA.
PLOT PLOT DFB1_1 WITH ID BY GRADE.
```

- The DATA LIST command defines the variables. The BEGIN DATA and END DATA commands indicate that the data (not shown) are inline. The VALUE LABELS and VARIABLE LABELS commands provide additional descriptive information for the variables.

- The COMPUTE command creates a sequential case number which is an additional identifier for each case. It will be used for plots.

- The LOGISTIC REGRESSION command identifies *GRADE* as the dependent variable and *GPA, TUCE,* and *PSI* as the independent variables. The CATEGORICAL subcommand is not used for the variable *PSI*, since *PSI* is already an indicator (0,1) variable.

- The PRINT subcommand requests that parameter estimates be displayed at every second iteration. By default, intermediate estimates are not displayed.
- The ID subcommand instructs that the casewise plot be labeled with the values of the variable *INITIAL*.
- The first METHOD subcommand enters the *GPA* variable into an equation which already contains the constant. (The constant can be suppressed with the ORIGIN subcommand.) Figure 1 contains the output when *GPA* is entered into the model.
- The second METHOD subcommand requests forward stepwise variable selection using the likelihood ratio as the criterion for variable removal. Only the variables *TUCE* and *PSI* are eligible for entry and removal. The variable *GPA* is already in the model and cannot be removed during the stepwise algorithm, since it is not included in the list of variables for FSTEP. If the variable list for FSTEP is not given, all independent variables are eligible for entry and removal.
- Figure 2 shows statistics for variables in the equation and those not in the equation when *PSI* is selected for entry into the model. It also shows the log likelihood for the model if *PSI* were removed. The message at the bottom of Figure 2 indicates that no additional variables meet the default entry and removal *p*-values, so model building terminates.
- The CLASSPLOT subcommand requests a plot of the estimated probabilities of receiving an A. Cases are identified on the plot by the first letter of the value label for the dependent variable. The plot when *PSI* is entered into the model containing the constant and *GPA* is shown in Figure 3.
- The SAVE subcommand requests that the change in coefficients when a case is eliminated from the analysis be saved. Three new variables named by default *DFB0_1* to *DFB2_1* are saved. The first variable corresponds to the constant, the second to *GPA*, and the third to *PSI*. Output from this step is shown in Figure 4.
- The CASEWISE subcommand requests the casewise listing shown in Figure 5. The variables *PGROUP* (the predicted group membership), *PRED* (the predicted probability of receiving an A), and *RESID* (the difference between the observed probability and that predicted by the model) are listed for all of the cases. Cases are identified by their value of *INITIAL*. Misclassified cases are marked with asterisks.
- The PLOT command requests a plot of the change in the coefficient for *GPA* when each case is removed from the analysis against the sequence number for each case. Each point is identified by the group to which it belongs. This plot is shown in Figure 6. Note the large change for the last case.

Figure 1   Statistics for model containing variable gpa

```
Beginning Block Number  1.  Method: Enter

Variable(s) Entered on Step Number
1..      GPA        ENTERING GRADE POINT AVERAGE

Estimation terminated at iteration number 4 because
Log Likelihood decreased by less than .01 percent.


              Iteration History:

Iteration   Log Likelihood      Constant           GPA
       1        -16.534755     -7.0342695      2.0561065
       3        -16.208908     -9.6927129      2.8369989

 -2 Log Likelihood         32.418
 Goodness of Fit           39.815

                     Chi-Square    df Significance

 Model Chi-Square          8.766     1      .0031
 Improvement               8.766     1      .0031

Classification Table for GRADE
                    Predicted
                 NOT A      A      Percent Correct
                   N  I   A
Observed         +------+------+
   NOT A     N   I  18  I   3  I    85.71%
                 +------+------+
   A         A   I   5  I   6  I    54.55%
                 +------+------+
                         Overall   75.00%

--------------------- Variables in the Equation ----------------------

Variable          B       S.E.     Wald     df     Sig      R    Exp(B)

GPA            2.8401    1.1270   6.3507      1    .0117   .3250  17.1168
Constant      -9.7032    3.6711   6.9861      1    .0082
```

Figure 2   Statistics for model containing variables gpa and psi

```
---------------------- Variables in the Equation ----------------------

Variable            B       S.E.      Wald     df      Sig      R     Exp(B)

GPA            3.0631    1.2228    6.2751      1    .0122   .3631  21.3948
PSI            2.3376    1.0408    5.0449      1    .0247   .3065  10.3565
Constant     -11.6007    4.2127    7.5830      1    .0059

--------------- Variables not in the Equation ----------------
Residual Chi Square        .459 with       1 df      Sig =  .4980

Variable            Score     df      Sig       R

TUCE                .4592      1    .4980    .0000

---------------- Model if Term Removed ------------------

Term        Log                                Significance
Removed     Likelihood     -2 Log LR    df     of Log LR

PSI            -16.209        6.165      1         .0130

No variables can be removed.

No variables can be added.
```

Figure 3   Histogram of predicted probabilities and group memberships

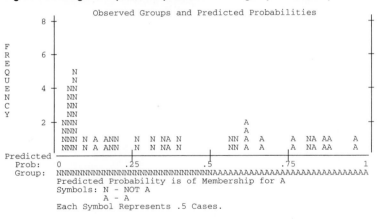

Figure 4   Saved variables

```
3 new variables have been created.
  Name          Contents

  DFB0_1        Dfbeta for the constant
  DFB1_1        Dfbeta for GPA
  DFB2_1        Dfbeta for PSI
```

Figure 5   Casewise listing

```
        ID  Observed
            GRADE      PGroup    Pred    Resid
am          S N          N      .0307   -.0307
cd          S N          N      .0602   -.0602
ez          S N          N      .1746   -.1746
rt          S N          N      .0656   -.0656
mk          S A          A      .6574    .3426
or          S N          N      .0552   -.0552
fs          S N          N      .0412   -.0412
rn          S N          N      .0568   -.0568
an          S N          N      .0895   -.0895
ds          S A          A      .6003    .3997
kb          S N          N      .0281   -.0281
rp          S N          N      .1929   -.1929
bz          S N          N      .3396   -.3396
ak          S A **       N      .1659    .8341
cl          S N          N      .3126   -.3126
ws          S N          N      .0389   -.0389
ms          S N          N      .0400   -.0400
dh          S N          N      .0506   -.0506
ae          S N **       A      .5730   -.5730
pp          S A          A      .6026    .3974
nn          S N          N      .0496   -.0496
oy          S A          A      .8612    .1388
ap          S N          N      .3988   -.3988
fu          S N **       A      .8159   -.8159
hk          S A          A      .8293    .1707
rt          S A **       N      .3556    .6444
mz          S A          A      .7542    .2458
gg          S N          N      .2527   -.2527
hi          S A          A      .8718    .1282
ln          S A          A      .9521    .0479
dp          S N **       A      .5579   -.5579
ss          S A **       N      .1254    .8746

            S=Selected U=Unselected cases
            ** = Misclassified cases
```

Figure 6   Plot of change in coefficient for variable gpa against case number

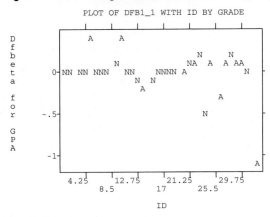

32 cases plotted.
A:A   N:NOT A $:Multiple occurrence

LOGLINEAR

You can use LOGLINEAR to analyze many types of designs for categorical variables. Combinations of variable specifications, CWEIGHT, CONTRAST, GRESID, and DESIGN subcommands can produce general loglinear models, logit models, quasi-independence models, logistic regressions on category variables, and others. The following examples demonstrate some of the types of models you can analyze. These examples have been obtained from books and articles on the analysis of categorical data. The examples use the WEIGHT command to replicate the published tables.

Example 1: Logit Model

The logit model is a special case of the general loglinear model in which one or more variables are treated as dependent and the rest are used as independent variables. Typically, logit models use dichotomous variables.

This example uses dichotomous variables to analyze data from *The American Soldier* (Stouffer et al., 1948). The researchers interviewed soldiers in training camps. The variables used in this example are:

- *PREF*—preference for training camps, where 1=stay in the same camp; 2=move to a northern camp; 3=move to a southern camp; 4=move, but undecided about location; and 5=undecided.

- *RACE*—race of soldier, where 1=black and 2=white.

- *ORIGIN, CAMP*—geographic origin and geographic location of camp, where 1=north and 2=south.

- *FREQ*—actual cell count obtained from the published table.

In this example, we transform the preference variable into the dichotomy north versus south. Typically, the first step in fitting a logit model is to use a saturated model and remove nonsignificant effects. This example fits only the significant effects in the interest of parsimony. The SPSS/PC+ commands are as follows:

```
SET WIDTH=WIDE.
TITLE "Stouffer's American Soldier".
DATA LIST FREE / RACE   ORIGIN   CAMP   PREF   FREQ.
BEGIN DATA
1 1 1 1 196
1 1 1 2 191
1 1 1 3  36
1 1 1 4  41
1 1 1 5  52
2 2 2 1 481
  ...
2 2 2 2  91
2 2 2 3 389
2 2 2 4  91
2 2 2 5  91
END DATA.
WEIGHT BY FREQ.
VARIABLE LABELS RACE 'RACE OF RESPONDENT'
    ORIGIN 'GEOGRAPHICAL ORIGIN'
    CAMP 'PRESENT CAMP'
    PREF 'PREFENCE FOR LOCATION'.
VALUE LABELS RACE 1 'BLACK' 2 'WHITE' /
    ORIGIN 1 'NORTH' 2 'SOUTH' /
    CAMP 1 'NORTH' 2 'SOUTH' /
    PREF 1 'STAY' 2 'GO NORTH' 3 'GO SOUTH'
    4 'MOVE UNDECIDED' 5 'UNDECIDED'.

* COLLAPSE CATEGORIES 1, 2, AND 3 INTO A DICHOTOMY.
COMPUTE DPREF=PREF.
IF (CAMP=1 AND PREF=1) DPREF=2.
IF (CAMP=2 AND PREF=1) DPREF=3.

VARIABLE LABELS DPREF 'PREFERENCE FOR LOCATION'.
VALUE LABELS DPREF 2 'NORTH' 3 'SOUTH'.

LOGLINEAR DPREF(2,3) BY RACE ORIGIN CAMP(1,2)
 /PRINT=DEFAULT ESTIM
 /DESIGN=DPREF, DPREF BY RACE, DPREF BY ORIGIN, DPREF BY CAMP,
    DPREF BY ORIGIN BY CAMP.
```

- The **SET WIDTH** command uses a wide format to permit listing of all the statistics, including percentages.

- The **DATA LIST** command reads the data in freefield format.

- Variable *FREQ* is the actual cell count obtained from the published table. The **WEIGHT** command weights each case (which represents a cell) back to the sample size.

- The **COMPUTE** and **IF** statements transform the first three categories of *PREF* into a dichotomy.

- The LOGLINEAR command specifies one design. The DESIGN subcommand specifies the dependent variable, as well as interactions involving the dependent variable. Note that this design is not the saturated model. If you specify a logit model with the keyword BY and do not use a DESIGN subcommand, LOGLINEAR automatically includes all the effects and interactions of independent factors. See Haberman (1979) for more details.

- The PRINT subcommand displays the frequencies and residuals table as well as the estimates for the parameters.

- Figure 1 and Figure 2 contain portions of the display for this example.

Figure 1 shows the final model fit. The chi-square statistics show a good fit, and all of the adjusted residuals are less than 1.

Figure 1   Model fit for Example 1

```
Observed, Expected Frequencies and Residuals

       Factor          Code        OBS. count & PCT.    EXP. count & PCT.     Residual   Std. Resid.   Adj

    DPREF         NORTH
    RACE          BLACK
      ORIGIN        NORTH
        CAMP          NORTH        387.00 (91.49)       390.64 (92.35)        -3.6431     -.1843
        CAMP          SOUTH        876.00 (77.80)       879.35 (78.09)        -3.3479     -.1129
      ORIGIN        SOUTH
        CAMP          NORTH        383.00 (58.65)       376.80 (57.70)         6.2000      .3194
        CAMP          SOUTH        381.00 (18.20)       380.21 (18.17)          .7909      .0406
    RACE          WHITE
      ORIGIN        NORTH
        CAMP          NORTH        955.00 (85.50)       951.36 (85.17)         3.6431      .1181
        CAMP          SOUTH        874.00 (63.15)       870.65 (62.91)         3.3479      .1135
      ORIGIN        SOUTH
        CAMP          NORTH        104.00 (37.14)       110.20 (39.36)        -6.2000     -.5906
        CAMP          SOUTH         91.00 ( 9.47)        91.79 ( 9.55)         -.7909     -.0825

    DPREF         SOUTH
    RACE          BLACK
      ORIGIN        NORTH
        CAMP          NORTH         36.00 ( 8.51)        32.36 ( 7.65)         3.6431      .6405
        CAMP          SOUTH        250.00 (22.20)       246.65 (21.91)         3.3479      .2132
      ORIGIN        SOUTH
        CAMP          NORTH        270.00 (41.35)       276.20 (42.30)        -6.2000     -.3731
        CAMP          SOUTH       1712.00 (81.80)      1712.79 (81.83)         -.7909     -.0191
    RACE          WHITE
      ORIGIN        NORTH
        CAMP          NORTH        162.00 (14.50)       165.64 (14.83)        -3.6431     -.2831
        CAMP          SOUTH        510.00 (36.85)       513.35 (37.09)        -3.3479     -.1478
      ORIGIN        SOUTH
        CAMP          NORTH        176.00 (62.86)       169.80 (60.64)         6.2000      .4758
        CAMP          SOUTH        870.00 (90.53)       869.21 (90.45)          .7909      .0268


Goodness-of-Fit test statistics

    Likelihood Ratio Chi Square =    1.44756     DF = 3   P =   .694
              Pearson Chi Square =    1.45707     DF = 3   P =   .692
```

Figure 2 shows the parameter estimates for the final model. To obtain regression-like (log-odds) coefficients, multiply the estimates by 2 (see Haberman, 1978).

Figure 2   Parameter estimates for Example 1

```
Estimates for Parameters

  DPREF

    Parameter        Coeff.         Std. Err.       Z-Value      Lower 95 CI      Upper 95 CI

         1         .1352217166        .01518        8.90608        .10546           .16498

  DPREF BY RACE

    Parameter        Coeff.         Std. Err.       Z-Value      Lower 95 CI      Upper 95 CI

         2         .1857281674        .01557       11.93145        .15522           .21624

  DPREF BY ORIGIN

    Parameter        Coeff.         Std. Err.       Z-Value      Lower 95 CI      Upper 95 CI

         3         .6195921388        .01687       36.72886        .58653           .65266

  DPREF BY CAMP

    Parameter        Coeff.         Std. Err.       Z-Value      Lower 95 CI      Upper 95 CI

         4         .3794390119        .01534       24.73658        .34937           .40950

  DPREF BY ORIGIN BY CAMP

    Parameter        Coeff.         Std. Err.       Z-Value      Lower 95 CI      Upper 95 CI

         5        -.0744977447        .01521       -4.89942       -.10430          -.04470
```

Use these coefficients to obtain log-odds coefficients and then use their anti-log to translate the model into odds rather than log odds. Table 1 shows the model coefficients.

Table 1   Model coefficients

Effect	Coefficient	Log Odds	Antilog
DPREF	0.135	0.270	1.311
DPREF by RACE	0.186	0.371	1.450
DPREF by ORIGIN	0.620	1.239	3.452
DPREF by CAMP	0.379	0.759	2.136
DPREF by ORIGIN by CAMP	-0.074	-0.149	0.862

The regression-like model implied by the coefficients can be expressed as

$$ln \, (F_{ijk1}/F_{ijk2}) \; = \; B + B\,(A)_i + B\,(B)_j + B\,(C)_k + B\,(BC)_{jk}$$

where F is an expected frequency andand

B equals	0.270
$B(A)_i$ equals	0.371 for $i = 1$
	-0.371 for $i = 2$
$B(B)_j$ equals	1.239 for $j = 1$
	-1.239 for $j = 2$
$B(C)_k$ equals	0.759 for $k = 1$
	-0.759 for $k = 2$
$B(BC)_{jk}$ equals	-0.149 for $j = k$
	0.149 for $j \neq k$

To evaluate the model in terms of odds rather than log odds, you can use an analogous multiplicative model, with the antilogs shown in Table 1 as coefficients. That is,

$$(F_{ijk1}/F_{ijk2}) = T^* T(A)_i^* T(B)_j^* T(C)_k^* T(BC)_{jk}$$

where

T equals	1.311
$T(A)_i$ equals	1.450 for $i = 1$
	1/1.450 for $i = 2$
$T(B)_j$ equals	3.452 for $j = 1$
	1/3.452 for $j = 2$
$T(C)_k$ equals	2.136 for $k = 1$
	1/2.136 for $k = 2$
$T(BC)_{jk}$ equals	0.862 for $j = k$
	1/1.862 for $j \neq k$

For example, consider someone whose race is black, who is originally from the north, and who is presently located in a northern camp. For this individual, i=j=k=1 because of the coding of the variables indicated at the beginning of this example. This person's observed odds of preferring northern versus southern camp location is 10.75 (91.49/8.51) from Figure 1. The expected odds given the model are 12.072 (92.35/7.65) from Figure 1. The model decomposes these expected odds into components (see Table 1)

$$12.072 = (1.311)(1.450)(3.452)(2.136)(0.862)$$

where the effects are interpretable.

- 1.311 is the mean or overall effect.
- 1.450 is the race effect indicating the net effect of being black versus white on preference of camp location. Other things being equal, blacks prefer northern camp locations by 1.450 to 1.

- 3.452 is the net effect of region of origin on present preference. Other things being equal, a person originally from the north prefers a northern camp location by 3.452 to 1.
- 2.136 is the net effect of present location on camp preference. Other things being equal, a person presently located in the north states a northern preference over twice as often as a southern preference.
- 0.862 is the interaction effect between region of origin and present camp location. The effect is negative, which means that the effect of being a northerner in a northern camp is less positive than is indicated by combining the main effect of being a northerner with the main effect of being in a northern camp.

Example 2: A General Loglinear Model

The general loglinear model has all dependent variables. This example uses the same data analyzed as in the first example. The general loglinear model treats all variables as jointly dependent. The following LOGLINEAR command is used to request this model:

```
LOGLINEAR DPREF(2,3) RACE ORIGIN CAMP(1,2)
  /PRINT=DEFAULT ESTIM
  /DESIGN=DPREF, RACE, ORIGIN, CAMP,
    DPREF BY RACE, DPREF BY ORIGIN, DPREF BY CAMP,
    RACE BY CAMP, RACE BY ORIGIN, ORIGIN BY CAMP,
    RACE BY ORIGIN BY CAMP,
    DPREF BY ORIGIN BY CAMP.
```

The LOGLINEAR command for the general loglinear model does not use the keyword BY in the first line. In this model, the DESIGN subcommand uses all the variables as main effects or as part of an interaction term. Compare this with the logit model shown in the first example, which uses the dependent variable and interactions involving the dependent variable.

Figure 3 and Figure 4 are the display produced by this example. Figure 3 shows that expected frequencies are identical to the logit model in the first example (Figure 1). However, observed and expected cell percentages differ. In the logit model, cell percentages sum to 100 across categories of the dependent variable within each combination of independent variable values. In other words, cell percentages in the logit model are comparable to row or column percentages in crosstabulation. In the general model, they sum to 100 across all categories and are comparable to total percentages in a crosstabulation.

Figure 3   Loglinear model fit for Example 2

Observed, Expected Frequencies and Residuals

Factor	Code	OBS. count & PCT.	EXP. count & PCT.	Residual	Std. Resid.	Adj. Resid.
DPREF	NORTH					
RACE	BLACK					
ORIGIN	NORTH					
CAMP	NORTH	387.00 (4.82)	390.64 (4.86)	-3.6431	-.1843	-.7714
CAMP	SOUTH	876.00 (10.90)	879.35 (10.94)	-3.3479	-.1129	-.4178
ORIGIN	SOUTH					
CAMP	NORTH	383.00 (4.77)	376.80 (4.69)	6.2000	.3194	.9994
CAMP	SOUTH	381.00 (4.74)	380.21 (4.73)	.7909	.0406	.1131
RACE	WHITE					
ORIGIN	NORTH					
CAMP	NORTH	955.00 (11.88)	951.36 (11.84)	3.6431	.1181	.7714
CAMP	SOUTH	874.00 (10.87)	870.65 (10.83)	3.3479	.1135	.4178
ORIGIN	SOUTH					
CAMP	NORTH	104.00 (1.29)	110.20 (1.37)	-6.2000	-.5906	-.9994
CAMP	SOUTH	91.00 (1.13)	91.79 (1.14)	-.7909	-.0825	-.1131
DPREF	SOUTH					
RACE	BLACK					
ORIGIN	NORTH					
CAMP	NORTH	36.00 (.45)	32.36 (.40)	3.6431	.6405	.7714
CAMP	SOUTH	250.00 (3.11)	246.65 (3.07)	3.3479	.2132	.4178
ORIGIN	SOUTH					
CAMP	NORTH	270.00 (3.36)	276.20 (3.44)	-6.2000	-.3731	-.9994
CAMP	SOUTH	1712.00 (21.30)	1712.79 (21.31)	-.7909	-.0191	-.1131
RACE	WHITE					
ORIGIN	NORTH					
CAMP	NORTH	162.00 (2.02)	165.64 (2.06)	-3.6431	-.2831	-.7714
CAMP	SOUTH	510.00 (6.35)	513.35 (6.39)	-3.3479	-.1478	-.4178
ORIGIN	SOUTH					
CAMP	NORTH	176.00 (2.19)	169.80 (2.11)	6.2000	.4758	.9994
CAMP	SOUTH	870.00 (10.82)	869.21 (10.82)	.7909	.0268	.1131

Goodness-of-Fit test statistics

```
Likelihood Ratio Chi Square =   1.44756    DF = 3   P =  .694
          Pearson Chi Square =   1.45707    DF = 3   P =  .692
```

Figure 4   Parameter estimates for Example 2

Estimates for Parameters

DPREF

Parameter	Coeff.	Std. Err.	Z-Value	Lower 95 CI	Upper 95 CI
1	.1352217166	.01518	8.90608	.10546	.16498

RACE

Parameter	Coeff.	Std. Err.	Z-Value	Lower 95 CI	Upper 95 CI
2	.0355803941	.01363	2.61113	.00887	.06229

ORIGIN

Parameter	Coeff.	Std. Err.	Z-Value	Lower 95 CI	Upper 95 CI
3	.0403904261	.01614	2.50201	.00875	.07203

CAMP

Parameter	Coeff.	Std. Err.	Z-Value	Lower 95 CI	Upper 95 CI
4	-.4480592813	.01614	-27.76919	-.47968	-.41643

DPREF BY RACE

Parameter	Coeff.	Std. Err.	Z-Value	Lower 95 CI	Upper 95 CI
5	.1857281674	.01557	11.93145	.15522	.21624

DPREF BY ORIGIN

Parameter	Coeff.	Std. Err.	Z-Value	Lower 95 CI	Upper 95 CI
6	.6195921388	.01687	36.72886	.58653	.65266

DPREF BY CAMP

Parameter	Coeff.	Std. Err.	Z-Value	Lower 95 CI	Upper 95 CI
7	.3794390119	.01534	24.73658	.34937	.40950

RACE BY CAMP

Parameter	Coeff.	Std. Err.	Z-Value	Lower 95 CI	Upper 95 CI
8	-.1364780340	.01413	-9.65595	-.16418	-.10878

RACE BY ORIGIN

Parameter	Coeff.	Std. Err.	Z-Value	Lower 95 CI	Upper 95 CI
9	-.4413477997	.01591	-27.73754	-.47253	-.41016

ORIGIN BY CAMP

Parameter	Coeff.	Std. Err.	Z-Value	Lower 95 CI	Upper 95 CI
10	-.0375668525	.01632	-2.30190	-.06955	-.00558

RACE BY ORIGIN BY CAMP

Parameter	Coeff.	Std. Err.	Z-Value	Lower 95 CI	Upper 95 CI
11	-.0885302170	.01359	-6.51497	-.11516	-.06190

DPREF BY ORIGIN BY CAMP

Parameter	Coeff.	Std. Err.	Z-Value	Lower 95 CI	Upper 95 CI
12	-.0744977447	.01521	-4.89942	-.10430	-.04470

Compare Figure 4 with Figure 2 in the first example. Note that identical results are produced for effects in common in the two models.

Example 3: A Multinomial Logit Model

The first two examples analyze Stouffer's data with "preference for location" transformed into a dichotomy. Example 3 uses the original five-category preference variable to demonstrate the multinomial logit model. This example uses orthogonal special contrasts to make desired comparisons among the categories of the dependent variable. The **LOGLINEAR** command is as follows:

```
LOGLINEAR PREF(1,5) BY RACE ORIGIN CAMP(1,2)
  /PRINT=DEFAULT ESTIM
  /CONTRAST(PREF)=SPECIAL(5*1,1 1 1 1 -4,3 -1 -1 -1 0,
    0 1 1 -2 0,0 1 -1 0 0)
  /DESIGN=PREF, PREF BY RACE, PREF BY ORIGIN, PREF BY CAMP,
    PREF BY RACE BY ORIGIN, PREF BY RACE BY CAMP,
    PREF BY ORIGIN BY CAMP, PREF BY RACE BY ORIGIN BY CAMP.
```

Figure 5 is the display of the parameter estimates for Example 3. This example fits the saturated model. If no **DESIGN** subcommand had been specified, the saturated model would have also included effects that are redundant when a logit model is specified. Parameter estimates for a multinomial model can be more interpretable when you specify special contrasts as in this example. The **CONTRAST** subcommand contrasts the movers and stayers versus the undecided, the movers versus the stayers, the decided versus the undecided, and northern versus southern camps.

Figure 5 Parameter estimates for Example 3

```
Estimates for Parameters

PREF
```

Parameter	Coeff.	Std. Err.	Z-Value	Lower 95 CI	Upper 95 CI
1	.1234825883	.00807	15.29520	.10766	.13931
2	.0724662120	.00826	8.77654	.05628	.08865
3	.2043174993	.01408	14.51506	.17673	.23191
4	.1282571558	.02068	6.20092	.08772	.16880

PREF BY RACE

Parameter	Coeff.	Std. Err.	Z-Value	Lower 95 CI	Upper 95 CI
5	-.0051416644	.00807	-.63687	-.02097	.01068
6	-.0063669961	.00826	-.77112	-.02255	.00982
7	.0062485789	.01408	.44391	-.02134	.03384
8	.0960361288	.02068	4.64311	.05550	.13658

PREF BY ORIGIN

Parameter	Coeff.	Std. Err.	Z-Value	Lower 95 CI	Upper 95 CI
9	-.0021584482	.00807	-.26736	-.01798	.01367
10	-.0586990400	.00826	-7.10917	-.07488	-.04252
11	-.0025353715	.01408	-.18012	-.03012	.02505
12	.6555140380	.02068	31.69248	.61497	.69605

PREF BY CAMP

Parameter	Coeff.	Std. Err.	Z-Value	Lower 95 CI	Upper 95 CI
13	-.0191848042	.00807	-2.37633	-.03501	-.00336
14	.0320805342	.00826	3.88534	.01590	.04826
15	.0038808442	.01408	.27570	-.02371	.03147
16	-.0156364228	.02068	-.75598	-.05618	.02490

PREF BY RACE BY ORIGIN

Parameter	Coeff.	Std. Err.	Z-Value	Lower 95 CI	Upper 95 CI
17	-.0033156723	.00807	-.41070	-.01914	.01251
18	-.0237329647	.00826	-2.87435	-.03992	-.00755
19	.0611636379	.01408	4.34517	.03357	.08875
20	-.0516750973	.02068	-2.49836	-.09221	-.01114

PREF BY RACE BY CAMP

Parameter	Coeff.	Std. Err.	Z-Value	Lower 95 CI	Upper 95 CI
21	.0030208725	.00807	.37418	-.01280	.01884
22	.1027873616	.00826	12.44880	.08660	.11897
23	-.0189810333	.01408	-1.34845	-.04657	.00861
24	.0076967580	.02068	.37212	-.03284	.04824

PREF BY ORIGIN BY CAMP

Parameter	Coeff.	Std. Err.	Z-Value	Lower 95 CI	Upper 95 CI
25	.0049220965	.00807	.60968	-.01090	.02075
26	.1316990028	.00826	15.95036	.11552	.14788
27	-.0090552616	.01408	-.64330	-.03664	.01853
28	-.0320161528	.02068	-1.54790	-.07256	.00852

PREF BY RACE BY ORIGIN BY CAMP

Parameter	Coeff.	Std. Err.	Z-Value	Lower 95 CI	Upper 95 CI
29	-.0008598058	.00807	-.10650	-.01668	.01496
30	.0217737066	.00826	2.63706	.00559	.03796
31	-.0115700249	.01408	-.82195	-.03916	.01602
32	.0406113662	.02068	1.96346	.00007	.08115

MANOVA

You can test different models with MANOVA. The following examples demonstrate some of the more commonly used MANOVA models.

Example 1: Analysis of Covariance Designs

This example shows how to use MANOVA for analysis of variance and covariance. The example comes from Winer et al. (1991).

The variables are:

- *A*—a factor that represents three methods of training.

- *X*—a covariate that is a score on an aptitude test.

- *Y*—a dependent variable that contains the scores on an achievement test on material covered in the training course. The test is given to the subjects after the training is complete.

The data are in an external file named *AMAN.DAT*. The SPSS/PC+ commands are as follows:

```
SET WIDTH=WIDE.
DATA LIST FILE='AMAN.DAT' / A 1 X Y 2-5.
MANOVA Y BY A(1,3)
  /PRINT=PARAM(ESTIM)
  /DESIGN.
MANOVA Y BY A(1,3) WITH X
  /PMEANS=VARIABLES(Y)
  /PRINT=PARAM(ESTIM)
  /DESIGN
  /ANALYSIS=Y
  /METHOD=SEQUENTIAL
  /DESIGN=X, A, A BY X
  /DESIGN=X WITHIN A, A.
```

- The SET command sets the display width to 132 characters to permit listing of all the statistics, including percentages.

- The DATA LIST command reads variables *A*, *X*, and *Y* from the data included in the file *AMAN.DAT*.

- The first MANOVA command specifies the first analysis—a one-way analysis of variance—using the default DESIGN subcommand. The PRINT subcommand requests that parameter estimates be included in the display.

- The second MANOVA command specifies the second through fourth analyses. The second is an analysis of covariance using the default DESIGN subcommand. The default analysis fits covariate *X* and factor *A* and assumes homogeneous slopes.

- The PMEANS subcommand displays predicted means for the second through fourth models. The PRINT subcommand requests that parameter estimates be included in the display.
- The third analysis tests the assumption of homogeneous slopes. If the A by X interaction is significant, you must reject the hypothesis of parallel slopes. The ANALYSIS subcommand specifies the dependent variable. The METHOD subcommand asks for sequential sums of squares. The DESIGN subcommand specifies effects, including the factor-by-covariate interaction.
- The fourth analysis fits separate regression coefficients in each group of the factor. As in the third analysis, the ANALYSIS subcommand specifies the dependent variable for the analysis. The WITHIN keyword on the DESIGN subcommand fits separate regression models within each of the three groups of factor A.

Portions of the display output are shown in Figure 1 through Figure 5. The exact appearance of printed display depends on the characters available on your printer.

- Figure 1 shows the display for the first analysis, including an analysis-of-variance table.
- Figure 2 shows the display for the second analysis, which includes the covariate X. MANOVA displays the analysis-of-variance table and regression statistics associated with X.
- Figure 3 shows the table of predicted means for the second analysis requested with the PMEANS subcommand. MANOVA displays the observed means, the adjusted means (which are adjusted for the covariate), and the estimated means (which are the cell means estimated with knowledge of A, not adjusted for the covariate).
- Figure 4 shows the analysis-of-variance table for the third analysis. Since the A by X interaction is not significant, the hypothesis of parallel slopes is not rejected. That is, we can assume that the effect of change in X on Y is the same across levels of A.
- Figure 5 shows the analysis-of-variance table for the fourth analysis. The X within A effect is the joint effect of the separate regressions. Since the third analysis shows the factor-by-covariate interaction is not significant, the second analysis (not the fourth) is the preferred solution.

Figure 1   Results for first analysis

```
Tests of Significance for Y using UNIQUE sums of squares
Source of Variation        SS       DF       MS        F  Sig of F

WITHIN CELLS             26.86      18      1.49
A                        36.95       2     18.48     12.38     .000

(Model)                  36.95       2     18.48     12.38     .000
(Total)                  63.81      20      3.19

R-Squared =          .579
Adjusted R-Squared = .532
```

- -

```
Estimates for Y
--- Individual univariate .9500 confidence intervals

A
```

Parameter	Coeff.	Std. Err.	t-Value	Sig. t	Lower -95%	CL- Upper
2	-1.8095238095	.37696	-4.80027	.00014	-2.60149	-1.01755
3	1.3333333333	.37696	3.53704	.00235	.54136	2.12530

Figure 2   Results for second analysis

```
Tests of Significance for Y using UNIQUE sums of squares
Source of Variation        SS       DF       MS        F  Sig of F

WITHIN CELLS             10.30      17       .61
REGRESSION               16.56       1     16.56     27.32     .000
A                        16.93       2      8.47     13.97     .000

(Model)                  53.51       3     17.84     29.43     .000
(Total)                  63.81      20      3.19

R-Squared =          .839
Adjusted R-Squared = .810
```

- -

```
Estimates for Y adjusted for 1 covariate
--- Individual univariate .9500 confidence intervals

A
```

Parameter	Coeff.	Std. Err.	t-Value	Sig. t	Lower -95%	CL- Upper
2	-1.3496598639	.25584	-5.27535	.00006	-1.88944	-.80988
3	.8380952381	.25825	3.24530	.00476	.29324	1.38295

- -

```
Regression analysis for WITHIN CELLS error term
--- Individual Univariate .9500 confidence intervals
Dependent variable .. Y
```

COVARIATE	B	Beta	Std. Err.	t-Value	Sig. of t	Lower -95%	CL- Upper
X	.7428571429	.5564957151	.14213	5.22671	.000	.44300	1.04272

Figure 3   Adjusted means for second analysis

```
Adjusted and Estimated Means
Variable .. Y
```

Factor	Code	Obs. Mean	Adj. Mean	Est. Mean	Raw Resid.	Std. Resid.
A	1	4.42857	4.88844	4.42857	.00000	.00000
A	2	7.57143	7.07619	7.57143	.00000	.00000
A	3	6.71429	6.74966	6.71429	.00000	.00000

Figure 4   Results for third analysis

```
Tests of Significance for Y using SEQUENTIAL Sums of Squares
Source of Variation        SS       DF       MS         F  Sig of F

WITHIN+RESIDUAL           9.63      15      .64
X                        36.58       1    36.58      56.94    .000
A                        16.93       2     8.47      13.18    .000
A BY X                     .67       2      .33        .52    .605

(Model)                  54.17       5    10.83      16.87    .000
(Total)                  63.81      20     3.19

R-Squared =             .849
Adjusted R-Squared =    .799
```

Figure 5   Results for fourth analysis

```
Tests of Significance for Y using SEQUENTIAL Sums of Squares
Source of Variation        SS       DF       MS         F  Sig of F

WITHIN+RESIDUAL           9.63      15      .64
X WITHIN A               47.48       3    15.83      24.64    .000
A                         6.69       2     3.35       5.21    .019

(Model)                  54.17       5    10.83      16.87    .000
(Total)                  63.81      20     3.19

R-Squared =             .849
Adjusted R-Squared =    .799
```

Example 2: Multivariate Multiple Regression and Canonical Correlation

MANOVA produces multivariate results, individual regression results, and analysis of residuals, although residual analysis is not as extensive as in REGRESSION. Since there is no canonical correlation procedure in SPSS/PC+, MANOVA can be used for canonical correlation analysis.

This example uses MANOVA for multivariate multiple regression and canonical correlation analysis. The data for this example come from Finn (1974) and were obtained from tests administered to 60 11th-grade students in a western New York metropolitan school.

The dependent variables are:

- *SYNTH*—a measurement of achievement.
- *EVAL*—another measurement of achievement.

There are three types of independent variables. The first is:

- *INTEL*—general intelligence as measured by a standard test.

The second type consists of three measures of creativity:

- *CONOBV*—consequences obvious, which involves the ability of the subject to list direct consequences of a given hypothetical event.

- *CONRMT*—consequences remote, which involves identifying more remote or original consequences of similar situations.
- *JOB*—possible jobs, which involves the ability to list a quantity of occupations that might be represented by a given emblem or symbol.

The third type of independent variable is a set of multiplicative interactions of the three creativity measures with intelligence to assess whether creativity has a greater effect on the achievement of individuals having high intelligence than on individuals of low intelligence. These variables are created using the SPSS/PC+ transformation language. For all independent variables, standardized scores are used. The data are in an external file named *AMAN.DAT*. The SPSS/PC+ commands are as follows:

```
SET WIDTH=WIDE.
DATA LIST FILE='AMAN.DAT' /
   SYNTH 1 EVAL 3 CONOBV 5-8(1) CONRMT 9-12(1)
   JOB 14-17(1) INTEL 19-23(1).
MISSING VALUE SYNTH TO INTEL(9.9).
DESCRIPTIVES INTEL CONOBV CONRMT JOB
  /OPTIONS=3 5.
COMPUTE CI1=ZCONOBV*ZINTEL.
COMPUTE CI2=ZCONRMT*ZINTEL.
COMPUTE CI3=ZJOB*ZINTEL.
MANOVA SYNTH EVAL WITH ZINTEL ZCONOBV ZCONRMT ZJOB CI1 CI2 CI3
  /PRINT=ERROR(SSCP COV COR)
        SIGNIF(HYPOTH STEPDOWN DIMENR EIGEN)
  /DISCRIM=RAW,STAN,ESTIM,COR,ALPHA(1.0)
  /RESIDUALS=CASEWISE PLOT
  /DESIGN.
```

- The SET command sets the display width to 132 characters to permit listing of all statistics, including percentages.
- The DATA LIST command names the file containing the data and defines six variables.
- The MISSING VALUE command declares the value 9.9 as user-missing for all the variables read from the data file.
- Option 3 on DESCRIPTIVES computes standardized scores for the intelligence and creativity measures. The new variables—*ZINTEL, ZCONOBV, ZCONRMT,* and *ZJOB*—are automatically added to the active file. Option 5 on DESCRIPTIVES specifies listwise deletion of missing values for the calculation.
- The COMPUTE commands compute three interaction variables—*CI1, CI2,* and *CI3*— from the standardized variables created with DESCRIPTIVES.
- The MANOVA specification names *SYNTH* and *EVAL* as joint dependent variables and specifies seven covariates—*ZINTEL, ZCONOBV, ZCONRMT, ZJOB, CI1, CI2,* and *CI3*.
- The PRINT subcommand requests several displays. The ERROR keyword prints the error sums-of-squares and cross-products (SSCP) matrix, the error variance-covariance matrix, and the error correlation matrix with standard deviations on the diagonal (Figure 6).

- The SIGNIF keyword has four specifications. HYPOTH prints the hypothesis SSCP matrix (Figure 6). STEPDOWN prints the Roy-Bargmann stepdown F tests for the dependent variables. DIMENR prints the dimension reduction analysis, and EIGEN prints the eigenvalues and canonical correlations (Figure 7).

- The DISCRIM subcommand requests a canonical analysis. The results correspond to canonical correlation analysis, since a set of continuous dependent variables is related to a set of continuous independent variables. The RAW keyword prints canonical function coefficients; the STAN keyword prints standardized canonical function coefficients; the ESTIM keyword produces effect estimates in canonical function space; the COR keyword prints correlations between the original variables and the canonical variables defined by the canonical functions; and the ALPHA keyword sets a cutoff value of 1.0 for the significance of the canonical functions in the analysis, thereby ensuring that MANOVA calculates all possible canonical functions. Two is the maximum possible in this analysis (Figure 8 and Figure 9).

- The RESIDUALS subcommand with keyword CASEWISE prints four casewise results for each dependent variable: the observed value of the dependent variable, the predicted value of the dependent variable, the residual value, and the standardized residual, where standardization consists of dividing the residual by the error standard deviation (Figure 11).

- The PLOT keyword on the RESIDUALS subcommand produces plots of the observed values, predicted values, and case number against standardized residuals, as well as normal and detrended normal probability plots for the standardized residuals (Figure 12 through Figure 14).

- The DESIGN subcommand specifies the model, which, in this example, is the default full factorial model.

Portions of the output are shown in Figure 6 through Figure 14. The exact appearance of printed display depends on the characters available on your printer.

- Figure 6 shows within-cells statistical results. The correlation of 0.37978 is the partial correlation of *SYNTH* and *EVAL*, taking into account the independent variable set. The two standard deviations are adjusted. The Bartlett test of sphericity leads to rejection of the hypothesis that the partial correlation between *SYNTH* and *EVAL* is zero. Figure 6 also shows the adjusted variance-covariance matrix, the error SSCP matrix, and the hypothesis SSCP matrix for the regression effect.

- Figure 7 shows the default display and the stepdown display. Both the multivariate and univariate test results indicate that the predictor set has a statistically significant impact on the dependent variables. While two dimensions are fit, it appears that one dimension will suffice. Of the two eigenvalues, the first eigenvalue has most of the variance associated with it, while the second eigenvalue has relatively little variability associated with it. Likewise, the first canonical correlation is moderately sized, while the second canonical correlation is negligible in magnitude. Provided that you accept the order of the criterion variables—*SYNTH*, then *EVAL*—the stepdown F

tests show that after taking *SYNTH* into account, *EVAL* does not contribute to the association with the predictors.

- Figure 8 shows canonical results for the two dependent variables. Recall that only the first canonical function is statistically significant. Correlations between the dependent variables and the first canonical variable are of similar magnitude. The part of the figure labeled *Variance explained by canonical variables of DEPENDENT variables* provides a redundancy analysis (Cooley & Lohnes, 1971).

- Figure 9 shows the analogous canonical results for the covariates. The correlations between covariates and the first canonical variable load most heavily on intelligence.

- Figure 10 shows the default display of the regression results for the two dependent variables.

- Figure 11 shows a portion of the casewise results for the synthesis variable produced by `RESIDUALS=CASEWISE`.

- Figure 12 shows two plots. The plot of observed versus predicted values for *SYNTH* reflects the multiple R for the model. The plot of observed values versus residuals shows how residuals vary in sign and magnitude across values of the dependent variable.

- Figure 13 shows two plots: the plot of predicted values versus residuals, and the plot of case number versus residuals. The latter plot is useful when there is some meaning to the order of cases in your file.

- Figure 14 shows the normal and detrended normal plots of the residuals.

Figure 6 Within-cells results and hypothesis SSCP

```
Adjusted WITHIN CELLS Correlations with Std. Devs. on Diagonal

                    SYNTH              EVAL

SYNTH               1.37049
EVAL                 .37978            1.51256

- - - - - - - - - - - - - - - - - - - - - - - - - - - - - - - - - - - - - - -

Statistics for ADJUSTED WITHIN CELLS correlations

Log(Determinant) =                  -.15575
Bartlett test of sphericity =      7.86554 with 1 D. F.
Significance =                       .005

F(max) criterion =                 1.21806 with (2,52) D. F.

- - - - - - - - - - - - - - - - - - - - - - - - - - - - - - - - - - - - - - -

Adjusted WITHIN CELLS Variances and Covariances

                    SYNTH              EVAL

SYNTH               1.87825
EVAL                 .78726            2.28783

- - - - - - - - - - - - - - - - - - - - - - - - - - - - - - - - - - - - - - -

Adjusted WITHIN CELLS Sum-of-Squares and Cross-Products

                    SYNTH              EVAL

SYNTH               97.66914
EVAL                40.93736          118.96726

- - - - - - - - - - - - - - - - - - - - - - - - - - - - - - - - - - - - - - -

Adjusted Hypothesis Sum-of-Squares and Cross-Products

                    SYNTH              EVAL

SYNTH               81.18086
EVAL                69.41264          67.21607
```

Figure 7   Test results and dimensionality statistics

Multivariate Tests of Significance (S = 2, M = 2 , N = 24 1/2)

Test Name	Value	Approx. F	Hypoth. DF	Error DF	Sig. of F
Pillais	.55946	2.88501	14.00	104.00	.001
Hotellings	1.05995	3.78553	14.00	100.00	.000
Wilks	.47077	3.33286	14.00	102.00	.000
Roys	.49886				

Note.. F statistic for WILKS' Lambda is exact.

- -

Eigenvalues and Canonical Correlations

Root No.	Eigenvalue	Pct.	Cum. Pct.	Canon Cor.	Sq. Cor
1	.99544	93.91374	93.91374	.70630	.49886
2	.06451	6.08626	100.00000	.24617	.06060

- -

Dimension Reduction Analysis

Roots	Wilks L.	F	Hypoth. DF	Error DF	Sig. of F
1 TO 2	.47077	3.33286	14.00	102.00	.000
2 TO 2	.93940	.55910	6.00	52.00	.761

- -

Univariate F-tests with (7,52) D. F.

Variable	Sq. Mul. R	Adj. R-sq.	Hypoth. MS	Error MS	F	Sig. of F
SYNTH	.45390	.38039	11.59727	1.87825	6.17450	.000
EVAL	.36102	.27500	9.60230	2.28783	4.19712	.001

- -

Roy-Bargmann Stepdown F - tests

Variable	Hypoth. MS	Error MS	StepDown F	Hypoth. DF	Error DF	Sig. of F
SYNTH	11.59727	1.87825	6.17450	7	52	.000
EVAL	2.32700	1.99625	1.16569	7	51	.339

Figure 8   Canonical results for dependent variables

```
Raw canonical coefficients for DEPENDENT variables
         Function No.

Variable                    1                    2

SYNTH                  .40444              -.59708
EVAL                   .22637               .66958

- - - - - - - - - - - - - - - - - - - - - - - - - - - - - - - - - - - - - -
Standardized canonical coefficients for DEPENDENT variables
         Function No.

Variable                    1                    2

SYNTH                  .70415             -1.03956
EVAL                   .40212              1.18946

- - - - - - - - - - - - - - - - - - - - - - - - - - - - - - - - - - - - - -
Correlations between DEPENDENT and canonical variables
         Function No.

Variable                    1                    2

SYNTH                  .94733              -.32027
EVAL                   .82794               .56081

- - - - - - - - - - - - - - - - - - - - - - - - - - - - - - - - - - - - - -
Variance explained by canonical variables of DEPENDENT variables

CAN. VAR.     Pct Var DEP     Cum Pct DEP     Pct Var COV     Cum Pct COV

     1           79.14597        79.14597        39.48249        39.48249
     2           20.85403       100.00000         1.26379        40.74628
```

Figure 9   Canonical results for the covariates

```
Raw canonical coefficients for COVARIATES
          Function No.

COVARIATE                    1                    2

ZINTEL                   .83827              -.13386
ZCONOBV                  .27415               .20994
ZCONRMT                  .19305               .47584
ZJOB                    -.07040              -.28276
CI1                     -.01401              1.06075
CI2                     -.07448              -.31847
CI3                      .20912              -.04711

- - - - - - - - - - - - - - - - - - - - - - - - - - - - - - - - - - -
Standardized canonical coefficients for COVARIATES
          CAN. VAR.

COVARIATE                    1                    2

ZINTEL                   .84396              -.13477
ZCONOBV                  .26569               .20347
ZCONRMT                  .19492               .48044
ZJOB                    -.06924              -.27810
CI1                     -.01177               .89105
CI2                     -.10225              -.43718
CI3                      .22014              -.04959

- - - - - - - - - - - - - - - - - - - - - - - - - - - - - - - - - - -
Correlations between COVARIATES and canonical variables
          CAN. VAR.

Covariate                    1                    2

ZINTEL                   .94646              -.09081
ZCONOBV                  .30260              -.06104
ZCONRMT                  .56188               .41804
ZJOB                     .57787              -.12674
CI1                      .22800               .85903
CI2                      .50900              -.00331
CI3                      .48168               .05619

- - - - - - - - - - - - - - - - - - - - - - - - - - - - - - - - - - -

Variance explained by canonical variables of the COVARIATES

CAN. VAR.    Pct Var DEP    Cum Pct DEP    Pct Var COV    Cum Pct COV

        1       15.53646       15.53646       31.14413       31.14413
        2         .81716       16.35362       13.48411       44.62824
```

Figure 10 Regression results

```
Regression analysis for WITHIN CELLS error term
--- Individual Univariate .9500 confidence intervals
Dependent variable .. SYNTH
```

COVARIATE	B	Beta	Std. Err.	t-Value	Sig. of t	Lower -95%	CL- Upper
ZINTEL	.9949136811	.5753166206	.21596	4.60696	.000	.56156	1.42827
ZCONOBV	.2905476453	.1617334120	.24316	1.19489	.238	-.19739	.77848
ZCONRMT	.1595804511	.0925413807	.23732	.67243	.504	-.31664	.63580
ZJOB	-.0431951386	-.0244002039	.27235	-.15860	.875	-.58970	.50331
CI1	-.1619248053	-.0781239341	.24173	-.66986	.506	-.64699	.32314
CI2	-.0430503230	-.0339435542	.21123	-.20380	.839	-.46692	.38082
CI3	.2500858250	.1512029091	.25475	.98169	.331	-.26111	.76128

```
Dependent variable .. EVAL
```

COVARIATE	B	Beta	Std. Err.	t-Value	Sig. of t	Lower -95%	CL- Upper
ZINTEL	.8379644061	.4749207675	.23835	3.51576	.001	.35969	1.31624
ZCONOBV	.3362698558	.1834612710	.26836	1.25303	.216	-.20224	.87478
ZCONRMT	.3172443564	.1803118473	.26192	1.21123	.231	-.20834	.84283
ZJOB	-.1424753726	-.0788810088	.30058	-.47400	.637	-.74563	.46068
CI1	.2455945571	.1161351087	.26679	.92057	.362	-.28975	.78094
CI2	-.1554740028	-.1201469506	.23313	-.66690	.508	-.62328	.31233
CI3	.2056840543	.1218837384	.28116	.73156	.468	-.35850	.76987

Figure 11 Casewise output

```
Observed and Predicted Values for Each Case
Dependent Variable.. SYNTH
```

Case No.	Observed	Predicted	Raw Resid.	Std Resid.
1	5.00000	2.82408	2.17592	1.58769
2	.00000	1.90538	-1.90538	-1.39029
4	4.00000	3.64830	.35170	.25662
5	1.00000	2.03041	-1.03041	-.75185
6	7.00000	4.20982	2.79018	2.03590
7	1.00000	1.95046	-.95046	-.69352
8	2.00000	2.03649	-.03649	-.02662
9	1.00000	1.76344	-.76344	-.55705
10	4.00000	3.86086	.13914	.10153
11	2.00000	2.01118	-.01118	-.00815
12	4.00000	3.81837	.18163	.13253
13	3.00000	2.88892	.11108	.08105
14	5.00000	5.17533	-.17533	-.12793
15	5.00000	4.41982	.58018	.42333
16	1.00000	1.56020	-.56020	-.40876
17	5.00000	4.65686	.34314	.25037
18	2.00000	2.58151	-.58151	-.42431
19	3.00000	1.20702	1.79298	1.30827

Figure 12 Observed values versus predicted values and residuals

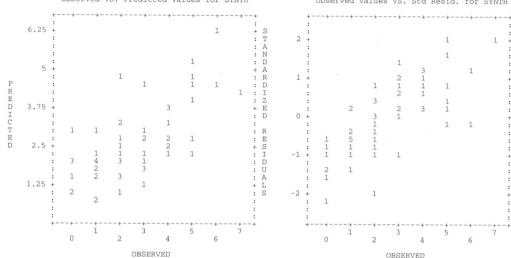

Figure 13 Residuals versus predicted values and case number

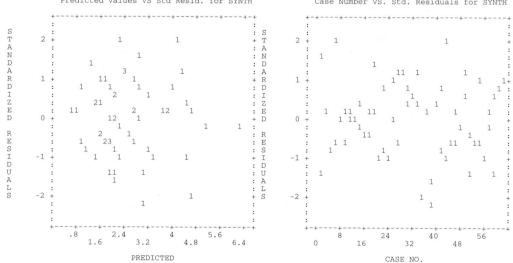

Figure 14 Normal and detrended normal probability plots

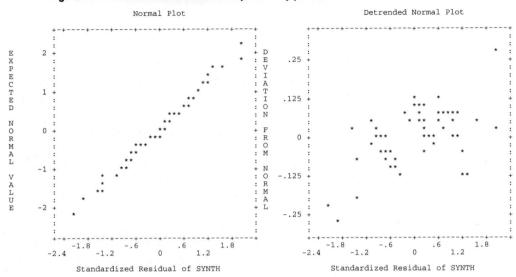

Example 3: Repeated Measures

This example is a repeated measures design using data from an experiment that studies the effects of four drugs on reaction time to a series of tasks (Winer et al., 1991). The subjects are trained in the tasks prior to the experiment so that the learning of the tasks does not confound the analysis. The experimenter observes each subject under each drug, and the order of administration of drugs is randomized. Since there are only five subjects in the analysis, the data are included inline. The SPSS/PC+ commands are as follows:

```
SET WIDTH=WIDE.
DATA LIST FREE/ DRUG1 DRUG2 DRUG3 DRUG4.
BEGIN DATA.
 30 28 16 34
 14 18 10 22
 24 20 18 30
 38 34 20 44
 26 28 14 30
END DATA.
MANOVA DRUG1 TO DRUG4
  /WSFACTORS=TRIAL(4)
  /CONTRAST(TRIAL)=SPECIAL(4*1, 1,-1,0,0,
                          1,1,0,-2, 1,1,-3,1)
  /PRINT=CELLINFO(MEANS)
         TRANSFORM
         SIGNIF(UNIV)
  /DESIGN.
```

- The SET command sets the width of the display to 132 characters to permit listing of all statistics, including percentages.
- The DATA LIST command defines four variables that will be read in freefield format from the inline data.
- The BEGIN DATA—END DATA commands surround the inline data.
- The MANOVA specification names *DRUG1* through *DRUG4* as four joint dependent variables. There are no between-subjects factors or covariates in the analysis.
- The WSFACTORS subcommand defines *TRIAL* as a within-subjects factor. The 4 in parentheses after the factor name indicates there are four drugs.
- The CONTRAST subcommand specifies a special set of contrasts for comparisons of the means across scores. The within-subjects factor requires orthogonal contrasts, which include difference, Helmert, and polynomial contrasts. If you do not specify orthogonal contrasts for the within-subjects factor, MANOVA takes your specified contrasts and orthonormalizes them.
- The first row of the special matrix is always the contrast for the overall mean and is typically a set of 1's. The remaining rows of the matrix contain the special contrasts signifying the desired comparisons between levels of the factor. The following comparisons are specified: (1) the mean of *DRUG1* versus the mean of *DRUG2*; (2) the means of *DRUG1* and *DRUG2* versus the mean of *DRUG4*; and (3) the means of *DRUG1*, *DRUG2*, and *DRUG4* versus the mean of *DRUG3*.
- The PRINT subcommand has three specifications. CELLINFO prints the means (Figure 15). TRANSFORM prints the orthonormalized transformation matrix, which directly reflects the contrasts on the within-subjects factor (Figure 16). SIGNIF(UNIV) prints the univariate *F* tests (Figure 21).
- The DESIGN subcommand specifies the model for the between-subjects factor. Since there is no between-subjects factor in this model, the DESIGN subcommand simply triggers the analysis.

Portions of the display output are shown in Figure 15 through Figure 22.

- Figure 15 shows the cell means and standard deviations. Inspection of the cell means provides a rationale for the special contrast used in the analysis. Notice that the means for *DRUG1* and *DRUG2* have the smallest difference. Then, the mean for *DRUG4* has a smaller difference from these two than does the mean for *DRUG3*. Finally, the mean for *DRUG3* is most different from the others. Note: If the width is not set wide (132 characters), the confidence intervals are not included in the display.
- Figure 16 shows the within-subjects design. The orthonormalized transformation matrix shows the contrasts on the means. The original contrasts on the CONTRAST subcommand are orthogonal. MANOVA normalizes the contrasts so that the sum of squares of any column of the matrix is 1.

- Figure 17 shows the beginning of the default display for multivariate repeated measures analysis. A message is displayed indicating that the variables are transformed.
- Figure 18 shows the test of significance for the between-subjects effect, which, in this example, is just the overall constant.
- Figure 19 shows the next cycle of the analysis, which is the test for the trial within-subjects effect. MANOVA jointly tests the three transformed variables, making this a multivariate test.
- Figure 20 shows Mauchly's test of sphericity, which is printed by default. This tests the hypothesis that the covariance matrix of the transformed variables has a constant variance on the diagonal and zeros off the diagonal.
- Figure 21 shows the multivariate tests of significance of the trial within-subjects effect. The multivariate tests are significant at the 0.05 level. The univariate F tests, the result of specifying SIGNIF(UNIV), reveal more detailed aspects of the pattern. Recall that the *T2* effect after transformation—the contrast between the means of *DRUG1* and *DRUG2*—is the first contrast of interest. The F statistic for this effect is not significant, which leads to the conclusion that these two drugs do not produce differences in reaction time. On the other hand, the transformed *T3* and *T4* effects are significant at the 0.01 level.
- Figure 22 shows the averaged test of significance for the drug effect; these are the univariate approach statistics. There are twelve error degrees of freedom for this test, while there are two error degrees of freedom for the multivariate tests. Given the error correlation results above, the averaged test is appropriate. The observed level of significance of this test is less than 0.0005, so the averaged F test corroborates the multivariate test results.

Figure 15 Cell means and standard deviations

```
Cell Means and Standard Deviations
  Variable .. DRUG1
                                   Mean   Std. Dev.        N    95 percent Conf. Interval

  For entire sample               26.400     8.764         5      15.519      37.281

  - - - - - - - - - -
  Variable .. DRUG2
                                   Mean   Std. Dev.        N    95 percent Conf. Interval

  For entire sample               25.600     6.542         5      17.477      33.723

  - - - - - - - - - -
  Variable .. DRUG3
                                   Mean   Std. Dev.        N    95 percent Conf. Interval

  For entire sample               15.600     3.847         5      10.823      20.377

  - - - - - - - - - -
  Variable .. DRUG4
                                   Mean   Std. Dev.        N    95 percent Conf. Interval

  For entire sample               32.000     8.000         5      22.067      41.933
```

Figure 16 Within-subjects design

```
Orthonormalized Transformation Matrix (Transposed)

                         T1              T2              T3              T4
DRUG1                .50000          .70711          .40825          .28868
DRUG2                .50000         -.70711          .40825          .28868
DRUG3                .50000          .00000          .00000         -.86603
DRUG4                .50000          .00000         -.81650          .28868
```

Figure 17 Constant within-subjects effect

```
Order of Variables for Analysis

  Variates      Covariates

  T1

  1 Dependent Variable
  0 Covariates

- - - - - - - - - -
Note..  TRANSFORMED variables are in the variates column.
        These TRANSFORMED variables correspond to the
        Between-subject effects.
```

Figure 18 Analysis of variance for CONSTANT

```
Tests of Between-Subjects Effects.

Tests of Significance for T1 using UNIQUE sums of squares
Source of Variation          SS       DF        MS          F  Sig of F

WITHIN CELLS             680.80        4    170.20
CONSTANT               12400.20        1  12400.20      72.86      .001
```

Figure 19 Trial within-subjects effect

```
Order of Variables for Analysis

  Variates      Covariates

  T2
  T3
  T4

  3 Dependent Variables
  0 Covariates

- - - - - - - - - -
Note..  TRANSFORMED variables are in the variates column.
        These TRANSFORMED variables correspond to the
        'TRIAL' WITHIN-SUBJECT effect.
```

Figure 20 Error correlation statistics

```
Tests involving 'TRIAL' Within-Subject Effect.


Mauchly sphericity test, W =        .18650
Chi-square approx. =                4.57156 with 5 D. F.
Significance =                      .470

Greenhouse-Geisser Epsilon =        .60487
Huynh-Feldt Epsilon =               1.00000
Lower-bound Epsilon =               .33333
```

Figure 21 Multivariate tests of significance

```
EFFECT .. TRIAL
Multivariate Tests of Significance (S = 1, M = 1/2, N = 0)

Test Name         Value   Approx. F Hypoth. DF   Error DF  Sig. of F

Pillais          .97707   28.41231       3.00       2.00      .034
Hotellings     42.61846   28.41231       3.00       2.00      .034
Wilks            .02293   28.41231       3.00       2.00      .034
Roys             .97707

- - - - - - - - - -
Univariate F-tests with (1,4) D. F.

Variable   Hypoth. SS   Error SS Hypoth. MS   Error MS         F  Sig. of F

T2            1.60000   26.40000    1.60000    6.60000    .24242      .648
T3          120.00000   12.00000  120.00000    3.00000  40.00000      .003
T4          576.60000   74.40000  576.60000   18.60000  31.00000      .005
```

Figure 22 Averaged test of significance

```
AVERAGED Tests of Significance for DRUG using UNIQUE sums of squares
Source of Variation          SS       DF        MS        F  Sig of F

WITHIN CELLS             112.80       12      9.40
TRIAL                    698.20        3    232.73    24.76      .000
```

NLR

The following example shows how to use NLR to do nonlinear estimation. The example includes a method for obtaining good initial estimates for NLR.

A Basic Nonlinear Model

Draper and Smith (1981) pose the following exercise: under adiabatic conditions, the wind speed Y is given by the nonlinear model

$$Y = a \ln (bX + c) + e$$

where

X = the nominal height of the anemometer
a = friction velocity
$b = 1 +$ (zero point displacement)/(roughness length)
$c = 1/$(roughness length)

The data are as follows:

X	Y
40	490.2
80	585.3
160	673.7
320	759.2
640	837.5

To arrive at good initial values, consider the model without the error term:

$$Y = a \ln (bX + c)$$

Simple algebraic manipulation transforms the model into linear form. First, divide both sides by a:

$$Y/a = \ln (bX + c)$$

Then, use the EXP function, which is the inverse of the natural logarithm:

$$exp (Y/a) = bX + c$$

The model is now in linear form. The dependent variable, $exp(Y/a)$, should be regressed on X to obtain estimates of b and c. To determine the value to use for a, you need to consider the magnitudes of the Y values. Recall that the transcendental number e is 2.7183 to four decimal places. Thus, e raised to the Y power, represented as *exp(Y)*, will be outside the bounds of machine storage if Y is at all large, as is the case here. Considering the scale of the Y variable, we decide to set a equal to 100 initially. If you choose naive initial values for a, b, and c, chances are you will get NLR off to a bad start. Having gone through the above exercise, however, we can confidently supply initial values to NLR.

The following SPSS/PC+ commands show how to arrive at initial estimates for NLR:

```
DATA LIST / X 1-3 Y 5-9.
BEGIN DATA
 40  490.2
 80  585.3
160  673.7
320  759.2
640  837.5
END DATA.

PLOT PLOT=Y WITH X.
COMPUTE EY=EXP(Y/100).
REGRESSION VAR=EY,X /DEP=EY /ENTER.
```

Figure 1 shows the plot of the Y versus X association. The relationship is nonlinear.

Figure 1   The functional form

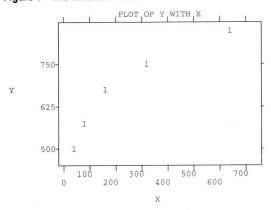

Figure 2 shows the regression used to get initial values for *b* and *c*.

Figure 2   Regression results

```
Multiple R              .99940
R Square                .99879
Adjusted R Square       .99839
Standard Error        69.22830

Analysis of Variance
                     DF      Sum of Squares       Mean Square
Regression            1        11886580.22650    11886580.22650
Residual              3           14377.67112        4792.55704

F =    2480.21675      Signif F =  .0000


----------------- Variables in the Equation ------------------

Variable              B         SE B       Beta         T    Sig T

X               7.065892      .141880    .999396    49.802   .0000
(Constant)   -223.259958    46.867778              -4.764   .0176
```

Recall that we set *a* to 100. The initial values for *b* and *c* are 7.07 and –223.26, respectively. The following commands show how to use NLR to estimate the model.

```
MODEL PROGRAM
    A=100 B=7.07 C=-223.26.
COMPUTE PRED=A*LN(B*X+C).
NLR Y WITH X/PRED=PRED/SAVE PRED.
PLOT
    FORMAT=OVERLAY
    /PLOT=PRED WITH X;Y WITH X.
```

Figure 3 shows the iteration history from NLR. NLR takes some time to get to a final solution, but an inspection of values as they change across iterations reveals that nothing is awry.

Figure 3   Iteration history

```
Iteration  Residual SS           A           B            C

     1     6714.647848   100.000000   7.07000000   -223.26000
   1.1     4077.992424   107.277280   2.67904252    -16.704306
     2     4077.992424   107.277280   2.67904252    -16.704306
   2.1       96.52824194 114.967093   2.28749099    -24.723034
     3       96.52824194 114.967093   2.28749099    -24.723034
   3.1        7.034306680 115.149369  2.31042749    -22.107125
     4        7.034306680 115.149369  2.31042749    -22.107125
   4.1        7.013266167 115.147452  2.31056492    -22.026881
     5        7.013266167 115.147452  2.31056492    -22.026881
   5.1        7.013265848 115.146861  2.31064761    -22.028816
     6        7.013265848 115.146861  2.31064761    -22.028816
   6.1        7.013265848 115.146865  2.31064717    -22.028804
     7        7.013265848 115.146865  2.31064717    -22.028804
   7.1        7.013265848 115.146867  2.31064679    -22.028796

Run stopped after 14 model evaluations and 7 derivative evaluations.
Iterations have been stopped because the relative reduction between successive
residual sums of squares is at most SSCON = 1.000E-08
```

Figure 4 shows the remaining NLR results. The analysis of variance for the regression shows that the fit of the final solution is very good. Using five data points to estimate a three-parameter model is a highly parameterized situation. This is reflected in the high correlations of the estimates. The standard error of the c coefficient is relatively large. This agrees with the iteration history shown in Figure 3, in which NLR began with an initial value of −223 and ended up with a final value of −22.

Figure 4　NLR results

```
Nonlinear Regression Summary Statistics        Dependent Variable Y

  Source                      DF  Sum of Squares  Mean Square

  Regression                   3   2314527.69673  771509.23224
  Residual                     2         7.01327       3.50663
  Uncorrected Total            5   2314534.71000

  (Corrected Total)            4      75525.34800

  R squared = 1 - Residual SS / Corrected SS =       .99991

                                             Asymptotic 95 %
                              Asymptotic    Confidence Interval
  Parameter     Estimate      Std. Error     Lower        Upper

  A         115.14686732    2.040553982  106.36707216 123.92666249
  B           2.310646787    .280311391    1.104564214   3.516729360
  C         -22.02879558    6.409408752  -49.60625565   5.548664482

Asymptotic Correlation Matrix of the Parameter Estimates

                    A          B          C

  A          1.0000     -.9963      .9666
  B          -.9963     1.0000     -.9802
  C           .9666     -.9802     1.0000
```

Figure 5 shows a plot of *PRED* versus *X* superimposed on a value of *Y* versus *X*. The fit is very good.

Figure 5　The fitted function

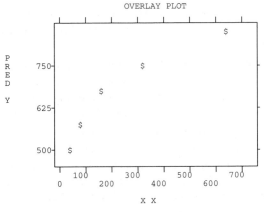

```
                        OVERLAY PLOT
                                               $

  P
  R       750-                    $
  E
  D                         $

  Y
          625-

                       $

          500-    $


              |   100      300      500      700
            0       200      400      600

                        X X

1:PRED WITH X   2:Y WITH X   $:Multiple occurrence
```

PROBIT

You can use PROBIT for a variety of dichotomous response models. The example shown here illustrates one of the most common applications: a dose-response model.

Dose-Response Model

The following shows the use of the Probit procedure to analyze an example from Finney (1971).

```
TITLE   "PROBIT ANALYSIS. DATA FROM 'PROBIT' BY FINNEY P.132".
DATA LIST / ROOT 1 X 3-7 N 9-11 R 13-15.
BEGIN DATA
1 148.0 142 142
1 100.0 127 126
1  48.0 128 115
1  12.0 126  58
2  62.0 125 125
2  46.0 117 115
2  31.0 127 114
2  14.8  51  40
2   3.8 132  37
2   0.0 129  21
END DATA.
PROBIT  R OF N BY ROOT(1,2) WITH X
  /MODEL = BOTH
  /NATRES
  /PRINT = ALL.
```

- The TITLE command sets up a title for the run.
- The DATA LIST command reads the variables *ROOT*, *X*, *N*, and *R* from the data included in the command file.
- The PROBIT command specifies that the number of responses is in variable *R* and the number of observations is in *N*. The response rate will be predicted from variable *X*. Two groups are defined by variable *ROOT*.
- The MODEL subcommand specifies both probit and logit response models.
- The NATRES subcommand requests an estimate of the natural response rate (or threshold) for each model. This specification requires that a control level be entered with the data. In this example, the control group is the last case, where *X* is 0.0.
- The PRINT subcommand requests all available output.
- The first data case shows 142 responses for the 142 observations with an *X* of 148.0 in the first group. The second-to-last case shows 37 responses for the 132 observations with an *X* of 3.8 in the second group. The last case has a value of 0.0 for predictor *X*, so the response rate used as the control level is 21 out of 129.

When both models are estimated, all output for the logit model is displayed before that for the probit model. Selected output from the logit model and all the output from the probit model are shown in Figure 1 through Figure 9. Figure 1 shows the case and model information displayed by PROBIT.

Figure 1   PROBIT case and model information

```
DATA   Information

        9 unweighted cases accepted.
        0 cases rejected because of out-of-range group values.
        0 cases rejected because of missing data.
        1 case is in the control group.
        0 cases rejected because LOG-transform can't be done.
Group Information

    ROOT      Level  N of Cases    Label
                 1            4        1
                 2            5        2


MODEL Information

      BOTH Probit and Logit models are requested.


Natural Response rate to be estimated

    The number of  subjects in the CONTROL group   129.0
    The number of responses in the CONTROL group    21.0
```

Parameter estimates for the logit and probit models are shown in Figure 2 and Figure 3. The number of iterations required to reach the convergence criterion is displayed first. If parameter estimates had failed to converge in the allotted iterations, PROBIT would have displayed an appropriate message and the estimates from the iterations that were completed (by default, the maximum number of iterations is 50 or $3(p+1)$, whichever is greater, where p is the number of parameters in the model).

Next, PROBIT displays parameter estimates with their standard errors. Three kinds of parameters are estimated: a regression coefficient, group intercepts, and a natural response rate. The regression coefficient for X is positive and large relative to its standard error. PROBIT produces separate intercept estimates for each group. Because no value labels are defined for *ROOT*, the actual values of the variable are used to label the subgroup intercepts. The second group has the greater response rate. Finally, PROBIT produces the estimate of the threshold or natural response rate.

Following the parameter estimates, PROBIT reports two chi-square statistics and their associated probabilities. The goodness-of-fit test is shown by default. It tests whether residuals are distributed homogeneously about the regression line. If this test is significant, PROBIT uses a heterogeneity factor to calculate confidence limits. A large chi-square can indicate that a different response model or predictor transformation is required. In this example, the probit model has the better fit. The PRINT subcommand requests all output, which includes the parallelism chi-square. This test indicates whether regression slopes differ between subgroups.

PROBIT estimated more than one parameter (excluding intercepts), so it automatically displays their covariance/correlation matrix. The diagonal entries (variances) simply equal the squares of the standard errors. The off-diagonal correlation and covariance terms indicate how much the estimate of the natural response rate depends on the estimate of the coefficient for X, and vice versa. Here, the two estimates are highly correlated. In multiple predictor models, this matrix is useful for examining multicollinearity.

Figure 2   Parameter estimates and covariances for logit model

```
Parameter estimates converged after 23 iterations.
Optimal solution found.

Parameter Estimates (LOGIT model:  (LOG(p/(1-p))) = Intercept + BX):

          Regression Coeff.   Standard Error     Coeff./S.E.

   X           5.42121             .68913           7.86674


          Intercept   Standard Error   Intercept/S.E.   ROOT
          -6.89404       1.20637         -5.71469          1
          -5.71387       1.11030         -5.14623          2

Estimate of Natural Response Rate = .239100  with  S.E. =    .07105

Pearson  Goodness-of-Fit  Chi Square =      8.653   DF = 5   P =  .124
         Parallelism Test Chi Square =      2.511   DF = 1   P =  .113

Since Goodness-of-Fit Chi square is significant, a heterogeneity
factor is used in the calculation of confidence limits.

Covariance(below) and Correlation(above) Matrices of Parameter Estimates

                    X    NAT RESP

X               .47490    .75954
NAT RESP        .03719    .00505
```

Figure 3   Parameter estimates and covariances for probit model

```
Parameter estimates converged after 21 iterations.
Optimal solution found.

Parameter Estimates (PROBIT model:  (PROBIT(p)) = Intercept + BX):

          Regression Coeff.   Standard Error     Coeff./S.E.

   X           3.02956             .41275           7.34001


          Intercept   Standard Error   Intercept/S.E.   ROOT
          -3.85967       .74033          -5.21347          1
          -3.17077       .68463          -4.63139          2

Estimate of Natural Response Rate = .229453  with  S.E. =    .08409

Pearson  Goodness-of-Fit  Chi Square =      5.707   DF = 5   P =  .336
         Parallelism Test Chi Square =       .958   DF = 1   P =  .328

Since Goodness-of-Fit Chi square is NOT significant, no heterogeneity
factor is used in the calculation of confidence limits.

Covariance(below) and Correlation(above) Matrices of Parameter Estimates

                    X    NAT RESP

X               .17036    .83934
NAT RESP        .02913    .00707
```

Figure 4 and Figure 5 show the observed and predicted frequencies from logit and probit models. PROBIT displays one row for each input case. The first column labels each case with the value of the grouping variable, *ROOT*. The second column shows the values for the log-transformed predictor, *X*. The procedure displays the number of subjects and the number of observed responses in the next two columns. The following two columns contain the number of responses predicted by the response model (*Expected Responses*) and the differences between the observed number of responses and those predicted (*Residual*). The probit response model in this example has smaller absolute residual values than the logit, indicating a better fit to the data. The final column (*Prob*) contains the predicted probability (or proportion) of responses for the predictor and group values in each row.

Figure 4　Observed and predicted frequencies for logit model

Observed and Expected Frequencies

ROOT	X	Number of Subjects	Observed Responses	Expected Responses	Residual	Prob
1	2.17	142.0	142.0	141.178	.822	.99421
1	2.00	127.0	126.0	125.172	.828	.98560
1	1.68	128.0	115.0	118.461	-3.461	.92548
1	1.08	126.0	58.0	55.098	2.902	.43728
2	1.79	125.0	125.0	123.294	1.706	.98636
2	1.66	117.0	115.0	113.834	1.166	.97294
2	1.49	127.0	114.0	118.747	-4.747	.93502
2	1.17	51.0	40.0	37.518	2.482	.73564
2	.58	132.0	37.0	38.697	-1.697	.29316

Figure 5　Observed and predicted frequencies for probit model

Observed and Expected Frequencies

ROOT	X	Number of Subjects	Observed Responses	Expected Responses	Residual	Prob
1	2.17	142.0	142.0	141.638	.362	.99745
1	2.00	127.0	126.0	125.638	.362	.98927
1	1.68	128.0	115.0	117.284	-2.284	.91628
1	1.08	126.0	58.0	55.855	2.145	.44330
2	1.79	125.0	125.0	123.851	1.149	.99081
2	1.66	117.0	115.0	114.207	.793	.97613
2	1.49	127.0	114.0	118.298	-4.298	.93148
2	1.17	51.0	40.0	37.089	2.911	.72724
2	.58	132.0	37.0	38.286	-1.286	.29005

Figure 6 displays the plot of probit-transformed response proportions against log-transformed values of the predictor, X. The plotting character (1 or 2) is the number of the group in which the observation appears. Because the default output width (80 columns) is used, the plot appears in compact form. In this plot, the relation of the variables appears linear, and the response rate appears greater in the second group.

Figure 6   PROBIT plot for single-predictor probit model

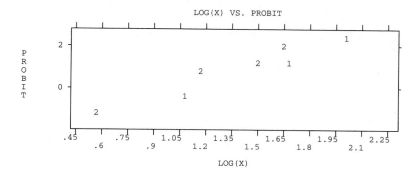

Figure 7 and Figure 8 present the confidence intervals for estimated effects of the predictor, X. For each group, PROBIT displays a table of estimated values for X to produce selected response rates from 0.01 to 0.99. Ninety-five percent fiducial confidence intervals are provided for these estimates (Finney, 1971). If the chi-square test had been significant, PROBIT would have used a heterogeneity factor to calculate the limits. The stimulus tolerance (the predictor estimate for a response rate of 0.50) is 18.69 in the first group and 11.32 in the second. PROBIT also displays effective levels and confidence limits for the log-transformed predictor.

Figure 7   Confidence intervals for effects by group in probit model

```
Confidence Limits for Effective X


ROOT          1            1

                          95% Confidence Limits
Prob          X            Lower        Upper

.01       2.65498          .27042        6.83381
.02       3.57925          .45382        8.47408
.03       4.27048          .61590        9.62952
.04       4.84679          .76635       10.55756
.05       5.35238          .90933       11.34993
.06       5.80938         1.04709       12.05110
.07       6.23071         1.18107       12.68638
.08       6.62465         1.31222       13.27171
.09       6.99689         1.44126       13.81783
.10       7.35154         1.56872       14.33238
.15       8.94775         2.19472       16.58986
.20      10.37440         2.82255       18.54405
.25      11.72273         3.47099       20.35084
.30      13.04327         4.15454       22.09245
.35      14.37114         4.88717       23.82356
.40      15.73574         5.68430       25.58819
.45      17.16579         6.56444       27.42824
.50      18.69303         7.55118       29.38955
.55      20.35614         8.67601       31.52830
.60      22.20608         9.98266       33.91979
.65      24.31465        11.53462       36.67318
.70      26.79000        13.42857       39.95943
.75      29.80783        15.82095       44.07049
.80      33.68188        18.98528       49.56246
.85      39.05217        23.45536       57.67033
.90      47.53144        30.47213       71.88697
.91      49.94064        32.42261       76.27568
.92      52.74684        34.66077       81.59132
.93      56.08180        37.26916       88.19706
.94      60.14915        40.37105       96.67943
.95      65.28488        44.16278      108.05516
.96      72.09504        48.98586      124.26607
.97      81.82441        55.51501      149.58632
.98      97.62637        65.38367      195.86921
.99     131.61283        84.47813      315.47613
```

Figure 8   Confidence intervals for effects by group in probit model

```
Confidence Limits for Effective X

ROOT          2           2

                           95% Confidence Limits
Prob          X          Lower          Upper
 .01      1.60829        .14392        4.33375
 .02      2.16819        .24184        5.36679
 .03      2.58691        .32853        6.09270
 .04      2.93601        .40910        6.67464
 .05      3.24228        .48576        7.17069
 .06      3.51912        .55969        7.60900
 .07      3.77435        .63166        8.00558
 .08      4.01298        .70218        8.37051
 .09      4.23847        .77162        8.71057
 .10      4.45331        .84026        9.03060
 .15      5.42024       1.17814       10.43013
 .20      6.28445       1.51822       11.63529
 .25      7.10123       1.87069       12.74384
 .30      7.90116       2.24356       13.80686
 .35      8.70554       2.64471       14.85775
 .40      9.53217       3.08293       15.92278
 .45     10.39844       3.56895       17.02631
 .50     11.32359       4.11660       18.19432
 .55     12.33104       4.74450       19.45792
 .60     13.45167       5.47890       20.85797
 .65     14.72897       6.35841       22.45272
 .70     16.22845       7.44286       24.33188
 .75     18.05655       8.83102       26.64624
 .80     20.40331      10.70018       29.67871
 .85     23.65645      13.40768       34.04922
 .90     28.79290      17.81434       41.50012
 .91     30.25231      19.07032       43.76653
 .92     31.95220      20.52579       46.49950
 .93     33.97240      22.23868       49.88396
 .94     36.43626      24.29442       54.22052
 .95     39.54731      26.82699       60.03382
 .96     43.67267      30.06526       68.33206
 .97     49.56639      34.45368       81.34536
 .98     59.13866      41.05465      105.27837
 .99     79.72648      53.67167      167.58370
```

You can compute the relative median potency (RMP) as the ratio of the stimulus tolerances in the two groups. The tolerances (from Figure 7 and Figure 8) are 18.69 and 11.32, which have a ratio of 1.65. The RMP and its confidence limits appear in Figure 9. The confidence limits do not include 1, so the difference is statistically significant.

Figure 9   Estimates of relative median potency (RMP) from probit model

```
Estimates of Relative Median Potency

                          95% Confidence Limits
ROOT         Estimate      Lower          Upper

1 VS.   2     1.6508      1.03667        3.80884
```

SURVIVAL

The data in this example are from a study of 647 cancer patients. The variables are:

- *TREATMNT*—the type of treatment received.
- *ONSETMO, ONSETYR*—month and year cancer was discovered.
- *RECURSIT*—recurrence status indicating whether a recurrence took place.
- *RECURMO, RECURYR*—month and year of recurrence.
- *OUTCOME*—status of patient at end of study: alive or dead.
- *DEATHMO, DEATHYR*—month and year of death, or, for those who are still presumed alive, the date of last contact.

Using these variables and the YRMODA function, the number of months from onset to recurrence and from onset to death or last contact are calculated. These new variables become the survival variables, with *TREATMNT* as the single control variable.

```
SET WIDTH=132.
DATA LIST FREE / TREATMNT  ONSETMO
        ONSETYR RECURSIT RECURMO RECURYR
        OUTCOME DEATHMO DEATHYR.
BEGIN DATA
(data records)
END DATA.

*TRANSFORM DATES TO DAYS FROM AN ARBITRARY TIME POINT.
COMPUTE   ONSDATE=YRMODA(ONSETYR,ONSETMO,15).
COMPUTE   RECDATE=YRMODA(RECURYR,RECURMO,15).
COMPUTE   DEATHDT=YRMODA(DEATHYR,DEATHMO,15).

*NOW COMPUTE ELAPSED TIME IN MONTHS FROM DIAGNOSIS TO
        LAST CONTACT OR DEATH.
COMPUTE   ONSSURV=(DEATHDT-ONSDATE)/30.

*COMPUTE TIME TO RECURRENCE.
IF  (RECURSIT EQ 0) RECSURV = ONSSURV.
IF  (RECURSIT NE 0) RECSURV = (RECDATE-ONSDATE)/30.

VARIABLE LABELS  TREATMNT 'PATIENT TREATMENT'
                 ONSSURV 'MONTHS FROM ONSET TO DEATH'
                   RECSURV 'MONTHS FROM ONSET TO RECURRENCE'.
VALUE LABELS  TREATMNT 1 'TREATMENT A' 2 'TREATMENT B'
              3 'TREATMENT C'.
SURVIVAL  TABLES = ONSSURV,RECSURV BY TREATMNT(1,3)
  /STATUS = RECURSIT(1,9) FOR RECSURV
  /STATUS = OUTCOME(3,4) FOR ONSSURV
  /INTERVALS = THRU 50 BY 5 THRU 100 BY 10
  /PLOT /COMPARE /CALCULATE=CONDITIONAL PAIRWISE.
```

- The SET command sets the page width to 132.
- The onset, recurrence, and death dates are transformed to days from a starting date using the YRMODA function on the COMPUTE command. The constant 15 is used as the day argument for YRMODA because only month and year were recorded, not the actual day.
- The first survival variable, *ONSSURV*, is the number of months between the date of death (or survival) and the date when cancer was discovered (*ONSDATE*). The number of days between the two events is divided by 30 to convert it from days to months.
- The second survival variable, *RECSURV*, is calculated conditionally using the IF command. For cases with *RECURSIT* values of 0, indicating that no recurrence took place, the length of time from onset to recurrence is equal to the length of time from diagnosis to last contact or death.
- The TABLES subcommand in SURVIVAL specifies two survival variables, *ONSSURV* and *RECSURV*, and one control variable, *TREATMNT*. The life table for *ONSSURV* is shown in Figure 1.
- The status variable for *RECSURV* is *RECURSIT*, with codes 1 through 9 indicating that the termination event, recurrence, took place. *OUTCOME* is the status variable for *ONSSURV* with codes 3 and 4 indicating death.
- The INTERVALS subcommand requests reporting at five-month intervals for the first 50 months, and at ten-month intervals for the remaining 50 months.
- The default plots are requested using PLOT. Figure 2 contains the plot of the survival function for *ONSSURV*.
- COMPARE with no specifications requests comparisons for all variables. The subgroup comparisons for *ONSSURV* are shown in Figure 3.
- Keyword CONDITIONAL on the CALCULATE subcommand requests approximate comparisons if memory is insufficient for exact comparisons. Keyword PAIRWISE requests that all pairs of treatments be compared. The pairwise comparisons for *ONSSURV* are shown in Figure 4.

Figure 1   Life table

```
LIFE TABLE
     SURVIVAL VARIABLE    ONSSURV    MONTHS FROM ONSET TO DEATH
              FOR         TREATMNT   PATIENT TREATMENT                    =    1   TREATMENT A
```

INTVL START TIME	NUMBER ENTRNG THIS INTVL	NUMBER WDRAWN DURING INTVL	NUMBER EXPOSD TO RISK	NUMBER OF TERMNL EVENTS	PROPN TERMINATING	PROPN SURVIVING	CUMUL PROPN SURV AT END	PROBABILITY DENSTY	HAZARD RATE	SE OF CUMUL SURVIVING	SE OF PROBABILTY DENS	SE OF HAZRD RATE
0.0	501.0	0.0	501.0	3.0	0.0060	0.9940	0.9940	0.0012	0.0012	0.003	0.001	0.001
5.0	498.0	1.0	497.5	16.0	0.0322	0.9678	0.9620	0.0064	0.0065	0.009	0.002	0.002
10.0	481.0	1.0	480.5	26.0	0.0541	0.9459	0.9100	0.0104	0.0111	0.013	0.002	0.002
15.0	454.0	0.0	454.0	17.0	0.0374	0.9626	0.8759	0.0068	0.0076	0.015	0.002	0.002
20.0	437.0	0.0	437.0	23.0	0.0526	0.9474	0.8298	0.0092	0.0108	0.017	0.002	0.002
25.0	414.0	1.0	413.5	25.0	0.0605	0.9395	0.7796	0.0100	0.0125	0.019	0.002	0.002
30.0	388.0	1.0	387.5	22.0	0.0568	0.9432	0.7354	0.0089	0.0117	0.020	0.002	0.002
35.0	365.0	1.0	364.5	24.0	0.0658	0.9342	0.6870	0.0097	0.0136	0.021	0.002	0.003
40.0	340.0	0.0	340.0	24.0	0.0706	0.9294	0.6385	0.0097	0.0146	0.022	0.002	0.003
45.0	316.0	1.0	315.5	14.0	0.0444	0.9556	0.6101	0.0057	0.0091	0.022	0.001	0.002
50.0	301.0	1.0	300.5	34.0	0.1131	0.8869	0.5411	0.0069	0.0120	0.022	0.001	0.002
60.0	266.0	0.0	266.0	22.0	0.0827	0.9173	0.4963	0.0045	0.0086	0.022	0.001	0.002
70.0	244.0	2.0	243.0	15.0	0.0617	0.9383	0.4657	0.0031	0.0064	0.022	0.001	0.002
80.0	227.0	3.0	225.5	24.0	0.1064	0.8936	0.4161	0.0050	0.0112	0.022	0.001	0.002
90.0	200.0	2.0	199.0	18.0	0.0905	0.9095	0.3785	0.0038	0.0095	0.022	0.001	0.002
100.0+	180.0	104.0	128.0	76.0	0.5938	0.4063	0.1538	**	**	0.019	**	**

**   THESE CALCULATIONS FOR THE LAST INTERVAL ARE MEANINGLESS.

THE MEDIAN SURVIVAL TIME FOR THESE DATA IS 69.18

Figure 2   Plot output for survival function

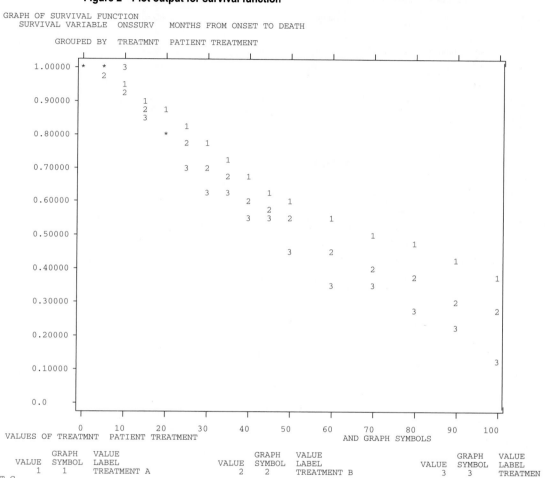

GRAPH OF SURVIVAL FUNCTION
    SURVIVAL VARIABLE   ONSSURV   MONTHS FROM ONSET TO DEATH

        GROUPED BY   TREATMNT   PATIENT TREATMENT

VALUES OF TREATMNT   PATIENT TREATMENT   AND GRAPH SYMBOLS

	GRAPH	VALUE			GRAPH	VALUE			GRAPH	VALUE
VALUE	SYMBOL	LABEL		VALUE	SYMBOL	LABEL		VALUE	SYMBOL	LABEL
1	1	TREATMENT A		2	2	TREATMENT B		3	3	TREATMEN

T C

Figure 3   Subgroup comparisons

```
COMPARISON OF SURVIVAL EXPERIENCE USING THE WILCOXON (GEHAN) STATISTIC
   SURVIVAL VARIABLE   ONSSURV   MONTHS FROM ONSET TO DEATH
       GROUPED BY   TREATMNT   PATIENT TREATMENT
```

OVERALL COMPARISON   STATISTIC   9.001   D.F.   2   PROB.   0.0111

GROUP	LABEL	TOTAL N	UNCEN	CEN	PCT CEN	MEAN SCORE
1	TREATMENT A	501	383	118	23.55	20.042
2	TREATMENT B	97	82	15	15.46	-67.412
3	TREATMENT C	26	24	2	7.69	-134.69

Figure 4   Pairwise comparisons

```
COMPARISON OF SURVIVAL EXPERIENCE USING THE WILCOXON (GEHAN) STATISTIC
   SURVIVAL VARIABLE   ONSSURV   MONTHS FROM ONSET TO DEATH
       GROUPED BY   TREATMNT   PATIENT TREATMENT
```

OVERALL COMPARISON   STATISTIC   9.001   D.F.   2   PROB.   0.0111

GROUP	LABEL	TOTAL N	UNCEN	CEN	PCT CEN	MEAN SCORE
1	TREATMENT A	501	383	118	23.55	20.042
2	TREATMENT B	97	82	15	15.46	-67.412
3	TREATMENT C	26	24	2	7.69	-134.69

PAIRWISE COMPARISON   STATISTIC   5.042   D.F.   1   PROB.   0.0247

GROUP	LABEL	TOTAL N	UNCEN	CEN	PCT CEN	MEAN SCORE
1	TREATMENT A	501	383	118	23.55	13.603
2	TREATMENT B	97	82	15	15.46	-70.258

PAIRWISE COMPARISON   STATISTIC   4.768   D.F.   1   PROB.   0.0290

GROUP	LABEL	TOTAL N	UNCEN	CEN	PCT CEN	MEAN SCORE
1	TREATMENT A	501	383	118	23.55	6.4391
3	TREATMENT C	26	24	2	7.69	-124.08

PAIRWISE COMPARISON   STATISTIC   0.766   D.F.   1   PROB.   0.3814

GROUP	LABEL	TOTAL N	UNCEN	CEN	PCT CEN	MEAN SCORE
2	TREATMENT B	97	82	15	15.46	2.8454
3	TREATMENT C	26	24	2	7.69	-10.615

Appendix A
Categorical Variable Coding Schemes

In many SPSS/PC+ procedures, you can request automatic replacement of a categorical independent variable with a set of contrast variables, which will then be entered or removed from an equation as a block. You can specify how the set of contrast variables is to be coded, usually on the CONTRAST subcommand. This appendix explains and illustrates how different contrast types requested on CONTRAST actually work.

Deviation

Deviation from the grand mean. In matrix terms, these contrasts have the form

mean	($1/k$	$1/k$	...	$1/k$	$1/k$)
df(1)	($1-1/k$	$-1/k$	...	$-1/k$	$-1/k$)
df(2)	($-1/k$	$1-1/k$	...	$-1/k$	$-1/k$)
.					
.			.		
.			.		
df(k-1)	($-1/k$	$-1/k$	...	$1-1/k$	$-1/k$)

where k is the number of categories for the independent variable and the last category is omitted by default. For example, the deviation contrasts for an independent variable with three categories are as follows:

(1/3	1/3	1/3)
(2/3	-1/3	-1/3)
(-1/3	2/3	-1/3)

To omit a category other than the last, specify the number of the omitted category in parentheses after the DEVIATION keyword. For example, the following subcommand obtains the deviations for the first and third categories and omits the second:

```
/CONTRAST(FACTOR)=DEVIATION(2)
```

Suppose that *factor* has three categories. The resulting contrast matrix will be:

```
( 1/3      1/3      1/3 )
( 2/3     -1/3     -1/3 )
(-1/3     -1/3      2/3 )
```

Simple

Simple contrasts. Compares each level of a factor to the last. The general matrix form is

mean	(1/k	1/k	...	1/k	1/k)
df(1)	(1	0	...	0	-1)
df(2)	(0	1	...	0	-1)
.		.			
.		.			
df(k-1)	(0	0	...	1	-1)

where k is the number of categories for the independent variable. For example, the simple contrasts for an independent variable with four categories are as follows:

```
( 1/4      1/4      1/4      1/4 )
( 1        0        0       -1 )
( 0        1        0       -1 )
( 0        0        1       -1 )
```

To use another category instead of the last as a reference category, specify in parentheses after the SIMPLE keyword the sequence number of the reference category, which is not necessarily the value associated with that category. For example, the following CONTRAST subcommand obtains a contrast matrix which omits the second category:

```
/CONTRAST(FACTOR) = SIMPLE(2)
```

Suppose that *factor* has four categories. The resulting contrast matrix will be:

```
( 1/4      1/4      1/4      1/4 )
( 1       -1        0        0 )
( 0       -1        1        0 )
( 0       -1        0        1 )
```

Helmert

Helmert contrasts. Compares categories of an independent variable with the mean of the subsequent categories. The general matrix form is

mean	(1/k	1/k	...	1/k	1/k)
df(1)	(1	-1/(k-1)	...	-1/(k-1)	-1/(k-1))
df(2)	(0	1	...	-1/(k-2)	-1/(k-2))
.		.			
.		.			
df(k-2)	(0	0	1	-1/2	-1/2)
df(k-1)	(0	0	...	1	-1)

where k is the number of categories for the independent variable. For example, an independent variable with four categories has a Helmert contrast matrix of the following form:

$$
\begin{pmatrix}
1/4 & 1/4 & 1/4 & 1/4 \\
1 & -1/3 & -1/3 & -1/3 \\
0 & 1 & -1/2 & -1/2 \\
0 & 0 & 1 & -1
\end{pmatrix}
$$

Difference

Difference or reverse Helmert contrasts. Compares categories of an independent variable with the mean of the previous categories of the variable. The general matrix form is

mean	(1/k	1/k	1/k	...	1/k)
df(1)	(-1	1	0	...	0)
df(2)	(-1/2	-1/2	1	...	0)
.		.			
.		.			
df(k-1)	(-1/(k-1)	-1/(k-1)	-1/(k-1)	...	1)

where k is the number of categories for the independent variable. For example, the difference contrasts for an independent variable with four categories are as follows:

$$
\begin{pmatrix}
1/4 & 1/4 & 1/4 & 1/4 \\
-1 & 1 & 0 & 0 \\
-1/2 & -1/2 & 1 & 0 \\
-1/3 & -1/3 & -1/3 & 1
\end{pmatrix}
$$

Polynomial

Orthogonal polynomial contrasts. The first degree of freedom contains the linear effect across all categories; the second degree of freedom, the quadratic effect; the third degree of freedom, the cubic; and so on for the higher-order effects.

You can specify the spacing between levels of the treatment measured by the given categorical variable. Equal spacing, which is the default if you omit the metric, can be specified as consecutive integers from 1 to k, where k is the number of categories. If the variable *drug* has three categories, the subcommand

```
/CONTRAST(DRUG)=POLYNOMIAL
```

is the same as

```
/CONTRAST(DRUG)=POLYNOMIAL(1,2,3)
```

Equal spacing is not always necessary, however. For example, suppose that *drug* represents different dosages of a drug given to three groups. If the dosage administered to the second group is twice that to the first group, and the dosage administered to the third group is three times that to the first group, the treatment categories are equally spaced and an appropriate metric for this situation consists of consecutive integers:

```
/CONTRAST(DRUG)=POLYNOMIAL(1,2,3)
```

If, however, the dosage administered to the second group is four times that given the first group, and the dosage given the third group is seven times that to the first, an appropriate metric is:

```
/CONTRAST(DRUG)=POLYNOMIAL(1,4,7)
```

In either case, the result of the contrast specification is that the first degree of freedom for *drug* contains the linear effect of the dosage levels and the second degree of freedom contains the quadratic effect.

Polynomial contrasts are especially useful in tests of trends and for investigating the nature of response surfaces. You can also use polynomial contrasts to perform nonlinear curve-fitting, such as curvilinear regression.

Repeated

Compares adjacent levels of an independent variable. The general matrix form is

mean	($1/k$	$1/k$	$1/k$	...	$1/k$	$1/k$)
df(1)	(1	-1	0	...	0	0)
df(2)	(0	1	-1	...	0	0)
.		.				
.		.				
df(k-1)	(0	0	0	...	1	-1)

where k is the number of categories for the independent variable. For example, the repeated contrasts for an independent variable with four categories are as follows:

```
(  1/4      1/4      1/4      1/4 )
(   1       -1        0        0 )
(   0        1       -1        0 )
(   0        0        1       -1 )
```

These contrasts are useful in profile analysis and wherever difference scores are needed.

Special

A user-defined contrast. SPECIAL allows entry of special contrasts in the form of square matrices with as many rows and columns as there are categories of the given independent variable. For MANOVA and LOGLINEAR, the first row entered is always the mean, or constant, effect and represents the set of weights indicating how to average other independent variables, if any, over the given variable. Generally, this contrast is a vector of ones.

The remaining rows of the matrix contain the special contrasts indicating the desired comparisons between categories of the variable. Usually, orthogonal contrasts are the most useful. Orthogonal contrasts are statistically independent and are nonredundant. Contrasts are orthogonal if:

• For each row, contrast coefficients sum to zero.

• The products of corresponding coefficients for all pairs of disjoint rows also sum to zero.

For example, suppose that *treatment* has four levels and that you want to compare the various levels of treatment with each other. An appropriate special contrast is

```
(   1        1        1        1 )     weights for mean calculation
(   3       -1       -1       -1 )     compare 1st with 2nd through 4th
(   0        2       -1       -1 )     compare 2nd with 3rd and 4th
(   0        0        1       -1 )     compare 3rd with 4th
```

which you specify by means of the following CONTRAST subcommand:

```
/CONTRAST(TREATMNT)=SPECIAL( 1   1   1   1
                             3  -1  -1  -1
                             0   2  -1  -1
                             0   0   1  -1 )
```

Each row except the means row sums to zero. Products of each pair of disjoint rows sum to zero as well:

Rows 2 and 3: $(3)(0) + (-1)(2) + (-1)(-1) + (-1)(-1) = 0$
Rows 2 and 4: $(3)(0) + (-1)(0) + (-1)(1) + (-1)(-1) = 0$
Rows 3 and 4: $(0)(0) + (2)(0) + (-1)(1) + (-1)(-1) = 0$

The special contrasts need not be orthogonal. However, they must not be linear combinations of each other. If they are, the procedure reports the linear dependency and ceases processing. Helmert, difference, and polynomial contrasts are all orthogonal contrasts.

Indicator

Indicator variable coding. Also known as dummy coding, this is not available in LOG-LINEAR or MANOVA. The number of new variables coded is $k - 1$. Cases in the reference category are coded 0 for all $k - 1$ variables. A case in the ith category is coded 0 for all indicator variables except the ith, which is coded 1.

Bibliography

Agresti, A. 1984. *Analysis of ordinal categorical data*. New York: John Wiley and Sons.
_____. 1990. *Categorical data analysis*. New York: John Wiley and Sons.
Aldrich, J. H., and F. D. Nelson. 1984. *Linear probability, logit, and probit models*. Beverly Hills, Calif.: Sage Publications.
Andrews, D. F., R. Gnanadesikan, and J. L. Warner. 1973. Methods for assessing multivariate normality. In: *Multivariate Analysis III*, P. R. Krishnaiah, ed. New York: Academic Press.
Atkinson, A. C. 1980. A note on the generalized information criterion for choice of a model. *Biometrika*, 67: 413–418.
Bacon, L. 1980. Unpublished data.
Bancroft, T. A. 1968. *Topics in intermediate statistical methods*. Ames: Iowa State University Press.
Barnard, R. M. 1973. Field-dependent independence and selected motor abilities. Ph.D. diss., School of Education, New York University.
Benedetti, J. K., and M. B. Brown. 1978. Strategies for the selection of log-linear models. *Biometrics*, 34: 680–686.
Bishop, Y. M. M., S. E. Fienberg, and P. W. Holland. 1975. *Discrete multivariate analysis: Theory and practice*. Cambridge, Mass.: MIT Press.
Bock, R. D. 1985. *Multivariate statistical methods in behavioral research*. Mooresville, Ind.: Scientific Software, Inc.
Brown, B. W., Jr. 1980. Prediction analyses for binary data. In: *Biostatistics Casebook*, R. G. Miller, B. Efron, B. W. Brown, and L. E. Moses, eds. New York: John Wiley and Sons.
Brown, M. B., and J. K. Benedetti. 1977. Sampling behavior of tests for correlation in two-way contingency tables. *Journal of the American Statistical Association*, 72: 309–315.
Burns, P. R. 1984. Multiple comparison methods in MANOVA. In: *Proceedings of the 7th SPSS Users and Coordinators Conference*. Chicago: ISSUE, Inc., 33–66.
_____. 1984. *SPSS-6000 MANOVA update manual*. Chicago: Vogelback Computing Center.
Churchill, G. A., Jr. 1979. *Marketing research: Methodological foundations*. Hinsdale, Ill.: Dryden Press.
Cochran, W. G., and G. M. Cox. 1957. *Experimental designs*. 2nd ed. New York: John Wiley and Sons.
Cohen, J. 1960. A coefficient of agreement for nominal scales. *Educational and Psychological Measurement*, 20: 37–46.
_____. 1977. *Statistical power analysis for the behavioral sciences*. New York: Academic Press.
Conover, W. J. 1980. *Practical nonparametric statistics*. 2nd ed. New York: John Wiley and Sons.

Cooley, W. W., and P. R. Lohnes. 1971. *Multivariate data analysis*. New York: John Wiley and Sons.

Daniel, C., and F. Wood. 1980. *Fitting equations to data*. Rev. ed. New York: John Wiley and Sons.

Davies, O. L. 1954. *Design and analysis of industrial experiments*. New York: Hafner Press.

Draper, N. R., and H. Smith. 1981. *Applied regression analysis*. New York: John Wiley and Sons.

Duncan, O. D. 1966. Path analysis: Sociological examples. *American Journal of Sociology*, 72: 1–16.

Elashoff, J. 1981. Data for the panel session in software for repeated measures analysis of variance. *Proceedings of the Statistical Computing Section*, American Statistical Association.

Everitt, B. S. 1977. *The analysis of contingency tables*. New York: Halsted Press.

_____. 1978. *Graphical techniques for multivariate data*. New York: North-Holland.

Eysenck, M. W. 1977. *Human memory: Theory, research and individual differences*. New York: Pergamon Press.

Finn, J. D. 1974. *A general model for multivariate analysis*. New York: Holt, Rinehart and Winston.

Finney, D. J. 1971. *Probit analysis*. Cambridge: Cambridge University Press.

Fisher, R. A. 1936. The use of multiple measurements in taxonomic problems. *Annals of Eugenics*, 7: 179–188.

Fox, J. 1984. *Linear statistical models and related methods: With applications to social research*. New York: John Wiley and Sons.

Freund, R. J. 1980. The case of the missing cell. *The American Statistician*, 34: 94–98.

Gilbert, E. S. 1968. On discrimination using qualitative variables. *Journal of the American Statistical Association*, 63: 1399–1412.

Gill, P. E., W. M. Murray, and M. H. Wright. 1981. *Practical optimization*. London: Academic Press.

Gill, P. E., W. M. Murray, M. A. Saunders, and M. H. Wright. 1984. Procedures for optimization problems with a mixture of bounds and general linear constraints. *ACM Transactions on Mathematical Software*, 10:3, 282–296.

_____. 1986. User's guide for NPSOL (version 4.0): A FORTRAN package for nonlinear programming. *Technical Report SOL 86-2*. Department of Operations Research, Stanford University.

Goldstein, M., and W. R. Dillon. 1978. *Discrete discriminant analysis*. New York: John Wiley and Sons.

Goodman, L. A. 1964. Simple methods of analyzing three-factor interaction in contingency tables. *Journal of the American Statistical Association*, 59: 319–352.

_____. 1978. *Analyzing qualitative/categorical data*. Cambridge, Mass.: Abt Books.

_____. 1984. *The analysis of cross-classified data having ordered categories*. Cambridge, Mass.: Harvard University Press.

Green, P. E. 1978. *Analyzing multivariate data*. Hinsdale, Ill.: Dryden Press.

Greenhouse, S. W., and S. Geisser. 1959. On methods in analysis of profile data. *Psychometrika*, 24: 95–112.

Haberman, S. J. 1978. *Analysis of qualitative data*. Vol. 1. New York: Academic Press.

_____. 1979. *Analysis of qualitative data*. Vol. 2. New York: Academic Press.

_____. 1982. Analysis of dispersion of multinomial responses. *Journal of the American Statistical Association*, 77: 568–580.

Hauck, W. W. and A. Donner. 1977. Wald's test as applied to hypotheses in logit analysis. *Journal of the American Statistical Association*, 72: 851–853.

Hays, W. L. 1981. *Statistics for the social sciences*. 3rd ed. New York: Holt, Rinehart and Winston.

Heck, D. L. 1960. Charts of some upper percentage points of the distribution of the largest characteristic root. *Annals of Mathematical Statistics*, 31: 625–642.

Hicks, C. R. 1973. *Fundamental concepts in the design of experiments*. 2nd ed. New York: Holt, Rinehart and Winston.

Hinds, M. A., and G. A. Milliken. 1982. Statistical methods to use nonlinear models to compare silage treatments. Unpublished paper.

Hoaglin, D. C., F. Mosteller, and J. W. Tukey. 1983. *Understanding robust and exploratory data analysis*. New York: John Wiley and Sons.

Hoerl, A. E., and R. W. Kennard. 1970. Ridge regression: Applications to nonorthogonal problems. *Technometrics*, 12: 69–82.

_____. 1970. Ridge regression: Biased estimation of nonorthogonal problems. *Technometrics*, 12: 55–67.

Hosmer, D. W., and S. Lemeshow. 1989. *Applied logistic regression*. New York: John Wiley and Sons.

Huberty, C. J. 1972. Multivariate indices of strength of association. *Multivariate Behavioral Research*, 7: 523–526.

Huynh, H., and L. S. Feldt. 1976. Estimation of the Box correction for degrees of freedom from sample data in randomized block and split-plot designs. *Journal of Educational Statistics*, 1: 69–82.

Huynh, H., and G. K. Mandevill. 1979. Validity conditions in repeated measures designs. *Psychological Bulletin*, 86: 964–973.

Judge, G. G., W. E. Griffiths, R. C. Hill, H. Lutkepohl, and T. C. Lee. 1985. *The theory and practice of econometrics*. 2nd ed. New York: John Wiley and Sons.

Kendall, M. G., and A. Stuart. 1973. *The advanced theory of statistics*. Vol. 2. New York: Hafner Press.

Kennedy, J. J. 1970. The eta coefficient in complex anova designs. *Educational and Psychological Measurement*, 30: 885–889.

Kirk, R. E. 1982. *Experimental design*. 2nd ed. Monterey, Calif.: Brooks/Cole.

Kleinbaum, D. G., L. L. Kupper, and H. Morgenstern. 1982. *Epidemiological research: Principles and quantitative methods*. Belmont, Calif.: Wadsworth, Inc.

Kvalseth, T. O. 1985. Cautionary note about R squared. *The American Statistician*, 39:4, 279–285.

Lachenbruch, P. A. 1975. *Discriminant analysis*. New York: Hafner Press.

Lee, E. T. 1992. *Statistical methods for survival data analysis*. New York: John Wiley and Sons.

Lee, E., and M. Desu. 1972. A computer program for comparing k samples with right-censored data. *Computer Programs in Biomedicine*, 2: 315–321.

Magidson, J. 1981. Qualitative variance, entropy, and correlation ratios for nominal dependent variables. *Social Science Research*, 10: 177–194.

Mantel, N., and W. Haenszel. 1959. Statistical aspects of the analysis of data from retrospective studies of disease. *Journal of the National Cancer Institute*, 22: 719–748.

McCullagh, P., and J. A. Nelder. 1989. *Generalized linear models*. 2nd ed. London: Chapman and Hall.

Miller, R. G. 1981. *Simultaneous statistical inference.* 2nd ed. New York: Springer-Verlag.

Milliken, G. A. 1987. A tutorial on nonlinear modeling with an application from pharmacokinetics. Unpublished manuscript.

Milliken, G. W., and D. E. Johnson. 1984. *Analysis of messy data.* Belmont, Calif.: Lifetime Learning Publications.

Montgomery, D. C., and E. A. Peck. 1982. *Introduction to linear regression analysis.* New York: John Wiley and Sons.

Morrison, D. F. 1976. *Multivariate statistical methods.* 2nd ed. New York: McGraw-Hill.

Mudholkar, G. S., Y. P. Chaubey, and C. C. Lin. 1976. Some approximations for the noncentral-F distribution. *Technometrics,* 18: 351–358.

Muller, K. E., and B. L. Peterson. 1984. Practical methods for computing power in testing the multivariate general linear hypothesis. *Computational Statistics and Data Analysis,* 2: 143–158.

Neter, J., W. Wasserman, and R. Kutner. 1985. *Applied linear statistical models.* 2nd ed. Homewood, Ill.: Richard D. Irwin, Inc.

Norusis, M. J., and SPSS Inc. 1989. *SPSS advanced statistics user's guide.* Chicago: SPSS Inc.

O'Brien, R. G. 1983. General Scheffé tests and optimum subeffects for linear models. Presented at the annual meeting of the American Statistical Association, August, 1983.

Olsen, C. L. 1976. On choosing a test statistic in multivariate analysis of variance. *Psychological Bulletin,* 83: 579–586.

Pillai, K. C. S. 1967. Upper percentage points of the largest root of a matrix in multivariate analysis. *Biometrika,* 54: 189–193.

Rao, C. R. 1973. *Linear statistical inference and its applications.* 2nd ed. New York: John Wiley and Sons.

Roy, J., and R. E. Bargmann. 1958. Tests of multiple independence and the associated confidence bounds. *Annals of Mathematical Statistics,* 29: 491–503.

Searle, S. R. 1971. *Linear models.* New York: John Wiley and Sons.

Snedecor, G. W., and W. G. Cochran. 1967. *Statistical methods.* 6th ed. Ames: Iowa State University Press.

Tatsuoka, M. M. 1971. *Multivariate analysis.* New York: John Wiley and Sons.

Timm, N. H. 1975. *Multivariate analysis with applications in education and psychology.* Monterey, Calif.: Brooks/Cole.

Tukey, J. W. 1977. *Exploratory data analysis.* Reading, Mass.: Addison-Wesley.

Van Vliet, P. K. J., and J. M. Gupta. 1973. THAM v. sodium bicarbonate in idiopathic respiratory distress syndrome. *Archives of Disease in Childhood,* 48: 249–255.

Wald, A. 1943. Tests of statistical hypotheses concerning several parameters with applications to problems of estimation. *Transcripts of American Mathematical Society,* 54: 426–482.

Winer, B. J., D. R. Brown, and K. M. Michels. 1991. *Statistical principles in experimental design.* 3rd ed. New York: McGraw-Hill.

Witkin, H. A., and others. 1954. *Personality through perception.* New York: Harper and Brothers.

Wright, S. 1960. Path coefficients and path regressions: Alternative or complementary concepts? *Biometrics,* 16: 189–202.

Index